THE C

WITH CONTINUAL REFERENCE TO SOCRATES

KIERKEGAARD'S WRITINGS, II

THE CONCEPT OF IRONY

WITH CONTINUAL REFERENCE TO SOCRATES

by Søren Kierkegaard

together with

NOTES OF SCHELLING'S BERLIN LECTURES

Edited and Translated
with Introduction and Notes by

Howard V. Hong and
Edna H. Hong

PRINCETON UNIVERSITY PRESS
PRINCETON, NEW JERSEY

Published by Princeton University Press, 41 William Street
Princeton, New Jersey 08540
In the United Kingdom: Princeton University Press, Chichester, West Sussex

Library of Congress Cataloging-in-Publication-Data
Kierkegaard, Søren, 1813-1855.
The concept of irony, with continual reference to Socrates.
(Kierkegaard's writings; 2)
Translation of: Om begrebet ironi.
Bibliography: p.
Includes index.
1. Irony. 2. Socrates. 3. Schelling, Friedrich Wilhelm Joseph von, 1775-1854. I. Hong, Howard Vincent, 1912- . II. Hong, Edna Hatlestad, 1913-. III. Title. IV. Series: Kierkegaard, Søren, 1813-1855. Works. English. 1978; 2.
B4373.042E5 1989 190 89-3642
ISBN 0-691-07354-6 ISBN 0-691-02072-8 (pbk.)

Second printing, with corrections, and first paperback printing, 1992

Preparation of this volume has been made possible in part by a grant from the Division of Research Programs of the National Endowment for the Humanities, an independent federal agency

Princeton University Press books are printed on acid-free paper, and meet the guidelines for permanence and durability of the Committee on Production Guidelines for Book Longevity of the Council on Library Resources

Designed by Frank Mahood

http://pup.princeton.edu

Printed in the United States of America

7 9 10 8

CONTENTS

HISTORICAL INTRODUCTION

On October 30, 1830, Søren Aabye Kierkegaard entered the University of Copenhagen. On September 29, 1841, he publicly defended his dissertation, *The Concept of Irony, with Continual Reference to Socrates*. For about eight of those eleven years, he appeared to be a typical perennial student. In the last three years, however, he not only completed intensive preparation for the climactic degree examination but wrote the 350-page dissertation and a considerable portion of Part II of *Either/Or*. In the midst of this concentrated work, he became engaged to Regine Olsen (September 10, 1840) and terminated the engagement within a fortnight after the dissertation defense.

Although the student years stretched out inordinately, Kierkegaard was not idle. He attended lectures and read extensively and intensively, but his mind was more preoccupied with his own creative thoughts than with formal study and completion of work for a degree. Four themes were of continuing interest: the ideas symbolized by Don Juan, Faust, the Master Thief, and the Wandering Jew.[1] During the period 1834-1838, he wrote a number of pieces for Johan Ludvig Heiberg's *Kjøbenhavns flyvende Post*,[2] an unpublished and unproduced play, *The Battle between the Old and the New Soap-Cellars*, and his first book, *From the Papers of One Still Living*[3] (on Hans Christian Andersen's *Only a Fiddler*). Journal entries from 1838 include indications of contemplated writing: "I would like to write a novella with my own mottoes. Motto:

[1] See Supplement, pp. 423-25, 429 (*Pap.* I A 11, C 66, A 72, C 69, 58; II A 597). See also *JP* I 769; II 1177-85 (*Pap.* II A 55; I A 88, 104, C 58, A 227, 292; II A 29, 50, 605); VII, pp. 28, 37, 60, 100.

[2] See "Articles from Student Days," *Early Polemical Writings*, *KW* I (*SV* XIII 5-39).

[3] Both *The Battle between the Old and the New Soap-Cellars* (*Pap.* II B 1-21) and *From the Papers of One Still Living* (*SV* XIII 46-92) are included in *Early Polemical Writings*, *KW* I.

Fantasy for a post horn";[4] "I would like to issue a publication for παράνεκροί [beside the dead]."[5]

Other journal entries and reading notes (on Jean Paul, Hamann, Wieland, Erdmann, Baur, and Grulich) from 1836 onward touch on Socrates, satire, humor, and irony,[6] and an entry dated September 25, 1837, reads, "Now I know a suitable subject for a dissertation: concerning the concept of satire among the ancients, the reciprocal relation of the various Roman satirists to each other."[7]

No extant journal entries touch specifically on the decision to write on irony, but two important entries on Kierkegaard's favorite teacher, philosophy professor Poul Martin Møller, point to a decision to write a substantial work. "I recall the words of the dying Poul Møller, which he often said to me while he lived and which, if I remember correctly, he enjoined Sibbern[8] to repeat (and in addition the words: Tell the little Kierkegaard that he should be careful not to lay out too big a plan of study, for that has been very detrimental to me): You are so thoroughly polemical that it is quite appalling."[9] Møller's death on March 13, 1838, seemed to be an activating and integrating occasion that brought Kierkegaard's far-ranging mind back to his initial resolve to write a dissertation. "Such a long period has again elapsed in which I have been unable to concentrate on the least little thing—now I must make another attempt. Poul Møller is dead."[10]

4 *JP* V 5290 (*Pap*. II A 683).

5 *JP* V 5295 (*Pap*. II A 690).

6 See Supplement, pp. 425, 436 (*Pap*. I A 125; II A 737). See also *JP* II 1669-1736.

7 See Supplement, pp. 434-35 (*Pap*. II A 166).

8 Frederik Christian Sibbern (1785-1872), professor of philosophy, University of Copenhagen, 1813-70.

9 *JP* VI 6888 (*Pap*. XI¹ A 225). See Supplement, pp. 432-33 (*Pap*. II A 102), for an entry on a conversation with Møller about irony and humor during the evening of June 30, 1837. In discussing what became Kierkegaard's dissertation, Møller possibly also had Kierkegaard in mind as his successor as professor of philosophy. See Troels Frederik Troels-Lund, *Bakkehus og Solbjerg*, I-III (Copenhagen: Gyldendal, 1920-22), III, p. 207; Eduard Geismar, *Søren Kierkegaard*, I-VI (Copenhagen: Gad, 1926-28), I, p. 89.

10 *JP* V 5302 (*Pap*. II A 209).

The second and even more important activating occasion was the death of his father, Michael Pedersen Kierkegaard. In September 1837, the twenty-four-year-old Søren had taken private quarters and lived somewhat estranged from his father. In the spring of 1838, there was a reconciliation[11] and for Søren an experience of "*indescribable joy*."[12] At the end of that summer, M. P. Kierkegaard died. Kierkegaard was profoundly shaken by his father's death and resolved to fulfill his father's hope and expectation for him. He decided to resume and complete work required for a degree, "a pursuit that does not interest me in the least and that therefore does not get done very fast,"[13] as he wrote in June 1835. But now he thought that he had no alternative.[14] Even though he felt as unfitted for the task as Sarah and Abraham were for parenthood,[15] he decided to take the plunge of disciplined preparation[16] in order to fulfill his father's wish.[17] In a conversation with an old friend, Hans Brøchner, Kierkegaard related that his father had once said to him, " 'It would be a good thing for you if I were dead. Then you might still perhaps become something. But as long as I live you will not.' "[18] Brøchner also records Kierkegaard's decision recounted in the same conversation: " 'So long as father lived, however, I was able to defend my thesis that I ought not to take it [the examination]. But when he was dead, I had to take over his part in the debate as well as my own, and then I could no longer hold out, but had to decide to read for the examination.' He did so, with great energy."[19] This decision meant that the work and the writing under way on irony were set aside until after the examination July 3, 1840, and a pil-

[11] See Supplement, p. 437 (*Pap*. II A 231, 233).

[12] See ibid.

[13] See Supplement, pp. 424, 437-38 (*Pap*. I A 72; II A 807).

[14] See Supplement, p. 438 (*Pap*. II A 422).

[15] See Supplement, p. 439 (*Pap*. II A 490).

[16] See Supplement, pp. 439-40 (*Pap*. II A 497, 534; III A 35).

[17] See Supplement, p. 440 (*Pap*. III A 73).

[18] Hans Brøchner, *Erindringer over Søren Kierkegaard* (Copenhagen: 1953), 7, p. 23; "The Recollections," *Glimpses and Impressions of Kierkegaard*, tr. T. H. Croxall (Digswell Place, Welwyn, Herts.: Nisbet, 1959), p. 11.

[19] Ibid., p. 10.

grimage of filial piety to Sæding, his father's birthplace, July 19-August 6, 1840.

Having made the decision to prepare for the examination, Kierkegaard wrote with some pathos in his journal:

> And you, too, my *lucida intervalla* [bright intervals], I must bid farewell, and you, my thoughts, imprisoned in my head, I can no longer let you go strolling in the cool of the evening, but do not be discouraged, learn to know one another better, associate with one another, and I will no doubt be able to slip off occasionally and peek in on you—Au revoir!
>
> S. K.
> formerly Dr. Exstaticus[20]

Another entry from the same time also reflects Kierkegaard's deliberate shift to the arduous task of completing his studies: "For a period of a year, a mile in time, I will plunge underground like the river Guadalquibir—but I am sure to come up again!"[21] What he came up to again after the examination and the Sæding pilgrimage was assiduous application to his work on the dissertation on irony.

In the absence of a dated manuscript of *The Concept of Irony* at any stage of writing and in the absence of dates in the few scattered notes, it is not possible to be precise about the time of the writing of *Irony*. Quite likely, however, a fair portion of the first part was written in 1838-1839 following discussions with Poul Martin Møller and before the clear decision to prepare for the degree examination. The rather complicated style of the first part is reminiscent of the style of *From the Papers of One Still Living* (1838). It is unlikely that the entire work could have been written in the eleven months between the Jutland pilgrimage and submission of the dissertation on June 3, 1841, a period that also coincides almost exactly with the engagement period with its attendant claims upon Kierkegaard's time and attention. In addition, Kierkegaard was

[20] *JP* V 5434 (*Pap*. II A 576).
[21] *JP* V 5397 (*Pap*. II A 497).

enrolled in the Royal Pastoral Seminary during the winter semester 1840-1841.[22]

On June 2, 1841, Kierkegaard sent a petition to the king requesting permission to submit his dissertation in Danish rather than in Latin. In the petition, he points out that Martin Hammerich and Adolph Peter Adler had been permitted the use of Danish in their dissertations submitted in 1836 and 1840. No mention is made of the permission granted in 1840 to Hans Lassen Martensen, whose name was omitted probably because he would participate in the faculty judgment of Kierkegaard's dissertation and because Martensen had been granted an honorary doctor's degree by Kiel University and therefore did not defend his dissertation for a Danish degree. In his petition, Kierkegaard stated that the discussion of irony in the modern period made Latin inappropriate. He pointed out in addition that he had taught Latin and that the public defense would be in Latin.

On September 16, 1841, copies of the dissertation were ready at the print shop, and on September 29 Kierkegaard defended it in a public colloquium for seven and one-half hours, from ten to two o'clock and four to seven-thirty. The official opponents were philosophy professor Frederik Christian Sibbern and Greek professor Peter Oluf Brønsted. The seven speakers from the audience included Kierkegaard's brother Dr. Peter Christian Kierkegaard, the official advocate, and Dr. Andreas Frederik Beck, who later wrote a review of *Irony*.[23] Very little is now known of what was said during that long discussion, but one member of the audience wrote home that Kierkegaard "played toss-in-a-blanket with the faculty."[24] Kierkegaard's public defense was his first and last participation in the official academic life of the University of Copenhagen.

[22] See *Kierkegaard: Letters and Documents*, Document XVI, *KW* XXV.

[23] *Fædrelandet*, 890, 897, May 29, June 5, 1842. See "Public Confession," *The* Corsair *Affair and Articles Related to the Writings*, pp. 9-12, *KW* XIII (*SV* XIII 404-05).

[24] Holger Frederik Rørdam, *Peter Rørdam*, I-III (Copenhagen: 1843), I, p. 79 (ed. tr.).

The criticism of the work by faculty readers prior to the public defense was more or less anticipated by the writer. "The ease of style will be censured," Kierkegaard wrote. "One or another half-educated Hegelian robber will say that the subjective is too prominent. . . . Moreover, whether I may have been too prolix at times, . . . let me be judged modestly and without any demands, but I will not be judged by boys."[25] "And if something should be found, particularly in the first part of the dissertation, that one is generally not accustomed to come across in scholarly writings, the reader must forgive my jocundity, just as I, in order to lighten the burden, sometimes sing at my work."[26] In the work itself, he concedes that "the form of the whole treatise . . . departs somewhat from the now widespread and in so many ways meritorious scholarly method."[27]

Sibbern, as dean of the philosophical faculty, was the first reader and approved the dissertation, although he advised a pruning of the style, a change of title to make Socrates even more central, and the addition of Latin theses. The other faculty readers agreed essentially with Sibbern. Brønsted, however, added that "it is the faculty's business only to render acknowledgment of *insight* and *knowledge* but *by no means* to bring about better taste in those who, according to their own insight and knowledge, ought to have better taste."[28] H. L. Martensen, in a very brief note, also voted for acceptance, although he, too, was critical of the style.[29]

On October 20, 1841, the *Magister Artium* diploma was issued. It should be noted that the *Magister* degree in the faculty of philosophy corresponded to the Ph.D. in the other faculties of the University of Copenhagen. This is reflected in the an-

[25] See Supplement, pp. 440-41 (*Pap.* III B 2).

[26] See Supplement, p. 441 (*Pap.* III B 3).

[27] P. 156.

[28] Quoted by Carl Weltzer in *Omkring Søren Kierkegaards Disputats, Kirkehistoriske Samlinger*, VI, 1949-50, pp. 297-98 (ed. tr.).

[29] See Hans Lassen Martensen, *Af mit Levnet*, I-III (Copenhagen: 1882-83), II, p. 142, where he writes of a discussion with Kierkegaard on the dissertation before its publication.

nouncement of *Søren Kierkegaards Doktordisputats* in the newspaper *Berlingske Tidende*, September 29, 1841. In 1854, the *Magister* degree with dissertation was abolished, and those with such a degree were declared to be doctors of philosophy. This change is indicated, for example, in the announcement of the death of "Dr. Søren Kierkegaard"[30] and in polemical pieces such as Nicolai Holten's *Polemiske Smuler eller en Smule Polemik mod Dr. Søren Kierkegaard.*[31]

Inasmuch as there is no record of the sale of the published dissertation, no inference about public interest in the work can be drawn, although there may have been a correlation between sales of the book and the large audience at the public colloquy. The number printed is also unknown, but it was customary to print dissertations in a much smaller number than 525 copies, the size of most other Kierkegaard editions. Printed at the cost of 182 rix-dollars, 4 marks, 8 shillings for the entire printing, paperbound copies were sold for 9 marks or 1½ rix-dollars (c. $7.50 at the 1973 level), with 25 percent going to the bookseller. No information on sales of the volume is available; a sale of 163 copies would have covered printing costs. The Latin theses required by the faculty were included in copies distributed within the university. They were not included in copies sold to the public. Such copies had a title page with a Greek quotation from Plato's *Republic*, whereas the university copies had a title page with a phrase about submission for the *Magister* degree and a space for writing the time of an eventual public colloquy.

The reception of *Irony* by reviewers during Kierkegaard's lifetime was scanty and supercilious—only two Danish reviews in fourteen years. The first review appeared in *The Corsair* on October 22, 1841.[32] The review was anonymous and ironically excessive in praise. Meïr Goldschmidt, the editor, was not satisfied with the review because it concentrated on the language and not on the substance of *Irony*, and therefore

[30] *Berlingske Tidende*, 304, November 16, 1855, p. 1.

[31] Published in Copenhagen in 1855.

[32] See Corsair *Affair*, pp. 91-93, *KW* XIII.

he added a postscript to the review.[33] The second review[34] was by Dr. Andreas Frederik Beck, who had spoken at the public defense of the dissertation. After eleven columns of summary, Beck praised the treatment of Xenophon and the absence of cramped scholastic terminology but in closing censured what he termed an attempted brilliance of wit and the use of allusions and references that were unclear to most readers, including the reviewer.[35] Another review[36] appeared in December 1855, about a month after Kierkegaard's death, as part of an article on Hegelianism in Denmark. Given that theme, the reviewer said, "Hegelianism ends with Kierkegaard, and nevertheless he never did entirely renounce Hegel."[37] The review also stated that the work "not only treats of irony but is irony."[38]

Kierkegaard's own estimate of *The Concept of Irony* is scarcely more rapturous than the reception it received at the time. Among the very few journal entries on *Irony* is a repentant word about what he had written concerning Socrates:

> *A Passage in My Dissertation*
>
> Influenced as I was by Hegel and whatever was modern, without the maturity really to comprehend greatness, I could not resist pointing out somewhere in my dissertation that it was a defect on the part of Socrates to disregard the whole and only consider numerically the individuals.
>
> What a Hegelian fool I was! It is precisely this that powerfully demonstrates what a great ethicist Socrates was.[39]

[33] See Meïr Aaron Goldschmidt, *Livs Erindringer og Resultater*, I-II (Copenhagen: 1877), I, p. 275; Corsair *Affair*, pp. 92-93, 139, *KW* XIII.

[34] *Fædrelandet*, 890, 897, May 29, June 5, 1842, col. 7133-40, 7189-91. The review appeared also in *Deutsche Jahrbücher für Wissenschaft und Kunst* (Halle), 222-23, May 29, June 5, 1842, pp. 885-91.

[35] For Kierkegaard's response, see "Public Confession," Corsair *Affair*, pp. 9-12, *KW* XIII (*SV* XIII 404-06).

[36] See Hans Friederich Helweg, *"Hegelianismen i Danmark," Theologisk Tidsskrift*, 2, 6, December 16, 23, 1855, col. 829-37, 841-43.

[37] Ibid., col. 829 (ed. tr.).

[38] Ibid., col. 830 (ed. tr.).

[39] See Supplement, p. 453 (*Pap*. X^3 A 477).

The two other critical references to *Irony* in the *Papirer* are in the same vein regarding the relation to Hegel:

> That the state in a Christian sense is supposed to be what Hegel taught—namely, that it has moral significance, that true virtue can appear only in the state (something I also childishly babbled after him in my dissertation),[40] that the goal of the state is to improve men—is obviously nonsense.
>
> The state is of the evil rather than of the good, a necessary evil, in a certain sense a useful, expedient evil, rather than a good.
>
> The state is human egotism on a large scale and in great dimensions—so far off was Plato when he said that in order to become aware of the virtues we should study them in the state.[41]
>
> The state is human egotism in great dimensions, very expediently and cunningly composed so that the egotisms of individuals intersect each other correctively. To this extent the state is no doubt a safeguard against egotism by manifesting a higher egotism that copes with all the individual egotisms so that these must egotistically understand that egotistically it is the most prudent thing to live in the state. Just as we speak of a calculus of infinitesimals, so also the state is a calculus of egotisms, but always in such a way that it egotistically appears to be the most prudent thing to enter into and to be in this higher egotism. But this, after all, is anything but the moral abandoning of egotism.[42]

In his dissertation, Magister Kierkegaard was alert enough to discern the Socratic but is considered not to have understood it, probably because, with the help of Hegelian philosophy, he has become super-clever and objective and positive, or has not had the courage to acknowledge the

[40] See pp. 229-35.

[41] See Plato, *Republic*, 368-369a; *Platonis quae exstant opera*, I-XI, ed. Friedrich Ast (Leipzig: 1819-32; *ASKB* 1144-54), IV, pp. 90-93; *The Collected Dialogues of Plato*, ed. Edith Hamilton and Huntington Cairns (Princeton: Princeton University Press, 1963), pp. 614-15.

[42] *JP* IV 4238 (*Pap*. XI² A 108).

negation. Finitely understood, of course, the continued and the perpetually continued striving toward a goal without attaining it means rejection, but, infinitely understood, striving is life itself and is essentially the life of that which is composed of the infinite and the finite.[43]

The last entry above is from a provisional draft of *Concluding Unscientific Postscript.* It is noteworthy that the pseudonymous author Johannes Climacus not only omits reference to *Irony* in the final copy but does not mention *Irony* at all in the section on the writings by Magister Kierkegaard and the pseudonymous writers.[44] *Irony* (as well as *From the Papers of One Still Living*) is also omitted from consideration in *On My Work as an Author* and *The Point of View for My Work as an Author.*[45]

Although Kierkegaard regarded *Either/Or*,[46] rather than *From the Papers* or *Irony*, as the beginning of his authorship, there are lines of continuity between them and later works. On a large scale, there is the formula of categories. In Part One of *Irony*, the Hegelian pattern is followed: possibility, actuality, and necessity. In Part Two,[47] Kierkegaard introduces his own pattern (noted also in a journal entry[48] from July 4, 1840) of the relation between possibility-actuality and concept (necessity). Existence as actuality combines two opposing factors, possibility and necessity, and thereby has a paradoxical character. This view is embodied in all of his subsequent writings.

The works most closely related to *Irony* are those closest in

[43] *JP* V 5796 (*Pap.* VI B 35:24).

[44] *Concluding Unscientific Postscript to* Philosophical Fragments, *KW* XII (*SV* VII 212-57).

[45] *KW* XXII (*SV* XIII 513-612).

[46] See *The Point of View for My Work as an Author*, in *The Point of View*, *KW* XXII (*SV* XIII 517): ". . . I now shall meet for the second time in literature my first work, the second edition of *Either/Or*, which I earlier was unwilling to have published." See also *Two Discourses at the Communion on Fridays*, *Without Authority*, *KW* XVIII (*SV* XII 267): "An authorship that began with *Either/Or* and advanced step by step . . .."

[47] See pp. 241-42.

[48] *JP* II 1587 (*Pap.* III A 1).

time, *From the Papers* (1838) and *Either/Or* (1843). In the first, the epic poet (novelist) is distinguished from the lyric poet by the role a comprehensive philosophy of life plays in giving organic coherence and depth to his epic productions.[49] In the dissertation, irony, controlled irony, is designated as the instrument of the poet who has gone beyond the first stage. "The more the poet has abandoned this [the immediacy of genius], the more necessary it is for him to have a totality-view of the world and in this way to be master over irony in his individual existence, and the more necessary it becomes for him to be something of a philosopher."[50]

If Part One of *Irony* is somewhat akin stylistically to *From the Papers*, *Either/Or* is a vast extension of the greater freedom in the style and in the play of ideas in Part Two of *Irony*. *Either/Or* as a whole and in its parts is clearly related to *Irony* also in substance. The first volume of *Either/Or* is the non-dissertation writer's sardonic development of the esthetic nihilism of romantic irony. The second volume and Judge William are the response of the ethical consciousness and the truly poetic. If Schlegel's *Lucinde* is regarded as the prime literary expression of romantic irony, *Either/Or* is in a sense Kierkegaard's *Vertraute Briefe contra Lucinde*,[51] with volume one as a witty, insightful, many-sided embodiment of the *Lucinde* stance[52] with a disclosure of its underlying despair, and volume two as a constructive approach that rescues the esthetic and the poetic from their self-anesthesia and destruction by transcending them and catching them up in the ethical consciousness.[53] Certain themes in *Irony* are developed in particular sections of *Either/Or:* Don Juan's sensuousness[54] in "The Musical Erotic," living poetically[55] in "The Seducer's Diary,"

[49] See *From the Papers of One Still Living*, *Early Polemical Writings*, *KW* I (*SV* XIII 73-74).
[50] P. 325.
[51] See p. 286 and note 97.
[52] See pp. 289-91.
[53] See pp. 300-01.
[54] See pp. 292-93.
[55] See pp. 288-89.

and the relation between substantiality and subjectivity[56] in the introduction to "The Tragic in Ancient Drama Reflected in the Tragic in Modern Drama." Certain important concepts embodied in a single word or phrase (for example, "transparency"[57] and the "absolute and eternal validity"[58]) are also developed further in *Either/Or*.

The theme of the first thesis (on the relation of Christ and Socrates) is the entire subject of *Philosophical Fragments* (1844), in which Socrates is presented as the highest representative of the relation between man and man with regard to essential truth and the teaching and learning of essential truth. Johannes Climacus then works out implications of the "if/then" question of going beyond Socrates or the relation of Socrates' recollection of eternal truth and eternal truth in time.

Similarly, the ramifications of other themes in *Irony*—immediacy, reflection, selfhood, subjectivity, objectivity, the esthetic, the ethical, the religious, and the transcendence of the human, individual and universal—are developed variously in the pseudonymous and the signed works. Thus the dissertation, although a work undertaken by Kierkegaard to some degree under external compulsion, was the seedbed of the entire authorship. This is emphasized in the comment Kierkegaard's friend Emil Boesen wrote to Hans Peter Barfod, an early editor of the *Papirer:* "It was only later that he really became clear about what he himself wanted and was able to do, and this breakthrough of the spirit occurred while he was writing *The Concept of Irony* and later during the engagement."[59]

Within the fortnight following the public defense of the dissertation, Kierkegaard conclusively terminated his engage-

[56] See pp. 262, 264, 270-71.

[57] See pp. 64, 74; *Either/Or*, II, pp. 160, 178-79, 189-90, 247-48, 252-54, 258, *KW* IV (*SV* II 146, 162, 171, 222, 227-28, 231). See also *The Sickness unto Death*, pp. 14, 124, 131, *KW* XIX (*SV* XI 128, 233, 241).

[58] See pp. 263-64, 326-29; *Either/Or*, II, pp. 206, 209, 231, 266, 269, *KW* IV (*SV* II 185, 188, 207, 239, 241).

[59] *Af Søren Kierkegaards Efterladte Papirer* [*E.P.*], I-IX, ed. Hans Peter Barfod and Hermann Gottsched (Copenhagen: 1869-81), I (1833-43), p. lii (ed. tr.).

ment to Regine Olsen (October 11, 1841; Regine's ring had been returned on August 11, 1841), and the day before the official royal authorization for the conferring of the degree was issued (October 26, 1841), he was on his way to hear Friedrich Wilhelm Joseph v. Schelling's lectures in Berlin.

For Kierkegaard, the Berlin episode was of threefold importance: the travel, the occasion, and the bracketed time for writing. Twice before, Kierkegaard had made a journey after crucial events had occurred: the Gilleleie journey and sojourn after his mother's death in 1834[60] and the Sæding pilgrimage after his father's death in 1838.[61] And now came the journey to Berlin following the rigors of the dissertation writing and defense and the tensions of the engagement. The first two journeys were "inland journeys,"[62] times of reflection. The Berlin journey and sojourn were more a time of instruction and production.

The occasion was the long-awaited "positive philosophy" of Schelling. In the *Papirer* there are only two early journal references to Schelling,[63] but Kierkegaard knew of Schelling's thought from H. L. Martensen's university lectures during the winter semester of 1838-1839,[64] and the auction catalog of Kierkegaard's library lists two Schelling works[65] published before 1841. The second journal entry indicates an estimate of Schelling[66] that must have heightened Kierkegaard's expectations for the Berlin lectures.

Georg Wilhelm Friedrich Hegel had died in 1831. In 1841, Schelling was appointed professor of philosophy at the University of Berlin with the task of combating Hegelianism.

[60] For Kierkegaard's reflections during that time, see especially *JP* V 5094 and note 109, 5100 (*Pap.* I A 63, 75).

[61] See Supplement, p. 440 (*Pap.* III A 34, 35, 73). See also *JP* V 5437-45, 5447-67, 5469-76 (*Pap.* III A 15-31, 40-72, 74-84).

[62] See *JP* II 1451; V 5726 (*Pap.* XI² A 171; V B 47:13).

[63] *JP* II 1190, 1589 (*Pap.* II A 31; III A 34).

[64] See *Pap.* II C 25 (suppl. vol. XII, pp. 313-20, 329-31).

[65] Schelling, *Philosophische Schriften*, I (Landshut: 1809; *ASKB* 763); *Vorlesungen über die Methode des academischen Studium* (Stuttgart, Tübingen: 1830; *ASKB* 764).

[66] "The view that Hegel is a parenthesis in Schelling seems to be more and more manifest; we are only waiting for the parenthesis to be closed."

Schelling regarded his own earlier philosophy as "negative" philosophy, the philosophy of "what," of essences. In Erlangen during the 1820s, Schelling had lectured also on "positive" philosophy. In the 1841-1842 lectures in Berlin, he proposed to consummate his philosophical program by developing positive philosophy, the philosophy of "that,"[67] a philosophy of nature, history, art, mythology, and religion, a philosophy of freedom, of existents, under the title *Philosophie der Offenbarung* [manifestation, revelation].[68]

Kierkegaard's high expectation for the lectures was shared by many throughout Europe. Among those present were Jakob Burkhardt, Swiss cultural historian, Friedrich Engels, one of Karl Marx's collaborators, and Russian philosopher Michael Bakunin. In a letter (December 14, 1841) to Emil Boesen, Kierkegaard wrote, "Schelling is lecturing to an extraordinary audience."[69] To Peter Johannes Spang, one of his teachers during Borgerdyds school days, he wrote:

> Schelling has commenced, but amidst so much noise and bustle, whistling, and knocking on the windows by those who cannot get in the door, in such an overcrowded lecture hall, that one is almost tempted to give up listening to him if this is to continue. I happened to sit between notable people—Prof. Werder[70] and Dr. Gruppe.[71] Schelling himself is

[67] See pp. 335-37.

[68] See pp. 335, 353-54, 375-77. The Berlin lectures were pirated by Heinrich Eberhard Gottlob Paulus prior to publication and published under the title *Die endlich offenbar gewordene positive Philosophie der Offenbarung oder Entstehungsgeschichte, wörtlicher Text, Beurtheilung und Berichtigung der v. Schellingischen Entdeckungen über Philosophie überhaupt, Mythologie und Offenbarung des dogmatischen Christenthums im Berliner Wintercursus von 1841-42. Der allgemeinen Prüfung vorgelegt von Dr. H.E.G. Paulus* (Darmstadt: 1843; repr. Frankfurt/M: Suhrkamp, 1977). Schelling brought suit against Paulus but lost the case. Schelling's revised edition appeared in 1858 under the title *Philosophie der Offenbarung*.

[69] See also *Letters*, Letter 54, p. 104, *KW* XXV.

[70] Karl Werder (1806-1893), German Hegelian philosopher, whose lectures on logic and metaphysics Kierkegaard attended in Berlin. See *JP* I 257; III 3285; V 5537 (*Pap*. III C 28, 30, 32); *Letters*, Letter 61, p. 119, *KW* XXV.

[71] Otto Friedrich Gruppe (1804-1876), German philosopher opposed to Hegelianism.

> a most insignificant man to look at; he looks like a tax collector, but he did promise to assist science, and us with it, to the flowering it has long deserved, to the highest it can attain. This would be gratifying enough for an old man, but for a young man it is always problematical to become contemporary with that rare flower at such an early age.[72] However, I have put my trust in Schelling and at the risk of my life I have the courage to hear him once more. It may very well blossom during the first lectures, and if so one might gladly risk one's life.[73]

To Professor Sibbern, Kierkegaard wrote:

> Schelling lectures to a select, numerous, and yet also an *undique conflatum auditorium* [audience blown together from everywhere]. During the first lectures it was almost a matter of risking one's life to hear him. I have never in my life experienced such uncomfortable crowding—still, what would one not do to be able to hear Schelling? His main point is always that there are two philosophies, one positive and one negative. The negative is given, but not by Hegel, for Hegel's is neither negative nor positive but a refined Spinozaism. The positive is yet to come.[74]

It was worth the risk—so thought Kierkegaard during the second lecture:

> I am so happy to have heard Schelling's second lecture—indescribably. I have been pining and thinking mournful thoughts long enough. The embryonic child of thought leapt for joy within me, as in Elizabeth,[75] when he mentioned the word "actuality"[76] in connection with the relation of philosophy to actuality. I remember almost every

[72] When he was twenty, Schelling (1775-1854) published his *Vom ICH als Prinzip der Philosophie, oder über das Unbedingte im menschlichen Wissen*, and, through the influence of Goethe, Schiller, and Fichte, was appointed professor of philosophy at Jena three years later.

[73] *Letters*, Letter 51, pp. 97-98, *KW* XXV.

[74] Ibid., Letter 55, p. 107.

[75] See Luke 1:41.

[76] See p. 335; *Either/Or*, I, p. 32, *KW* III (*SV* I 16).

> word he said after that. Here, perhaps, clarity can be achieved. This one word recalled all my philosophical pains and sufferings. —And so that she, too, might share my joy, how willingly I would return to her, how eagerly I would coax myself to believe that this is the right course. —Oh, if only I could! —now I have put all my hope in Schelling . . . .[77]

As time went on, however, Kierkegaard's estimate of Schelling's lectures decreased. To Emil Boesen, he wrote January 16, 1842: "Schelling's most recent lectures have not been of much significance."[78] On February 6, he wrote to Boesen: "I have completely given up on Schelling. I merely listen to him, write nothing down either there or at home."[79] To his brother Peter Christian, he wrote in February:

> Dear Peter,
>
> Schelling talks the most insufferable nonsense. If you want to get some idea of it, I must ask you—for your own punishment, even though voluntarily assumed—to submit yourself to the following experiment. Imagine Pastor R[othe]'s[80] harebrained philosophy, his whole accidental character in the scholarly world; imagine in addition the late Pastor Hornsyld's[81] persistence in the betrayal of learning; imagine these combined and then add the insolence in which no philosopher has outdone Schelling; keep all this vividly in your poor brain, and then walk out to the workhouse in Our Savior's parish or to the work halls at Ladegaarden,[82] and you will have an idea of the Schelling philosophy and of the circumstances in which it is presented. To

[77] *JP* V 5535 (*Pap*. III A 179).

[78] *Letters*, Letter 62, p. 125, *KW* XXV.

[79] Ibid., Letter 68, p. 138.

[80] Waldemar Henrik Rothe (1777-1857), whose dissertation had been reviewed by J. L. Heiberg in *Perseus*, I, 1837, pp. 1-89. See p. 2 and note 2.

[81] Jens Hornsyld (1757-1840), a frequent contributor to *Theologisk Maanedsskrift*, ed. Nicolai Frederik Severin Grundtvig and Andreas Gottlob Rudelbach.

[82] A Copenhagen workhouse for indigents and criminals.

> make matters worse, he has now gotten the idea of lecturing longer than is customary, and therefore I have gotten the idea that I will not attend the lectures as long as I otherwise would have. Question: Whose idea is the better? —In other words, I have nothing more to do in Berlin. My time does not allow me to ingest drop by drop what I would hardly willingly open my mouth to swallow all at once. I am too old to attend lectures, just as Schelling is too old to give them. His whole doctrine of potencies[83] betrays the highest degree of impotence.
>
> I shall leave Berlin as soon as possible. I am coming to Copenhagen. A stay there is necessary for me so that I can bring a little order into my affairs again. You see how strange it is. I have never in my life felt like traveling as much as I do now. I owe that to Schelling. Had Schelling not lectured in Berlin, I would not have gone, and had Schelling not been so nonsensical, I would probably never have traveled again. Now I have learned that it is worthwhile to travel, but *nota bene*, not for the sake of studying. But I can talk about that with you in Copenhagen. I cannot now set out on a proper journey abroad. All things must have their particular stages with me. I shall leave Copenhagen again as soon as I have finished a little work I am engaged in.[84]

Kierkegaard's progressive disappointment with the lectures was due to Schelling's virtual abandonment of his initial distinction between *quid sit* [what it is] and *quod sit* [that it is]. The lectures culminated in a historical philosophy of mythology and religion. At least for Kierkegaard, there was scarcely the seed of existentialism sometimes claimed for the Berlin lectures.[85] To paraphrase the first Latin thesis of *The Concept of Irony: similitudo Kierkegaardem inter et Schellingem in dissimilitu-*

[83] See pp. 336-40, 372-97.

[84] *Letters*, Letter 70, p. 141, *KW* XXV. The "little work" was *Either/Or*. See p. 81.

[85] See Frederick Copleston, *A History of Philosophy*, I-IX (Westminster, Md., and New York: Newman, 1946-75), VII, pp. 147-48.

dine praecipue est posite.[86] Besides attending the Schelling lectures and carefully rewriting his notes in his room at Mittelstrasse 61, *eine Treppe hoch*, Kierkegaard heard lectures by Philipp Marheineke, Karl Werder, and Henrich Steffens.[87] His great omission was the philosopher Friedrich Adolph Trendelenburg, of whom he later wrote:

> The first time I was in Berlin, Trendelenburg was the only one I did not take the trouble to hear—to be sure, he was said to be a Kantian. And I practically ignored the young Swede traveling with me who intended to study only under Trendelenburg. Oh, foolish opinion to which I also was in bondage at the time.[88]

Although Kierkegaard was satisfied with only the first of his purposes in journeying to Berlin, the recreational value of travel, and disappointed with the second, the Schelling lectures, he must have been greatly pleased with the yield of the third, the bracketed time for writing. To Emil Boesen, he wrote (February 6) more specifically about "the little work I am engaged in," to which he had alluded in his letter to Peter Christian:

> My dear Emil,
>
> Schelling talks endless nonsense both in an extensive and an intensive sense. I am leaving Berlin and hastening to Copenhagen, but not, you understand, to be bound by a new tie, oh no, for I feel more strongly than ever that I need my freedom. A person with my eccentricity should have his freedom until he meets a force in life that, as such, can bind him. I am coming to Copenhagen to complete Either/Or. It is my favorite idea, and in it I exist. You will see that this idea is not to be made light of. In no way can my life yet be

[86] See p. 5. In Anton Mirko Koktanek, *Schellings Seinslehre und Kierkegaard* (Munich: Oldenbourg, 1962), p. 65, Karl Jaspers is quoted (*Die geistige Situation der Zeit* [Berlin: Gruyter, 1931], p. 145) as saying that Schelling is " '*erst entdeckbar, wenn man von Kierkegaard kommt*' " [discoverable only if one comes from Kierkegaard].

[87] See *Letters*, Letters 49, 51, 55, *KW* XXV.

[88] *JP* V 5978 (*Pap.* VIII¹ A 18).

> considered finished. I feel I still have great resources within me.
>
> I do owe Schelling something. For I have learned that I enjoy traveling, even though not for the sake of studying. As soon as I have finished Either/Or, I shall fly away again like a happy bird. I must travel. Formerly I never had the inclination for it, but first I must finish Either/Or, and that I can do only in Copenhagen.
>
> What do you think of that? Probably you have missed me at times, but have a little patience and I shall soon be with you. My brain has not yet become barren and infertile, words still flow from my lips, and this eloquence of mine, which you at least appreciate, has not yet been stilled.[89]

February 4, 1842, is the last date given on a summary of a Schelling lecture. On March 6, 1842, Kierkegaard arrived in Copenhagen from Kiel on the steamship *Christian VIII*. His Berlin sojourn had been invigorating and productive, and he came home so eager to continue his writing that by April 14 he finished "The Seducer's Diary,"[90] the latter portion of Part I of *Either/Or*, and before the end of the year the entire manuscript was ready for the printer. On February 15, 1843, appeared this pseudonymous, ironical, philosophical-poetic sequel (although unrecognizable as such to most readers) to Magister Kierkegaard's ironical dissertation on the concept of irony.

[89] *Letters*, Letter 69, p. 139, *KW* XXV.
[90] See *Pap*. III B 168:3.

THE CONCEPT OF IRONY
WITH CONTINUAL REFERENCE TO SOCRATES

---

by Søren Kierkegaard

XIII 96 *Dissertationem hanc inauguralem Philosophorum in Universitate Hauniensi Ordo dignam censuit, quae una cum thesibus adjectis rite defensa auctori gradum Magisterii artium acquirat.*

Dabam d. XVI Julii MDCCCLI.[1]

F. C. Sibbern,[2]
h. a. Decanus fac. philos.

[The Faculty of Philosophy of the University of Copenhagen has judged this inaugural dissertation worthy, which, together with the additional theses, having been duly defended, acquires for the author the degree of Master of Arts.[3]

July 16, 1851

F. C. Sibbern,

Current Dean of the Faculty of Philosophy]

THESES, XIII 97

DISSERTATIONI DANICAE DE NOTIONE IRONIAE

ANNEXAE

QUAS

AD JURA MAGISTRI ARTIUM
IN UNIVERSITATE HAFNIENSI RITE OBTINENDA
die XXIX Septemb.
HORA 10[4]
PUBLICO COLLOQUIO DEFENDERE CONABITUR.[5]

Severinus Aabye Kierkegaard,
theol. cand.

MDCCCLXI.[6]

[THESES,
attached to
the dissertation in Danish on the Concept of Irony
which
Søren Aabye Kierkegaard, B.Th.,
will endeavor to defend in a public colloquium
September 29
10 o'clock
in order to obtain in the appointed manner
the degree of Master of Arts
1861]

THESES XIII 99

I. Similitudo Christum inter et Socratem in dissimilitudine praecipue est posita.

II. Xenophonticus Socrates in utilitate inculcanda subsistit, nunquam empiriam egreditur nunquam ad ideam pervenit.

III. Si quis comparationem inter Xenophontem et Platonem instituerit, inveniet, alterum nimium de Socrate detraxi[s]se, alterum nimium eum evexi[s]se, neutrum verum invenisse.

IV. Forma interrogationis, quam adhibuit Plato, refert negativum illud, quod est apud Hegelium.

V. Apola[o]gia Socratis, quam exhibuit Plato aut spuria est, aut tota ironice explicanda.

VI. Socrates non solum ironia usus est, sed adeo fuit ironiae deditus, ut ipse illi succumberet.

VII. Aristophanes in Socrate depingendo proxime ad verum accessit.

VIII. Ironia, ut infinita et absoluta negativitas, est levissima XIII 100
et maxime exigua subjectivitatis significatio.

IX. Socrates omnes aequales ex substantialitate tanquam ex naufragio nudos expulit, realitatem subvertit, idealitatem eminus prospexit, attigit non occupavit.

X. Socrates primus ironiam introduxit.

XI. Recentior ironia inprimis ad ethicen revocanda est.

XII. Hegelius in ironia describenda modo ad recentiorem non ita ad veterem attendit.

XIII. Ironia non tam ipsa est sensus expers, tenerioribus animi motibus destituta, quam aegritudo habenda ex eo, quod alter quoque potiatur eo, quod ipsa concupierit.

XIV. Solgerus non animi pietate commotus, sed mentis invidia seductus, quum negativum cogitare et cogitando subigere nequiret, acosmismum effecit.

XV. Ut a dubitatione philosophia sic ab ironia vita digna, quae humana vocetur, incipit.

[I. The similarity between Christ and Socrates consists essentially in their dissimilarity.

II. The Xenophontic Socrates stops with an emphasis on the useful; he never goes beyond the empirical, never arrives at the idea.

III. If a comparison is made between Xenophon and Plato, one will find that the first takes too much from Socrates, the second raised him too high; neither of them finds the truth.

IV. The form of interrogation employed by Plato corresponds to the negative in Hegel.

V. Socrates' defense, as presented by Plato, is either spurious or is to be interpreted altogether ironically.

VI. Socrates not only used irony but was so dedicated to irony that he himself succumbed to it.

VII. Aristophanes has come very close to the truth in his depiction of Socrates.

VIII. Irony as infinite and absolute negativity is the lightest and weakest indication of subjectivity.

IX. Socrates drove all his contemporaries out of substantiality as if naked from a shipwreck, undermined actuality, envisioned ideality in the distance, touched it, but did not take possession of it.

X. Socrates was the first to introduce irony.

XI. The more recent irony belongs essentially under ethics.

XII. Hegel in his description of irony has considered only the more recent form, not so much the ancient.

XIII. Irony is not so much apathy, devoid of the more tender emotions of the soul; instead, it must rather be regarded as vexation at the possession also by others of that which it desires for itself.

XIV. Solger, not moved by piety of soul but seduced by envy of mind because he could not think the negative or subdue it by thought, adopted acosmism.

XV. Just as philosophy begins with doubt, so also a life that may be called human begins with irony].[7]

Part One

THE POSITION OF SOCRATES VIEWED AS IRONY

[8]If there is anything that must be praised in modern philosophical endeavor in its magnificent manifestation, it certainly is the power of genius with which it seizes and holds on to the phenomenon. Now if it is fitting for the phenomenon, which as such is always *foeminini generis* [of the feminine gender], to surrender to the stronger on account of its feminine nature, then in all fairness one can also demand of the philosophical knight a deferential propriety and a profound enthusiasm, in place of which one sometimes hears too much the jingling of spurs and the voice of the master. The observer ought to be an amorist; he must not be indifferent to any feature, any factor. But on the other hand he ought to have a sense of his own predominance—but should use it only to help the phenomenon obtain its full disclosure. Therefore, even if the observer does bring the concept along with him, it is still of great importance that the phenomenon remain inviolate and that the concept be seen as coming into existence [*tilblivende*] through the phenomenon.[9]

Before I proceed to an exposition of the concept of irony, it is necessary to make sure that I have a reliable and authentic view of Socrates' historical-actual, phenomenological existence with respect to the question of its possible relation to the transformed view that was his fate through enthusiastic or envious contemporaries. This becomes inescapably necessary, because the concept of irony makes its entry into the world through Socrates.[10] Concepts, just like individuals, have their history and are no more able than they to resist the dominion
of time, but in and through it all they nevertheless harbor a XIII
kind of homesickness for the place of their birth. Indeed, phi- 106
losophy can now on one side no more disregard the recent history of this concept than it can stop with its earliest history, no matter how copious and interesting. Philosophy continually demands something more, demands the eternal, the

true, compared with which even the most sterling existence is in itself just a fortunate moment. On the whole, the relation of philosophy to history is like that of a father confessor to a penitent and therefore like him ought to have a sensitive, perceptive ear for the secrets of the penitent but, having examined the whole sequence of confessed sins, is then also able to make this manifest to the penitent as something else. Just as the individual making a confession is certainly able not only to reel off the incidents of his life chronologically but also to relate them entertainingly but still does not comprehend them himself, so history certainly is also able to declare the eventful life of the human race with pathos and in a loud voice but must leave it to the senior* (philosophy) to explain it and is then able to relish the delightful surprise that at first is almost unwilling to acknowledge the copy provided by philosophy but gradually, to the degree that it familiarizes itself with this philosophical view, eventually regards this as the actual truth and the other as apparent truth.

Thus there are these two elements that constitute the essential issue [*Mellemværende*[12]] between history and philosophy. Both of them ought to have their rights so that, on the one XIII 107 hand, the phenomenon has its rights** and is not to be intimidated and discouraged by philosophy's superiority, and philosophy, on the other hand, is not to let itself be infatuated by

* Some may take exception to my calling philosophy the senior, but I am assuming, of course, that the eternal is older than the temporal, and even though philosophy in many ways comes later than history, it in fact instantly makes such a monumental step that it passes the temporal, considers itself to be the eternal *prius* [first][11] and, reflecting ever more deeply about itself, recollects itself further and further back in time into eternity, does not recollect it into eternity in reverie but, more and more awake, recollects it not as the past but recollects the past as a present.

** Philosophy relates itself in this respect to history—in its truth, as eternal life to the temporal according to the Christian view—in its untruth, as eternal life to the temporal according to the Greek and the antique view in general. XIII 107 According to the latter view, eternal life began when one drank of the river Lethe in order to forget the past;[13] according to the former, eternal life is attended by the bone-and-marrow-piercing consciousness of every idle word that is spoken.[14]

the charms of the particular, is not to be distracted by the superabundance of the particular. The same holds for the concept of irony: philosophy is not to look too long at one particular side of its phenomenological existence and above all at its appearance but is to see the truth of the concept in and with the phenomenological.

It is common knowledge, of course, that tradition has linked the word "irony" to the existence of Socrates, but it by no means follows that everyone knows what irony is. Moreover, if through an intimate acquaintance with Socrates' life and way of living someone gained a notion of his singularity, he still would not therefore have a total concept of what irony is. In saying this, we are by no means nourishing the distrust of historical existence that would identify becoming [*Vordelsen*] with a falling away from the idea,[15] since it is much more the unfolding of the idea. This, to repeat, is far from our intention, but on the other hand neither can one assume that a specific element of existence as such would be absolutely adequate to the idea. In other words, just as it has been correctly pointed out that nature is unable to adhere to the concept[16]—partly because each particular phenomenon contains but one element, and partly because the whole sum of natural existence is still always an imperfect medium that engenders longing [*Forlængsel*] rather than gratification[17]—so also something similar can legitimately be said about history, inasmuch as every single fact does indeed evolve, but only as an element, and the whole sum of historical existence is still not the completely adequate medium of the idea, since it is the idea's temporality and fragmentariness (just as nature is its spatiality) that long for the backward-looking repulse emanating, face to and against face,[18] from the consciousness.

This must be enough on the difficulty inherent in any philosophical conception of history and the care that therefore ought to be taken. Special situations, however, may be attended with new difficulties, which is especially the case in the present inquiry. For example, what Socrates himself prized so highly, namely, standing still and contemplating[19]—in other words, silence—this is his whole life in terms of world history.

XIII 108 He has left nothing by which a later age can judge him; indeed, even if I were to imagine myself his contemporary, he would still always be difficult to comprehend. In other words, he belonged to the breed of persons with whom the outer as such is not the stopping point. The outer continually pointed to something other and opposite. He was not like a philosopher delivering his opinions in such a way that just the lecture itself is the presence of the idea, but what Socrates said meant something different.[20] The outer was not at all in harmony with the inner[21] but was rather its opposite, and only under this angle of refraction[22] is he to be comprehended. Therefore, the question of a view in regard to Socrates is quite different from what it is in regard to most other people. Because of this, Socrates can of necessity be comprehended only through a combined reckoning. But since we are now separated from him by centuries, and even his own age could not apprehend him in his immediacy, it is easy to see that it becomes doubly difficult for us to reconstruct his existence, inasmuch as we must strive to comprehend an already complicated view by means of a new combined reckoning. If we now say that irony constituted the substance of his existence (this is, to be sure, a contradiction, but it is supposed to be that), and if we further postulate that irony is a negative concept,[23] it is easy to see how difficult it becomes to fix the picture of him—indeed, it seems impossible or at least as difficult as to picture a nisse[24] with the cap that makes him invisible.

I XIII 109

The View Made Possible

We shall now move to a summary of the views of Socrates provided by his closest contemporaries. In this respect there are three who command our attention: Xenophon, Plato, and Aristophanes. I cannot fully agree with Baur,* who thinks that, along with Plato, Xenophon should be most highly regarded. Xenophon stopped with Socrates' immediacy and thus has definitely misunderstood him in many ways;**
whereas Plato and Aristophanes have blazed a trail through XIII 110
the tough exterior to a view of the infinity that is incommensurable with the multifarious events of his life. Thus it can be said of Socrates that just as he walked through life continually between a caricature and the ideal, so after his death he continues to stroll between those two. As for the relation between Xenophon and Plato, Baur is correct in saying on page 123: "Zwischen diesen Beiden tritt uns aber sogleich eine Differenz entgegen, die in mancher Hinsicht mit dem bekannten Verhältnisz verglichen werden kann, welches zwischen den synoptischen Evangelien und dem des Johannes stattfindet. Wie die synoptischen Evangelien

* F. C. Baur, *Das Christliche des Platonismus oder Sokrates und Christus*[25] (Tübingen: 1837).

** I cite, as an example, the person who ate nothing but meat *(Memorabilia,* III, 14, 2).[26] There are two alternatives here: either this is one of those infinitely profound ironies that treat the most trivial matters with deep earnestness and precisely thereby most penetratingly mock everything; or it is nonsense, one of Socrates' weak moments when an ironic nemesis made him sink down into the sphere of the exceedingly trivial (more on that later[27]). But neither alternative is the case with Xenophon; his version ends with the youth presumably not sinking so far into melancholy that he gave up eating meat altogether, τὸ μὲν ὄψον οὐκ ἐπαύσατο ἐσθίων, but became so morally improved that he ate bread with it (ἄρτον δὲ προσέλαβεν).

zunächst mehr nur die äussere, mit der jüdischen Messias-Idee zusammenhängende, Seite der Erscheinung Christi darstellen, das johanneische aber vor allem seine höhere Natur und das unmittelbar Göttliche in ihm ins Auge faszt, so hat auch der platonische Sokrates eine weit höhere ideellere Bedeutung als der xenophontische, mit welchem wir uns im Grunde immer nur auf dem Boden der Verhältnisse des unmittelbaren praktischen Lebens befinden [Yet we instantly encounter a difference between these two that in many respects may be likened to the well-known relation between the Synoptic Gospels and the Gospel of John. Just as the Synoptic Gospels present primarily only the external aspect of Christ's appearance, the aspect connected with the Jewish idea of the Messiah, whereas the Gospel of John above all captures his higher nature and the immediately divine within him, so also the Platonic Socrates does indeed have an ideal significance far higher than the Xenophontic Socrates, with whom we in effect always find ourselves on the flat and even level of conditions belonging to the immediate practical life]." Baur's comment is not only striking but also to the point when one remembers that Xenophon's view of Socrates differs from the Synoptic Gospels in that the latter merely recorded the immediate, accurate picture of Christ's immediate existence[28] (which, please note, did not signify anything else* than what it was), and insofar

* Christ himself declares: "ἐγώ εἰμι ἡ ὁδὸς καὶ ἡ ἀλήθεια καὶ ἡ ζωή [I am the way, the truth, and the life],"[29] and as for the apostles' view of him, it was palpable—not an ingenious work of art. "Ὃ ἀκηκόαμεν, ὃ ἑωράκαμεν τοῖς ὀφθαλμοῖς ἡμῶν, ὃ ἐθεασάμεθα, καὶ αἱ χεῖρες ἡμῶν ἐψηλάφησαν [That which we have heard, which we have seen with our eyes, which we have looked upon, and our hands have handled]" (I John 1:1). For this reason, Christ also declares that kings and princes have longed to *see him*,[30] whereas Socrates, as already noted, was invisible to his age. Socrates was invisible and visible only through hearing (*loquere ut videam te* [speak so that I may see you]).[31] On the whole, Socrates' existence was apparent, not transparent. So much for Christ's existence. As for what he said, one could always take him at his word; his words were life and spirit. Socrates could only be misunderstood through his words,
XIII and he was enlivening only by way of negativity. —On the whole, I could
111 wish (if this wish were not already outside the scope of this study) that I

as Matthew's seeming to have an apologetic objective, the XIII 111
question at that time was to reconcile Christ's life with the idea of the Messiah, whereas Xenophon is dealing with a man whose immediate existence means something else than meets the eye at first glance, and insofar as he mounts a defense of him, he does this only in the form of an appeal to a subtilizing, right-honorable age. On the other hand, the comment about Plato's relation to John is also correct if one simply holds fast to the position that John found and immediately perceived in Christ everything that he, precisely by restraining himself to silence, presents in all its objectivity, because his eyes were opened to the immediate divinity in Christ; whereas Plato creates his Socrates by means of poetic productivity, since Socrates, precisely in his immediate existence, was only *negative*.

But first an exposition of each one separately.

XENOPHON

As a preliminary, we must recall that Xenophon had an objective (this is already a deficiency or an irksome redundancy*)—namely, to show what a scandalous injustice it was for the Athenians to condemn Socrates to death. Indeed, Xenophon succeeded in this to such a singular degree that one would be more inclined to believe that it was Xenophon's objective to prove that it was foolishness or an error on the part of the Athenians to condemn Socrates, for Xenophon defends Socrates in such a way that he renders him not only innocent but also altogether innocuous—so

---

would be permitted within the sphere of this inquiry to explore the relation between Socrates and Christ,[32] about which Baur in the book just cited has said so much that is noteworthy, despite the fact that there still is always a modest little asthmatic doubt in me that the similarity consists in dissimilarity[33] and that there is an analogy only because there is a contrast.

* Xenophon had so much distrust both of Socrates and of the truth in general that he did not dare allow Socrates to stand on his own feet and therefore was always ready to urge how unfair, how unjust it was of the Athenians, how completely different it appeared to him.[34]

much so that we wonder greatly about what kind of daimon must have bewitched the Athenians to such a degree
XIII 112 that they were able to see more in him than in any other good-natured, garrulous, droll character who does neither good nor evil, does not stand in anyone's way, and is so fervently well-intentioned toward the whole world if only it will listen to his slipshod nonsense. And what *harmonia praestabilita* [preestablished harmony][35] in lunacy, what higher unity in madness is there not inherent in Plato's and the Athenians' uniting to put to death and immortalize such a good-natured bourgeois as that? This, after all, would be an incomparable irony upon the world. Plato and the Athenians must have felt almost as uncomfortable with Xenophon's irenic intervention as one feels at times in an argument when—just as the point in dispute, precisely by being brought to a head, begins to be interesting—a helpful third party kindly takes it upon himself to reconcile the disputants, to take the whole matter back to a triviality. Finally, by eliminating all that was dangerous in Socrates, Xenophon actually reduced him totally *in absurdum*, in recompense, probably, for Socrates' having done this so often to others.

What makes it even more difficult to get a clear notion of Socrates' personality from Xenophon's account is the *total lack of situation.* The base on which the specific conversation moves is just as invisible and shallow as a straight line, just as monotonous as the single-color background that children and Nürnberg painters customarily use in their pictures. Yet situation was immensely important to Socrates' personality, which must have given an intimation of itself precisely by a secretive presence in and a mystical floating over the multicolored variety of exuberant Athenian life and which must have been explained by a duplexity of existence, much as the flying fish in relation to fish and birds. This emphasis on situation was especially significant in order to indicate that the true center for Socrates was not a fixed point but an *ubique et nusquam* [everywhere and nowhere],

in order to accentuate the Socratic sensibility, which upon the most subtle and fragile contact immediately detected the presence of idea, promptly felt the corresponding electricity present in everything, in order to make graphic the genuine Socratic method, which found no phenomenon too humble a point of departure from which to work oneself up into the sphere of thought. This Socratic possibility of beginning anywhere, actualized in life (although it no doubt would most often be overlooked by the crowd, for whom the way they ever came upon this or that subject always
remains a riddle, because their discussions often end and XIII
begin in a stagnating* village pond), this unerring Socratic 113
magnifying glass for which no subject was so compact that he did not immediately discern the idea** in it (not gropingly but with immediate sureness, and yet also with a practiced eye of his own for the apparent foreshortenings of

* For Socrates nothing was static in this sense; what we read in the Gospel story about the water in the pool of Bethesda[36] also holds true for his view of knowledge—it was healing only when it was agitated.

** Inasmuch as I am here interpreting Socrates' view of the relation of idea to phenomenon as a positive one, thereby prompting the alert reader to find me guilty of a self-contradiction with respect to my later conception of this relation according to the Socratic point of view, I take the liberty of just a few comments. In the first place, it is based on Socrates' polemic against the Sophists, who were totally unable to cope with actuality [*Virkelighed*], whose speculation finally became so high-flying and their eloquence so hyperbolized that in the end they could say nothing at all because of an excess of ideas. In contrast to this, Socrates always dwelt on the lowest aspects of life, on food and drink, on shoemakers, tanners, on shepherds and pack asses, and by forcing the Sophists down into this sphere, he compelled them to recognize their own pretense. But, in the second place, existence [*Existens*] itself for Socrates was still only metaphor, not an element in the idea, and this shows his idea to be abstract. This is strengthened even more by the fact that he had no qualitative determinants with respect to the phenomenon's relation to the idea; to him one thing was just as good as another because everything was always metaphor and only metaphor—just as one must also regard it as a sign of having the idea only in abstraction when one finds that God is just as perceptibly present in a straw as in world history, since it all boils down to his really being present nowhere, and finally the idea Socrates had was always the dialectical, the logical idea—more on that later.[37]

perspective, and thus he did not attract the subject to him by subreption but simply kept the same ultimate prospect in sight, while for the listener and observer it emerged step by step), this Socratic modest frugality that formed such a sharp contrast to the Sophist's empty noise and unsatiating gorging—all this one might wish that Xenophon had let us perceive. And what life would then have come into the
XIII 114 presentation if in the midst of the bustling work of the artisans and the braying of the pack-asses one had discerned the divine woof with which Socrates interlaced the web of existence. If through the boisterous noise of the marketplace one had heard the divine fundamental harmony[38] that resounded through existence [*Tilværelse*] (since for Socrates every single thing was a metaphorical and not inappropriate symbol of the idea), what an interesting conflict there would have been between the earthly life's most routine forms of expression and Socrates, who seemed to be saying the very same thing. This importance of situation is not lacking in Plato, however, although it is purely poetical, and thus demonstrates precisely its own validity and the lack in Xenophon.

But just as Xenophon on the one hand lacks an eye for situation, so on the other he lacks an ear for rejoinder. Not that the questions Socrates asks and the answers he gives are incorrect—on the contrary, they are all too correct, all too stubborn, all too tedious.* With Socrates, rejoinder was not an immediate unity with what had been said, was not a flowing out but a continual flowing back, and what one misses in Xenophon is an ear for the infinitely resonating reverse echoing[40] of the rejoinder in the personality (for as a rule the rejoinder is straightforward transmission of thought by way of sound).

* Therefore, if Xenophon's understanding of Socrates is correct, I believe that in sophisticated, inquisitive Athens people would rather have wanted Socrates done away with because he bored them than because they feared him. Admittedly, the fact that Socrates bored them would have been just as valid a reason to execute him as Aristides' justice was a valid reason for the Athenians to exile him.[39]

The more Socrates tunneled under existence [*Existents*], the more deeply and inevitably each single remark had to gravitate toward an ironic totality, a spiritual condition that was infinitely bottomless, invisible, and indivisible. Xenophon had no intimation whatever of this secret. Allow me to illustrate what I mean by a picture. There is a work that represents Napoleon's grave. Two tall trees shade the grave. There is nothing else to see in the work, and the unsophisticated observer sees nothing else. Between the two trees there is an empty space; as the eye follows the outline, suddenly Napoleon himself emerges from this nothing, and now it is impossible to have him disappear again. Once the eye has seen him, it goes on seeing him with an almost alarming necessity. So also with Socrates' rejoinders. One hears his words in the XIII
same way one sees the trees; his words mean what they say, 115
just as the trees are trees. There is not one single syllable that gives a hint of any other interpretation, just as there is not one single line that suggests Napoleon, and yet this empty space, this nothing, is what hides that which is most important. Just as in nature we find sites so remarkably arranged that those who stand closest to the one who is speaking cannot hear him and only those standing at a specific spot, often at some distance, can hear, so also with Socrates' rejoinders, if we only bear in mind that at this point to hear is identical with understanding and not to hear with misunderstanding. It is these two fundamental defects I must in a provisional way point out in Xenophon, and yet situation and rejoinder are the combination that makes up the personality's ganglionic and cerebral system.

We proceed now to a *collection of observations* found in Xenophon and attributed to Socrates. Generally speaking, these observations are so scrubby and stunted that it is not difficult but is deadening for the eye to take in the whole lot at one glance. Only rarely does an observation rise to a poetic or a philosophic thought; and despite the beautiful language, the exposition has exactly the same flavor as the profundities of our *Folkeblad*[41] or the heavenly parish-clerk[42] caterwauling of a nature-worshiping normal-school student.*

XIII 116 Proceeding now to the Socratic observations preserved by Xenophon, we shall attempt to trace their possible family resemblance, even though they often seem to be children of different marriages.

* Only rarely does one hear in this degenerate prose a comment that still has a remnant of its heavenly origin, although always with a disturbing additive. As an example, I shall for Xenophon's sake quote *Mem.*, I, 1, 8. Socrates is speaking of the things that human sagacity itself can do, and then adds: "τὰ δὲ μέγιστα τῶν ἐν τούτοις ἔφη τοὺς θεοὺς ἑαυτοῖς καταλείπεσθαι· οὔτε γάρ τοι τῷ καλῶς ἀγρὸν φυτευσαμένῳ δῆλον ὅστις καρπώσεται κτλ [but the deepest secrets of these matters the gods reserved to themselves; you may plant a field well; but you know not who shall gather the fruits etc.]."[43] The Socratic is in this suggestion of the contrast between the rush and pressure of human activity and what is accomplished even within the boundaries that define human activity. The Socratic way is first of all to sketch the territory that is inaccessible to human knowledge (para. 6: "περὶ δὲ τῶν ἀδήλων ὅπως ἀποβήσοιτο, μαντευσομένους ἔπεμπεν, εἰ ποιητέα [but if the consequences could not be foreseen, he sent them to the oracle to inquire whether the thing ought to be done]") and there-
XIII 116 after to suggest what human beings themselves are capable of accomplishing, and then, when the mind is resting at anchor in this security, suddenly to rouse it up by showing that even here they are unable to achieve anything, by thawing the ice, as it were, in which they had become icebound and settled as if on the mainland, and to let them again drift with the current. But we must not miss the irony, because it is precisely this that wrests from them this conclusion. But this is lacking in Xenophon, since this observation is introduced with the words τὰ δὲ μέγιστα [but the deepest] (of course, Socratically it would have read: the little difficulty still remaining etc.). On the other hand, neither must we be without the possibility of, the disposition to, and the threat of a dogmatic view that must have been peculiar to Socrates. In order to substantiate his remark that especially in finite matters the gods had kept the greatest for themselves, Socrates shows that no one knows his future fate and that as a consequence this ignorance is a rock upon which every shrewd insurance can run aground. We might rather have expected that Socrates, precisely when to all appearances he makes people self-active, would have emphasized that they were never the deity's co-workers[44] at all, that all their bustling activity was a nothing or merely a receiving, so that even if they dug with machines instead of with hand tools and ploughed furrows six feet deep, they still would not find fruitfulness in the earth if the deity did not will it. For the ignorance of one's finite fate, which Socrates here points out as the human race's common lot, was of course never unfamiliar to men, whereas this total incapacity, which in the realm of doing is the proper analogy to total igno-

We trust that the readers will agree with our statement that XIII 117
the empirical determinant is the polygon,[48] that the intuition is the circle, and that the qualitative difference[49] between them will continue forevermore. In Xenophon, gadding observation always wanders about in the polygon, presumably often victim of its own deception, when, just by having a good distance yet to go, it believes that it has found the true infinity and, like an insect crawling along a polygon, falls off because what appeared to be an infinity was only an angle.

In Xenophon, one of the points of departure for Socratic teaching is the useful. But the useful is simply the polygon, which corresponds to the interior infinity of the good emanating from and returning to itself, indifferent to none of its own elements but moving in all of them and totally in all of

---

rance in the realm of knowledge, always needed the injunctions of a Socrates. —Someone could of course argue that in the very passage just mentioned there is reference to the hidden possibility in the secret deliberations of the gods, to the outcome that the contrast is between what cannot be the object of any calculation whatever and what at first glance surely seems to lend itself to calculation. But in any case everyone will surely admit that irony is lacking here and that doing it as just suggested would give far more Socratic insight into the nature and being of man, because then Socrates would place man in collision not with chance but with necessity. Of course, it was possible that hail could destroy the farmer's crop, but that there should be no germination capacity in the earth, despite all the human operations, if the deity did not will it so—this is a still more profound negation. The one is a conception of possibility as possibility, the other an attempt to make even actuality appear as a XIII 117
hypothetical possibility. —To cite another example where Socrates, even in the Xenophon version, seems to approach irony, there is the well-known dialogue with Critias and Charmides in *Mem.*, I, 2. But here Socrates is moving more in the territory of the Sophists (para. 36: "μηδ' ἀποκρίνωμαι οὖν, ἔφη, ἄν τίς με ἐρωτᾷ νέος, ἐὰν εἰδῶ, οἷον, ποῦ οἰκεῖ Χαρικλῆς; ἤ, ποῦ ἐστι Κριτίας [Am I to give no answer, then, if a young man asks me something that I know?—for instance, 'Where does Charicles live?' or 'Where is Critias?']").[45] Consequently this is only as ironic as Sophists can be but is still qualitatively different from irony. More on this later.[46] Strangely enough, Charicles is actually more witty than Socrates—at least his well-known answer far outdoes him: "φυλάττου, ὅπως μὴ καὶ σὺ ἐλάττους τὰς βοῦς ποιήσῃς [Watch, else *you* may find the cattle decrease]."[47] —I have elaborated these two examples in some detail in order to show that, even when Xenophon wanders closest to a view of Socrates, one still does not come to see his two faces but merely something that is neither the one nor the other.

them and totally in each one. The useful has an infinite dialectic and also an infinite spurious dialectic. In other words, the useful is the external dialectic of the good, its negation, which detached becomes in itself merely a kingdom of shadows where nothing endures but everything formless and shapeless liquifies and volatilizes, all according to the observer's capricious and superficial glance, in which each individual existence is only an infinitely divisible fractional existence in a perpetual calculation. (The useful mediates everything for its own ends, even the useless, since, just as nothing is absolutely use-
XIII ful, neither can anything be absolutely useless, because the ab-
118 solutely useful is merely a fleeting element in the fitful changes of life.) This universal view of the useful is developed in the dialogue with Aristippus[50] (*Mem.*, III, 8). Whereas in Plato it is Socrates in particular who always takes his subject from the accidental concretion in which his associates see it and leads it on to the abstract,[51] in Xenophon it is Socrates in particular who demolishes Aristippus's admittedly weak attempt to approach the idea. It is unnecessary to elaborate further on this dialogue, since Socrates' opening attitude simultaneously makes manifest the skilled fencer and the rules for the entire investigation. To Aristippus's question whether he knew anything good, he answers (para. 3): "ἆρά γε, ἔφη, ἐρωτᾷς με, εἴ τι οἶδα πυρετοῦ ἀγαθόν [Are you asking if I know of anything good for a fever?]," whereby the discursive *raisonnement* [reasoning, line of argument] is immediately suggested. The whole dialogue then proceeds along this path with an imperturbability that does not circumvent the apparent paradox (para. 6): "ἆρ' οὖν, ἔφη, καὶ κόφινος κοπροφόρος καλόν ἐστιν; Νὴ Δί', ἔφη, καὶ χρυσῆ γε ἀσπὶς αἰσχρὸν, ἐὰν πρὸς τὰ ἑαυτῶν ἔργα ὁ μὲν καλῶς πεποιημένος ᾖ, ἡ δὲ κακῶς [Is a dung-basket beautiful then? Of course, and a golden shield is ugly, if the one is well made for its special work and the other badly]." Although I have quoted this dialogue only as an example and thus must essentially take my stand on the total impact that is the vital force in the example, I shall nevertheless, having also cited it as an example *instar omnium* [worth them all, i.e., typical], call to mind the difficulty with respect to the manner in which

Xenophon introduces this dialogue. He implies, namely, that it was a captious question on Aristippus's part, in order to embarrass Socrates with the infinite dialectic implicit in the good when understood as the useful. He suggests that Socrates saw through this trick. Thus it is conceivable that Xenophon preserved this whole dialogue as an example of Socrates' gymnastics. It might seem that possibly there was still a dormant irony in Socrates' whole deportment, that by seeming to enter unsuspectingly into the trap Aristippus had set for him he thereby demolished his cunning plot and made Aristippus the one who against his will had to advance the argument he had calculated that Socrates would have stressed. But anyone who knows Xenophon will surely find this highly improbable, and for additional ease of mind Xenophon has also provided a completely different reason why Socrates behaved in this manner—namely, "in order to benefit those around him." From this it is obvious, according to Xenophon's view, that XIII
Socrates is in dead earnest when he takes the inspiring infinity 119
of the inquiry back down to the underlying spurious infinity of the empirical.[52]

The commensurable in general is Socrates' proper arena, and for the most part his activity consists of encircling all of man's thinking and doing with an insurmountable wall that shuts out all traffic with the world of ideas. Study of the sciences must not transgress this cordon of health either (*Mem.*, IV, 7).[53] One should learn enough geometry* to help to see to it that one's fields are correctly measured; the further study of astronomy is deprecated and he advises against the speculations of Anaxagoras—in short, every science is reduced *zum Gebrauch für Jedermann* [for use by everyone].

* Compare this with the importance Socrates in *Republic* VII assigns to geometry and its influence on thought, leading it away from becoming to being, "for when geometry compels us to intuit being, it benefits us, but when becoming, then not." See Ast's edition of Plato, vol. IV, p. 404.[54] But becoming (γένεσις) is obviously the empirical multiplicity, and immediately thereafter he says the same thing about astronomy; he thinks that these sciences purge and awaken a psychic sense more valuable than a thousand eyes and therefore censures astronomers as well as musicians for stopping with empirical kinetics and empirical harmonics.

The same thing happens in every other sphere. His nature observations are altogether run-of-the-mill, finite teleology in a variety of patterns. —His conception of friendship cannot be accused of fanaticism. He does, of course, believe that no horse* or ass has as much value as a friend, but it by no means follows as a matter of course that several horses and several asses should not have just as much worth as one friend. And this is the same Socrates of whom Plato, in order to describe his whole interior infinity in relation to friends, uses a sensate-
XIII 120 intellectual phrase such as παιδεραστεῖν μετὰ φιλοσοφίας [to love young boys according to the love of wisdom],[56] and Socrates himself says in the *Symposium* that the only thing he understands is ἐρωτικά [love].[57] And then, when in *Mem.*, III, 11, we hear Socrates talking with that dubious lady, Theodoté, and bragging about the love potions he has to draw young men to himself, we are just as disgusted with him as with an aged coquette who still believes herself capable of captivating—indeed, we are even more disgusted, because we cannot perceive the possibility of Socrates' ever having been capable of it. —We find the same finite pedestrianism with respect to life's multifarious pleasures, whereas Plato so magnificently credits Socrates with a kind of divine health that makes immoderation an impossibility for him and yet does not take from him but specifically bestows upon him the fullest measure of pleasure.** When Alcibiades tells us in the *Symposium* that he has never seen Socrates drunk, he is also suggesting that this was an impossibility for Socrates, as we do in fact in the *Symposium* see him drink everybody else under the table.[59] Xenophon, of course, would have explained this by saying that he never transgressed the *quantum satis* [sufficient amount] of an experientially tried and tested rule. Thus Xenophon portrays in Socrates not that beautiful, harmonious unity of natural determinant and freedom indicated in the term σωφροσύνη

* *Mem.*, II, 4; I, 3, 14.[55]

** *Symposium* (tr. by Heise, p. 97): "And when there was high living, he was the one who really knew how to enjoy it; he exceeded all primarily in drinking, to which he first had to be urged, and yet, the most extraordinary thing of all, no one has ever seen Socrates drunk."[58]

[self-control] but a graceless composite of cynicism and bourgeois philistinism. —His view of death is just as deficient, just as narrowhearted. This is evident in Xenophon where Socrates perceives the joy in his imminent death to be his being freed from the frailties and burdens of old age (*Mem.*, IV, 8, 8). In the *Defense*, we of course find some more poetic features, as in para. 3,[60] where Socrates suggests that he has been preparing his defense throughout his whole life. Yet it must also be pointed out that not even when Socrates declares he XIII
will not defend himself does Xenophon envision him in a pre- 121
ternatural magnitude (such as, for example, Christ's divine silence before his accusers) but sees it merely as motivated by his daimon's concern—perhaps inexplicable to Socrates—for his posthumous reputation. And when we are informed by Xenophon (*Mem.*, I, 2, 24) that Alcibiades was a quite worthy fellow as long as he fraternized with Socrates but later became dissolute, we wonder more at his remaining so long in Socrates' company than at his becoming dissolute later, because after an intellectual Christiansfeld[61] like that, after a reform school of restrictive mediocrity such as that, he might indeed become rather ravenous for pleasure. Consequently, in Xenophon's view of Socrates, we have the caricaturing shadowcast that corresponds to the idea in its manifold manifestation. Instead of the good, we have the useful, instead of the beautiful the utilitarian, instead of the true the established, instead of the sympathetic the lucrative, instead of harmonious unity the pedestrian.

Finally, with respect to irony,* there is not one trace of it in Xenophon's Socrates. Instead, sophistry makes its appearance. But sophistry is precisely the everlasting duel of knowledge with the phenomenon in the service of egotism, which can never terminate the duel in a decisive victory because the phenomenon rises up again as quickly as it falls, and since only the knowledge that like a rescuing angel snatches the phenom-

* The ironic in Xenophon is never the floating of irony blissfully resting in itself but is a means of education, therefore at times encouraging to those from whom Socrates is actually expecting something (*Mem.*, III, 5, 24), at times only castigating (*Mem.*, III, 6).

enon from death and translates it from death to life* can win, [sophistry] finally sees itself saddled with the endless hosts of phenomena. But the Chladni figure[63] corresponding to this monstrous polygon, the life's quiet interior infinity corresponding eternally to this noise and uproar, is either the system or irony as the "infinite, absolute negativity,"[64] with the
XIII difference, of course, that the system is infinitely eloquent,
122 irony infinitely silent. Thus we perceive that also here Xenophon has very consistently come to the opposite of the Platonic view.

There are sophisms enough in *Memorabilia*,** but for one thing they lack *pointe* [sting] (for example, the short sentences in *Mem.*, III, 13), and for another they lack the ironic infinite elasticity, the secret trap-door† through which one suddenly plunges down—not one thousand fathoms, as did the schoolmaster in *Alferne*,[67] but into irony's infinite nothing. On the other hand, his sophisms equally fail to approximate a view. As an example, I cite *Mem.*, IV, 4,[68] the dialogue with Hippias. Here, too, it is apparent how Socrates carries a question only to a certain point, without letting it answer itself in an opinion. In other words, after justice has been defined as iden-

* Therefore all knowledge requires courage, and only the person who has the courage to sacrifice his life saves his life; to everyone else the same thing happens that happened to Orpheus, who wanted to descend into the underworld in order to bring back his wife, but the gods showed him the mere shadow of her, because they regarded him as a sentimental zither player who did not have the courage to sacrifice his life for love.[62]

** *Mem.*, IV, 2, a whole web of sophisms, especially para. 22.

† A notable exception is *Mem.*, IV, 4, 6: "ἔτι γὰρ σὺ, ἔφη, ὦ Σώκρατες, ἐκεῖνα τὰ αὐτὰ λέγεις, ἃ ἐγὼ πάλαι ποτέ σου ἤκουσα; καὶ ὁ Σωκρατης, ὃ δέ γε τούτου δεινότερον, ἔφη, ὦ Ἱππία, οὐ μόνον ἀεὶ τὰ αὐτὰ λέγω, ἀλλὰ καὶ περὶ τῶν αὐτῶν· σὺ δ' ἴσως διὰ τὸ πολυμαθὴς εἶναι περὶ τῶν αὐτῶν οὐδέποτε τὰ αὐτὰ λέγεις ['How now?' he cried in a tone of raillery, 'still the same old sentiments, Socrates, that I heard from you so long ago?' 'Yes, Hippias,' he replied, 'always the same, and—what is more astonishing—on the same topics too! You are so learned that I daresay you never say the same thing on the same subjects.']" As is well known, the same remark by Polus[65] and the same reply by Socrates are found in the *Gorgias*,[66] and it cannot be denied that what Xenophon added, "διὰ τὸ πολυμαθὴς εἶναι [because of your wide learning]," presumably does not make the irony more profound but only more sparkling.

tical with the lawful and doubt about the lawful (with respect to laws being changed, see para. 14) seems to be quieted by the observation about the lawful as recognized by all at all times (the law of God), he nevertheless stops with some specific examples in which the peculiar consistency of sin is obvious. Likewise in the example of ingratitude quoted in para. 24, whereby the thought had to be traced back to the *harmonia praestabilita* [preestablished harmony][69] with which existence is imbued, the observation stops with the superficiality that the ungrateful person loses friends etc. and does not rise up into the more perfect order of things, where there is no change or shadow of variation,[70] where reprisal strikes without being
stopped by any finiteness. As long as we stop with taking only XIII
the external into account, it is conceivable, for example, that 123
hobbling justice will not catch up with the ungrateful person.

This completes my view of Socrates as he stands and walks in Xenophon's puppet box, and in conclusion I only ask my readers, insofar as they have been bored, not to place the blame solely upon me.

PLATO

In the previous pages, the readers have no doubt caught many a stolen glimpse of the world that will now be the object of our inquiry. We do not deny it, but it is due in part to the eye, which by staring long at one color involuntarily forms its opposite, in part to my own perhaps somewhat youthful infatuation with Plato, in part also to Xenophon himself, who might have been a second-rate fellow were it not for the chinks in his presentation, which Plato so fits and fills that in Xenophon *eminus et quasi per transennas* [at a distance and as if through a lattice] one catches sight of Plato. To be honest, this was my longing, but it certainly did not diminish during the reading of Xenophon. Dear critic, allow me just one sentence, one guileless parenthesis, in order to vent my gratitude, my gratitude for the relief I found in reading Plato. Where is balm to be found if not in the infinite tranquillity with which, in the quiet of the night, the idea soundlessly, solemnly, gently, and

yet so powerfully unfurls in the rhythm of the dialogue, as if there were nothing else in the world, where every step is deliberated and repeated slowly, solemnly, because the ideas themselves seem to know that there is time and an arena for all of them? Indeed, when was repose ever more needed in the world than in our day, when the ideas accelerate one another with insane haste, when they merely give a hint of their existence [*Tilværelse*] deep down in the soul by means of a bubble on the surface of the sea, when the ideas never unfurl but are devoured in their delicate sprouts, merely thrust their heads
XIII into existence but then promptly die of grief, like the child
124 Abraham à Santa Clara tells of, who in the moment it was born became so afraid of the world that it rushed back into its mother's womb.[71]

Introductory Observations[72]

Just as a system appears to have the possibility of making every element a point of departure, but this possibility never becomes an actuality because every element is essentially determined *ad intra* [inwardly], held and carried by the system's own conscience*—so every view, and above all a religious view, actually has a specific external point of departure, something positive, which in relation to the particular manifests itself as a higher causality and in relation to the derived manifests itself as the *Ursprüngliche* [original]. The individual continually seeks to move from the account and through the account back to the contemplative repose that only personality gives, to the confident devotedness that is the cryptic reciprocity of personality and sympathy. Presumably I need but remind the reader that a primitive personality such as that, such a *status absolutus*[74] [independent status] of the personality, in contrast to the *status constructus* [conjoined status] of the race, is given and can be given only once. But we must not disregard the fact that the analogy to this, history's repeated

* Within the system every particular element acquires a meaning different from the one it has outside the system; it has, as it were, *aliud in lingua promtum, aliud pectore clausum* [one ready on the tongue, another locked in the breast].[73]

attempt at this infinite leap,[75] also has its truth. *What Plato saw in Socrates* was such a personality, an *immediate conveyor of the divine* such as this. The essential impact of such an original personality upon the race and its relation to the race fulfill themselves partly in a communication of life and spirit (when Christ breathes upon the disciples and declares: Receive the Holy Spirit[76]), partly in a release of the individual's locked-up powers (when Christ says to the paralytic: Stand up and walk[77]) or, more correctly, it fulfills itself through both simultaneously. Consequently, the analogy to this can be double, XIII 125
either positive, that is, stimulating, or negative, that is, aiding the paralytic, the individual diffused in himself, to achieve the original resilience, only protectively and watchfully allowing the individual reinvigorated in this way to come to himself.* But in both analogies the relation to a personality such as that is for the second person not merely inciting but epoch-making, is a spring of eternal life unexplainable to the individual himself. We may say either that it is the word that creates or the silence that begets and gives birth to the individual.[79] The reason I have cited these two analogies may not at this moment be obvious to the reader, but I trust that it will become obvious later. That Plato saw the unity of these two elements in Socrates or, more correctly, illustrated their unity in Socrates cannot be denied; that a second view, which perceived a metaphor of Socrates' delivering activity in the fact that Socrates' mother, Phaenarete, was a midwife,[80] has accentuated the other side of the analogy—this everyone knows.

But what is the relation between the Platonic and the actual Socrates? This question cannot be dismissed. Socrates flows

* That this relation of the personality is a relation of love [*Kjærlighed*], you will, I am sure, agree with me—indeed, that it actually calls to mind the species of it that in Plato is always attributed to Socrates, "pederasty," referring, of course, to youth's first awakening from the sleep of childhood and the coming to oneself—and that it provides a not unsuitable clue to the partiality with which Socrates viewed and really enjoyed his pupil's minor frailties. Thus in the *Symposium* (Heise, p. 21) we read: "These do not love boys but only those in whom the spiritual development has begun, which usually occurs in the first period of youth."[78]

through the whole fertile territory of Platonic philosophy; he is present everywhere in Plato. At this point I shall not examine more closely how much this grateful pupil not only believed he owed Socrates but also how much this adoring youth with youthful ardor wished to owe him—because he cherished nothing unless it came from Socrates or unless he at least was co-owner and co-knower of these love-secrets [*Elskovs-Hemmeligheder*] of knowledge, because there is for the kindred spirit a self-expression that is not constricted by the limitations of the other but is expanded and is endowed with a preternatural magnitude in the other's conception, since thought does not understand itself, does not love itself until it is caught up
XIII 126 in the other's being, and for such harmonious beings it becomes not only unimportant but also impossible to determine what belongs to each one, because the one always owns nothing but owns everything in the other. Just as Socrates so beautifully binds men firmly to the divine by showing that all knowledge is recollection,[81] so Plato feels himself so inseparably fused with Socrates in the unity of spirit that for him all knowledge is co-knowledge with Socrates. That this need to hear his own professions from the mouth of Socrates after the latter's death must have become even more acute, that for him Socrates had to rise transfigured from his grave to an even more intimately shared life, that the confusion between mine and thine had to increase now, since for Plato, however much he humbled himself, however inferior he felt about adding anything to Socrates' image, it was still impossible not to mistake the poetic image for the historical actuality—all this is certainly obvious.

After this general observation, I believe it appropriate to point out here that even the ancients were aware of this question of the relation between the actual Socrates and Plato's poetic version, and that the division of the dialogues as found in Diogenes Laertius into δραματικοί and διηγηματικοί [dramatic . . . narrative][82] contains a kind of answer. Consequently the diegematic [narrative] dialogues are supposed to be the ones that are closest to the historical view of Socrates. To this group belong the *Symposium* and the *Phaedo*, and even their outer form reminds us of their significance in this respect, as Baur correctly observes in the above-mentioned work (p. 122):[83] "Eben deszwegen scheinen die Dialoge der andern Art, die diegematischen, bei welchen der eigentliche Dialog nur in einer Erzählung gegeben wird, wie Plato im Gastmahl alles dem Apollodor in den Mund legt, in Phaedon den [dem] Phaedon, den [dem] Echekrates und einige[n] andere[n], was Socrates an seinem letzten Tage zu seinen Freunden gesprochen, und was sich mit ihm zugetragen, erzählen läszt, durch ihre Form von selbst zu verstehen zu geben, dass sie einen mehr historischen Charakter an sich tragen [In dialogues of the second kind, the diegematic, the dialogue as such is rendered only through a narrative, for instance, in the banquet scene, the *Symposium*, where Plato places the entire story in the mouth of Apollodorus, and in the *Phaedo*, where he has Phaedo relate to Echecrates and a few others what Socrates had said to his friends during his last day and all that had occurred. Thus by their external form these dialogues automatically seem to suggest a more intrinsic historical character]."

Whether this historical element in the form is merely a matter of the scenic setting and the contrast to the dramatic dialogues is due to the fact that the dramatic element (what Baur calls *die äuszere Handlung* [the external action]) is Plato's free XIII
poetizing, or whether it is due to the fact that the contents of 127
diegematic dialogues are mainly Socrates' own thoughts and the contents of the dramatical dialogues are Plato's views reflected into Socrates, I am unable to determine. I must once again, however, not only endorse but also copy what Baur[84] so correctly said: "Wenn nun aber auch Plato mit Rücksicht auf diesen historischen Grund, diesen Dialogen gerade diese Form gab, so kann doch hieraus auf den historischen Charakter des Ganzen nicht geschlossen werden [But even though Plato, with attention to this historical basis, gave these dialogues precisely this form, nothing can be concluded from this with regard to the historical character of the whole]."

And thus we come now to the important problem: in the Platonic philosophy, what belongs to Socrates and what belongs to Plato, a question we cannot dismiss, however painful it is to divorce them, closely united as they are. At this point I must lament that Baur has left me in the lurch, for after having shown the necessity of Plato's espousing in part the folk consciousness (in this he sees the significance of the mythical) and in part Socrates' personality as the positive point of departure, he nevertheless ends the whole inquiry by declaring that method* remains the essential significance of Socrates. But since method in its absolute, necessary relation to idea is still not evident in Plato, the question inevitably arises: *In what relation did Socrates stand to Plato's method?*

It is, therefore, important to give some consideration to method in Plato. Surely everyone believes that dialogue did not become the dominant form in Plato by accident but that there is a deeper reason. At this point I cannot elaborate on the relation between a dichotomy as found in Plato and the kind of trichotomy[85] the modern and in a stricter sense speculative development insists upon. (This will be touched upon in the discussion of the relation between the dialectical and the mythical elements,[86] a dichotomy in Plato's earlier dialogues.) Nor can I take the time, even if I were to show the necessity of a dichotomy for the Greeks and thereby acknowledged its relative validity, to show its relation to the absolute method as well. Presumably the Socratically disciplined dialogue is an at-
XIII 128 tempt to allow the thought itself to emerge in all its objectivity, but the unity of successive conception and intuition, which only the dialectical trilogy makes possible, is, of course, lacking. The method is essentially one of simplifying life's multifarious complexities by leading them back to an ever more abstract abbreviation. Since Socrates commences most of his inquiries not at the center but on the periphery, in the motley variety of life endlessly interwoven within itself, an exceptional degree of art is needed to unravel not only itself but also the abstract of life's complications and those of the Sophists as well. The art we are describing here is, of course,

* Since it would be too lengthy to quote Baur, may I refer the reader to the section beginning on page 90 and ask him to read pages 90, 91, and 98.

the rather well known Socratic art of *asking questions** or, to recall the necessity of dialogue for Platonic philosophy, the art of *conversing*. This is why Socrates so frequently and with such profound irony points out to the Sophists that they do indeed know how to speak but do not know how to converse.[88] In contrasting speaking and conversing, he specifically censures the self-seeking element in eloquence that craves what could be called abstract beauty, *versus rerum inopes nugaeque canorae* [verses void of thought, and sonorous trifles],[89] that sees in the expression itself, dissociated from its relation to an idea, an object for pious veneration. On the other hand, conversing forces the one speaking to stick to the subject** —that is, XIII 129

* The opposite of this is the Sophists' reputed skill in being able to *answer* questions; thus their greed to be asked questions so that their wisdom can really gush forth, so that they "can set full sail and before a smacking breeze take flight out upon the deeps of truth where one loses sight of land."[87] As an example of this, I can use the beginning of the *Gorgias*, where both Gorgias and particularly Polus are as uneasy as cows that have not been milked at the proper time.

** See *Symposium* (Heise, pp. 60 bot. and 61 top). "Agathon: 'I cannot contradict you, Socrates; it is indeed as you say.' Socrates: 'It is the truth, dear Agathon, that you cannot contradict, but Socrates very easily.' "[90] See *Protagoras* (Heise, p. 152). "Protagoras: 'But what difference does it make? Therefore, if you wish, let justice be pious and piety just.' Socrates: 'No, not so, I said, for I do not demand that this "If you like" or "If you think so" be subjected to the test but my true meaning and yours, and by this I understand XIII 129
that the matter is tested best.' "[91] *Protagoras* (Heise, p. 160): "When he (Protagoras) had said this, those present loudly applauded, because he had spoken so beautifully. But I said: 'I am a very forgetful man, and if someone speaks so long, I completely forget what the discourse is about. So just as you, if I were hard of hearing, would consider it necessary to speak more loudly to me than to the others if you wanted to talk to me, so now, too, since you have met a forgetful man, you will cut down your answers and make them shorter if I am to follow you.' "[92]

See *Gorgias* (Heise, p. 21): "Socrates, ... 'but you must not be surprised if I promptly ask you again about one thing or another, even though it seems altogether clear. For, as stated, I do not ask about it for your sake but in order that we can bring our investigation to a conclusion in a consistent way and not form the habit of taking the words from each other's mouth, although we only guess each other's meaning, and in order that we may be able to advance your view in the way you find most appropriate.' "[93] —Hence this stubbornness in sticking to the subject, which does not allow itself to be disturbed by

when the conversation is not regarded as identical with eccentric antiphonal singing, in which everyone sings his part with-
XIII 130 out regard to the other and there is a resemblance to conversation only because they do not all talk at once. This concentricity of conversation is expressed more definitely when conceived in the form of question and answer. Therefore, what it means to ask questions must be developed in more detail.

To ask questions denotes in part the individual's relation to the subject, in part the individual's relation to another individual. In the first case, it is an effort to free the phenomenon from any finite relation to the individual. Inasmuch as I ask a

---

anything. See *Gorgias* (Heise, p. 68): "Socrates: 'Amiable Polus, now you want to frighten me again instead of refuting me, just as before when you called up witnesses against me.' " Further on: "Is this a new way of conducting an argument, to laugh at what one says instead of refuting it?"[94] —Thus whether or not several are of the same opinion does not enter into the consideration—only whose opinion is the correct one. Polus adduces that those present agree with him and requests Socrates to ask them. *Gorgias* (Heise, p. 68): " 'O Polus, I am no politician. When it fell to my lot last year to sit on the Council because my tribe was presiding and it was my duty to gather votes, I prompted general laughter because I did not know how. Therefore you must not ask me to gather the votes of those present. For I only know how to call up one witness for what I say, namely, the one with whom I am speaking, and the others I ignore.' "[95] (In contrast to this Socratic earnestness, which attaches itself to its subject as alertly and assiduously as a prison guard to his prisoner, on one particular occasion we see him more in search of the easy partings and meetings in the conversation, along with the eroticism im-
XIII 130 plicit in this. Phaedrus scolds him in the *Symposium* [Heise, II, p. 47]: " 'O dear Agathon, if you answer Socrates, he will not care at all about what happens if he just has one to talk with, particularly someone handsome.' "[96] —Ordinarily the conversation of lovers is diametrically opposite to the proper discussion of something; thus it is as upbuilding to the lovers as it is dull and uninteresting to a third person.) Hence, in the *Phaedrus* (Ast, I, p. 148, 237 c) Socrates gives this Eulenspiegelian advice: "περὶ παντός, ὦ παῖ, μία ἀρχὴ τοῖς μέλλουσι καλῶς βουλεύεσθαι, εἰδέναι δεῖ, περὶ οὗ ἂν ᾖ ἡ βουλή, ἢ παντὸς ἁμαρτάνειν ἀνάγκη [My boy, if anyone means to deliberate successfully about anything, there is one thing he must do at the outset. He must know what it is he is deliberating about; otherwise he is bound to go utterly astray]"[97]—much like the important advice Eulenspiegel[98] gave the tailors, telling them to knot the thread in order not to lose the first stitch.[99]

question, I know nothing and am related altogether receptively to my subject. In this sense, Socratic questioning is clearly, even though remotely, analogous to the negative in Hegel,[100] except that the negative, according to Hegel, is a necessary element in thought itself, is a determinant *ad intra* [inwardly]; in Plato, the negative is made graphic and placed outside the object in the inquiring individual. In Hegel, the thought does not need to be questioned from the outside, for it asks and answers itself within itself; in Plato, thought answers only insofar as it is questioned, but whether or not it is questioned is accidental, and how it is questioned is not less accidental. Although such a question form is supposed to free the thought from every solely subjective determinant, nevertheless in another respect it succumbs entirely to the subjective as long as the questioner is seen only in an accidental relation to what he is asking about. But if asking questions is seen as a necessary relation to its subject, then asking becomes identical with answering. And just as Lessing[101] has already wittily distinguished between replying to a question and answering it, XIII 131
so there is a similar contradistinction fundamental to the difference proposed by us, namely, the contradistinction between asking [*spørge*] and interrogating [*udspørge*]; hence the true relation comes to be the relation between interrogating and answering.* Admittedly there is still always something subjective about it, but if it is borne in mind that the reason for the individual's asking thus and so is found not in his arbitrariness** but in the subject, in the relation of necessity that joins them together, then this also will disappear.

In the second case [the relation of the individual to another individual], the subject is an account to be settled between the one asking and the one answering, and the thought development fulfills itself in this rocking gait (*alterno pede*),[102] in this limping to both sides. This, too, is of course a kind of dialec-

* Their identity is beautifully expressed in the German language, where the word for "to question closely" [*udfritte*] is *aushorchen* [to sound out].

** Just as a divining rod [*Ønskeqvist*, wishing twig] mysteriously communicates with the water hidden in the earth and wishes only where there is water.

tical movement, but since the element of unity is lacking, inasmuch as every answer contains a possibility of a new question, it is not the truly dialectical evolution. This understanding of questioning and answering is identical with the meaning of dialogue, which is like a symbol of the Greek conception of the relation between deity and man, where there certainly is a reciprocal relation but no element of unity (neither an immediate nor a higher unity), and genuine duality is really lacking also, because the relation empties itself in mere reciprocity—like a *pronomen reciprocum* [reciprocally retroactive pronoun] it does not have the nominative but only *casus obliqui* [dependent cases][103] and only in the dual and plural forms.

If what has been said so far is accurate, then it is manifest that the intention in asking questions can be twofold. That is, one can ask with the intention of receiving an answer containing the desired fullness, and hence the more one asks, the deeper and more significant becomes the answer; or one can ask without any interest in the answer except to suck out the apparent content by means of the question and thereby to leave an emptiness behind. The first method presupposes, of course, that there is a plenitude; the second that there is an emptiness. The first is the *speculative* method; the second the *ironic*. Socrates in particular practiced the latter method. When
XIII the Sophists, in good company, had befogged themselves in
132 their own eloquence,* it was Socrates' joy to introduce, in the
most polite and modest way of the world, a slight draft** that

* See *Gorgias*, p. 38. "Socrates: 'I request, O Polus, that you spare us the long speeches that you already sought to use at times.' Polus: 'What? Am I not to be allowed to speak as much as I wish?' Socrates: 'It certainly would be very hard, my dear friend, if you should come to Athens, where reigns the greatest freedom of speech in all Greece, and you alone were not to have the right to make use of it.' "[104]

** See *Protagoras*, pp. 145 and 146 middle. [Socrates]: "Now then, Protagoras, only one small thing is lacking for me to have everything, if you will give me an answer to *this*."[105] But this "this" is what everything depends upon. —Or take another example, Socrates' defense (Ast, VIII, p. 98): " Ὅ τι μὲν ὑμεῖς, ὦ ἄνδρες Ἀθηναῖοι, πεπόνθατε ὑπὸ τῶν ἐμῶν κατηγόρων, οὐκ, οἶδα· ἐγὼ δ'οὖν καὶ αὐτὸς ὑπ' αὐτῶν ὀλίγου ἐμαυτοῦ ἐπελαθόμην· οὕτω πιθανῶς ἔλεγον [I do not know

in a short time expelled all these poetic vapors. These two methods do in fact have a strong resemblance, especially for the kind of observation that pays attention only to the element; indeed, this similarity becomes even greater because Socrates' questioning was essentially aimed at the knowing subject for the purpose of showing that when all was said and done they knew nothing whatever. Every philosophy that begins with a presupposition naturally ends with the same presupposition, and just as Socrates' philosophy began with the presupposition that he knew nothing, so it ended with the presupposition that human beings know nothing at all; Platonic philosophy began in the immediate unity of thought and XIII
being and stayed there. The direction that manifested itself in 133
idealism as reflection upon reflection manifested itself in Socrates' questioning. To ask questions—that is, the abstract relation between the subjective and the objective—ultimately became the primary issue for him.

I shall attempt to explain what I mean by examining more closely one of Socrates' statements in Plato's *Apology*. On the whole, the entire *Apology* is splendidly suited for attaining a clear concept of Socrates' ironic activity.* On the occasion of

---

what effect my accusers have had upon you, gentlemen, but for my own part I was almost carried away by them—their arguments were so convincing]."[106] Even in the *Symposium*, against Agathon (Heise, p. 54): "My dear sir, how embarrassing for me and everyone else to come forth after such a beautiful and rich discourse! Not everything was equally worthy of admiration, but who could hear the many beautiful words and modes of expression in the conclusion without being transported? . . . . . In my innocence, I believed that one ought to present the truth about every object one wanted to praise; . . . . . But this, as I observe, is not the true way in which to praise; that consists in attributing to the object as many and as beautiful characteristics as possible, whether it possesses them or not."[107] See *Protagoras*, pp. 170 bottom and 171 top.[108]

* Indeed, the whole *Apology* in its totality is an ironic work, inasmuch as most of the accusations boil down to a nothing—not to a nothing in the usual sense of the word, but to a nothing that Socrates simply passes off as the content of his life, which again is irony, and likewise his proposal about being entertained in the prytaneum or being fined a sum of money,[109] and mainly the fact that it really does not contain any defense at all but is in part a leg-pulling of his accusers and in part a genial chat with his judges.[110] This also

the first charge by Meletus that Socrates is guilty of blasphemy, Socrates himself mentions the well-known declaration by the oracle at Delphi that he was the wisest man. He tells how this statement perplexed him for a moment, how he tried to test whether the oracle had spoken the truth by going to one of the most highly esteemed wise men. This wise man was a statesman, but Socrates soon found out that he was ignorant. Thereupon he went to a poet, but when he asked him for a detailed explanation of his own poems he discovered that he, too, did not know anything about them, either. (On this occasion he also suggests that the poem must be regarded as a divine inspiration that the poet understood no more than prophets and soothsayers understand the beautiful things they say.) Finally he went to the artisans, and they certainly knew something, but since they were trapped in the illusion that they understood other things also, they fell into the same category as the others. In short, Socrates explains how he circumnavigated the whole empire of intelligence and found the whole domain to be bounded by an Oceanus[112] of illusory knowledge. We see how thoroughly he has understood his
XIII 134 task, how he has conducted the test with every intelligent power, and he himself finds this confirmed by the fact that his three accusers represented the three great powers whose nothingness he had already disclosed in their personal manifestations. Meletus made his appearance on behalf of the poets, Anytus on behalf of the artisans and statesmen, Lycon on behalf of the orators. Indeed, he considers it his divine calling, his mission, to walk around among his countrymen and foreigners so that when he hears of someone who is supposed to be wise and it does not appear to be true, he can come to the aid of the deity and show that the man is not wise.*[113] For this

---

tallies with the familiar story that he received and read through a speech for the defense written by Lysias but declared that, although it certainly was an excellent speech, he did not feel called upon to use it.[111]

* He includes all, especially his countrymen, in this act of refuting: "ταῦτα καὶ νεωτέρῳ καὶ πρεσβυτέρῳ, ὅτῳ ἂν ἐντυγχάνω, ποιήσω, καὶ ξένῳ καὶ ἀστῷ· μᾶλλον δὲ τοῖς ἀστοῖς, ὅσῳ μοι ἐγγυτέρω ἐστὲ γένει· ταῦτα γὰρ κελεύει ὁ θεός, εὖ ἴστε [I shall do this to everyone I meet, young or old, foreigner or fellow citizen, but

reason he had no time* to achieve something important, nei- XIII
ther in public nor in private affairs, but by reason of this divine 135
service he is a pauper in every respect.

But I return to that passage in the *Apology*. Socrates points to the joy of meeting after death the great men who have lived before him and shared his own fate, and he goes on to say: "καὶ δὴ καὶ τὸ μέγιστον, τοὺς ἐκεῖ ἐξετάζοντα καὶ ἐρευνῶντα, ὥσπερ τοὺς ἐνταῦθα, διάγειν, τίς αὐτῶν σοφός ἐστι καὶ τίς οἴεται μέν, ἔστι δ'οὔ [And above all I should like to spend my time there, as here, in examining and searching people's minds, to find out who is really wise among them, and who only thinks that he is]."[117] (Ast, VIII, p. 156, 41 b.) Here we stand at a

---

especially to you, my fellow citizens, since you are closer to me in kinship. This, I assure you, is what my God (the god) commands . . .]."[114] (See Ast, VIII, p. 128, 30 a.) He says that many attached themselves to him because it is not uninteresting to see people who fancy that they know something being convinced that they know nothing: "ἐμοὶ δὲ τοῦτο, ὡς ἐγώ φημι, προστέτακται ὑπὸ τοῦ θεοῦ πράττειν καὶ ἐκ μαντείων καὶ ἐξ ἐνυπνίων καὶ παντὶ τρόπῳ ᾧπέρ τίς ποτε καὶ ἄλλη θεία μοῖρα ἀνθρώπῳ καὶ ὁτιοῦν προσέταξε πράττειν [This duty I have accepted, as I said, in obedience to God's (the god's) commands given in oracles and dreams and in every other way that any other divine dispensation has ever impressed a duty upon man]."[115] (Ast, VIII, p. 136, 33 c.)

* In contrast to this, bear in mind Xenophon's presentation, in which Socrates is so very busy making good citizens of his pupils. Therefore, in Plato's *Apology*, Socrates stresses the importance of being a private citizen, and this is in total harmony with Socrates' otherwise negative relation to life. To be a private citizen in Greece meant something quite different from living as a man of private means these days, for according to the Greek mentality every single individual saw his life encompassed and carried by the political life in a far deeper sense than in our times. This is why Callicles (in the *Gorgias*) criticizes Socrates for continuing to have anything to do with philosophy, since Callicles believes that philosophizing is like stuttering, excusable only in children, and that an elder who continues to philosophize deserves to be punished for it (see Heise, p. 99): "For as I said earlier, however magnificent he may be, it cannot be otherwise than that he will become unmanly, since he absents himself from the heart of the city and shuns public meetings, in which, as the poet XIII
says, men first distinguish themselves, and spends the rest of his life in a cor- 135
ner, where he sits whispering something in the ears of three or four youths without ever expressing himself in a free, noble, and powerful way."[116] — Presumably I scarcely need remind the alert reader of the strong resemblance between this discourse by Callicles and the scholarly moderation Xenophon has Socrates endorse.

crucial point. It is undeniable that here Socrates almost lapses into the ridiculous in this zeal for spying on people that does not even allow him peace after death. And who, indeed, can keep from smiling when he imagines the somber shades of the underworld and Socrates right there in the middle, indefatigably interrogating them and showing them that they know nothing. Admittedly, it might seem that Socrates himself thought that some of them perhaps were wise, for he says that he will test which of them is wise and which imagines himself to be so and yet is not. But for one thing it must be remembered that this wisdom is neither more nor less than the ignorance* described, and for another that he declares that he is going to test them there just as he has those here; this suggests that it presumably will go no better with those great men in that *tentamen rigorosum* [rigorous examination] than it went
XIII with the great men here in life. Here, then, we see irony in all
136 its divine infinitude, which allows nothing whatever to endure. Like Samson,[120] Socrates grasps the pillars that support knowledge and tumbles everything down into the nothingness of ignorance. That this is genuinely Socratic everyone will certainly admit, but Platonic it will never become. Here, then, I have arrived at one of the duplexities in Plato and the very clue I shall pursue in order to find the unalloyed Socratic.

The previously mentioned distinction between asking questions in order to find the content and asking questions in order to humiliate now appears in a more definite form as the relation between the abstract and the mythical in Plato's dialogues.

In order to clarify this more precisely, I shall examine a few dialogues in greater detail to show how the abstract can ter-

* As to there being a lingering question of a knowledge of something other than this ignorance, a faint clue, a fugitive suggestion of a positive knowledge, Socrates himself says in *Symposium* (Heise, p. 10): "My wisdom is a poor kind and of an ambiguous nature, like a dream,"[118] and in the *Apology* construes the Delphic oracle's declaration as follows: "ὅτι ἡ ἀνθρωπίνη σοφία ὀλίγου τινός ἀξία ἐστὶ καὶ οὐδενός [human wisdom has little or no value]."[119] See Ast, VIII, p. 112, 23 a.

minate in irony and how the mythical can herald a more copious speculation.

In the Earliest Platonic Dialogues the Abstract Terminates in Irony

SYMPOSIUM

The dialogues *Symposium* and *Phaedo* provide turning points in the view of Socrates, since, as is so often repeated, the one presents the philosopher in life, the other in death. The two kinds of presentation previously designated as the dialectical and the mythical[121] are in the *Symposium*. The mythical account begins when Socrates withdraws and introduces the Mantinean seeress Diotima[122] as the one speaking. To be sure, Socrates remarks at the close that he himself was convinced by Diotima's discourse and that he is now trying to convince others of the same[123]—in other words, he makes us doubtful as to whether this discourse, even if at second hand, is not actually his own. Nevertheless, one still cannot draw from this any further conclusion as to the historical relation of the mythical to Socrates. This dialogue also tries in another way to attain fullness of knowledge by having the abstract conception of love exemplified finally in the person of Socrates through the drunken Alcibiades' speech;[124] but this speech, of course, cannot provide us with any further clarification regarding the issue of Socratic dialectic. How that is related to the dialectical development in this dialogue will now be scru- XIII 137
tinized more closely.

But anyone who has read this dialogue with any attention at all will surely agree with the earlier comment that the method is one of "simplifying life's multifarious complexities by leading them back to an ever more abstract abbreviation."[125] The final presentation of the essence of Eros by no means inhales what the previous development had exhaled, but reflection, in a continual ascent, mounts higher and higher above the atmospheric air until breathing almost stops in the pure ether of the abstract. Accordingly, the earlier discourses are regarded not as components in the final conception but rather as a terrestrial gravity from which thought must more and more be freed. While the different presentations do not stand in any necessary relation to the final one, they do, however, have a mutual relation to one another in that they are discourses about love springing from the heterogeneous viewpoints found in life with which the speakers, like allied powers, surround the whole territory constituting the real nature of love, which in the Socratic view proves to be as invisible as the mathematical point, inasmuch as it is abstract, and from which point the various relative and warped views cannot be deduced. Thus all these speeches are like a sliding telescope; the one presentation ingeniously merges into the other and in the process is so lyrically effervescent that it is like wine in crystal so artfully polished that it is not only the bubbling wine in it that intoxicates but also the infinite refraction, the light that blazes forth when one looks down into it. Although the relation between the dialectical and the mythical is not as markedly conspicuous in the *Symposium* as it is, for example, in the *Phaedo* and although for that reason is less useful for my purpose, it nevertheless does have the advantage that it so definitely accentuates what Socrates himself says and what he has heard from Diotima.

Phaedrus begins.[126] He describes the eternal in Eros. Eros is victorious even over time, as is indicated by the fact that he has no parents; in man he is victorious not merely over all the pettymindedness (by means of that inspiring modest blush) but also over death, and thus brings his beloved object back from the underworld and is rewarded by the gods, who are deeply moved by this themselves. Pausanias concentrates on the dual nature of Eros, yet not in such a way that this duality is understood in a negative unity, as in Diotima's presentation,
XIII where Eros is a son of Poros [plenty] and Penia [poverty]. The
138 one, heavenly love, is the motherless daughter of Uranus; the other, vulgar love, is far younger, has sexual difference as its source. He goes on to discuss the meaning of the heavenly pederasty that loves the spiritual in man and thus is not dragged down and debased by the sexual. Aristophanes, in a spasm of hiccoughs, declares that it is up to the physician

Eryximachus either to banish his hiccoughs or to speak in his place. Thereupon Eryximachus begins. He continues, so he himself thinks, Pausanias's comments, but he actually perceives the dichotomy of love from a position totally different from that of Pausanias. Whereas Pausanias stopped with two kinds of love, whose difference he had tried to describe, Eryximachus regards the issue in the light of there being two factors present in every element of love and demonstrates this especially in nature as seen from his medical, scientific viewpoint. Thus love is the unity in hostile factors, and because Asclepius understood how to infuse love into the most opposite factors (hot and cold, sour and sweet, dry and wet), he became the creator of the art of medicine. The same thing is repeated everywhere in nature; the seasons, weather, etc. also depend on expressions of love. So it is also with respect to sacrifices and everything involved in the gift of prophecy, since this constitutes the communion between gods and human beings. His whole speech is a kind of improvisation on the philosophy of nature.*

After Aristophanes has overcome his hiccoughs (suggesting a relation of opposites different from the one described earlier
by the physician, since he is freed from hiccoughing by sneez- XIII
ing), he takes the floor and bases the relation of opposites im- 139
plicit in love more deeply than any of the previous speakers in illustrating it by the opposition of the sexes and by the bisecting of human beings undertaken by the gods.[129] Indeed, he even suggests the possibility that the gods might get a notion

* Incidentally, there is something unclear in Eryximachus's speech; he disregards on the one hand the necessity of the immediate element of unity, the bond of unity that encircles the duplexity, despite his quoting of Heraclitus's words that what is in conflict with itself is in unison with itself just as in the tuning of a lyre or the tensioning of a bow.[127] On the other hand, the dichotomized Eros still remains for him, and likewise for Pausanias, something merely external, an external division, and it is not the reflection of the duality present in love and proceeding from it with necessity. Thus love at times is the relation of opposites as such, at times a kind of personal relation to opposites, at times an empty *prius* [antecedent] outside this antagonism, at times something standing over against the opposites. In short, his speech is a blend of tradition and nature poetry.[128]

to divide human beings up even more if they should be discontented with what they are, one half of a human being, "since we, sliced like flounders, have become two out of one."[130] And now he gives his whimsicality free play both in describing the original indifference of the sexes and the consequent human condition and in perceiving with deep irony the negative element in love, the yearning for union. During this Aristophanic exposition, one involuntarily comes to think of the gods, who most likely had the time of their lives watching these half-human beings who in endless confusion among themselves sought to become whole human beings.

After Aristophanes, the tragedian Agathon speaks; his speech is more organized. He points out that the others have not been eulogizing the god as much as congratulating humankind for the blessings the god bestows; but as to the nature of the one who dispenses all these blessings, no one has yet touched on that subject. Therefore Agathon aims to show what the god himself is like and what the blessings he bestows upon others are. His whole speech is an ode to Eros; he is the youngest of the gods (since he is perpetually young and keeps company with young people); he is the most delicate of them (for he lives in the softest thing of all, in the hearts and souls of the gods and of human beings and shuns anyone of hard disposition); his coloring is utterly lovely (for he continually lives among flowers) etc. etc. He has bestowed upon humankind mastery in every art, for only those whom Eros inspired became famous.

Since it would take me too far to go into a more detailed examination of the relation between these different speeches, I will now turn to the last speaker, that is, Socrates. In his simplicity, he had believed that one ought to state the truth about every object one wished to eulogize; this was essential, and after that one ought to select the most attractive points and to display them in the worthiest manner. . . . . . "But I note that this was not the true way to eulogize; it consists in attributing to the object as many beautiful qualities as possible, whether they belong to it or not. If they are false, it makes
XIII 140 no difference, because the task was, so it seems, this, that each

of us should give a specious, not a genuine, eulogy on Eros."[131] In his customary way, Socrates now gets down to the business of asking questions. He begins with one of those genuinely Socratic squeezing-out questions: whether Eros by nature is love of something or of nothing. But then if love also desires that which is its object, it does not, of course, possess it but is in want of it, also if this want is considered identical with the wish for continued future possession, since one does indeed desire what one does not have when one also desires to keep in the future what one has. Consequently, love is the want of and desire for what one does not have, and so if love is love of the beautiful, then Eros is in want of beauty and does not possess it. If the good is also the beautiful, then Eros also is in want of the good. The same process was carried out with every idea, and we see how Socrates does not peel off the husk in order to get to the kernel but scoops out the kernel. This is the end of Socrates' presentation, inasmuch as what follows is merely an account. If the reader has not yet seen what I wanted him to see, I hope that both he and I will succeed if he continues to give me his attention.

Socrates began his speech with some irony, but this was merely, if I may say so, an ironic figure (formulation), and he really would not deserve the name of ironist if his distinguishing trait were merely the brilliant knack he had for speaking ironically just as others spoke gibberish. The previous speakers had said very much about love, of which a large part, admittedly, did not pertain to the subject, but the presumption still remained that there were many things to say about love. Now Socrates develops the theme for them. Love, you see, is desire, a want, etc. But desire, want, etc. are nothing. Now we see the method. Love is continually disengaged more and more from the accidental concretion in which it appeared in the previous speeches and is taken back to its most abstract definitions, wherein it appears not as love of this or that or for this or that, but as love for something it does not have, that is, as desire, longing. Now in a certain sense this is very true, but in addition love is also infinite love. When we say that God is love, we are saying that he is the infinitely self-communicating; when we speak of continuing in love, we are speaking of participation in a fullness. This is the substance in love. The XIII 141 desiring and the longing are the negative in love, that is, the immanent negativity. Desire, want, longing, etc. are love's infinite subjectivizing[132]—to use a Hegelian expression that calls to mind precisely what must be called to mind here. This definition is also the most abstract, or rather it is the abstract itself, not in the ontological sense but in the sense of what lacks content. One can, of course, either understand the abstract as that which constitutes everything, track it down in its own silent movements, and let it determine itself toward the concrete and unfold itself in it. Or one may start from the concrete and with the abstract *in mente* [in mind][133] find it in and [draw it] out of the concrete. But neither is the case with Socrates. He does not call the relationship [of love] back to the categories. His abstract is a totally empty designation. He starts with the concrete and arrives at the most abstract and there, where the investigation should begin, he stops. The conclusion he comes to is actually the indefinable qualification of pure being: love *is*—because the addendum, that it is longing, desire, is no definition, since it is merely a relation to a something that is not given. In the same way, one could also take knowledge back to a totally negative concept by defining it as appropriation, acquisition, because this, after all, is manifestly the sole relation of knowledge to the known, but beyond that it is also possession. But just as the abstract in the sense of the ontological has its validity in the speculative, so the abstract as the negative has its truth in the ironic.

Here once again we meet a duplexity in Plato: the dialectical development is carried out until it disappears in the purely abstract. Then a new kind of development begins that would deliver the idea, but since the idea as such does not stand in a necessary relation to the dialectical, it becomes apparent that the whole evolution probably does not belong to one. But, on the other hand, neither can one thing be attributed arbitrarily to the one, another to the other, just so each one acquires something. The view of Socrates and the view of Plato—namely, *the ironical* (since the dialectical as such does not con-

stitute a view that stands in an essential relation to personality) and *the speculative*—however different they may have been, XIII
must have had *essential points of conjunction*. To what extent the 142
issue is advanced by the exposition presented by Socrates, following Diotima, and what significance may be attributed to the dichotomy of love and the beautiful (whereby the negative factor is placed outside and the positive factor is a lethargic and lazy quietism, whereas a trichotomy would promptly regard them in and with each other and therefore would not risk what happens to Diotima, namely, that the beautiful once again becomes the beautiful as such, becomes something purely abstract, as will be apparent later)—all this I shall go into in greater detail in discussing the exposition of the mythical[134] in the dialogues.

I alluded earlier to the general comment that in the *Symposium* a complement is sought to what is lacking in the dialectical view [of love] by having love exemplified in the person of Socrates, and thus the eulogies on love end in a eulogy on Socrates. Now even if the exemplification of the idea in a personality is a mere element in the idea itself, it nevertheless does as such still have its importance in the exposition. Precisely because the dialectical movement in Plato is not the idea's own dialectic, it remains alien to the idea, no matter in what ingenious *pas* [steps] it proceeds. Thus while the other speakers, like blindman's buffs, groped for the idea, the drunken Alcibiades grasps it with immediate certainty. Furthermore, it must be noted that Alcibiades' being intoxicated seems to suggest that only in an intensified immediacy is he secure in the love-relation that must have caused him in a sober state all the alarming and yet so sweet suspense of uncertainty. If we consider the nature of the love-relation that has come about between Socrates and Alcibiades, we certainly have to agree with Alcibiades when he tells how Socrates mocked him for his love and then adds: "And he has treated not only me in this manner, but also Charmides, Glaucon's son, and Euthydemus, the son of Diocles, and many others whom he, seemingly the lover, deceived in such a way that instead of the lover he became the beloved."[135] Alcibiades is incapable of tearing himself

away from him. He attaches himself to Socrates with vehement passion: "When I hear him my heart beats more violently than the Corybantes',[136] and tears pour out while he speaks."[137] Other orators cannot possibly affect him in this way; he resents his enslaved state—indeed, life in this state
XIII 143 seems unbearable to him. He avoids him as if he were a Siren, plugs his ears[138] lest he remain sitting at his side and grow old—indeed, he often even wishes that Socrates were dead, and yet he knows that it would be far more painful for him if that were to happen. He is like someone bitten by a snake—indeed, he is bitten by something more painful and in the most painful place, namely in the heart or in the soul. That the love-relation that has come about between Socrates and Alcibiades was an intellectual relation scarcely needs mentioning. But if we ask what it was in Socrates that made such a relation not merely possible but inevitable (Alcibiades correctly observes that not only he but almost every one of Socrates' associates had this relation to him), I have no other answer than that it was Socrates' irony. In other words, if their love-relation had involved a rich exchange of ideas, or a copious outpouring on the one side and a grateful receiving on the other, then they would, of course, have had the third in which they loved each other—namely, in the idea, and a relation such as that would never have given rise to such a passionate agitation. But precisely because it is the nature of irony never to unmask itself and also because a Protean[139] change of masks is just as essential, the infatuated youth must inevitably experience so much torment.* But just as there is something deterring about irony, it likewise has something extraordinarily seductive and fascinating. Its masquerading and mysteriousness, the telegraphic communication it prompts because an ironist always has to be understood at a distance, the infinite sympathy it presupposes, the fleeting but indescribable instant of understanding that is immediately superseded by the anxiety of mis-

* The ironist lifts the individual up and out of immediate existence. This is his liberating function, but thereafter he lets him float like Mohammed's coffin, which, according to legend, floats between two magnets—the one attracting and the other repelling.

understanding—all this holds one prisoner in inextricable bonds. Inasmuch as the individual at first feels liberated and broadened by the contact with the ironist when he opens himself up to this individual, the next moment he is in his power, and this is probably what Alcibiades means when he mentions how they have been deluded by Socrates in that he became the beloved instead of the lover. Since, in the next place, it is essential for the ironist never to articulate the idea as such but XIII
only casually to suggest it, to give with one hand and take 144
away with the other, to hold the idea as personal property, the relation naturally becomes even more exciting. In this manner there quietly develops in the individual the disease that is just as ironic as any other wasting disease and allows the individual to feel best when he is closest to disintegration. The ironist is the vampire who has sucked the blood of the lover and while doing so has fanned him cool, lulled him to sleep, and tormented him with troubled dreams.

The question could now be raised: Why this whole exposition? My reply: The intention is twofold. In the first place, to show that even in Alcibiades' view of Socrates irony is his essential aspect; in the second place, to suggest that the love-relation that has developed between Socrates and Alcibiades and what we can learn from it about the nature of love are negative.

With respect to the first point, we must recall that some have thought they could prove the necessity of an enormous abundance of the positive in Socrates by adducing the enthusiasm with which Alcibiades discusses his relation to him.* It might be important to look more closely for a moment at the nature of this enthusiasm. In the sphere of emotions, this enthusiasm seems to parallel what La Rochefoucauld calls *la fievre de la raison* [the fever of reason][140] in the sphere of understanding. Given the possibility that something else could have evoked this enthusiasm in Alcibiades (I have tried to show in

* *Anticipando* [in anticipation], I remind the reader that this same issue will repeat itself in another form when I come to consider whether it is necessary to assume a fullness of the positive in Socrates in order to explain the circumstance that so many philosophical schools originated with him.

the foregoing that irony is capable of doing it), it certainly would have to be suggested in Alcibiades' eulogy. Let us see if it is. Alcibiades stresses the Silenus side of Socrates: "Socrates says that he is ignorant and knows nothing. Is not this character of his Silenus-like? Of course, for with this he has merely changed his external appearance, like a carved image of Silenus, but if he is opened up, what a wealth of wisdom you will see in him—believe me, dear drinking companions! . . . . . He pretends to people and always has his joke with
XIII 145 them. But when he was in earnest and his inner being opened, I do not know if anyone saw the divine images in his soul. I beheld them once, and they seemed to me so divine, golden, inordinately beautiful and admirable that I promptly resolved to do everything that Socrates commanded."[141] On this, the following may be said. On the one hand, it is difficult to see what Alcibiades really means, and it is not totally unreasonable to suppose that Alcibiades did not fully realize what he was saying about Socrates. On the other hand, Alcibiades himself suggests that Socrates very seldom opened up in this way. Pressing Alcibiades' account further, we see that he uses the words "I beheld them once." He beheld these divine images. If we think of anything in this connection, we certainly must think of the divine presence of the personality who supported the irony, but this says nothing more about Socrates than can be said of him as an ironist. But moments of transfiguration such as this do indeed demonstrate at most only the presence of a divine fullness κατὰ κρύψιν [hidden][142] in such a manner that one cannot say that it was the fullness of the positive that was inspiring. Furthermore, if we remember that Socrates' proper sphere was discourse, dialogue, then there really seems to be a kind of emphasis in Alcibiades' use of the expression "to behold," just as it is also remarkable to hear him say: "In the foregoing, I forgot that his speeches also resemble those opened Sileni."[143] This also seems to suggest that Alcibiades was primarily in love with Socrates' personality, his harmonious nature, which nevertheless fulfilled itself in a negative self-relation to the idea and an omphalopsychic staring at oneself. Admittedly, Alcibiades says that when one saw

these discourses opened up, they were first the most intelligent and then the most divine, and they contained the most ethical metaphors and had the broadest range. But if this had been the dominant feature or at least the rather conspicuous feature in Socrates' discourses, then there is no explanation for the source of all the passionate agitation, all the demonic in his love, since one would rather have expected that his association with Socrates would have been instrumental in developing in him the incorruptible manners and bearing of a serene spirit. Consequently, we see the whole thing end with Socrates again seesawing Alcibiades out into the surging sea with his irony, and despite his intoxication, his enthusiasm, and his inflated words, his relation to Socrates is as close as it ever was. XIII 146
Indeed, Alcibiades must reconcile himself to the fact that just as he "in sensual desire laid himself under Socrates' mantle, took this godlike and truly admirable man in both arms and lay that way the whole night, but scorned, jeered at, and mocked despite his beauty, did not rise from the couch beside Socrates otherwise than if he had been lying with a father or a brother,"[144] just so he also must reconcile himself here to Socrates' repulsing him once again with the remark that he had delivered this whole speech out of jealousy of Agathon: "Your whole speech tended to separate Agathon and me from each other, since you think that I ought not love anyone other than you and that Agathon ought not be loved by anyone other than you."[145]

In regard to the second point, the nature of love as embodied in Socrates, we shall by this presentation satisfy ourselves that theory and practice in him were in harmony. The love described here is that of irony, but irony is the negative in love; it is love's incitement. In the domain of intelligence it is what lovers' games and quarrels are in the realm of baser love. It is beyond dispute, we are again reminded, that there is in the ironist an *Urgrund* [primordial ground], an intrinsic value, but the coin he issues does not have the specified value but, like paper money, is nothing, and yet all his transactions with the world take place in this kind of money. The fullness in him is a qualification of nature; therefore in him it is neither the fullness in immediacy as such nor the fullness acquired through reflection.[146] Just as it takes a high degree of healthiness to be sick, and yet the healthiness is not detected in the positive fullness but in the vitality with which it continually feeds the sickness, so also with the ironist and the positive fullness in him. It does not unfurl into the fullness of beauty—indeed, the ironist even tries to conceal the diver's connection with the atmospheric air that nourishes him.

Before leaving the *Symposium*, however, I have one more comment to make. Baur makes the beautiful observation that at the end of the *Symposium* Agathon and Aristophanes (the discursive elements) finally become drunk and Socrates alone keeps himself sober as the unity of the comic and the tragic;
XIII he also recalls the analogy (inappropriate, in my opinion) that
147 Strauss draws between the ending of the *Symposium* and Christ's transfiguration on the mountaintop.[147] The extent to which Socrates may be said to constitute the *unity* of the comic and the tragic depends obviously on the extent to which irony itself is this unity. If we imagine that Socrates, after all the others were drunk, became immersed in himself, as was his practice, he could furnish us, because of this gazing into vacancy to which he so often abandoned himself, with a sculptural image of the abstract unity of the comic and the tragic in question here. In other words, gazing can signify either contemplative preoccupation (this would be closest to Platonic gazing) or, as we say, gazing can signify what we call thinking about nothing until "nothing" becomes almost visible. Presumably Socrates could provide a higher unity of that kind, but this unity is the abstract and negative unity in nothingness.

PROTAGORAS

I shall now proceed to discuss the *Protagoras* in a similar manner in order to show how the whole dialectical movement, which is prominent here, ends in the totally negative. Before doing so, however, I must make a more general comment somewhere with respect to Plato's dialogues, and I believe this the right place, inasmuch as the *Protagoras* is the first dialogue to provide occasion for it. When Plato's dialogues are

to be classified, I believe it best to follow Schleiermacher's division[148] between the dialogues in which the dialogical is the main element and the tireless irony at times disentangles, at times tangles, the disputation and the disputants, and the constructive dialogues, which are characterized by an objective, methodical style. To the latter group belong the *Republic*, *Timaeus*, and *Critias*. Both tradition and the internal character of these dialogues place them last in the phase of development. In these dialogues, the question method has had its day, and the one who answers functions more as an attesting or a parish clerk with his "yes" and "amen"—in short, there is no conversation anymore. Irony, too, has in some measure disappeared. But if we now bear in mind how necessary it was for Socrates to carry on a conversation and that he always offers XIII 148
only the choice between his asking and the other's answering or the other's asking and his answering,* we certainly see an

* Yet it should be noted that through long habit the asking of questions has become so necessary to Socrates that even when he allows the other permission to do so it lasts no more than one, two, or three rounds before Socrates answers in the form of a question and once again begins asking the questions. He sees to it that the question method is properly observed and that there is no confusion of it with the rhetorical method of questioning. For example, in the *Gorgias:* "Polus: Do you think, then, that in the cities the good rhetoricians are regarded as flatterers and despised as bad people? Socrates: Is that a question you are presenting or the beginning of a speech? . . . . . Polus: What? Could they not, like tyrants, put to death whomever they will and deprive anyone of his fortune and banish from the state whomever it seems best? Socrates: By the dog, Polus, from all that you say, I am unsure as to whether it is your own opinion you are presenting or whether you are questioning me."[149] —At the end of the *Gorgias*,[150] where Socrates, having silenced the Sophists, continues the inquiry alone, he does it in the form of a conversation with himself. In the *Crito*, where the personified laws and the state themselves contribute to the conversation, they say, "Do not be surprised at our question, Socrates, but answer it, since, after all, you are accustomed to speak in question and answer."[151] In the *Apology*, he also conducts his defense in the form of question and answer and even calls attention to it. Cf. Ast, VIII, p. 122, 27 a-b: "σὺ δὲ ἡμῖν ἀπόκριναι, ὦ Μέλιτε. ὑμεῖς δὲ, ὅπερ κατ' ἀρχὰς ὑμᾶς παρῃτησάμην, μέμνησθέ μοι μὴ θορυβεῖν, ἐὰν ἐν τῷ εἰωθότι τρόπῳ τοὺς λόγους ποιῶμαι [You, Meletus, will oblige us by answering my questions. Will you all kindly remember, as I requested at the beginning, not to interrupt if I conduct the discussion in my customary way?]."[152]

essential difference between Plato and Socrates, whether or not Plato had a conscious understanding of it or rendered it directly and faithfully. Consequently, I shall have very little to do with these constructive dialogues, inasmuch as they cannot contribute much to the view of Socrates' personality as it actually was or as Plato imagined it to be. Anyone who knows anything about these dialogues will surely sense the utterly external relation the person speaking has to the subject, so much so that the name Socrates has practically become a *nomen appellativum* [common name] that merely designates the one speaking, the one expounding. Add to this the fact that when the umbilical cord that joins the speech to the speaker is cut, the continued use of the dialogue form turns out to be
XIII 149 entirely accidental and one is almost amazed that Plato, who in the *Republic*[153] disapproves of the poetic rendition in contrast to the simple narrative, has not allowed the presentation of dialogue to be superseded by a stricter methodical form.

Many of these earliest dialogues end without a conclusion, or, as Schleiermacher remarks, all the dialogues before the *Republic* that discuss one virtue or another do not find the right explanation. See Schleiermacher's *Platons Werke*, III^{1}, p. 8: "So behandelte Protagoras die Frage von der Einheit und von der Lehrbarkeit der Tugend, aber ohne den Begriff derselben aufzustellen, so ist im Laches von der Tapferkeit die Rede und im Charmides von der Besonnenheit. Ja da auch in der Frage von der Gerechtigkeit der Gegensatz zwischen Freund und Feind ein bedeutendes Moment bildet, mögen wir auch des Lysis hier gedenken [Thus the *Protagoras* treated the question of the unity and communicability of virtue, but without defining the idea of virtue itself; thus in the *Laches* courage is discussed, and in the *Charmides*, discretion. And since, in the question of justice, the opposition between friend and enemy forms an important element, even the *Lysis* might occur to the mind on the present occasion]."[154] Indeed, the fact that they end without a conclusion may be specified even more explicitly by saying that they end with a negative conclusion. As an example of this, we shall use the *Protagoras* as well as the first book of the *Republic*, which, according to Schleiermacher,[155] also ends without a conclusion. This, however, is very important for the present inquiry, for if we are to find the Socratic at all it must be sought in the earliest dialogues.

As for the *objective* in the dialogue *Protagoras*, whether it aims to make a running start at a definitive answer to the problems (of the unity of virtue and the possibility that it can be taught) posed in the dialogue, or whether, as Schleiermacher assumes, it does not consist in any single point and consequently is incommensurable with the concerns touched on in the dialogue and, in a state of suspension throughout the whole dialogue, is not completed until, by way of the successive disappearance of each specific point, the Socratic method, purified and rejuvenated, emerges clearly—I shall not determine this here but say only that I can readily agree with Schleiermacher,[156] provided the reader bears in mind that in my opinion the method consists not in the dialectical in the form of the question as such, but in the dialectical sustained by irony, springing from irony and returning to irony. Thus at the end of the dialogue Socrates and the Sophist are left—as
the Frenchman actually says of only one person: *vis-à-vis au* XIII
rien [facing nothing].[157] They stand face-to-face like the two 150
bald men, who, after a long, drawn-out quarrel, finally found a comb. For me, of course, the essential thing in this dialogue is its altogether ironic structure. The fact that no definite answer is achieved to the issues raised would, of course, fit what Schleiermacher says, that the dialogue ends without a conclusion, but that, after all, would not be ironical, since the interruption of the inquiry at this point could be due in part to something totally accidental, of which an entire infinitude can be imagined, or it could be connected with a deep longing to be liberated from the earlier unproductive labor pains by an accomplished delivery, in other words, when the dialogue could become conscious of itself as an element in a total inquiry.

Thus the dialogue would presumably end without a conclusion, but this "without a conclusion" is by no means synonymous with a negative conclusion. A negative conclusion always denotes a conclusion, and only irony can provide a negative conclusion in its purest and most unadulterated form. Even skepticism always posits something, whereas irony, like that old witch, continually makes the very tantalizing attempt to eat up everything first of all and thereupon to eat up itself—or, as in the case of the witch, eats up its own stomach.[158]

The dialogue is therefore very well aware of this lack of a conclusion—indeed, it seems to take a certain pleasure in the fascinating game of demolition and does not relish only the annihilation of the Sophist. Socrates himself says, "The present outcome of our conversations seems, like a human being, to reproach us and to laugh at us and, if it could speak, would say: 'What strange people you are, Socrates and Protagoras.' "[159] That is, after the two antagonists have tried every kind of grappling, following Protagoras's abandonment of his epideictic discourse, in that Socrates asks the questions at first and Protagoras answers, and then the latter asks the questions and the former answers, and finally Socrates once again is the questioner and Protagoras the answerer, and thus, to use a possibly illuminating expression, they have repeatedly weighed salt with each other, there is the curious turn that Socrates defends what he has wanted to attack and Protagoras attacks what he has wanted to defend. The whole dialogue is reminiscent of the well-known argument between a Catholic and a Protestant that ended with their convincing each other,
XIII so that the Catholic turned Protestant and the Protestant
151 turned Catholic,*[160] except that here the ridiculous is taken up in the ironic consciousness.

* The anecdote I refer to here provides the second form of an ironic negative result, for here the irony is due to arriving at an actual conclusion. But since the actual conclusion is wholly personal and as such is neutral to the idea, and since the Catholic convert presumably will in turn have the same persuasive power over the newly hatched Protestant as the latter had over him in the first lap, and so on, we perceive the possibility of a never-ending dispute that for the disputants is at all times convincing despite the fact that neither of them has a conviction at any time. There is only the relation of correspondence between them, so that the moment A is Catholic B becomes Protestant, and the moment B becomes Catholic A becomes Protestant, which means,

At this point I would like to consider a possible objection that could be raised, all the more so since only an alert reader can raise it. It might seem as if it were Plato who was using the ironic lever here to tilt not only Protagoras but also Socrates up into the air in a right lively toss-in-the-blanket, and however funny this could look in such a hurly-burly, I must expressly on Socrates' behalf decline such an interpretation. It is indeed Socrates himself who makes the remark, and the equivocal (vying with his ironic earnestness) ironic smile with which he has introduced his ironic amazement that the whole game had this result, his surprise at seeing Protagoras find what he with certainty knew Protagoras had to find, since he himself had hidden it—all this cannot possibly escape the reader who has any sympathy at all.

So much for the total structure or form of the dialogue. If we now consider the content, that is, the issues interwoven in the dialogue, which, like the *meta* [pillar] on the racetrack, constitute the fixed points around which the contestants move, moving ever closer and closer to them, speeding ever faster and faster past one another, then I believe that a similar negative irony will be found in the whole dialogue.

This is particularly the case with the first question, whether
virtue is one. Socrates raises the question whether justice, self- XIII
control, piety, etc. are parts of virtue or only names of one 152
and the same thing; and next, whether they are parts in the same way as the mouth, nose, eyes, and ears are parts of the face, or instead are like the gold particles, which do not differ intrinsically from one another or from the whole lump but only with respect to largeness and smallness. Without becoming involved in a detailed discussion of the many sophistries mustered up by both sides, I will simply indicate that Socrates' argumentation aims essentially at wiping out the relative unlikeness among the different virtues in order to save the unity; whereas Protagoras continually focuses on the apparent qualitative unlikeness, but therefore the bond is lacking that is able

---

of course, that neither of them changes his *habitus* [inner disposition] but each of them changes his suit [*Habit*].

to encircle and hold together this rich multiplicity. Thus the idea of mediation never dawns for him; he gropes in its twilight when, hoping to reclaim the unity, he clings to the subjectivized idea of mediation, which depends upon the identity of likeness and unlikeness. Generally speaking, he says, all things resemble one another in a certain respect. In one way even white resembles black and hard resembles soft, and so it is with all other seemingly extreme opposites. But according to Socrates the unity of virtue* is like a tyrant who does not
XIII 153 have the courage to rule over the actual world but first murders all his subjects in order to be able to rule proudly and with perfect security over the silent kingdom of pale shadows. That is, if piety is not justice, Socrates argues, then to be pious is the same as being not just, that is, unjust, that is, impious. Now anyone can see the sophistry in Socrates' argumentation. But what I must particularly point out is that this unity of virtue becomes so abstract, so egotistically closed up in itself, that it only becomes the rock upon which the individual virtues, like well-freighted sailing vessels, run aground and are smashed to pieces. Like a soft whisper, a shudder, virtue skims through its own qualifications without becoming audible, to say nothing of being articulated in any of them, just as

* Since, as we know, *opposita juxta se posita magis illuscescunt* [opposites placed beside each other are clearer], I will cite the positive understanding of the unity of virtue that can presumably be regarded as Platonic and surely is not a fruit of the kind of dialectical development touched on here but belongs to a totally different order of things. See the *Republic* (Ast, 445 c): "Καὶ μήν, ἦν δ'ἐγώ, ὥσπερ ἀπὸ σκοπιᾶς μοι φαίνεται, ἐπειδὴ ἐνταῦθα ἀναβεβήκαμεν τοῦ λόγου, ἓν μὲν εἶναι εἶδος τῆς ἀρετῆς, ἄπειρα δὲ τῆς κακίας [And truly, said I, now that we have come to this height of argument, I seem to see as from a point of outlook that there is one form of excellence, and that the forms of evil are infinite],"[161] . . . . . where the positive unity of virtue is clearly the rich fullness of the happy life and the contrast to it is the unhappy shattering, multiple dissipation of wickedness, its many-tongued self-contradiction. See the *Republic*, 444 d: " 'Αρετὴ μὲν ἄρα, ὡς ἔοικεν, ὑγίειά τέ τις ἂν εἴη καὶ κάλλος καὶ εὐεξία τῆς ψυχῆς, κακία δὲ νόσος τε καὶ αἶσχος καὶ ἀσθένεια [Virtue, then, as it seems, would be a kind of health and beauty and good condition of the soul, and vice would be disease, ugliness, and weakness]."[162] Here the positive is the vegetative plenitude of health. But, of course, it is very easy to see that both these definitions are immediate, since they both lack the dialectic of temptation.

if I were to imagine that each soldier would forget the password the moment he whispered it into his neighbor's ear. And if I then imagined an endless row of soldiers, the password would not exist in the proper sense at all—such would almost be the case with this unity. The definition of virtue as one in the sense that Socrates maintains is clearly in the first place no qualification at all, since it is the most weakly inspired statement of its existence possible, and I take the opportunity to refer the reader for further enlightenment to Schleiermacher's penetrating judgment (in his dogmatics)[163] of the significance of the attribute of God that he is one. In the next place, it is a negative definition, since the unity it establishes is as unsocial as possible. The ironic consists in this, that Socrates tricks Protagoras out of every concrete virtue, and when he is to lead it back to unity, he completely volatilizes it. The sophistical is that by which he is able to do this. Thus we simultaneously have the irony carried by a sophistical dialectic and a sophistical dialectic resting in irony.

With regard to the second thesis, whether virtue can be taught,[164] as Protagoras believes, or cannot be taught, as Socrates believes, the former, of course, puts too much stress on the separate element, in that he would have the one virtue develop entirely at the expense of the other and yet would have virtue as unity be present in the individual concerned, and thus he crowns the one who is still on the racetrack. Socrates, on the other hand, so insists upon unity that despite his owning an immense capital he is poor, because he cannot make it productive. The Socratic thesis that virtue cannot be taught
seems to contain a high degree of positivity, since it traces vir- XIII 154
tue back either to a natural qualification or to something fatalistic. Yet in another sense virtue understood as immediate harmony, as well as virtue in its fatalistic διασπορά [dispersion], is an utterly negative qualification. On the other hand, to say that virtue can be taught must be understood as meaning either that an original emptiness in man is gradually filled through teaching (but this is a contradiction, since something that is absolutely foreign to man can never be brought into him) or that an inner condition of virtue gradually unfolds

through successive teaching, and consequently it presupposes the original presence of virtue. The misunderstanding of the Sophist is that he presumes to want to impart something to man; the Socratic misunderstanding, on the other hand, is to deny categorically that virtue can be taught. That this Socratic conception is negative is obvious; it expressly denies life, development—in short, history in its most universal and widest sense. The Sophist denies the original presence; Socrates denies the subsequent history.

If we now inquire further and ask to what more universal view this Socratic outlook may be traced, in what totality it rests, then it obviously is in the meaning ascribed to recollection; but recollection is in fact the retrograde development and thus the opposite of what, strictly speaking, is called development. Thus we have not just a negative qualification in the thesis that virtue cannot be taught, but also an ironic negative qualification moving in an entirely opposite direction. Virtue is so far from being teachable that, on the contrary, it is far behind the individual, and one might fear that it had been forgotten. It would be Platonic to fortify existence by the upbuilding thought that man is not driven empty-handed out into the world, by calling to mind his abundant equipment through recollection. It is Socratic to disparage all actuality and to direct man to a recollection that continually retreats further and further back toward a past that itself retreats as far back in time as that noble family's origin that no one could remember. Admittedly, Socrates does not adhere to this thesis, but, as we shall now see, what he puts in its place is no less ironic.

Up until now, I have interpreted the thesis that virtue can or cannot be taught in the sense of having experience; I have understood it as pertaining to the school of experience in which virtue is taught. We noted that whereas the Sophist had man going to school continually because he held fast (or, more correctly, at every moment abandoned and loosened) only
XIII what was discontinuous in experience, so that man, like stu-
155 pid Gottlieb,[165] never learned from experience, Socrates made
virtue so astringent and narrow that, because of this, it never

came to have experience. Socrates, however, searches deeper to show that virtue is one—that is, he wants to discover that other in which all virtues, so to speak, love one another, and this then becomes knowledge. But this thought is by no means carried through to the depth of a careless Pelagianism[166] that is characteristic of the Greek mentality, so that sin becomes ignorance, misunderstanding, and infatuation, and the element of will therein—pride and defiance—is disregarded. But because Socrates, in order to secure a footing, argues *e concessis* [on the basis of the opponent's premises], he posits the good as the pleasurable, and the knowledge he reclaims in this manner becomes an art of measurement, a subtle sensibleness in the sphere of pleasure. But a knowledge of that sort basically cancels itself because it continually presupposes itself. Thus while the irony touched on earlier is manifest throughout the dialogue in the fact that Socrates, who maintained that virtue could not be taught, nevertheless reduces it to knowledge and consequently proves the opposite, and the same thing happens to Protagoras, irony is also to be seen in his positing a knowledge that cancels itself, as stated before, because the endless calculating of the circumstances of pleasure impedes and stifles pleasure itself. As a result, we see that the good is the pleasant, the pleasant depends upon enjoyment, enjoyment depends upon knowledge, knowledge upon an endless measuring and sorting out—in other words, the negative lies in the perpetually necessary, inherently disastrous discontent in a limitless empiricism; the ironic lies in the "*Velbekomme!*",[167] so to speak, that Socrates wishes Protagoras. Thus in a certain sense Socrates comes once again to his first thesis, that virtue cannot be taught, since the limitless sum of experience is like a heap of utterly mute letters—the more it grows, the less it can be pronounced. The ironic to the first power lies in the erection of a kind of epistemology that annihilates itself; the ironic to the second power lies in Socrates' pretending that by accident he found himself defending Protagoras's thesis, although he in fact crushes it by the defense itself. It would, indeed, be altogether unreasonable to assume that the Platonic Socrates would have propounded the thesis that the good is the pleasant and the evil the unpleasant for any other reason than to crush it.

XIII 156

PHAEDO

I shall now move to a consideration of the *Phaedo*, a dialogue in which the mythical is more conspicuous, just as the dialectical was found unalloyed in the *Protagoras*. In this dialogue, demonstrations of the immortality of the soul are advanced, about which a quotation from Baur (p. 112) will suffice for the time being: "Dieser Glaube (an die Fortdauer der Seele nach dem Tode) gründet sich auf die Beweise, welche Plato den Socrates entwickeln läszt, diese Beweise selbst aber, wenn wir sie näher betrachten, führen uns wieder auf etwas anderes zurück, was in der unmittelbarsten Beziehung zu der Person Sokrates steht [This belief (in the continuance of the soul after death) is based upon the demonstrations that Plato has Socrates develop, but more closely considered these demonstrations themselves once again lead us back to something else that stands in the most immediate relation to the person of Socrates]."

But before examining the nature of these demonstrations, I shall contribute my bit to answering the question about the *kinship* between the *Symposium* and the *Phaedo*. As is well known, Schleiermacher[168] and later our own Heise[169] placed these two dialogues in the closest correlation, inasmuch as they assume that these dialogues embrace the whole Socratic existence beyond the world as well as in the world, and in integrating these dialogues into the whole cycle of Platonic dialogues they regarded the two dialogues as providing the positive element to the *Sophist* and to the *Statesman* (since these dialogues in their opinion did not achieve their aim—to delineate the nature and essence of the philosopher), which certainly must be true of the Sophist's relation to these dialogues, since the Sophist must be the very negation of the philosopher. Ast* thinks otherwise. In his book *Platon's Leben und*

* *Stallbaum*[170] also takes exception to this correlation and is of the opinion that the *Phaedo* must be closely associated with the *Phaedrus*, *Gorgias*, and *Re-*

Schriften[172] (Leipzig: 1816), he assigns the *Phaedo* to the first series of Platonic dialogues, the so-called Socratic dialogues, of which he numbers four: *Protagoras*, *Phaedrus*, *Gorgias*, and *Phaedo* (see p. 53). He notes in regard to the relation among these four dialogues: "und zwar ist der Phädon, wenn der Protagoras und Phädros wegen der Vorherrschaft des Mimischen und Ironischen zur Komödie sich hinneigen, entschieden tragisch: Erhabenheit und Rührung sein Charakter [if the *Protagoras* and the *Phaedrus* may be said to tend toward comedy because the mimical and the ironical are dominant, then, admittedly the *Phaedo* is decidedly tragic and characterized by sublimity and compassion]" (p. 157). Furthermore, he ob- XIII 157
serves that Schleiermacher has completely misunderstood the spirit of the Platonic composition by linking the *Phaedo* to the *Symposium:* "Im *Symposion* wird der hellenische Weise als vollendeter Erotiker dargestellt, im Phädon dagegen verschwindet der heitere, himmlisch-schöne Hellenismus, und der griechische Socrates wird zum indischen Brahminen idealisirt, der einzig in der Sehnsucht nach Wiedervereinigung mit Gott lebt, dessen Philosophie also Betrachtung des Todes ist. . . . . . Er (der Geist) flieht die den Geist trübende und störende Sinnlichkeit, und schmachtet nach Erlösung aus den Fesseln des ihn einkerkernden Körpers [In the *Symposium*, the Hellenic sage is presented as a consummate eroticist; but in the *Phaedo*, the bright, divinely beautiful sky of Hellenism disappears as the Greek Socrates is idealized into an Indian Brahmin, whose life is but a yearning for reunion with God, whose philosophy is thus a contemplation of death. . . . . . It (the spirit) flees from the sensuousness besetting and distressing it and pines for release from the bodily shackles imprisoning it]" (pp. 157, 158).

Quite obviously there is on first consideration a rather significant difference between the *Phaedo* and the *Symposium*, but it cannot be denied, on the other hand, that Ast completely *isolates* the *Phaedo* and that his attempt to put it together with

---

public, but he does not elaborate further and refers readers to Ast. See *praefatio ad Phaedonem*, p. 19.[171]

the *Phaedrus*, *Protagoras*, and *Gorgias* by designating it as tragic and rife with pathos actually does not harmonize with what he himself says about the dark, Oriental mysticism that forms a contrast to the bright, divinely beautiful Hellenism that arches over the *Symposium*. Although the *Phaedo* is tragic, the Grecian sky could really shine upon it just as beautifully, just as calmly, just as cloudlessly, since, after all, it had witnessed many a tragedy, and neither did it therefore become overcast and cloudy nor the air become as heavy and close as that of the Orientals. But if it is not Greek in this way, then it is futile to try to incorporate it into Plato, to say nothing of ranking it with others.

As for Schleiermacher's conception, one cannot deny that the view of life advanced in the *Symposium* and the view of death offered in the *Phaedo* do not completely harmonize, as one can perceive even in the mere fact that the *Phaedo* makes death the point of departure for a view of life, whereas the *Symposium* holds to a view of life in which death is not admitted as a factor.

Now these two views can by no means be regarded to be so favorably disposed toward each other that they could mesh into one another without a third view. This third view must be either a speculative view that is able to vanquish death, or it is the irony that in the *Symposium* made love the substance of life but then took it back again with the other hand by interpreting love negatively as longing, the irony that here [in the *Phaedo*] views life as retrospective, always wanting to go back into the nebulosity from which the soul emerged or, more correctly, into a formless, infinite transparency. In the
XIII 158 *Phaedo*, death is clearly viewed altogether negatively. To be sure, death is and always remains a negative factor, but as soon as it is understood only as factor, then the positive therein, the emancipating metamorphosis, will also triumphantly survive the negative.[173] When at this point I declare myself for *irony* (despite even such statements as those on page 27: "At least, said Socrates, I do not think that anyone who hears our conversation—even if he were a comedy writer—would dare say that I am indulging in poor talk and speaking about things that

do not concern me"[174]), it perhaps at first glance may seem very unreasonable to some, but on closer inspection perhaps quite acceptable. In other words, the speculative unity cannot be invisibly and imperceptibly present in this way, but the ironic unity certainly can.

When I say that irony is an essential element in the *Phaedo*, I do not mean, of course, the ironic ornamentations scattered throughout this dialogue, inasmuch as they, however meaningful they might be and however much they progressively expand on closer consideration, are able to be at most only a hint of the ultimate view that permeates the entire dialogue. I shall quote a few examples. "Yet you and Simmias seem to wish very much to extend this thesis further, and like children you seem to fear that the wind will really blow it (the soul) away and disperse it when it leaves the body, particularly if by chance one does not die during still weather but during a heavy storm" (p. 42).[175] Socrates chides Crito for asking him how he wishes to be buried and adds that Crito presumably thinks that everything he has said about wanting to depart to the glories of the blessed, "whatever they may be," was said only to comfort his pupils and himself. "You must post security with Crito for me—the opposite of the one that he posted with the judges for me. He gave assurance that I would definitely remain, but you can assure him that I definitely shall not remain when I am dead but shall go away" (p. 119).[176] Yet ironic statements such as these are quite compatible with the presumed earnestness and the deep pathos that are supposed to permeate this entire dialogue; however, one really ought not deny that they show up to far better advantage when one discerns the quiet, secret developing of irony in them.

My first contribution to the support of my position, however, is a defense of my claim that the spirit in this dialogue is genuinely Greek and not Oriental. Insofar as I can grasp Oriental mysticism, whatever dying away [*Hendøen*] is to be XIII
found there consists in a relaxation of the soul's muscular 159
strength, of the tension that constitutes consciousness, in a disintegration and melancholic relapsing lethargy, in a softening whereby one becomes heavier, not lighter, whereby one is

not volatilized but is chaotically scrambled and then moves with vague motions in a thick fog. Therefore the Oriental may indeed wish to be liberated from the body and feel it as something burdensome, but this is really not in order to become more free but in order to become more bound, as if he wished for the vegetative still life of the plant instead of locomotion. It is wishing for the foggy, drowsy wallowing that an opiate can procure rather than for the sky of thought, wishing for an illusory repose in a consummation connected with a *dolce far niente* [sweet idleness] rather than for the energy of action.[177] But the Grecian sky is high and arched, not flat and burdensome; it rises ever higher, does not anxiously sink down; its air is light and transparent, not hazy and close. Therefore the longings to be found here tend to become lighter and lighter, to be concentrated in an ever more volatile sublimate, and tend not to evaporate in a deadening lethargy. Consciousness does not want to be soaked to softness in vague qualifications but to be stretched more and more. Thus the Oriental wants to go back behind consciousness, the Greek to go over and beyond the sequence of consciousness. But this sheer abstractness that it desires becomes ultimately the most abstract, the lightest of all—namely, nothing.

And here we stand at a point of coincidence of the two views, one that arises either from the subjective mysticism or from the irony. That the existence resulting from the successive dying to [*Afdøen*] is understood altogether abstractly in the *Phaedo* will surely be obvious to anyone who has read this dialogue. To point this out a bit more explicitly may not be amiss, however. This may be done partly by showing how Socrates views the nature of the soul, insofar as the right view of the soul must actually contain within itself, must be impregnated with, the right demonstration of its immortality, and partly by analyzing more carefully the various statements with respect to the soul's future how. In this latter inquiry, I shall *subsidialiter* [for assistance] refer to the *Apology*, which, as an expressly historical document, may be able to direct us on our way.

Just one comment before proceeding to these investigations—namely, because of the importance such a question as the immortality of the soul must always have, there is something dubious about its being treated incidentally in Platonism, that is, on the occasion of Socrates' death. Thus I shall XIII 160 begin with the first investigation, or with the question of how Socrates *views the nature of the soul*, and this leads us into a closer examination of the *demonstrations* he advances for its immortality.*

* Here I shall touch briefly on two other demonstrations that appear more indirectly in the *Phaedo*. The *first* comes at the very beginning of the dialogue, where Socrates warns against suicide and calls to mind the words of the Mystery rite to the effect that we human beings are on a kind of guard duty and must not absolve ourselves or slip away.[178] If this observation had been allowed to concentrate upon its rich content, if it had been expanded to the concept of human beings as the deity's co-workers[179] and the real existence before God implied in that concept, then this observation would contain a view, even though in a popular and more upbuilding than demonstrative form, that would emerge in the idea's regeneration with a speculative bearing. But this does not happen. In response to Cebes' genuinely Greek remark that if one really adhered to this thought one would continue to cling to life instead of wishing, as philosophers do according to Socrates,[180] to die, would cling to life in order not to get away from the power of the gods, Socrates answers that he, too, would be afraid to die if he did not believe he would meet other gods who are also good,[181] a rather obscure answer, because this indeed fixes a chasmal abyss between this life and a next life and, since death always becomes a withdrawal from the power of the gods of this life, the ambiguous relation to them still remains. Not until one recognizes that it is the same god who has led one by the hand through life and in the moment of death lets go, as it were, in order to open his arms and receive in them the yearning soul,[182] not until then is the demonstration fully developed in conceptual form. —The *second* indirect demonstration is purely personal. The gladness, the bold confidence, the dauntlessness with which Socrates goes to his death, the indifference with which he practically disregards it, are very inspiring, of course, both to those contemporary witnesses and to those who through them have over the centuries become witnesses[183] to his death. He sends Xanthippe away in order not to hear screaming and wailing.[184] He jests about how quickly the pleasant follows upon the unpleasant: "because I felt a pain in my leg from the chain, the pleasant feeling now seems to follow."[185] It appeals to his sense of the comic that the pleasant and the unpleasant are like two bodies attached to the same head, and he adds that it would have been a task for Aesop, "who, if he had thought of it, would have made up this fable: that the god wanted to XIII 161 stop their continued quarreling, and when he found that it was impossible, he fastened them together by their extremities."[186] He picks up the poison cup

XIII 161 By way of introduction to the argumentation proper, Socrates first of all informs us of the meaning of the philosophers' wish to die. If death, as acknowledged, is a separation of soul and body and, furthermore, if genuine knowledge depends upon an abstraction from the lower sense perceptions, since by way of any sense perception one never encounters that which constitutes the essential nature of a thing, that by which it is what it is, such as magnitude, health, strength, etc. (see p. 17),[188] then one readily comprehends that the philosophers are bound to wish (see p. 20)[189] to have as little as possible to do with the body; indeed, they are bound to wish to be purified by death and freed from the foolishness of the body in order to complete what they have already sought to do here in life (see p. 18)[190]—to hunt down the pure essence of things with pure thought. But obviously the soul is here understood just as abstractly as the pure essence of the things that are the object of its activity. And even if philosophy ever so energetically seeks to scare this pure essence of things out of all its hiding places, a serious doubt remains as to whether anything else will really show up other than the purely abstract (health, magnitude, etc.), which as such in its contrast to the concrete is nothing.

It follows, then, that in order to become really congruent with its object the soul in its cognitive activity must become nothing to the same degree. Indeed, the soul must ever and always become lighter and lighter to such a degree that only the souls that have cultivated too much affiliation with the body will for this reason (see p. 50)[191] be weighed down and
XIII 162 dragged back to the visible world, fearing the formless and the

---

with the same dignity, the same zest for life with which he would have picked up a foaming goblet at a banquet. He asks the jailer: "What do you think? Does one dare pour out some of this drink as a sacrifice? Is it permitted or not?"[187] All this is fine, but if one also bears in mind that he still does not really know what the shape of the next life will be or whether there will be a next life, if amid this poetry we hear the prosaic calculating that it can never do any harm to assume another life and other things that will be made clear at the proper place, then one sees that the persuasive power of this argument is considerably limited.

world of spirit, and hovering around tombstones and graves like shadowy apparitions. Souls that have not been completely released but are still involved in the visible world (which is why they are also visible) must appear to us as such apparitions. Presumably there is no objection to regarding ghosts as incomplete existences, but when the "formless" is set as the ideal, it is apparent how negatively everything is conceived and how the soul comes to be nothing. Thus if one will accept the dilemma posited by Socrates (see p. 20),[192] that one must assume one of two things, that we shall either never come to comprehension or not until after death, then one certainly will also be rather dubious about the Socratic compromise. I have lingered a bit longer on this introductory probing to give some idea of what to expect in the observations to come. It would take too long to marshal all the arguments and examine each one, and I refer to Baur and Ast those readers who do not wish to follow them in their development through the discussion but wish to see them, as far as possible, in their complete scholarly formulation.

It seems more important, however, to point out that the particular arguments advanced do not always harmonize. To be specific, if the argument based on the observation that opposites come from opposites[193]—and that among the units of the opposites there are two currents, the first flowing to the second and the second flowing back to the first—is placed together with the argument based on a consideration of the preexistence of the soul as manifested in the nature and essence of recollection,[194] with the aim thereby to assure continuity, then it seems to me that either the concept of the preexistence of the soul excludes the idea of its coming into existence or, if preexistence is to be kept in harmony with the view of becoming, then it must be assumed that Socrates has demonstrated the resurrection of bodies. But this, of course, completely contradicts the rest of his theory. No doubt there will always be a discrepancy between these two arguments, one that cannot be removed by the ambiguity in the first argument about the real nature of death or by the surreptitious presupposition (to which Baur justifiably takes exception) that death is not

the cessation of life but just another kind of existence (see *op. cit.*, p. 114). Now, one can certainly agree with Baur when he disputes the evidential weight of these arguments and thinks
XIII 163 that they are only an analytic exposition of the concept of the soul and that consequently immortality derives from them only to the extent that it is already presupposed in the concept of the soul. Yet one must not disregard that the hard thing the soul becomes here does not stand here as a point of departure, as is usual with the good, the beautiful, etc., but as a conclusion, that it is precisely when reflection wants to grasp the essence of the soul that the soul appears as impenetrable, and it is not by virtue of the soul's impenetrability that the profusion of arguments eventuates. In other words, this is a negative conclusion and the other a positive presupposition, as I must once again point out.

If we now turn to what the nature of the soul must be, what specific existence it must have, insofar as the answer to these questions is to be gained from the conception of it implied in the argument for its immortality drawn from the nature and essence of recollection, we also come to the most abstract qualifications. To be specific, the impact of sense impressions leads one to certain universal concepts—for example, equality (see pp. 33ff.),[195] the in-and-for-itself beauty, the good, justice, piety, etc.—indeed, to all those characteristics "that we designate in our questions as well as in our answers as that which is" (see p. 37).[196] These universal concepts are not attained through the atomistic observations of experience or by the usurpations of induction—on the contrary, they continually presuppose themselves. "Consequently, either we are born with this knowledge and we possess it throughout our whole lives, or they of whom we say that they learn something basically only recollect it, and therefore to learn is a recollecting" (see p. 38).[197]

Here the speculatively unexplained (indeed, anything speculative is at first glance paradoxical) synthesis of the temporal and the eternal is poetically and religiously set at ease. What we confront here is not the eternal self-presupposing of self-consciousness that allows the universal to enclose the particular, the individual, tightly and constrictively—on the contrary, the universal flutters loosely around it. The *punctum saliens* [salient point] in the argumentation really amounts to this—that just as the ideas exist before palpable things, so the soul exists before the body. In and by itself, this no doubt sounds rather acceptable, but as long as there is no explanation as to how ideas exist before things and in what sense they do, we see that the "just as" around which everything revolves becomes the abstract equal sign between two unknown quantities.

As for believing in further enlightenment through closer examination of the given quantity on one side of the equal XIII 164
sign, a belief already strengthened by the thought that the discussion is of the in-and-for-itself good, beauty, justice, piety, this is suppressed again when we consider that the preexistence of the soul indeed depends on the preexistence of equality etc. If it goes no better with the preexistence of the soul than with universal concepts such as these, then it is easy to see that it vanishes into this infinite abstraction just as they do. Presumably it is possible to make a transition from this point to a positive view, in the form of either a victorious speculation or a definite loss of faith, but this does not happen; and what the reader must absorb as an eternal *in mente* [in mind][198] even in the most minor calculation in this whole study is that this point is not the nothing as the point of departure but the nothing arrived at by way of strenuous reflection.

And one can go even further. Suppose a concept could be joined to this existence of the ideas outside any concretion, the question would still remain: In what relation to this would the preexisting soul then be placed? In its life on earth, its activity was to lead the particular back to this universal, but the concrete relation of the particular to the universal as given in and with individuality was apparently out of the question. The connection between these two powers achieved by the soul was altogether transitory, in no way permanent. Consequently, to that extent the soul in its earlier existence would then have to be totally volatilized in the world of ideas, as so aptly articulated by Plato when he says that upon its transition

into the physical life the soul forgets these ideas,[199] because this forgetting is precisely the night that precedes the day of consciousness and is the center of gravity, which is indeed infinitely vanishing, a nothing, from which the universal gradually crystallizes out the particular. Thus forgetting is the eternal limiting presupposition that is infinitely negated by the eternally combining presupposition of recollection. But the fact that the Platonic doctrine needs the two extremes of abstraction, totally abstract preexistence and the equally abstract postexistence, that is, immortality, simply shows that the soul must be understood altogether abstractly and negatively also in its temporal existence. Plato's belief that life on this earth shades off (to use a term both pictorial and musical) on both sides might lead one to the view that the life on this earth is
XIII the full center, but this is by no means the case here in the
165 *Phaedo*. On the contrary, this life is the incomplete, and the formless is that toward which longing aspires.*

We end up with conclusions just as abstract when we work our way through the rest of the demonstrations to the view of the soul that is the basis for them. —The noncompounded cannot be disintegrated, cannot perish. But the compounded is subject to disintegration in the same manner as it is compounded. Since the soul belongs to the noncompounded, it follows that it cannot be disintegrated. But this whole train of thought is altogether deceptive since it moves on the quaggy ground of tautology. Thus we must follow Socrates as he elucidates the analogies. The uncompounded is that which always remains invariable. Does that being, that entity itself to which we in our discussion attribute genuine being, he asks (p. 44),[200] always remain invariable or is it at times this and at other times different? The in-and-for-itself equality, beauty, and everything that has genuine being—can this ever undergo

* Just as in the *Symposium* it is longing that constitutes the substance, so also here. However, in the *Symposium* it is the longing that desires to possess, while in the *Phaedo* it desires to lose, but both qualifications are equally negative, since both longings are ignorant of the what into which the one wishes to hurl itself and into which the other wishes to be volatilized by dying to [*Afdøen*].

any change whatever? "These things are always exactly the same, are formless, and cannot be seen."[201]

Now, the soul has the greatest similarity to what is divine, immortal, rational, homogeneous, indissoluble, and is ever self-consistent and invariable; whereas the body has the greatest similarity to that which is human, mortal, irrational, multiform, dissoluble, and never self-consistent (p. 47).[202] But here we come to an equally abstract view of the existence of the soul and its relation to the body. To be more specific, this view is by no means guilty of tangibly assigning the soul a specific place in the body, but on the other hand it does disregard, and completely, the soul's relation to the body, and the soul, instead of moving freely in the body produced by it, continually tries to sneak out of the body. The metaphor Cebes later uses as an objection to the immortality of the soul (insofar as this was concluded from the view that since the body, which nevertheless is the weaker, continues, then the soul, which is the stronger, must necessarily continue), that
this is like saying of a deceased old weaver that the man is not XIII
dead but must certainly be somewhere, and as proof adducing 166
that the suit he had worn and which he himself had woven was intact and not destroyed (p. 61)[203]—this metaphor, I say, if properly used with an accentuation of the ingeniousness of comparing the soul to a weaver, would already lead to far more concrete concepts. That the soul is not compounded is quite admissible, but as long as there is no more explicit answer to the question in what sense it is not compounded and, in another sense, to what extent it is a summary of qualifications, the definition of the soul naturally becomes totally negative, and its immortality becomes just as *langweilig* [boring] as the eternal number one.

The situation turns out to be no better with the last argument, which is built on the thesis that whatever continues to exist does so through its participation in the idea, and that every idea intrinsically rules out the opposite (p. 97[204]: "Or must we not say that three will rather succumb and suffer anything than to tolerate being three and also becoming even") and also that this ruling out holds not only for the idea but also for everything that belongs under the idea. The soul is the life principle, but life is the opposite of death and consequently the soul can never assimilate the idea's (i.e., life's) opposite (i.e., death); therefore it is immortal. But at this point the idea heads further and further *gerade ins Blaue hinein* [straight out into the wild blue yonder] of abstraction. For as long as the relation of contrast between life and death goes unexplained, the relation of soul to body is also understood altogether negatively, and the life of the soul apart from the body in every case remains indeterminate and without predication.

But if the nature of the soul is understood that abstractly, one can figure out in advance what elucidation to expect with regard to the question of the *how* of the future existence of the soul. By this I do not mean topographical and statistical surveys of the new world, nor a fantastic potpourri, but speculative transparency with respect to this question. Indeed, the Apostle John also says that we do not know how we shall be,[205] but this, of course, is in the vein of an experience beyond this world. But the speculative elucidation that there is a resurrection of bodies was an obvious conclusion for him, not in
XIII 167 order to escape a difficulty but because he himself found rest in it. On the other hand, it is stated even in the mythical part of this dialogue that the continuance or resurrection of bodies is something that only the ungodly have to fear, whereas they who are adequately purified by philosophy will in the coming time live altogether without bodies (p. 117).[206] The only attempt made to resist this unrestrained leap of abstraction out "into the wide world" and to obtain real existence that does not permit thought to capsize and life to be volatilized is the ethical harmony, the moral melody, that will provide the natural law constitutive of everything in the new order of things, will provide, if I may put it in one short phrase, the just retribution that will be the moving principle in everything. Indeed, when this view comes to be honored and respected, immortality will not be a phantom existence and eternal life will not be a *Schattenspiel an der Wand* [shadow play on the wall]. But not even in the mythical part of the dialogue is this worked out completely. How far it is worked out will be ex-

amined later; at this point just bear in mind that it is attempted only in the mythical part of the dialogue.

Now, thought can once again turn back to the point momentarily out of view—the negative *what* and the equally negative *how*, which in the dialectical development in the *Phaedo* declare themselves as the positive answer to the question of the nature of the soul, insofar as this incloses within itself the demonstration of its immortality. That the whole observation ends negatively, that life dies away in the distant, fading echo (*Nachhall* [reverberation] is to me a preferable word), could be due to the subjective Platonic position, which—dissatisfied with the idea's immediacy in existence, for example, as rendered in the blissful satisfaction of the classical—now tries to grasp it as given in reflection and therefore clasps the cloud instead of Juno.[207] This subjective view adds nothing that was not there before but even deprives it of something—namely, actuality. Rosenkrantz[208] has correctly observed somewhere that the fuller life is, the more exuberantly it burgeons, the paler and more insubstantial is immortality. Homer's heroes[209] sigh for the very humblest station in actual life and
wish to trade the underworld's realm of shades for it. In Plato, XIII
immortality becomes even slighter, indeed, almost to the 168
point of being blown away, and yet the philosopher wishes to forsake actuality, yes, as far as possible to be dead already while still alive. This, then, is the tragic self-contradiction of the subjective position.

But this still does not bring us to see the ironical, and yet this is what I am trying to show as far as possible. That irony can be like this to a T, that in a superficial examination irony can even be confused with it, will surely be admitted by anyone who knows what a small, invisible character irony is. Accordingly, this again is one of the points of coincidence between Plato and Socrates. Thus, by accentuating in particular the pathos that frequently appears in this dialogue, someone may assign everything to Plato, to the enthusiasm that surely is underpaid in terms of the conclusion. On the other hand, however, it is certainly undeniable that in the dialogue a kind of uncertainty prevails that indicates that irony is involved in one way or another. No matter how negligible the conclusion, it nevertheless could very well be expressed with all the conviction of enthusiasm. This uncertainty is perceptible in several places in the *Phaedo*, and these passages gain importance when linked to the *Apology*, which, if the purely Socratic is sought, must be assigned a preeminent place as a historical document.

Before proceeding to this documentation, however, I must pause to consider somewhat more closely the longing for death attributed to the philosopher in the *Phaedo*, inasmuch as the view that life essentially consists in dying to can be understood both morally and intellectually. It has been understood morally in Christianity, which did not stop with the purely negative, either, because to the same degree a person dies to the one, the other has a divine increase,[210] and when this other has assimilated, so to speak, and appropriated and thereby refined all the germinating power in the body of sin, which must be mortified, then this, too, gradually shrivels up and dries out, and as it cracks and crumbles the full-grown God-man arises out of it, created after God [*efter Gud*][211] in the righteousness and holiness of truth. Insofar as Christianity also assumes a more perfect knowledge related to this regeneration, this is nevertheless only secondary and mainly only to the extent that knowledge was formerly infected with the contamination of sin. The Greek mentality understands this dying to intellectually, that is, purely intellectually, and here one also
XIII 169 recognizes at once paganism's carefree Pelagianism.

To be on the safe side, allow me to point out what in all likelihood most readers realize. On the one hand, in Christianity that which is to be died to is understood in its positivity as sin, as a realm that all too convincingly proclaims its validity to everyone who languishes under its laws; on the other hand, that which is to be born and is to arise is understood just as positively. In the intellectual dying to, that which is to be died to is something indifferent; that which is to grow during this dying to is something abstract.

The relation between these two important views is somewhat as follows. The one says that we should refrain from unwholesome food, control desire, and then good health will come; the other says that we are to stop eating and drinking, and then one can have the hope of gradually becoming nothing. Thus we see that the Greek is more of a rigorist than the Christian, but therefore his view is also untrue. According to the Christian view, the moment of death is the last struggle between day and night; death, as is so beautifully expressed in the Church, is birth.[212] In other words, the Christian does not dwell upon the struggle, the doubt, the pain, the negative, but rejoices in the victory, the certitude, the blessedness, the positive.

Platonism wants one to die to sensate knowing in order to be dissolved by death into the kingdom of immortality, where the in-and-for-itself equality, the in-and-for-itself beauty, etc., live in the stillness of death. This is articulated even more strongly by Socrates when he declares that a philosopher's desire is to die and *to be dead*.[213] But to desire death in and for itself this way cannot be based on enthusiasm, provided this word is respected and is not applied, for example, to the madness sometimes seen in one who wishes for extinction, a desire that must be based on a kind of weariness with life. As long as it cannot be said that the content of this wish is really discerned, enthusiasm can still be present; whereas if the desire has its basis in a certain apathy or if the person wishing to die is himself aware of what he is wishing, then life-weariness is dominant. In my view, that well-known epitaph by Wessel, "At last he could not be bothered to live,"[214] contains irony's perception of death. But he who dies because he cannot be bothered to live certainly would not wish for a new life either,
since that would indeed be a contradiction. Obviously the lan- XIII
guor that desires death in this sense is a snobbish sickness 170
found only in the highest social circles and in its perfectly unalloyed state is just as great as the enthusiasm that sees in death the transfiguration of life. Ordinary human life moves drowsily and vaguely between these two poles. Irony is a healthiness insofar as it rescues the soul from the snares of relativity; it is a sickness insofar as it cannot bear the absolute except in the form of nothing, but this sickness is an endemic disease

that only a few individuals catch and from which fewer recover.

As for the irony in the *Phaedo*, this must be grasped, of course, in the moment when irony as intuition breaches the bastion that separates the waters of heaven and of earth and unites with the total irony that annihilates the individual. This point is just as hard to fix as the point between thawing and freezing, and yet the *Phaedo*, if one is willing to use my proposed gauge of *point de vue*, lies precisely between these two qualifications of irony. I shall now proceed to a documentation insofar as this is possible. In this respect, my intention is by no means to conceal that any such documentation continually presupposes a something, the totality of intuition that transcends the specific, the "Let there be" of creation[215] that in every work of man does not come until afterward, in the moment when the invisible becomes perceptible in the visible. To be specific, if it were a subjective mysticism, of which Socrates was not a victim (since this term would indeed already suggest a consciousness), but whose cornucopious overflowing, as it were, overwhelmed him, then we presumably would not hear at the same time a doubting, uncertain calculation of probability. That this takes place surely no one who has read the *Phaedo* carefully will deny, and even less anyone who has only casually skimmed the *Apology*. It must be left to individual judgment whether such remarks can be brought into harmony with the pathos of a Plato or, what amounts to the same thing, put into tune with a Socrates altogether identified with Plato, or whether it does not rather indicate a difference that is just as unlike as it is like and just as like as it is unlike. That this is the case with an immediate speculation and irony has already been intimated above, and the inquiry will also come back to this frequently.

Socrates himself declares in the *Phaedo* that the primary aim of his endeavors to demonstrate the immortality of the soul really is to become convinced himself that this is so and adds: "I reckon, dear friend—and you see how selfish I am—that if
XIII what I assume is true, it is still excellent to be convinced of it,
171 but if there is nothing after death, I will at least during the time

before my death be less burdensome to my companions because of complaints, and furthermore this folly of mine will not last long—for that would indeed be an evil—but in a short time will vanish" (Heise's translation, p. 69).[216] Now these words sound from a totally different world, and it certainly is not only the exclamation θέασαι ὡς πλεονεκτικῶς [see how selfish I am] that conceals the irony. The thought that one might become absolutely nothing through death (εἰ δὲ μηδέν ἐστι τελευτήσαντι; *sin post mortem sensus omnis atque ipse animus exstinguitur* [but nothing remains for the dead; but if after death all consciousness and the soul itself are extinguished], see Stallbaum, p. 133) does not horrify him at all. On the other hand, he does not take it along in order, terrified by this conclusion, to drive the eccentric thought home again, but he actually does jest with it and, should the worst come to worst, would rather be snatched out of this error, "for to remain in it would indeed be an evil," and thereby be totally annihilated. But what expressly characterizes irony is the abstract standard by which it levels everything, by which it controls every inordinate emotion, thus does not set the pathos of enthusiasm against the fear of death but finds that it is a curious hypothesis to surmise total extinction in this way. This must be a *locus classicus* [standard illustrative passage] of the *Phaedo*; the scattered similar touches of irony found here and there would require a much too detailed treatment for me to embark on it. Moreover, the *Apology* now calls for attention.

APOLOGY

The *Apology* will be used for a dual purpose: first, to use its comments on the immortality of the soul to support our argumentation drawn from the *Phaedo* in which we tried to let the dialectic in this dialogue round itself off in irony and, second, on the basis of its total structure, to let Socrates' position become apparent as irony.

Provided one does not assume with Ast[217] that the *Apology* is not by Plato but by some unknown orator, it is a matter of indifference for this investigation whether one maintains with
Schleiermacher that this defense actually was delivered in this XIII 172

manner by Socrates* or with Stallbaum that it presumably was not delivered in this manner but that Plato in working on this speech tried to come as close to the historical Socrates as possible. Stallbaum declares *(praefatio ad apologiam Socratis*, p. 4[219]): "quae (sc. sententia) si vera est, nemo, opinor, mirabitur, quod Plato non eam, quam alias, verborum sententiarumque sublimitatem in hoc libro adhibuit. Nam quum Socratem ita demum sibi videretur recte defendere, si illum, qualis in vita fuerit, talem in judicio dicentem faceret, non licebat ei arbitratu suo agere, sed debebat videre, quid Socratis ingenio et moribus conveniret, et quid loci ac temporis rationibus esset accommodatum [if this (thought) is true, I think no one will marvel at the fact that Plato does not apply the loftiness of words and thoughts in this book that he does in other places. For since he rightly seems to defend Socrates so precisely as he saw it, if he were to portray him speaking in the courtroom just as he was in life, he would not be permitted to plead at his own discretion, but he would have had to look to what was fitting in regard to the genius and character of Socrates and what would have been appropriate to the circumstances of place and time]." If anyone wishes to become informed about the large number of authors who have come out against Ast, their names are conveniently listed in the same passage in Stallbaum. For me the most important point is that an authentic picture of the actual Socrates is seen in the *Apology*. Ast, who found loftiness and pathos predominant in the *Phaedo*, can, of course, only be indignant over the manner in which Socrates conducts himself here, and this is one of the reasons he declares the *Apology* to be spurious. But if one assumes

* See Schleiermacher, *Platons Werke* (Berlin: 1818, I[2]): "Nichts ist demnach wahrscheinlicher, als dasz wir an dieser Rede von der wirklichen Vertheidigung des Socrates eine so treue Nachschrift aus der Erinnerung haben, als bei dem geübten Gedächtnisz des Platon und dem nothwendigen Unterschiede der geschriebenen Rede von der nachlässig gesprochenen nur möglich war [Accordingly, nothing is more probable than that in this speech we have as true a copy from recollection of the actual defence of Socrates as the practised memory of Plato, and the necessary distinction between a written speech and one negligently delivered, could render possible]."[218]

with the majority—indeed, a clear majority of interpreters—that the *Apology* is authentic, then one is really obliged to find something other than the usual way of confining oneself to the assurance that there is nothing in the *Apology* that is alien to Plato's spirit, whether this assurance seeks its strength in being set forth interrogatively or assertively. Ast's objections are really too important to be dispatched* in this way, and, if he is right, one is tempted also to allow that he is right in pre- XIII
ferring Xenophon's *Apology* to Plato's.[220] 173

Here, however, the issue will be not the *Apology* as a whole but the passages in which Socrates develops his view of death. As the difficulty of explaining them Platonically increases, the likelihood of seeking the right explanation in irony also increases. All these passages manifest Socrates' complete incertitude, but, please note, not as if this incertitude had disquieted him; no, on the contrary, this game with life, this giddiness, with death showing itself at one time as infinitely significant and at another time as nothing, is what appeals to him. On the front of the stage, then, is Socrates—not as someone who rashly brushes away the thought of death and clings anxiously to life, not as someone who eagerly goes toward death and magnanimously sacrifices his life; no, as someone who takes delight in the alternation of light and shadow found in a syllogistic *aut/aut* [either/or][221] when it almost simultaneously manifests broad daylight and pitch darkness, manifests the infinitely real and the infinitely nothing; as someone who on behalf of his audience also takes delight in the fact that these two points are like the pleasure and the pain joined together at the top (see *Symposium*[222]), and yet on that account does not crave certainty with the soul's fervent longing but with a kind of inquisitiveness longs for the solution of this riddle. Socrates

* I recall from my early youth, when the soul demands the lofty, the paradigmatical, how when reading the *Apology* I felt disappointed, deceived, and depressed because it seemed to me that all the poetical, the courage that triumphs over death, was here wretchedly replaced by a rather prosaic reckoning executed in such a way that one could believe that Socrates wanted to say: When all is said and done, this whole affair doesn't concern me much at all. Later I learned to understand it otherwise.

is very aware that his syllogisms do not provide an exhaustive answer to the question, but just the speed with which the infinite contrast appears and disappears delights him. The background, receding infinitely, forms the infinite possibility of death.

Thus in the *Apology* the most pathos-filled outbursts are usually followed by argumentation that blows away the foam of eloquence and discloses that underneath there is nothing XIII whatever. Socrates points out how foolish it would be for 174 him, whom the god charged to live as a lover of wisdom (φιλοσοφοῦντα [loving wisdom, philosophizing][223]) and to explore and examine himself and others, how foolish it would be for him to abandon his post out of fear of death. Now comes the reason (see Ast, p. 126, 29 a): "τὸ γάρ τοι θάνατον δεδιέναι, ὦ ἄνδρες, οὐδὲν ἄλλο ἐστὶν ἢ δοκεῖν σοφὸν εἶναι, μὴ ὄντα· δοκεῖν γὰρ εἰδέναι ἐστιν ἃ οὐκ οἶδεν· . . . . . καὶ τοῦτο πῶς οὐκ ἀμαθία ἐστὶν αὕτη ἡ ἐπονείδιστος ἡ τοῦ οἴεσθαι εἰδέναι ἃ οὐκ οἶδεν [For let me tell you, gentlemen, that to be afraid of death is only another form of thinking that one is wise when one is not; it is to think that one knows what one does not know . . . . . and this ignorance, which thinks that it knows what it does not, must surely be ignorance most culpable]."[224] In this respect, too, Socrates feels that he has an advantage over others, for since he knows nothing at all about death he does not fear it. Now this is not only a sophism but also irony.[225] In other words, as he emancipates people from the fear of death, in recompense he gives them the alarming idea of an unavoidable something about which nothing whatever is known, and, to find repose in that, one certainly must be habituated to being built up by the quietude inherent in nothing. Therefore, as he remarks elsewhere, it would be unreasonable of him to choose something else that he definitely knew to be an evil (for example, prison) out of fear of suffering the penalty Meletus thinks he has deserved (see Ast, VIII, p. 146, 37 b): "ὅ φημι οὐκ εἰδέναι οὔτ' εἰ ἀγαθὸν οὔτ' εἰ κακόν ἐστιν [when, as I said, I do not know whether it is a good thing or a bad]."[226]

At the end of the *Apology*, however, an attempt is made to

show that to die is a good. But this observation is once again an *aut/aut*, and since the view that death is nothing whatever emerges in conjunction with the one *aut*, the extent to which one can share the joy that encircles both these continents like the ocean certainly becomes somewhat doubtful. See Ast, VIII, p. 154, 40 c-e: "Ἐννοήσωμεν δὲ καὶ τῇδε, ὡς πολλὴ ἐλπίς ἐστιν ἀγαθὸν αὐτὸ εἶναι. δυοῖν γὰρ θάτερόν ἐστι τὸ τεθνάναι· ἢ γὰρ οἷον μηδὲν εἶναι μηδ' αἴσθησιν μηδεμίαν μηδενὸς ἔχειν τὸν τεθνεῶτα, ἤ, κατὰ τὰ λεγόμενα, μεταβολή τις τυγχάνει οὖσα καὶ μετοίκησις τῆς ψυχῆς τοῦ τόπου τοῦ ἐνθένδε εἰς ἄλλον τόπον. καὶ εἴτε δὴ μηδεμία αἴσθησίς ἐστιν, ἀλλ' οἷον ὕπνος, ἐπειδάν τις καθεύδων μηδ' ὄναρ μηδὲν ὁρᾷ, θαυμάσιον κέρδος ἂν εἴη ὁ θάνατος. ἐγὼ γὰρ ἂν οἶμαι, εἴ τινα ἐκλεξάμενον δέοι ταύτην τὴν νύκτα, ἐν ᾗ οὕτω κατέδαρθεν ὥστε μηδ' ὄναρ ἰδεῖν, καὶ τὰς ἄλλας νύκτας τε καὶ ἡμέρας τὰς τοῦ βίου τοῦ ἑαυτοῦ ἀντιπαραθέντα ταύτῃ τῇ νυκτὶ, δέοι σκεψάμενον εἰπεῖν, ὁπόσας ἄμεινον καὶ ἥδιον ἡμέρας καὶ νύκτας ταύτης τῆς νυκτὸς βεβίωκεν ἐν τῷ ἑαυτοῦ βίῳ, οἶμαι ἂν μὴ ὅτι ἰδιώτην τινά, ἀλλὰ τὸν μέγαν βασιλέα εὐαριθμήτους ἂν εὑρεῖν αὐτὸν ταύτας πρὸς τὰς ἄλλας ἡμέρας καὶ νύκτας. εἰ οὖν τοιοῦτον ὁ θάνατός ἐστι, κέρδος ἔγωγε λέγω. καὶ γὰρ οὐδὲν πλείων ὁ πᾶς χρόνος φαίνεται οὕτω δὴ εἶναι ἢ μία νύξ. εἰ δ' αὖ οἷον ἀποδημῆσαί ἐστιν ὁ θάνατος ἐνθένδε εἰς ἄλλον τόπον, καὶ ἀληθῆ ἐστι τὰ λεγόμενα, ὡς ἄρα ἐκεῖ εἰσὶν ἅπαντες οἱ τεθνεῶτες, τί μεῖζον ἀγαθὸν τούτου εἴη ἄν, ὦ ἄνδρες δικασταί [We should reflect that there is much reason to hope for a good result on other grounds as well. Death is one of two things. Either it is annihilation, and the dead have no consciousness of anything, or, as we are told, it is really a change—a migration of the soul from this place to another. Now if there is no consciousness but only a dreamless sleep, death must be a marvelous gain. I suppose that if anyone were told to pick out the night on which he slept so soundly as not even to dream, and then to compare it with all the other nights and days of his life, and then were told to say, after due consideration, how many better and happier days and nights than this he had spent in the course of his life—well, I think that the Great King himself, to say nothing of any private person, would find these days and nights easy to count in comparison with the rest. If death is like this, then I call it a gain, because the whole time, if you look at it in this way, can be regarded as no more than one single night. If on the other hand death is a removal from here to some other place, and if what we are told is true, that all the dead are there, what greater blessing could there be than this, gentlemen?]."[227] The latter must also be joyful, because then one escapes those judges who pretend to be judges and comes to judges who deserve to be judges—such as Minos, Rhadamanthus, Aeacus, and Triptolemus.[228]

Thus, on the one horn of the dilemma, he believes that to become nothing whatever by death is θαυμάσιον κέρδος [a marvelous gain]—indeed, his words take on an intensity when he declares that not merely a private person but the Great King himself would have but few days to compare to this. A sleep of the soul such as this and a nothing such as this must eminently appeal to the ironist, who right here has the absolute
XIII face-to-face with life's relativity, but an absolute so light that
176 he cannot overstrain himself on it since he has it in the form of
nothing. On the other horn of the dilemma, he elaborates on how superb it would be in the underworld to come to grips with the great men of the past and to chat with them pleasantly about their fate but above all to ask them questions and examine them*—remarks the ironic nature of which I have touched on earlier.[229]

Hence just a few comments at this point. It is clear, in the first place, that these remarks cannot easily be reconciled with the expectations voiced in the *Phaedo* of becoming disembodied and, in the second place, that this joy is very hypothetical, since the other possibility is indeed so close at hand, that is, not a hairbreadth away. This hypothesis in toto evaporates into thin air, and Socrates makes no attempt to actualize the one half of it any more than he does the other. The previously quoted words from the *Phaedo* presumably do contain an attempt, for Socrates believes that it is the most attractive alternative, since then a person will be less burdensome to his

* Here immortality and eternal life are understood as infinite progress, as an eternal interrogation.

friends; but the reader will undoubtedly find in this observation a shrewdness about life and an irony that daringly ventures to trick death. The *Apology* ends with the same ambiguity (42 a): "'Αλλὰ γὰρ ἤδη ὥρα ἀπιέναι, ἐμοὶ μὲν ἀποθανουμένῳ, ὑμῖν δὲ βιωσομένοις· ὁπότεροι δὲ ἡμῶν ἔρχονται ἐπὶ ἄμεινον πρᾶγμα, ἄδηλον παντὶ πλὴν ἢ τῷ θεῷ [Now it is time that we are going, I to die and you to live, but which of us has the happier prospect is unknown to anyone but the god]."[230] Now if this is true of the view of death itself in the *Apology*, then the probability of my interpretation of the *Phaedo* thereby increases, if the possibility is established that the *Phaedo* can simultaneously be Socratic and Platonic.

I shall now proceed to a more specific scrutiny of the *Apology* in order to show that in its totality it is irony. With that in mind, I will let Ast[231] speak for a moment, hoping that, by means of the enormous pressure the weight of his comments must necessarily have, the reader's soul will gain adequate resilience to permit the irony to surface. "Diese männliche Standhaftigkeit des Socrates (that Ast finds in Xenophon's XIII
presentation) hat der Redner nach seiner Weise so übertrieben, 177
dasz sie als die geist- und gemüthloseste Gleichgültigkeit erscheint. Nach der Verurtheilung nemlich läszt er den Socrates nicht über den Ausspruch der Richter, sondern über die Zahl der beiderseitigen Stimmen sich wundern, und die kaltblütige Berechnung anstellen, dasz er entkommen seyn würde, wenn nur drei Stimmen anders gefallen wären, und dasz Melitos, wenn nicht Anytos und Lykon mit ihrer Anklage hinzugekommen wären, tausend Drachmen erlegen müszte, weil ihm der fünfte Theil der Stimmen nicht zugefallen wäre. Noch auffallender ist diese Gleichgültigkeit da, wo Socrates vom Tode redet; immer versichert er, dasz er sich vor dem Tode nicht fürchte, aber worauf gründet sich diese Furchtlosigkeit? Auf nichts; also ist sie leere Prahlerei . . . . . Konnte Platon, der Verfasser des Phädon, den Socrates so über den Tod reden lassen, und ihm eine solche wahrhaft gemeine, geist- und gefühllose ja fast lächerliche Gleichgültigkeit zuschreiben . . . . . Und gleichwohl will dieser gefühl- und gemüthlose Socrates noch den Erregten und Begeisterten spielen, indem er

sich zu prophezeien unterfängt [The speaker has in his own way exaggerated this masculine steadfastness of Socrates . . . . . so much so that it appears to be the most spiritless and heartless indifference. After the verdict he does not allow Socrates to wonder at the pronouncement of the judges, but merely at the number of votes on each side. He then has Socrates make the cold-blooded calculation that he would have been acquitted if only three votes[232] had gone the other way, and that if Anytus and Lycon had not come forward with their additional accusations, Meletus would have had to pay a thousand drachmas for not having obtained one fifth of the votes. But this indifference is even more noticeable when Socrates speaks of death. He continually asserts that he has no fear of death, but upon what is this fearlessness based? On nothing; it is thus empty ostentation . . . . . Could Plato, the author of the *Phaedo*, allow Socrates to speak in this way about death, and could he attribute to him such a truly vulgar, spiritless and listless, almost ludicrous indifference? . . . . . And yet this listless and spiritless Socrates seeks to play the part of the inspired enthusiast inasmuch as he ventures to prophesy]" (pp. 487, 488). Now this whole Astian interpretation is not supposed to stand here in boredom as a loose and vacant quotation; on the contrary, I hope that it will become an active laborer in the vineyard,[233] for I am counting upon the perspectival angle of perception in which the irony will become apparent to some of the readers and also show to better advantage. In other words, as the earnestness that predominates in Ast strides with measured steps into the neutral *Apology*, irony sits quietly waiting, watching with eyes never closed, continually in motion, participating in every skirmish, although the reader may not perceive it until the moment it casts its net over him and traps him. If, therefore, my commentary should be such a large-holed net that the reader can easily slip through it, or so frail that it cannot hold him, then especially a few parts of the quotation from Ast will be both sufficiently fine-drawn and sufficiently strong, and the stridency in the other part of the quotation will also have its great importance, since it will be the noise that drives the reader to

the point where he must be captured. For example, the passage—"und gleichwohl will dieser gefühl- und gemüthlose Sokrates noch den Erregten und Begeisterten spielen, indem er sich zu prophezeien unterfängt [and yet this listless and spiritless Socrates seeks to play the part of the inspired enthusiast inasmuch as he ventures to prophesy]"—is not only far superior to my whole commentary in its fascinating cunning and brawn, but I regard it as absolutely irresistible to anyone who disagrees with Ast in rejecting the *Apology*. Many another
specific comment by Ast will fortify the wavering and unsta- XIII
ble reader and will be dangerous for anyone who is still scan- 178
dalized by the thought that irony is supposed to explain the *Apology*. Page 488: "Auch im Vortrage verräth sich der Redner, nicht nur in der Entgegensetzung der Gedanken (wie: ἀλλ' ἐν πενίᾳ μυρίᾳ εἰμὶ διὰ τὴν τοῦ θεοῦ λατρείαν, worin das Niedre mit dem Hohen, der klägliche Ton mit dem stolzen Gefühle so contrastirt, dasz uns der Satz fast ein Lächeln abnöthigt), sondern auch der Worte; denn die damaligen Redner gefielen sich, nach dem Vorbilde des Gorgias und Lysias, in spielenden Antithesen [The speaker betrays himself in his delivery not only by opposing thoughts (e.g., 'but I am in utter poverty by reason of my devotion to the god,' in which the lower is set in such contrast to the high, and the complaining tone in such contrast to the feeling of pride, that the statement almost draws a smile from us), but also by opposing words; for orators at that time flattered themselves with antitheses that trifle in the manner of Gorgias and Lysias]."

This seems to be the right point for a consideration of the attacks on the ironic interpretation Ast made a bit earlier in the same study.[234] To be specific, I dare not let go unchallenged the observation that the irony in the *Apology* might not be Platonic. The alert student of Plato will find in him two kinds of irony. The one is the quickening force integral to the investigation; the other arrogates, if possible, lordship to itself. Thus, since there is irony in the *Apology*, one cannot summarily reject it, as Ast does, because it is not Platonic irony, because it is indeed possible that Socrates' irony was different from Plato's and therefore possible that the *Apology* is a historical document. In proceeding to scrutinize more closely Ast's attempt to show that the irony found in the *Apology* is not Platonic or, as one in agreement with Ast might rather say, that there is no irony whatever in the *Apology*, I must, of course, call attention to something disadvantageous in regard to my own point of view: namely, that irony has been handled under a separate rubric and that Ast has not carried out his various attacking operations in a mutually clarifying way and in the awareness that they must concentrate in one main attack on one point, and that this is whether there is irony in the *Apology*, not in this or that point, but in its entirety.

What significance Socrates could attribute to an arraignment before the judgment seat of the Athenian people and how ridiculous he must have thought it would be to have to defend himself before such judges are intimated in a comment he makes in *Gorgias* (Heise, p. 188): "And what I said to Polus can be used for me, namely, that I would be judged as was a
XIII physician who was prosecuted by a cook before a jury of chil-
179 dren."[235] It has already been suggested that the *Apology* must be regarded as irony in its very design, since, after all, the grievous charges about all the new teaching Socrates was introducing in Athens were bound to stand in a very strange and essentially ironic relation to his defense that he knew nothing and thus could not possibly introduce new teachings. The irony obviously consists in there being no point of contact whatever between the charge and the defense. If Socrates had tried to show that he adhered to the old or, provided he was introducing something new, that this was the truth, then everything would have been in order. But Socrates does not refute his accusers but instead wrests the charge itself from them, exposing the whole thing as a false alarm, and the accusers' hundred-pound cannons, which are supposed to smash the accused to pieces, are fired in vain, since there is absolutely nothing that can be annihilated. The whole situation calls to mind a profoundly witty verse by Baggesen.* But

* And no one, not any mother's wight,
Can slay with a vengeance one who has died;

the ironic design in the *Apology* shows up from another side also. To Socrates, who despite the Sophists' distortions and terror tactics was accustomed to stick to a question with a stubbornness and equally fearless courage alarming to the Sophists, it must have seemed an extremely ridiculous *argumentum ad hominem* [argument directed against the opponent's personal circumstances] the Athenians had concocted—that he should be put to death. According to Socrates' view, the accusers either had to persuade him that he was wrong or allow themselves to be persuaded, whereas this matter of whether he should or should not be put to death or at least be fined or not fined was altogether irrelevant. Thus here again there was no reasonable connection between the crime and the punishment. If to that is added the point that this question, altogether unrelated to the issue, was to be decided in an altogether external manner, by a poll, a method of making XIII
decisions that had always been the object of Socrates' special 180
interest, and about which he somewhere else remarked that he himself was utterly ignorant[237]—then one is forced to admit the justice of the seemingly naïve and good-natured but icy irony with which he, ignoring this dreadful argument, amiably talks with the Athenians about the likelihood that he would be acquitted, indeed (something that naturally must appear equally ridiculous to him), that a fine would be imposed upon Meletus.[238] It is, therefore, simply a new irony for him at the end to wish to speak a few words to those who had acquitted him,[239] since obviously these were just as much involved in the voting as the others. And yet there is in the *Apology* an irony even loftier than the previous ironies, an irony that pulls down Socrates himself, inasmuch as Socrates so altogether unilaterally insisted on knowledge, with the result

---

Though the thief himself the dust must bite,
All advantage would be on his side.[236]

Please note the last two lines, for just as the thief would have had the advantage by actually being put to death, so Socrates, who knew nothing, would in a way have had the advantage if his accusers could prove that he not only knew something but even knew something new.

that every crime becomes an error and every punishment thereby totally incongruous, and inasmuch as the polemical force with which he argued this view[240] took an extremely ironic revenge upon him, since he himself in a way is felled by an argument as ridiculous as a death sentence.

To me it is indisputable that everything described here definitely constitutes ironic situations and that certainly anyone who read the *Apology* with the assumption that Socrates had never lived but that a poet had wanted to embody the intriguing elements in an indictment and condemnation such as this would feel the irony, but since we are dealing with historical events, many readers will presumably lack the courage to dare believe this.

When it comes to an account of the irony diffused in the *Apology*, to which I now turn, I find myself in a bit of difficulty. I could try to chase together a host from every corner, but, to say nothing of the fact that the lengthy argumentation necessary for each point would bore the reader, I also believe that that whole section, instead of coming like a soft whisper, as is the nature of irony, would come whistling. To have to demonstrate irony through additional research at every single point would, of course, rob it of the surprise, the striking—in short, would enervate it. Irony requires strong contrast and
XIII would utterly vanish in such boring company as argumenta-
181 tion. Therefore, I shall quote Ast again, since with extraordinary mastery he has laid his hands on all their ambiguous points in order with them to demonstrate, by scaring the reader out of his wits, that the *Apology* is spurious; and since I invest the text with his pathos, in the notes I shall permit myself a little hint that I hope will be sufficient for the reader.

There is an etching of the ascension of the Madonna.[241] In order to raise heaven as high as possible, there is drawn across the bottom a dark line, over which two angels peek up at her. Similarly, by quoting Ast's words in the text,[242] I shall elevate his words as high as possible, and in order to heighten his pathos even more, I shall draw a line over which at times irony's roguish face will be allowed to peek. Ast, p. 477ff.: "Die Freimüthigkeit, mit welcher er den Socrates sprechen läszt, ist

nicht jene edle, aus dem Bewusztseyn der Unschuld und Rechtschaffenheit fliessende, welche sich, durch Verläumdung angereizt, als Stolz verkündet, sondern prahlerische Selbsterhebung; denn Socrates setzt sich nur herab, um sich indirect desto mehr zu erheben." (In a note to this, Ast comments: "der Verfasser der Apologie kann selbst nicht umhin, dieses anzudeuten, S. 82:[243] μὴ θορυβήσητε μηδέν, ἂν δόξω τι ὑμῖν μέγα λέγειν.[a]) Dieses ist nicht die Platonische Ironie, sondern Geringschätzung anderer, die den eitlen Zweck hat, sich selbst zu erheben. Socrates sagt (z. B. S. 68), wenn man denjenigen einen Redner nenne, der die Wahrheit spreche, so sei er allerdings ein Redner, nur nicht auf die Art, wie die anderen (worin der Sinn versteckt liegt, er sei ein eigentlicher oder wahrhafter Redner, die anderen hingegen blosz Scheinredner). Ebenso enthalten die Worte ἴσως μὲν γάρ τι χείρων, ἴσως δὲ βελτίων ἂν εἴη (ἡ λέξις) (S. 71) verstecktes Selbstlob. Noch XIII
unverkennbarer ist die falsche Ironie in der Stelle (S. 84-91), 182
wo Socrates die Wahrhaftigkeit jenes Orakelspruches, der ihn für den weisesten erklärt habe, darzuthun sucht[b]; das Eitle und Prahlerische liegt schon in der Ausführlichkeit, mit der Socrates davon redet. Ebenso erklärt Socrates, er sei ein berühmter und ausgezeichneter Mann (S. 81. 90. 136), und seine Bestimmung eine göttliche[c] (S. 120); er sei der gröszte Wohlthäter der Stadt[d] (S. 116. 119. 142); deszhalb werde ich verläumdet und beneidet (107) u. s. f. Ferner schreibt er sich Weisheit zu[e] (S. 82. 83. 84 ff.), und spricht von der Weisheit der Sophisten in einem skeptischen Tone[f], der nur Hochmuth andeutet. Denn was ist es anders, wenn man sich selbst herabsetzt, zugleich aber alle andere erniedrigt, als eine rednerische Selbsterhebung, die, wenn man ihr eine ernste Absicht unterlegt, als eitle Prahlerei erscheint, wenn man sie aber für unbefangene, absichtlose Freimüthigkeit nimmt, eine Naivität verräth, die durch den nicht beabsichtigten Contrast der Selbstverachtung und der Selbsterhebung[g] (wenn sich Socrates z. B. für unwissend erklärt, zugleich aber für weiser als alle andere, sich selbst also, den unwissenden, zum weisesten erhebt) fast in das Komische übergeht? Hat also der Verfasser der Apologie die Absicht gehabt, den Socrates als Ironiker zu

XIII 183 schildern, so hat er ihn in das Gegentheil vom Platonischen Socrates in einen prahlerischen Sophisten umgewandelt; wollte er ihm aber eine unbefangene, absichtlose Freimüthigkeit leihen, so hat er die Naivität übertrieben und seinen Zweck verfehlt, weil die Gegenseite der Selbstherabsetzung, die Selbsterhebung, zu hervorstechend und grell ist, als dasz man glauben könnte, es sei mit der Selbstherabsetzung ernstlich gemeint; jene Anspruchlosigkeit ist daher nur affectirt, und die Selbstherabsetzung blosz scheinbar, weil sie von der ihr nachfolgenden Selbsterhebung überwogen wird. In diesem Scheinwesen eben erkennen wir am meisten den Redner, der, an das Antithesenspiel gewöhnt, das erste durch das zweite gegenüberstehende wieder aufzuheben pflegt. Eben so hat unser Apologiker gerade das Schönste in seiner Rede, was ihm als Thatsache vorlag, jene Aeusserungen nehmlich der edlen und stolzen Freimüthigkeit und Seelengrösze des Socrates, in Schein gewendet, indem er es durch den Gegensatz wieder aufhebt; dieser Gegensatz ist die Besorgnisz, die Richter, auf deren Geneigtheit alles ankam, zu erzürnen[h]; wes-
XIII 184 halb er eben allemal die Gründe seiner Aeuszerung so weitläufig und mit fast ängstlicher Sorgfalt auseinandersetzt, um ja nichts zu sagen, was keinen Grund für sich hätte und die Richter unwillig machen könnte. Diese Besorgnisz und Furcht, die der Freimüthigkeit immer gegenübertritt, hebt sie nicht diese wieder auf und verwandelt sie in Schein? Der wahrhafte Freie und Seelenstarke wird, ohne Rücksicht auf etwas anderes als die Wahrheit seiner Aussage, und unbekümmert, wie man diese aufnehme, so reden, wie ihm Bewusztseyn und Erkenntnisz gebieten. Eben so bekennt Socrates, dasz er seine Ankläger und Widersacher fürchte (S. 72, 86). Erkennen wir darin des Socrates Seelengrösze und durch nichts zu schreckende Wahrheitsliebe wieder, wie er sie z. B. in der Unterredung mit dem Kritias und Charikles, die sein Verderben beabsichtigen, beim Xenophon (*Denkw. d. Socr.* 1, 2, 33 ff.) an den Tag legt? Socrates stellt sich ferner, als spreche er nicht zu seiner Vertheidigung, sondern in der Absicht, die Richter zu überreden, dasz sie ihn nicht verurtheilen möchten, damit sie sich nicht am Geschenke der Gottheit versündigten (S. 121).

Wenn ihr mir folgt, setzt her hinzu (S. 122), so werdet ihr meiner schonen. Wer erkennt nicht darin die rednerische Wendung? Die Bitte und der Wunsch, losgesprochen zu werden, wird versteckt und erscheint als wohlgemeinter Rath, nicht gegen die Götter zu freveln und ihr Geschenk zu verschmähen. Also ist jene Aeuszerung des Socrates, dasz er nicht für sich (um seine Lossprechung zu bewirken) sondern für die Athenäer spreche, ebenfalls blosz rednerisch d. h. Schein und Täuschung[i]) [The bold confidence with which he allows Soc- XIII 181
rates to speak is not the noble kind of confidence flowing from a consciousness of innocence and uprightness and which, when incited by slander, displays itself as pride. No, it is merely ostentatious self-exaltation. For Socrates debases himself only in order indirectly to exalt himself even more. (In a note to this, Ast comments: The author of the *Apology* cannot refrain from suggesting this himself, 20 e: 'Do not interrupt me with noise, even if I seem to you to be boasting.'[a]) Now this is not Platonic irony but merely a contempt for others that has the vain intention of exalting itself. Socrates says, for example (17 b), that if someone who speaks the truth is called an orator, then he is certainly an orator, but not in the same way as the others (implying that he is a genuine or true orator, the others merely apparent orators). Similarly, the reference to his manner of speech (18 a): 'For perhaps it might be worse and perhaps better,' contains concealed self-glorification. Even XIII 182
more unmistakable is the false irony in the passage (21 b–22 e) where Socrates undertakes to demonstrate the truthfulness of the oracle in pronouncing him the wisest of men,[b] for the conceit and the boastfulness are indeed present in the circumstantiality with which Socrates discusses it. Likewise, Socrates declares himself to be an exceptional person of renown (20 c,

[a] This is completely analogous to Socrates' decision to prophesy, and the icy earnestness with which he draws the Athenians out upon thin ice is totally harmonious with the explanation he gives later of his importance for the Athenian people, how he was a divine gift.

[b] This is the renowned journey of exploration Socrates made—not to find something but to convince himself that there was nothing to find.

23 a, 34 e), and his calling divine[c] (31 a). He is the greatest benefactor of the city[d] (30 a, 30 e, 36 d), and on this account am I slandered and envied (28 a) etc. Further, he attributes wisdom to himself[e] (20 d, 20 e, 21 b ff.), and speaks of the Sophists' wisdom in a skeptical tone[f] signifying arrogance. For what is it except oratorical self-exaltation when a person disparages himself, yet at the same time debases all others? If granted a serious intent, this self-exaltation appears as vain prattling, and if taken as artless and aimless boldness, it exhibits a naïveté that, through the unintentional contrast of self-abasement and self-exaltation,[g] nearly slips into the comical (for example, when Socrates declares himself to be ignorant yet at the same time wiser than all others, and hence exalts himself, the ignorant, as the wisest). Thus, if the author of the
XIII 183 *Apology* intended to portray Socrates as an ironist, he has transformed him into a boastful Sophist, the reverse of the Platonic Socrates; but if he intended to confer upon Socrates an artless and designless boldness, he has exaggerated the naïveté and missed the mark, because the self-exaltation, the reverse of self-abasement, is too obtrusive and glaring for anyone to believe the latter was earnestly intended. Thus the modesty is only affected and the self-abasement merely feigned, since it is outweighed by the subsequent self-exaltation. In this phantom we do recognize for the most part the speaker who, accustomed to the play of antitheses, takes his usual pleasure in abrogating the first by means of its opposite, the second. In this way, and again by abrogating it by means

[c] In other words, he is like a gadfly.

[d] Indeed, he even wants to be supported at public expense.

[e] Namely, that he knows nothing.

[f] But yet with all the courtesy in the world.

[g] This is patently the subtly ironic rippling of muscles. He delights in knowing that he knows nothing, and he finds himself boundlessly disencumbered by it, whereas the others are slaving themselves to death for pennies. Socrates never understands ignorance speculatively but finds it so comfortable, so portable. He is an *Asmus omnia secum portans* [Asmus carrying everything with him],[244] and this *omnia* is nothing. Indeed, the happier he is over this nothing—not as result but as boundless freedom—the more profound his irony.

of its opposite, our apologist has shammed the most beautiful part of his speech and transmogrified into show that which lay before him as fact, namely, those expressions of the noble and proud confidence and magnanimity of Socrates; and here the abrogating opposite is the concern about not angering the judges, upon whose favor everything depended.[h] Accordingly, he always explicates the grounds for his statements so XIII
diffusely and with almost anxious solicitude so as to say noth- 184
ing unfounded that might annoy the judges. Now, do not this fear and concern, which always contrapose bold confidence, abrogate the latter and transmogrify it into mere show and deception? A truly free and magnanimous person will speak as consciousness and knowledge bid him without regard for anything but the truth of his statement and untroubled by how it is received. By the same token, Socrates admits that he fears his accusers and adversaries (18 b, 21 e). Do we here recognize again the Socratic magnanimity and love of truth that, fearing nothing, are exhibited, for example, in Xenophon's rendering (*Mem.* I, 2, 33ff.) of the conversation with Critias and Chari-

[h] In a note to this passage, Ast says: "Daher das häufige [Therefore the frequent]: 'μὴ θορυβεῖτε, μὴ θορυβήσητε, καί μοι μὴ ἄχθεσθε λέγοντι τἀληθῆ [Cease interrupting, do not interrupt, be not offended if I tell the truth].' "[245] He believes that the author of the *Apology* had in mind the actual historical event that Socrates was interrupted several times but that he now has Socrates anticipate these interruptions and thus changes the actual θορυβεῖν [to disturb] to an apparent one. He [Ast] thereby fails to recognize how genuinely Socratic this apprehensive gentleness really is that continually quiets the Athenians so as not to shock them by the great and extraordinary thing he has to say. Now this great thing is the importance he has for the Athenians—to say it bluntly, that he is a divine gift—which is more closely defined by saying that he is a gadfly. Cf. 30 e. Socrates cautions the Athenians not to condemn him, not on his behalf but on their own: "μή τι ἐξαμάρτητε περὶ τὴν τοῦ θεοῦ δόσιν ὑμῖν ἐμοῦ καταψηφισάμενοι, ἐὰν γὰρ ἐμὲ ἀποκτείνητε, οὐ ῥᾳδίως ἄλλον τοιοῦτον εὑρήσετε, ἀτεχνῶς, εἰ καὶ γελοιότερον εἰπεῖν, προσκείμενον τῇ πόλει ὑπὸ τοῦ θεοῦ ὥσπερ ἵππῳ μεγάλῳ μὲν καὶ γενναίῳ, ὑπὸ μεγέθους δὲ νωθεστέρῳ καὶ δεομένῳ ἐγείρεσθαι ὑπὸ μύωπός τινος [to save you from misusing the gift of God (the god) by condemning me. If you put me to death you will not easily find anyone to take my place. It is literally true, even if it sounds rather comical, that God (the god) has specially appointed me to this city, as though it were a large thoroughbred horse which because of its great size is inclined to be lazy and needs the stimulation of some stinging fly]."[246]

cles, whose aim is Socrates' ruin? Furthermore, Socrates pretends not to be speaking in his own defense, but rather with the intent of convincing his judges that they should not condemn him, lest they sin against a gift of the deity (30 d). If you take my advice, he adds (31 a), you will spare my life. Now, who does not recognize this as a rhetorical device? The request and the wish to be acquitted are concealed and appear as benevolent counsel in favor of not offending the gods and disdaining their gift. Thus Socrates' statement about speaking not for himself (in order to bring about his acquittal) but for the Athenians is again merely rhetorical, that is, mere show, deception, and deceit.[i]]"

The Mythical in the Earlier Platonic Dialogues as a Token of a More Copious Speculation

This concludes the discussion of the dialectical in Plato insofar
XIII 185 as it was necessary for the present study. I have deliberately allowed this whole analysis to end with the *Apology* in order to consolidate whatever was wavering and unstable in the course of the previous argumentation. The mythical will now be the object of consideration, and as I try to forget the overall aim of the undertaking in order that this consideration may be as unbiased as possible, I must beg the reader to concentrate to the same degree on the fact that the duplexity implicit in the misrelation between the dialectical and the mythical is one of the keys, one of the clues, that will lead, it is hoped, to separating what time and intimacy had apparently made inseparable.

Now, at first the mythical may be looked upon with indifferent eyes, may be regarded as merely a change in presentation, another kind of discourse without there necessarily being anything essential about the relation between the two kinds of discourse; indeed, some of Plato's comments could seem to hint at this. For example, as Protagoras prepares to

[i] This is all entirely correct, because Socrates is far too ironically indifferent to involve himself in earnest with the Athenians, and this is why he sometimes pretends to be passionately intrepid and sometimes timid and discouraged.

demonstrate that virtue can be taught, he says (Heise, p. 130): "Well, Socrates, I will not keep it for myself, but as the elder speaking to the younger, shall I cloak the demonstration in a myth or present it in a treatise?"[247] And when he has finished, he says (p. 145): "So, Socrates, by both myth and arguments, I have now demonstrated that virtue can be taught."[248] Thus we see that here the mythical discourse is distinguished from the investigative in such a way that the mythical is considered the less perfect, designed for the young. We see that these two kinds of discourses are not indispensable to each other, since their necessity for each other would first be seen in the higher unity in which they themselves are visible and actual as detached elements. These two kinds of presentation are seen not in relation to the idea but in relation to the listener; they are like two languages—the one less articulated, more childlike and soft, the other more developed, more sharp-edged and hard. But since they are not seen in their relation to the idea, a third language, a fourth, etc., a whole assortment of such forms of presentation is conceivable.

In addition, according to this view, myth is entirely in the power of the presenter. It is his free creation; he can subtract or add accordingly as it seems to him to be beneficial to the listener. But this cannot possibly hold true with the mythical in Plato. Here the mythical has a far more profound meaning,
as one will realize if one notices that the mythical in Plato has XIII
a history. Thus in the first and earliest dialogues it is either 186
completely absent, in which case its opposite reigns supreme, or it is present in connection with—and yet in another sense without connection with—its opposite, the abstract. Thereupon it utterly vanishes in a whole cycle of dialogues where the dialectical is present, although in a different sense than in the earlier dialogues, and finally it emerges again in the last Platonic works, but in a more profound connection with the dialectical.

With regard, then, to the mythical in Plato, for the time being I am led back to the dialogues I just left, because there one finds the mythical in combination with its opposite, the abstract dialectic. For example, *Gorgias*,[249] where, after the

Sophists have fought with the rage of despair and ever more "shamelessly," where, after Polus has surpassed Gorgias in insolence and Callicles Polus, the whole thing ends[250] with a mythical exposition of the state after death.* But what is the nature of the mythical here, since it is obvious that in these dialogues it is not so much Plato's free composition, tractable and obedient to him, as it is instead something that overwhelms him and since it is to be considered not so much a secondary account for younger or less gifted listeners as a presentiment of something higher.

In his understanding of the mythical, Stallbaum** clearly

* Moreover, this myth appears in three places in Plato. See Stallbaum, *ad Phaedonem*, p. 177: "Narrat Olympiodorus tertiam hujus dialogi partem vocari νεκυίαν, quo nomine constat rhapsodiam Odysseae Homericae ab veteribus dictam esse. Platonis autem cum tres sint νεκυῖαι s. fabulae de inferis, in Phaedone, Gorgia, de republica, singulaeque singulis invicem lucem affundant, omnes inter se diligenter comparandae sunt [Olympiodorus narrates that the third part of this dialogue is called a myth of the underworld, by which name it is well known that the rhapsody of the Homeric *Odyssey* (Book XI) was called by the ancients. However, since there are three myths of the underworld in Plato, i.e., stories concerning the underworld, in the *Phaedo*, *Gorgias*, and *Republic*,[251] and since each one sheds light in turn upon each of the others, all ought to be compared diligently with one another]."

** See *prefatio ad Phaedonem*, p. 16: "quum autem rerum difficultatem tan-
XIII tam esse intelligeret, ut multa divinari potius animo, quam mente intelligi ac
187 dilucide explicari posse viderentur, mirum non est, etiam in hoc libro subtilissimis rerum disputationibus intextas esse mythicas et fabulosas narrationes, quae locum obtineant demonstrationis et certorum argumentorum . . . . . Nam verissime Eberhardus Script. Miscell., p. 382,[252] haec scripsit: 'Man kann als gewisz annehmen, Plato habe sich bisweilen der Mythen im Gegensatz des Raisonnements oder der Vernunftbeweise bedient, da wo von Gegenständen die Rede war, die ausser dem Gesichtkreise der menschlichen Vernunft und Erfahrung liegen, oder wo ihm die Vernunftbeweise selbst noch zu schwer waren, oder wo sie ihm für die Fassungskraft seiner Zuhörer zu schwer schienen.' " Cfr. *ad Phaedonem*, p. 177: "Saepenumero enim videtur mythicis illis narrationibus usus esse, quo significaret, argumentum, quod attigisset, ita esse comparatum, ut suspicionibus magis et conjecturis esset indulgendum, quam ratiociniis ac disputationibus confidendum. Quod ubi facit, iis fabulis et narrationibus, quae apud Graecos erant vulgo celebratae, sic plerumque utitur, ut non solum abjiciat aut mutet, quae consilio suo parum accommodata erant. sed simul etiam civium suorum superstitionem corrigat et removere studeat. Ex qua re intelligitur, quodnam aliud etiam consilium in usu mythorum Plato secutus sit. Voluit enim ineptam illam plebis superstiti-

takes the position suggested earlier. He regards it in part as an XIII
accommodation or, to use an expression that is certainly ap- 187
propriate in this connection, a συγκατάβασις [condescension], XIII
since this word, after all, suggests that Plato in the mythical 188
condescends to the listener instead of assuming as we do that the mythical is something higher—indeed, something lying beyond Plato's subjective authority. He also connects it to the folk consciousness, which before Plato maintained the idea in such a frame. But neither observation is effectively developed to the point of a sharp and significant distinction between what was understood by means of rational inferences and what was grasped by intimation or to a truly reassuring settlement of the boundary disputes between tradition and Plato. Baur (*op. cit.*, pp. 90-98) sees the traditional in the mythical and agrees with Ackermann[253] in placing the poets and oracles

---

onem sensim tollere, aut certe emendare. Denique etiam mythos eo consilio adhibuisse videtur, ut animos aequalium coeca superstitione oppressos sensim quasi praepararet ad purioris sapientiae doctrinam percipiendam [However, since he understood that the difficulty of things was so great that many things
seemed able to be divined by the soul rather than understood or explicated XIII
clearly by the mind, it is no wonder that, even in this book, stories and myth- 187
ical narrations that hold the place of demonstration and sure arguments have been interwoven with the most subtle disputations of things . . . . . For Eberhard, *Script. Miscell.*, p. 382, has written these things most truly: 'It may be regarded as certain that Plato has sometimes employed the myth in opposition to *raisonnements*, for example, when the subject under discussion transcends the competence of human reason and experience, or when the demonstrations of reason were too difficult for him, or when they seemed to him to be too difficult for the comprehension of his listeners.' " See *ad Phaedonem*, p. 177: "Often he seems to have used these mythical presentations in order to suggest that the topic under discussion was of such a nature that one should give oneself over to presentiments and premonitions, rather than put one's confidence in demonstrations and explanations. When he does this, he generally uses those myths and fables commonly known among the Greeks, yet in such a way that he not only changes and discards what does not conform to his purpose, but also corrects the superstitiousness of his fellow citizens and attempts to remove it. And here is seen the additional purpose Plato had in his use of myths. He desired to revoke the foolish superstitions of the common people gradually, or at least to correct them. Finally, he seems also to have employed myths for the purpose of gradually preparing the minds of his contemporaries, so oppressed by blind superstition, to receive a purer doctrine of wisdom]."

in the same relation to Plato as the prophets in the Old Testament had to the apostles and evangelists. On the one hand, the devout veneration, the filial piety with which Plato embraced the religious consciousness of his native land's past, should be seen in the mythical in his writings; on the other hand, the noble momentary distrust of his own constructions, which, of course, is the reason he does not want to make any laws about worship in the *Republic*[254] but leaves that to the Delphic Apollo. Ast* has a more complete view, except that it is not actually based upon observation and has the character more of a wish than of an achievement.

Apparently Baur as well as Ast failed to see the inner history of the mythical in Plato. Whereas in the earlier dialogues this forms a contrast to the dialectical so that when the dialectical
XIII is silent the mythical lets itself be heard or rather be seen, in
189 the later dialogues it appears in a more friendly relation to the
dialectical—that is, Plato has mastered it or, in other words, the mythical becomes the metaphorical. Simply to explain the mythical as the traditional, as Baur does, simply to have Plato seek a point of departure for ethical-religious truths in the

* See *Platon's Leben*, p. 165: "Das Mythische ist gleichsam die theologische Basis der platonischen Speculation: die Erkenntnisz wird durch das Dogma gebunden und befestigt, und der Geist aus dem Gebiete der menschlichen Reflexion zur Anschauung des höheren unendlichen Lebens emporgeführt, wo er sich, seiner Endlichkeit und irdischen Selbstheit vergessend, in die unergründliche Tiefe des Göttlichen und Ewigen versenkt. Man könnte sagen, dasz in den platonischen Gesprächen die philosophischen Darstellungen nur den Zweck haben, den Geist auf die höhere Betrachtung hinzuleiten und zur Anschauung der in den Mythen sinnbildlich geoffenbarten Unendlichkeit und Göttlichkeit vorzubereiten, gleichwie in den Mysterien auf die Vorbereitung und Einweihung erst die eigentliche Beschauung (ἐποπτεία) folgte [The mythical is, so to speak, the theological basis of Platonic speculation: knowledge becomes bound and consolidated through dogma and the mind is led out of the sphere of human reflection upward toward an intuition of the higher life of infinity, where, forgetting its finite and earthly selfhood, it immerses itself in the unfathomable deep of the divine and eternal. It may be said that in the Platonic dialogue the philosophical presentation merely serves the purpose of leading the mind to a higher view and preparing it for the intuition of the infinite and divine that is metaphorically manifested in the myth, just as in the mysteries the actual beholding (viewing face-to-face)[255] followed only upon preparation and initiation]."

higher authority implicit in poetry and oracles, will not do. The first books of the *Republic*[256] utterly disparage the validity of the utterances of the poets, argue and warn strongly against them, and disapprove of the depictive (i.e., the fictive) interpretation in contrast to the strictly narrative version; indeed, in the tenth book of the *Republic*,[257] Plato wants the poets banished from the country. Simply by itself, therefore, this will not do. The necessary rectification, however, comes through a consideration of the metamorphosis of the mythical in Plato. This emerges most clearly in the earliest dialogues. Whereas the dialectical here provides a completely abstract and sometimes negative conclusion, the mythical will provide much more. But if we ask what the mythical is basically, one may presumably reply that it is the idea in a state of alienation, the idea's externality[258]—i.e., its immediate temporality and spatiality as such. The mythical in the dialogues does indeed bear this mark throughout. The enormous spans of time the soul traverses according to the presentation in the *Phaedrus*[259] and the capacious infinity that is graphically presented in the *Gorgias*[260] and the *Phaedo*[261] as the soul's existence after death are myths. This is easily explained. The dialectical clears the terrain of everything irrelevant and then attempts to clamber up to the idea, but since this fails, the imagination reacts. Weary of the dialectical work, the imagination begins to dream, and from this comes the mythical. During this dreaming, the idea either floats by quickly in an endless succession or it stands still and expands until infinitely present in space. Thus the mythical is the enthusiasm of imagination in the service of speculation and, to a certain degree, is what Hegel calls pantheism of the imagination.*[262] It has validity in the mo- XIII 190

* When the mythical is understood in this way, it might seem as if it were being confused with the poetical, but please note that the poetical is conscious of itself as the poetical, has its reality [*Realitet*] in this ideality, and does not want to have any other reality. The mythical, however, consists in the neither-nor-ness and duplexity, the intermediate state out of which the interests of consciousness have not as yet struggled. The poetic is a hypothetical statement in the subjunctive mood; the mythical is a hypothetical statement in the XIII 190
indicative mood.[263] This duplexity, the indicative statement and the hypothetical form, which wavers between being neither subjunctive nor indicative and both subjunctive and indicative, is a sign of the mythical. As long as the

ment of contact and is not brought into relation with any re-
XIII 191 flection. One will realize this as well by considering the *Gorgias* and the *Phaedo*. The mythical presentation of the soul's existence after death is related neither to a historical reflection as to whether it actually is this way, whether Aeacus, Minos, and Rhadamanthus do sit and judge, nor to a philosophical

---

myth is taken for actuality, it is really not myth; it does not become myth until the moment it touches a reflecting consciousness; and insofar as it now has a speculative substance and applies itself to the imagination, the mythical presentation results. But in one sense the period of the myth is over as soon as the question of a mythical presentation arises, but since reflection has not as yet been permitted to annihilate it, the myth still exists, and just as it is taking its leave and departing, it raises itself up from the earth, but in farewell it reflects itself once again in the imagination, and this is the mythical presentation. Erdmann declares (*Zeitschrift für spekulative Theologie*, ed. Bruno Bauer, III, 1, p. 26): "Ein Faktum oder auch eine Reihe von Faktis, welche eine religiöse Idee auch nicht sind aber bedeuten, nennen wir einen religiösen Mythus. Der religiöse Mythus ist ein Faktum oder eine Reihe von Faktis, welche einen religiösen Inhalt in der sinnlich zeitlichen Form darstellen, die aber (und darin besteht ihr Unterschied von der Geschichte) nicht eine nothwendige Manifestation der Idee selbst sind, sondern in einem äuszerlichen Verhältnisz zu ihr stehen. Deswegen sind die Mythen nicht *wahr*, wenn sie auch Wahrheit enthalten sollten, sie sind *ersonnen*, wenn auch nicht durch Reflexion, sie sind keine wirklichen Fakta, sondern fingirt [A fact or a series of facts that are not a religious idea but do signify one, we call a religious myth. A religious myth is a fact or a series of facts that presents religious content in sensuous and temporal form, a form, however, that is not a necessary manifestation of the idea itself (and in this lies its difference from history), but merely externally related to it. Hence the myths are not *true*, though they are supposed to contain truth; they are *fabricated*, though not by reflection; and they are not actual facts, but invented]." But that the myths are not true is, of course, reserved for a later, a more truthful moment of time to perceive. But the imagination, to which their truth or falsity is a matter of indifference, views them with philosophic interest and, just as in the present situation, tired of the work of dialectics, rests in them. In one way it poetizes them itself—this is the poetical; in another way it does not poetize them, and this is the nonpoetical; the unity of these is the mythical, when it is understood as the mythical presentation. Thus when Socrates declares in the *Phaedo*[264] that no one can claim that the myth is true, this is the element of freedom; the individual feels free and emancipated from the myth. But when he still thinks that one should risk believing it, this is the element of dependence. In the first case, he can play helter-skelter with the myth, as he pleases, subtract from it and add to it; in the latter case, it overwhelms him when he surrenders to it, and the unity is the mythical presentation.

reflection as to whether it is truth. If the dialectic that is equivalent to the mythical may be characterized as desire, craving, as the glance that looks at the idea desiringly, then the mythical is the idea's flourishing embrace. The idea descends and hovers over the individual like a beneficent cloud. Provided, however, that there is in this individual's condition a faint indication, a remote intimation, of a reflecting consciousness, a secret, almost inaudible whisper, there is at every moment a possibility that the mythical will undergo a metamorphosis.

In other words, as soon as consciousness puts in its appearance, it turns out that these mirages were not the idea. Now that the consciousness has awakened, if the imagination once again is nostalgic for those dreams, the mythical steps forth in a new form, that is, as metaphor. The change that has now taken place is that the mythical has been taken into the consciousness, not as the idea but as a mirroring of the idea. So it is, I think, with the mythical presentations in the constructive dialogues. Provisionally, the mythical is taken up into the dialectical, is no longer in conflict with it, is no longer sectarianly self-contained; it alternates with the dialectical,* and in this way the dialectical and also the mythical are raised to a higher order of things. For this reason, it is acceptable for the mythical to have something of the traditional. The traditional is like the lullaby that also constitutes an element in the dream; yet it is authentically mythical precisely in the moments when the spirit wanders away and no one knows whence it comes or whither it goes.[265]

A similar view of the mythical may be attained by starting out from the metaphorical. To be specific, when in a reflective age the metaphorical is found very rarely and sparsely in a reflective presentation, much like an antediluvian fossil reminding us of another kind of life that doubt has eroded, one will XIII 192
perhaps marvel that the metaphorical could ever have played so great a role. But as the metaphor gains more and more ground, accommodates more and more in itself, it invites the

* Because Plato never arrived at the speculative train of thought at all, the mythical, or rather the metaphorical, can always still be an element in the presenting of the idea. Plato's sphere is not thought but representation.

onlooker to rest in it, to anticipate a pleasure to which restless reflection perhaps would lead one by a long detour. When the metaphor finally acquires such dimensions that all existence becomes visible in it, this is the retrograde movement toward the mythical. Nature philosophy frequently provides examples of this. For example, H. Steffens' preface to *Karrikaturen des Heiligsten*[266] is that kind of grand and ambitious metaphor in which nature-existence becomes a myth about the existence of spirit. Thus the metaphor overwhelms the individual—he loses his freedom, or rather he sinks into a state in which he does not have reality, because the metaphor now is not a free production and an artistic creation, and however busily thought inspects the particulars, however ingenious it is in making associations, however cozily it adapts its existence to them, it is still unable to separate the whole from itself and make it appear light and fleeting in the sphere of pure poetry. This shows how the mythical, too, may affirm itself in an isolated individual. The prototype of this must, of course, have affirmed itself in the development of nations, but it must be remembered that it continues to be myth only so long as this selfsame process repeats itself in the nations' consciousness, which, itself dreaming, reproduces the myth of its past. Any attempt to take the myth historically already indicates that the reflection has awakened and is destroying the myth. Like the fairy tale, myth reigns only in the twilight of the imagination; whereas mythical elements can very well sustain themselves for a time after the historical interest has awakened and the philosophical interest comes to consciousness.

If the mythical in Plato is of this kind, then it is not difficult to answer the question: Does the mythical belong to Plato or to Socrates? I believe that I dare answer for myself and my readers: It *does not belong* to Socrates. But if it is kept in mind, something that antiquity does indeed bear out, that it was from a productive life as a poet that Socrates called the twenty-year-old Plato back to abstract self-knowledge*—then it cer-

* Karl Friedrich Hermann, *Geschichte und System der platonischen Philosophie*[267] (Heidelberg: 1839), pt. 1, p. 30 and note 54.

tainly is quite natural that the poetic element in his active pas- XIII
sivity and passive activity was bound to manifest itself in con- 193
trast to the famished Socratic dialectic and that it was bound to appear most strongly and most isolated in the writing that was either contemporary with Socrates or at least closest to him. This is indeed the case, inasmuch as the mythical stands on its rights most stubbornly and rebelliously in the earlier dialogues, whereas in the constructive dialogues it has submitted to the mild rule of an encompassing consciousness. Therefore those who have a somewhat more intimate acquaintance with Plato presumably will agree with me in having the more strictly Platonic development begin with the dialectic that appears in the *Parmenides* and the other dialogues in this cycle and ends in the constructive dialogues. But it has already been pointed out that the dialectic in these dialogues is essentially different from the dialectic described so far. Therefore, in relation to the whole Platonic development, the mythical in the first dialogues is to be regarded as a kind of preexistence of the idea, and if one draws together what has been advanced here, one could perhaps call the mythical in the earlier dialogues the unripe fruit of speculation, and since ripening is a fermentation process, the subsequent authentic Platonic dialectic can no doubt be appropriately compared to this. The fruit of speculation, however, never fully ripens in Plato because the dialectical movement is never fully accomplished.

I shall now briefly examine the mythical component of a few dialogues. It would be superfluous to point out that one cannot call it the mythical simply because reference is made to some myth or other, because to quote a myth in a presentation does not necessarily make the presentation mythical; nor does using a myth do so, because the using of it simply indicates that one is beyond it; nor does making the myth an object of faith make the presentation mythical, because the mythical addresses itself not chiefly to cognition but rather to the imagination, requires that the individual lose himself in it, and the presentation does not become mythical until it flutters in this manner between the imagination's production and reproduction.

It is assumed that the mythical presentation in the *Symposium* begins with Diotima's story.[268] Now, this is not mythical because reference is made to the myth about Eros's having been born of wealth [*Poros*] and poverty [*Penia*], since also in the earlier speeches the legends about the origin of Eros had not gone unnoticed. Here, however, the characterization of
XIII 194 Eros is negative: Eros is an intermediate being, is neither rich nor poor. At this level we have not gone beyond the Socratic development. But this negative element, which is the eternal restlessness of thinking, continually dividing and combining, this negative element that thought cannot hold on to since it is the propelling element in thought[269]—this negative element stops here and relaxes before imagination, expands before intuition. Therein resides the mythical. Anyone who has anything to do with abstract thinking will certainly have noticed how seductive it is to want to maintain something that actually is not, except when it is annulled. But this is a mythical tendency. In other words, what happens is that the idea is kept under the qualifications of time and space, understood altogether ideally.* Thus the addition given to the dialectical movement by the mythical presentation described before is that it lets the negative be seen.

In one sense, however, the mythical presentation thereby provides less, impedes the thought process and discloses itself not as a completion of the inaugurated process but as a completely new beginning. The more it seeks to expand contemplation and the more copious it wants to make it, the more it

* What gives space reality [*Realitet*] is the organic process of nature; what gives time reality is the plenitude of history. In the mythical, both time and space have merely the reality of the imagination. In the Indian myths, for example, this is seen in the childish squandering of time, which, since it wants to say so much, says nothing at all, because the standard of measure it uses is immediately robbed of its validity. To say that a king has reigned for 70,000 years is, after all, self-annulling, because the temporal category is used and yet no reality is attributed to it. With complete arbitrariness, time and space are confused and interchanged in this ideality.

manifests its contrast to the purely negative dialectic, but it also departs further from real thinking, fascinates thought, and makes it sentimental and soft. The other way whereby the mythical component of this dialogue provides more than the dialectical is that it advances the beautiful as the object of Eros. We now have, therefore, a genuinely Platonic dichotomy, which, as noted earlier, suffers from all the troubles of a dichotomy because it has the negative outside itself and the unity achieved can never hypostatize itself. In a closer examination of the nature of the beautiful, a host of qualifications is stripped off by way of a dialectical movement. Successively the object of love is: beautiful bodies—beautiful souls—beautiful observations—beautiful knowledge—the beautiful. The beautiful is now defined not merely negatively as something
that will appear in a far more glorious light than gold, clothes, XIII
beautiful boys and adolescents, but Diotima adds (Heise, p. 195
81): "But what would we think if someone had the good fortune of beholding that beauty itself, sheer, pure, unalloyed, not clad in human flesh and hues or other mortal vanity, but the divine beauty itself in the unity of its essence?"[270] The mythical clearly consists in this, that beauty in and by itself must be *beheld*. Even though the feminine interpreter [Diotima] has renounced all mortal taint and trappings, it is clear that these will return in the world of imagination and provide the mythical drapery. So will it always be with *das Ding an sich* [the thing in itself][271] if one cannot cast it away and consign it to oblivion; but instead, because one has managed to exclude it from thinking, one will now allow imagination to repair and make good the loss.

This position, of course, is very reminiscent of the Kantian position. I shall briefly touch on the difference. To be sure, Kant stopped at this *an sich* of things, but he either went on dauntlessly trying to grasp it by way of subjective thinking and, since grasping it was impossible, then had the obviously great advantage, the rather ironic good fortune, of always hoping; or he discarded it, tried to forget it. On the other hand, insofar as he at times wants to maintain it, he develops the mythical, and thus his whole view of "radical evil,"[272] for

example, is really a myth. The evil, namely, with which thought cannot cope is placed outside thought and is handed over to imagination. In the mythical part of the *Symposium*, Plato the poet daydreams and visualizes everything the dialectician Socrates was seeking; in the world of dreams, irony's unhappy love finds its object. Plato's placement of this presentation in the mouth of Diotima certainly cannot make it a mythical presentation; whereas it is intrinsic to the mythical (something the imagination generally favors) that the object is placed outside, is distanced in order to be drawn back again, just as a fairy tale should not be related to one's own experience, but one thrusts it away and tries to make the present tense of imagination all the more attractive by way of a time contrast. As a matter of fact, Ast[273] also points out that Diotima is a pure fabrication, and Baur's comment[274] that Plato has chosen the mythical form of presentation in order to give
XIII 196 his philosophizing inquiry positive support in a form familiar to the folk consciousness certainly explains too little and interprets the relation of the mythical to Plato altogether externally.

In considering the mythical presentation of the state of the soul after death as described in the *Gorgias* and the *Phaedo*, we find a certain disparity between the two views. In the *Gorgias*, Socrates does, it is true, emphasize several times*[275] that he believes it and confesses his faith in it contrary to those who perhaps "would regard and spurn this account as an old wives' tale,"[276] but one nevertheless perceives in his next remarks that it is more important to him to maintain the idea of justice than to preserve the myth, since he himself admits that it is only natural to spurn such accounts if by investigation one can find something better and truer. Again, the mythical consists not so much in the reference to the legend about Minos, Aeacus, and Rhadamanthus but rather in adherence to making the decree of judgment visible before the imagination or in the way

* That Socrates is the speaker also in the mythical part of the dialogues does not disprove the correctness of the division of the dialectical and the mythical established here, because, as is well known, Plato is never in evidence as speaking but always uses Socrates' name.

the imagination itself reproduces it for itself. In the *Phaedo*, however, Socrates himself suggests how things stand with regard to the entire conception (Heise, p. 117): "Of course, it is not proper for a reasonable man to insist that things are as I have presented them, but I think it is proper to assume that the circumstances of our souls and their dwellings are like this or something similar, since the soul is clearly immortal, and it is worth the effort to venture to believe that things are actually like this. The venturesome deed is noble, and one ought to conjure forth such things for oneself. And that is why I have dwelt so long on this tale."[277] The proper terms are also used here—namely, that it is a venturesome deed to believe it and that one ought to conjure forth such things for oneself. The presentation of the many and extensive periods of time that the soul, all in relation to its quality, must pass through, the enormous dimensions of the underworld into which we see the soul vanish, accompanied by its daemon, the various kinds of abodes, the wave of Tartarus that hurls the soul into Co-
cytus or Pyriphlegethon, the assembly of these souls in the XIII
Acherusian lake, from which they cry out and call to those 197
they have either slain or wronged—all this is very properly mythical. But the mythical resides in the power it gains over the imagination as one, wishing to conjure it forth, evokes visions that overwhelm oneself. The speculative thought that goes busily about, so to speak, in this twilight is divine justice, the harmony in the world of spirit, of which the laws of nature in the universe are but a metaphor.

REPUBLIC, BOOK I

Before proceeding to explain my choice of the dialogues I have examined, I must make one more choice. Before leaving the details of Plato, I must first examine the first book of the *Republic* more closely. Schleiermacher, in his introduction to the *Republic*, makes some observations on the relation of this dialogue to the earlier ethical dialogues: "Wenn wir Platos Meinung ganz verstehen wollen, dürfen wir nicht aus der Acht lassen, dasz diese ganze Aehnlichkeit unseres Werkes mit den ältern ethischen Gesprächen auch am Ende dieses ersten

Buches gänzlich verschwindet . . . . . Auch die Methode ändert sich gänzlich; Socrates tritt nicht mehr fragend als der Nichtwissende auf, der nur im Dienste des Gottes die grössere Unwissenheit aufsucht, sondern als einer, der gefunden hat, trägt er in strengem Zusammenhange fortschreitend die gewonnenen Einsichten mit. Ja auch dem Style nach tragen nur noch die nächsten Reden der beiden Brüder, als den Uebergang bildend, eine Aehnlichkeit mit dem bisherigen, hernach nichts mehr von dialogischer Pracht und reizender Ironie, sondern bündige Strenge allein soll den Preis gewinnen. Der gesammte Apparat der jugendlicheren Virtuosität glänzt hier noch einmal im Eingang, und erlischt dann auf immer, um so verständlich als möglich zu gestehen, dasz alles Schöne und Gefällige dieser Art doch auf dem Gebiete der Philosophie nur in vorbereitenden, mehr spornenden und anregenden als fördernden und befriedigenden Untersuchungen seinen Ort habe, dasz aber, wo eine zusammenhängende Darstellung von den Resultaten philosophischer Forschung gegeben werden soll, solcher Schmuck mehr abziehend wirken als die vollständige Auffassung fördern würde [If we would completely understand Plato's meaning, we must not overlook the fact that all this resemblance between the work before us and the other ethical dialogues completely vanishes also at the end of Book I . . . . . Even the method is completely changed—Socrates no longer comes forward with questions in the character of a man who is ignorant and only seeks greater ignorance in the service of the god, but as one who has already found what he seeks, he advances onward, bearing along with him in strict connection the insights he has acquired. Yes, even in point of style, it is only the immediately succeeding speeches of the two brothers, as constituting the transition, that bear any resemblance to what has gone before, no dialogic embellishment or enticing irony is hereafter to gain the prize, but solid strictness of argument alone. The whole store of the youthful virtuoso glitters here once more in the introduction, and is then extinguished forever, in order to make it understood as well as possible that all that is beautiful and pleasing of this kind occupies a place in the province of philosophy only in

preparatory investigations, the object of which is more to stimulate and excite than to advance and come to satisfactory conclusions; and that when a connected exposition of the results of philosophical investigations is to be given, such embellishment would contribute more to distract the mind than assist the perfect comprehension of the subject]" (Schleiermacher, *Platons Werke*, III^{1}, pp. 9, 10[278]). Thus it will be beneficial to dwell once more on the nature of the presentation* XIII 198
and *in specie* [in particular] on its relation to the idea. In other words, if one cannot deny that there is an essential difference between the first book of the *Republic* and the ones that follow, if one agrees with Schleiermacher's observations, then one of course thinks back to the first dialogues and the form that must have been influenced by Socrates, and then this section of the *Republic* will provide occasion for sanctioning *in compendio* [in summary], if possible, the survey given above. Two things are especially noteworthy: the first book does not merely end without a conclusion, as Schleiermacher thinks, but rather with a negative conclusion; here again irony is an essential element.

For the sake of completeness, we shall now consider irony both in its particular manifestations and in its definitive endeavor. The latter, of course, is the primary consideration, but nevertheless it will be of some significance to see that even its particular manifestations are unrelated to the idea, that the an-

* Inasmuch as I generally agree with Schleiermacher's observations, I would rather not become involved in an explanation of how Plato in one of his latest works turns his mind to the whole Socratic dialectic and irony, something he had abandoned in a not inconsiderable number of intervening dialogues and to which he does not return anymore. However, since the explanation is so close at hand, I shall find a place for it here. The first book of the *Republic* deals expressly with the questions examined in the first dialogues. Therefore it was quite natural for Plato to wish to recall Socrates very vividly, and since in the *Republic* he sought to embody his total view, he found it appropriate to run through briefly the development in the earliest dialogues and to supply a kind of introduction, which for the reader of the *Republic* is presumably far from being an introduction but, regarded as a recapitulation, can always be of interest to the reader of Plato and must have been of great sentimental value to the grateful pupil.

nihilation of distortions and biases does not take place in order to let the truth appear but in order to begin something just as distorted and biased. This is important in order to see that even the particular manifestations of irony have not denied their origin and kinship, that they are busy journeymen, the sly scouts and unbribable informers, who work in their master's service. But this master is nothing else than the total irony that looks out over the total nothing when all the minor skirmishes have been fought and all the ramparts demolished
XIII and becomes aware that there is nothing left or rather that
199 what is left is nothing. So this first book of the *Republic* is very vividly reminiscent of the earlier dialogues. The result of the dialogue is reminiscent of the *Protagoras*, the internal plan is reminiscent of the *Gorgias*, and there is a striking similarity between Thrasymachus and Callicles. The insolence that Socrates in the *Gorgias* so admires in Callicles, who believes that Gorgias and Polus have been vanquished because they have not had the boldness to say flatly that most people share their view that to do wrong is best when it is done only for gain, but that people have a certain modesty about saying it, just as it is also the fainthearted who have devised this means of defense—this insolence we again find complete in Thrasymachus.* The manner in which Thrasymachus, who has been waiting impatiently for a long time to get to speak, finally opens fire[280] is reminiscent of the violent attacks by Polus and Callicles.[281] Socrates' first ironic display (*Republic*, 336 d)[282] (καὶ ἐγὼ ἀκούσας ἐξεπλάγην καὶ προσβλέπων αὐτὸν ἐφοβούμην· καί μοι δοκῶ, εἰ μὴ πρότερος ἑωράκη αὐτὸν ἢ ἐκεῖνος ἐμέ, ἄφωνος ἂν γενέσθαι· νῦν δέ, ἡνίκα ὑπὸ τοῦ λόγου ἤρχετο ἐξαγριαίνεσθαι, προσέβλεψα αὐτὸν πρότερος, ὥστε αὐτῷ οἷός τ' ἐγενόμην ἀποκρίνασθαι καὶ εἶπον ὑποτρέμων Ὦ Θρασύμαχε, μὴ χαλεπὸς ἡμῖν ἴσθι· [And I, when I heard him, was dismayed, and look-

* Cf. 348 d. To the question whether he calls justice goodness and injustice badness, he replies: No! the opposite, which he then modifies; to the question whether he calls justice badness, he replies: οὐκ, ἀλλὰ πάνυ γενναίαν εὐήθειαν· τὴν ἀδικίαν ἄρα κακοήθειαν καλεῖς; Οὐκ, ἀλλ' εὐβουλίαν, ἔφη [No, but a most noble simplicity or goodness of heart. Then do you call injustice badness of heart? No, but goodness of judgment].[279]

ing upon him was filled with fear, and I believe that if I had not looked at him before he did at me I should have lost my voice. But as it is, at the very moment when he began to be exasperated by the course of the argument, I glanced at him first, so that I became capable of answering him, and said with a slight tremor, Thrasymachus, don't be harsh with us]) is reminiscent of a similar passage in the *Gorgias*.[283] The biting manner in which Socrates evasively mocks Thrasymachus's thesis (τὸ δίκαιον οὐκ ἄλλο τι εἶναι ἢ τὸ τοῦ κρείττονος ξυμφέρον [the just is nothing else than the advantage of the stronger]) by advancing the skeptical theory (338 c): εἰ Πολυ-
δάμας ἡμῶν κρείττων ὁ παγκρατιαστὴς καὶ αὐτῷ συμφέρει τὰ βόεια XIII
κρέα πρὸς τὸ σῶμα, τοῦτο τὸ σιτίον εἶναι καὶ ἡμῖν τοῖς ἥττοσιν 200
ἐκείνου ξυμφέρον ἅμα καὶ δίκαιον [if Polydamas, the pancratist, is stronger than we are and the flesh of beef is advantageous for him, for his body, this viand is also for us who are weaker than he both advantageous and just][284] is a clear analogy to the way in which Socrates ridicules the thesis of Callicles that the strongest (i.e., the most knowledgeable, i.e., the best) should have the most.* On the whole, the irony in this whole first book is so excessive and ungovernable, sparkles so inordinately, frolics with such wantonness and fieriness that one certainly has an intimation of the enormous muscular strength a corresponding dialectic must have; but since all these efforts still do not have any relation to the idea, the Sophists and the thought processes in this whole first book have a certain resemblance to the grotesque figures that appear and the equally grotesque leaps that are made in a *Schattenspiel*

* Socrates is of the opinion that the one who is most knowledgeable about food and drink should have the most, and when Callicles answers (Heise, p. 111): "Your talk always revolves around food and drink and physicians and other nonsense, but I have none of all that in mind," Socrates goes on to say, "I understand you, but perhaps the one who knows the most will have the most clothes, and the one who is the best weaver have the largest wardrobe and will go about wearing the most clothes and the most beautiful clothes." Callicles: "Oh, you and your clothes!" Socrates: "But the one who is the best and knows the most about shoes obviously must have the most shoes, and perhaps the shoemaker ought to walk in shoes with the most and the largest soles" etc.[285]

an der Wand [shadow play on the wall]. And yet the Sophists conduct the whole business with an earnestness and supreme effort that form a glaring contrast to the nothingness of the result, and it is almost impossible to keep from laughing when Socrates says (350 d): Ὁ δὴ Θρασύμαχος ὡμολόγησε μὲν πάντα ταῦτα, οὐχ ὡς ἐγὼ νῦν ῥαδίως λέγω, ἀλλ᾽ ἑλκόμενος καὶ μόγις, μετὰ ἱδρῶτος θαυμαστοῦ ὅσου, ἅτε καὶ θέρους ὄντος [Thrasymachus made all these admissions not as I now lightly narrate them, but with much balking and reluctance and prodigious sweating, it being summer].[286] The particular expressions of irony here are of course not in the service of the idea, are not its messengers who collect the scattered parts into a whole; they do not collect but scatter, and each new beginning is not an unfolding of what went before, is not an approach to the idea, but is devoid of deeper connection with the foregoing and devoid of any relation to the idea.

XIII As for the contents of this first book, I shall try to give a
201 survey of it as full as required and as condensed as possible. Socrates and Glaucon had gone to the Piraeus in order to be present at the Βενδίδεια [festival of Bendis].[287] On the way home, they are invited to the aged Cephalus's house. Socrates accepts the invitation, and a conversation quickly develops between him and Cephalus. The dominant tone of this part is idyllically charming. Socrates expresses his gratitude that the old gentleman wants to spend time with him, inasmuch as someone who has traveled far on life's way must necessarily be able to give advice on many things to someone who is just setting out. With reference to Cephalus's having both received and earned a rather considerable fortune, Socrates turns his attention to resolving the question whether justice on the whole is truth and paying back what one owes, or whether there may not be cases in which it becomes unjust to pay back what one owes. (For example, if one were to give back to a friend a sword, received when he was in his right mind, if that friend becomes mentally deranged.) At this point, Cephalus stops and hands the discussion over to the others, whereupon Polemarchus, his son and heir (ὁ τοῦ λόγου κληρονόμος [the inheritor of the argument]), picks up the thread. He advances

the thesis: "τὸ τὰ ὀφειλόμενα ἑκάστῳ ἀποδιδόναι δίκαιόν ἐστι [that it is just to pay everyone what is owed him]" and goes on to elucidate that it is to do good to friends and evil to enemies, and explains ὀφειλόμενον [what is due] by τὸ ἑκάστῳ προσῆκον [what befits each one].[288] This expression τὸ προσῆκον [what befits someone] provides Socrates with the occasion to unfold a total skepticism, derived from the world of knowledge, and inasmuch as it is manifest that to give everyone τὸ προσῆκον depends upon thorough knowledge, the territory of justice is reduced exceedingly. Thereupon he turns the whole matter in such a way that justice is seen to be useful only when one is not using something, and consequently justice becomes useful in the useless. Up until now, Thrasymachus has been silent but has been impatiently waiting for his chance to break in, and now he lunges at Socrates with the violence of a madman and, after venting his fury over the way Socrates was making fun of them, says: φημὶ γὰρ ἐγὼ εἶναι τὸ δίκαιον οὐκ ἄλλο τι ἢ τὸ τοῦ κρείττονος ξυμφέρον [I affirm that the just is
nothing else than the advantage of the stronger].[289] Socrates XIII
pretends to be discountenanced, but after some banter aimed 202
at diverting Thrasymachus's attention from the main question he resumes the same tactics he had so successfully used against Polemarchus. Socrates once again takes refuge in the sphere of knowledge. The word κρείττων [stronger] is now the stumbling block. If this is understood of the stronger without reference to whether a specific person or power in the state is meant, then, since the laws of the state are made for a distinct advantage in both cases, it certainly would be possible, inasmuch as the lawgiver is not infallible, for the laws to be detrimental to the stronger instead of being in his best interest. Thrasymachus, however, believes this argument must collapse when one considers that just as a physician is a physician not by virtue of his failures but by virtue of his successes, so also a lawgiver in the true sense of the word will know how to promulgate such laws as are truly designed for his own advantage. Thrasymachus is speaking, therefore, not of a so-called ruler but of someone who in the strict sense, indeed, in the strictest sense, is ruler (τὸν ἀκριβεῖ λόγῳ—τὸν τῷ ἀκριβεστάτῳ

λόγῳ ἄρχοντα ὄντα [in the precise sense—the most precise sense of the word]).[290] But precisely this, that the concept is interpreted *sensu eminentiori* [in the eminent sense] in this way, gives Socrates the occasion for a new doubt—namely, that with the art of ruling it is presumably the same as with any other art when it is practiced truly: it admits no alien motive, firmly and fixedly concentrates on its object, and consequently does not squint for advantage. Socrates had brought the discussion to this point—and one cannot deny the rightness of his conception of the line of the inquiry, ὅτι ὁ τοῦ δικαίου λόγος εἰς τοὐναντίον περιειστήκει [that his formula of justice had suffered a reversal of form][291]—when Thrasymachus has a new attack of fury and like one possessed, egocentrically lost in a garrulous monologue, vents himself in a new stream of what Socrates would call insolence, the gist of which is as follows: when he speaks of doing wrong he does not mean doing wrong on a small scale—on the contrary, the more grandiose the wrong, the more perfect it is and the more advantageous it is to the one who does the wrong. Having finished this diatribe, he wanted to depart, but the others present detained him.

XIII Socrates turns again to his previous view, and shows that
203 every art must be understood in its ideal endeavor, that the parasite of finite teleology that wants to attach itself to it must be rejected. Every art has its own distinctive objective, its own usefulness, which is nothing other than to promote the interests of those entrusted to its care. Thrasymachus adheres to his thesis and explains further that justice is nothing but simplicity and injustice is sagacity. Socrates now prompts Thrasymachus to affirm that injustice is wisdom and virtue. Thereupon Socrates bears down on the thesis that injustice is wisdom, and by way of some analogies from the sphere of knowledge he again ousts Thrasymachus from the entrenched position he had taken behind his bold paradox. The just person does not, of course, want more than the just but certainly wants more than the unjust; but the unjust person wants to have an advantage over both the just and the unjust. Likewise an artist does not want to have an advantage over another art-

ist, but certainly over someone who is not an artist; a physician does not want to have an advantage over the physician, but certainly over someone who is not a physician. Generally speaking, the expert does not want to have an advantage over another expert, but certainly over the nonexpert. The nonexpert, however, wants to have an advantage over the expert as well as the nonexpert. Ergo, the just person is judicious and good; the unjust person, injudicious and evil. Now, of course, the discussion is in stride, and the rest of the book is by no means stingy about predicating every possible good with regard to justice. These predicates, however, are primarily external description; they are to be regarded as a kind of police poster that can help someone with a clue for an arrest but does not contain any definitions. Thus they do set thought in motion but let it float in the abstract and do not satisfy it with positive fullness. Thus when at the end Socrates wants to have Thrasymachus ratify the result: Οὐδέποτ᾽ ἄρα, ὦ μακάριε Θρασύμαχε, λυσιτελέστερον ἀδικία δικαιοσύνης [Never, then, most worshipful Thrasymachus, can injustice be more profitable than justice], one can in a certain sense forgive Thrasymachus the scornful reply: Ταῦτα δή σοι, ἔφη, ὦ Σώκρατες, εἰστιάσθω ἐν τοῖς Βενδιδείοις [Let this complete your entertainment, Socrates, at the festival of Bendis].[292] But Socrates also has too much of an overview of the course of the conversation not to discern that the whole line of procedure has been rather desultory. Therefore he concludes with the observation
(354 b): ἀλλ᾽ ὥσπερ οἱ λίχνοι τοῦ ἀεὶ παραφερομένου ἀπογεύον- XIII
ται ἁρπάζοντες, πρὶν τοῦ προτέρου μετρίως ἀπολαῦσαι, καὶ ἐγώ 204
μοι δοκῶ οὕτω, πρὶν ὃ τὸ πρῶτον ἐσκοποῦμεν εὑρεῖν, τὸ δίκαιον ὅ, τι ποτ᾽ ἔστιν, ἀφέμενος ἐκείνου ὁρμῆσαι ἐπὶ τὸ σκέψασθαι περὶ αὐτοῦ εἴτε κακία ἐστὶ καὶ ἀμαθία εἴτε σοφία καὶ ἀρετή, καὶ ἐμπεσόντος αὖ ὕστερον λόγου ὅτι λυσιτελέστερον ἡ ἀδικία τῆς δικαιοσύνης, οὐκ ἀπεσχόμην τὸ μὴ οὐκ ἐπὶ τοῦτο ἐλθεῖν ἀπ᾽ ἐκείνου· ὥστε μοι νυνὶ γέγονεν ἐκ τοῦ διαλόγου μηδὲν εἰδέναι· ὁπότε γὰρ τὸ δίκαιον μὴ οἶδα ὅ ἐστι, σχολῇ εἴσομαι εἴτε ἀρετή τις οὖσα τυγχάνει εἴτε καὶ οὔ, καὶ πότερον ὁ ἔχων αὐτὸ οὐκ εὐδαίμων ἐστὶν ἢ εὐδαίμων [But just as gluttons snatch at every dish that is handed along and taste it before they have properly enjoyed

the preceding, so I, methinks, before finding the first object of our inquiry—what justice is—let go of that and set out to consider something about it, namely whether it is vice and ignorance or wisdom and virtue. And again, when later the view was sprung upon us that injustice is more profitable than justice, I could not refrain from turning to that from the other topic. So that for me the present outcome of the discussion is that I know nothing. For if I don't know what the just is, I shall hardly know whether it is a virtue or not, and whether its possessor is or is not happy].[293]

Anyone looking at the overall movement in this first book will surely acknowledge that this is *not* the dialectic of the idea but rather a question dialectically evolving from the speakers' fatuities, and that this first book achieves the possibility of asking with speculative energy: What is justice? Thus one must agree with Schleiermacher[294] that the book ends without a conclusion. Incidentally, this could seem completely accidental. In other words, if a work such as Plato's *Republic*, which consists of ten books in which the exposition of the idea of justice is the main subject, does not promptly produce the conclusion in the first book, one could find this altogether appropriate. But such is not the case. The big difference between the first and the following books must not be overlooked, nor the fact that the second book begins all over again from the beginning. Add to this the fact that the first book is conscious of not arriving at a result and that it does not run away from this consciousness but clings to it and rests in it, then it certainly cannot be denied that this first book not only ends without a conclusion* but ends with a negative conclusion. And

* It cannot be denied that Socrates touches on a few more positive thoughts in the course of the conversation. But here again the positive is understood in
XIII 205 all its abstraction and to that extent is only a negative qualification. To lift up every art into an ideal sphere in this way,[295] into a higher order of things, where it is performed only for its own sake, unaffected by any earthly defilement, is a very positive thought in and by itself, but it is also so abstract that in relation to every particular art it is a negative qualification. The positive thought, the actual πλήρωμα [fullness], would be given only upon the appearance of that wherein it desires itself. The negative qualification that it does not desire anything else would follow the positive qualification like a shadow, as

just as this in itself is ironic, so also Socrates' concluding observation bears an unmistakably ironic stamp. XIII 205 If I have not been shadowboxing, then my observation on the first book of the *Republic* will be substantiated in everything said previously, just as what was said previously, insofar as it was still suspended, will gain its footing in this final inquiry; and my whole structure by no means needs to become ramshackle, because the one part simultaneously rests upon and sustains the other.

I must, however, place primary stress upon the first book of the *Republic*. In one way or another, Plato must have been aware of the difference between this first book and the following ones, but since a whole intermediate cycle of dialogues is totally different from it, he must have meant something by it. This is one side. The other side is that this first book is very reminiscent of the earlier dialogues. These must have been under Socrates' influence and personal dominance in a totally different sense than the later dialogues were. The conclusion from this is that the best and surest way to a view of Socrates is through these first dialogues and the first book of the *Republic*.

A Justifying Retrospection XIII 206

As far as the choice of dialogues is concerned, I have continually had regard for only one thing—namely, to limit myself to the dialogues that according to common opinion would disclose to me, even though fragmentarily, a view of the *actual Socrates*. Most scholars, in their grouping of the dialogues, have a first division (and to me this is the primary concern);

---

a perpetually nullified possibility of such a desire. Here the relation is in a sense reversed, for it is propounded as the positive, that the art is not performed for the sake of something else. One can presumably say that justice ought to be desired for the sake of justice alone, but in order for there to be any real progression in the thought, justice in the first place must be displayed in justice in the second place; the ambitious restlessness in justice in the first place must have found its rest and reassurance in justice in the second place. Therefore, as long as one does not know what justice is, the thought that justice ought to be desired for its own sake alone of course becomes a negative thought.

all of them are closely connected with Socrates, not simply because they are closest to him in time, for that, after all, would be a totally external qualification, but also because they are assumed to be most kindred to him in spirit, even though not all scholars explicitly call them the Socratic dialogues, as Ast does.* Furthermore, not all scholars agree on which dialogues should be assigned to this first division, but all of them include the *Protagoras* and most of them the *Gorgias*, which is adequate for me. Ast places the *Phaedo* in this group as well.[296] Many scholars oppose him on this. Most of them, however, agree again in assigning special significance to the *Symposium* and *Phaedo* in the conception of Socrates. Insofar as Ast is in opposition to Schleiermacher's views on the connection between the *Phaedo* and the *Symposium*[297] (presented in the appropriate place in this treatise[298]), this protest, to be sure, does put an obstacle in my way, but since he does, however, reckon the *Phaedo* among the "Socratic" dialogues, I can with some modification follow Schleiermacher and his adherents on this point. Most scholars agree in assigning historical significance
XIII in the stricter sense to the *Apology*, and consequently I must,
207 as I have done, lay primary stress upon it. Finally, under the auspices of Schleiermacher, I have tried to affirm the special importance of the first book of the *Republic* for this inquiry.

If in my choice of dialogues I have in one respect kept in

* "In den Gesprächen der ersten Reihe lebte Platon noch ganz in der Socratik; hier hatte er den Zweck, die Socratik gegen die verderblichen Grundsätze der damaligen Sophisten (Protagoras), Redner und Schriftsteller (Phaedrus), und Politiker (Gorgias) geltend zu machen, und im Gegensatze zu ihr nicht nur ihre Nichtigkeit und Gehaltlosigkeit, sondern auch ihre Schädlichkeit zu zeigen [In the dialogues belonging to the first group, Plato's life was still totally absorbed in the Socratic. Here his purpose was to uphold the validity of the Socratic over against the corrupt tenets of the Sophists (*Protagoras*), the orators and writers (*Phaedrus*), as well as the statesmen (*Gorgias*), of the day; in opposing these, he sought to demonstrate not only their nullity and insubstantiality but also their perniciousness]" (pp. 53-54). This observation by Ast is acceptable if one does not forget that the polemic in evidence here is not a positive polemic thundering at teachers of false doctrines with the pathos of earnestness, but a negative polemic that in a far more subtle but also far more forceful way undermines them, coolly and inflexibly watches them sink down into absolutely nothing.

mind the conclusions of scholarly researchers, adapted myself to them as far as possible, leaned upon them as much as they allowed me to, I have also, on the other hand, endeavored to ascertain their correctness by an unbiased examination of a large portion of Plato. That irony and dialectic are the two great forces in Plato everyone will surely admit, but that there is a double kind of irony and a double kind of dialectic cannot be denied, either. There is an irony that is only a *stimulus* for thought, that quickens it when it becomes drowsy, disciplines it when it becomes dissolute. There is an irony that is itself the activator and in turn is itself the terminus striven for. There is a dialectic that in perpetual movement continually sees to it that the question does not become entrapped in an incidental understanding, that is never weary and is always prepared to set the issue afloat if it runs aground—in short, that always knows how to keep the issue in suspension and precisely therein and thereby wants to resolve it. There is a dialectic that, in proceeding from the most abstract ideas, wants to let these display themselves in more concrete qualifications, a dialectic that wants to construct actuality with the idea. Finally, in Plato there is yet another element that is a necessary supplement to the deficiency in both the great forces. This is the mythical and the metaphorical. The first kind of dialectic corresponds to the first kind of irony, the second kind of dialectic to the second kind of irony; to the first two corresponds the mythical, to the last two the metaphorical—yet in such a way that the mythical is not indispensably related to either the first two or the last two but is more like an anticipation engendered by the one-sidedness of the first two or like a transitional element, a *confinium* [border territory], that actually belongs neither to the one nor to the other.

Either it must be assumed that these positions lie within Plato's range, that he himself has primarily experienced the first stage separately, has let it unfold within itself, until the second stage began to assert itself and after gradually developing under the first ended by entirely superseding it; the first stage is not absorbed into the second—in the second stage everything is new. If both positions are to be ascribed to Plato, the first XIII 208 must be designated as skepticism, as a kind of introduction that nevertheless does not lead into the subject, as a running start that nevertheless does not reach the goal. Furthermore, an injustice is thereby done to the first position: it is not allowed to consolidate inwardly but is razed as much as possible in order to make easier the transition to the second. If this is done, the phenomenon is altered; if not, the difficulty of containing both of them primarily in Plato becomes all the greater. Moreover, this completely shoves aside the importance of Socrates, and such an interpretative venture would conflict with all history, since in this way all that Plato would have to thank Socrates for would be the name Socrates, which in Plato plays just as essential a role as it would play an accidental role according to this conception. *Or* it must be assumed that one of these positions belongs primarily to Socrates, secondarily to Plato, consequently that Plato has only reproduced it. —As to which of these two positions belongs to Socrates, there can be no doubt. It must be the first. As suggested above, its distinctive features are: irony in its total endeavor,* dialectic in its negatively liberating activity.**

Insofar as I may not have adequately managed in the above to justify this position on the basis of Plato, the reason, apart from what is due to my own lack of ability, is that Plato only reproduced it. But just as [Socratic] irony must have been able to exert a powerful influence on a poetic temperament such as
XIII 209 Plato's, so it must also have become equally difficult for him to explain this influence and to reproduce the irony in its totality, and in this reproduction to avoid adding a positive content so as to make sure that it did not become in this position what it later is in him—a negative power in the service of a

* It might seem that the first stage could be designated as pure dialectic and Socrates could thus be understood only as a dialectician. Schleiermacher did in fact do this in his well-known treatise,[299] but dialectic as such is a much too impersonal category to encompass a figure such as Socrates; on the other hand, whereas dialectic infinitely expands and emanates into the extremities, irony leads it back into personality, rounds it off in personality.

** To this extent it is quite appropriate that Aristotle denies to Socrates dialectic in the proper sense of the word.[300]

positive idea. If this is the case, then one will indeed see the correctness of regarding, as all the above suggested, the expressions in the first dialogues, which vacillate between a positive and a negative position, as an ambiguous preliminary glimpse, the mythical part of these dialogues as an anticipation, and the cycle of dialogues to which the *Parmenides*, *Theaetetus*, *Sophist*, and *Statesman* belong as the beginning of authentic Platonism.

A difficulty always remaining for me is obviously that it is possible really to understand the first position only by way of discriminating observation, inasmuch as Plato's reproduction is not entirely free of a certain double illumination. This can be very easily explained, because there is often a deceptive similarity between irony and subjective thinking. With regard to the first in the relation between one personality and another, provided that it is liberating, it is obvious that it can be both negatively and positively liberating, as already explained in the foregoing.[301] Because irony cuts the bonds that restrain speculation, helps it to shove off from the purely empirical sandbanks and to venture out upon the ocean, this is a negatively liberating activity. Irony is in no sense a partner in the expedition. But insofar as the speculating individual feels liberated and an abundance spreads out before his observing eyes, he may readily believe that he also owes all this to irony and his gratitude may wish to owe everything to it. Now, up to a point there is some truth in this confusion, since all intellectual property naturally exists only in relation to the consciousness that possesses it. Thus a personality is a necessary point of departure in the positions of both irony and subjective thinking; the activity of this personality becomes liberating in both of these positions, but the position of irony is negative, whereas that of reasoning is positive. Therefore, Plato was liberating for his pupils in a different sense than Socrates was for Plato; but it became necessary also for Plato's pupils to include him in their thinking, because his speculation remained purely subjective, and he himself did not retire into the shadows while the idea as such moved before the listener. On the other hand, Plato's relation to Socrates was not continually sus-

XIII 210 tained; later he was liberated not so much by Socrates as he liberated himself in himself, even though his memory was too faithful and his gratitude too fervent ever to forget him. However much Socrates is still the main character in the constructive dialogues, this Socrates is still only a shadow of the one who appears in the first dialogues, a recollection that Plato, no matter how precious it was to him, nevertheless freely transcended, indeed, freely and poetically created.

As for form, dialogue is equally necessary for both positions. It expressly indicates the *I* and its relation to the world; but in the one case it is the *I* that continually devours the world, and in the other it is the *I* that wants to take up the world; in the one case the *I* is continually talking itself out of the world, and in the other it is continually talking itself into the world; in the one position it is a questioning that consumes the answer, and in the other a questioning that develops the answer. As for method, this is the dialectical method, in both positions the abstractly dialectical. Of course, as such it does not exhaust the idea. What is left over is, in the one position, nothing; that is, in the other position the negative consciousness into which the abstract dialectic is taken is a beyond, an abstract qualification, but one that is maintained positively. If irony is beyond subjective thinking, it is beyond[302] it to the extent that it is a fulfilled position that turns back into itself; whereas subjective thinking has a frailty, a weakness, through which a higher position must work itself forward. In another sense, irony is a lower position insofar as it lacks this possibility, insofar as it remains inaccessible to every challenge, refuses to become involved any more with the world, but is itself enough. Since both positions are subjective, both of them naturally reside to a certain degree in the sphere of approximation philosophy, yet without becoming lost in it, whereby they would sink down into altogether empirical positions. The means by which the one position goes beyond actuality is the negative, that is, the consciously absorbed negation of the validity of experience; the other position has a positivity in the form of an abstract qualification. The one maintains recollection negatively and retrogressively in contrast to the current of life; the other maintains recollection forward[303] in its outflowing into actuality.*

XIII 211 But since I am in the process of showing this misunderstanding to be possible, of carrying on my investigation of it, some reader may be thinking a bit ironically that it is rather a misunderstanding on my part, that the whole thing is a false alarm. The difficulty such a reader has in mind is obviously this: to explain how Socrates conceivably could have mystified Plato so that the latter took seriously what Socrates had said ironically. Indeed, the difficulty for me could be increased by recalling that on the whole Plato understood irony very well, something that even his latest writings indicate. To this latter objection, may I say that my subject is of course not the individual manifestations of irony but Socratic irony in its total design. But to conceive of irony in this way takes an altogether unique mental disposition that is qualitatively distinguished from every other. In particular, a very creative poetic temperament is scarcely qualified to grasp it *sensu eminentiori* [in the eminent sense], although a temperament such as this may very well be attracted to individual manifestations of irony without suspecting the infinitude concealed here, may have fun with it without any notion of the prodigious daemon dwelling in the empty wastelands[304] of irony.

To the first objection, I would answer, for one thing, that it would always be rather difficult for a Plato to understand Socrates completely and, for another (and this is my main response), that one cannot look for a mere representation of Socrates in Plato and that it has never occurred to any reader of Plato to look for this. But if Plato, as most scholars agree, has not merely represented Socrates but has poetically created him, then everything is here that one could want for removing this difficulty. No more than one dares to draw the conclusion (from the fact that in the later dialogues Plato lets Socrates do the talking) that Socrates' dialectic is actually so constituted as

* The detailed development of all these similarities and dissimilarities, of all these points of coincidence, is to be found in the appropriate places in the foregoing portion.

it is in the *Parmenides* and that his conceptualizing is just as it is found in the *Republic*, no more can one justifiably conclude from the depiction in the first dialogues that Socrates' position actually was as described there.

Some reader might be willing to admit this; indeed, he might be waiting impatiently for me to finish this comment in order to plague me with a new objection. If in the previous
XIII 212 examination of the particular dialogues I have tried to show the total endeavor of this irony, then Plato must certainly have understood it, inasmuch as it is found in his presentation. By way of answer, in the discussion above I have, for one thing, merely tried to establish the possibility of my view of Socrates. Therefore, in several places I have kept the view in suspension, suggested that there could be an alternative. For another, I have argued *principaliter* [primarily] from the *Apology*. But in this dialogue we do have, according to the view of the great majority, a historical representation of Socrates' actuality; and yet here, too, I have had to conjure up the spirit of irony, so to speak, and let it gather itself and disclose itself in its complete totality.

Xenophon and Plato

If Plato's view of Socrates were to be expressed in a few words, it could be said that he provides him with the idea. Where the empirical ends, Socrates begins; his function is to lead speculation out of finite qualifications, to lose sight of finitude and steer out upon the Oceanus where ideal striving and ideal infinity recognize no alien considerations but are themselves their infinite goal. Thus, just as the lower sense perception turns pale before this higher knowledge—indeed, becomes a delusion, a deception by comparison—just so every consideration of a finite goal becomes a disparagement, a profanation of the holy. In short, Socrates has gained ideality, has conquered those vast regions that hitherto were a *terra incognita* [unknown land]. For this reason, he disdains the useful, is indifferent to the established [*Bestaaende*], is an out-and-out enemy of the mediocrity that in empiricism is the highest, an object of pious worship, but for speculation a troll changeling.

But if we remember the conclusion we arrived at through Xenophon, namely, that here we found Socrates busily functioning as an apostle of finitude, as an officious bagman for mediocrity, tirelessly recommending his one and only saving secular gospel, that here we found the useful rather than the good, the useful rather than the beautiful, the established rather than the true, the lucrative rather than the sympathetic, pedestrianism rather than harmonious unity, then one will surely admit that these two conceptions cannot very well be joined.

Either Xenophon must be charged with sheer arbitrariness, XIII
with an incomprehensible hatred of Socrates that sought sat- 213
isfaction in such slander, or an equally incomprehensible idiosyncrasy must be attributed to Plato because of his opposition, which just as puzzlingly resulted in changing Socrates into conformity with himself. If we momentarily let the actuality of Socrates be an unknown quantity, one may say of these two interpretations that Xenophon, like a huckster, has deflated his Socrates and that Plato, like an artist, has created his Socrates in supranatural dimensions.

But what was Socrates actually like? What was the point of departure for his activity? The answer to this must, of course, also help us out of the dilemma in which we have been situated until now. The answer is: Socrates' existence is irony. Just as this answer, in my opinion, removes the problem, so the fact that it removes the problem makes it the right answer as well—thus it simultaneously appears as a hypothesis and as the truth. In other words, the point, the line that makes the irony into irony, is very difficult to grasp. Along with Xenophon, therefore, one can certainly assume that Socrates was fond of walking around and talking with all sorts of people because every external thing or event is an occasion for the ever quick-witted ironist; along with Plato, one can certainly let Socrates touch on the idea, except that the idea does not open up to him but is rather a boundary. Each of these two interpretations has, of course, sought to give a complete characterization of Socrates—Xenophon by pulling him down into the lower regions of the useful, Plato by elevating him into the supramundane regions of the idea. But the point, one that lies between, invisible and so very difficult to grasp securely, is irony. On the one hand, the manifold variety of actuality is the very element of the ironist. On the other hand, his passage across actuality is floating and ethereal; he is continually just touching the ground, but since the real kingdom of ideality is still foreign to him, he has not as yet emigrated to it but seems always to be on the point of departure. Irony oscillates between the ideal *I* and the empirical *I*; the one would make Socrates a philosopher, the other a Sophist; but what makes him more than a Sophist is that his empirical *I* has universal validity.

XIII 214

ARISTOPHANES

Aristophanes' view of Socrates will provide just the necessary contrast to Plato's and precisely by means of this contrast will open the possibility of a new approach for our evaluation. Indeed, it would be a great lack if we did not have the Aristophanic appraisal of Socrates; for just as every process usually ends with a parodying of itself,[305] and such a parody is an assurance that this process has outlived its day, so the comic view is an element, in many ways a perpetually corrective element, in making a personality or an enterprise completely intelligible. Therefore, even though we lack direct evidence about Socrates, even though we lack an altogether reliable view of him, we do have in recompense all the various nuances of misunderstanding, and in my opinion this is our best asset with a personality such as Socrates.

Plato and Aristophanes do have in common an ideality of depiction, but at opposite poles; Plato has the tragic ideality, Aristophanes the comic. What motivated Aristophanes to view Socrates this way, whether he was bribed to do it by Socrates' accusers, whether he was embittered by Socrates' friendly relations with Euripides, whether through him he opposed Anaxagoras's speculations about nature, whether he identified him with the Sophists, in short, whether any finite and mundane motivation determined him in his view is totally

irrelevant to this study, and insofar as it should provide an answer on this point, it would, of course, have to be negative, since it acknowledges the conviction that Aristophanes' conception is ideal and thereby already freed from any such concerns, does not cringingly creep along the ground but, free and light, takes flight above it. Simply to apprehend the empirical actuality of Socrates, to bring him on stage as he walked and stood in life, would have been beneath the dignity of Aristophanes and would have changed his comedy into a satirical poem; on the other hand, to idealize him on a scale whereby he became completely unrecognizable would lie entirely outside the interest of Greek comedy. That the latter was XIII 215
not the case is attested by antiquity,[306] which recounts that the performance of *The Clouds* was honored in this respect by the presence of its severest critic, Socrates himself, who to the public's delight stood up during the performance so that the theater crowd could see for themselves the fitting likeness. We certainly must agree with the perspicacious Rötscher* that such a purely eccentric ideal view would not lie within the interest of Greek comedy, either. He has so excellently explained how the essence of comedy consisted expressly in viewing actuality ideally, in bringing an actual personality on stage, yet in such a way that this one is indeed seen as a representative of the idea, which is why we find also in Aristophanes the three great comic paradigms: Cleon, Euripides, and Socrates,[308] whose roles comically represent the aspiration of the age in its three trends. Just as the scrupulously detailed view of actuality filled the distance between the audience and the stage, so also the ideal view in turn separated these two forces to the extent to which art must always do this. That Socrates in actual life presented many comic sides, that he, to put it bluntly once and for all, was to a certain degree a *Sonderling* [eccentric]** cannot be denied; neither can it be denied XIII 216

* Heinrich Theodor Rötscher, *Aristophanes und sein Zeitalter, eine philologisch-philosophische Abhandlung zur Alterthumsforschung.*[307] Berlin: 1827.

** Cf. Johann Georg Sulzer, *Nachträge zu Sulzers allgemeiner Theorie der schönen Künste,*[309] VII, 1, p. 162: "Leider kennen wir den Socrates nur aus den verschönernden Gemählden eines Plato und Xenophon, indesz geht aus die-

that this is enough justification for a comic poet; but there is no denying, either, that this would not have been enough for an Aristophanes.

Thus, even though I cannot help ranging myself behind the deservedly exultant Rötscher,[310] who so triumphantly leads the idea through and out of its battle with the misunderstandings of earlier views, even though I cannot help agreeing with him that only insofar as Aristophanes saw in Socrates the representative of a new principle did he become a comic figure for him, there still remains a second question, whether the earnestness he so definitely claims for this play does not make him somewhat at odds with the irony he otherwise attributes to Aristophanes. There is yet another question, whether

---

sen so manches hervor, was Befremden erregt und auf einen seltsamen Mann hindeutet. Die Leitung eines unsichtbaren Genius, deren der Weise sich zu erfreuen glaubte, seine Zurückgezogenheit und Versenkung in sich selbst, die sogar im Lager tagelang dauerte und allen seinen Zeltgenossen auffiel, seine Unterhaltungen, deren Gegenstand, Zweck und Wendungen sich durch so viel Eigenthümlichkeiten auszeichneten, sein vernachlässigtes Aeuszere und sein in vielen Hinsichten ungewöhnliches Betragen—alles diesz muszte ihm nothwendig in den Augen der Menge den Anstrich eines Sonderlings geben [Unfortunately, we know Socrates only from Plato's and Xenophon's embellished portraits, from which a great deal follows, however, that seems strange and suggests a peculiar person. The guidance of an invisible daimon in which the philosopher was pleased to believe, his withdrawal and absorption into himself lasting for days even while at camp and quite to the astonishment of fellow campers, his conversation, whose object, aim, and manner were distinguished by so much that was odd, his neglected exterior and in many respects unusual behavior—all this must inevitably have given him the appearance of an eccentric in the eyes of the crowd]." —Also p. 140, where the author observes that if we knew Socrates more accurately, Aristophanes would no doubt be given even more credence: "wir würden uns dann unfehlbar über-
XIII zeugen, dasz er, bei allen seinen groszen Tugenden und herrlichen Eigen-
216 schaften, doch die Fehler und Gebrechen der Menschheit im reichen Maasze an sich trug, dasz er, wie so gar mehrere unverdächtige Winke vermuthen lassen, in noch mancher Rücksicht zu der Classe der Sonderlinge gehörte, seine Lehrart von dem Vorwurfe der Weitschweifigkeit und Pedanterei nicht frei war [We would then be unmistakably convinced that in spite of his many virtues and splendid qualities he still had the faults and defects of humanity in great measure, that, as several reliable indications suggest, he belonged in many respects to the class of eccentrics, and that his mode of teaching was not exempt from the reproach of verbosity and pedantry]."

Rötscher has not seen and therefore let Aristophanes see too much in Socrates. He certainly can be called the representative of a new principle—both because he personally represented a new position and because his liberating activity inevitably had to evoke a new principle; but it by no means follows that Socrates can very well be confined a little more within this admission. In Rötscher's view, Socrates becomes so towering that one does not see Plato at all. But all this will be discussed later. Assuming that irony was constitutive in Socrates' life, one will certainly admit that this affords a much more comic side than would be the case if the principle of subjectivity, the principle of inwardness, along with the whole train of ensuing ideas, were taken to be the Socratic principle, and if the authorization of Aristophanes were to be sought in the earnestness with which he as an advocate of early Greek culture had to try to destroy this modern monstrosity. This earnestness bears down too heavily, just as it also restricts the comic infinity, which as such recognizes no limits. Irony, on the other hand, is simultaneously a new position and as such is absolutely polemical toward early Greek culture. It is a position that continually cancels itself; it is a nothing that devours everything, and a something one can never grab hold of, something that is and XIII
is not at the same time, but something that at rock bottom is 217
comic. Therefore, just as irony surmounts everything by seeing its misrelation to the idea, so it capitulates to itself, because it continually goes over and beyond itself and yet remains in the idea.

It is of importance first of all to be satisfied that the Socrates brought on stage by Aristophanes is the actual Socrates. Just as ancient tradition fortifies this conviction, there are various traits found in this play that either are historically certain or at least prove to be altogether analogous to what we otherwise know about Socrates. With vast philological scholarship and much discernment, Süvern has tried to show the unity of the Aristophanic Socrates and the actual Socrates by means of just such a series of individual traits.* Rötscher, too, has provided

* J. W. Süvern, *Ueber Aristophanes Wolken*[311] (Berlin: 1826), pp. 3ff.

a collection of such data, if not on the same scale, yet adequate for the purposes of this study. It is found in the above-mentioned work, pp. 277ff. In the second place, it is of importance to see the principle, the idea, that Aristophanes lets us glimpse in Socrates, who is presented as its transparent representative.

But for this to be achieved, it is necessary to give a brief summary of the play itself, its plot and action. I can embark on this investigation all the more hopefully since I have a Hegelian at the head, and one must always grant that they have a genius for clearing the way, a police authority that promptly knows how to disperse all sorts of learned mobs and dubious historical conspiracies. In the first place, the chorus, which usually represents the moral substance in our play,[312] has dressed itself in a symbol.* Rötscher looks for the irony in the consciousness of this on the part of the chorus itself, which seems ever ready to leap out of its hiding place, as it were, and indeed does so at the end as it mocks Strepsiades, who has been tricked by them. Whether the irony lies in this, whether this earnestness,** which is fighting to rescue the substantial
XIII 218 consciousness of the state from the emptiness of the modern monstrosity, restricts the poetic infinity and heedlessness of irony, whether or not the whole finale of the play, even if it were a just nemesis, is effected at the expense of irony—without assuming, something that no one as far as I know has hitherto maintained, that precisely the revenge Strepsiades takes by burning down the building (φροντιστήριον [Thinkery], l. 94) by its inexpediency was a new comic motif, and that the rather witty lines,† which in one sense are too good to be his,

* See the excellent discussion of the history of the chorus in Aristophanes in Rötscher, pp. 50-59.

** Aristophanes himself acknowledges this earnestness in the first parabasis.[313]

† See ll. 1495-96:

ὅ τι ποιῶ; τί δ' ἄλλο γ' ἢ
διαλεπτολογοῦμαι ταῖς δοκοῖς τῆς οἰκίας.
[What am I at? I'll tell you.
I'm splitting straws with your house-rafters here].

l. 1503: ἀεροβατῶ, καὶ περιφρονῶ τὸν ἥλιον.
[I walk on air, and contemplate the Sun].

should be explained as a kind of ecstatic madness in which he, beside himself, raved and with comic cruelty destroyed and exterminated the disease with which he himself was infected—all this I shall not go into.* But if we bypass this, it XIII
becomes all the more important to dwell on a consideration of 219
the symbol in which the poet has mantled the chorus—*the clouds*. This cannot, of course, have been chosen accidentally, and thus the task is to find out the poet's idea therein. Obviously it symbolizes the whole empty, meaningless activity going on in the φροντιστήριον [Thinkery], and it is therefore with profound irony that Aristophanes, in the scene where Strepsiades is supposed to be initiated into this wisdom, has Socrates invoke the clouds,[314] the aeriform reflection of his own hollow interior. Clouds superbly characterize the utterly flabby thought process,** continually fluctuating, devoid of

* As a matter of fact, the irony is far more clear-cut and freeborn in an earlier passage where Strepsiades actually lets himself be convinced by Pheidippides' sophisms that he is right and that he (Strepsiades) ought to be flogged. See ll. 1437-39:

> ἐμοὶ μὲν, ὦνδρες ἥλικες, δοκεῖ λέγειν δίκαια·
> κἄμοιγε συγχωρεῖν δοκεῖ τούτοισι τἀπιεικῆ.
> κλάειν γὰρ ἡμᾶς εἰκός ἐστ᾽, ἢν μὴ δίκαια δρῶμεν
> [Good friends! I really think he has some reason to complain.
> I must concede he has put the case in quite a novel light:
> I really think we should be flogged unless we act aright!]

The relation between the two kinds of discourse, the good and the bad, is viewed with infinite irony, for in response to the comment that the bad always wins, Strepsiades implores Socrates to tutor Pheidippides in the bad above all else. See ll. 882-85:

> ὅπως δ'ἐκείνω τὼ λόγω μαθήσεται,
> τὸν κρείττον', ὅστις ἐστι, καὶ τὸν ἥττονα,
> ὃς τἄδικα λέγων ἀνατρέπει τὸν κρείττονα·
> ἐὰν δὲ μὴ, τὸν γοῦν ἄδικον πάσῃ τέχνῃ.
> [So now, I prithee, teach him both your Logics,
> The Better, as you call it, and the Worse
> Which with the worse cause can defeat the Better;
> Or if not both, at all events the Worse].

** It is quite in keeping with this when in nature the αἰθέριος δῖνος [ethereal XIII
vortex][315] becomes the constitutive principle instead of the well-molded fig- 219
ures of the blessed gods, and the totally negative dialectic is splendidly characterized as a whirlwind.

footing and devoid of immanental laws of motion, that takes all kinds of shapes with the same aberrant variability of the clouds: at times resembling mortal women, at times a centaur, a panther, a wolf, a bull, etc.[316]—resembling them but, please note, not actually being them, since the clouds are nothing but fog or the dim, self-affecting, infinite possibility of becoming anything that is supposed to be, yet unable to make anything remain established, the possibility that has infinite dimensions and seems to encompass the whole world but still has no content, can accept anything but retains nothing. In a way, it is sheer arbitrariness on Socrates' part to call the clouds goddesses, and it is far more reasonable for Strepsiades to assume them to be fog, mist, and smoke (see l. 330). But just as their emptiness is manifested in themselves, so it is also manifested in the community, the state, which they nourish and protect, and which Socrates himself describes as a bunch of street-corner loafers[317] and aimless idlers who sing praises to the
XIII 220 clouds.* Indeed, the corresponding relation between the

* See ll. 331-34:

οὐ γὰρ μὰ Δί' οἶσθ' ὁτιὴ πλείστους αὗται βόσκουσι σοφιστὰς,
θουριομάντεις, ἰατροτέχνας, σφραγιδονυχαργοκομήτας,
κυκλίων τε χορῶν ᾀσματοκάμπτας, ἄνδρας μετεωροφένακας,
οὐδὲν δρῶντας βόσκουσ' ἀργοὺς, ὅτι ταύτας μουσοποιοῦσιν
[O, then I declare, you can't be aware
 that 'tis these who the sophists protect,
Prophets sent beyond sea, quacks of every degree,
 fops signet-and-jewel-bedecked,
Astrological knaves, and fools who their staves
 of dithyrambs proudly rehearse—
'Tis the Clouds who all these support at their ease,
 because they exalt them in verse].

XIII 220 And therefore their gifts are also commensurate. See ll. 316-18:

ἥκιστ', ἀλλ' οὐράνιαι Νεφέλαι, μεγάλαι θεαὶ ἀνδράσιν ἀργοῖς·
αἵπερ γνώμην καὶ διάλεξιν καὶ νοῦν ἡμῖν παρέχουσι
καὶ τερατείαν καὶ περίλεξιν καὶ κροῦσιν καὶ κατάληψιν
[No mortals are there, but Clouds of the air,
 great Gods who the indolent fill:
These grant us discourse, and logical force,
 and the art of persuasion instil,
And periphrasis strange, and a power to arrange,
 and a marvellous judgement and skill].

clouds and the world to which they belong is expressed even more specifically—something interpreters in my opinion have so far overlooked—in the statement: γίγνονται πάνθ' ὅ τι βούλονται [the clouds assume whatever shape they wish] (l. 348), so when they see a shaggy-haired fellow, they assume the shape of a centaur, and when they see an embezzler, they assume the shape of a wolf (ll. 349-52). Although this is described as an absolute power of the clouds, yes, even though Socrates himself remarks that they assume such shapes in order to mock, it can just as well be regarded as an impotence in them, and the Aristophanic irony no doubt resides in the mutual impotence—the impotence of the subject, who in wanting the objective obtains only his own likeness, and the impotence of the clouds, which merely catch the likeness of the subject but reproduce it only as long as they see it. That this is a superb description of the purely negative dialectic that continually remains in itself, never goes out into the qualifications of life or of the idea, and therefore does indeed rejoice in a freedom that scorns the chains that continuity lays on,* the dialectic that is a power only in the most abstract sense, a king without a country who delights in the sheer possibility of renouncing everything in the moment of specious possession of everything, although the possession as well as the renunciation is illusory, a dialectic that is not embarrassed by the
past, is not inclosed by its ironbound consequences, is not un- XIII 221
easy about the future because it so quickly forgets that even the future is practically forgotten before it is experienced, a dialectic that regrets nothing, desires nothing, is unto itself

* In this exposition I have mainly focused on the intellectual aspect, because this obviously is closest to Greek culture. To be sure, a similar dialectic, the arbitrary, manifests itself in an even more lamentable form in the ethical sphere, but in this respect I also believe that the characteristic features of one's own age are sometimes given too much attention in interpreting the transitional period of Greek culture in Aristophanes' day. Hegel is quite correct in saying (*Geschichte der Philosophie*, II, p. 70): "Wir dürfen es den Sophisten nicht zum Verbrechen machen, dasz sie nicht das Gute zum Princip gemacht haben, es ist die Richtungslosigkeit der Zeit [We must not make criminals of the Sophists for failing to turn the good into a principle; this is the aimlessness of the age]."[318]

enough, and leaps over everything as recklessly and casually as a straying child—this, I am sure, no one will deny.

The consciousness of this nothingness, due to the fact that the chorus simultaneously is a symbol and yet is ironically aware of being over and above it and of having a totally different reality [*Realitet*], Rötscher attributes only to the chorus, the poet, and the informed spectator and adds on page 325: "Dem von diesem Gegensatze nicht wissenden hingegen ist nothwendig der wahrhafte Sinn verborgen, und er erblickt in ihnen nur das Symbol, nimmt diese Gestalt, in welche sich derselbe wissentlich hüllt, für sein wahrhaftes Wesen, und giebt sich ihm vertrauungsvoll und arglos hin, nicht ahnend, dasz er nur ein Schein sei, welcher ihm für die Wahrheit geboten wird. Die Schuld des Subjects besteht aber gerade darin, dasz es sich arglos diesen täuschenden Mächten hingiebt, und unwissend ist über das Wesen, welches diesen Schein herauskehrt [But to the one who remains ignorant of this contrast, the true meaning is inevitably concealed, and he perceives in them merely the symbol, takes the shape in which it consciously mantles itself to be its true essence, and trustfully and artlessly surrenders himself to it, never suspecting that he is offered only an illusion instead of the truth. But the fault of the subject consists in surrendering himself artlessly to these deceptive forces and in remaining ignorant of the essence that displays this appearance]."[319]

Yet this pertains more to the whole internal economy of the play, whereas at this point it becomes more necessary to see if one cannot, by following the symbol of the chorus depicted as clouds, find out something more about the nature of what it metaphorically designates. The chorus represents clouds, but the clouds in turn represent different objects and at the beginning of this play have the form of women. But Socrates obviously speaks very facetiously about these forms of the clouds, which adequately indicates that they have no validity for him. What he worships, that for which he uses the predicate "goddess," is therefore the formless vapor mass, what Strepsiades very correctly designates as fog, mist, smoke.[320] Consequently, what he keeps is formlessness as such. Therefore, all the forms the clouds assume are just like so many predicates that can be stated in such a way that they are all arranged together but devoid of relation to one another, devoid of inner sequence, constituting nothing—in short, like so many predicates that can be rattled off. Just as we saw earlier in our investigation that Socrates arrived at the idea but in such a way that no predicate disclosed or betrayed what it actually was, but all the predicates were witnesses that were silenced before its splendor, so in my opinion does Aristophanes suggest the same relation between Socrates and the clouds. What remains when the various cloud forms are allowed to vanish is the vapor mass itself, which is a very good designation for Socrates' idea. The clouds always appear in a form, but Socrates XIII 222 knows that the form is the unessential and that the essential lies behind the form, just as the idea is the true and the predicate as such means nothing. But that which is the true in this way never becomes an actual predicate; it never does exist.* Furthermore, if we consider the symbol of the chorus, clouds, and see therein Socrates' thoughts objectively** envisioned in it, see them as thoughts presumably produced by the individual but nevertheless also as thoughts adored by this individual as objective (divine), then precisely by the hovering of the clouds over the earth, by their multitude of forms, there is suggested the contrast between the subjective and the objectivity of early Greek culture, in which the divine really had a

* If some reader happens to think that I find too much in Aristophanes, I will gladly concede this if he in recompense will dispose of the difficulty that is bound to arise if one examines more closely the curious relation in which the subject stands to the clouds. Here there obviously are two factors to be noted: the chorus has enveloped itself in its symbol, the clouds, but in turn these clouds have taken the form of women.

** This is why it is set forth as a creed, which like any creed contains both the subjective and the objective side—for example, l. 424: τὸ Χάος τουτὶ καὶ τὰς Νεφέλας (the objective), καὶ τὴν γλῶτταν (the subjective), τρία ταυτὶ [And *my* creed you'll embrace, *I believe in wide space, in the Clouds . . . , in the eloquent Tongue . . . , these three*], and there is great comic force in Aristophanes' having Socrates swear by the same powers; see l. 627:

μὰ τὴν Ἀναπνοήν, μὰ τὸ Χάος, μὰ τὸν Ἀέρα
[Never by Chaos, Air, and Respiration].

firm foothold on the earth in definite, distinct, eternal forms. Thus there is a very profound harmony between the clouds as the objective power that cannot find an abiding place on earth, whose approach to the earth is always at a distance, and the subject, Socrates, who floats above the earth in a basket and struggles to rise into these regions, because he fears that the force of gravity will pull down his thoughts or, to drop the metaphor, that actuality will absorb, will crush, the delicate subjectivity (ἡ φροντὶς λεπτή [the delicate thought]).*[321] But
XIII 223 we shall return to this matter later when, focusing not on the chorus but on the character in action, we shall examine more closely the relevance Socrates' peculiar situation has to the idea.

The chorus symbolizes the whole new order that wants to oust early Greek culture, and thus the question whether Aristophanes, behind the mask of Socrates, wanted to mock the Sophists can best be answered here. Of course, it must by no means be assumed that Aristophanes merely kept Socrates' name and otherwise produced a sketch that did not resemble him in the least. But if one bears in mind that in a certain sense Socrates and the Sophists held the same position and that Socrates actually struck at their very roots by carrying through their position, by destroying the halfness in which the Soph-

* See ll. 227-34:

Σ: οὐ γὰρ ἄν ποτε
ἐξεῦρον ὀρθῶς τὰ μετέωρα πράγματα,
XIII 223 εἰ μὴ κρεμάσας τὸ νόημα καὶ τὴν φροντίδα
λεπτὴν καταμίξας εἰς τὸν ὅμοιον ἀέρα.
εἰ δ' ὢν χαμαὶ τἄνω κάτωθεν ἐσκόπουν,
οὐκ ἄν ποτ' εὗρον. οὐ γὰρ ἀλλ' ἡ γῆ βίᾳ
ἕλκει πρὸς αὑτὴν τὴν ἰκμάδα τῆς φροντίδος.
πάσχει δὲ ταὐτὸ τοῦτο καὶ τὰ κάρδαμα
[SO. Most true.
I could not have searched out celestial matters
Without suspending judgement, and infusing
My subtle spirit with the kindred air.
If from the ground I were to seek these things,
I could not find: so surely doth the earth
Draw to herself the essence of our thought.
The same too is the case with water-cress].

ists set their minds at ease, so that Socrates by defeating the Sophists was thereby in a certain sense himself the greatest Sophist,* one already perceives a possibility for Aristophanes to identify him with the Sophists. This identification did indeed lend itself to being carried through with a profound irony. It certainly would be irony worthy of an Aristophanes to perceive Socrates, the Sophists' most ill-tempered enemy, not as their opponent but as their teacher, which in a certain sense he indeed was. And the strange confusion that someone who opposes a trend may himself be considered its representative precisely because he in some measure belongs to it conceals so much intentional or unintentional irony that one ought not lose sight of it completely. Enough on that subject. Moreover, it is only insofar as the chorus is assumed as the
criterion that Socrates vanishes among the Sophists; if we fol- XIII
low the personal portrayal of him in the play itself, he emerges 224
adequately distinguished.

The action in the play may be described rather briefly, so much more so in this study since here it is only a matter of relating the action to the extent that the plot thereby displays Aristophanes' view of Socrates. A simple farmer, Strepsiades, has come into financial straits through an unwise marriage. His son, Pheidippides, through his passion for horses, has been very helpful in ruining his father. Strepsiades, continually agitated by the thought of his debt, continually troubled over getting out of it, looks around in vain for a way out, when suddenly the thought of the new wisdom beginning to assert itself in Athens and of its ability to argue everything in or out of existence awakens in him, to his amazed joy, the hope of finding in it his rescue. His first intention is to let Pheidippides enjoy the fruits of this modern erudition, but since the latter proves unwilling, he resolves to go to the φροντιστήριον [Thinkery] himself. He meets one of the students, who gives him a most favorable idea of the school. As an honest, upright farmer, Strepsiades is taken aback by Socrates' nu-

* Thus the predicate that the clouds apply to him is very expressive (l. 359): λεπτοτάτων λήρων ἱερεῦ [high priest of this most subtle nonsense].

merous strokes of ingenuity, by his many shrewd questions and answers, but a masterstroke on the part of Socrates, which is very close to his own ideas, wipes out his vacillation, and in impatient enthusiasm he demands to be taken to Socrates.*
XIII 225 After a preliminary ordeal designed to divest him of the out-

* See ll. 177-83:

Μ. κατὰ τῆς τραπέζης καταπάσας λεπτὴν τέφραν,
κάμψας ὀβελίσκον, εἶτα διαβήτην λαβών,
ἐκ τῆς παλαίστρας θοἰμάτιον ὑφείλετο.
Σ. τί δῆτ' ἐκεῖνον τὸν Θαλῆν θαυμάζομεν;
ἄνοιγ' ἄνοιγ' ἀνύσας τὸ φροντιστήριον,
καὶ δεῖξον ὡς τάχιστά μοι τὸν Σωκράτη.
μαθητιῶ γάρ· ἀλλ' ἄνοιγε τὴν θύραν

[STU. He sprinkled on the table—some fine ash—
He bent a spit—he grasped it compass-wise—
And—filched a mantle from the Wrestling School.
ST. Good heavens! Why Thales was a fool to this!
O open, open, wide the study door,
And show me, show me, show me Socrates.
I die to be a student. Open, open]!

XIII 225 If the reader will remember that Strepsiades later comes home from the φροντιστήριον without a mantle,[322] he certainly will sense the comic element in the fact that Strepsiades, who had been hoping to share in the booty (a mantle) himself, comes home not only without any proceeds but without even having what he had owned before—a mantle. And yet, considering what Strepsiades himself says, this is getting off rather well, inasmuch as in the instructional period he is afraid that Socrates will speculate him out of existence (ll. 717-22):

καὶ πῶς; ὅτε μου
φροῦδα τὰ χρὴματα, φρούδη χροιὰ,
φρούδη ψυχὴ, φρούδη δ'ἐμβάς·
καὶ πρὸς τούτοις ἔτι τοῖσι κακοῖς φρουρᾶς ᾄδων
ὀλίλου φροῦδος γεγένημαι

[Why, what can I do?
Vanished my skin so ruddy of hue,
Vanished my life-blood, vanished my shoe,
Vanished my purse, and what is still worse
As I hummed an old tune till my watch should be past,
I had very near vanished myself at the last].

And it is also apparent in the chorus's suggestion to Socrates that everything is designed, as we say, to skin Strepsiades (ll. 810-12):

Χορός.

σὺ δ' ἀνδρὸς ἐκπεπληγμένου καὶ φανερῶς ἐπηρμένου
γνοὺς ἀπολάψεις, ὅ τι πλεῖστον δύνασαι, ταχέως·

moded mentality in which he had hitherto walked and stood (ingeniously suggested by his having to undress* when he is to enter the φροντιστήριον) after a solemn initiation, which, if it could make any impression upon Strepsiades at all, would inevitably confuse his concepts completely, he obtains permission to enter the φροντ. and is now shown the same path to the knowledge of the truth that Socrates himself has fol- XIII
lowed: heedless of the surroundings to become immersed in 226
himself,** which for Strepsiades naturally becomes a very frugal meal, as scarcely satisfying as the repast to which the stork invited the fox was for the fox, who was merely a fasting witness to the way its host, storklike, drank deeply from the long-necked bottle.[323] Therefore, Strepsiades is soon found to be incapable of being remodeled, whereupon he is dismissed. But he has by no means surrendered his hope of fulfilling his wish by this route. Too modest to think that the fault could be in the teacher, he looks for it in himself and consoles himself with the thought of his promising son, Pheidippides, who, although skeptical of the samples of wisdom Strepsiades reports, at last succumbs to his pleas and lets himself be accepted in the φροντιστήριον. It goes better with the son, and the father brings gifts to Socrates in gratitude for the enormous progress the son has made. However, the threatening actuality comes closer and closer and finally appears in the grave forms of two creditors. Beside himself with joy over Pheidippides' dialectical ability to move boundary marks†

[Chorus.

But now that you have dazzled and elated so your man,
Make haste and seize whate'er you please as quickly as you can].

* See ll. 497-99:

ΣΩ. ἴθι νυν, κατάθου θοἰμάτιον.
ΣΤ. ἠίκηκά τι;
ΣΩ. οὒκ, ἀλλὰ γυμνοὺς εἰσιέναι νομίζεται
[SO. Put off your cloak.
ST. Why, what have I done wrong?
SO. O, nothing, nothing: all go in here naked].

** Here we have the Aristophanic view of the well-known Socratic standing still and staring.

† See ll. 1178-85:

XIII 227 trusting in the still not forgotten shrewd questions and answers he himself has learned in the φροντ., he rashly dares to confront these two calamitous representatives of a grievous actuality. Pasias and Amymias, however, are financiers enough not to be put off by such shrewdness; they still have so much confidence in actuality that they have no qualms about coming into their own, if not by dialectic, then by going to court.

Meanwhile, if Strepsiades can momentarily indulge in the

Φ. φοβεῖ δὲ δὴ τί;
Σ. τὴν ἔνην τε καὶ νέαν.
Φ. ἔνη γάρ ἐστι καὶ νέα τις ἡμέρα;
Σ. εἰς ἥν γε θήσειν τὰ πρυτανεῖά φασί μοι.
Φ. ἀπολοῦσ' ἄρ' αὔθ' οἱ θέντες· οὐ γὰρ ἔσθ' ὅπως
μί' ἡμέρα γένοιτ' ἂν ἡμέραι δύο.
Σ. οὐκ ἂν γένοιτο;
Φ. πῶς γάρ; εἰ μή πέρ γ' ἅμα
αὑτὴ γένοιτ' ἂν γραῦς τε καὶ νέα γυνή

[PH. What is it ails you?
ST. Why the Old-and-New day.
PH. And is there such a day as Old-and-New?
ST. Yes: that's the day they mean to stake their gages.
PH. They'll lose them if they stake them. What! do you think
That one day can be two days, both together?
ST. Why, can't it be so?
PH. Surely not; or else
A woman might at once be old and young].

"The Athenians' month consisted of thirty days; the first twenty were numbered forward from the first to the twentieth, but the rest backward from the month following. Thus the twenty-first was called the tenth, the twenty-sixth the fifth, the twenty-ninth the second. The thirtieth was called the old and the new; the first was called the new moon" (*Aristophanes's Komedier*,[324] translated by Johan Krag, Odense: 1825, p. 233 note). —On this last day of the month, interest was to be paid, and thus it was a day of terror for Strepsiades. But see, this agitation was now over for him, thanks to the cleverness of Pheidippides, who had the ability to cancel actuality and to prove that the day did not exist at all. I have deliberately pointed out this sophism as an example of the dialectic taught in the φροντ., because it is parodically reminiscent of the Socratic dialectic based essentially on the theory that one cannot enunciate two opposite predicates about the same thing and because with great comic force it not only claims to have validity in the world of thought but claims authority to negate actuality itself.[325]

joy of having fulfilled his desire, the poet has still reserved for him a slight bonus, an utterly unexpected surplus resulting from the great strides Pheidippides has made under the Socratic instruction. Pheidippides has also gone beyond an actuality that Strepsiades, after all, does not wish to see shaken, one totally different from the due-date actuality. By means of this dialectic, filial respect for and obedience to the father follow the same path as the due day. Strepsiades is unable to withstand the force of Pheidippides' syllogisms, which, just as they previously manifested themselves as actuality-destroying, now manifest themselves in the most forceful way of the world as actuality-positing, since thrashings are, as they say, durable goods and make themselves evident in a fashion that leaves no doubt. And just as Pheidippides previously showed himself sufficiently devoid of conscience to support his father in defaulting on the loan, so he now develops an almost exaggerated conscientiousness about paying an installment, an XIII 228
advance payment on the debt of beatings with which his fond father had overwhelmed him. Too late, Strepsiades discovers the corruption in the new wisdom. Revenge is awakened; it throws itself upon its prey, who in turn storms into the φροντιστήριον, burns it down, and the play ends.

This is the briefest possible summary of the structure of the play. The comic element obviously lies in the something that Strepsiades craves as the fruit of speculation, the something that in his opinion must result from all these movements. To be specific, just as in the sphere of intelligence the movements Socrates makes prove to be meaningless, prove unable to establish anything, the same thing becomes even more apparent in the world of Strepsiades, who has come upon the desperate idea that in a finite and mundane sense something will result from all this,* who hopes—to use one of modern philosophy's XIII 229

* This seems to be the place to include an interpretation of the much disputed lines quoted earlier[326] about the mantle that Socrates, according to the pupil, filched from the fencing school. As for the *vita ante acta* [earlier life] of this interpretation, see Rötscher, pp. 284-88.[327] —Süvern[328] has refuted Reisig's explanation[329] and in its place has himself found a characterization of the well-known Socratic distraction, and because there is a suggestion that it took

slogans—to speculate into his own pockets the Kantian one hundred dollars[331] or, failing that, to speculate away his debt.* The irony lies in the something he speculates himself into—if not immediately then at least intermediately through Pheidippides: the conscious beatings, however unexpected, that still

---

place at a mathematical demonstration, he linked it to the Socratic narrow-mindedness, for which we have Xenophon to thank, according to whom Socrates thought that mathematics ought to be learned only to the extent that it could be used in everyday life. Rötscher is of the opinion that no specific episode is referred to but that it merely stands as the supreme, the most brilliant characterization of the *Gewandtheit* [adroitness] that Strepsiades in his straitened circumstances so greatly needed. But when, in order to accentuate the Socratic cunning, Rötscher insists that Socrates had stolen the mantle from the Palaestra, a crime for which according to Solon's law the death penalty was mandatory, I believe that he misses in these lines the real point, to which in other statements he comes so very close. Aristophanes presumably wanted to ironize over the negative dialectic that bleeds to death in altogether vacuous imaginary constructions [*Experimenter*], and to which he now with even more profound irony attributes a *creative power* by having him seem to produce an actuality by means of spurious demonstrations, yet in such a way
XIII that since this actuality is a finite and worldly thing the performance borders
229 on theft. In the same way it can be explained, as is remarked in a note to the same portion, that Socrates' friend Chaerephon is often honored by the comedians with the nickname κλέπτης [thief]. The words introducing the episode—"He sprinkled some fine ash on the table, then he bent a spit"—seem to be the introduction to an act of creation, and then, with all the greater effect and with all the surprise of the sudden, come the words: "He filched" etc. — However one interprets the significance of this passage in the whole play, it will never be clear how this tour de force is supposed to remedy the need. The pupil tells Strepsiades that, since they did not have any supper, Socrates performed the operation described and filched a mantle from the wrestling school. But for one thing it is not apparent how this took care of getting supper, unless it is assumed that Socrates sold it and thereby obtained what was needed; for another, it is not apparent what his pilfering the mantle from the wrestling school is supposed to mean. In a note in Hermann's edition[330] (Leipzig: 1798, p. 33), there is a variant reading, namely, ἐκ τραπέζης [from the table]. He also calls attention to another problem—that the definite article is not appropriate here, since it is not a matter of a particular mantle, but he fails to solve the difficulty.

* In this respect, we cannot deny Strepsiades a commendable tenacity, for although he comes home from the φροντ. without having learned anything because of his senility (see l. 855), although he had lost both his mantle and his sandals (l. 857: Σ. ἀλλ' οὐκ ἀπολώλεκ', ἀλλὰ καταπεφρόντικα [I have not lost them, but studied them away]), trusting in Pheidippides' natural talents, he still does not give up his faith and belief in the new wisdom.

come with an inevitability that is impossible to escape. Strepsiades can certainly rejoice temporarily over all these ingenious moves, but what his sober soul craves is "*die Nutzanwendung* [practical application]," which in fact does not fail to XIII
appear, even if it comes where he had least expected it. 230

But if we try to find what the point of view is that shines through in this parody, we cannot say that it is the position of subjectivity, because this always yields something, yields the whole world of abstract ideality, but what is described here is a purely negative position, which yields nothing. The profound observations expounded dissolve like a thunderclap into nothing; on the other hand, that Strepsiades wants to have something tags along like a parodying shadow—but, please note, something finite, a finite advantage that this point of view is just as incompetent to supply as it is incompetent to supply the intellectual dividend it makes a show of producing. If it is assumed, therefore, that Socrates' whole activity was ironizing, it is also apparent that in wanting to interpret him in the comic vein Aristophanes proceeded quite correctly, for as soon as irony is related to a conclusion, it manifests itself as comic, even though in another sense it frees the individual from the comic. Neither is the dialectic, of which there are many examples, a genuine philosophical dialectic; it is not the kind of dialectic described earlier as characteristic of Plato but is an entirely negative dialectic. Now, if Socrates had had that Platonic subjective dialectic, it would certainly have been fallacious and it would not have been comic, even though sufficiently funny, for Aristophanes to interpret him in this way (since the comic must, of course, have some truth in it); whereas if Socrates' dialectic had been, for one thing, armed with sophisms and polemically directed against the Sophists and, for another, negatively aimed toward the idea, then Aristophanes' view[332] is appropriate precisely as comic. The same naturally holds true also of the symbol of the chorus, clouds. If it had been the ideal richness of the subjective they were supposed to symbolize, it would have been false, despite the fact that Aristophanes' view is comic, to have the individual relate to it as superficially as Aristophanes does. The ironist, however, is obviously very casual even with the idea; he is completely free under it, for the absolute to him is nothing.

As we proceed now to the next element in the play, the characters, and our main concern, the character of Socrates, it is immediately apparent that Aristophanes has not identified him with the Sophists, not only by his having made Socrates recognizable by a variety of minor traits (this is the point
XIII 231 Rötscher[333] particularly emphasizes), but also and mainly by his describing Socrates' position as one of complete isolation. This certainly is entirely correct. Socrates does indeed have pupils in the play, just as he did in life, but they are not involved in any relationship with him or, more correctly, he is not involved in any relationship with them;* he does not become attached to them, but, analogously to his earlier described relationship with Alcibiades, he continually hovers freely above them, enigmatically attracting and repelling. The significance of his immersion in himself never becomes clear to them, since the subtleties that seek to betray something about it are totally irrelevant. Aristophanes has recapitulated everything pertaining to the various periods in Socrates' life, including also the Anaxagorean speculations on nature that had preoccupied Socrates for a time, according to the *Phaedo*,[335] but which he had subsequently abandoned. Since there is no trace of an idea in many scenes,** I shall bypass them, because they contain nothing but foolish subtleties or slapstick jugglery and the swaggering that goes with such practical jokes—in short, a lot of what one could designate as leg-pulling. The atheistic observations about nature, which so frequently produce a highly comic effect in contrast to Strepsiades' rather naïve popular superstitions,† will have a kind of

* This is why he also says in Plato's *Apology*[334] that he had never been anyone's teacher or accepted any pupils.

** It merits attention that it was very well planned on Aristophanes' part to have Socrates play a larger role at the beginning of the play than at the end, to have Strepsiades' education take place before the eyes of all while Pheidippides' education takes place offstage, thereby representing the old and modern points of view in equally comic personalities, each as ridiculous as the other.

† See ll. 368ff.,[336] where Socrates explains rain, that it is the clouds that rain,

significance later. Three things are of primary importance, however: first, the understanding of Socrates as a personality; second, the description of what becomes the first consideration in his teaching, the dialectical; and finally, the exposition of his position.

As for the first, it already contains proof that Aristophanes XIII has not identified Socrates with the Sophists, inasmuch as 232 Sophistry is the undisciplined and wild jumping about of egotistical thought; the Sophist is its panting priest. And just as the eternal idea in Sophistry disintegrates into an infinitude of thoughts, so this throng of thoughts is appropriately symbolized by a throng of Sophists.* In other words, it is not necessary to think of a Sophist as singular, whereas an ironist is always singular, because the Sophist falls under the category of species, genus, etc., whereas the ironist falls under the rubric of personality. The Sophist is always busily preoccupied, always reaching for something ahead of him, whereas the ironist at every moment leads this back into himself; but precisely this taking back, and thereby the reverse current it sets up, is the qualification of personality. The sophism is therefore a serving element in irony, and whether the ironist frees himself by means of the sophism or wrests something from others, he nevertheless takes both elements into his consciousness—that is, he enjoys.

But enjoyment is expressly a qualification of personality, even if the ironist's enjoyment is the most abstract of all, is the

---

and Strepsiades says (l. 373): καίτοι πρότερον τὸν Δί' ἀληθῶς ᾤμην διὰ κοσκίνου οὐρεῖν [Yet before, I had dreamed that the rain-water streamed from Zeus and his chamber-pot sieve].

* This is also why the solemn stillness by which every new world-historical point of view is characterized (all such things pass off so quietly that it seems as if they did not occur in the world at all but took place outside it) is followed by the shrill chorus of Sophists, a buzzing and humming of marvelous insects, which in endless movements and positions [*Mellemhverandre*][337] have a touch-and-go, in-and-out, up-and-down relation to themselves and to each other. As a rule, they come in enormous crowds, like the grasshoppers over Egypt, suggesting that world-thought is once again about to emancipate itself from the coercion of personality in order to dissipate itself in a terrain like that of the Rhine at its mouth.

most empty, the mere outline, the weakest intimation of the enjoyment that possesses the absolute content—that is, bliss. Thus while the Sophist runs around like a busy man of business, the ironist, proud and self-contained, goes about—enjoying. Aristophanes does in fact suggest this. When he has the chorus declare its preference for Socrates, he also has it distinguish Socrates from another special pet, Prodicus.[338] The chorus now makes the following distinction: it approves of Prodicus because of his wisdom and insight but approves of Socrates "because he swaggers down the street, looking
XIII 233 sideways, and bareleggedly puts up with so much hardship and casts a grand look at us."*

That Aristophanes makes Socrates a comic character is quite in order, but he nevertheless gives him the pliability that is characteristic of a personality, the self-containedness that therefore needs no circle of associates but is a monologue made visible. Surely no one believes that Aristophanes intended to portray an accidental actuality, such as Socrates' hulk of a body, his notoriously big feet (which Socrates himself considered an indulgent gift of nature because they were so wonderful to stand upon), his deep-set eyes (with which, as he himself notes, he can look around so superbly), the unprepossessing exterior[339] with which nature so ironically had supplied him and which Socrates himself viewed with so much irony; surely everyone believes that in these lines by the chorus Aristophanes wanted to suggest an idea. But an out-

* See ll. 360-63:

Χορός: οὐ γὰρ ἂν ἄλλῳ γ' ὑπακούσαιμεν τῶν νῦν μετεωροσοφιστῶν
πλὴν ἢ Προδίκῳ, τῷ μὲν σοφίας καὶ γνώμης οὕνεκα, σοὶ δὲ,
ὅτι βρενθύει τ' ἐν ταῖσιν ὁδοῖς καὶ τὠφθαλμὼ παραβάλλεις,
κἀνυπόδητος κακὰ πόλλ' ἀνέχει κἀφ' ἡμῖν σεμνοπροσωπεῖς
[Chorus: Since there is not a sage for whom we'd engage
our wonders more freely to do,
Except, it may be, for Prodicus; he
for his knowledge may claim them, but you,
For that sideways you throw your eyes as you go,
and are all affectation and fuss;
No shoes will you wear, but assume the grand air
on the strength of your dealings with us].

standing personality such as this is not a symbol even for a merely subjective speculation, in which, precisely because the empirical *I* vanishes and the ideal qualities of the pure *I* unfold, the individual to a certain extent vanishes. The ironist, on the other hand, is a prophecy about or an abbreviation of a complete personality.

In the next place, with respect to the Socratic dialectic as delineated in the play, it must be borne in mind, of course, that this can be a matter of discussion only insofar as it can be construed purely intellectually; whereas we have nothing at all to do with the altogether immoral conduct in which such a dialectic can become an active collaborator in the service of a corrupted will. Up to a point, Aristophanes himself must have been aware of this; if not, I really do not see how Aristophanes XIII 234 can be saved from the old accusation of having slandered Socrates. Even though Aristophanes with ever so much justification depicted Socrates as a representative of a principle that threatened early Greek culture with destruction, it nevertheless would always be an injustice to charge Socrates with corrupting the morals of the youth, with introducing a dissoluteness and superficiality that both the old and the new Greek culture must necessarily abominate. It would be an injustice not merely because Socrates had acquired a prescriptive title to being the most honest man in Greece, but mainly because without a doubt Socrates' position was so abstractly intellectual (something already sufficiently manifest in the well-known definition of sin as ignorance) that with regard to a view of him I think it would be more correct if one eliminated some of the bombast about his virtue and his noble heart but at the same time considered his life immune to all the charges of corrupting the morals. Let Rötscher[340] inflate as much as he wishes the earnestness with which Aristophanes laid hold of his task in *The Clouds*—Aristophanes is not exonerated thereby, unless one wishes to accentuate the comic element consisting in Aristophanes' having become so earnest about something that only a later perversity could make it as corrupt as it did become. Aristophanes does in fact seem to ascribe that kind of intellectual neutrality to Socrates by having honesty and dishonesty appear—when Pheidippides is supposed to be initiated into the Socratic teaching—as two forces confronting each other with Socrates standing outside both of them as the neutral possibility.[341]

The dialectic displayed here is manifestly an idle vagabond who on occasion thoroughly tracks down the stupidest things and spends time and energy on the most foolish hairsplitting (λόγων ἀκριβῶν σχινδαλάμους [the nice hairsplittings of subtle logic], l. 130). Indeed, it sometimes becomes so stagnant and lethargic that it takes more the form of an ingenious riddle-solving or a kind of hypothesizing cleverness that is generally the object of the insipid admiration of idle and empty heads, at times even becomes absorbed in such futilities with a kind of morbid earnestness (which is why the whole school is called μεριμνοφροντισταὶ [deep thinkers], l. 101). Then at other times this dialectic wants to seize upon something great and significant, but nevertheless the very instant this shows
XIII 235 itself it leaps back from it again.*

* See ll. 700-04. The chorus[342] is addressing Strepsiades:

φρόντιζε δὴ καὶ διάθρει, πάντα τρόπον τε σαυτὸν
στρόβει πυκνώσας.
ταχὺς δ', ὅταν εἰς ἄπορον πέσῃς,
ἐπ' ἄλλο πήδα
νόημα φρενός

[Now then survey in every way,
with airy judgement sharp and quick:
Wrapping thoughts around you thick:
And if so be in one you stick,
Never stop to toil and bother,
Lightly, lightly, lightly leap,
To another, to another].

If it is not seeing too much in these lines, they may be taken as a characterization of the desultory dialectic that allows the idea to become a solid body it cannot penetrate but from which it leaps away. Moreover, the tenacity Socrates commends proves to be such that it simply perpetuates the problem but does not solve it. See ll. 743-45:

ἔχ' ἀτρέμα· κἂν ἀπορῇς τι τῶν νοημάτων,
ἀφεὶς ἄπελθε· κᾆτα τὴν γνώμην πάλιν
κίνησον αὖθις αὐτὸ καὶ ζυγώθρισον

[Hush: if you meet with any difficulty
Leave it a moment: then return again
To the same thought: then lift and weigh it well].

Between these two extreme points lies the dialectic activity whose validity is actualized in dividing. That is, while the essentially philosophic dialectic, the speculative, unites, the negative dialectic, because it relinquishes the idea, is a broker who continually makes transactions in a lower sphere; that is, it separates.* Thus it presupposes only two qualifications in the pupil, the possession of which by Strepsiades is the object of XIII
Socrates' inquiry**—whether or not Strepsiades has a good 236
memory and a natural capacity for speaking.† Indeed, Strepsiades' answer to the first question—that he has a good memory in a double sense, for if someone owes him something he has an exceedingly good memory, but if he himself owes somebody something, then he is very forgetful[344]—actually contains a very pertinent metaphorical characterization of this kind of dialectic. But this dialectic has, of course, no content, and this is superbly indicated by Socrates' urging Strepsiades not to believe in the gods but only in the great empty space and the tongue[345]—a perfect designation of the boisterous twaddle that is apropos of nothing and reminds me of a line in the Grimms' *Irische Elfenmärchen*, where reference is made to people with an empty head and a tongue like the tongue in a church bell.[346]

Finally, regarding Socrates' position, Aristophanes has

* This is why Socrates asks Strepsiades, when he is to be instructed, what he would like to learn about those things of which until then he had learned nothing (ll. 637-38):

ᾄγε δὴ, τί βούλει πρῶτα νυνὶ μανθάνειν
ὧν οὐκ ἐδιδάχθης πώποτ' οὐδέν; εἰπέ μοι.
πότερα περὶ μέτρων ἢ περὶ ἐπῶν ἢ ῥυθμῶν

[Attend to me: what shall I teach you first
That you've not learnt before? Which will you have,
Measures or rhythms or the right use of words]?

If grammar instruction is denoted by the term ἔπος [epic poetry] and if Socrates acts like a Per Degn[343] with his linguistic hairsplitting, we must also remember that we are dealing with a hilarious comic parody and that this may well suggest a corresponding dialectical hairsplitting based upon language.

** See ll. 482 and 486.

† Consequently, the fruits of instruction correspond perfectly to this, for XIII
Socrates promises (l. 260): 236

"λέγειν γενήσει τρίμμα, κρόταλον, παιπάλη
[You'll be the flower of talkers, prattlers, gossips]."

understood its peculiar difficulty very correctly. He has let us perceive how very emphatically Socrates was able to say: δός μοι ποῦ στῶ [Give me a place to stand].[347] Consequently, much to Strepsiades' amazement, he has allotted Socrates space in the φροντ. [Thinkery] in a suspended basket (κρεμάθρα, l. 218). Whether he is in a basket suspended from the ceiling or staring omphalopsychically into himself and thereby in a way freeing himself from earthly gravity, in both cases he is hovering. But it is precisely this hovering that is so very significant; it is the attempted ascension that is accomplished only when the whole realm of the ideal opens up, when this staring into oneself allows the self to expand into the universal self, pure thought with its contents. The ironist, to be sure, is
XIII 237 lighter than the world, but on the other hand he still belongs to the world; like Mohammed's coffin, he is suspended between two magnets. Now if Socrates' position had been that of subjectivity, inwardness, it would have been inappropriate in terms of the comic to view him as Aristophanes does. Compared with the substantiality of early Greek culture, subjectivity certainly is in suspension, but it is infinitely in suspension, and in terms of the comic it would have been more appropriate to present Socrates as infinitely vanishing and to have accentuated the comic in Strepsiades' inability to catch a glimpse of him rather than to present him suspended in a basket, because the basket is in a way the basis for the empirical actuality that the ironist needs, whereas subjectivity in its infinity gravitates to itself—that is, it is infinitely in suspension.

Summarizing what has been said here about Aristophanes' *The Clouds*, I think that if one agrees with Rötscher's designation of Socrates' position as that of subjectivity,[348] Aristophanes' view of Socrates will be found to be more true in terms of the comic and consequently more just,* and likewise

* Hegel, after having shown how the Socratic dialectic destroys all the concrete qualifications of the good at the expense of the good itself as the empty, contentless universal, and with the aid thereof, also notes that it is Aristophanes who has understood Socrates' philosophy merely from its negative side (*Geschichte der Philosophie*, II, p. 85).[349] But, of course, if there had been a Platonic positivity in Socrates, then, however much freedom the Greeks al-

one will also see a way to remove some of the difficulties that otherwise would remain in this Aristophanic play if one defines this position more specifically as an ironic position—that is, allows the subjectivity to pour out in its profusion, but prior to this lets it egotistically terminate in irony.

Xenophon, Plato, Aristophanes

With regard to Aristophanes' relation to Xenophon and Plato, there are elements of the views of both in Aristophanes. Plato tried to fill up the cryptic nothing that actually constitutes the point in Socrates' life by giving him the idea; Xenophon tried to do it with the prolixities of the useful. Aristophanes has not XIII 238
viewed this nothing as the ironic freedom in which Socrates indulged but has viewed it in such a way that he always merely shows its implicit emptiness. Therefore, instead of the eternal fullness of the idea, Socrates attains the most ascetic scantiness in a self-immersion that never brings up anything from the depths, an immersion that, even if it goes down into the underworld of the soul (psychologically, one could dwell on the words in Aristophanes referring to the students of natural science in the new school, l. 192: οὗτοι δ' ἐρεβοδιφῶσιν ὑπὸ τὸν Τάρταρον [They're diving deep into the deepest secrets]), always comes back—empty-handed. Instead of the useful,*

---

lowed their comedy writers, Aristophanes undeniably has overstepped the boundary, the boundary the comic itself possesses, the requirement that it must be true to the comic point of view.

* Whereas in Xenophon the useful vacillates between being commensurate with the good and the beautiful and thus is more of an intellectual than an ethical concept, in Aristophanes the useful is perceived only ethically in its contrast to the good and in its unity with the bad. Xenophon does not have Socrates accept payment for his teaching[350] and thereby suggests that his instruction was incommensurate with any such evaluation, suggests the dubious relation of Socrates' instruction to any external appraisal (since in one sense it was too good and in another too poor for that). Aristophanes not only lets him accept payment but has him veritably plunder his pupils.[351] If one is unwilling to see in this latter trait one of the ethical charges that become difficult to justify, or a flippant hilarity that needs excusing, then one may see in it a symbol of the ironist's relation to the individual, since in this relationship he subtracts more than he gives and intellectually does what Socrates did to

which is, after all, one kind of view, there emerges here the advantageous, which involves only the particular in its relation to the individual watching out solely for his own interest and—the meddlesome (see ll. 177-79).[353] Moreover, the observations on nature that Aristophanes puts in Socrates' mouth are occasionally reminiscent of the Xenophontian studies in natural history if one simply overlooks the charge of irreligiousness that appears in Aristophanes.*

XIII 239 Consequently, with respect to Plato Aristophanes has subtracted, and with respect to Xenophon has added, but since in the latter case it is a matter only of negative quantities, this adding is in one sense also a subtracting. If we now allow the lines (which in this discussion are always drawn with a sharp eye on the reciprocal relation of these three authors) to emerge more clearly and set the limits of the unknown quantity, the position that simultaneously fits and fills the intervening space, it will look something like this: its relation to the idea is negative—that is, the idea is the boundary of the dialectic. Continually in the process of leading the phenomenon up to the idea (the dialectical activity), the individual is thrust back or flees back into actuality; but actuality itself has only the validity of continually being the occasion for wanting to go beyond actuality—yet without its taking place; whereas the individual takes the *molimina* [efforts] of this subjectivity back into himself, incloses them within himself in a personal satisfaction; but this position is precisely that of irony.

Strepsiades in a physical sense by having him come naked into the φροντ. and likewise run naked out of it.[352]

* Some readers may upbraid me for having become guilty of an anachronism by classifying these three interpretations more according to their relation to the idea (the purely historical—the ideal—the comic) than according to time. I think, however, that I am correct in suspending the chronological consideration. But this does not necessarily mean that I want to deprive the Aristophanic view of the weight it does have because it is closest to Socrates in time. The historical importance it derives from that is increased even more by the report that Plato sent *The Clouds* to Dionysius the Elder and also gave him to understand that he could become acquainted with the Athenian state from it.[354]

The treatise has now reached a point of rest; one mode of investigation is behind us. If I were to state in a few words its nature, its significance as a factor in the whole context, I would say that it is to make possible a view of Socrates. Xenophon, Plato, and Aristophanes have viewed Socrates not only in the ordinary sense in which this term is taken with reference to an intellectual phenomenon, but in a far more special sense they have not reproduced him but interpreted XIII 240
him.*

Consequently, we must use them rather cautiously, must take care to stop them the instant they carry us away. But to that end it becomes necessary, lest one become guilty oneself of arbitrariness, to have the help of someone, which is why I myself have continually tried to be a third party against each one.[355] Then I have allowed the whole development to reach a point of final confrontation. I have thereby procured a possibility of being able to explain the discrepancy among these three views by a view of Socrates corresponding to it. But with all this I still have come no further than the possibility, for even though the explanation propounded is able to reconcile the opposing powers, it by no means follows that this explanation is therefore entirely correct. If, however, it could not reconcile them, then it could not possibly be correct. Now, however, it is possible.

During this whole investigation, I have continually had something *in mente* [in mind], namely, the final view, without thereby laying myself open to the charge of a kind of intellectual Jesuitism or of having hidden, sought, and then found what I myself had found long ago. The final view has hovered over each exploration simply as a possibility. Every conclusion has been the unity of a reciprocity: it has felt itself drawn to what it was supposed to explain and what it is supposed to explain is drawn to it. In a certain sense it has come into exis-

* Wherever it is a matter of reconstructing a phenomenon by means of what could be a view in the stricter sense of the word, there is a double task: one must indeed explain the phenomenon and in so doing explain the misunderstanding, and through the misunderstanding one must attain the phenomenon and through the phenomenon break the spell of the misunderstanding.

tence by means of this reflecting, although in another sense it existed prior to it. But this can scarcely be otherwise, since the whole is prior to its parts.[356] If it has not come into existence, then at least it is born again. I hope, however, that the fair and reasonable reader will recognize this as circumspection on my part, even though the form of the whole treatise thereby departs somewhat from the now widespread and in so many ways meritorious scholarly method. If I had posed the final view first of all and in each particular portion had assigned each of these three considerations its place, then I would easily have lost the element of contemplation, which is always important but here doubly so, because by no other way, not by immediate observation, can I gain the phenomenon.

XIII From this point on, the investigation will take another
241 form. I shall deal with some phenomena that as historical facts do not need to be provided through a mistaken view but merely need to be kept in their inviolate innocence and thereupon explained. Here again the final view is a necessary *prius* [antecedent], although in another sense it results from this. This section could be called The Actualization of the View, because it actualizes itself through all these historical data.

II XIII 242

The Actualization of the View

THE DAIMON OF SOCRATES

It will be obvious at the outset that I have now entered a different sphere. Here the issue is not Plato's or Xenophon's view of Socrates, provided that one is not so unreasonable as to think it was all a fiction on the part of Plato and Xenophon. It must now be taken as a fact that Socrates has assumed such a daimon, and from certain comments to be found on the subject* we must try to get an idea about it and harmonize it with our whole view of Socrates. This Socratic daimon has always been a *crux philologorum* [a cross for the philologists], a difficulty that nevertheless has had an effect more tempting than forbidding and, because of its mysterious magic, even fascinating. Thus from time immemorial there has been a strong tendency to talk about it (since "what, indeed, would we rather listen to than such fairy tales?"[357]), but the matter usually ends there. The curiosity that is titillated by mystery is satisfied by getting a name for it; profundity is gratified by having someone say with solemn countenance: What is there to say? If readers wish to make the acquaintance of a perfect masterpiece in this regard, one so rounded off that it practi- XIII 243
cally rolls right out of the subject, may I refer them to an article found in Funcke,**[358] an article that ends with just as much thoroughness as it begins, and the middle of which is no less thorough than its beginning and its end. Likewise, a Dane of kindred spirit, Magister Block, in his introduction to his translation of Xenophon's *Memorabilia* could not resist the temptation to explain the noteworthy phenomenon; he is of

* Consequently, these comments are rather to be found in the historical writings in the stricter sense of the word.

** *Neues Real-Schullexikon* von Funcke, II, pp. 643ff.

the opinion that Socrates himself believed that he had such a daimon, and "that this feeling was a presentiment or a kind of fanaticism that to some extent had its roots in his vivid imagination and his delicate nervous system."*[359]

But first a presentation of the facts. Xenophon as well as Plato discusses this peculiarity. As Ast correctly observes (p. 483[361]), the word τὸ δαιμόνιον [the daimonion] is neither simply adjectival in such a way that one must complete it by understanding ἔργον, σημεῖον [deed, sign] or something similar; nor is it substantive in the sense that it designates a special or unique being. Therefore, we see that this word expresses something entirely abstract, as is also evidenced by the double way in which it is used and the double connection in which it appears. Sometimes it reads: τὸ δαιμόνιόν μοι σημαίνει [the daimonion manifests itself to me] and elsewhere: δαιμόνιόν τι or τὸ δαιμόνιον γίγνεται [something daimonian . . . the daimonion comes]. The first thing to note, then, is that this word denotes something abstract, something divine, something that precisely in its abstraction is above definition, is unutterable and indescribable, since it allows no vocalization.[362]

If we next inquire about the way it functions, we learn that it is a voice that can be heard, yet no one ventures to insist on
XIII this, as if it made itself known in words, since it functions
244 altogether instinctively. As for its functioning, Plato's and Xenophon's reports vary. According to Plato, it warns, deters, commands abstention (see *Phaedrus*, 242 b–c; *Apology*, 31 d; *Alcibiades*, 103 a, 124 c; *Theages*, 128 d). According to Xenophon, it orders, prompts as well as commands doing something (see *Memorabilia*, I, 1, 4; IV, 8, 1; *Apology*, 12). On this point, Ast believes that we ought to rely on Xenophon more than on Plato and proceeds to disconcert anyone who refuses to be satisfied with this judgment by citing the following pas-

* The modern age, too, has been very preoccupied with this daimon, and I see in a book by Heinsius that a psychiatrist [*Galelæge*] in Paris by the name of Lelut has been so opinionated as to claim: "*que Socrate etait affecté de la folie, qu'en language technique on appelle hallucination*" [Socrates was afflicted with the madness that in technical language is called hallucination].[360] The book is titled *Du demon de Socrate. Par* F. Lelut. Paris: 1836.

sage (from his point of view absolutely correct and adequately convincing): "An sich schon ist es unglaublich, dasz das Daemonion als göttliche Andeutung oder Ahndung blosz abgemahnt habe; denn sollte Socrates nur ein Vorgefühl des Unrechten, Unglücklichen u. s. w. gehabt haben, nicht auch eine lebendige Ahndung des Glücklichen, die ihn nicht blosz zum Handeln antrieb, sondern auch mit begeisterter Hoffnung erfüllte [Properly considered, it is unbelievable that the daimonion as a divine intimation or presentiment merely warned; for should Socrates have had only a presentiment of injustice, misfortune, etc. and not also a lively presentiment of prosperous conditions, one that not only incited him to action but also filled him with enthusiastic hope]?" But that is Ast's problem.

What I, on the other hand, would like to point out to the reader is significant for the whole conception of Socrates: namely, that this daimonian is represented only as warning, not as commanding—that is, as negative and not as positive. If there is a choice between Xenophon and Plato, I think that one must rather side with Plato, with whom the invariable predicate for the activity of this daimonian is that it only warns,* and regard Xenophon's amendment as lack of thought on the part of Xenophon, who, without an intimation of the significance that could be hidden in this, in his wisdom thought that if the daimonian warned, then it surely must prompt as well. The relation of the daimonian thereby falls much more under the rubric of the trivial, and naturally the superficial "partly this, partly that, now here, now there" must have been more appealing to Xenophon. His flabbiness can be explained much more easily than Plato's tension, since XIII 245
the former just takes merely good-natured simplemindedness, but the latter takes a high degree of boldness and arbitrariness. Moreover, in the passage in the *Apology*[365] where Socrates, in order to defend himself against Meletus's accusation, refers to

* Both Plutarch (*Plutarchi Chaeronensis opuscula*,[363] ed. H. Stephanus, II, pp. 241, 243) and Cicero (*De divinatione*,[364] I, 54) have preserved several stories about the activity of this daimonian, but in all of them it manifests itself only as warning.

this daimonian, it is clear that he has become aware of how significant it is that the daimonian merely warned. On this basis, he explains the remarkable circumstance that he, who privately was always ready to give advice (ἰδίᾳ περιϊὼν καὶ πολυπραγμονῶν [going around and privately busying myself]), was never involved in matters of the state. But this is, as it were, the visible disclosure of the negative relation of the daimonian to Socrates, because in turn this had the express effect of making him relate negatively to actuality or, in the Greek sense, to the state. If the daimonian had been prompting as well, then precisely thereby he would have been qualified to be involved with actuality.* This is essentially linked to the question: Was Socrates, as his accusers claimed, in conflict with the state religion by the assumption of this daimonian? Obviously he was. For one thing, it was an entirely polemic relation to the Greek state religion to substitute something completely abstract** for the concrete individuality of the gods. For another, it was a polemical relation to the state reli-
XIII 246 gion to substitute a silence in which a warning voice was audible only on occasion, a voice that (and this is about the most fundamental polemic) never had a thing to do with the substantial interests of political life, never said a word about them, but dealt only with Socrates' and at most his friends' completely private and particular affairs—to substitute this for the Greek life permeated, even in the most insignificant man-

* It must be kept in mind that this passage is found in the *Apology*, which, on the whole, may be assumed to be historically reliable. This must be kept in mind so that one may be convinced that I am not dealing here with a Platonic view but work on a factual basis.

** Even if we discount the irony in which he invests his proof and the indirect polemic concealed therein, Socrates' attempt to defend himself by showing the necessity of assuming daimonions if one assumes something daimonian[366] is practically worthless. For even if one generally and consequently also *in casu* [in this case] has to admit the correctness of the view that theism must be deduced syllogistically from pantheism, it by no means follows that Socrates thereby cleared himself before the state, because the state had not acquired its gods by way of syllogism, and Socrates was well able to relate himself indifferently—that is, irreligiously—to the result he was at all times able to produce on demand.

ifestations, by a god-consciousness, to substitute a silence for this divine eloquence echoed in everything.

If we turn now from the previously mentioned pharisaical scholars, who strain at a gnat and swallow a camel,[367] to the most recent scholarly studies along this line, an essential difference is immediately apparent in that the latter have gone to the center of the problem and therefore seek not so much to explain as to comprehend. As long as the difficulty of the daimonian in Socrates is dealt with separately, as long as it is considered from the outside, it naturally remains inexplicable, even though precisely thereby it is necessary for and indispensable to a host of conjecture makers; but if one considers it from the inside, then that which appears as an insurmountable barrier proves to be a necessary boundary that stops the rapid flight of the eye and thereby of thought, forces it back from the periphery to the center, and thereby to comprehend.

One of Hegel's* statements expresses in a general sense and yet very pregnantly how to understand the daimonian: "Socrates, indem er es der Einsicht, der Ueberzeugung anheimgestellt hat, den Menschen zum Handeln zu bestimmen, hat das Subject als entscheidend gegen Vaterland und Sitte gesetzt, und sich somit zum Orakel im griechischen Sinne gemacht. Er sagte, dasz er ein δαιμόνιον in sich habe, das ihm rathe, was er thun solle, und ihm offenbare, was seinen Freunden nützlich sei [Socrates, in assigning to insight, to conviction, the determination of men's actions, posited the Individual as capable of a final moral decision, in contraposition to Country and to Customary Morality, and thus made himself an Oracle, in the Greek sense. He said that he had a daimon(ion) within him that counseled him what to do, and revealed to him what was advantageous to his friends]."[368]

Rötscher (p. 254)[369] also, according to Hegel, interprets it quite correctly: "Mit diesem Princip der freien Entscheidung des Geistes aus sich selber, und dem groszen Bewusztsein, dasz Alles vor das Forum des Denkens gezogen werden müsse, um dort seine Bestätigung zu empfangen, hängt auch

* *Vorlesungen über die Philosophie der Geschichte*, 2 ed., p. 328.

die im Alterthum schon vielfach besprochene Erscheinung des Genius des Socrates zusammen. In diesem Dämon ist uns der eben ausgesprochene Gedanke der inneren Entscheidung vor die Vorstellung gebracht [Related to this principle of the free decision of mind by itself, and the immense awareness that everything must be drawn before the forum of thought and there receive its confirmation, is the phenomenon of Socrates' genius—so frequently discussed even in antiquity. In this daimon the notion of inward decision, mentioned above, is set before us through representation]."

In the *Philosophy of Right*[370] also, Hegel discusses this dai-
XIII 247 mon of Socrates. See para. 279: "Im Dämon des Socrates können wir den Anfang sehen, dasz der sich vorher nur jenseits seiner selbst versetzende Wille sich in sich verlegte und sich innerhalb seiner erkannte,—der Anfang der sich wissenden und damit wahrhaften Freiheit [In the 'divine sign' of Socrates we see the will which formerly had simply transferred itself beyond itself now beginning to apply itself to itself and so to recognize its own inward nature. This is the beginning of a self-knowing and so of genuine freedom]." The place, however, where Hegel discusses this in most detail is, of course, in his *Geschichte der Philosophie* (II, pp. 94ff., 103ff.). Although Hegel becomes involved in making analogies,*[371] thereby solving the problems associated with this phenomenon, yet

* "Bei Sterbenden, im Zustande der Krankheit, der Katalepsie kann es kommen, dasz der Mensch Zusammenhänge kennt, Zukünftiges oder Gleichzeitiges weisz, was nach dem verständigen Zusammenhang für ihn durchaus verschlossen ist. . . . . . Das Nähere in Ansehung des Dämonion des Socrates ist mithin eine an den Somnambulismus, an diese Gedoppelheit des Bewusztseins hingehende Form; und bei Socrates scheint sich auch ausdrücklich etwas von der Art, was magnetischer Zustand ist, gefunden zu haben, da er öfter (im Lager) in Starrsucht, Katalepsie, Verzückung verfallen sein soll [It may happen that at death, in illness and catalepsy, men know of circumstances future or present, which, in the understood relations of things, are altogether unknown. . . . . . The further investigation of this Genius consequently presents to us a form which passes into somnambulism, into this double of consciousness; and in Socrates there clearly appears to be something of the kind, or something which is magnetic, for, as we already mentioned, he is said to have often fallen into fits of staring, trances, and catalepsy]."[372]

the objective of his entire investigation and its conclusion were that it be comprehended.

Socrates' position, then, is that of subjectivity, of inwardness, which reflects upon itself and in its relation to itself detaches and volatilizes the established [*Bestaaende*] in the flood of thought that surges over it and carries it away while it itself recedes again into thought. Replacing the grace to be ashamed (αἰδως), which powerfully but mysteriously kept the individual tied to the lead string of the state, there now came the decisiveness and self-assurance of subjectivity. Hegel says on page 96: "Der Standpunkt des griechischen Geistes ist nach der moralischen Seite als unbefangene Sittlichkeit bestimmt. Der Mensch hatte ein solches Verhältnisz noch nicht, sich so in sich zu reflektiren, aus sich [sich] zu bestimmen [The standpoint of the Greek mind was determined in its moral aspect as natural morality. Man did not yet have the condition of reflecting into himself, of determining by himself]."[373] In early Greek culture, the laws had for the individual the venerableness of tradition, as the laws sanctioned by the gods. Corresponding to this tradition were time-honored customs. But while the laws defined the universal, early Greek culture also demanded a decision in particular instances, both in political and in private matters. The oracle served this purpose (p. 97): "Diesz Moment ist wesentlich, dasz das Volk so nicht das Beschlieszende ist, das Subject diesz noch nicht auf sich nahm, sondern sich von einem Andern, Aeuszeren bestimmen liesz; wie denn XIII
Orakel überall nothwendig sind, wo der Mensch sein Inneres 248
noch nicht so unabhängig, so frei weisz, dasz er die Entschlieszung nur aus sich selbst nimmt,—und diesz ist der Mangel der subjectiven Freiheit [In essence this element means that the people lacks the power of decision, that the subject is not yet ready to assume this power but can be determined by an other, by something external; and oracles are necessary wherever man does not yet know himself inwardly as being sufficiently free and independent to make a decision solely on his own—and this is a lack of subjective freedom]."[374]

Instead of the oracle, Socrates now has his daimon. The daimonian in this case now lies in the transition from the oracle's external relation to the individual to the complete inwardness of freedom and, as still being in this transition, is a subject for representation. Page 95: "Das Innere des Subjects weisz, entscheidet aus sich; diesz Innere hat bei Socrates noch eine eigenthümliche Form gehabt. Der Genius ist noch das Bewusztlose, Aeuszerliche, das entscheidet; und doch ist es ein Subjectives. Der Genius ist nicht Socrates selbst, nicht seine Meinung, Ueberzeugung, sondern ein Bewusztloses; Socrates ist getrieben. Das Orakel ist zugleich nichts Aeuszerliches, sondern sein Orakel. Es hat die Gestalt gehabt von einem Wissen, das zugleich mit einer Bewusztlosigkeit verbunden ist." P. 96: "Diesz ist nun der Genius des Socrates; es ist nothwendig, dasz dieser Genius an Socrates erschienen ist." P. 99: "Das Dämonion steht demnach in der Mitte zwischen dem Aeuszerlichen der Orakel und dem rein Innerlichen des Geistes; es ist etwas Innerliches, aber so, dasz es als ein eigener Genius, als vom menschlichen Willen unterschieden vorgestellt wird,—nicht als seine Klugheit, Willkür [The inwardness of the subject knows and decides by itself, but in Socrates this inwardness had a unique form. The daimon is still the unconscious, the external, that decides; yet it is also something subjective. The daimon is not Socrates himself, nor his opinion, nor his conviction, but it is something unconscious; Socrates is impelled. Besides, this oracle is nothing external but is his own oracle. It had a form of knowledge that was concomitant with a state of unconsciousness. P. 96: So this is the daimon of Socrates, and it is necessary that this daimon appear in Socrates. P. 99: Accordingly, the daimonian stands midway between the externality of oracles and the pure inwardness of mind; it is something inward and yet presented as a separate daimon, as distinct from human will, and not as his own prudence and choice]."[375]

But since this daimon intervened only in very particular situations in Socrates' career, Hegel also shows that its disclosures are extremely insignificant in comparison with the disclosures of his spirit and mind.* Cf. p. 106: "Diesz Dämonion

* Cf. p. 98: "Wenn Einer das Zukünftige voraus weisz im Somnambulismus oder im Sterben, so sieht man diesz für eine höhere Einsicht an; näher

des Socrates hat übrigens auch nicht das Wahrhafte, Anundfürsichseiende betroffen, sondern nur Particularitäten; und diese dämonischen Offenbarungen sind so weit geringfügiger, als die seines Geistes, seines Denkens [Besides, this daimon of Socrates did not pertain to anything true, to being-in-and-for-itself, but only to particularities; and these daimonian disclosures are far inferior to those of his mind, his thought]."[377]

This concludes my exposition of Hegel's presentation, and, XIII 249
here as always when one has Hegel along (Caesar and his good fortune[378]), I have thereby acquired a footing from which I can safely start out on an excursion to see whether there might be some particular worthy of note to which I can safely return whether or not I have found anything. We have already seen that in many ways Socrates' position presumably was that of subjectivity, yet such that the subjectivity did not disclose itself in its full opulence, such that the idea became the boundary from which Socrates turned back into himself in ironic satisfaction. As we have seen, the daimonian is a qualification of subjectivity also in its relation to the Greek mentality. But subjectivity is not consummated in it; it still has something external (Hegel mentions that this daimonian must not be called conscience[379]).

If, in the next place, we remember that this daimonian was

---

betrachtet sind es aber nur Interessen der Individuen, Particularitäten. Will Einer heirathen, oder ein Haus bauen u.s.f.: so ist der Erfolg nur für dieses Individuum wichtig; dieser Inhalt ist nur particular. Das wahrhaft Göttliche, Allgemeine ist die Institution des Ackerbaues selbst, der Staat, die Ehe, gesetzliche Einrichtungen; gegen diesz ist das etwas Geringes, dasz ich weisz, dasz, wenn ich zu Schiffe gehe, ich umkommen werde oder nicht. Es ist eine Verkehrung, die auch in unserer Vorstellung leicht vorkommt; das zu wissen, was recht, was sittlich ist, ist viel etwas Höheres als solche Particularitäten zu wissen [Foreseeing the future in somnambulism or at death is regarded as a higher kind of insight; but upon closer examination this merely amounts to the interests of individuals, mere particularities. If someone wishes to marry or build a house etc., the outcome is important only for this individual, the content merely particular. The truly divine and universal is the institution of agriculture itself, the state, marriage, legal institutions. Compared with these, it is a trivial matter to know whether or not I shall perish by going to sea. This is an aberration that may easily occur to us in our figures of thought. Knowing what is right and ethical is much higher than knowing such particularities]."[376]

concerned only with particular situations and merely spoke warningly, we perceive here, too, that subjectivity is halted in its outpouring, that it closes itself off in a particular personality. The daimonian was sufficient for Socrates, and with it he could manage; but this is a qualification of personality, but of course only the egotistical satisfaction of one particular personality. Here again Socrates proves to be one who is ready to leap into something but never in the relevant moment does leap into this next thing but leaps aside and back into himself.

If we now add to this the polemic consciousness into which Socrates absorbed his whole relation to his contemporaries, the infinite albeit negative freedom in which he lightly and freely breathed, under the vast horizon intimated by the idea as boundary, the security provided for him by the daimonian against being perplexed by all the happenings in life, then Socrates' position once again manifests itself as irony.

As a rule, irony is understood ideally, is assigned its place as a vanishing element in the system, and is therefore treated very briefly. For this reason it is not easy to comprehend how a whole life can be taken up with it, since, after all, the content of this life must be regarded as nothing. But we forget that a position is never as ideal in life as it is in the system; we forget that irony, just as any other position in life, has its spiritual trials, its battles, its retreats, its victories. Thus doubt is also a
XIII 250 vanishing element in the system, but in actuality, where doubt is carried out in continual conflict with everything that rises up and wants to hold out against it (καθαιρῶν πᾶν ὕψωμα ἐπαιρόμενον . . . . . καὶ αἰχμαλωτίζων πᾶν νόημα εἰς τὴν ὑπακοὴν) [destroying every proud obstacle . . . . . and taking every thought captive in obedience][380]), doubt has much content in another sense. This is the purely personal life with which science and scholarship admittedly are not involved, even though a somewhat more intimate acquaintance with it would free them from the tautological *idem per idem* [the same with the same] from which such views often suffer. Whatever the case may be, grant that science and scholarship are right in ignoring such things; nevertheless, one who wants to understand the individual life cannot do so. And since Hegel himself

says somewhere that with Socrates it is not so much a matter of speculation as of individual life,[381] I dare to take this as sanction for my procedural method in my whole venture, however imperfect it may turn out because of my own deficiencies.

THE CONDEMNATION OF SOCRATES

Everyone will promptly perceive that here we are dealing with something factual, and therefore the issue cannot be a view as with Xenophon, Plato, and Aristophanes, for whom the actuality of Socrates was the occasion for and a factor in a presentation that sought to round off and to transfigure his person ideally—something that the solemnity of the state could not possibly enter into, and therefore its conception [of Socrates] is *sine ira atque studio* [without anger and partiality].[382] To a certain extent, this is indeed based upon the accusers' view, but however savagely they resented him, they still had to try as far as possible to adhere to the truth. Moreover, the accusation is only one element in the state's view of Socrates; it is the external occasion for the state to become conscious* in a special sense of this particular individual's relation to itself.
Whether the Athenian state committed a glaring injustice in XIII 251
condemning Socrates, whether we are right in voluntarily joining the scholarly professional mourners and the crowd of shallow but lachrymose humanitarians whose blubbering and sighing because such a good man, such an honest human

* Socrates, too, became very conscious of this, and in the *Apology* he
presses upon the judges' consciousness the question of his activity as brought XIII 251
up by the accusation. See 20 c: ὑπολάβοι ἂν οὖν τις ἴσως: 'Αλλ', ὦ Σώκρατες, τὸ σὸν τί ἐστι πρᾶγμα; πόθεν αἱ διαβολαί σοι αὗται γεγόνασιν; οὐ γὰρ δήπου σοῦ γε οὐδὲν τῶν ἄλλων περιττότερον πραγματευομένου, ἔπειτα τοσαύτη φήμη τε καὶ λόγος γέγονεν, εἰ μή τι ἔπραττες ἀλλοῖον ἢ οἱ πολλοί. λέγε οὖν ἡμῖν, τί ἐστιν, ἵνα μὴ καὶ ἡμεῖς περὶ σοῦ αὐτοσχεδιάζωμεν [Here perhaps one of you might interrupt me and say, But what is it that you do, Socrates? How is it that you have been misrepresented like this? Surely all this talk and gossip about you would never have arisen if you had confined yourself to ordinary activities, but only if your behavior was abnormal. Tell us the explanation, if you do not want us to invent it for ourselves].[383]

being, paragon, and cosmopolitan all rolled into one, became a victim of the meanest envy, whose blubbering and sighing, I say, still echo through the centuries; or whether the Athenian state was completely justified in condemning Socrates; or whether we with a clear conscience dare indulge in joy over the bold and vigorous brushstrokes of the modern scholarship[384] that sketches Socrates as a tragic hero who was simultaneously right and wrong and the Grecian state as an articulated order of things—all this we shall not discuss further here.

The accusation against Socrates is a historical document.* It is in two parts, each of which will be examined closely.

XIII 252

1. *Socrates Does Not Accept the Gods Accepted by the State, and He Introduces New Deities.*

This accusation, as we see, has two points: he does *not* accept the gods of the state and introduces new ones. The latter point has already been considered in connection with Socrates' daimon. Mention was also made there of the questionable value of the dialectical movement with which he, in his defense before the court, intends to derive the objective, under the rubric of personality, out of the abstract category of inwardness (the daimonian). But the main point, which I trust became clear, in that discussion was that the daimonian indicated Socrates' completely negative relation to the established order with respect to religion—not primarily because he introduced something new, for in that case his negative relation would appear more and more as a shadow following his positivity, but rather because he rejected the established order, inclosed him-

* According to Diogenes Laertius, Favorinus, Plutarch's contemporary and friend, had read the indictment in the Metroön. The Greek text reads as follows: Τάδε ἐγράψατο καὶ ἀντωμόσατο Μέλιτος Μελίτου Πιτθεὺς Σωκράτει Σωφρονίσκου 'Αλωπεκῆθεν· ἀδικεῖ Σωκράτης, οὓς μὲν ἡ πόλις νομὶζει θεοὺς οὐ νομίζων, ἕτερα δέ καινὰ δαιμόνια εἰσηγούμενος, ἀδικεῖ δὲ καὶ τοὺς νέους διαφθείρων· τίμημα θάνατος [This indictment and affidavit is sworn by Meletus, the son of Meletus of Pitthos, against Socrates, the son of Sophroniscus of Alopece: Socrates is guilty of refusing to recognize the gods recognized by the state, and of introducing other new divinities. He is also guilty of corrupting the youth. The penalty demanded is death].[385]

self within himself, egotistically confined himself within himself.

With regard to the first point, we must not see this rejection as a result of a cold, prudent, prosaic view of nature, which was not unfamiliar to the Athenians and which also at this time had provided the occasion for exiling some individuals because of suspected atheism.[386] Socrates had nothing to do with such things, and even though he had been influenced earlier by Anaxagoras, he soon freed himself from this influence, as Plato[387] in fact informs us several times, inasmuch as he gave up the study of nature for the study of man. To say, therefore, that Socrates did not accept the gods accepted by the state does not mean that he was an atheist. On the contrary, Socrates' nonacceptance of the national gods was essential to his whole position, which he himself theoretically characterized as ignorance.* But ignorance is a true philosophical XIII 253 position and at the same time is also completely negative. In other words, Socrates' ignorance was by no means an empirical ignorance; on the contrary, he was a very well informed person, was well read in the poets and philosophers, had much experience in life, and consequently was not ignorant in the empirical sense. In the philosophic sense, however, he was ignorant. He was ignorant of the ground of all being, the eternal, the divine—that is, he knew that it was, but he did not know what it was. He was conscious of it, and yet he was not conscious of it, inasmuch as the only thing he could say about it was that he did not know anything about it. But this says in other words the same thing that we previously designated as follows: Socrates had the idea as boundary. Thus he must have found it very easy to refute the accusers' allegation that he did not accept the gods the state accepted. His response, Socratically appropriate, to this had to be: How can I be accused of

* Here the difficulty of the accusers' position is readily perceived, because every time they made a positive complaint it was easy for Socrates to shatter it by means of this ignorance, and his accusers really ought to have charged him precisely with his ignorance, since particularly in the Greek state and to a certain extent in every state there is indeed an ignorance that must be regarded as a crime.

this? Since I know nothing at all, I also, of course, do not know whether I accept the gods the state accepts. Here it becomes apparent how this relates to the question whether a positive knowledge has established itself behind this ignorance.

In one of his treatises,* Schleiermacher calls attention to the fact that when Socrates went about in the service of the oracle in order to show people that they knew nothing, he could not possibly have known only that he knew nothing, because behind that he must indeed have known what knowledge is. He then goes on to show how Socrates is actually the founding father of dialectic. But this again is a positivity that on closer inspection is a negativity. To recall an earlier comment, Socrates arrived at the idea of dialectic but did not have the dialectic of the idea. And this, even in Plato's opinion, is a negative position. Therefore, in the dichotomy in the *Republic*,[388] where the dialectical appears, the good as the corresponding positive also appears; likewise in the dichotomy where love functions as the negative, the beautiful corresponds to it as the
XIII 254 positive.[389] Now, it is certainly true that in this continually implied negativity, which is perpetually postulated and at the same time revoked, there is a rich and profound positivity the moment it has a chance to come to itself, but Socrates continually kept it merely in this possibility that never became actuality.

A person will indeed be persuaded of the truth of this statement if he carefully reads through Plato's *Apology*, which in its description of Socrates' ignorance is so pregnant that all one has to do is be quiet and listen while it speaks. He compares his own wisdom with that of Evenus of Paros, who charged five minae for his teaching. He considers him lucky because of the positivity he must have had since he was paid so much and answers the question about his own wisdom (20 d): ποίαν δὴ σοφίαν ταύτην; ἥπερ ἐστὶν ἴσως ἀνθρωπίνη σοφία. τῷ ὄντι γὰρ κινδυνεύω ταύτην εἶναι σοφός [What kind of wis-

* *"Ueber den Werth des Socrates als Philosophen,"* in *Abhandlungen der Königlichen Academie der Wissenschaften* (Berlin: 1814–15), pp. 51-68.

dom do I mean? Human wisdom, I suppose. It seems that I really am wise in this limited sense].[390] He believes, however, that the others must have a higher wisdom: οὗτοι δὲ τάχ' ἄν, οὓς ἄρτι ἔλεγον, μείζω τινὰ ἢ κατ' ἄνθρωπον σοφίαν σοφοὶ εἶεν [Presumably the geniuses whom I mentioned just now are wise in a wisdom that is more than human].[391] Here the predicate "human,"* which is attributed to wisdom in contrast to a wisdom that is more than human, is extremely significant. To be specific, when subjectivity by means of its negative power has broken the spell in which human life lay in the form of substantiality, when it has emancipated man from his relation to God just as it freed him from his relation to the state, then the first form in which this manifests itself is ignorance. XIII 255
The gods take flight, taking the fullness with them, and man remains as the form, as that which is to receive the fullness into itself, but in the sphere of knowledge a situation such as this is correctly interpreted as ignorance. This ignorance is in turn quite consistently called human wisdom, because here man has come into his own right, but this right is precisely the right not to be merely man as such. In comparison, the wisdom of the other teachers had much more content, although in another sense, of course, much less, and thus Socrates' comments on their superabundance are not without a certain irony.

This view is confirmed for Socrates by the pronouncement

* This may be compared with Xenophon's *Apology*, para. 15, where the discussion is about the pronouncement of the same Delphic oracle to Chaerephon. It reads: Ὡς δ'αὖ ταῦτ' ἀκούσαντες οἱ δικασταὶ ἔτι μᾶλλον ἐθορύβουν εἰκότως, αὖθις εἰπεῖν τὸν Σωκράτην· ἀλλὰ μείζω μὲν, ὦ ἄνδρες, εἶπεν ὁ θεὸς ἐν χρησμοῖς περὶ Λυκούργου τοῦ Λακεδαιμονίοις νομοθετήσαντος, ἢ περὶ ἐμοῦ· λέγεται γὰρ εἰς τὸν ναὸν εἰσιόντα προσειπεῖν αὐτόν· φροντίζω πότερα θεόν σε εἴπω, ἢ ἄνθρωπον. ἐμὲ δὲ θεῷ μὲν οὐκ εἴκασεν, ἀνθρώπων δὲ πολλῷ προέκρινεν ὑπερφέρειν [When the jurors, naturally enough, made a still greater tumult on hearing this statement, he said that Socrates again went on: And yet, gentlemen, the god uttered in oracles greater things of Lycurgus, the Lacedaemonian law-giver, than he did of me. For there is a legend that, as Lycurgus entered the temple, the god thus addressed him: 'I am pondering whether to call you god or man.' Now Apollo did not compare me to a god; he did, however, judge that I far excelled the rest of mankind].[392]

of the Delphic oracle, which sees the very same thing* from the divine point of view. And just as the oracle was generally proportionate to the corresponding human consciousness, just as in an earlier age it gave advice with divine authority and in a later age engaged in proposing scientific problems,** so we see a *harmonia praestabilita* [preestablished harmony][395] also in the Delphic oracle's pronouncement about Socrates. The misunderstanding that he was hiding a knowledge behind this ignorance was known to Socrates as well, but he regarded it
XIII 256 as a misunderstanding. He explains how his efforts to convince have been able to arouse much animosity toward him and adds (23 a): οἴονται γάρ με ἑκάστοτε οἱ παρόντες, ταῦτα αὐτὸν εἶναι σοφόν, ἃ ἂν ἄλλον ἐξελέγξω [This is due to the fact that whenever I succeed in disproving another person's claim

* As Socrates tells it, the Delphic oracle's pronouncement expressly signifies (23 a): ὅτι ἡ ἀνθρωπίνη σοφία ὀλίγου τινὸς ἀξία ἐστὶ καὶ οὐδενός . . . . . ὥσπερ ἂν εἴποι: ὅτι οὗτος ὑμῶν, ὦ ἄνθρωποι, σοφώτατός ἐστιν, ὅστις, ὥσπερ Σωκράτης, ἔγνωκεν, ὅτι οὐδενὸς ἄξιός ἐστι τῇ ἀληθείᾳ πρὸς σοφίαν [that human wisdom has little or no value . . . . . as if he would say to us, The wisest of your men is he who has realized, like Socrates, that in respect of wisdom he is really worthless].[393] Just as the oracle was always merely the occasion for the interpreting consciousness, so this Delphic pronouncement found its interpretation in Socrates.

** See Hegel, *Geschichte der Philosophie*, II, p. 173: "Plato selbst brachte es in der Mathematik bald zu hoher Fertigkeit. Es wird ihm die Lösung des delischen oder delphischen Problems zugeschrieben, das vom Orakel aufgegeben wurde, und sich, ähnlich dem pythagoräischen Lehrsatze, auf den Kubus bezieht: Nämlich die Verzeichnung einer Linie anzugeben, deren Kubus gleich sei der Summe von zwei gegebenen Kubis. Dieses erfordert Konstruction durch zwei Kurven. Bemerkenswerth ist, welche Art von Aufgaben die Orakel jetzt gemacht haben. Es war bei einer Seuche, wo man sich an das Orakel wandte, und da gab es diese ganz wissenschaftliche Aufgabe;—es ist eine Veränderung im Geiste der Orakel, die höchst merkwürdig ist [Plato himself soon attained to high proficiency in mathematics. To him is attributed the solution of the Delian or Delphic problem, which was proposed by the oracle, and, like the Pythagorean dogma, has reference to the cube. The problem is to draw a line, the cube of which will be the sum of two given cubes. This requires a construction through two curves. The nature of the tasks then set by the oracle is very curious; on this particular occasion application has been made to the oracle in a time of pestilence, and it responded by proposing an entirely scientific problem—the change indicated in the spirit of the oracle is highly significant]."[394]

to wisdom on a given subject, the bystanders assume that I know everything about that subject myself].[396] But we see also how he objects to this misunderstanding and how incorrect he considers the conclusion that he must know something just because he can convince others that they know nothing.

What kept Socrates from a speculative absorption in the remotely intimated positivity behind this ignorance was, of course, the divine call that he had to convince every individual of the same thing. He had come not to save the world but to judge it.[397] His life was dedicated to that, and it was this activity that also kept him from taking part in the affairs of the state.[398] The Athenians could take his life—to this he would submit—but an acquittal on the condition that he give up this divine mission he would never accept,[399] since that would be an attempt to murder him in an intellectual and spiritual sense. He was the eternal counsel for the prosecution who on behalf of the divine adamantly constrained payment of the divine claim down to the last farthing.[400] What nemesis was formerly in relation to the distinguished, the prominent, was thoroughly and totally carried out in Socrates' ironic activity related to mankind as such.

But Socrates did not stop with a philosophical consideration of mankind; he addressed himself to each one individually, wrested everything from him, and sent him away empty-handed. It was as if the angry gods* had turned away from human beings, had taken everything with them, and now were going to leave human beings to themselves. But in another sense it was the human beings who had turned away from the gods and become absorbed in themselves. Yet this, of course, is only a moment of transition. In many ways, man was still on the right road, and therefore what Augustine says about sin may be said about this: *beata culpa* [happy fault].[402] The heavenly host of gods rose from the earth and vanished from mortal sight, but this very disappearance was the con- XIII 257

* Later the gods became reconciled; therefore, in the *Timaeus*, Plato derives the origin of the world from the goodness of God, who did not know envy but wished to make the world like himself as much as possible.[401]

dition for a deeper relationship. Therefore, Rötscher is very correct in saying (p. 253): "Von hier aus erhellt es auch, welche Bewandnisz es mit der so vielfältig gemiszbrauchten Socratischen Unwissenheit hat, deren man sich so häufig als eine gute Apologie der eigenen Ignoranz, wie als Wehr gegen die Anerkennung des wahrhaften Wissens bedient hat. Das Wissen, dasz er nichts wisse, ist nämlich nicht etwa, wie es gewöhnlich vorgestellt wird, das reine leere Nichts, sondern das Nichts des bestimmten Inhalts der bestehenden Welt. Das Wissen der Negativität alles endlichen Inhalts ist seine Weisheit, durch welche getrieben er in sich geht, und dies Erforschen seiner Innerlichkeit als das absolute Ziel ausspricht, der Beginn des unendlichen Wissens, aber auch nur erst der Beginn, da sich noch keinesweges dies Bewusztsein erfüllt hat, sondern erst die Negation alles Endlichen und Bestehenden ist [This also sheds light on what might be the case with the much abused Socratic ignorance, which has frequently served no less as a good apology for one's own ignorance than as a defense against the recognition of true knowledge. The knowledge that he knew nothing is not at all the pure, empty nothing one usually takes it to be, but the nothingness of the determinate content of the world as it is. The knowledge of the negativity of all finite content is his wisdom, through which he is drawn into himself, and he expresses this exploration of his own inwardness as his absolute goal, as the beginning of infinite knowledge, yet merely the beginning, since this consciousness has nowise been consummated but is only the negation of everything established in a finite sense]."[403] Hegel also observes (p. 60): "So lehrte also Socrates die, mit denen er umging, wissen, dasz sie nichts wissen; ja was noch mehr ist, er sagte selber, er wisse Nichts, docirte also auch nicht. Wirklich kann man auch sagen, dasz Socrates nichts wuszte; denn er kam nicht dazu, eine Philosophie zu haben und eine Wissenschaft auszubilden. Dessen war er sich bewuszt; und es war auch gar nicht sein Zweck, eine Wissenschaft zu haben [Thus Socrates taught those with whom he associated to know that they knew nothing; indeed, what is more, he himself said that he knew nothing and therefore taught nothing. It may actually be said that Socrates knew nothing, for he did not reach the scientific construction of a systematic philosophy. He was conscious of this, and it was also not at all his aim to establish a science]."[404]

Socrates certainly indicated a new direction; he gave the age its direction (taking this word not so much in a philosophic as in a military sense). He went around to each one individually in order to find out if that person had a sound position; nevertheless, his activity was intended not so much to draw their attention to what was to come as to wrest from them what they had. This he accomplished, as long as the campaign lasted, by cutting off all communication with the besieged through his questions, which starved the garrison out of opinions, conceptions, time-honored traditions, etc. that up until now had been adequate for the person concerned. When he had done this to the individual, the devouring flame of envy (using this word metaphysically) was momentarily slaked, the annihilating enthusiasm of negativity momentarily satisfied, and he relished the joy of irony to its fullest, relished it doubly, because he felt himself divinely authorized, was convinced of his calling. But naturally this was only for a moment; soon he XIII 258
was back to his task* again.

For him, the negativity implicit in his ignorance was not a conclusion, not a point of departure for a more profound speculation, but the speculative element in the idea, whereby he had infinitely circumnavigated existence, was the divine authority by virtue of which he practiced in the realm of the particular. This ignorance was the eternal victory over the

* But this, of course, is his activity regarded ideally. In his life, the energy of this wrath (using this word metaphysically) may very well have been relieved by a kind of indolence, a kind of collapsing into himself, at which time he accepted in advance and *in abstracto* the pleasure that really should be acquired *in concreto*, until the divine call echoed within him again and he was ready again to come to the aid of the deity in the persuasion of human beings. Thus Socrates' standing still and staring, the subject of so much discussion and mentioned also in our discussion, is best conceived of as a state of dreaming in which the negativity became clear to him and he was intoxicated, so to speak, by its emptiness. Although he usually went around and associated with both his countrymen and aliens, in such moments he stood still and stared.

phenomenon, which no particular phenomenon or the sum of all phenomena could wrest from him, but by virtue of it he triumphed over the phenomenon at every moment. In this way he admittedly freed the single individual from every presupposition, freed him as he himself was free; but the freedom he personally enjoyed in ironic satisfaction the others could not enjoy, and thus it developed in them a longing and a yearning. Therefore, while his own position rounds itself off in itself, this position when absorbed into the consciousness of others becomes only the condition for a new position. The reason Socrates could be satisfied in this ignorance was that he had no deeper speculative craving. Instead of speculatively setting this negativity to rest, he set it far more to rest in the eternal unrest in which he repeated the same process with each single individual. In all this, however, that which makes him into a personality is precisely irony.

Naturally this theoretical ignorance, for which the eternal nature of the divine remained a mystery, must have had its counterpart in a similar religious ignorance of the divine dispensations and direction in human life, a religious ignorance that seeks its upbuilding and discloses its piety in a total ignorance, just as, for example, in a far more concrete develop-
XIII ment Schleiermacher[405] sought the upbuilding in the feeling
259 of absolute dependence. Naturally this also conceals a polemic and dismays anyone who has found his repose in one or another finite relation to the divine. This is reminiscent of the passage from Xenophon's *Memorabilia*[406] quoted earlier, where Socrates explains how the gods have kept for themselves what is most important, namely, the outcome, so that all human striving is vanity, accomplishing nothing. This appears also in the Platonic dialogue *Alcibiades II*,[407] where Socrates speaks about the significance of prayer and where he urges extreme caution in praying to the gods for something lest they grant this prayer and later it may turn out to be of no benefit at all to mankind. To be sure, this caution seems to imply the possibility that a man is able in certain cases to see what is serviceable and consequently dares to pray for it. But it must be remembered both that Socrates by no means assumes (even presupposing that a man knew what was best for

him and prayed for it) the gods therefore will grant it, which suggests an even deeper doubt about what is really best for man, and that this caution degenerates into anxiety, which is not alleviated until the prayer is neutralized. This is evident in his praising a verse of a poem that reads:

> Give us the good, O Zeus,
> Whether we pray for it or not;
> Even when we pray for it,
> Avert the evil from us.[408]

But herein we see the divine removed from man in a religious sense just as much as it was theoretically, and the term for it once again is ignorance.*

It is customary to characterize Socrates' position also with the well-known phrase: γνῶθι σαυτόν [know yourself].[409] This XIII
phrase, somewhat like the word "truth" in Christian termi- 260
nology, unquestionably contains an ambiguity that serves precisely to recommend it, since it is just as applicable to a theoretical as to a practical position. In modern scientificity, however, this phrase is often torn completely out of the complex of ideas to which it belongs and for some time now has been vagabonding in literature unchallenged. Here, then, is an attempt to bring it back to its native soil, that is, an attempt to show what it signified for Socrates, or how Socrates made fruitful the thought implicit in this phrase. Now it is certainly true that the phrase γνῶθι σαυτόν can designate subjectivity in its fullness, inwardness in its utterly infinite wealth, but for Socrates this self-knowledge was not so copious; it actually contained nothing more than the separating, the singling out, of what later became the object of knowledge. The phrase "know yourself" means: separate yourself from the other. Precisely because this self did not exist prior to Socrates, it was once again an oracular pronouncement corresponding to Soc-

* To prevent any misunderstanding and, if possible, to illuminate this comment from a completely different position, may I point out that in the Christian consciousness prayer has its absolute validity; the Christian knows what to pray for, knows that when he prays for it he will absolutely be listened to, but this is expressly grounded in his knowing himself to be in a real relationship with his God.

rates' consciousness that commanded him to know himself. But it was reserved for a later age to go deeply into this self-knowledge. But if we understand it in this way, as required by Socrates' opposition to the Greek substantiality, we see that Socrates again has a completely negative result. This principle, "know yourself," is entirely congruous with the ignorance previously described. The reason he could continue to insist upon this negative point is the same as before, because his life task and interest were to affirm it—not speculatively, for then he would have had to go further, but to affirm it practically against every single human being. Therefore he placed individuals under his dialectical vacuum pump, pumped away the atmospheric air they were accustomed to breathing, and left them standing there. For them, everything was now lost, except to the extent that they were able to breathe ethereal air. Socrates, however, had nothing more to do with them but hastened on to new ventures.

But if we return for a moment to the situation that prompted this whole investigation, the accusation against Socrates, it is obvious that Socrates was in conflict with the view of the state—indeed, that from the viewpoint of the state his offensive had to be considered most dangerous, as an attempt to suck its blood and reduce it to a shadow. Moreover, it is also clear that he would unavoidably draw official atten-
XIII 261 tion to himself, because it was not a scholarly still life to which he was devoting himself. On the contrary, with the enormous elasticity of a world-historical viewpoint, he tipped one individual after the other out of the substantial actuality of the state. But once he was accused, the state could not be satisfied with the defense supposedly derived from his declared ignorance, because, from the state's point of view, this ignorance naturally had to be considered an offense.

But if his position was negative theoretically, then it was no less negative practically, because he was unable to contract any real relationship to the established order.* Naturally this was

* As a matter of fact, Socrates had done military service in three battles (the siege of Potidaea, the campaign in Boeotia near Delium, the battle of Am-

due to his theoretical stance. He had found his way out of the other (according to the Greek view, the state), but then he could not find his way into the state, either. In the *Apology*,[413] he himself tells how his divine mission had robbed him of the time and opportunity to devote himself to political affairs and declares that it is necessary for him to live as a private person.

When we take into account that even in our countries, where the state, precisely because it has undergone a far deeper mediation, allows subjectivity a much greater latitude than that which the Greek state could allow, when we take into account, I say, that even in our countries someone living on private means is always a dubious person, we may infer from that how the Greek state must have regarded Socrates' attempt to go his own way and live as a private person. And if Professor Heinsius[414] thinks he has adequately answered Forchhammer's comment by asking if anyone agrees with Forchhammer, may I modestly venture to respond to Professor Heinsius and say that I find what Forchhammer portrays XIII
on page 6 as Socrates' activity is both well described and cor- 262
rectly perceived as heresy against the state: "Er zupfte in jeder Stoa, an jeder Straszenecke, auf jedem Spaziergang die Athenischen Jünglinge am Mantel, und *fragte* so lange, bis sie mit dem beschämenden Gefühl des Nichtwissens, aber auch mit Zweifel an dem, was sie bisher für Göttlich gehalten, ihn verlieszen, oder sich gänzlich in seine Lehre begaben [On every stoa, on every street corner, on every walk, Socrates tugged the Athenian youths by the mantle and kept asking questions until they took their leave, not only with a shameful feeling of knowing nothing, but also with doubts about what they had previously regarded as divine, or else devoted themselves entirely to his teaching]."[415] What I consider good in Forchhammer's description is his account of how Socrates hung about

---

phipolis);[410] later he was a member of the council and had the rank of presiding officer[411] for just one day. Despite this, however, he had totally emancipated himself from the proper civic relationship to the state. Xenophon does, it is true, justify this by having him say: "If I form good citizens, then I am multiplying the services I owe my fatherland,"[412] but this, of course, is part of Xenophon's narrowness, with which we are already familiar.

the streets and boulevards instead of taking his place in the state or being a citizen in the Greek sense, how he exempted himself from carrying the burdens of the state and was satisfied to lead a private life. Thus his position in life was altogether predicateless.* I do not mean this, of course, in the odious sense that he was not chancellor or cabinet secretary, but since he did not have any connection with the state, the
XIII 263 state on its part could not predicate anything about his whole life and activity.

Later we see how Plato, too, called the philosopher away from actuality, how he wanted the buoyant forms of ideas to beckon him away from the tangible and wanted the philosopher to live apart from the noise of the world. But this was not the case with Socrates. To be sure, Socrates was something of an enthusiast about knowledge, just as it is usually the abstract that is the most conducive to enthusiasm, but still this did not distance him from life—on the contrary, he was in very lively contact with it, but his relation to it was his purely

* He even prides himself on this in the *Apology*, where he maintains that his life has been active but also incommensurate with the standards of the state (the latter, of course, he says polemically against the state, and because he very ironically blends everything together [*mellem hverandre*], he easily fools a superficial consideration). He tells that he has never cared about making money, about household matters, about military, civic, and other seats of honor and public offices (but from the viewpoint of the state this is considered not at all praiseworthy); he has never cared about political parties and conspiracies (here is the confusing element, for his nonparticipation must of course be considered praiseworthy by the state, and furthermore, there is striking irony in the careless way he lumps together proper civic life in the state with mobs and partisan politics). On the other hand, he has privately sought to do the single individual the greatest service, but this obviously means that he has entered into only purely personal relations with the individuals; see *Apology* 36 b-c.[416] —A similar blending of everything is also found elsewhere in the *Apology*,[417] where he speaks with much pathos about how everyone should remain where either he himself has placed himself, thinking it best for him, or the state has placed him, for it is precisely the latitude of arbitrariness he postulates here that naturally from the state's point of view must be restricted considerably. The confusion becomes even greater when he proceeds to argue on the basis of the few instances when he remained at his assigned place in service to the state. The state, of course, would always be appreciative of this; what is dubious is his taking it upon himself to choose a place.

personal relation to individuals, and his exchange with them consummated itself as irony. For him, therefore, people were of infinite importance,* and if he was rigid and inflexible about subordinating himself to the state, he was equally flexible, equally supple, in his associations with people, was just as great a virtuoso in casual contacts. He conversed equally well with tanners, tailors, Sophists, politicians, poets, with young and old, conversed equally well with them about everything, because wherever he went he found a task for his irony.** But in all this he was not a good citizen and certainly did not make others so.†

Whether the position taken by Socrates was actually supe- XIII
rior to the state's, whether he truly was divinely authorized, 264
of that world history must judge, but if it is to judge fairly, it must also admit that the state was authorized to judge Socra-

* Although Socrates did not especially fetch philosophy down from the sky and bring it into the houses, as Cicero thinks,[418] but rather brought people out of their houses and up from the netherworld in which they lived, it nevertheless may very well have happened that he himself, despite all his virtuosity, became bogged down sometimes and during a lengthy talk with every Tom, Dick, and Harry may even have lost the irony, lost sight of the ironic thread and momentarily wandered off into more or less triviality. So much for an earlier comment on Xenophon's view.[419]

** Thus when Phaedrus (in the dialogue of the same name) is amazed that Socrates is so unfamiliar with the region that he has to be led around like a stranger, indeed, that he almost seems never to have set foot outside the city gates, Socrates replies: ξυγγίγνωσκέ μοι, ὦ ἄριστε· φιλομαθὴς γάρ εἰμι· τὰ μὲν οὖν χωρία καὶ τὰ δένδρα οὐδέν μ' ἐθέλει διδάσκειν, οἱ δ'ἐν τῷ ἄστει ἄνθρωποι [You must forgive me, dear friend; I'm a lover of learning, and trees and open country won't teach me anything, whereas men in the town do].[420]

† The method he used— ἐπιχειρῶν ἕκαστον ὑμῶν πείθειν μὴ πρότερον μήτε τῶν ἑαυτοῦ μηδενὸς ἐπιμελεῖσθαι, πρὶν ἑαυτοῦ ἐπιμεληθείη . . . . . μήτε τῶν τῆς πόλεως, πρὶν αὐτῆς τῆς πόλεως [I tried to persuade each one of you not to think more of practical advantages than of his mental and moral well-being . . . . . or in general to think more of advantage than of well-being in the case of the
state] (*Apology*, 36 c)[421]—was, of course, totally upside down for Greek cul- XIII
ture, just as the thesis—Be concerned first about the state before you concern 264
yourself with its specific affairs—reminds one of the revolutionary strivings[422] that in our day manifest themselves not so much in tangible things as in thoughts (the thoughts of single individuals, of course) and their usurped sovereignty.

tes. In a certain sense, he was revolutionary, yet not so much by doing something as by not doing something; but a partisan or leader of a conspiracy he was not. His irony saved him from that, for just as it deprived him of due civic sympathy for the state, due civic pathos, it also freed him from the morbidity and the imbalance required for being a partisan. On the whole, his position was far too personally isolated, and every relationship he contracted was too loosely joined to result in anything more than a meaningful contact. He stood ironically above every relationship, and the law for the relationship was a continual attraction and repulsion. His connection with the single individual was only momentary, and he himself was suspended high above all this in ironic contentment. Pertinent to this is a charge made against Socrates in recent times, that he was an aristocrat (see Forchhammer).[423] Naturally this must be understood in the intellectual sense, and then Socrates cannot be acquitted of the charge. The ironic freedom he enjoyed because no relationship was strong enough to bind him and he continually felt himself free above it, the enjoyment of being sufficient unto himself, to which he abandoned himself—all this suggests something aristocratic.

Diogenes, as is well known, has been compared to Socrates and called a "furious Socrates."[424] Schleiermacher believed that he should rather be called a caricatured Socrates but tried to find a similarity between them in the independence from sensual pleasure that they both sought to acquire.[425] But this is surely too little. If one bears in mind, however, that Cynicism is negative enjoyment (in relation to Epicureanism), that Cynicism enjoys the absence, the lack of desire, is not unac-
XIII 265 quainted with it but seeks satisfaction in not giving in to it, and therefore instead of ending in desire always turns back into itself and enjoys the lack of enjoyment, an enjoyment strongly reminiscent of what ironic satisfaction is in the intellectual sense. If one takes all this into consideration and then applies it intellectually to the complexities of political life, the likeness will surely not be inconsiderable. True freedom, of course, consists in giving oneself to enjoyment and yet preserving one's soul unscathed. In political life, true freedom

naturally consists in being involved in the circumstances of life in such a way that they have an objective validity for one and through all this preserving the innermost, deepest personal life, which certainly can move and have its being under all these conditions but yet to a certain degree is incommensurate with them.

But if we turn back for a moment to the circumstance that provided the occasion for our entering into this discussion, namely, Socrates' arraignment, it is clear that Socrates as a citizen was not a point on the periphery of the state gravitating toward its center but rather a tangent continually touching the peripheral complexities of the state. Moreover, it is apparent that in his relation to the state one should not attribute to him the negative virtue of not doing evil (a negativity that in the Greek sense must be regarded as a crime); rather, by bringing others into the same situation, he actually did do evil. There is one more point to remember. He did not contract a deeper relation with others, those whom he had lifted out of their natural position (he was not a partisan), but at the same time he was ironically beyond them.

But if it was impossible for Socrates to accommodate to the manifold concretion of the state, and if it became doubtful that he could accomplish anything with average Athenian citizens, whose life over the years was formed by the life of the state, in the youth, whom the state, looking to its future, protected, he nevertheless had a nursery where his ideas could thrive, inasmuch as young people always live more universally than adults. Thus it was altogether natural for Socrates to turn his attention mainly to the youth. This provides the transition to the second charge.

2. *Socrates Seduces the Youths.*

In Plato's *Apology* (26 a),[426] Socrates argues in his defense that
he must do it either knowingly or unknowingly (ἑκών—ἄκων). XIII
But since it would be foolish to assume that he did it know- 266
ingly, inasmuch as he certainly must be well aware that sooner or later he would have to suffer because of it, then he must be assumed to do it unknowingly, and in that case it would be

unreasonable to order him punished, since his accusers should rather petition that he be censured and reprimanded—this defense, I say, everyone undoubtedly can see is not particularly weighty, because in this way any crime could be explained away and made into an error.[a]

Hegel's treatment[427] of this particular charge is so excellent that I shall be as brief as possible about everything on which we can agree, lest I bore the more knowledgeable readers with what they already know from him. Against Meletus's general charge that he seduced the youths, Socrates stakes his whole life; the charge is then made more specific—that he weakened children's respect for their parents.[b] This is elucidated further by a special exchange between Socrates and Anytus with respect to Anytus's son.[c] Socrates' defense essentially ends up with the general thesis that the most competent ought to be preferred to the less competent. For example, in the choosing of a general, preference would be given not to the parents but to the experts in warfare.[d] Thereupon Hegel propounds as indefensible in Socrates' conduct this moral interference of a third party in the absolute relation between parents and children, an intrusion that seems to have prompted (to limit the proof to a specific factual instance) the young man mentioned above, Anytus's son, to become dissatisfied with his position.[e]

XIII 267 This is as far as Hegel goes and we with him, for we have actually come quite far with this Hegelian view. But the case may still be regarded from another side. The state, of course, has fully agreed with Socrates that the more competent ought to be preferred to the less competent. But it by no means follows that the state can leave it up to each individual to decide

[a] I have purposely stressed this *raisonnement* [line of reasoning], because it gives us a clue to how Socrates' moral philosophy was constituted (something that will be investigated later), because it reveals that his moral philosophy had the defect of being founded on an altogether abstract epistemology.

[b] Xenophon, *Mem.*, I, 2, 49;[428] Xenophon, *Apology*, para. 20.[429] This can also be compared to Pheidippides' behavior toward his father in Aristophanes.[430]

[c] Xenophon, *Apology*, para. 29-31.[431]

[d] Xenophon, *Apology*, 20-21;[432] *Mem.*, I, 2, 51.[433]

[e] See Hegel, *op. cit.*, p. 109.[434]

whether or to what extent he is the most competent, to say nothing of allowing the single individual, simply because he deems himself the most competent, to propagate this competence of his with no concern for the state. As the whole in which the family lives and moves, the state can suspend to a certain degree the absolute relation between parents and children, can to a certain degree use its authority to make stipulations regarding the children's education, but this is precisely because the state ranks higher than the family, which is within the state. But the family in turn ranks higher than the single individual, especially in regard to its own affairs. Vis-à-vis the family, therefore, the single individual, just because he believes himself to be the most competent, cannot without further ado be authorized on his own responsibility to extend his competence. Vis-à-vis the single individual, therefore, the child's relation to its parents is an absolute.*

Just as Socrates by way of irony rose above the validity of the substantial life of the state, so also family life had no validity for him. For him the state and the family were a sum of individuals, and therefore he related to the members of the state and the family as to individuals; any other relation was unimportant to him. Thus we see how the thesis that the most competent ought to be preferred to the less competent (it really ought to read: The person who considers himself the most competent ought to push himself ahead of the one he considers less competent; after all, Socrates was not preferred except perhaps by the youths, who as the ones to be instructed could not be granted any vote) becomes essentially immoral precisely by its total abstraction. Here, then, is another example of how the celebrated Socratic moral philosophy was XIII 268

* Throughout this discussion, I have considered only the relation as such between Socrates and the young people he wanted to instruct. I have paid no attention at all to the harm his instruction might have done. Whatever can be said on that subject has already been developed above. My objective here is to stress the unwarranted aspect of Socrates' unceremonious arrogation as teacher. From the standpoint of the state, the divine authority he claimed is worthless, since by completely isolating himself he had placed himself outside the sanction of the state.

constituted. The defect is definitely due to the abstract position he took with regard to knowledge.

By not accepting money for his instruction, Socrates may have thought to make recompense for the harm done by his unauthorized intrusion. It is a familiar fact that Socrates was quite proud of not taking money for his teaching* and often spoke of it with considerable bravado.[436] Undeniably this most frequently was said with deep irony directed at the Sophists, who charged so much that in the opposite sense their instruction became almost incommensurate with money and monetary value. But on closer inspection there may be something more here than meets the eye. It may also have its basis in the irony with which he understood his own teaching. Just as his wisdom, by his own statement, was of an ambiguous nature, so also was his instruction. And just as he himself says of ship pilots in the *Gorgias:* "he who practices this art (the art of piloting) and has done us so great a favor (by transporting us safely) disembarks and paces humbly back and forth alongside his ship. For he is able, I think, to reflect that it is exceedingly difficult to determine which of the passengers he has benefited by not letting them be drowned on the way and which he has harmed,"[437] so also he might say the same of the instruction by which he transferred individuals from one part of the world to another. And just as he in the same passage praises the art of piloting for accepting, in contrast to rhetoric, a very modest payment although accomplishing the same as rhetoric, so he can also boast that in contrast to the Sophists he takes no payment. Thus in and by itself his refusal to accept money for his instruction can certainly not be regarded as anything so extraordinarily superior, nor can it automatically be regarded as an absolute sign of the absolute worth of his instruction. It is no doubt true that all genuine
XIII 269 instruction is incommensurate with money, and it is no doubt true that it becomes utterly ludicrous if the payment is allowed to have a decisive influence on the instruction, as if, for ex-

* Aristophanes differs; he has him accept not only money for his teaching but even sacks of flour.[435]

ample, a logic teacher had logic for three rix-dollars and logic for four rix-dollars, but it by no means follows from this that it is intrinsically wrong to accept money for his instruction. The practice of being paid for teaching did indeed begin with the Sophists, and to that extent one can very well understand Socrates' conduct and his ironic polemicizing against it; but, to repeat, Socrates' behavior here may also conceal an irony about his own teaching, as if he were to say: To be quite honest, this has a strange connection with my knowledge, for since I know nothing, it is easy to see that I cannot accept payment for imparting this wisdom to others.

Turning back for a moment to the circumstance that gave us an occasion for making this analysis, the charges against Socrates, we easily perceive that his crime (from the standpoint of the state) was that he neutralized the validity of family life, slackened the law of nature according to which the individual member of the family rests in the whole family—namely, respect.

If one wanted only to track down the accusation, one could stop here; but anyone who makes the view of Socrates the object of his inquiry must go one step further. Although Socrates committed a crime against the state by this kind of unauthorized intrusion into families, it is nevertheless conceivable that through the absolute significance of his teaching, through the intimate way he related to his students, solely with their best interest in mind, he could have repaired the damage done by his importunate interference. We shall now see whether his relation to his pupils has the earnestness and his teaching the pathos that could be required of such a teacher. But these are totally lacking in Socrates. One could not think of Socrates as someone who under the celestial vault of ideas elevated his pupils through the intuition of their eternal essence, as someone who impregnated the youths with the rich fullness of a vision, as someone who ethically laid an enormous responsibility upon his own shoulders and watched over them with fatherly concern, reluctantly let them go but never lost sight of them, as someone who, to recall a previous expression, loved them in the idea. In relation to others, Socrates' character was too negatively rounded off for such things to take place.

XIII 270 He certainly was an amorist of the highest order, had an extraordinary enthusiasm for knowledge—in short, had all the seductive gifts of the mind; but communicate, fill up, enrich—this he could not do. In this sense, one perhaps would dare to call him a seducer, since he infatuated the youths, awakened longings in them but did not satisfy them, let them flare up in the thrilling joy of contact but never gave them strong and nourishing food. He deceived them all just as he deceived Alcibiades, who himself says, as was mentioned earlier,[438] that instead of being the lover Socrates was the beloved. And what does this mean other than that he attracted youth to himself, but when they looked up to him, wanted to find a point of rest in him, wanted, forgetting all else, to seek reassurance in his love, wanted themselves to cease to be and to be only in being loved by him—then he was gone, the spell was broken. Then they felt the deep pain of unhappy love, then they felt that they were deceived, that it was not Socrates who loved them but they who loved Socrates and yet were not able to tear themselves away from him. For more resourceful natures, of course, this might have been neither so perceptible nor so painful. He had turned his pupils' gazes inward, and therefore in gratitude the gifted ones were bound to feel that they owed it to him; they were bound to feel all the more grateful the more they saw that they had themselves to thank for their rich resources and not Socrates. Thus his relation to his pupils was certainly stimulating, but by no means personal in the positive sense. What stood in the way here was once again his irony.

If someone wants to adduce as contrary instances the love with which Xenophon and Plato regarded Socrates, my answer is, first, that I have indeed pointed out that Socrates' pupils might very well love him—indeed, might not even be able to tear themselves away from this love—and, second, and this is the more concrete answer, that Xenophon was too limited in resources to perceive this and Plato too rich. Every time Plato felt how much he possessed, he had to think involuntar-

ily of Socrates; therefore he loved Socrates in the idea, which he certainly did not owe to Socrates but which Socrates had nevertheless helped him to obtain. Therefore, in the *Apology*, Socrates quite correctly says: ἐγὼ δὲ διδάσκαλος μὲν οὐδενὸς πώποτ' ἐγενόμην· εἰ δέ τις ἐμοῦ λέγοντος, καὶ τὰ ἐμαυτοῦ πράττοντος, ἐπιθυμοῖ ἀκούειν, εἴτε νεώτερος, εἴτε πρεσβύτερος, οὐ- XIII 271
δενι πώποτε ἐφθόνησα [I have never set up as any man's teacher, but if anyone, young or old, is eager to hear me conversing and carrying out my private mission, I never grudge him the opportunity] (*Apology*, 33 a).*[439]

As for Socrates' closer relations to his pupils, his relation to Alcibiades must be an example *instar omnium* [worth them all]. This reckless, sensate, ambitious, talented young person must naturally have been a highly flammable material for Socrates' ironic sparks. We have seen earlier how this relation continually remained at the same point precisely through Socrates' irony, how it was held at the abstract, vacillating initiation of a relation, was held at the zero point and never increased in strength and inwardness, so that while the intensity increased on both sides, this intensity nevertheless was so exactly balanced that the relation remained the same and Alcibiades' growing vehemence continually found its master in Socrates' irony.

Thus, in an intellectual sense, we can say of Socrates' relation to the youths that he looked at them with desire.[440] But just as his desire did not aim to possess the youths, neither was his course of action so designed. He did not set out with fine words, with long oratorical effusions, with huckstering trumpeting of his own wisdom. On the contrary, he went about quietly. He was seemingly indifferent to the young men; his questions did not pertain to his relation to the youths. He dis-

* Socrates presumably says this primarily to refute the charge that in the intimate circle of his pupils he discussed things entirely different from those discussed when someone else was present. In this respect, one may certainly concede to Socrates that he was always the same, but nevertheless his words do indicate how loose his relation was to the youths, inasmuch as this relation was bound up with nothing more than accidental contacts in the sphere of knowledge.

cussed some subject that was personally important to them, but he himself remained completely objective; and yet underneath this indifference to them they felt, more than they saw, the piercing sidelong glance that instantly pierced their souls like a dagger. It seemed as if he had secretly listened to the most intimate conversations of their souls, as if he constrained them to speak aloud about them in his presence. He became their confidant without their quite knowing how it had happened, and while throughout all this they were completely changed, he remained unbudgingly the same. And then, when all the bonds of their prejudices were loosened, when all
XIII their intellectual sclerosis was softened, when his questions
272 had straightened everything out and made the transformation possible, then the relation culminated in the meaningful moment, in the brief silvery gleam [*Sølvblink*][441] that instantly illuminated the world of their consciousness, when he turned everything upside down for them at once, as quickly as a glance of the eye [*Øieblik*] and for as long as a blink of the eye, when everything is changed for them ἐν ἀτόμω, ἐν ῥιπῆ ὀφθαλμοῦ [in a moment, in the twinkling of an eye].[442]

There is a story about an Englishman who traveled in order to see the sights.[443] When he came to a mighty forest and found a place where he could open up an amazing vista by having the intervening woods cut, he hired people to saw through the trees. When everything was ready, when the trees were sawed through for toppling, he climbed up to this spot, took out his binoculars, gave the signal—the trees fell, and his eyes instantaneously delighted in the enchanting view, which was even more seductive because in almost the same moment he had the opposite. So also with Socrates. By means of his questions, he quietly sawed through for toppling the primeval forest of substantial consciousness, and when everything was ready—look, then all these formations vanished, and the eyes of the soul delighted in a vista such as they had never seen before. Most likely the youths enjoyed this happiness, but Socrates stood as the ironic spectator who enjoyed their amazement. But this work of sawing through the trees often took a long time. In this, Socrates was indefatigable. But when it was accomplished, in the same instant the relation had reached its peak. He did not give more, and while the young man now felt inseparably bound to Socrates, the relation changed so that, as Alcibiades aptly describes it, Socrates became the beloved rather than the lover. If we understand his relation in this way, we are vividly reminded of the art he himself claimed to possess—the art of midwifery.[444] He helped the individual to an intellectual delivery; he cut the umbilical cord of substantiality. As an *accoucheur* [obstetrician], he was unrivaled, but more than that he was not. Nor did he assume any real responsibility for the later lives of his students, and here again Alcibiades provides us with an example *instar omnium*.*

If we take the word in its intellectual meaning, we can call
Socrates an amorist and express it even more warmly by re- XIII
calling those well-known words in the *Phaedrus* (249 a): παι- 273
δεραστεῖν μετὰ φιλοσοφίας [passion for a loved one joined with the love of wisdom].[445] At this point we may touch briefly on Socrates' being charged with pederasty, an accusation that has not been allowed to die over the years, because in every generation there has been some research scholar who felt constrained to defend Socrates' honor on this matter. Since I am not at all interested in replying to this charge, it is not my purpose to present a defense of Socrates, but if the reader is willing to understand it metaphorically,** I believe that in this there is new evidence of Socrates' irony.

In the eulogy Pausanias delivers in the *Symposium*, there appears the following statement: "This Eros (the inferior, whose worshipers, first of all, love women as well as boys; moreover, in those they love, they love the body more than the soul) also descends from the goddess who is much younger than the other and owes her existence to a union of both sexes: the other is a son of the heavenly one, who does not come from the female, but only from the male sex . . . . . therefore those who are inspired by this Eros seek the male sex, because they

* Cf. Forchhammer, *op. cit.*, p. 42ff.

** Those who cannot understand this intellectually, I refer on this point to Johannes M. Gesner's *Socrates sanctus Paederasta*;[446] see *Commentarii societatis regiae scientiarum Gottingensis*, Tom. II, *ad annum MDCCLII*, pp. 1-31.

love that which by nature possesses greater vigor and intellect."[447] In these words there is already an adequate description of the intellectual love that is bound to be present in a people as esthetically developed as the Greeks, where the individuality was not infinitely reflected in itself but instead was what Hegel so significantly calls "beautiful individuality,"[448] in which the conflict in the individuality was not split so deeply as to allow the true love to be the higher unity. But when this intellectual love preferably seeks its object among the youths, it is thereby suggested that it loves possibility but avoids actuality. But this manifests precisely its negative character. Despite this, it may very well have a high degree of enthusiasm—in fact, this is why it can have it. Enthusiasm is not always bound up with endurance; on the contrary, enthusiasm is a
XIII 274 consuming zeal in the service of possibility. Therefore, an ironist is always an enthusiast, except that his enthusiasm never accomplishes anything, for he never goes beyond the category of possibility.

In this sense Socrates loved the youths. But as is apparent, this is a negative love. No doubt his relation to the youths was not without meaning, but, as pointed out earlier, when the relation was to gain a deeper meaning, it was over—that is, the relation to the youths was the beginning of a relation. That this relation, however, could last for a time, that the young man could very well feel attached to Socrates after the latter had detached himself from him—this I have tried to show above. But if we bear in mind that this relation between Socrates and the youths is the last possibility to show a positive relation, if we bear in mind how much could be demanded in that respect of the man who, having emancipated himself from every other real relation, had concentrated on this one, if we bear all this in mind, we shall be unable to explain the negativity described here unless we assume that Socrates' position was irony.*

* History has preserved an additional relation Socrates entered into with another person—his relation to Xanthippe. Everyone, of course, perceives that Socrates was not exactly a model husband, and the interpretation of his relation to her attributed to Socrates, according to Xenophon[449]—that he had

We go back to the indictment and the ensuing condemnation of Socrates. The judges declared him guilty, and if, more or less disregarding the points of the complaint, we were to describe his crime in one word, we could call it *apragmosyne* [indolence] or indifferentism. Admittedly he was not idle, and admittedly he was not indifferent to everything, but in his relation to the state he was indifferent precisely by way of his private practice. Consequently, Socrates was declared guilty, but the punishment was still not determined. With Greek humaneness, the accused was permitted to stipulate the punishment himself, within certain limits, of course. Hegel relates in
detail what was wrong with Socrates' conduct. He shows that XIII
Socrates was deservedly condemned to death, that his crime 275
was refusing to recognize the sovereignty of the nation and asserting instead his subjective conviction over against the objective judgment of the state. His refusal in this respect may very well be regarded as moral greatness, but he nevertheless brought his death upon himself; the state was just as justified in condemning Socrates as he was in emancipating himself, and Socrates thereby became a tragic hero.* So far Hegel.

Following the *Apology* very closely, we shall now attempt to give an account of his conduct. One would think that the freedom to stipulate his own punishment must have been most welcome to Socrates, for just as his course of life had shown itself to be incommensurate with common standards, his punishment also was bound to be the same, and it was entirely consistent for him to think that the only punishment he could impose upon himself was a fine,[452] because, if he had had money, it would have been no loss for him to lose it—in other words, because the punishment *in casu* [in the case] would cancel itself. Therefore, it was also entirely consistent

the same benefit from this shrewish woman as trainers have from wild horses, the benefit of learning to constrain them, that for him she was an exercise in controlling mankind, for when he had finished with her he would easily be able to tolerate other people—this view, I say, does not indicate much conjugal love, but certainly a considerable measure of irony. See Forchhammer, p. 49 and note 43.[450]

* See Hegel, *op. cit.*, pp. 113ff.[451]

for him to suggest that the judges be content with the little bit he could pay, entirely consistent, because, since money on the whole had no reality [*Realitet*] for him, the punishment would be the same whether he paid a large amount of money or little—that is, the punishment would amount to nothing. Consequently, the only punishment he considered appropriate was the punishment that was no punishment.

We shall now pursue in detail this instructive portion[453] of the *Apology*. He begins by expressing his amazement at being convicted by such a small majority; by this he indicates that he does not see in the state's sentence an objectively valid view in contrast to the particular subject. To a certain degree, the state does not exist at all for him; he dwells merely on the numerical. He seems to have no intimation that a quantitative decision can shift over into a qualitative one. He dwells on the oddity that three votes[454] decide the outcome, and, to stress the oddity even more, he supposes the extreme opposite: If Anytus and Lycon had not gone along, he says, then Meletus himself would have been fined a thousand drachmae. Here we see again how Socrates' irony makes him disparage every ob-
XIII 276 jective qualification of his life. The judges are a number of individuals, their verdict has only numerical value, and if the majority pronounce him guilty, then Socrates thinks that nothing more nor less is said thereby than that such and such a number of individuals have condemned him. Now, anyone can clearly see here the entirely negative view of the state.

An ironic fate wills that Socrates himself shall stipulate the punishment. What gives this situation such extraordinary ironic elasticity is the enormous contrasts: the sword of the law hangs by a horsehair over Socrates' head,[455] a human life is at stake, the people are solemn, sympathetic, the horizon dark and cloudy—and now Socrates is as absorbed as an old arithmetician in finishing the problem, in getting his life to conform to the state's conception, a problem as difficult as squaring a circle, since Socrates and the state turn out to be absolutely heterogeneous quantities. It would indeed be comic to see Socrates try to conjugate his life according to the paradigm of the state, inasmuch as his life was entirely irregular, but the situation becomes even more comic because of the *dira necessitas* [cruel constraint of necessity][456] that under penalty of death bids him find a likeness in this unlikeness. It is always comic when two things that cannot possibly be related are placed in relation to each other, but it is even more comic when the pronouncement is made: If you cannot find any relation, then you must die. In its complete isolation, Socrates' life is bound to appear entirely heterogeneous with every qualification of the state, and for this reason the thought process, the dialectic with which Socrates seeks to bring about a relation, also manifests the most extreme contrasts.

He is pronounced guilty by the state. Now the question is what punishment he has deserved. Since Socrates, however, feels that his life is utterly incomprehensible to the state, it is apparent that he could just as well deserve a reward. He proposes, therefore, that he be maintained at public expense in the prytaneum.* If the state, however, should not feel called upon to reward him in this way, he will accommodate himself to it and ponder what punishment he could have deserved. To avoid the death sentence insisted upon by Meletus, he could XIII
choose a fine or exile. But he is unable to make a choice, for 277
what could prompt him to choose one of these two? Fear of death? That would be unreasonable, for he in fact does not know whether death is a good or an evil.[457] So it seems that Socrates himself thinks that death would be the most appropriate punishment, precisely because no one knows whether it is an evil—that is, because here the punishment, just as before with the fine, cancels itself. A fine or exile he could not choose, because in the first case he would be jailed, since his financial situation would not allow him to pay it. In the second case, he is very well aware that he is even less fitted for living in another state than in Athens, so that in a short time he would be banished also from that state etc. Consequently, he cannot choose a fine or exile. Why? Because they would bring

* Since his life as such is incommensurate with a conception of the state and thus he can just as little deserve reward as punishment, he provides *subsidialiter* [for assistance] a second reason—namely, that he is a poor man who needs peace and quiet.

suffering upon him, but he cannot accept that, because it is undeserved, and as he himself says: καὶ ἐγὼ ἅμ' οὐκ εἴθισμαι ἐμαυτὸν ἀξιοῦν κακοῦ οὐδενός [Besides, I am not accustomed to think of myself as deserving punishment].[458] Insofar as there is a question of what punishment, broadly speaking, he has deserved, his answer is: That which is no punishment, that is, either death, since no one knows whether it is a good or an evil, or a fine, provided they will be satisfied with a fine of the amount he can afford to pay, since money has no value for him. But as for a more specialized punishment, a punishment that would be felt by him, he finds that every such punishment is inappropriate.

Thus we see how Socrates' position is entirely negative toward the state, how he does not fit into it at all; but we see it even more clearly in the moment when he, charged because of the course of his life, would most likely have to become aware of his misrelation to the state. Despite this, with the sword hanging over his head, he nevertheless undauntedly carries through his position. His delivery, however, does not have the powerful pathos of enthusiasm; his bearing does not have the absolute authority of personality; his indifference is not a blissful relaxation in his own repletion. We find nothing of all this, but we do find a most consistently sustained irony that lets the objective power of the state break up on the rock-firm negativity of irony. The objective power of the state, its claims upon the activity of the individual, the laws, the courts—everything loses its absolute validity for him. He divests himself of all of them as imperfect forms; he rises ever
XIII 278 more lightly, sees it all disappear beneath him in his ironic bird's-eye view, and he himself hovers over it in ironic contentment, borne up by the absolute self-consistency of infinite negativity. In this way he becomes alien to the whole world to which he belongs (however much he belongs to it in another sense); the contemporary consciousness has no predicate for him—nameless and indefinable, he belongs to another formation. What bears him up is the negativity that still has engendered no positivity. This explains why even life and death lose their absolute validity for him. Yet in Socrates we have

the actual, not the apparent, pinnacle of irony, because Socrates arrived at the idea of the good, the beautiful, the true only as the boundary—that is, came up to ideal infinity as possibility. Much later, however, after these ideas have acquired their actuality and personality its absolute *pleroma* [fullness], when subjectivity again isolates itself, when the infinite negativity again opens its chasm in order to swallow this actuality of the spirit, irony manifests itself in a more alarming form.[459]

XIII 279

III

The View Made Necessary

For the observer, Socrates' life is like a magnificent pause in the course of history: we do not hear him at all; a profound stillness prevails—until it is broken by the noisy attempts of the many and very different schools of followers to trace their origin in this hidden and cryptic source. With Socrates the stream of historical narrative, just like the river Guadalquivir,[460] drops underground for some distance, only to rush out again with renewed power. He is like a dash[461] in world history, and the ignorance about him, due to the lack of opportunity for direct observation, is an invitation not so much to bypass him as to conjure him forth with the aid of the idea, to make him become visible in his ideal form—in other words, to become conscious of the idea that is the meaning of his existence in the world, of the phase in the development of the world spirit that is symbolically indicated by the singularity of his existence in history.

Just as he himself in a certain sense exists and yet again does not exist in world history, so his significance in the development of the world spirit[462] is precisely to be and yet not to be, or not to be and yet to be: he is the nothing from which the beginning must nevertheless begin. He is not, because he is not the object of immediate apprehension, to which corresponds in the intellectual sense the negation of the immediacy of substantiality. He is, because for thought he is, which corresponds to the emergence of the idea in the world of mind—but, please note, the idea in its abstract form, its infinite negativity. Thus, the form of his existence in history is not a per-
XIII 280 fectly adequate pictorial indication of his intellectual significance.

Therefore, if in the first section of this dissertation I tried to apprehend Socrates through *via negationis* [the way of negation], in the second section I shall try to apprehend him through *via eminentiae* [the way of idealization].[463] The point of this, of course, is not to tear Socrates out of his historical context—on the contrary, it is to see him properly in that context. Nor is the point of this that Socrates is supposed to be so divine that he cannot find a foothold on earth—the historian who has reached adulthood and the age of discrimination is as little served by such characters as the Indian maiden was served by lovers of that kind.* "Socrates ist aber nicht wie ein Pilz aus der Erde gewachsen, sondern er steht in der bestimmten Continuität mit seiner Zeit [But Socrates did not grow like a mushroom out of the ground; on the contrary, he stands in definite continuity with his time],"[465] a certain man says; but despite this continuity, one must remember that he cannot be completely explained by his past, that if we in one sense regard him as a logical conclusion to the premises of the past, there is more in him than was in the premises, the *Ursprüngliche* [original] that is necessary if he is truly to be a turning point.[466] Plato has expressed this several places by saying that Socrates was a divine gift. Socrates himself also says this in the *Apology* (30 d): νῦν οὖν ὦ ἄνδρες Ἀθηναῖοι, πολλοῦ δέω ἐγὼ ὑπὲρ ἐμαυτοῦ ἀπολογεῖσθαι, ὥς τις ἂν οἴοιτο, ἀλλ' ὑπὲρ ὑμῶν, μὴ ἐξαμάρτητε περὶ τὴν τοῦ θεοῦ δόσιν ὑμῖν, ἐμοῦ καταψηφισάμενοι [For this reason, gentlemen, so far from pleading on my own behalf, as might be supposed, I am really pleading on yours, to save you from misusing the gift of God (the god) by condemning me],[467] and in 31 a: ὅτι δ'ἐγὼ τυγχάνω ὢν τοιοῦτος οἷος

* "In der Episode *Nala* aus dem Gedichte *Mahabharata* wird erzählt, wie eine Jungfrau in ihrem 21sten Jahre, in dem Alter, in welchem die Mädchen selbst das Recht haben einen Mann zu wählen, unter ihren Freiern sich einen aussucht. Es sind ihrer fünf; die Jungfrau bemerkt aber, dasz vier nicht fest auf ihren Füszen stehen, und schlieszt ganz richtig daraus, dasz es Götter seien. Sie wählt also den fünften, der ein wirklicher Mensch ist [In the episode *Nala* in the poem *Mahabharata*, we have a story of a virgin who in her twenty-first year—the age at which the maidens themselves have the right to choose a husband—makes a selection from among her wooers. There are five of them, but the maiden remarks that four of them do not stand firmly on their feet and from this infers correctly that they are gods. She therefore chooses the fifth, who is a veritable man]." See Hegel, *Philosophie der Geschichte*, p. 185.[464]

ὑπὸ τοῦ θεοῦ τῇ πόλει δεδόσθαι κ.τ.λ. [If you doubt whether I am really the sort of person who would have been sent to this city as a gift from God (the god) etc.].[468] This expression, that Socrates was a divine gift, is indeed especially significant in that it points out that he was altogether appropriate for his
XIII 281 age, for why should the gods not give good gifts, and also recalls that he was more than the age could give to itself.

But since Socrates provides a turning point in this way, it becomes necessary to consider the age before him and the age after him.

To give a historical account of the decline of the Athenian state at this point seems to me rather superfluous, and that I am right about this surely everyone will agree who is not infected with the lunacy from which a good many younger research scholars seem to suffer, a lunacy that manifests itself as tragic, not comic, in continually telling the same story.[469] Precisely because it is a turning point in history, Hegel talks about it again and again; sometimes his task is to describe it, and sometimes he uses it as an example. Therefore, everyone who has read anything at all of Hegel must be familiar with his views on this, and I shall not vex people by repeating what no one can say so well as Hegel himself.[470] If the reader wants a full-flavored and more detailed presentation that shows how Athens decayed more and more after Pericles, who in a way was an abnormal phenomenon himself, who in his lifetime had stemmed the evil and held it back, a presentation that carries the principle of decay through the different spheres of the state, may I refer him to Rötscher, pp. 85ff.[471]

But I cannot refrain from one comment. In many ways, the Athens of this period calls to mind what Rome was at a later time. Intellectually, Athens was the heart of Greece. Thus when Greek culture approached its disintegration, all the blood rushed back violently into the chambers of the heart. Everything concentrated in Athens—wealth, luxury, opulence, art, science, recklessness, the enjoyment of life*—in

* Ὅπου γὰρ ἐὰν ᾖ τὸ πτῶμα, ἐκεῖ συναχθήσονται οἱ ἀετοί [Wherever the body is, there the eagles will be gathered together]. Matthew 24:28.

short, everything that, as the city hastened toward its ruin, could also help to glorify it and illuminate one of the most brilliant intellectual dramas conceivable. There was a restlessness in Athenian life; there was a palpitation of the heart intimating that the hour of disintegration was at hand. But from the other side, that which was the condition for the decline of the state proved to have immense significance for the new principle that was to appear, and the disintegration and decay became indeed the fertile soil of the new principle. The evil principle in the Greek state now was the arbitrariness of finite
subjectivity[472] (i.e., unwarranted subjectivity)—arbitrariness XIII 282
in all its numerous, variegated forms.

Only *one form* will be the object of closer scrutiny here, that is, Sophistry. This is indeed the troll that wreaks havoc in the domain of thought, and its name is legion.[473] We shall consider these Sophists; in them Socrates had the present or past that had to be destroyed. We shall see what it was like and then consider what Socrates must have been like to be able to destroy them so radically. Reflection begins with the Sophists, and to that extent Socrates always has something in common with them, and in relation to Socrates the Sophists could be called false messiahs.

The *Sophists** represent knowledge separating itself in its XIII 283

* Here again Hegel has provided excellent expositions. Yet it seems to me that the more prolix study, found in his *Geschichte der Philosophie*,[474] does not always hang together and at times has the character of a collection of random comments that frequently do not quite fall under the stated rubrics. But to the short sketch (in his *Philosophie der Geschichte)*, as related to the more prolix presentation, a remark Hegel himself made somewhere[475] is applicable: the mind [*Aand*] is the best epitomizer. This sketch is so pertinent and clear that I shall quote it. It is found on p. 327: "Mit den Sophisten hat das Reflectiren über das Vorhandene und das Räsonniren seinen Anfang genommen. Eben diese Betriebsamkeit und Thätigkeit, die wir bei den Griechen im praktischen Leben und in der Kunstausübung sahen, zeigte sich bei ihnen in dem Hin- und Hergehen und Wenden in den Vorstellungen, so dasz, wie die sinnlichen Dinge von der menschlichen Thätigkeit verändert, verarbeitet, verkehrt werden, ebenso der Inhalt des Geistes, das Gemeinte, das Gewuszte hin- und herbewegt, Object der Beschäftigung und diese Beschäftigung ein Interesse für sich wird. Die Bewegung des Gedankens, und das innerliche Ergehen darin, diesz interesselose Spiel wird nun selbst zum Interesse. Die gebildeten So-

motley multiplicity from substantial morality by means of the awakening reflection. On the whole, they represented the separated culture for which a need was felt by everyone for whom the fascination of immediacy had faded away. Their wisdom was "*ein fliegendes Blatt* [a fly sheet],"[477] which was not kept

---

phisten, nicht Gelehrte oder wissenschaftliche Männer, sondern Meister der Gedankenwendung setzten die Griechen in Erstaunen. Auf alle Fragen hatten sie eine Antwort, für alle Interessen politischen und religiösen Inhalts hatten sie allgemeine Gesichtspunkte, und die weitere Ausbildung bestand darin,
XIII Alles beweisen zu können, in Allem eine zu rechtfertigende Seite aufzufinden.
283 In der Demokratie ist es das besondere Bedürfnisz, vor dem Volke zu sprechen, ihm etwas vorstellig zu machen, und dazu gehört, dasz ihm der Gesichtspunkt, den es als wesentlichen ansehen soll, gehörig vor die Augen geführt werde. Hier ist die Bildung des Geistes nothwendig, und diese Gymnastik haben die Griechen sich bei ihren Sophisten erworben. Es wurde aber nun diese Gedankenbildung das Mittel, seine Absichten und Interessen bei dem Volke durchzusetzen: der geübte Sophist wuszte den Gegenstand nach dieser und jener Seite hin zu wenden, und so war den Leidenschaften Thür und Thor geöffnet. Ein Hauptprincip der Sophisten hiesz: 'der Mensch ist das Maasz aller Dinge'; hierin, wie in allen Aussprüchen derselben, liegt aber die Zweideutigkeit, dasz der Mensch der Geist in seiner Tiefe und Wahrhaftigkeit, oder auch in seinem Belieben und besonderen Interessen sein kann. Die Sophisten meinten den blosz subjectiven Menschen, und erklärten hiemit das Belieben für das Princip dessen, was recht ist, und das dem Subjecte Nützliche für den letzten Bestimmungsgrund [With the Sophists began the process of reflection on the existing state of things, and of ratiocination. That very diligence and activity which we observed among the Greeks in their practical life, and in the achievement of works of art, showed itself also in the turns and windings which these ideas took; so that, as material things are changed, worked up, and used for other than their original purposes, similarly the essential being of spirit—what is thought and known—is variously handled; it is made an object about which the mind can employ itself, and this occupation becomes an interest in and for itself. The movement of Thought—that which goes on within its sphere (without reference to an extrinsic object)—a process which had formerly no interest—acquires attractiveness on its own account. The cultivated Sophists, who were not erudite or scientific men but masters of subtle turns of thought, excited the admiration of the Greeks. For all questions they had an answer; for all interests of a political or religious order they had general points of view; and in the ultimate development of their art, they claimed the ability to prove everything, to discover a justifiable side in every
XIII position. In a democracy it is a matter of the first importance to be able to
283 speak in popular assemblies—to urge one's opinions on public matters. Now this demands the power of duly presenting before them that point of view

from flapping about either by a prominent public figure or by integration into a coherent system of knowledge. Their external conduct corresponded to this completely. They were here, there, and everywhere, as is said of bad money. They roamed from city to city like troubadours and wandering students[478] in the Middle Ages, set up their schools, lured young people to come, and they came, inveigled by the trumpeted news that these men knew and could demonstrate everything.*

On the whole, what they wanted to impart to people was not so much an insight into the particular sciences but a universal culture, and Protagoras's declaration is very reminiscent of the warning by Mephistopheles in Goethe's *Faust*[480] against studies in various faculties. He expressly assures the young people that they need not fear that he, like the other Sophists, will lead them against their will back to the branches of knowledge they specifically wished to avoid. Therefore, he would not instruct them in arithmetic, astronomy, etc.—no, he would make cultured men of them, he would give them the proper instruction for becoming competent politicians and XIII 284
no less competent in their private lives. Thus we see also in the *Gorgias*[481] how this universal culture manifests itself as the science that in public life can excel all other sciences, so that he who possesses it possesses the master key whereby he can open all doors. This universal culture reminds us of what is offered for sale in our time by scholarly vendors of indul-

---

which we desire them to regard as essential. For such a purpose, intellectual culture is needed, and this discipline the Greeks acquired under their Sophists. This mental culture then became the means, in the hands of those who possessed it, of enforcing their views and interests on the Demos: the expert Sophist knew how to turn the subject of discussion this way or that way at pleasure, and thus the doors were thrown wide open to all human passions. A leading principle of the Sophists was that 'Man is the measure of all things'; but in this, as in all their apophthegms, lurks an ambiguity, since the term 'Man' may denote Spirit in its depth and truth, or in the aspect of mere caprice and private interest. The Sophists meant Man simply as subjective and intended, in this dictum of theirs, that mere liking was the principle of Right, and that advantage to the individual was the ground of final appeal]."[476]

* The introduction to the *Protagoras*[479] vividly pictures the conduct of some of the Sophists.

gences under the name of enlightenment. Inasmuch as the Sophists' main interest, next to earning money, was to gain influence in political affairs, their wanderings bring to mind the holy pilgrimages and pious pageantry that now are the order of the day in the political world and by which the political traveling salesmen try to impart to people in the shortest possible time the requisite political background to enable them to talk.

The immediate consciousness, secure and confident as it relies upon what it receives from the past, like a sacred treasure, scarcely ever notices that life is full of contradictions. Reflection, on the other hand, discovers this at once. It discovers that what is supposed to be absolutely certain, determinative for men (laws, customs, etc.), places the individual in conflict with himself; it also discovers that all this is something external to a person, and as such he cannot accept it. Consequently, it shows the error, but it also has available the remedy for it—it teaches how to give reasons for everything. Thus it gives people an adroitness, a competence in classifying every particular instance under certain universal instances; it places at the disposal of each individual a rosary of *loci communes* [general propositions], by repeated recital of which he is in the position of always being able to say something about the particular, make some observations about it, state some reasons for or against. The more such categories one has, the more expert one is in using them, the more educated one is. This was the culture provided by the Sophists. Although they did not give instruction in the particular sciences, the universal culture they practiced, the drilling with which they trained people, nevertheless seems to be most comparable to the capsule information that a tutor tries to convey to those being tutored. In one sense this universal culture is very rich and in another very meager. It deceives itself and others and does not detect at all that it always uses the same magnitudes; it deceives both itself and others, just as Tordenskjold[482] deceived others by having
XIII 285 the same troops who had paraded down one street parade down the next street.[483] Therefore, in relation to the immediate consciousness, which in all innocence accepts with child-

like simplicity whatever is offered, this culture is negative, and it is too shrewd to be innocent; in relation to thought, however, it is highly positive. In its first form, this education shakes the foundations of everything, but in its second form it enables every pupil of integrity to make everything firm and fast again. The Sophist, therefore, demonstrates that everything is true. In one sense, the thesis that everything is true was valid also for early Greek culture—the actual had absolute validity. But in Sophistry, reflection is awakened; it shakes the foundations of everything, and it is then that Sophistry lulls it to sleep again with reasons. By means of *raisonnements*,[484] this hungry monster is satisfied, and thus together with the Sophists the thinker seems able to demonstrate everything, for they could give reasons for everything, and by means of reasons they could at any time whatever make anything whatever true.

Now, it is no doubt true that the thesis "Everything is true," placed in the sphere of reflection, in the very next instant shifts over into its opposite: Nothing is true. But this next moment did not come for Sophistry, precisely because it lived in the moment. What enabled Sophistry to rest there was that it lacked a comprehensive consciousness; it lacked the eternal moment in which it would have to give an account of the whole. Since reflection had shaken the foundations of everything, Sophistry assumed the role of remedying the momentary need. Thus reflection in Sophistry was checked in its precarious outflowing and was controlled at every moment, but the security that bound it was the particular subject.

It appeared, therefore, as if Sophistry were able to constrain the ghost that it itself had raised. But when the foundations of everything have been shaken, what can then become the firm ground that is to save the situation? Either it is the universal (the good etc.), or it is the finite subject, his propensities, desires, etc. The Sophists seized the latter expedient. Therefore, freely ranging thought, which to a certain degree already announces its presence in reflection if it is not arbitrarily stopped, lives like a slave in Sophistry, and every time it raises its head to look around freely, it is bound by the individual in

the service of the moment. The Sophist has hamstrung it, so to speak, so that it cannot run away from him. Now reflection has to mold bricks,[485] construct buildings, and do other slave work; it lives subjugated and oppressed under the yoke of the thirty tyrants (the Sophists). Hegel notes in his *Geschichte der Philosophie*, II, p. 5: "Der Begriff, den die Vernunft im Anaxa-
XIII 286 goras als das Wesen gefunden, ist das einfache Negative, in welches alle Bestimmtheit, alles Seiende und Einzelne sich versenkt. Vor dem Begriffe kann nichts bestehen; er ist eben das prädikatlose Absolute, ihm ist schlechthin Alles nur Moment; für ihn giebt es, um sich so auszudrücken, nichts Niet- und Nagelfestes. Eben der Begriff ist diesz flieszende Uebergehen Heraklits, diesz Bewegen, —diese Kausticität, der nichts widerstehen kann. Der Begriff also, der sich selbst findet, findet sich als die absolute Macht, welcher Alles verschwindet;—und jetzt werden alle Dinge, alles Bestehen, alles für fest Gehaltene flüssig. Diesz Feste—sei es nun eine Festigkeit des Seins, oder Festigkeit von bestimmten Begriffen, Grundsätzen, Sitten, Gesetzen—geräth in Schwanken und verliert seinen Halt. Grundsätze u. s. f. gehören selbst dem Begriffe, sind als Allgemeines gesetzt; aber die Allgemeinheit ist nur ihre Form, der Inhalt, den sie haben, geräth, als etwas Bestimmtes, in Bewegung. Diese Bewegung sehen wir in den sogenannten Sophisten werden . . . . . [The Notion, which reason has found in Anaxagoras to be real existence (*sic*), is the simple negative into which all determination, all that is existent and individual sinks. Before the Notion nothing can exist, for it is simply the predicateless absolute to which everything is clearly a moment only; for it there is thus nothing so to speak permanently fixed and sealed. The Notion is just the continual change of Heraclitus, the movement, the causticity, which nothing can resist. Thus the Notion which finds itself, finds itself as the absolute power before which everything vanishes; and thereby all things, all existence, everything held to be secure, is now made fleeting. This firm ground—whether it be a security of natural Being or the security of definite conceptions, principles, customs, and laws—becomes vacillation and loses its stability. As universal, such principles, &c., cer-

tainly themselves pertain to the Notion, yet their universality is only their form, for the content which they have, as determinate, falls into movement. We see this movement arising in the so-called Sophists . . . . .]."[486]

It seems, however, that Hegel makes the Sophistic movement too grandiose, and therefore the distrust one may have about the correctness of his view is strengthened even more by the presence, in his subsequent discussion of Sophistry, of various points that cannot be harmonized with it; likewise, if this were the correct interpretation of Sophistry, there is much in his conception of Socrates that would make it necessary to identify Socrates with them. Now, it is undoubtedly true that Sophistry harbors in itself a secret very dangerous to itself, but it refuses to become conscious of it, and the Sophists' pompous, confident parading, their matchless self-sufficiency (all of which we learn from Plato), is proof enough that they thought themselves able to satisfy the demands of the times, not by shaking the foundations of everything but, after having shaken the foundations, by making it all secure again. In a finite view, the frequently repeated Sophistic thesis: πάντων χρημάτων μέτρον ἄνθρωπον εἶναι [man is the measure of all things]* contains a positivity, but a more profound view sees XIII 287

* This Sophistic thesis can provide a very interesting contribution to the fate of quotations in their frequently long and difficult passage through life. Certain quotations resemble stock characters in comedies; merely an incidental and fleeting intimation of their existence is needed for one to recognize them at once. The person who scoops his wisdom from magazines, journals, prefaces to books, and booksellers' blurbs easily acquires a great number of XIII 287
what could be called casual acquaintances. But as it turns out, one knows the external man but is usually totally ignorant of his origin, history, situation, etc. —This Sophistic thesis is now a stock figure in modern literature's world of quotations. Hegel,[487] however, took the liberty of interpreting it to mean that man is the goal[488] toward which everything strives. This was a bold act of rape for which one can easily forgive Hegel, since he himself so often reminds us of the significance it had in the mouths of the Sophists. However, a good many Hegelians, for want of being parties to the good, have preferred to be parties to the evil and have widely circulated this false currency. In Danish, the ambiguity of the word *Maal* [measure, goal] is tempting for the person who does not know that it is a Sophistic thesis; for this reason I chose to quote it in the Greek from Plato's *Theaetetus*, 152 a (Ast, II).[489]

it as ultimately negative. On the whole, the Sophists considered themselves to be *physicians* to the age.

In Plato, therefore, we always find that whenever the Sophists are obliged to make a statement about which art they possess, the invariable answer is: the art of public speaking. But it is in precisely this sphere that the positivity of the Sophists manifests itself. The public speaker's concern is always with a particular case; here it is a matter of seeing something from the front, from behind, of chattering up one side and down the other. On the other hand, he is dealing with a great number of individuals. Here the Sophists taught how to work upon the emotions and passions. It was always a matter of the particular case and of victory in the particular case, and of this the Sophist was sure. An analogy may throw some light on this positivity in Sophistry. Casuistry hides exactly the same kind of secret that Sophistry hides. In casuistry, incipient reflection is halted. As soon as this reflection is permitted to emerge, it demolishes casuistry immediately. And yet casuistry is indeed a positivity, even though a more profound consideration sees its negativity. The casuist is secure and calm; he feels that he not only is able to help himself but is able to
XIII 288 help others as well. If someone doubts and then turns to a casuist, he always has seven pieces of advice, seven answers right at hand. This is certainly a high degree of positivity. That this is an illusion and that the casuist nourishes the sickness he wants to cure is undoubtedly the case, but he is not conscious of it.

In my discussion of the dialogue *Protagoras*,[490] I have adequately stressed the relation between Socrates' view and the Sophists'. Protagoras has a host of virtues, a positive assortment; for Socrates, virtue is one and only one. This Socratic thesis is certainly negative in comparison with Protagoras's abundance, but it is also speculative; it is the negative infinity in which each particular virtue is free. Protagoras's thesis that virtue can be taught is certainly positive; it contains a high degree of confidence in existence and in the Sophistic art. On the other hand, the Socratic thesis that virtue cannot be taught is negative, but it is also speculative, for it signifies the eternal self-positing infinity in which all learning is encompassed. Thus Protagoras is continually positive, but only apparently so, and Socrates is continually negative, but up to a point this, too, is only apparent. He is positive to the extent that the infinite negativity contains within itself an infinity; he is negative because for him the infinity is not a disclosure but a boundary.*

This, then, was the positivity from which Greece was to be XIII 289 liberated—a positivity that was just as vapid in theory as it was ruinous in practice. For this to occur thoroughly, however, a radical cure was necessary, and to that end the sickness had to burn itself out so that no susceptibility still remained in the body. Now, these Sophists were Socrates' born enemies, and if we ask what qualifications he had to have in order to keep a tight rein on them, it is impossible not to be momentarily overjoyed at the ingeniousness in world history, because Soc-

* Although the dialectic of Gorgias (who, incidentally, refused to be branded a Sophist[491]) takes the Sophistic skepticism still further, even he was to a certain degree more positive than Socrates. The three well-known theses[492] he sets forth in his work on nature certainly do contain a skepticism that not only undertakes to show the relativity of being or its not-in-and-for-itself being, its being for another, but also forces its way even into the qualifications of being; nevertheless, the way he perceives being is still infected with a positivity in comparison with infinite, absolute negativity. As Hegel says of Gorgias's dialectic in general: "diese Dialectik ist allerdings unüberwindbar für denjenigen, der das (sinnliche) Seyende als Reelles behauptet [This dialectic is undoubtedly impregnable to those who maintain sensuous Being to be real]" (p. 41).[493] To be sure, the positivity I generally have attributed to the Sophists has acquired a somewhat different meaning here, but it must be remembered that Gorgias ranked the highest of the Sophists and thus cannot be denied a certain scientific scholarliness. Nevertheless, compared with Socrates, he is positive precisely because he had a presupposition, whereas the infinite negativity is the pressure that gives subjectivity the elas- XIII 289 ticity that is the condition for ideal positivity. In Plato's *Gorgias*, the theses maintained by Gorgias, Polus, and Callicles "with increasing insolence"[494] are also positive in comparison with Socrates' view and positive in the sense in which I have generally used the term with regard to the Sophists. The thesis[495] that justice is what the stronger wants is positive compared with the negativity in which the inner infinity of the good is intimated. The thesis that it is better to do wrong than to suffer wrong is positive compared with the negativity in which the divine providence is dormant.

rates and the Sophists are, as is said, made for each other and on a scale rarely found. Socrates is so equipped and armed that it is impossible to fail to appreciate that he is going to war with the Sophists. If Socrates had had a positivity to advance, the result would have been that he and the Sophists would have talked together, since the wisdom of the Sophists was just as tolerant as the piety of the Romans and had no objection to there being one more Sophist, one more shop.

But such was not to be the case. The sacred was not to be taken in vain; the temple had to be cleansed before the sacred would once again take a seat there. Truth demands silence before it will raise its voice, and Socrates was to bring about this silence. For this reason, he was purely negative. If he had had any positivity, he would never have been so merciless, never such an ogre as he was and as he was obliged to be in order not to fall short of his mission in the world. For this he was indeed equipped. If the Sophists had an answer for everything, then he could pose questions; if the Sophists knew everything,
XIII 290 then he knew nothing at all; if the Sophists could talk without stopping, then he could be silent—that is, he could converse.* If the Sophists' pageant was pompous and pretentious, then Socrates' appearance was quiet and modest; if the Sophists' mode of living was sumptuous and self-indulgent, his was simple and abstemious; if the Sophists' goal was influence in the state, Socrates was reluctant to have anything to do with political affairs; if the Sophists' instruction was priceless, then Socrates' was, too, in the opposite sense; if the Sophists wished to sit at the head of the table, Socrates was content to sit at the foot; if the Sophists wanted to be regarded as somebodies, Socrates preferred to be a nobody. All this can, of course, be understood as examples of Socrates' moral strength, but it would perhaps be more correct to see it as an indirect polemic against the odious abuses of the Sophists, a polemic born of the inner infinity of irony. In one sense, admittedly, we may speak of Socrates' moral strength, but the

* The loquacity[496] and long speeches of the Sophists are like a sign of the positivity they possessed.

point he reached in this respect was rather the negative qualification that subjectivity intrinsically determines itself, but he lacked the objectivity in which subjectivity in its intrinsic freedom is free, the objectivity that is not the limiting but the enlarging boundary of subjectivity. The point he reached was primarily the ideal infinity's internal self-consistency in the abstraction wherein it is a qualification just as much metaphysical as esthetic and moral. The thesis Socrates so often advances—that sin is ignorance—is already adequate evidence of this. It is the infinite, nonchalant freedom of subjectivity that we see in Socrates, but this is precisely the irony.

At this point, I trust that two things are apparent—namely, that irony has a world-historical validity and that Socrates is not depreciated by my interpretation of him but really becomes a hero,[497] so that he is seen going about his business, so that he becomes visible to the one who has eyes to see, audible to the one who has ears to hear.[498] Early Greek culture had outlived itself, a new principle had to emerge, but before it could appear in its truth, all the prolific weeds of misunderstanding's pernicious anticipations had to be plowed under, destroyed down to the deepest roots. The new principle must contend; world history needs an *accoucheur* [obstetrician]. Socrates fills this place. He himself was not the one who was to XIII 291
bring the new principle in its fullness; in him it was only κατὰ κρύψιν [cryptically] present; he was to make its advancement possible. But this intermediate stage, which is not the new principle and yet is that (*potentia non actu* [potentially, not actually]), is precisely irony. But irony, in turn, is the glaive, the two-edged sword that he swung like an avenging angel over Greece.

In the *Apology*,[499] Socrates himself correctly understood this. There he says that he is like a gift of the gods and more specifically defines himself as a gadfly, which the Greek state, like a great and noble but lazy horse, needed. How his practice completely corresponded to this has already been discussed adequately above. But irony is the very incitement of subjectivity, and in Socrates irony is truly a world-historical passion. In Socrates, one process ends and with him a new one begins.

He is the last classical figure, but he consumes this sterling quality and natural fullness of his in the divine service by which he destroys classicism. But his own classicism makes it possible for him to sustain the irony. This is what I earlier called the divine healthiness that Socrates must have possessed.

XIII 292 For the reflective individuality,* every natural qualification is simply a task, and through and out of life's dialectic emerges the transfigured individuality as the personality who at every

* It certainly might seem that Socrates was a reflective individuality, and the dubious aptitudes suggested by his appearance seem to indicate not so much that he was what he was as that he became what he was. It might be possible, however, to conceive of this as more in line with the ugly exterior he himself describes with so much irony. It is well known that Zopyrus[500] made physiognomic studies of Socrates. The truth of the whole art of physiognomy, however, is based upon the thesis that essence is and is only insofar as it is in appearance, or that appearance is the truth of essence, essence is the truth of appearance. Now, essence is surely the negation of appearance, but it is not the absolute negation, since thereby essence itself would actually have disappeared. But to a certain degree, this is irony; it negates the phenomenal, not in order to posit by means of this negation, but negates the phenomenal altogether. It runs back instead of going out; it is not in the phenomenon but seeks to deceive with the phenomenon; the phenomenon exists not to disclose the essence but to conceal it. If one bears in mind that in happy Greece essence
XIII 292 and phenomenon were united as an immediate, natural qualification, then one also perceives that as this harmony is broken, the separation must be cut so deep that a unity in a higher form is brought about. In that case, it might be possible that Socrates interpreted this contradiction between his essence and his appearance ironically. He considered it entirely appropriate that his exterior suggested something quite different from his interior. Even though stress is laid on the moral freedom that negated all these preposterous natural contours, the incongruity still remains insofar as his moral striving never made him able to regenerate his exterior. Thus Socrates will always be a difficult task for physiognomy: if the element of self-determination is stressed, there remains the problem that Socrates' exterior did not essentially change; if heredity is stressed, then Socrates is indeed a stumbling block for the whole art of physiognomy. (Mehring, *"Ideen zur wissensch. Begründung d. Physiognomik,"* in Fichte's journal,[501] II, 2, 1840, p. 244, stresses the factor of self-determination but does not stress the difficulty.) But if we rather bear in mind the ironic delight Socrates took in being so equipped by nature that everyone inevitably was mistaken about him, there will be no need to go any deeper into physiognomic profundities.

moment is victorious and yet is still fighting. The reflective individuality never acquires the equanimity that encompasses the beautiful individuality, because it is to some extent a product of nature and has in itself the sensate as an essential element. The beautiful individuality's harmonious unity is disturbed by irony, and to a certain degree it is also disturbed in Socrates; in him it is destroyed, negated, at every moment. This also explains the view of death discussed earlier. But above this destruction, the ironic ataraxia (to recall an expression from skepticism)[502] towers higher and higher.

Just as with the Jews, who were, after all, the chosen people, the skepticism of the law had to pave the way, by its negativity had to consume and cauterize, so to speak, the natural man so that grace would not be taken in vain,[503] so also with the Greeks, the people who in the secular sense can certainly be called the chosen, the happy people, whose native land was XIII 293
the land of harmony and beauty, the people in whose development the purely human passed through its qualifications, the people of freedom—so also with the Greeks in their carefree, intelligible world, the silence of irony had to be the negativity that prevented subjectivity from being taken in vain. For just like the law, irony is a demand, an enormous demand, because it rejects reality [*Realitet*] and demands ideality.* It is clear that ideality is already in this desire, even though only as possibility, because intellectually that which is desired is always in the desire already, inasmuch as the desire is regarded as the agitation of the desired itself in the desiring. And just as irony is reminiscent of the law, so the Sophists are reminiscent of the Pharisees, who in the realm of the will operated in the very same way as the Sophists in the realm of knowledge.

What Socrates did with the Sophists was to give them the next moment, the moment in which the momentarily true dissolved into nothing—in other words, he let the infinite devour the finite. But Socrates' irony was not turned against

* But precisely because this demand was authentic in that period of world history, Socrates' irony is world-historically authorized and does not have the sickliness and egotism it has in a much later period,[504] when, after ideality has been given in fullest measure, it insists on an exaggerated sublimate[505] of it.

only the Sophists; it was turned against the whole established order. He demanded ideality from all of it, and this demand was the judgment that judged and condemned Greek culture. But his irony was not the instrument he used in the service of the idea; irony was his position—more he did not have. If he had had the idea, his annihilating activity would not have been so radical. The one who proclaimed the law was not the one who also brought grace; the one who laid down the demand in all its rigor was not the one who could satisfy the demand. But it must be borne in mind that between Socrates' demand and its satisfaction there was not the chasmic abyss such as that fixed between law and grace. In Socrates' demand, the satisfaction was κατὰ δύναμιν [potentially] present. The world-historical formation thereby became quite well rounded. In the previously cited treatise (p. 54), Schleiermacher points out that Plato is much too complete for a beginning from scratch,
XIII 294 and makes the point in contrast to Krug[506] and Ast,[507] who bypassed Socrates and began with Plato. But irony is the beginning, and yet no more than the beginning; it is and it is not, and its polemic is a beginning that is just as much an ending, for the destruction of the earlier development is just as much the ending of this as it is the beginning of the new development, since the destruction is possible only because the new principle is already present as possibility.

We now proceed to show in Socrates the other side of the bifrontic character implicit in every historical beginning: we must look at his relation to the development that traces its beginning back to him.* —It is a familiar fact that not only Plato but also a multiplicity of schools regarded this point** as the

* Plato interpreted his relation to Socrates with equal beauty and piety in the well-known statement that he thanked God for four things—that he was born a human being and not an animal, a male and not a female, a Greek and not a barbarian, but principally because he was born a citizen of Athens and a contemporary of Socrates.[508]

** See Christian A. Brandis, *"Grundlinien der Lehre des Socrates," Rheinisches Musäum* (Bonn: 1827), p. 119: "Aber eine so grosze Anzahl sehr begabter Männer hat kein Philosoph des Alterthums in dem Maasze für sich und für Erforschung der Wahrheit gewonnen, wie Socrates, keiner wie er, eine *Mannichfaltigkeit* von *Schulen* veranlaszt, die in Lehre und Lehrweise höchst ver-

source of their wisdom. It might seem as if it were necessary, in order to explain this phenomenon, to assume a high degree of positivity in Socrates. I have already tried to show how particularly the relation to Alcibiades can be explained very well
without assuming such a positivity—indeed, that an explana- XIII
tion is possible only on the assumption that it was not present. 295
I also tried to show what kind of magic irony possessed in order to captivate the mind.

I now go on to similar observations to show how once again irony can explain this phenomenon—indeed, that this phenomenon requires irony as its explanation. Hegel (*Geschichte der Philosophie*, II, p. 126)[510] notes that Socrates has been reproached for the derivation of so many diverse philosophies from his teaching; he replies that this was on account of the indefiniteness and abstraction of his principle. To upbraid Socrates for this simply indicates the desire that he should have been different from what he actually was. In other words, if the Socratic position had included the limitation that every intermediate positivity must necessarily have, then it most certainly to all eternity would have been impossible that so many descendants could try to claim their right of primogeniture. If, however, his position was infinite negativity, then it is easily explained, since this contains within itself the possibility of everything, the possibility of the whole infinity of subjectivity.

---

schieden unter einander, sich in der Ueberzeugung vereinigten, dem Socrates ihre leitenden Grundsätze zu verdanken. Unter den philosophischen Schulen, deren von einigen zehn, von andern neun, als ethische i.e.: Socratische bezeichnet wurden, fand sich ausser der Epicuräischen schwerlich eine, die solche Bezeichnung verschmäht haben würde [No philosopher of antiquity has won for himself and for the pursuit of truth such a great number of extremely gifted men as did Socrates, none other has given occasion to a *multiplicity of schools* so different from one another in doctrine and mode of teaching, yet united in the conviction that they owe their guiding principles to Socrates. Among these philosophical schools, of which some have designated ten (others nine) as ethical, that is, Socratic, scarcely one, except the Epicurean, would have found such a designation disdainful]."[509] (The nine Socratic schools are the Academic, Megaric, Eretrean, Elean, Peripatetic, Cyrenaic, Cynic, Stoic, and Epicurean.)

In discussing the three Socratic schools (Megaric, Cyrenaic, and Cynic), Hegel notes (p. 127)[511] that all three schools are very different from one another and adds that this alone clearly shows that Socrates had no positive system. Not only did he have no positive system, but he was also devoid of positivity. I shall try to show this later in connection with the way in which Hegel reclaims for him the idea of the good; here it suffices to say that even the good he had only as infinite negativity. In the good, subjectivity legitimately possesses an absolutely valid goal for its striving, but Socrates did not start from the good but arrived at the good, ended with the good, which is why it is entirely abstract for him.*

XIII 296 But if Hegel's comments are restricted in this way, they must also be extended by stressing the prodigious elasticity inherent in this infinite negativity. It does not suffice to say that from the heterogeneity of the Socratic schools the conclusion may be drawn that Socrates had no positive system; but it must be added that by its pressure the infinite negativity has made all positivity possible, has been an infinite incitement and stimulation for positivity. Just as in daily life Socrates could begin anywhere, so his significance in the world-historical development is to be the infinite beginning that contains

* Hegel, too, seems to agree, but he is not always consistent (p. 124): "Socrates selbst war nicht darüber hinausgekommen, dasz er für das Bewusztsein überhaupt das einfache Wesen des Sichselbstdenkens, das Gute, aussprach und die bestimmten Begriffe vom Guten untersuchte, ob sie das, dessen Wesen sie ausdrücken sollten, gehörig ausdrückten, die Sache durch sie in der That bestimmt sei. Das Gute wurde als Zweck für den handelnden Menschen gemacht. Dabei liesz er die ganze Welt der Vorstellung, überhaupt das gegen-
XIII 296 ständliche Wesen, für sich liegen, ohne einen Uebergang von dem Guten, dem Wesen des Bewuszten als eines solchen, zu dem Ding zu suchen, und das Wesen als Wesen der Dinge zu erkennen [Socrates himself did not come so far that he expressed for consciousness generally the simple essence of self-thought, the Good, and investigated the determinate concepts of the Good, whether they properly expressed that of whose essence they should express, and whether in fact the matter was determined by them. The Good was made the end of the man acting. He thereby left the whole world of idea, objective existence in general, resting by itself, without seeking a passage from the Good, from the essence of the conscious as such to the thing, and without recognizing the essence as the essence of things]."[512]

within itself a multiplicity of beginnings. Thus as beginning he is positive, but as mere beginning he is negative. Consequently, his relation here is the reverse of what it was with regard to the Sophists. But the unity thereof is precisely irony.

It is also apparent, therefore, that the three Socratic schools are united in the abstractly universal,* however differently they otherwise interpret this. But this has the very ambiguity that it can both polemically turn against the finite and be stimulative for the infinite. Just as in his association with his pupils (if I may be permitted to use this expression)[514] Socrates was indispensable to them for keeping the investigation continually on the move, so also in the world-historical sense his significance was that he set the ship of speculation afloat. But that requires an infinite polemic, a power to clear away every hindrance that may halt its movement. He himself, however, does not go on board but only prepares the ship for embarkation. He himself still belongs to an older formation, and yet a new one begins with him.** He discovers within himself the other continent in the same sense as Columbus had discovered America before he went aboard and actually discovered it. Therefore, his negativity forestalls any backsliding just as much as it accelerates the actual discovery. And just as his in- XIII 297
tellectual mobility and enthusiasm in daily association were inspiring to his pupils, so the enthusiasm of his position is the actuating energy in the subsequent positivity.

In the preceding sections, it has become apparent that Socrates, in his relation to the established order of things, was entirely negative, that he is suspended in ironic satisfaction above all the qualifications of substantial life. It has also become apparent that with regard to the positivity the Sophists claimed and with their multiplicity of reasons tried to anchor and to

* For Hegel's account of the principles of these schools, see pp. 127 and 128.[513]

** Compare this with our concluding remark on page 209 [p. 196]: "In this way he (Socrates) becomes alien to the whole world to which he belongs; the contemporary consciousness has no predicate for him—nameless and indefinable, he belongs to another formation."

make into an established order, Socrates once again related himself negatively and in ironic freedom was aware of being over and above it. His whole position, therefore, rounds itself off in the infinite negativity that turns out to be negative in relation to both a previous and a subsequent development, although in another sense it is positive in both relations—that is, infinitely ambiguous. Against the established order of things, the substantial life of the state, his whole life was a protest. He became involved with the Sophists in their attempt to create a surrogate for the established order. Their reasons could not hold back the gale wind of his infinite negativity, which instantly blew away all the polypous ramifications by which the particular and empirical subject clung fast and swept them out into the infinite Oceanus in which the good, the true, the beautiful, etc. confined themselves in infinite negativity. So much for the relations in which his irony manifested itself. As for the way in which it disclosed itself, it emerged both partially, as a mastered element in the development of discourse, and totally and in all its infinity, whereby it finally sweeps Socrates away with it.

APPENDIX XIII 298

Hegel's View of Socrates

What remains now is to compare the view of Socrates given in this dissertation with earlier perceptions; what remains is to let it test itself in the world. But it is by no means my intention to reel off every possible view or by way of a kind of historical survey to follow the pattern of the youngest followers of a certain modern school, who once again have chosen the form of a fairy tale as a model by always rehearsing the whole lesson at the beginning of each new part.[515] Surely everyone perceives the unreasonableness of going so far back that Brucker[516] or Tychsen[517] would have to be included, or of being so conscientious as to include Krug's reminiscences.[518] To begin with Schleiermacher's well-known treatise* would

* The task that Schleiermacher assigned himself, to evaluate Socrates' worth as a philosopher, is already sufficient proof that any absolutely exhaustive result is not to be expected. With Socrates (to bring up again a previously quoted remark by Hegel,[519] which strangely enough is by Hegel) it is a question not so much of philosophy as of the individual life. What Schleiermacher reclaims for Socrates is the idea of knowledge, and this is also the positivity XIII
(as stated above) that Schleiermacher thinks Socrates hides behind his igno- 299
rance. Schleiermacher says (p. 61): "Denn woher anders konnte er auch, was Andere zu wissen glaubten, für ein Nichtwissen erklären, als nur vermöge einer richtigeren Vorstellung vom Wissen und vermöge eines darauf beruhenden richtigeren Verfahrens. Und überall wo er das Nichtwissen darlegt, sieht man, er geht von diesen beiden Merkmalen aus, zuerst dasz das Wissen in allen wahren Gedanken dasselbe sei, also auch jeder solche Gedanke die eigenthümliche Form desselben an sich tragen müsse, und dann dasz alles Wissen Ein Ganzes bilde. Denn seine Beweise beruhen immer darauf, dasz man von Einem wahren Gedanken aus nicht könne in Widerspruch verwickelt werden mit einem andern, und dasz auch ein von Einem Punkte aus abgeleitetes durch richtige Verknüpfung gefundenes Wissen nicht dürfe widersprechen einem von einem andern Punkte auf gleiche Weise gefundenen, und indem er an den gangbaren Vorstellungen der Menschen solche Widersprüche aufdeckte, suchte er in Allen, die [ihn] irgend verstehen oder auch nur ahnen konnten, jene Grundgedanken aufzuregen [For how else was he able to announce as

XIII 299 already be starting from the beginning, although I cannot even agree with Brandis[527] that Schleiermacher was the first to make a breakthrough.

XIII 300 Hegel clearly provides a turning point in the view of Socrates. Therefore, I shall begin with Hegel and end with Hegel,

---

mere ignorance what others believed themselves to know if it were not for a more correct conception of knowledge and a more correct procedure based on this? Wherever he expounds this ignorance, he is seen to proceed by way of two criteria: first, knowledge in all true thought is the same, and consequently every such thought must intrinsically bear its own unique form; and second, all knowledge constitutes a totality. Hence, his proofs always depend upon the fact that whoever proceeds from a true thought cannot become entangled in a contradiction with another true thought, and that knowledge derived through valid inferences from one point cannot contradict knowledge gained in the same way from another point. And by uncovering such contradictions in the customary ideas of men, Socrates sought to stir up this fundamental thought in everyone who could somehow understand him or at least had an inkling]."[520] Further on (p. 63), he attributes method to Socrates and understands this according to the *Phaedrus*[521] as having the double task: "zu wissen, wie man richtig vieles zur Einheit zusammenfasse und eine grosze Einheit auch wieder ihrer Natur gemäsz in mannigfaltiges theile [to know how to synthesize correctly multiple components into a unity and, in turn and in accordance with its nature, to divide a larger unity into multiple parts]." If we scrutinize what is suggested here, we see that there is nothing that is incompatible with our whole view. What is stressed here is the very idea of consistency, the law upon which the domain of knowledge rests; but it is still understood so negatively that the principle it contains, one that Socrates also used, is *principium exclusi medii inter duo contradictoria* [the principle of the excluded middle between two contradictories]. The whole that all knowledge is supposed to form is once again conceived so negatively that it actually is infinite negativity. The two tasks of the method are also negative, because the unity under which the multifarious are comprehended is the negative unity in which it disappears, and the separation by which the unity is dissolved is the negativity of discursiveness. But this, indeed, is what we have understood as the essential in Socrates' dialectic, that it establishes the infinite self-consistency of the ideal. What is lacking in Schleiermacher, however (al-
XIII 300 though it is in some measure unfair to demand this of him since he himself has limited his task), is an awareness of Socrates' significance as personality. Baur, in his so frequently quoted book,[522] is excellent on this, and the whole view that the similarity between Socrates and Christ, if anything, must be sought in the validity they both had as personalities is a very productive view. But the main point is to insist on the infinite dissimilarity that still remains within this similarity. That irony is a qualification of personality has been indicated frequently in the foregoing. It has the returning-into-itself that characterizes personality; it searches back into itself, incloses itself within itself.

without giving attention to his predecessors, since they, insofar as they have any significance, have been corroborated by his view, or to his successors, since they have only relative value in comparison with Hegel. Just as his presentation of the historical usually cannot be charged with wasting time on wrangling about minutiae, so it focuses with prodigious intellectual intensity upon specific, crucial, central battles. Hegel apprehends and comprehends history in its large formations. Thus Socrates is by no means permitted to stand still like *ein Ding an sich* [a thing in itself],[528] but he must step forth whether he wishes to or not.

The difficulty implicit in the establishment of certainty about the phenomenal aspect of Socrates' life does not bother Hegel. He generally does not acknowledge such trivial concerns. And when the troubled augurs report that the sacred hens will not eat, he replies with Appius Claudius Pulcher, XIII
"Then they must drink"—and so saying throws them overboard.[529] 301
Although he himself observes that with respect to Socrates it is a matter not so much of philosophy as of the individual life, there is nothing at all in his presentation of Socrates in *Geschichte der Philosophie* to illuminate the relations of the three different contemporary views of Socrates.* He uses one single dialogue from Plato**[531] as an example of the

But in this movement, irony comes back empty-handed. Its relation to the world is not one in which the relation is an element in the content of personality; its relation to the world is a continuous nonrelation to the world, a relation in which, the moment the relation is to begin, it pulls back with a skeptical reserve (ἐποχή[523]); but this reserve is the personality's reflex in itself, which is indeed abstract and without content. Therefore, the ironic personality is actually only the outline of a personality. Thus one sees that there is an absolute dissimilarity between Socrates and Christ,[524] because the immediate fullness of deity resided in Christ,[525] and his relation to the world is so absolutely real a relation that the Church is conscious of itself as members of his body.[526]

* Aristophanes is an exception, but more of this in the appropriate place.[530]

** In connection with this dialogue, he makes just one very general observation (p. 69): "So in der Art endigen sich eine Menge xenophontischer und platonischer Dialoge, und lassen uns in Ansehung des Resultats (Inhalts) ganz unbefriedigt. So der Lysis: Was Liebe und Freundschaft unter den Menschen verschaffe; so wird die Republik eingeleitet mit der Untersuchung, was das Gerechte sei. Diese Verwirrung hat nun die Wirkung, zum Nachdenken zu

Socratic method without explaining why he chose this particular one. He uses Xenophon's *Memorabilia* and *Apology*, and also Plato's *Apology*, quite uncritically. On the whole, he does not like much fuss, and does not cast a benevolent eye even upon Schleiermacher's efforts to order the Platonic dialogues so that one great idea moves through them all in successive development. He says[533] (p. 179): "Das Literarische, das Kritische Herrn Schleiermachers, die kritische Sonderung, ob die einen oder die andern Neben-Dialoge ächt seien,—(über die groszen kann ohnehin nach den Zeugnissen der Alten kein Zweifel sein),—ist für Philosophie ganz überflüssig, und gehört der Hyper-Kritik unserer Zeit an [Moreover, it is quite superfluous for philosophy, and belongs to the hypercriticism of our times, to treat Plato from a literary point of view, as Schleiermacher does, critically examining whether one or another of the minor dialogues is genuine or not (the testimony of the ancients leaves no doubt about the important ones)]." Anything like this is effort wasted on Hegel, and when the phenomena are paraded, he is in too much of a hurry and is too aware of the great importance of his role as commander-in-chief of world history to take time for more than the royal glimpse he allows to glide over them.

Although he is thereby spared considerable prolixity, he also misses some things that in a complete account would be a necessary element. This is why something that suffers the injustice of being overlooked in this way sometimes intrudes
XIII elsewhere in order to claim its due. Thus in Hegel's discussion
302 of Plato's system there appear various loosely scattered remarks claiming to be absolute because the whole context in which they would have manifested themselves in their relative truth (but therefore all the more justified) is destroyed. Page

führen; und diesz ist der Zweck des Socrates. Diese blosz *negative* Seite ist die Hauptsache [A number of dialogues end in the same manner, both in Xenophon and Plato, leaving us quite unsatisfied as to the conclusion (contents). It is so in the *Lysis:* what do love and friendship secure for men; similarly the *Republic* commences by inquiring what justice is. This confusion now has the effect of leading to reflection, and this is Socrates' aim. This purely *negative* side is the main thing]."[532]

184: "Was von dem in den Dialogen Dargestellten dem Socrates oder dem Platon angehöre, bedarf keiner weiteren Untersuchung. So viel ist gewisz, dasz wir aus Platos Dialogen sein System vollkommen zu erkennen im Stande sind." Page 222: "Diese Dialectik (i.e., whose result is merely negative) sehen wir bei Plato häufig, Theils in den mehr eigentlich socratischen,* moralischen Dialogen, Theils auch in den vielen Dialogen, welche sich auf die Vorstellung der Sophisten von der Wissenschaft beziehen." Page 226: "Die Dialectik in dieser höheren Bestimmung (as that which resolves the contrasts in the universal, so that this resolution of the contradiction is the affirmative) ist die eigentlich platonische."** Page 230: "Viele Dialoge enthalten so nur negative Dialectik; das ist die socratische Unterredung [(184) There is, therefore, no need to inquire further as to what belongs to Socrates in the dialogues and what belongs to Plato. This much is certain—we are perfectly able to understand Plato's system from his dialogues. (222) We find this dialectic (. . .) a great deal in Plato, both in the more really Socratic* and moralizing dialogues, and in many dialogues which relate to the conceptions of the Sophists in regard to science. (226) Dialectic in this higher sense (. . .) is the really Platonic.** (230) Many dialogues contain merely negative dialectic, and this is the Socratic conversation]." These separate observations are in complete agreement with what I tried to point out in the first section of this study. But since they are such casual remarks, I cannot go on adducing them.

The discussion proper of Socrates is found in *Geschichte der Philosophie* (XVIII, pp. 42-122),[534] and it is to this I shall now proceed. This discussion by Hegel is remarkable in that it ends as it begins—with the person of Socrates. Even though in various places Hegel seems to want to reclaim a positivity for him, and even though he attributes to him the idea of the

* By means of the predicate "more really Socratic," Hegel here makes a distinction between the dialogues, without indicating, however, how satisfied he is with the philological endeavors.

** In calling this dialectic "the really Platonic," he is creating a contrast to another dialectic that is not as really Platonic.

good, it nevertheless turns out that the individual, in relation to the good, is arbitrarily self-determining, and that the good as such has no absolute binding power. On page 93 it says, "Das Subject ist das Bestimmende, das Entscheidende. Ob guter oder schlechter Geist entscheide, bestimmt jetzt das Subject [The subject is the determining and deciding principle. Whether the mind deciding is good or bad, the subject
XIII now determines]."[535] (In other words, the subject stands freely
303 above that which must properly be regarded as determinative for him; he stands freely above it not only in a moment of choice but at every instant, since arbitrariness constitutes no law, no constancy, no content.) [*Pages 93-94, continued:*] "Der Punkt der Entscheidung aus sich selbst fing an, bei Socrates aufzugehen; dieses war bei den Griechen bewusztloses Bestimmen. Bei Socrates wird dieser entscheidende Geist in das subjective Bewusztseyn des Menschen verlegt; und die Frage ist nun zunächst, wie diese Subjectivität an Socrates selbst erscheint. Indem die Person, das Individuum zum Entscheidenden wird, so kommen wir auf diese Weise auf Socrates *als Person*, als Subject zurück; und das Folgende ist nun eine Entwickelung seiner persönlichen Verhältnisse [The point of deciding within oneself began to unfold with Socrates; with the Greeks this was an unconscious determination. With Socrates the deciding spirit is situated in the subjective consciousness of man, and now the next question is how this subjectivity appears in Socrates himself. Because the person, the individual, now gives the decision, we return in this way to Socrates *as person*, as subject, and what follows is a development of his personal relations]."

The form in which subjectivity now manifests itself in Socrates is the daimonian, but since Hegel himself correctly points out that the daimonian is still not conscience, one sees how subjectivity in Socrates vibrates between the finite subjectivity and the infinite, since in conscience the finite subject makes itself infinite. Page 95: "Gewissen ist die Vorstellung allgemeiner Individualität, des seiner selbst gewissen Geistes, der zugleich allgemeine Wahrheit ist. Der Dämon des Socrates ist die ganz nothwendige andere Seite zu seiner Allgemeinheit;

wie ihm diese zum Bewusztseyn kam, so auch die andere Seite, die Einzelnheit des Geistes. Sein *reines Bewusztseyn* stand *über beiden Seiten.* Welcher Mangel in dieser Seite, werden wir sogleich bestimmen: nämlich der Mangel des Allgemeinen ist ersetzt selbst mangelhaft, auf eine einzelne Weise, nicht Wiederherstellung des Verdorbenen für das Negative [Conscience is the representation of universal individuality, of the mind certain of itself, which is at the same time universal truth. The daimon of Socrates is the entirely necessary other side of his universality; as this came to consciousness in him, so also the other side, the individuality of mind. His *pure consciousness* stands *over both sides.* We shall promptly specify the lack of this side: namely, the lack of the universal is amended in an individual manner that is itself lacking, not a reinstatement of corruption in the place of the negative]."[536] But that his pure consciousness stood above both sides is clearly what I have expressed by saying that he had the idea of the good as the infinite negativity.

The many excellent particular comments found in this section of Hegel and the pregnancy of thought that characterizes him would be difficult to discuss coherently, inasmuch as so much is often put together that it is hard to find the coherence.[537] Various things have already been used previously in this dissertation. However, when I consider the Hegelian account in its totality and consider it in relation to the modification I have advanced, I believe that it all can best be dealt
with under one rubric: In what sense is Socrates the founder XIII
of morality?[538] Under this rubric, the most important ele- 304
ments of Hegel's view [of Socrates] will be discussed.

In What Sense Is Socrates the Founder of Morality?

In very general terms, Hegel describes Socrates' importance in the development as follows (p. 43): "Socrates spricht nun das Wesen als das allgemeine Ich aus, *als das Gute*, das in sich selbst ruhende Bewusztseyn; das Gute, als solches, frei von der seyender Realität, frei gegen das Verhältnisz des Bewusztseyns zu seyender Realität—es sey einzelnes sinnliches Bewusztsein (Gefühl und Neigungen),—oder endlich frei von dem theoretisch über die Natur speculirenden Gedanken, der ob zwar er Gedanke, doch noch die Form des Seyns hat, Ich bin darin nicht als meiner gewisz [Socrates expresses essence as the universal I, *as the good*, the consciousness resting in itself; the good as such, free from existent reality, free toward the relation of consciousness to existent reality—it is individual sensuous consciousness (feeling and inclination)—or finally free from the theoretically speculative thought about nature, which, if it is indeed thought, still has the form of Being and in which I am not certain of my existence]."[539] Thus Socrates has arrived at being-in-and-for-itself as the being-in-and-for-itself for thought. This is the one element; the other is that this good, this universal, must be recognized by me.

Lest more be read into this than is there according to Hegel, it is necessary to say a little about his teaching. That Socrates' teaching, in Hegel's opinion, was negative, was intended to be negative, was designed to shake up and not to firm up, that in Socrates the negative is not immanental in a positivity, but is self-oriented, is already apparent in the several scattered quotations I have given and from a multitude of observations found in the section treating particularly of Socrates, but it comes out ever more clearly in the way in which Hegel discusses Aristophanes' view of Socrates. On page 85,[540] he makes the comment that it is Aristophanes who has interpreted Socratic philosophy from the negative side, whereby the whole established order vanishes in the indefinite universal. He notes that it could not occur to him to justify or simply to excuse Aristophanes. Page 89: "Die Uebertreibung, die man dem Aristophanes zuschieben könnte, ist, dasz er diese Dialectik zur ganzen Bitterkeit der Conseqvenz fortgetrieben hat; es kann jedoch nicht gesagt werden, dasz dem Socrates Unrecht geschehen mit dieser Darstellung. Aristophanes hat durchaus *nicht Unrecht*, ja man musz sogar seine Tiefe bewundern, die Seite des Dialectischen des Socrates als eines Negativen erkannt und (nach seiner Weise freilich) mit so festem
XIII 305 Pinsel dargestellt zu haben . . . . . Socrates' Allgemeinheit hat die negative Seite des Aufhebens der Wahrheit (Gesetze), wie sie im unbefangenen Bewusztseyn ist; —diesz Bewusztseyn

wird so die reine Freiheit über den bestimmten Inhalt, der ihm als an sich galt [The exaggeration which may be ascribed to Aristophanes is that he drove this dialectic to its bitter end; yet it cannot be said that injustice is done to Socrates by this representation. Aristophanes was *not unjust* in this; indeed, one must admire his depth in having recognized the dialectical aspect in Socrates as being negative and in having presented it (though after his own way) so forcibly . . . . . Socrates' universality has the negative aspect of the annulment of truth (laws) as it is in natural consciousness; —this consciousness thus becomes the pure freedom over the determinate content, which for him was valid in itself]."[541]

That his teaching was negative is also articulated in another way by Hegel in the observation that his philosophy actually was not speculative philosophy but "ein *individuelles Thun* [an *individual doing*]" (p. 53).[542] In order to evoke this individual action he moralized: "es ist aber nicht eine Art und Weise von Predigen, Ermahnen, Dociren, düsteres Moralisiren u. s. f. [but its nature and method are not that of preaching, exhorting, teaching, of a dry moralizing etc.]" (p. 58).[543] Anything like that was not in accord with Greek urbanity. This moralizing manifested itself, however, in his prompting everyone to think about his duties. He entered into the interests of the young and old, shoemakers, blacksmiths, Sophists, politicians, citizens of every kind, whether they were domestic interests (bringing up children) or intellectual interests, and directed their thinking away from the specific incident to the universal, the in-and-for-itself truth and beauty (p. 59).[544]

Here, then, we have the significance of his moralizing, and here it is clear what Hegel means when he, in line with the tradition of antiquity, calls Socrates the founder of morality. However, the rather familiar meaning of morality as found in Hegel must not be neglected. He distinguishes between *morality* [*Moralitet*] and *ethics* [*Sædelighed*].[545] But ethics is in part unreflected ethics such as ancient Greek ethics, and in part a higher determination of it such as manifests itself again after having recollected itself in morality. For this reason, in his *Philosophie des Rechts* he discusses morality before proceeding to ethics.[546] And under morality he discusses in the section "Good and Conscience" the moral forms of evil, hypocrisy, probabilism, Jesuitism, the appeal to the conscience, irony.[547] Here the moral individual is the negatively free individual. He is free because he is not bound by another, but he is negatively free precisely because he is not limited in another. When the individual by being in his other is in his own, then for the first time he is in truth (i.e., positively) free, affirmatively free. Therefore, moral freedom is arbitrariness; it is the possibility of good and evil.

Hegel himself says this in *Philosophie des Rechts* (p. 184):
XIII 306 "Das Gewissen ist als formelle Subjectivität schlechthin diesz auf dem Sprunge zu seyn, ins Böse umzuschlagen [The conscience as formal subjectivity is simply to be on the verge of slipping into evil]."[548] In the old Greek culture, the individual was by no means free in this sense but was confined in the substantial ethic; he had not as yet taken himself out of, separated himself from, this immediate relationship, still did not know himself. Socrates brought this about, but not in the sense of the Sophists, who taught the individual to constrict himself in his own particular interests; he brought the individual to this by universalizing subjectivity, and to that extent he is the founder of morality. He maintained, not sophistically but speculatively, the importance of consciousness. He arrived at being-in-and-for-itself as the being-in-and-for-itself for thought; he arrived at the definition of knowledge that made the individual alien to the immediacy in which he had previously lived. The individual should no longer act out of fear of the law but with a conscious knowledge of why he acted. But this, as we shall see, is a negative definition, negative toward the established order as well as negative toward the deeper positivity, which, as speculative, conditions negatively.

This is also manifest in connection with the definition of the concept of virtue. Hegel goes through Aristotle's view of Socrates' definition of virtue, and we shall follow him. On page 77 he quotes Aristotle as saying: "Socrates hat besser von der Tugend gesprochen, als Pythagoras, aber auch nicht ganz richtig, da er die Tugenden zu einem Wissen (ἐπιστήμας)

machte. Diesz ist nämlich unmöglich. Denn alles Wissen ist mit einem Grunde (λόγος) verbunden, der Grund aber ist nur im Denken; mithin setzt er alle Tugenden in die Einsicht (Erkenntnisz). Es widerfährt ihm daher, dasz er die alogische—empfindende—Seite der Seele aufhebt: nämlich die Leidenschaft (πάθος) und die Sitte (ἦθος) [Socrates spoke better of virtue than did Pythagoras, but not quite justly, for he made virtues into a science (ἐπιστήμας). But this is impossible, since, though all knowledge has some basis (λόγος) this basis exists only in thought. Consequently, he places all the virtues in judgment (cognition). Hence it comes to pass that he does away with the irrational-feeling part of the soul, that is, inclination (πάθπος) and habit (ἦθος)]."[549] Hegel goes on to say that this is a good criticism: "Wir sehen, dasz dasjenige, was Aristoteles an der Bestimmung der Tugend bei Socrates vermiszt, die Seite der subjectiven Wirklichkeit—heutiges Tages Herz—ist [We see that what Aristotle misses in the determination of virtue in Socrates is the side of subjective actuality which we now call the heart]."[550] Thus what virtue lacks is a qualification of being, whether this is viewed in relation to the individual subject or in a higher sense is regarded as actualized in the state. But Socrates destroyed the immediate, substantial political consciousness and did not arrive at the idea of the state, and as a result virtue can be defined only in this abstract way and has its reality neither in the state nor in the full per- XIII
sonality* yielded only by the state. 307

On page 78, Hegel quotes Aristotle further as saying: "Socrates habe einer Seits ganz richtig geforscht, anderer Seits aber unrichtig. Dasz die Tugend Wissenschaft sey, sey unwahr, aber dasz sie nicht ohne Einsicht (ohne Wissen) sey,

* Socrates is customarily cited as a paragon of virtue, and Hegel also holds to this view. On page 55 he says, "Socrates war ein Musterbild moralischer Tugenden: Weisheit, Bescheidenheit, Enthaltsamkeit, Mäszigung, Gerechtigkeit, Tapferkeit, Unbeugsamkeit, feste Rechtlichkeit gegen Tyrannen und δῆμος, entfernt von Habsucht, Herrschsucht [Socrates was a model of the moral virtues: of wisdom, discretion, temperance, moderation, justice, courage, inflexibility, firm sense of rectitude in relation to tyrants and people; he was removed from cupidity and despotism]."[551] This is undoubtedly true, but the

darin habe er recht. Er habe die Tugend zum Logos gemacht; wir aber sagen sie ist mit dem Logos [Socrates in one respect worked on right lines, but not in the other. For to call virtue scientific knowledge is untrue, but to say that it is not without scientific basis (without knowledge) is right. Socrates made virtue into perceptions (*Logos*), but we say that virtue exists
XIII 308 with perception]."*[553] Once again Hegel says that this is a very accurate definition. It is one side, that the universal begins with thought, but it is part and parcel of virtue as character that a person is that, and that involves the heart, temperament, etc. Consequently, there are two sides: the universal and the actualizing individuality, the real spirit [*reale Aand*].

---

very predicate "moral" that Hegel applies to these virtues already indicates that they nevertheless lacked the deep earnestness that every virtue acquires only when it is ordered in a totality. But since the state had lost its significance for Socrates, his virtues are not civic virtues but personal virtues—indeed, to define them more sharply, they are imaginatively constructed virtues. The individual stands freely above them. If Socrates is therefore free of the prudery that is so often manifest in strict moralists, and if we must agree with Hegel when he says (p. 56) "dasz wir uns Socrates durchaus nicht in der Weise von der Litanei der moralischen Tugend zu denken haben [that we have not to think of Socrates throughout after the fashion of the litany of moral virtues],"[552] then it becomes just as certain that all such virtues have reality for the individual only as imaginary constructions. He stands freely above them, can dispense with them when he wants to, and insofar as he does not do so, it is because he does not want to, but that he does not want to is again because he does not want to—he never feels a deeper commitment to them than that. To that extent, it may fairly be said that these virtues do not involve the individual's earnestness, even though he takes the matter ever so seriously, provided one does not deny that every arbitrary exercise essentially lacks earnestness and is nothing other than Sophistry in the realm of action.

* With respect to Socrates, the thesis that virtue is knowledge can also be elucidated from another side if we remember the other thesis, that sin is ignorance,[554] a Socratic thesis we have already referred to several times. The thesis that virtue is knowledge contains not only, as already treated, a negative qualification in contrast to the uncommitted and natural ethics [*Sædelighed*], which in all innocence does not know what it is doing, but also an indication of the infinite consistency of the good, whereby in its abstract movement it goes beyond every finite qualification. This is seen even more clearly in the
XIII 308 thesis that sin is ignorance, because this implies that sin is inconsistency. Sin stops somewhere, falls away, and does not remain in the infinity that the good has. When virtue as a qualification of knowledge detaches itself from the im-

Here we have come once again to the point where the sense in which Socrates had a positivity will become evident. That is, we have come back to the point we left in the discussion of his teaching. This involved letting the universal manifest itself in contrast to the particular. Thus, the first qualification with regard to the Socratic principle is the major one, even though it is still only formal: that consciousness draws from itself what constitutes truth (see p. 71).[555] This is the principle of subjective freedom: that one carries consciousness within oneself. The universal thereby comes to be visible. But the universal has a positive and a negative side (p. 79).

We shall now see how successful Hegel was in demonstrating a positive side to Socrates' conception of the universal, or perhaps we should turn back to a comment by Hegel (p. 70) that by way of a kind of caption—"Diesz ist kurz die Manier—(und die Philosophie)—des Socrates [this, in short, is the method—(and the philosophy)—of Socrates]"—has already announced itself as an observation that ought to be credited with exceptional value. To this he adds: "Es scheint, als hätten wir noch nicht viel von der socratischen Philosophie dargelegt, indem wir uns nur an das Princip gehalten haben; diesz ist aber die Hauptsache, dasz das Bewusztseyn des Socrates selbst erst zu diesem Abstracten gekommen ist. *Das Gute* ist das Allgemeine . . . . .. Es ist ein in sich concretes Princip, das aber in seiner concreten Bestimmung noch nicht dargestellt ist; und in dieser abstracten Haltung liegt der Mangel des so- XIII
cratischen Princips. Affirmatives läszt sich *nicht* angeben; denn 309
es hat keine weitere Entwickelung [It now seems as if we had not yet shown forth much of the Socratic philosophy, for we

mediate ethics, it assumes an ideal form that corresponds to the ideal infinity of the good. In the substantial ethics, virtue is limited at all times, knows in the ideality of ethics that it is taken up into the infinity of the good, knows itself in the infinity in which the good knows itself. But all these are still always abstract, negative qualifications as long as one stops with qualifications of pure knowledge, even though it is the infinite, absolute negativity. The thesis that sin is ignorance and inconsistency is true from a totally abstract, metaphysical position that regards everything only according to its infinite intrinsic consistency.

have merely kept to the principle; but the main point with Socrates is that his knowledge for the first time reached this abstraction. *The good* is the universal . . . . .. It is a principle, concrete within itself, which, however, is not yet manifested in its concrete qualification, and in this abstract attitude we find what is wanting in the Socratic principle. It can *not* be formulated positively, because it has no further development]."[556]

In comparison with the Sophists, Socrates has taken a giant stride in arriving at the in-and-for-itself good. The Sophists stopped with the infinite refraction of the good in the multiplicity of the useful and the advantageous. But please note that he arrived at this; he did not proceed from it. Consequently, the universal has a positive and a negative side. The reality of ethics has become shaky, and this came to consciousness in Socrates. He raised ethics to insight, but this means precisely to bring to consciousness the fact that in their definiteness, their immediacy, ethical customs and laws are shaky; this "ist die Macht des Begriffs, welche diesz unmittelbare Seyn und Gelten derselben, die Heiligkeit ihres Ansichseyns aufhebt [is the power of the Notion which sublates the determinate existence and the immediate value of moral laws and the sacredness of their implicitude]."[557]

As an example of the fact that the universal has a positive side in Socrates ("er zeigte ihnen [the young men] das Gute und Wahre in dem Bestimmten, in das er zurückging, da er es nicht bei dem blosz Abstracten bewenden lassen wollte [he showed them (. . .) the good and true in what is determined, going back into it because he did not wish to remain in mere abstraction]"), Hegel quotes from Socrates' conversation with the Sophist Hippias (Xenophon, *Memorabilia*, IV, 4, 12-16, 25[558]). Here Socrates generally affirms the thesis that it is the just who obey the laws, and against the argument that laws, after all, cannot be absolute since people and sovereigns often change them, he affirms the thesis by presenting the analogy that those who make war also in turn make peace. Here he says in general that the best and the happiest state is the one in which the citizens are of one mind and obey the laws. Hegel

sees in this an affirmative content. But the reason Socrates has something affirmative here is that he does not carry through his position, he does not continue on to the in-and-for-itself good, at which he does actually arrive. Here he lets the established order [*Bestaaende*] continue, and as a result this is not the positivity that follows from his infinite negation but a positivity that precedes it. Yet by this movement he does indeed go beyond the immediate Greek culture, since he does, after all, take the laws up into reflection and thereby takes them out of their immediate givenness, but this still is actually no more than a simulated movement and is by no means the genuine Socratic movement. Thus whatever positivity there is here cannot decide anything with regard to the question of the extent to which Socrates maintained a positivity or to which the universal became concrete for him. Hegel, too, senses this, as we see from his comments on pp. 79 middle, 81 bottom, and XIII 310
82 top.

Hegel also cites examples of the negative side, and since we now have seen that the positive side was not positive in the same sense as the other was negative, we see that Socrates has advanced the universal only as the negative. Hegel cites an example from Xenophon and adds (p. 83): "Hier sehen wir die negative Seite, dasz Socrates das wankend macht, was der Vorstellung sonst fest war. Nicht lügen, nicht betrügen, nicht rauben gilt in der unbefangenen Vorstellung für recht,—diesz ist ihr das Feste; aber durch die Vergleichung dieses für fest Gehaltenen mit Anderem, das ihr ebenso fest als wahr gilt, zeigt sich, dasz sie sich widersprechen,—und jenes Feste wird wankend, es gilt nicht mehr für fest. Das Positive, was Socrates an die Stelle des Festen setzt, ist eines Theils im Gegensatze wieder dieses, den Gesetzen zu gehorchen: wir sehen ganz das Allgemeine, Unbestimmte, und 'den Gesetzen gehorchen' versteht nun jeder, der diesz hört, eben die Gesetze ausgedrückt, wie die allgemeine Vorstellung derselben sich bewuszt ist, nicht lügen, nicht betrügen; aber diese Gesetze sind eben diesz, dasz sie so im Allgemeinen Lügen, Betrügen, Rauben als Unrecht aufstellen,—Bestimmungen, die für den Begriff nicht aushalten [Here we see the negative side, namely, that Socrates renders shaky what has hitherto been fixed and firm to representational reflection. To refrain from lying, deceiving, and stealing is regarded as right—as something fixed and firm—to this natural reflection; but then the comparison of the fixed and the firm with something else of equal truth and fixity shows that they contradict each other. Hence, what has formerly been fixed and firm becomes shaky and is no longer valid as fixed and firm. The positive that Socrates sets in the place of the fixed and the firm, and partly in opposition to it, is once again this: to obey the laws. Here we see the universal, the indeterminate; and by the phrase 'to obey the laws,' everyone who hears it will indeed understand the laws expressed in such a way that the universal representational reflection is conscious of them, that is, do not lie, do not deceive. But these very laws establish lying, deceiving, and stealing as universally wrong—as determinants that cannot withstand the concept]." Page 85: "Hier sehen wir also das Allgemeine so bestimmt, realisirt: allgemeines Nennen der Gesetze; in Wahrheit aber, da diese verschwindende Momente sind: das unbestimmte Allgemeine, und *den Mangel* seiner Unbestimmtheit *noch nicht* ergänzt [Here we see the universal determined and realized: a general announcement of laws. But inasmuch as these laws are vanishing elements, we see in truth the indeterminate universal, and *the deficiency* of its indeterminateness *as yet* incomplete]." Hegel then proceeds to show (pp. 90 top ff.) "wie dem Socrates selbst das Realisirende des Allgemeinen erschien [the mode in which the actualization of the universal appeared to Socrates himself]." Here the subject shows itself to be the deciding factor, as that which arbitrarily determines itself within itself. But the limiting of the universal that takes place thereby is one that the subject himself arbitrarily posits at every moment. It is possible for this curtailment of the universal to remain fast and not be occasional, for the universal to be acknowledged in its determinateness, only in a total system of actuality. But this Socrates lacks. He negated the state, but he did not come back again to the state in a higher form in which the infinite he negatively required is affirmed.

We see, therefore, how Socrates can very well be called the founder of morality in the sense Hegel thinks of it, and that his position still could have been irony. The good as task, when the good is understood as the infinitely negative, corresponds to the moral, that is, the negatively free subject. The moral individual can never actualize the good; only the posi- XIII
tively free subject can have the good as the infinitely positive, 311
as his task, and fulfill it. If we wish to include the qualification of irony, which Hegel so frequently stresses, that for irony nothing is a matter of earnestness,[559] then this can also be claimed for the negatively free subject, because even the virtues he practices are not done with earnestness, provided that—and Hegel certainly would agree with this—true earnestness is possible only in a totality in which the subject no longer arbitrarily decides at every moment to continue his imaginary construction but feels the task to be something that he has not assigned himself but that has been assigned to him.*

It is upon this point—to show Socrates as the founder of morality—that Hegel unilaterally concentrates his view of Socrates. It is the idea of the good he wants to claim for Socrates, but he gets into trouble thereby since he must show how Socrates interpreted the good. The real difficulty with Hegel's view of Socrates is centered in the continual attempt to show how Socrates interpreted the good, and what is even more wrong in the view, as I see it, is that it does not accurately adhere to the direction of the trend in Socrates' life. The movement in Socrates is toward arriving at the good. His significance in the world development is to arrive there (not to have arrived there at some time). His significance for his contemporaries is that they arrived there. Now, this does not mean that he arrived there almost toward the end of his life, but that his life was a continual arriving at the good and having others arrive at this. But in so doing he also arrived at the

* In Plato's *Republic*,[560] dialectic corresponds to the good (just as love corresponds to the beautiful). Thus it is entirely legitimate for Aristotle[561] to declare Socrates devoid of dialectic. He lacked the dialectic that can allow the contrary to stand, but precisely this is necessary if the good is to manifest itself as the infinitely positive.

true, that is, the true in-and-for-itself, at the beautiful, that is, the beautiful in-and-for-itself, in general, at being-in-and-for-itself as the being-in-and-for-itself for thought. He arrived at this and was continually arriving at this. Therefore, he did not just moralize but on the whole let the being-in-and-for-itself become visible in the qualifications of the manifold. He spoke with artists about the beautiful, let the beautiful in-and-for-
XIII 312 itself work itself out (*via negationis*[562]) of the qualifications of being in which it had been hitherto. The same with the true.

This he did not do once and for all but did it with each individual. He began anywhere and quickly was in full swing clearing each one. But as soon as he had taken one person across, he immediately came back. No actuality could resist him, but what became visible was ideality in the most evanescent intimation of the slightest limitation—that is, ideality as infinitely abstract. Just as Charon[563] took people across from the fullness of life to the shadowy land of the underworld, just as he, lest his frail boat be overloaded, had the travelers divest themselves of all the manifold qualifications of concrete life, of titles, honors, purple robes, pompous words, sorrows, anxieties, etc., until only the sheer human being remained, so Socrates also shipped individuals from reality [*Realitet*] to ideality; and the ideal infinity as the infinite negativity was the nothing into which he had the entire multiplicity of reality disappear. Inasmuch as Socrates continually let being-in-and-for-itself become visible, it might seem that here, at least, was his earnestness. But precisely because he only arrived at it, had being-in-and-for-itself only as the infinitely abstract, he had the absolute in the form of nothing. By way of the absolute, reality became nothing, but in turn the absolute was nothing. But in order to be able to hold him fast at this point, in order never to forget that the content of his life was to make this movement at every moment, we must recollect his significance as a divine missionary. Although Socrates himself places much weight on his divine mission, Hegel has ignored this. As for the continual temptation to attribute something more to him, this is due to the failure to see that world-historical individualities are great precisely because their entire lives belong to the world and they, as it were, have nothing for themselves. But this is also why the world has all the more for which to thank them.

In Hegel's description of the Socratic method, there are particularly two forms of it that become subjects for discussion: his irony and his midwifery.[564] The space Hegel gives to irony is itself sufficient indication that he views irony in Socrates XIII 313 more as a controlled element, a way of associating with people, and this is confirmed by explicit statements. How this must be understood and to what extent Hegel is right in this will now be the object of investigation. With this, I proceed to the second part of the dissertation, namely: the concept of irony.

Part Two

THE CONCEPT OF IRONY

INTRODUCTION

The object of investigation in this part has already been given to a certain extent in the first part, insofar as this permitted one aspect of the concept to appear in the form of contemplation. Therefore, in the first part I have not so much assumed the concept as I have let it come into existence while I sought to orient myself in the phenomenon. In so doing, I have found an unknown quantity, a position that appeared to have been characteristic of Socrates. I have called this position irony, but in the first part of the dissertation the term for it is of minor importance; the main thing is that no factor or feature has been slighted, also that all the factors and features have grouped themselves into a totality. Whether or not this position is irony will first be decided now as I come to that point in developing the concept in which Socrates must fit if his position was really irony at all. But just as I dealt in the first part of the dissertation solely with Socrates, so in the development of the concept it will become apparent in what sense he is a factor in the development of the concept—in other words, it will become apparent whether the concept of irony is absolutely exhausted in him or whether there are other modes to be inspected before we can say that the concept has been adequately interpreted.

Therefore, just as in the first part of the dissertation the concept always hovered in the background with a continual craving to take shape in the phenomenon, just so in this part of the dissertation the phenomenal manifestation of the concept, as
a continual possibility to take up residence among us, will ac- XIII 318
company the progress of the discussion. These two factors are inseparable, because if the concept were not in the phenomenon or, more correctly, if the phenomenon were not understandable, actual, only in and with the concept, and if the phenomenon were not in the concept or, more correctly, if from the outset the concept were not understandable, actual, in and

with the phenomenon, then all knowledge would be impossible, inasmuch as I in the first case would be lacking the truth and in the second case the actuality.

Now, if irony is a qualification of subjectivity, we shall promptly see the necessity of two manifestations of this concept, and actuality has indeed attached the name to them. The first one, of course, is the one in which subjectivity asserts its rights in world history for the first time. Here we have Socrates, that is, we are hereby shown where we should look for the concept in its historical manifestation. But once having made its appearance in the world, subjectivity did not vanish again without a trace, the world did not sink back again into the earlier form of development; on the contrary, the old vanished and everything became new. For a new mode of irony to be able to appear now, it must result from the assertion of subjectivity in a still higher form. It must be subjectivity raised to the second power, a subjectivity's subjectivity, which corresponds to reflection's reflection. With this we are once again world-historically oriented—that is, we are referred to the development that modern philosophy attained in Kant and that is completed in Fichte, and more specifically again to the positions that after Fichte sought to affirm subjectivity in its second potency. Actuality bears out that this hangs together properly, for here again we meet irony. But since this position is an intensified subjective consciousness, it quite naturally is clearly and definitely conscious of irony and declares irony as its position. This was indeed the case with Friedrich Schlegel,[1] who sought to bring it to bear in relation to actuality; with Tieck,[2] who sought to bring it to bear in poetry; and with Solger,[3] who became esthetically and philosophically conscious of it. Finally, here irony also met its master in Hegel.[4] Whereas the first form of irony was not combated but was pacified by subjectivity as it obtained its rights, the second form of irony was combated and destroyed, for inasmuch as subjectivity was unauthorized it could obtain its rights only by being annulled.

If these observations are adequate for orientation in the history of the concept of irony, this by no means implies that an

interpretation of this concept, insofar as it seeks a stronghold
and support in what was developed earlier, is not fraught with
difficulty. Insofar as we seek a thorough and coherent devel- XIII 319
opment of this concept, we shall soon be convinced that it has
a strange history or, more correctly, no history. In the period
after Fichte, when it was especially current, we find it mentioned again and again, suggested again and again, presupposed again and again. However, if we are looking for a clear exposition, we look in vain.* Solger laments that A. W. v. Schlegel in his *Vorlesungen über dramatische Kunst und Litteratur*,[6] where, if anywhere, we would expect to find adequate information, cursorily mentions it but once. Hegel** laments that with Solger it was the same and no better with Tieck.

* *Solgers nachgelassene Schriften und Briefwechsel*, ed. Ludwig Tieck and Friedrich v. Raumer, II, p. 514 (in a critique of A. W. v. Schlegel's lectures): "Es war dem Rec. höchst auffallend, der Ironie, in welcher er den wahren Mittelpunct der ganzen dramatischen Kunst erkennt, so dasz sie auch beim philosophischen Dialog, wenn er einigermaszen dramatisch seyn soll, nicht zu entbehren ist, in dem ganzen Werke nur Einmal erwähnt zu finden, Th. II. Abth. 2, S. 72, und noch dazu um ihr alle Einmischung in das eigentliche Tragische zu untersagen; und doch erinnert er sich an frühere Aeuszerungen des Verfassers, welche sich an diese Ideen wenigstens sehr anzunähern schienen. Die Ironie ist aber auch das gerade Gegentheil jener Ansicht des Lebens, in welcher Ernst und Scherz, wie sie der Verfasser annimmt, wurzeln [As reviewer I was stunned by finding irony (which I regard as the true focus of all dramatic art and also as indispensable to philosophical dialogue if it is to be properly dramatic) mentioned only once in the entire work (pt. II, sec. 2, p. 72) and then for the sake of prohibiting irony from any and all intermingling in the genuinely tragic. And yet the reviewer can recall previous statements of this author that at least appear to approximate this idea. But irony is the very opposite of that view of life in which, as the author supposes, seriousness and jest are rooted]."[5]

** Hegel, *Werke*, XVI, p. 492 (in a review of Solger's posthumous writings): "Dasselbe ist Solger'n begegnet; in den speculativen Expositionen der höchsten Idee, die er in der oben angeführten Abhandlung mit dem innersten Geistesernste giebt, *erwähnt* er der Ironie *gar nicht*, sie, welche mit der Begeisterung auf's Innigste vereint, und in deren Tiefe Kunst, Religion und Philosophie identisch seyen. Gerade dort, hätte man geglaubt, müsse der Ort seyn, wo man in's Klare gesetzt finden werde, was es denn mit dem vornehmen Geheimnisse, dem groszen Unbekannten—der Ironie—für eine philosophische Bewandtnisz habe [The same happened with Solger; in the speculative exposition of the highest Idea, which in the above-mentioned work is

Since they all lament, why should I not also lament? My lament is that it is just the reverse with Hegel. At the point in all his systems where we could expect to find a development of irony, we find it referred to. Although, if it all were copied, we would have to concede that what is said about irony is in one sense not so inconsiderable, in another sense it is not
XIII much, since he says just about the same thing on every point.
320 Add to this the fact that he directs his attack against the particular and often disparate ideas we have attached to the word "irony," and as a result, since usage is not constant, his polemic is not always entirely clear. Yet I am far from being able to lament justifiably over Hegel in the same sense as Hegel laments over his predecessors. There are excellent observations especially in his review of Solger's posthumous writings (in vol. XVI of his collected works). And even if the presentation and characterization of negative positions (since *loquere, ut videam te* [speak, so that I may see you] is particularly pertinent to the characterization of these positions) are not always as exhaustive, as rich in content, as we could wish, Hegel knows all the better how to deal with them, and thus the positivity he asserts contributes indirectly to his characterization. While the Schlegels and Tieck had their major importance in the polemic with which they destroyed a previous development, and while precisely for this reason their position became somewhat scattered, because it was not a principal battle they won but a multitude of skirmishes, Hegel, on the other hand, has absolute importance by defeating with his positive total view the polemic prudery, the subjugation of which, just as Queen Brynhild's virginity required more than an ordinary husband, required a Sigurd.[8] Jean Paul also mentions irony frequently, and some things are found in his *Aesthetik*,[9] but without any philosophic or genuinely esthetic authority. He

---

presented with the most intense intellectual earnestness, he *does not even mention* irony, that very irony that is in intimate union with enthusiasm and in whose depth art, religion, and philosophy are identical. Here, if anywhere, one would have expected to find a lucid presentation of what might philosophically be the case with that exclusive secret, that great unknown—irony]."[7] See the same place for Hegel's comments concerning Tieck.

speaks mainly as an esthetician, from a rich esthetic experience, instead of actually giving grounds for his esthetic position. Irony, humor, moods seem for him to be different languages, and his characterization is limited to expressing the same thought ironically, humorously, in the language of moods—somewhat as Franz Baader[10] at times, after having described some mystical theses, then translates them into mystical language.

But since the concept of irony has often acquired a different meaning in this way, the point is that one is not to use it altogether arbitrarily either knowingly or unknowingly; the point
is that, having embraced the ordinary use of language, one XIII
comes to see that the various meanings the word has acquired 321
in the course of time can still all be included here.

There was a time, and not so long ago, when one could score a success also here with a bit of irony, which compensated for all other deficiencies and helped one get through the world rather respectably, gave one the appearance of being cultured, of having a perspective on life, an understanding of the world, and to the initiated marked one as a member of an extensive intellectual freemasonry. Occasionally we still meet a representative of that vanished age who has preserved that subtle, sententious, equivocally divulging smile, that air of an intellectual courtier with which he had made his fortune in his youth and upon which he had built his whole future in the hope that he had overcome the world.[11]

Ah, but it was an illusion! His watchful eye looks in vain for a kindred soul, and if his days of glory were not still a fresh memory for a few, his facial expression would be a riddle to the contemporary age, in which he lives as a stranger and a foreigner.[12] Our age demands more; it demands, if not lofty pathos then at least loud pathos, if not speculation then at least conclusions, if not truth then at least persuasion, if not integrity then at least protestations of integrity, if not feeling then at least verbosity about feelings. Therefore, it also coins a totally different kind of privileged faces. It will not allow the mouth to be defiantly compressed or the upper lip to quiver mischievously; it demands that the mouth be open, for how, indeed, could one imagine a true and genuine patriot who is not delivering speeches; how could one visualize a profound thinker's dogmatic face without a mouth able to swallow the whole world; how could one picture a virtuoso on the cornucopia of the living word without a gaping mouth? It does not permit one to stand still and to concentrate; to walk slowly is already suspicious; and how could one even put up with anything like that in the stirring period in which we live, in this momentous age, which all agree is pregnant with the extraordinary? It hates isolation; indeed, how could it tolerate a person's having the daft idea of going through life alone—this age that hand in hand and arm in arm (just like itinerant journeymen and soldiers) lives for the idea of community?*

But even if irony is far from being the distinctive feature of our age, it by no means follows that irony has totally disappeared. Our age is not an age of doubt, either, but nevertheless many manifestations of doubt still survive, in which one can, as it were, study doubt, even though there is a qualitative difference between speculative doubt and common doubt about this or about that.[14] In oratory, for example, there frequently appears a figure of speech with the name of irony and the characteristic of saying the opposite of what is meant. Already here we have a quality that permeates all irony—namely, that the phenomenon is not the essence but the opposite of the essence. When I am speaking, the thought, the meaning, is the essence, and the word is the phenomenon. These two elements are absolutely necessary, and it is in this sense that Plato[15] has said that all thinking is a discourse. Now, truth demands identity, for if I had the thought without the word, then I would not have the thought; and if I had the word without the thought, then I would not have the word, either—just as one cannot say of children and deranged people that they speak. If I next consider the speaking subject, I once again have a qualification that permeates all irony—namely, the subject is negatively free. When I am aware as I speak that what I am saying is what I mean and that what I have said adequately expresses my meaning, and I assume that the person to whom I am talking grasps my meaning completely, then I am bound in what has been said—that is, I am positively free therein. Here the old verse is appropriate: *semel emissum volat irrevocabile verbum* [the word once let slip flies beyond recall].[16] I am also bound with respect to myself and cannot free myself any time I wish. If, however, what I said is not my meaning or the

* This is not meant to depreciate or deprecate the earnest efforts of the age, but it is certainly to be wished that the age were more earnest in its earnestness.[13]

opposite of my meaning, then I am free in relation to others and to myself.

XIII 323 The ironic figure of speech cancels itself, however, inasmuch as the one who is speaking assumes that his hearers understand him, and thus, through a negation of the immediate phenomenon, the essence becomes identical with the phenomenon. If it sometimes happens that an ironic figure of speech such as this is misunderstood, this is not the fault of the one who is speaking, except insofar as he has come to grips with such a crafty fellow as irony, who likes to play tricks just as much on friends as on foes. In fact, we say of such an ironic turn of speech: Its earnestness is not in earnest. The remark is so earnest that it is shocking, but the hearer in the know shares the secret lying behind it. But precisely thereby the irony is once again canceled. It is the most common form of irony to say something earnestly that is not meant in earnest. The second form of irony, to say as a jest, jestingly, something that is meant in earnest, is more rare.* But, as was mentioned, the ironic figure of speech cancels itself; it is like a riddle to which one at the same time has the solution.

The ironic figure of speech has still another property that characterizes all irony, a certain superiority[18] deriving from its not wanting to be understood immediately, even though it wants to be understood, with the result that this figure looks down, as it were, on plain and simple talk that everyone can promptly understand; it travels around, so to speak, in an exclusive incognito and looks down pitying from this high position on ordinary, prosaic talk. In everyday affairs, the ironic figure of speech appears especially in the higher circles as a prerogative belonging to the same category as the *bon ton* [good form] that requires smiling at innocence and looking upon virtue as narrow-mindedness, although one still believes in it up to a point.

Just as kings and princes speak French, the higher circles

* This most frequently happens in connection with a certain despair and thus is often found in humorists, for example, when Heine[17] waggishly ponders which is worse, a toothache or a bad conscience, and declares himself for the first.

(this, of course, must be understood according to an intellectual ordering of rank) speak ironically so that lay people will not be able to understand them, and to that extent irony is in the process of isolating itself; it does not wish to be generally understood. Consequently, irony does not cancel itself here. Moreover, it is only a secondary form of the ironic vanity[19] that desires witnesses in order to assure and reassure itself of XIII 324
itself, just as it also is only an inconsistency irony has in common with every negative position that irony, which is isolation according to its concept, seeks to form a society and, when it cannot elevate itself to the idea of community, tries to actualize itself in conventicles. This is why there is just as little social unity in a coterie of ironists as there is real honesty in a band of thieves.

Leaving this aspect of irony through which it opens itself to the inner circle and looking at irony in relation to the uninitiated, in relation to those against whom the polemic is directed, in relation to the existence it ironically interprets, we see that ordinarily it has two modes of expression. Either the ironist identifies himself with the odious practice he wants to attack, or he takes a hostile stance to it, but always, of course, in such a way that he himself is aware that his appearance is in contrast to what he himself embraces and that he thoroughly enjoys this discrepancy.

When it comes to a silly, inflated, know-it-all knowledge, it is ironically proper to go along, to be enraptured by all this wisdom, to spur it on with jubilating applause to ever greater lunacy, although the ironist is aware that the whole thing underneath is empty and void of substance. Over against an insipid and inept enthusiasm, it is ironically proper to outdo this with scandalous praise and plaudits, although the ironist is himself aware that this enthusiasm is the most ludicrous thing in the world. Indeed, the more successful the ironist is in beguiling, the further his fakery proceeds, the more joy he has in it. But he relishes this joy in private, and the source of his joy is that no one realizes his deception. —This is a form of irony that appears only rarely, although it is just as profound as the irony that appears under the form of opposition and is easier to carry through. On a small scale, it is sometimes seen used against a person about to be afflicted with one or another fixed idea, or against someone who imagines himself to be a handsome fellow or has especially beautiful sideburns or fancies himself to be witty or at least has said something so witty it cannot be repeated enough, or against someone whose life is wrapped up in a single event, to which he comes back again and again, and which he can be prompted to tell at any time merely by pressing the right button etc.

In all these cases, it is the ironist's joy to seem to be caught
XIII in the same noose in which the other person is trapped. It is
325 one of the ironist's chief joys to find weak sides such as this everywhere, and the more distinguished the person in whom it is found, the more joy he has in being able to take him in, to have him in his power, although that person himself is unaware of it. Thus at times even a distinguished person is like a puppet on a string for the ironist, a jumping-jack he can get to make the motions he wants it to make by pulling the string. Strangely enough, it is the weaker sides of the human being more than the good sides that come close to being Chladni figures that continually become visible when made to vibrate properly; they seem to have an intrinsic, natural necessity, whereas the good sides, to our dismay, so often suffer from inconsistencies.

But, on the other hand, it is just as characteristic of irony to emerge in an antithetical situation. Faced with a superfluity of wisdom and then to be so ignorant, so stupid, such a complete Simple Simon[20] as is possible, and yet always so good-natured and teachable that the tenant farmers of wisdom are really happy to let someone slip into their luxuriant pastures; faced with a sentimental, soulful enthusiasm, and then to be too dull to grasp the sublime that inspires others, yet always manifesting an eager willingness to grasp and understand what up until now was a riddle—these are altogether normal expressions of irony. And the more naïve the ironist's stupidity appears to be, the more genuine his honest and upright striving seems, the greater his joy. Thus we perceive that it can be just as ironic to pretend to know when one knows that one does not know as to pretend not to know when one knows that one knows. —Indeed, irony can manifest itself in a more indirect way through an antithetical situation if the irony chooses the simplest and dullest of persons, not in order to mock them but in order to mock the wise.[21]

In all these cases, irony manifests itself rather as the irony that comprehends the world, seeks to mystify the surrounding world, seeking not so much to remain in hiding itself as to get others to disclose themselves. But irony can also be in evidence when the ironist tries to mislead the outside world concerning himself. In our day, when the civic and social situation practically makes every secret love affair impossible, XIII
when the city or neighborhood usually has already read the 326
banns for the happy pair many times from the pulpit before the pastor has done it once; in our day, when society would consider itself robbed of one of its most precious prerogatives if it did not have the absolute power to tie the love knot and also at its own request (not at the pastor's) to speak out against it, with the result that a love affair is first validated by public discussion, and a relationship entered into without the town's knowing about it is almost considered invalid or at least a shameful invasion of its rights, just as undertakers regard suicide as an inadmissible sneaking out of the world—in our day, I say, it may certainly at times seem necessary for someone to cheat if he does not want the town to assign itself the honorable task of proposing marriage for him so that all he needs to do is present himself with the conventional demeanor of someone who is proposing *(ad modum* [in the manner of] Peder Erik Madsen[22]), wearing white gloves and carrying an outlined sketch of his life prospects, together with other charms and amulets (not to forget a most deferential reminder) to be used in the final assault. Now, if there are circumstances of a primarily more external nature that make a certain secrecy necessary, the mystification to be used becomes more and more outright dissimulation. But the more the individual sees these mystifications as episodes in his own love affair, the more exuberant he is in his joy over drawing people's attention to a totally different point, the more pro-

nounced is the irony. The ironist relishes the whole infinity of love, and the amplification others seek by having confidants he obtains by having highly trusted associates who still know nothing.

Similar mystifications are sometimes also necessary in literature, where one is surrounded on all sides by a crowd of alert literati who discover authors the way Mrs. Matchmaker arranges matches. The less it is an external reason (family reasons, timidity, regard for promotion, etc.) that makes someone decide to play the game of secrecy, the more it is a kind of inner infinity that desires to emancipate its creation from every finite relation to itself, wants to see itself freed from all the condolences of fellow sufferers and from all the congratulations of the tender, loving brotherhood of authors—the
XIII 327 more pronounced is the irony. If it goes so far that one can get some cackling rooster who would so very much like to lay an egg to support imputed paternity, half evading, half encouraging people in their error, then the ironist has won the game. If one sometimes wishes to take off the garments (something some one or other can easily be tempted to do in our day) everyone obsequiously must put on and wear according to his station in society; if one now and then at least wants to know that one has the advantage over convicts of daring to appear dressed in something other than the uniform of the penitentiary—then a certain mystification becomes necessary here also. Now, the more it is a finite reason that makes someone decide upon a mystification such as this, as when a merchant travels incognito to promote the closing of a business venture, a king in order to take his pursers by surprise, a police officer for a change to come as a thief in the night,[23] a subordinate public official afraid of his superiors, etc.—the more it approaches outright dissimulation. However, the more it is an urge to be a human being once in a while and not always and forever the chancellor, the more poetic infinity there is in it, and the more skillfully the mystification is carried out, the more pronounced is the irony. And if one is totally successful in hoaxing people, perhaps even to the point of being arrested

as a suspicious character or becoming entangled in an interesting family situation, the ironist has achieved what he desires.

But in all these and similar incidents, the salient feature of the irony is the subjective freedom that at all times has in its power the possibility of a beginning and is not handicapped by earlier situations. There is something seductive about all beginnings, because the subject is still free, and this is the enjoyment the ironist craves. In such moments, actuality loses its validity for him; he is free and above it. This is something the Roman Catholic Church has realized at certain points, and therefore in the Middle Ages it tended to rise above its absolute reality at certain times and to view itself ironically—for example, at the Feast of the Ass, the Feast of Fools, the Easter
Comedy,[24] etc. A similar feeling was the basis for allowing the XIII
Roman soldiers to sing satirical songs about the victor. There 328
was simultaneously an awareness of the prestige of life and the reality of glory, and at the very same time there was an ironical detachment beyond it. Likewise, without needing the mockery of a Lucian,[25] there was much irony in the lives of the Greek deities; not even the heavenly actuality of the gods was spared the sharp blasts of irony. Just as much of life now is not actuality and just as there is something in personality that at least momentarily is incommensurate with actuality, so also there is a truth in irony. Add to this the fact that heretofore we have more or less viewed irony as a momentary manifestation and thus in all these instances are still unable to speak of pure irony or of irony as a position. But the further we extend consideration of the relation between actuality and subject, which has been asserted here only occasionally, the closer we shall approach the point where the irony manifests itself in its usurped totality.

A diplomat's view of the world is ironic in many ways, and Talleyrand's famous statement that man did not acquire speech in order to reveal his thoughts but in order to conceal them[26] contains a profound irony about the world and from the angle of political prudence corresponds entirely to another genuinely diplomatic principle: *mundus vult decipi, decipiatur ergo* [the world wants to be deceived; therefore let it be deceived].[27] Still this does not necessarily mean that the diplomatic world views existence ironically; on the contrary, there is much it earnestly wants to affirm.

The difference, therefore, between all the manifestations of irony suggested here is merely a quantitative difference, a more or less, whereas irony *sensu eminentiori* [in the eminent sense] qualitatively differs from the irony described here in the same way that speculative doubt differs qualitatively from common, empirical doubt. Irony *sensu eminentiori* is directed not against this or that particular existing entity but against the entire given actuality at a certain time and under certain conditions. Thus it has an intrinsic apriority, and it is not by successively destroying one portion of actuality after another that it arrives at its total view, but it is by virtue of this that it destroys in the particular instance. It is not this or that phe-
XIII 329 nomenon but the totality of existence that it contemplates *sub specie ironiae* [under the aspect of irony]. To this extent we see the correctness of Hegel's view of irony as infinite absolute negativity.[28]

However, before we go on to discuss this in more detail, it seems best to orient ourselves in the conceptual milieu to which irony belongs. To that end we must distinguish between what could be called executive irony* and contemplative irony.

* Also belonging to executive or, as it could be called, dramatic irony, is nature's irony—that is, provided the irony is not conscious in nature but is conscious only to the one who has an eye for it, to whom it seems as if nature, like a person, were playing its joke on him or confiding its grief and pain to him. This discrepancy is not intrinsic to nature—it is too natural and far too naïve for that, but it appears in nature to the person who is ironically advanced. In his *Symbolik des Traumes* (Bamberg: 1821), Schubert has an engaging selection of many such ironic features in nature. He notes (p. 38) that nature, with profound mockery, "Klage mit Lust, Fröhlichkeit mit Trauer wunderlich paart, gleich jener Naturstimme, der Luftmusik auf Ceylon, welche im Tone einer tiefklagenden, herzzerschneidenden Stimme, furchtbar lustige Menuetten singt [curiously joins lament with merriment, joy with sorrow, like that voice of nature on Ceylon, the air music, which sings a frightfully merry minuet in the tones of a profoundly plaintive, heartrending voice]."[29] He points out nature's ironic juxtaposition of outrageous extremes (p. 41): "Unmittelbar auf den vernünftigen gemäszigten Menschen, folgt in

We shall first consider what we ventured to call executive XIII 330 irony. Insofar as irony asserts contradistinction in all its various nuances, it might seem that irony would be identical with dissimulation.* For the sake of conciseness, the word "irony" is customarily translated as "dissimulation." But dissimulation denotes more the objective act that carries out the discrepancy between essence and phenomenon; irony also denotes the subjective pleasure as the subject frees himself by means of irony from the restraint in which the continuity of life's conditions

---

der Ideenassociation der Natur der tolle Affe, auf den weisen, keuschen Elephanten das unreine Schwein, auf das Pferd der Esel, auf das häszliche Cameel die schlanken Reharten, auf die mit dem gewöhnlichen Loos der Säugthiere unzufriedne, dem Vogel nachäffende Fledermaus, folgt in verschiedener Hinsicht die Maus, die sich kaum aus der Tiefe herauswagt [In nature's association of ideas, the rational and moderate human being is immediately succeeded by the ridiculous ape, after the wise and pure elephant comes the unclean swine, after the horse the ass, after the hideous camel the slender deer, and after the bat, dissatisfied with the ordinary lot of the mammal and imitating the bird, comes the mouse, which, dissatisfied in a different sense, scarcely ventures forth from the depths]." Now all such things are not in nature, but the ironic subject sees them in nature. Similarly, we can also interpret all sensory illusions as irony on the part of nature. But it takes a consciousness that is itself ironic to become aware of this. The more polemically developed an individual is, the more irony he will also find in nature. Therefore, such a view of nature belongs more to the romantic than to the classical trend. It was difficult for Greek harmoniousness to find such sarcasm in nature. I shall illustrate this with an example. In happy Greece, nature seldom witnessed anything but the soft and gentle harmonies of an even-tempered psyche, for even Greek sorrow was beautiful, and therefore Echo was a friendly nymph. But in Norse mythology, where nature resounded with wild lament, where the night was not light and clear but dark and foggy, full of anxiety and terror, where grief was assuaged not by a quiet recollection but XIII 330 by a deep sigh and everlasting oblivion, there Echo was a troll. Thus in Norse mythology, Echo is called *Dvergmaal* or *Bergmaal* (see Grimm, *Irische Elfenmärchen*, p. LXXVIII; *Færøiske Qvæder* [Randers: 1822], p. 464).[30] This irony in nature has been placed in a footnote because only the humorous individual actually perceives it, since it is actually only through the contemplation of *sin* in the world that the ironic interpretation of nature really emerges.[31]

* Irony is interpreted in this way by Theophrastus. See *Theophrasti Characteres*,[32] ed. Ast, ch. 1, p. 4: περὶ εἰρωνείας [concerning irony]. Here irony is defined as follows: προσποίησις ἐπὶ χεῖρον πράξεων καὶ λόγων (*simulatio dissimulatioque fallax et fraudulenta*) [false and fraudulent dissimulation and concealment].

holds him—thus the ironist can literally be said to kick over the traces. Add to this the fact that dissimulation, insofar as it is brought into relation to the subject, has a purpose, but this purpose is an external objective foreign to the dissimulation itself. Irony, however, has no purpose; its purpose is immanent in itself and is a metaphysical purpose. The purpose is nothing other than the irony itself. If, for example, the ironist appears as someone other than he actually is, his purpose might indeed seem to be to get others to believe this; but his actual purpose still is to feel free, but this he is precisely by means of irony—consequently irony has no other purpose but is self-motivated. We readily perceive, therefore, that irony differs from Jesuitism,[33] in which the subject is, to be sure, free to choose the means to fulfill his purpose but is not at all free in the same sense as in irony, in which the subject has no purpose.

Insofar as it is essential for irony to have an external side that is opposite to the internal, it might seem that it would be iden-
XIII tical with hypocrisy.[34] Indeed, irony is sometimes translated
331 in Danish as *Skalkagtighed* [roguishness], and a hypocrite is usually called an *Øienskalk* [eye-rogue]. But hypocrisy actually belongs to the sphere of morality. The hypocrite is always trying to appear good, although he is evil. Irony, on the other hand, lies in the metaphysical sphere, and the ironist is always only making himself seem to be other than he actually is; thus, just as the ironist hides his jest in earnestness, his earnestness in jest (somewhat like the sounds of nature on Ceylon[35]), so it may also occur to him to pretend to be evil, although he is good. Only remember that the moral categories are actually too concrete for irony.

But irony also has a theoretical or contemplative side. If we regard irony as a minor element, then irony, of course, is the unerring eye for what is crooked, wrong, and vain in existence. Regarded in this way, irony might seem to be identical with mockery, satire, persiflage, etc. There is, of course, a resemblance insofar as irony sees the vanity, but it diverges in making its observation, because it does not destroy the vanity; it is not what punitive justice is in relation to vice, does not have the redeeming feature of the comic but instead reinforces vanity in its vanity and makes what is lunatic even more lunatic. This is what could be called irony's attempt to mediate the discrete elements—not into a higher unity but into a higher lunacy.[36]

If we consider irony as it turns against all existence, here again it maintains the contradiction between essence and phenomenon, between the internal and the external. It might seem now that as the absolute negativity it would be identical with doubt. But one must bear two things in mind—first, that doubt is a conceptual qualification, and irony is subjectivity's being-for-itself; second, that irony is essentially practical, that it is theoretical only in order to become practical again—in other words, it has to do with the irony of itself and not with the irony of the situation. Therefore, if irony gets an inkling that there is something more behind the phenomenon than meets the eye, then precisely what irony has always insisted upon is this, that the subject feel free, so that the phenomenon never acquires any reality [*Realitet*] for the subject. Therefore, the movement is continually in the opposite direction. In doubt, the subject continually wants to enter into the object, and his unhappiness is that the object continually eludes him. In irony, the subject continually wants to get outside the object, and he achieves this by realizing at every moment that the XIII 332
object has no reality. In doubt, the subject is an eyewitness to a war of conquest in which every phenomenon is destroyed, because the essence must continually lie behind it. In irony, the subject is continually retreating, talking every phenomenon out of its reality in order to save itself—that is, in order to preserve itself in negative independence of everything.

Finally, insofar as irony, when it realizes that existence has no reality [*Realitet*], pronounces the same thesis as the pious mentality, irony might seem to be a kind of religious devotion. If I may put it this way, in religious devotion the lower actuality [*Virkelighed*], that is, the relationships with the world, loses its validity, but this occurs only insofar as the relationships with God simultaneously affirm their absolute reality. The devout mind also declares that all is vanity,[37] but this is only insofar as through this negation all disturbing factors are set aside and the eternally existing order comes into view. Add to this the fact that if the devout mind finds everything to be vanity, it makes no exception of its own person, makes no commotion about it; on the contrary, it also must be set aside so that the divine will not be thrust back by its opposition but will pour itself into the mind opened by devotion. Indeed, in the deeper devotional literature, we see that the pious mind regards its own finite personality as the most wretched of all.

In irony, however, since everything is shown to be vanity, the subject becomes free. The more vain everything becomes, all the lighter, emptier, and volatilized the subject becomes. And while everything is in the process of becoming vanity, the ironic subject does not become vain in his own eyes but rescues his own vanity. For irony, everything becomes nothing, but nothing can be taken in several ways. The speculative nothing is the vanishing at every moment with regard to the concretion, since it is itself the craving of the concrete, its *nisus formativus* [formative impulse]; the mystic nothing is a nothing with regard to the representation, a nothing that nevertheless is just as full of content as the silence of the night is full of sounds for someone who has ears to hear.[38] Finally, the ironic nothing is the dead silence in which irony walks again and haunts (the latter word taken altogether ambiguously[39]).

The World-Historical Validity of Irony, XIII 333 the Irony of Socrates

If we turn back to the foregoing general description of irony as infinite absolute negativity, it is adequately suggested therein that irony is no longer directed against this or that particular phenomenon, against a particular existing thing, but that the whole of existence has become alien to the ironic subject and the ironic subject in turn alien to existence, that as actuality has lost its validity for the ironic subject, he himself has to a certain degree become unactual. The word "actuality," however, must here primarily be understood as historical actuality—that is, the given actuality at a certain time and in a certain situation. This word can be understood metaphysically—for example, as it is used when one treats the metaphysical issue of the relation of the idea to actuality, where there is no question of this or that actuality but of the idea's concretion, that is, its actuality—and the word "actuality" can also be used for the historically actualized idea. The latter actuality is different at different times. By this it is in no way meant that in the sum total of its existence the historical actuality is not supposed to have an eternal and intrinsic coherence, but for different generations separated by time and space the given actuality is different. Even though the world spirit in any process is continually in itself, this is not the case with the generation at a certain time and the given individuals at a certain time in the same generation. For them, a given actuality does not present itself as something that they are able to reject, because the world process leads the person who is willing to go along and sweeps the unwilling one along with it.[40] But insofar as the idea is concrete in itself, it is necessary for it to become continually what it is—that is, become concrete. But this can occur only through generations and individuals.

In this way, a contradiction appears, by means of which the world process takes place. The given actuality at a certain time is the actuality valid for the generation and the individuals in that generation, and yet, if there is a reluctance to say that the process is over, this actuality must be displaced by another actuality, and this must occur through and by individuals and the generation. Catholicism was the given actuality for the generation living at the time of the Reformation, and yet it was also the actuality that no longer had validity as such. Con-
XIII sequently, one actuality collides here with another actuality.
334 Herein lies the profoundly tragic aspect of world history. At one and the same time, an individual may be world-historically justified and yet unauthorized. Insofar as he is the latter, he must become a sacrifice; insofar as he is the former, he must prevail—that is, he must prevail by becoming a sacrifice. Here we see how intrinsically consistent the world process is, for as the more true actuality presses onward, it nevertheless itself esteems the past; it is not a revolution but an evolution. The past actuality shows itself to be still justified by demanding a sacrifice, the new actuality by providing a sacrifice. But a sacrifice there must be, because a new element must actually emerge, since the new actuality is not just a conclusion to the past but contains something more in itself; it is not a mere corrective of the past but is also a new beginning.

At any such turning point in history, two movements must be noted. On the one hand, the new must forge ahead; on the other, the old must be displaced. Inasmuch as the new must forge ahead, here we meet the prophetic individual who spies the new in the distance, in dim and undefined contours. The prophetic individual does not possess the future—he has only a presentiment of it. He cannot claim it, but he is also lost to the actuality to which he belongs. His relation to it, however, is peaceful, because the given actuality senses no clash. Then comes the tragic hero in the strict sense. He battles for the new and strives to destroy what for him is a vanishing actuality, but his task is still not so much to destroy as to advance the new and thereby destroy the past indirectly. But the old must be superseded; the old must be perceived in all its imperfec-

tion. Here we meet the ironic subject. For the ironic subject, the given actuality has lost its validity entirely; it has become for him an imperfect form that is a hindrance everywhere. But on the other hand, he does not possess the new. He knows only that the present does not match the idea. He is the one who must pass judgment. In one sense the ironist is certainly prophetic, because he is continually pointing to something impending, but what it is he does not know. He is prophetic, but his position and situation are the reverse of the prophet's. The prophet walks arm in arm with his age, and from this position he glimpses what is coming. The prophet, as was noted above, is lost to his generation, but essentially that is the case only because he is preoccupied with his visions. The ironist, however, has stepped out of line with his age, has turned XIII 335
around and faced it. That which is coming is hidden from him, lies behind his back, but the actuality he so antagonistically confronts is what he must destroy; upon this he focuses his burning gaze. The words of Scripture, "The feet of those who will carry you out are at the door,"[41] apply to his relation to his age. The ironist is also a sacrifice that the world process demands, not as if the ironist always needed in the strictest sense to fall as a sacrifice, but his fervor in the service of the world spirit consumes him.[42]

Here, then, we have irony as the infinite absolute negativity. It is negativity, because it only negates; it is infinite, because it does not negate this or that phenomenon; it is absolute, because that by virtue of which it negates is a higher something that still is not. The irony establishes nothing, because that which is to be established lies behind it. It is a divine madness that rages like a Tamerlane[43] and does not leave one stone upon another.[44] Here, then, we have irony. To a certain degree, every world-historical turning point must have this formation also, and it certainly would not be without historical interest to track this formation through world history. Without engaging in this, I shall merely cite as examples taken from the period closest to the Reformation, Cardanus, Campanella, and Bruno.[45] To some extent, Erasmus of Rotterdam[46] was also an example of irony. In my opinion, the significance of this formation has not received sufficient attention hitherto—all the more strange, since Hegel has treated the negative with such decided partiality. But the negative in the system corresponds to irony in the historical actuality. In the historical actuality, the negative exists, which is never the case in the system.

Irony is a qualification of subjectivity. In irony, the subject is negatively free, since the actuality that is supposed to give the subject content is not there. He is free from the constraint in which the given actuality holds the subject, but he is negatively free and as such is suspended, because there is nothing that holds him. But this very freedom, this suspension, gives the ironist a certain enthusiasm, because he becomes intoxicated, so to speak, in the infinity of possibilities, and if he
XIII 336 needs any consolation for everything that is destroyed, he can have recourse to the enormous reserve fund of possibility. He does not, however, abandon himself to this enthusiasm; it simply inspires and feeds his enthusiasm for destroying.

But since the ironist does not have the new in his power, we might ask how, then, does he destroy the old, and the answer to that must be: he destroys the given actuality by the given actuality itself; but it should be remembered nevertheless that the new principle is present within him κατὰ δύναμιν [potentially], as possibility.* But by destroying actuality by means of actuality itself, he enlists in the service of world irony. In his *Geschichte der Philosophie* (II, p. 62), Hegel says: "Alle Dialectik läszt das gelten, was gelten soll, als ob es gelte, läszt die innere Zerstörung selbst sich daran entwickeln—allgemeine Ironie der Welt [All dialectic allows as valid that which is to be valid as if it were valid, allows the inner destruction to develop in it—the universal irony of the world],"[48] and in this the world irony is very accurately interpreted.

Precisely because every particular historical actuality is continually but an element in the actualization of the idea, it car-

* Like water in relation to what it reflects, the negative has the quality of showing as high above itself that which it supports as it shows beneath itself that which it is battling;[47] but the negative, like the water, does not know this.

ries within itself the seeds of its own downfall. This appears very clearly particularly in Judaism, whose significance as a transitional element is especially remarkable. It was already a profound irony over the world when the law, after having declared the commandments, added the promise: If you obey these, you will be saved,[49] since it turned out that people could not fulfill the law, and thus a salvation linked to this condition certainly became more than hypothetical. That Judaism destroyed itself by itself is expressly shown in its historical relation to Christianity. If, without entering into a study of the significance of Christ's coming, we merely keep this as a turning point in world history, then one cannot miss the ironic formation there as well. This time it is provided by John the Baptizer. He was not the one who was supposed to come;[50] he did not know what was to come—and yet he destroyed Judaism. Thus he destroyed it not by means of the new but by means of Judaism itself. He required of Judaism what Judaism wanted to give—justice, but this it was unable to give, and thereby it foundered. Consequently, he let Judaism continue XIII
to exist and at the same time developed the seeds of its own 337
downfall within it. Nevertheless, the personality of John the Baptizer recedes completely into the background; in him we see the irony of the world in its objective shape, so to speak, so that he becomes but an instrument in its hand.

But in order for the ironic formation to be perfectly developed, it is required that the subject also become conscious of his irony, feel negatively free as he passes judgment on the given actuality, and enjoy this negative freedom. So that this might take place, the subjectivity must be in an advanced stage or, more correctly, as the subjectivity asserts itself, irony emerges. Face-to-face with the given actuality, the subjectivity feels its power, its validity and meaning. But as it feels this, it rescues itself, as it were, from the relativity in which the given actuality wants to keep it. Insofar as this irony is world-historically justified, the subjectivity's emancipation is carried out in the service of the idea, even if the ironic subject is not clearly conscious of this. This is the genius of justified irony. It holds true of unjustified irony that whoever wants to save his soul must lose it.[51] But only history can judge whether the irony is justified or not.

But just because the subject views actuality ironically, it in no way means that he conducts himself ironically as he asserts his view of actuality. For example, there has been sufficient talk in modern times about irony and about the ironic view of actuality, but this view has rarely taken ironic form. But the more this happens, so much the more certain and inevitable is the downfall of the actuality, so much greater is the superiority of the ironic subject over the actuality he wishes to destroy, and so much more free is he also. Here he quietly carries out the same operation as world irony. He permits the established to remain, but for him it has no validity; meanwhile, he pretends as if it did have validity for him, and under this mask he leads it to its certain downfall. To the extent that the ironic subject is world-historically justified, there is here a unity of genius and artistic presence of mind.

But if irony is a qualification of subjectivity, then it must manifest itself the first time subjectivity makes its appearance in world history. Irony is, namely, the first and most abstract qualification of subjectivity.[52] This points to the historical turning point where subjectivity made its appearance for the first time, and with this we have come to Socrates.

XIII 338 The nature of Socrates' irony has been sufficiently covered in the first part of this investigation. For him, the whole given actuality had entirely lost its validity; he had become alien to the actuality of the whole substantial world. This is one side of irony, but on the other hand he used irony as he destroyed Greek culture. His conduct toward it was at all times ironic; he was ignorant and knew nothing but was continually seeking information from others; yet as he let the existing go on existing, it foundered. He kept on using this tactic until the very last, as was especially evident when he was accused. But his fervor in this service consumed him, and in the end irony overwhelmed him; he became dizzy, and everything lost its reality. To me, this view of Socrates and of the significance of his position in world history seems to be so well balanced that I hope it finds acceptance with some readers. But since Hegel declares himself against viewing Socrates' position as irony,[53] it becomes necessary to look at the objections found here and there in his books.

Before proceeding to this, however, I shall try as well as I can to explain a weakness from which Hegel's whole understanding of the concept of irony seems to suffer. Hegel always discusses irony in a very unsympathetic manner; in his eyes, irony is anathema. Hegel's appearance coincides with Schlegel's most brilliant period. But just as the irony of the Schlegels had passed judgment in esthetics on an encompassing sentimentality, so Hegel was the one to correct what was misleading in the irony. On the whole, it is one of Hegel's great merits that he halted or at least wanted to halt the prodigal sons of speculation on their way to perdition. But he did not always use the mildest means for this, and when he called out to them his voice was not always gentle and fatherly but at times was harsh and schoolmasterly. The partisans of irony gave him the most trouble; he soon gave up hope of their salvation and now treats them as irreclaimable and obdurate sinners. He takes every opportunity to talk about these ironists XIII 339
and always in the most unsympathetic manner. Indeed, Hegel looks down with immense scorn and superiority on those whom he often calls "superior people."[54] But the fact that Hegel became irritated with the form of irony closest to him naturally impaired his interpretation of the concept. Explanation is often lacking—but Schlegel is always reprimanded.[55] In no way does this mean that Hegel was not right about the Schlegels and that the Schlegelian irony was not on a very dubious wrong road. All it says is that Hegel has surely conferred a great benefit through the earnestness with which he takes a stand against any isolation, an earnestness that makes it possible to read much that he has written with much invigoration and considerable edification.[56] But on the other hand, it must be said that by his one-sided attack on the post-Fichtean irony he has overlooked the truth of irony, and by his identifying all irony with this, he has done irony an injustice. As soon as Hegel mentions the word "irony," he promptly thinks of Schlegel and Tieck, and his style is immediately marked by a

certain resentment. What was wrong and unwarranted with Schlegel's irony as well as Hegel's good services in this respect will be discussed in the appropriate place. We turn now to his view of Socrates' irony.

We called attention earlier to the fact that Hegel, in his description of Socrates' method, stresses two forms: his irony and his midwifery. His discussion of this is found in *Geschichte der Philosophie*, II, pp. 59-67.[57] Although the discussion of Socratic irony is very brief, Hegel nevertheless uses the occasion to rant against irony as a general principle and on page 62 adds: "Friedrich von Schlegel ist es, der diese Gedanken zuerst aufgebracht, Ast hat es nachgesprochen [It was Friedrich von Schlegel who first brought forward this idea, and Ast repeated it]"; and then follow the earnest words that Hegel customarily delivers on such an occasion. Socrates pretends to be ignorant, and in the role of being taught he teaches others. P. 60: "Dieses ist dann die Seite der berühmten *socratischen Ironie*. Sie hat bei ihm die subjective Gestalt der Dialectik, sie ist Benehmungsweise im Umgang; die Dialectik ist Gründe der Sache, die Ironie ist besondere Benehmungsweise von Person zu Person [This, then, is the aspect of the celebrated Socratic irony. In him it has the subjective form of dialectic, it is a way of dealing with people; the dialectic is the reasons of things, the irony is a special way of dealing person to person]." But inasmuch as just before that Hegel noted that Socrates uses the same irony "wenn er die Manier der Sophisten zu Schanden machen will [when he wishes to bring the manner of the Sophists into dis-
XIII 340 repute]," we promptly encounter a difficulty here, because in the one instance he does indeed want to teach, but in the other merely to disgrace. Hegel then points out that this Socratic irony seems to contain something false but thereupon shows the correctness of his conduct. Finally he shows the real meaning of Socratic irony, the greatness in it—namely, that it seeks to make abstract conceptions concrete and developed. He goes on to add (p. 62): "Wenn ich sage, ich weisz, was Vernunft, was Glaube ist, so sind diesz nur ganz abstracte Vorstellungen; dasz sie nun concret werden, dazu gehört, dasz sie explicirt werden, dasz vorausgesetzt werde, es sey nicht bekannt, was

es eigentlich sey. Diese Explication solcher Vorstellungen bewirkt nun Socrates; und diesz ist das wahrhafte der socratischen Ironie [In saying that I know what reason is, what belief is, these remain but quite abstract conceptions; in order to become concrete, they must indeed be explicated and presupposed to be unknown in terms of what they really are. Socrates effected the explications of such conceptions, and this is the truth of Socratic irony]."

But this confuses everything; the description of Socratic irony completely loses its historical weight, and the passage quoted is so modern that it hardly reminds us of Socrates. To be specific, Socrates' undertaking was by no means one of making the abstract concrete, and the examples cited are certainly very poorly chosen, because I do not think that Hegel would be able to cite analogies of this unless he were to take the whole of Plato and plead the continual use of Socrates' name in Plato, whereby he would come into conflict with both himself and everyone else. Socrates' undertaking was not to make the abstract concrete, but to let the abstract become visible through the immediately concrete. In a refutation of these Hegelian observations, it is sufficient to remember two things: first, the double nature of the irony we found in Plato (for it is obviously the irony we have called Platonic irony that Hegel meant and that on page 64 he identifies with Socratic irony); second, the principle of movement in Socrates' whole life—that it proceeded not from the abstract to the concrete but from the concrete to the abstract and continually arrived at this. Thus, when Hegel's whole examination of Socratic irony ends in such a way that Socratic irony becomes identified with Platonic irony and both ironies become (p. 64) "mehr Manier der Conversation, die gesellige Heiterkeit, als dasz jene reine Negation, jenes negative Verhalten darunter verstanden wäre [more a manner of conversation, sociable pleasantry, and not that pure negation, not the negative attitude]," this comment has indeed already been answered.

Hegel's description of Socrates' art of midwifery does not fare much better. Here he develops the significance of Socrates' asking questions, and this discussion is both beautiful and

true, but the distinction we made earlier between asking in order to get an answer and asking in order to disgrace is over-
XIII 341 looked here. At the end, the example of the concept "to become" that he chooses is once again totally un-Socratic, unless he intends to find a Socratic development in the *Parmenides*.

As for Hegel's ever really discussing Socrates' tragic irony,[58] one must bear in mind that it is not the irony of Socrates but the world's irony with Socrates. Therefore, it cannot shed any light on the question of Socratic irony.

In his review of the works of Solger,[59] Hegel again points out on page 488 the difference between Schlegelian irony and Socratic irony. That there is a difference we have fully conceded and shall point out in more detail in the appropriate place, but it is by no means to be concluded from this that Socrates' position was not irony. Hegel upbraids Friedrich Schlegel because, with his lack of judgment with regard to the speculative and his neglect of it, he has wrenched the Fichtean thesis on the constitutive validity of the ego out of its metaphysical context, wrenched it out of the domain of thought, and applied it directly to actuality, "zum Verneinen der Lebendigkeit der Vernunft und Wahrheit, und zur Herabsetzung derselben zum Schein im Subject und zum Scheinen für Andere [in order to deny the vitality of reason and truth and to relegate these to an illusory status in the subject and to illusion for others]."[60] He then points out that in order to designate this vitiation of truth into appearance, the name of innocent Socratic irony has been allowed to be vitiated. If the similarity is based particularly on the circumstance that Socrates always introduced his inquiry with the declaration that he knew nothing, in order to disgrace the Sophists, then the outcome of this conduct is always something negative and without any scientific-scholarly conclusion. In that case, Socrates' protesting that he knew nothing is given in dead earnest and consequently is not ironic. I shall not at this point become further involved in the issue that arises here from Hegel's showing that Socrates' teaching ended without a conclusion, if we compare this with what he advanced earlier about Socrates' making the abstract concrete through his ironic teaching, but on the other hand I shall in a little detail investigate how earnest Socrates really was about his ignorance.

As pointed out earlier, when Socrates declared that he was ignorant, he nevertheless did know something, for he knew about his ignorance; on the other hand, however, this knowledge was not a knowledge of something, that is, did not have any positive content, and to that extent his ignorance was XIII 342 ironic, and since Hegel has tried in vain, in my opinion, to reclaim a positive content for him, I believe that the reader must agree with me. If his knowledge had been a knowledge of something, his ignorance would merely have been a conversational technique. His irony, however, was complete in itself. Inasmuch, then, as his ignorance was simultaneously earnest and yet again not earnest, it is on this prong Socrates must be held. To know that one is ignorant is the beginning of coming to know, but if one does not know more, it is merely a beginning. This knowledge was what kept Socrates ironically afloat.

When Hegel next hopes to show that Socrates' ignorance was not irony by pointing out that Socrates was in earnest about his ignorance, it seems to me that here again Hegel is not consistent. To be specific, if irony is going to advance a supreme thesis, it does as every negative position does—it declares something positive and is earnest about what it says. For irony, nothing is an established order; it plays helter-skelter *ad libitum* [at will] with everything; but when it wants to declare this, it says something positive, and to that extent its sovereignty is thereby at an end. Therefore, when Schlegel or Solger says: Actuality is only appearance, only semblance, only vanity, a nothing, he obviously is saying this in earnest, and yet Hegel assumes it to be irony. The difficulty here is that, strictly speaking, irony actually is never able to advance a thesis, because irony is a qualification of the being-for-itself subject, who in incessant agility allows nothing to remain established and on account of this agility cannot focus on the total point of view that it allows nothing to remain established. Schlegel's and Solger's consciousness that finitude is a nothing is obviously just as earnestly intended as Socrates' ignorance.

Ultimately the ironist always has to posit something, but what he posits in this way is nothing. But then it is impossible to be earnest about nothing without either arriving at something (this happens if one becomes speculatively earnest about it) or despairing (if one takes it personally in earnest). But the ironist does neither, and thus we can also say that he is not in earnest about it.

Irony is the infinitely light playing with nothing that is not terrified by it but even rises to the surface on occasion. But if one does not speculatively or personally take nothing in ear-
XIII nest, then one obviously is taking it lightly and thus does not
343 take it in earnest. If Hegel thinks that Schlegel was not in earnest in holding that existence is a nothing devoid of reality [*Realitet*], then there certainly must have been something that did have validity for him, but in that case his irony was merely a form. Therefore we can say of irony that it is earnestness about nothing—insofar as it is not earnestness about something. It continually conceives of nothing in contrast to something, and in order to free itself of earnestness about anything, it grasps the nothing. But it does not become earnestness about nothing, either, except insofar as it is not earnestness about anything.

So it is also with Socrates' ignorance; his ignorance is the nothing with which he destroys any knowledge. This is best seen in his view of death. He is ignorant of what death is and of what there is after death, whether there is anything or nothing at all; consequently, he is ignorant. But he does not take this ignorance greatly to heart; on the contrary, he genuinely feels quite liberated in this ignorance. Consequently, he is not in earnest about this ignorance, and yet he is altogether earnest about being ignorant. —I believe, therefore, that everyone will agree with me that there is nothing in these Hegelian observations to preclude the assumption that Socrates' position was irony.

We shall now summarize what was stressed in the first part of this dissertation as characteristic of Socrates' position, namely: that the whole substantial life of Greek culture had lost its validity for him, which means that to him the established actuality was unactual, not in this or that particular aspect but in its totality as such; that with regard to this invalid actuality he let the established order of things appear to remain established and thereby brought about its downfall; that in the process Socrates became lighter and lighter, more and more negatively free; consequently, that we do indeed perceive that according to what is set forth here Socrates' position was, as infinite absolute negativity, irony. But it was not actuality in general that he negated; it was the given actuality at a particular time, the substantial actuality as it was in Greece, and what his irony was demanding was the actuality of subjectivity, of ideality.

On this issue, history has judged Socrates to be world-historically justified. He became a sacrifice. This is certainly a tragic fate, but nevertheless Socrates' death is not basically tragic; and the Greek state really comes too late with its death sentence. On the other hand, the execution of the death sentence has little upbuilding effect, because death has no reality XIII 344 for Socrates. For the tragic hero, death has validity; for him, death is truly the final battle and the final suffering. Therefore the age he wanted to destroy can in that way satisfy its fury for revenge. But obviously the Greek state could not find this satisfaction in Socrates' death, since by his ignorance Socrates had frustrated any more meaningful connection with the thought of death. Admittedly the tragic hero does not fear death, but still he knows it as a pain, as a hard and harsh course, and to that extent it has validity if he is condemned to die; but Socrates knows nothing at all, and thus it is an irony over the state that it condemns him to death and believes that it has inflicted punishment upon him.

Irony after Fichte

It was in Kant, to call to mind only what is generally known, that modern speculative thought, feeling itself mature and come of age, became tired of the guardianship in which it had lived hitherto under dogmatism and, like the prodigal son, went to its father and demanded that he divide and share the inheritance with it.[61] The outcome of this division of the inheritance is well known, and also that speculation did not have to go abroad in order to squander its resources, because there was no wealth to be found. The more the *I* in criticism became absorbed in contemplation of the *I*, the leaner and leaner the *I* became, until it ended with becoming a ghost, immortal like Aurora's husband.[62] The same thing happened to the *I* as to the raven who, fooled by the fox's praise of its person, lost the cheese.[63] Because reflection was continually reflecting about reflection, thinking went astray, and every step it advanced led further and further, of course, from any content. Here it became apparent, as it does in all ages, that if one is going to speculate, one had better be facing in the right direction. Speculative thought utterly failed to see that what it was seeking was in its own seeking, and when it would not look for it XIII 345 there, it was not to be found in all eternity. Philosophy walked around like a man who is wearing his glasses and nevertheless is looking for his glasses—that is, he is looking for something right in front of his nose, but he does not look right in front of his nose and therefore never finds it.

But that which is external to experience, which like a hard body collided with the experiencer, whereupon they parted with the force of the collision—*das Ding an sich*,[64] which never ceased to test the experiencing subject (just as a certain school[65] in the Middle Ages believed that the visible signs in Holy Communion were present in order to test faith)—this externality, this *Ding an sich*, constituted the weakness in

Kant's system. Indeed, it became a question whether the *I* itself is not a *Ding an sich*.

This question was raised and answered by Fichte.[66] He removed the difficulty with this *an sich* by placing it within thought; he infinitized the *I* in *I-I*. The producing *I* is the same as the produced *I*. *I-I* is the abstract identity. By so doing he infinitely liberated thought. But this infinity of thought in Fichte is, like all Fichte's infinity (his ethical infinity is ceaseless striving for the sake of this striving itself; his esthetic infinity is ceaseless producing for the sake of this producing itself; God's infinity is ceaseless development for the sake of the development itself), negative infinity, an infinity in which there is no finitude, an infinity without any content. When Fichte infinitized the *I* in this way, he advanced an idealism beside which any actuality turned pale, an acosmism in which his idealism became actuality even though it was Docetism. In Fichte, thought was infinitized, subjectivity became the infinite, absolute negativity, the infinite tension and urge.

Because of this, Fichte has significance for science and scholarship. His *Wissenschaftslehre* [theory of knowledge][67] infinitized knowledge. But he infinitized it negatively, and thus instead of truth he obtained certainty, not positive but negative infinity in the *I*'s infinite identity with itself; instead of positive striving, that is, happiness [*Salighed*], he obtained a negative striving, that is, an ought. But precisely because Fichte had the negative, his position had an infinite enthusiasm, an infinite elasticity. Kant lacks the negative infinity, Fichte the positive. For this reason Fichte has an absolute gain from the method; with him science and scholarship became a XIII 346
whole out of one part.

But since Fichte in his *I-I* insisted on abstract identity in this way and in his ideal kingdom would have nothing to do with actuality, he achieved the absolute beginning, and proceeding from that, as has so frequently been discussed, he wanted to construct the world. The *I* became the constituting entity. But since the *I* was merely formally understood and consequently negatively, Fichte actually went no further than the infinite, elastic *molimina* [efforts] toward a beginning. He has the infinite urge of the negative, its *nisus formativus* [formative impulse], but possesses it as a fieriness that cannot get started; possesses it as a divine and absolute impatience, as an infinite power that still accomplishes nothing because there is nothing to which it can be applied. It is a potentiation, an exaltation as strong as a god who can lift the whole world and yet has nothing to lift.

The starting point for the problem of philosophy is hereby brought to consciousness. It is the presuppositionless with which it must begin, but the prodigious energy of this beginning goes no further. In other words, in order for thought, subjectivity, to acquire fullness and truth, it must let itself be born; it must immerse itself in the deeps of substantial life, let itself hide there as the congregation is hidden in Christ;[68] half fearfully and half sympathetically, half shrinking back and half yielding, it must let the waves of the substantial sea close over it, just as in the moment of inspiration the subject almost disappears from himself, abandons himself to that which inspires him, and yet feels a slight shudder, for it is a matter of life and death. But this takes courage, and yet it is necessary, since everyone who wants to save his soul must lose it.[69] But this is not the courage of despair, as Tauler so beautifully says in an even more concrete situation:

> *Doch dieses Verlieren, dies Entschwinden*
> *Ist eben das echte und rechte Finden*
> [Yet this loss, this vanishing,
> Is indeed the genuine and proper finding].[70]

As is known, Fichte later abandoned this position, which had many admirers and few adherents, and in some of his works tried in a more upbuilding manner to quiet and lessen the earlier πληροφορία [full assurance].[71] On the other hand, it
XIII 347 appears from the works published posthumously[72] by his son that Fichte also tried to become lord and master of that negative infinity by concentrating upon the very essence of consciousness. Since that does not pertain to this study, I shall deal with one of the positions related to the earlier Fichte—namely, with the Schlegelian and Tieckian irony.

In Fichte, subjectivity became free, infinite, negative. But in order for subjectivity to get out of this movement of emptiness in which it moved in infinite abstraction, it had to be negated; in order for thought to be able to become actual, it had to become concrete. This brings up the question of metaphysical actuality. This Fichtean principle that subjectivity, the *I*, has constitutive validity, is the sole omnipotence, was grasped by Schlegel and Tieck, and on that basis they operated in the world. In this there was a twofold difficulty. In the first place, the empirical and finite *I* was confused with the eternal *I*; in the second place, metaphysical actuality was confused with historical actuality. Thus a rudimentary metaphysical position was summarily applied to actuality. Fichte wanted to construct the world, but he had in mind a systematic construction. Schlegel and Tieck wanted to obtain a world.*

Here we perceive that this irony was not in the service of the world spirit. It was not an element of the given actuality that must be negated and superseded by a new element, but it was all of historical actuality that it negated in order to make room for a self-created actuality. It was not subjectivity that should forge ahead here, since subjectivity was already given in world situations, but it was an exaggerated subjectivity, a subjectivity raised to the second power. We also perceive here that this irony was totally unjustified and that Hegel's hostile behavior toward it is entirely in order.

Irony** now functioned as that for which nothing was estab- XIII
lished, as that which was finished with everything, and also as 348
that which had the absolute power to do everything. If it allowed something to remain established, it knew that it had the

* But this ironic endeavor by no means ended with Tieck and Schlegel; on the contrary, in Young Germany[73] it has a crowded nursery. In fact, in the general development of this position, considerable attention is directed to this Young Germany.

** Throughout this whole discussion I use the terms "irony" and "ironist"; I could just as well say "romanticism" and "romanticist." Both terms say essentially the same thing; the one is more reminiscent of the name with which the faction christened itself; the other, the name with which Hegel christened it.

power to destroy it, knew it at the very same moment it let it continue. If it posited something, it knew it had the authority to annul it, knew it at the very same moment it posited it. It knew that in general it possessed the absolute power to bind and to unbind.[74] It was lord over the idea just as much as over the phenomenon, and it destroyed the one with the other. It destroyed the phenomenon by showing that it did not correspond to the idea; it destroyed the idea by showing that it did not correspond to the phenomenon. Both were correct, since the idea and the phenomenon are only in and with each other. And during all this, irony saved its carefree life, since the subject, man, was able to do all this, for who is as great as Allah, and who can endure before him?

But actuality (historical actuality) stands in a twofold relation to the subject: partly as a gift that refuses to be rejected, partly as a task that wants to be fulfilled. Irony's misrelation to actuality is already sufficiently intimated by the essentially critical stance of irony. Both its philosopher (Schlegel) and its poet (Tieck) are critical. Thus the seventh day—which in our age is supposed finally to have arrived in so many ways—is used not to rest from the historical work but to criticize. But criticism as a rule precludes sympathy, and there is a criticism to which nothing is established any more than anyone is innocent to a suspicious policeman. But the old classics were not criticized, consciousness was not criticized as it was by Kant, but actuality itself was criticized. Now, there certainly may have been much in actuality that needed criticism, and evil in the Fichtean sense of the word, apathy and indolence, may very well have gained the upper hand, and its *vis inertiae* [force of inertia] may very well have needed chastisement. In other words, there may well have been much in existence that had
XIII to be cut away precisely because it was not actuality, but it was
349 utterly indefensible for irony to aim its criticism at all actuality
for that reason. That Schlegel was critical, I need only remind the reader; but that Tieck also was critical, anyone will certainly agree if he also agrees that Tieck has embodied his polemic against the world in his dramas and that it takes a polemically mature individual to understand them, a circum-

stance that has made his plays less popular than they, considering their genius, deserve to be.

But when I said earlier that actuality offers itself partly as a gift, the individual's relation to a past is thereby implied. This past will now claim validity for the individual and will not be overlooked or ignored. For irony, however, there really never was a past. This was due to its refusal to be involved in metaphysical inquiries. It confused the eternal *I* with the temporal *I*. But the eternal *I* has no past, and as a result the temporal *I* does not have one, either. But to the extent that irony is good-natured enough to assume a past, this past must be of such a nature that irony can have a free hand with it and play its game with it. Thus it was the mythical part of history, legend and fairy tale, that mainly found favor in its eyes. The actual history, however, in which the authentic individual has his positive freedom because therein he possesses his premises, had to be set aside. To that end, irony acted just as Hercules did when he was fighting with Antaeus, who could not be conquered as long as he kept his feet on the ground. As we all know, Hercules lifted Antaeus up from the ground and thereby defeated him. Irony dealt with historical actuality in the same way. In a twinkling, all history was turned into myth—poetry—legend—fairy tale. Thus irony was free once again.

Now, it again made its choice and played helter-skelter as it pleased. It took special delight in Greece and the Middle Ages. It did not, however, lose itself in historical views, which it knew to be *Dichtung und Wahrheit*.[75] Sometimes it lived in Greece under the beautiful Greek sky, lost in the present-tense enjoyment of harmonious Greek life, lived therein so that it had its actuality there. But when it became tired of that, it shoved this arbitrarily posited actuality so far away from itself that it vanished altogether. For irony, Greek culture had no validity as a world-historical element but had validity and absolute validity for it because it was pleased to have it so.

Sometimes it hid away in the primeval forest of the Middle Ages, listened to the secret-laden whispering of the trees, and
built nests in their leafy tops or hid in its dark hollows—in XIII 350
short, it sought its actuality in the Middle Ages in the com-

pany of knights and troubadours, fell in love with a noble maiden on a spirited horse with a falcon trained for the hunt on her outstretched right arm. But if this love affair lost its validity, then the Middle Ages receded far back into the infinite and faded more and more in ever dimmer outlines on the backdrop of consciousness. For irony, the Middle Ages did not have its validity as a world-historical element but had validity and absolute validity for it because it was pleased to have it so.

The same is repeated in all theoretical spheres. One religion or another was momentarily the absolute for it, but it also was very well aware that the reason it was the absolute was that irony itself wanted it so—period. In the next moment, it wanted something else. Therefore it taught, just as it is taught in *Nathan der Weise*,[76] that all religions are equally good, Christianity perhaps the worst, and then for a change it was itself pleased to be Christian.

It was the same with regard to knowledge. It judged and denounced every scholarly position, was always passing judgment, was always on the judgment seat, but never investigated. It continually stood above the object, and this, of course, was quite natural, because only now was actuality supposed to begin. In other words, irony refused to be involved in the metaphysical question of the idea's relation to actuality, but the metaphysical actuality lies beyond time and consequently could not possibly be the actuality irony wanted to have, could not possibly be given in time.

It is against this judging and denouncing conduct on the part of Friedrich Schlegel that Hegel declaims in particular (*Werke*, XVI, p. 465[77]). In this connection, Hegel's great service to the understanding of the historical past cannot be sufficiently acknowledged. He does not reject the past but comprehends it; he does not repudiate other scholarly positions but vanquishes them. Thus Hegel put a stop to all this continual chatter that now world history was going to begin, as if it were going to begin at precisely four o'clock or at least by five o'clock. And if one or another Hegelian has attained such enormous world-historical momentum that he cannot stop

but at a dreadful speed steers to the back of beyond, then Hegel is not to blame for that. And when it comes to contemplation, if even more can be done than Hegel has done, no one XIII
who has any concept of the meaning of actuality would be so 351
ungrateful as to go beyond Hegel so fast that he forgets what he owes to him, that is, if he has been familiar with him at all.

With regard to what authorizes irony to behave as described, it must be said that it is because irony knows that the phenomenon is not the essence. The idea is concrete and therefore must become concrete, but the idea's becoming concrete is precisely the historical actuality. In this historical actuality, every single link has its validity as an element. But irony does not acknowledge this relative validity. For irony, historical actuality sometimes has absolute validity, sometimes none at all; because it has, after all, taken upon itself the significant assignment of bringing about actuality.

But for the individual actuality is also a task that wants to be fulfilled. Here one would expect that irony would properly have to show its advantageous side; since it has gone beyond all given actuality, one would think that it must have to have something good to put in its place. But this is by no means the case, for just as irony managed to defeat the historical actuality by placing it in suspension, so irony itself has become suspended. Its actuality is only possibility. In order for the acting individual to be able to accomplish his task by fulfilling actuality, he must feel himself integrated in a larger context, must feel the earnestness of responsibility, must feel and respect every reasonable consequence.

Irony is free from this. It knows it has the power to start all over again if it so pleases; anything that happened before is not binding, and just as irony in infinite freedom enjoys its critical gratification in the theoretical realm, so it enjoys in the realm of practice a similar divine freedom that knows no bonds, no chains, but plays with abandon and unrestraint, gambols like a leviathan[78] in the sea. Irony is indeed free, free from the sorrows of actuality, but also free from its joys, free from its blessing, for inasmuch as it has nothing higher than itself, it can receive no blessing, since it is always the lesser that is blessed by the greater.[79] This is the freedom that irony craves. Therefore it watches over itself and fears nothing more than that some impression or other might overwhelm it, because not until one is free in that way does one live poetically, and, as is well known, irony's great requirement was to live poetically.[80]

XIII 352 But by "living poetically" irony understood something other and something more than what any sensible person who has any respect for a human being's worth, any sense for the originality in a human being, understands by this phrase. It did not take this to mean the artistic earnestness that comes to the aid of the divine in man, that mutely and quietly listens to the voice of what is distinctive in individuality, detects its movements in order to let it really be available in the individual and to let the whole individuality develop harmoniously into a pliable form rounded off in itself. It did not understand it to be what the pious Christian thinks of when he becomes aware that life is an upbringing, an education, which, please note, is not supposed to make him into someone completely different (for the Christian's God does not have the infinite negative omnipotence of the Mohammedan's, for whom a man as large as a mountain, a fly as large as an elephant, is just as possible as a mountain as little as a man and an elephant as little as a fly, since everything can just as well be something entirely different from what it is) but is specifically supposed to develop the seeds God himself has placed in man, since the Christian knows himself as that which has reality for God. Here, in fact, the Christian comes to the aid of God, becomes, so to speak, his co-worker in completing the good work God himself has begun.[81]

By the phrase "living poetically," irony not only registered a protest against all the contemptibleness that is nothing but a miserable product of its environment, against all the commonplace people who, sorry to say, populate the world in such numbers, but it wanted something more. In other words, it is indeed one thing to compose oneself poetically; it is something else to be composed poetically. The Christian lets himself be poetically composed, and in this respect a simple Christian lives far more poetically than many a brilliant intellectual. But also the person who in the Greek sense poetically composes himself recognizes that he has been given a task. Therefore it is very urgent for him to become conscious of what is original in him, and this originality is the boundary within which he poetically composes, within which he is poetically free. Thus the individuality has an objective that is its absolute objective, and its activity is aimed precisely at the fulfillment of this objective and the enjoyment of itself in and with this fulfillment, that is, its activity is to become *für sich* [for itself] what it is *an sich* [in itself].

But just as commonplace people do not have any *an sich* but
can become anything, so also the ironist has none. But this is
not simply because he is merely a product of his environment.
On the contrary, he stands above his whole environment, but
in order really to live poetically, really and thoroughly to be
able to create himself poetically, the ironist must have no *an* XIII
sich. In this way, irony itself lapses into that which it is fighting 353
the hardest, because an ironist comes to have a certain resemblance to an altogether commonplace person, except that the ironist has the negative freedom with which he stands, poetically creating, above himself. Therefore the ironist frequently becomes nothing, because what is not true for God is true for man—out of nothing comes nothing. But the ironist continually preserves his poetic freedom, and when he notices that he is becoming nothing, he includes that in his poetizing; and, as is well known, it is part and parcel of the poetic poses and positions in life that irony promoted—indeed, to become nothing at all is the most superior of them all. In the poetry of the romantic school, therefore, a *Taugenichts* [good-for-nothing][82] is always the most poetic character, and what the Christians so often speak about, especially in troubled times—becoming a fool in the world[83]—this the ironist actualized in his own way, except that he feels nothing akin to martyrdom, because to him this is the supreme poetic enjoyment.

But the infinite poetic freedom, already suggested by the inclusion of becoming nothing at all, manifests itself in a more positive manner also, inasmuch as the ironic individual has

looked over a multitude of destinies, usually in the form of possibility, has familiarized himself with them poetically before he ends with nothing. In irony, just as in the world according to Pythagorean teaching,[84] the soul is always on pilgrimage, except that it does not take such a long time. But even though irony is behind with respect to time, it perhaps has the advantage in the multitude of destinies, and certainly many an ironist, before finding rest in nothing, has run through much stranger *fata* [destinies] than the rooster presented in Lucian, which had first been Pythagoras himself, then Aspasia, the dubious beauty from Miletus, then Crates the Cynic, then a king, a beggar, a satrap, a horse, a jackdaw, a frog, and a thousand other things too numerous to mention, and finally a rooster, and that more than once, because it found the most pleasure in being a rooster.[85] For the ironist, everything is possible. Our God is in heaven and does whatever he pleases;[86] the ironist is on earth and does whatever he desires. But we cannot blame the ironist for finding it so difficult to become something, because when one has such a prodigious multitude of possibilities it is not easy to choose. For
XIII 354 a change, the ironist finds it proper to let fate and chance decide. Therefore he counts on his fingers as children do: *Edelmann, Bettelman* [nobleman, beggar],[87] etc. But since for him all such destinies have only the validity of possibility, he can run through the whole scale almost as fast as children do.

What takes the ironist's time, however, is the solicitude he employs in dressing himself in the costume proper to the poetic character he has poetically composed for himself. Here the ironist is very well informed and consequently has a considerable selection of masquerade costumes from which to choose. At times he walks around with the proud air of a Roman patrician wrapped in a bordered toga, or he sits in the *sella curulis*[88] with imposing Roman earnestness; at times he conceals himself in the humble costume of a penitent pilgrim; then again he sits with his legs crossed like a Turkish pasha in his harem; at times he flutters about as light and free as a bird in the role of an amorous zither player. This is what the ironist means when he says that one should live poetically; this is what he achieves by poetically composing himself.

But we turn back to the earlier comment that it is one thing to let oneself be poetically composed and another thing to compose oneself poetically. An individual who lets himself be poetically composed does have a definite given context into which he has to fit and thus does not become a word without meaning because it is wrenched out of its associations. But for the ironist, this context, which he would call a demanding appendix, has no validity, and since it is not his concern to form himself in such a way that he fits into his environment, then the environment must be formed to fit him—in other words, he poetically composes not only himself but he poetically composes his environment also.[89] The ironist stands proudly inclosed within himself, and just as Adam had the animals pass by, he lets people pass before him and finds no fellowship for himself. In so doing, he continually collides with the actuality to which he belongs. Therefore it becomes important for him to suspend what is constitutive in actuality, that which orders and supports it: that is, morality [*Moral*] and ethics [*Sædelighed*].[90]

Here we have come to the point that has been the particular object of Hegel's attack. Everything established in the given actuality has nothing but poetic validity for the ironist, for he, after all, is living poetically. But when the given actuality loses its validity for the ironist in this way, it is not because it is an antiquated actuality that must be replaced by a truer actuality, but because the ironist is the eternal *I* for which no actuality is XIII 355
adequate. Here we also perceive the implications of the ironist's placing himself outside and above morality and ethics, something that even Solger[91] declaims against in pointing out that this is not what he means by irony. It cannot really be said that the ironist places himself outside and above morality and ethics, but he lives far too abstractly, far too metaphysically and esthetically to reach the concretion of the moral and the ethical. For him, life is a drama, and what absorbs him is the ingenious complication of this drama. He himself is a spectator, even when he himself is the one acting. Thus he infinitizes

his *I*, volatilizes it metaphysically and esthetically, and while his *I* sometimes contracts as egotistically and narrowly as possible, at other times it flaps about so loosely and disintegratedly that the whole world can be encompassed in it. He is inspired by self-sacrificing virtue the way a spectator is inspired by it in a theater; he is a severe critic who knows very well when this virtue becomes insipid and inauthentic. He himself repents, but he repents esthetically, not ethically. In the moment of repentance, he is outside and above his repentance, testing to see whether it is poetically appropriate, whether it could do as a line in the mouth of a poetic character.

As the ironist poetically composes himself and his environment with the greatest possible poetic license, as he lives in this totally hypothetical and subjunctive way, his life loses all continuity. He succumbs completely to mood. His life is nothing but moods.[92] Now it is certainly true that to have mood can be something very genuine and that no mortal life is so absolute that it does not know the contrasts involved therein. In a sound and healthy life, however, the mood is just an intensification of the life that ordinarily stirs and moves within a person. An earnest Christian, for example, is well aware that there are moments when he is more profoundly and vitally gripped by the Christian life than he usually is, but he does not therefore become a pagan when the mood passes. Indeed, the more soundly and earnestly he lives, the more he will become master of his moods, that is, the more he will humble himself under them and thereby save his soul.

But since there is no continuity in the ironist, the most contrasting moods succeed one another. At times he is a god, at times a grain of sand. His moods are just as occasional as the incarnations of Brahma. And the ironist, who considers him-
XIII self free, thereby falls under the horrible law of world irony
356 and drudges along in the most frightful slavery. But the ironist is a poet, and that is why, although he is sport for the whims of world irony, it does not always appear so. He poetizes everything, poetizes his moods, too. In order genuinely to be free, he must have control of his moods; therefore one mood must instantly be succeeded by another. If it so happens that

his moods succeed one another so nonsensically that even he notices that things are not going quite right, he poetizes. He poetizes that it is he himself who evokes the mood; he poetizes until he becomes so intellectually paralyzed that he stops poetizing. Thus the mood itself has no reality for the ironist, and he seldom vents his mood except in the form of contrast. He hides his sorrow in the superior incognito of jesting; his happiness is muffled up in bemoaning. At times he is on the way to the monastery, and along the way he visits Venusberg;[93] at times he is on the way to Venusberg, and along the way he prays at a monastery. Irony's scientific-scholarly endeavor also ends up in mood. It is especially for this that Hegel criticizes Tieck, and it is also present in his correspondence with Solger. At times he has a clear grasp of everything, at times he is seeking; at times he is a dogmatician, at times a doubter, at times Jacob Böhme, at times the Greeks,[94] etc.—nothing but moods.

But since there always must be a bond that ties these contrasts together, a unity in which the enormous dissonances of these moods resolve themselves, upon closer inspection one will reveal this unity in the ironist. Boredom[95] is the only continuity the ironist has. Boredom, this eternity devoid of content, this salvation devoid of joy, this superficial profundity, this hungry glut. But boredom is precisely the negative unity admitted into a personal consciousness, wherein the opposites vanish. That both Germany and France at this time have far too many such ironists and no longer need to be initiated into the secrets of boredom by some English lord, a traveling member of a spleen club, and that a few of the young breed in Young Germany and Young France would long ago have been dead of boredom if their respective governments had not been paternal enough to give them something to think about by having them arrested—surely no one will deny. If anyone de- XIII
sires an excellent picture of an ironist who by the very duality 357
of his existence lacked existence, I will call attention to Asa-Loki.[96]

We perceive here how irony continues to be totally negative in that in the realm of theory it establishes a misrelation between idea and actuality, between actuality and idea, and in the realm of practice between possibility and actuality, between actuality and possibility. —In order to demonstrate this further in the historical manifestation of irony, I shall examine its most important representatives in some detail.

FRIEDRICH SCHLEGEL

The subject for discussion here is Friedrich Schlegel's celebrated novel *Lucinde*,*[97] the gospel of Young Germany[98] and the system for its *Rehabilitation des Fleisches* [rehabilitation of the flesh], which was an abomination to Hegel.[99] But this discussion is not without its difficulties, because, inasmuch as *Lucinde* is a very obscene book, as is well known, by citing some parts of it for more detailed consideration I run the risk of making it impossible for even the purest reader to escape altogether unscathed. I shall, however, be as circumspect and careful as possible.

Lest an injustice be done to Schlegel, one must bear in mind the many degradations that have crept into a multitude of life's relationships and have been especially indefatigable in making love as tame, as housebroken, as sluggish, as dull, as useful and usable as any other domestic animal—in short, as unerotic as possible. To that extent, we would be very obligated to Schlegel if he should succeed in finding a way out, but unfortunately the climate he discovered, the only climate in which love can really thrive, is not a more southern climate compared with ours in the north but is an ideal climate nowhere to be found. Therefore it is not just the tame ducks and geese of domestic love that beat their wings and raise a dreadful cry when they hear the wild birds of love swishing by over their
XIII 358 heads,[100] but it is every more profoundly poetic person whose longings are too powerful to be bound by romantic spider webs, whose demands upon life are too great to be satisfied by writing a novel, who precisely on poetry's behalf must reg-

* *Lucinde*, a novel by Friedrich v. Schlegel (second unaltered edition, Stuttgart: 1835).

ister his protest at this point, must try to show that it is not a way out that Friedrich Schlegel found but a wrong way he strayed into, must try to show that living is something different from dreaming.

If we examine more closely what it is that Schlegel was combating with his irony, presumably no one will deny that there was and is much in the ingress, progress, and egress of the marriage relationship that deserves a correction such as this and that makes it natural for the subject to want to be liberated. There is a very narrow earnestness, an expediency, a miserable teleology, which many people worship as an idol that demands infinite endeavor as its legitimate sacrifice. Thus in and of itself love is nothing but becomes something only through the intention whereby it is integrated with the pettiness that creates such a furor in the private theaters of families. "Absichten haben, nach Absichten handeln, und Absichten mit Absichten zu neuer Absicht künstlich verweben; diese Unart ist so tief in die närrische Natur des gottähnlichen Menschen eingewurzelt, dasz er sichs nun ordentlich vorsetzen und zur Absicht machen musz, wenn er sich einmahl ohne alle Absicht, auf dem innern Strom ewig flieszender Bilder und Gefühle frei bewegen will [To have intentions, to act according to intentions, to weave one intention artificially into another intention so as to arrive at another: still this perversion is rooted so deeply in godlike man's idiotic nature that if he wants to move freely and for once completely unintentionally on the inner stream of eternally flowing images and feelings, he actually has to intend consciously and formally to do so]" (p. 153).[101] "Freilich wie die Menschen so lieben, ist es etwas anders. Da liebt der Mann in der Frau nur die Gattung, die Frau im Mann nur den Grad seiner natürlichen Qvalitäten und seiner bürgerlichen Existenz und beide in den Kindern nur ihr Machwerk und ihr Eigenthum [To be sure, the way people usually love is quite another thing. With them, the man loves only the species in the woman, and the woman only the degree of the man's natural gifts and his social position, and they love their children only for being their own bungling creations and their property]" (p. 55).[102] "O! es ist wahr, meine

Freundin, der Mensch ist von Natur eine ernsthafte Bestie [Oh, it's true, my dear—man is inherently a serious beast]" (p. 57).[103]

There is a moral prudery, a straitjacket, in which no reasonable person can move. In God's name, let it break to pieces. Conversely, there are the moonlit theater marriages of an exaggerated romanticism for which nature at least can have no purpose and whose unproductive labor pains and weak embraces[104] are of no more service to Christian than to pagan countries. Just give irony a free rein against anything like that. But Schlegel does not limit his attack to only that kind of falsity.

There is a Christian view of marriage that in the very hour
XIII of the wedding has had the boldness to pronounce the curse
359 before giving the benediction. There is a Christian view that places everything under sin, knows no exception, spares nothing, neither the child in the womb nor the most beautiful of women. There is an earnestness in this view too high to be grasped by the bustling laborers in prosaic, everyday life, too rigorous to let itself be mocked by marital improvisers.

Those days are over and gone—those days when human beings lived so happily without sorrows and cares, so innocently, when everything was so human, when the gods themselves set the tone and sometimes laid down their heavenly dignity in order fraudulently to gain the love of a mortal woman, when someone who softly and secretly stole away to a tryst could fear or be flattered to see a god among his rivals—the times when the heavens high and beautiful arched overhead as a friendly witness to happy love or quiet and grave hid it in the solemn peacefulness of night, when everything lived for love alone and for the happy lovers everything in turn was but a myth about love.

Here is the difficulty, and it is from this point of view that we must form an estimate of Schlegel's efforts and those of the younger and older romantics. Those times are past, and yet the longing of romanticism yearns to go back to them; it does not make *peregrinationes sacras* [holy pilgrimages] in that direction but *profanas* [profane]. Now, if it were possible to

reconstruct a vanished age, we still would have to reconstruct it in all its purity, Greek culture, for example, in all its naïveté. But this romanticism does not do. It is not really Greek culture that it reconstructs but an unknown part of the world that it discovers. And not only this, but its enjoyment is extremely refined, because it not only wishes to enjoy naïvely but in its enjoyment also wants to be conscious of the destruction of the given morality. The point, so to speak, of its enjoyment is to smirk at the morality under which others, so it thinks, are sighing, and herein resides the free play of ironic arbitrariness. By means of the spirit, Christianity has set flesh and spirit* at variance, and either the spirit has to negate flesh or the flesh has to negate the spirit. Romanticism wants the latter, and its XIII
difference from Greek culture is that in its enjoyment of the 360
flesh it also enjoys the negation of the spirit. In so doing, it thinks it is living poetically, but I hope to show that the poetic is the very thing it misses, because true inward infinity comes only through resignation, and only this inner infinity is truly infinite and truly poetic.

Schlegel's *Lucinde* is an attempt to suspend all ethics [*Sædelighed*][107] or, as Erdmann rather aptly expresses it: "Alle sittliche Bestimmungen sind nur Spiel, es ist willkührlich für den Liebenden, ob die Ehe Monogamie, ob Ehe *en quatre* ist u. s. f. [All ethical qualifications are mere play, and to the lover it is an arbitrary matter whether marriage is monogamous, whether marriage is *en quatre* (in fours) etc.]."**

If it were possible to imagine *Lucinde* as a whole to be merely a caprice, a whimsical darling child of arbitrariness, kicking its legs like little Wilhelmine[108] without a care for her dress or for what the world thinks; if it were merely a hilarious playfulness that took joy in setting everything on its head, in

* By no means does Christianity want thereby to destroy the sensuous,[105] for it teaches that not until the resurrection will there be neither taking nor giving in marriage, but it also calls attention to the husband who did not have time to come to the great wedding because he himself was going to be married.[106]

** Johann Eduard Erdmann, *Vorlesungen über Glauben und Wissen* (Berlin: 1837), p. 86 (ed. tr.).

turning everything upside down; if it were merely witty irony over all the ethics that is identical with custom and habit—who, then, would be so laughable as not to want to laugh at it, who, then, would be such a surly slug that he would not have the time of his life relishing it?

But this is by no means the case. On the contrary, *Lucinde* has a highly doctrinaire character, and a certain melancholy earnestness that runs through it seems to come from the fact that its hero has arrived too late at the knowledge of this glorious truth and that a part of his life has thus gone unused. Thus the "brazenness"[109] to which this novel so often returns and which it seems to call for is not a whimsical, momentary suspension of the objectively valid, so that the word "brazenness" used here is itself a flippancy, as is so often the case when a strong word is deliberately used—no, this brazenness is what we plainly and bluntly call brazenness, but it is so charming and interesting that by comparison morality, modesty, and decency, which at first glance have something appealing about them, appear to be very insignificant characters. Anyone who has read *Lucinde* through will admit that it actually does have a kind of doctrinaire character. If anyone wishes to deny it, will he please explain the difficulty that arises from the fact that Young Germany has been so utterly mistaken about it. Should someone succeed in explaining that, may I remind him that Schlegel, as is well known, be-
XIII came a Catholic later in his life and as such discovered that the
361 Reformation was the second Fall of man, which adequately indicates that he had been in earnest with *Lucinde*.

What *Lucinde* attempts, then, is to *annul* all ethics [*Sædelighed*][110]—not only in the sense of custom and usage, but all the ethics that is the validity of spirit, the mastery of the spirit over the flesh. Thus it will become apparent that it completely corresponds to what we earlier described as irony's special endeavor: to cancel all actuality and substitute for it an actuality that is no actuality. Therefore, it is entirely in order that the girl, or rather the woman, in whose arms Julius finds rest, that Lucinde "also was one of those who had a decided bent for the romantic and who do not live in the ordinary world but in a self-created and self-conceived world" (p. 96),[111] one of those, therefore, who essentially have no other actuality than the sensate, and it is also entirely in order that one of Julius's great tasks is to picture to himself an eternal embrace,[112] presumably as the one and only true actuality.

If, then, we regard *Lucinde* as a kind of catechism of love, it demands of its disciples "was Diderot die Empfindung des Fleisches nennt, eine seltene Gabe [what Diderot calls the sensitivity of the flesh, a rare gift]" and is committed to developing it into that higher artistic sense of voluptuousness (pp. 29 and 30),[113] and Julius appears as the priest in this divine worship "not without unction," as the one "zu wem der Witz selbst durch eine Stimme vom geöffneten Himmel herab sprach: Du bist mein lieber Sohn, an dem ich Wohlgefallen habe [to whom Wit himself has spoken with a voice coming down from the open heavens: You are my beloved son in whom I find favor]" (p. 35),[114] as one who cries out to himself and others: "*Weihe dich* selbst ein und verkündige es, dasz die Natur allein ehrwürdig und die Gesundheit allein liebenswürdig ist [Consecrate thyself and proclaim to the world that nature alone is worthy of being honored, and health alone of being loved]" (p. 27).

What it wishes is the naked sensuousness in which spirit is a negated element; what it resists is the spirituality in which sensuousness is an assimilated element. This being so, it is wrong to present the little two-year-old Wilhelmine, "die geistreichste Person ihrer Zeit oder ihres Alters [the cleverest person for her age—or of her time]" (p. 15), as its ideal, since in her sensuousness spirit is not denied, inasmuch as spirit is not yet present. On the whole, it wishes nakedness and thus hates the northern cold; it points the finger of scorn at the narrowmindedness that cannot tolerate nakedness. Whether it is a narrowmindedness or whether the veil of apparel is not rather a beautiful picture of how all sensuousness ought to be, XIII 362
for if sensuousness is ruled by spirit, it is not naked—I shall not go into that subject further but only point out that we still forgive Archimedes for running stark naked through the streets of Syracuse, and surely this is not because of the mild

southern climate but because his intellectual joy, his εὕρηκα, εὕρηκα [I have found (it), I have found (it)],[115] was adequate attire.

The confusion and disorder that *Lucinde* wishes to bring about in all that is established is illustrated in the novel itself by the most complete confusion in construction. Thus, at the very beginning, Julius declares that along with the rest of the rules and regulations of reason and ethics, he has abandoned also a sense of time (p. 3),[116] and further on he says: "Für mich und für diese Schrift, für meine Liebe zu ihr und für ihre Bildung in sich, ist aber kein Zweck zweckmässiger, als der, dasz ich gleich Anfangs das was wir Ordnung nennen vernichte, weit von ihr entferne und mir das Recht einer reizenden Verwirrung deutlich zueigne und durch die That behaupte [No purpose, however, is more purposeful for myself and for this work, for my love for it and for its own structure, than to destroy at the very outset all that part we call order, remove it, and claim explicitly and affirm actually the right to a charming confusion]" (p. 5).[117] He hopes to achieve the purely poetic in this manner, and as he abandons all understanding and lets fantasy alone prevail,* the power of the imagination may succeed (for him and the reader, too, if he wants to do likewise) in securing this movement and positioning [*Mellemhverandre*] in a simple, eternally moving image. —Despite this confusion I shall try to give a kind of order to my presentation and focus the whole on a particular point.

* This (letting fantasy alone prevail) is repeated throughout *Lucinde*. Who would be so inhuman as not to be able to enjoy the free play of fantasy, but that does not imply that all of life should be abandoned to imaginative intuition. When fantasy alone gains the upper hand in this way, it exhausts and anesthetizes the soul, robs it of all moral tension, makes life a dream. But this is essentially what *Lucinde* attempts to promote, and its position is fundamentally described on page 153 in the following words: "Es ist der Gipfel des Verstandes, aus eigner Wahl zu schweigen, die Seele der Phantasie wieder zu geben und die süszen Tändeleien der jungen Mutter mit ihrem Schooszkinde nicht zu stören [The acme of intelligence is choosing to keep silent, restoring the soul to the imagination, and not disturbing the sweet dalliance of the young mother and her baby]."[118] This clearly means that when the understanding has reached its apex, its order should give way to fantasy, which now alone is to prevail and not be an interlude in the task of life.

The hero in this novel, Julius, is no Don Juan (who by means of his sensate genius as a necromancer casts a spell on everything; who acts with an immediate authority; who XIII 363
shows that he is lord and master, an authority that words cannot describe but that can be suggested by a few absolutely imperative bow strokes by Mozart; who does not seduce but by whom all would like to be seduced, and if their innocence were restored to them would want to be seduced again; a daimon who has no past, no history of development, but like Minerva immediately steps forward fully armed[119]) but a personality trapped in reflection, who develops only in a successive process. In "*Lehrjahre der Männlichkeit* [Apprenticeship for Manhood]," we learn more of his history. "Pharao zu spielen mit dem Anscheine der heftigsten Leidenschaft und doch zerstreut und abwesend zu seyn; in einem Augenblick von Hitze alles zu wagen und, sobald es vorloren war, sich gleichgültig wegzuwenden: das war nur eine von den schlimmen Gewohnheiten, unter denen Julius seine wilde Jugend verstürmte [Playing cards with the appearance of being passionately involved and yet detached and inattentive; in one moment of feverish excitement wagering everything, and having lost that, turning away indifferently: this was only one of the bad habits in which Julius spent his wild and stormy youth]" (p. 59).[120]

The author believes that by this one trait he has adequately described Julius's life. We quite agree. Julius is a young man who is internally disrupted and by this very disruption has acquired a vivid idea of that black art that in a few seconds is able to make a person many, many years older—a young man who by means of this interior disruption apparently possesses an enormous power, just as the ardor of despair gives rise to authentic strength—a young man who a long time ago already began his grand finale[121] but still raises his goblet with a certain dignity and charm, with a worldly intellectual ease, and concentrates all his power in one single breath in order by a brilliant exit to cast a glorifying light over a life that has been worthless and will not be missed—a young man who has had a long acquaintance with the thought of suicide but whose storms of soul have not granted him time to make up his mind. Now it is love that must rescue him. After having been at the point of seducing a young and innocent girl[122] (incidentally, an adventure of no further significance to him, for she obviously was too innocent to be able to satisfy his inquisitiveness), he finds the instructor he needs in Lisette, a teacher who has long been initiated into the nocturnal mysteries of love, whose public instruction Julius tries in vain to limit to private instruction for himself alone.

XIII 364 The portrait of Lisette[123] is perhaps the best executed one in the whole novel, and the author has treated it with a marked preference and done everything to cast a poetic light over it. As a child she had been more melancholy than thoughtless but already at that time was demonically aroused by sensuousness (page 78).[124] Later she had been an actress, but only for a short time, and always made fun of her incompetence and the boredom she had endured. At last she had devoted herself totally to the service of sensuousness. Next to independence, she had an inordinate love of money, which she nevertheless knew how to use with taste. At times she allowed her favors to be paid for with money, at times with the satisfaction of her whimsical preference for some individual. Her boudoir was simple and devoid of all the customary furniture, except for the large and expensive mirrors on all sides and between them voluptuous paintings by Corregio and Titian. Instead of chairs, genuine oriental rugs and groups of half-life-sized marble statues. Here she often sat Turkish fashion all day long, alone, her hands idle in her lap, for she abhorred all feminine work. She regaled herself only from time to time with sweet-smelling things and during this time had stories, travel accounts, and fairy tales read to her by her attendant, a handsome, supple boy she herself had seduced in his fourteenth year. She paid only slight attention to the reading, except when there was something laughable or a general comment she also considered true, for she disregarded anything else, had no sense for anything but reality, and thought all poetry ridiculous.

This is Schlegel's depiction of a life, however corrupt it is, that nevertheless seems to claim to be poetic. Especially predominant here is the superior indolence that cares for nothing at all, that does not care to work but scorns every feminine occupation, does not care to engage its mind but merely lets it be engaged, that disperses and exhausts all the powers of the soul in soft enjoyment, and lets consciousness itself evaporate into a loathsome gloaming. But still it was enjoyment, and to enjoy, after all, is to live poetically. Indeed, the author seems to want to ascribe something poetic to her distributing her favors without always having regard for money; at those times when it was not money that determined her choice, he seems to want her wretched love to be glorified by a mirroring of the devotion that only innocent love possesses, as if it were more XIII 365 poetic to be a slave to whims than a slave to money.

So there she sits in this voluptuous room and is lost to external consciousness; the great mirrors reflecting her image on all sides provide the only consciousness she has left. Therefore, when speaking of herself, she was in the habit of calling herself Lisette and frequently said that if she could write she would write her story as if it were that of someone else; she generally preferred to speak of herself in the third person. However, in no way was this because her exploits on earth were as world-historical as a Caesar's,[125] so that her life did not belong to her but to the world, but it was because this *vita ante acta* [earlier life] was too heavy for her to bear. To collect her thoughts about it, to let its threatening shapes pass judgment on her—that would be too earnest to be poetic. But to let this miserable life become volatilized in vague outlines, to stare at it as at something that did not concern her—that she would do. She wanted to grieve over this unhappy, lost girl; she might even offer her a tear, but that this girl was she herself—that she wanted to forget.

It is a weakness to want to forget, but in the effort to do so there may at times stir an energy suggestive of something better, but to want to live over again poetically in such a way that repentance does not prick because, after all, the question is about someone else altogether, and yet the enjoyment is heightened by this secret participation—this is horrible, soft cowardice. And yet it is this collapsing into an esthetic stupe-

XIII 366 faction* that actually comes out in the whole of *Lucinde* as a sign of what it is to live poetically and, as it lulls the deeper *I* into a somnambulant state, gives the arbitrary *I* free rein in ironic self-satisfaction.[132]

This will now be examined in a little more detail. There have been enough attempts to show that books like *Lucinde* are immoral [*umoralsk*], and "alas!" and "alack!" have frequently been sounded over such books, but as long as the author has been openly allowed to claim and the reader secretly

* This is enunciated especially in an "Idyll of Idleness,"[126] where the highest perfection is assigned to sheer and unalloyed passivity. "Je schöner das Klima ist, je passiver ist man. Nur Italiener wissen zu gehen, und nur die im Orient verstehen zu liegen; wo hat sich aber der Geist zarter und süszer gebildet als in Indien? Und unter allen Himmelsstrichen ist es das Recht des Müszig-gangs, was Vornehme und Gemeine unterscheidet, und das eigentliche Princip des Adels [The more beautiful the climate, the more passive one is. Only Italians know how to walk, and only Orientals how to repose. And where has the spirit taken a more delicate and a sweeter form than in India? And in all parts of the earth it is the right to idleness that distinguishes the superior from the inferior classes. It is the intrinsic principle of aristocracy]" (p. 42).[127] "The highest, most perfect life is nothing other than pure vegetating."[128] Plant life is on the whole the ideal to which it strives; therefore Julius writes to Lucinde: "Wir beide werden noch einst in Einem Geiste anschauen, dasz wir Blüthen Einer Pflanze oder Blätter Einer Blume sind, und mit Lächeln werden wir dann wissen, dasz was wir jetzt nur Hoffnung nennen, eigentlich Erinnerung war [There will come a time when the two of us will perceive in a single spirit that we are blossoms of a single plant or petals of a single flower, and then we will know with a smile that what we now call merely hope is really remem-
XIII 366 brance]" (p. 11).[129] Hence longing itself assumes the form of vegetative still life. " 'Julius,' fragte Lucinde, 'warum fühle ich in so heiterer Ruhe die tiefe Sehnsucht?' 'Nur in der Sehnsucht finden wir die Ruhe,' antwortete Julius. 'Ja die Ruhe ist nur das, wenn unser Geist durch nichts gestört wird, sich zu sehnen und zu suchen, wo er nichts höheres finden kann, als die eigene Sehnsucht' (p. 148). Julius: 'Die heilige Ruhe fand ich nur in jenem Sehnen, Freundinn.' Lucinde: 'Und ich in dieser schönen Ruhe jene heilige Sehnsucht' (p. 150) ['Julius,' Lucinde asked, 'why do I feel this deep sense of yearning amid this happy peace?' 'Only in yearning do we find peace,' replied Julius. 'Yes, there is peace only when our spirit remains completely undisturbed in its yearning and seeking after itself, only when it can find nothing higher than its own yearning'] (p. 148).[130] [Julius: 'I found holy peace only in that yearning, my love.' Lucinde: 'And I that holy yearning only in this lovely peace']" (p. 150).[131]

to believe that they are poetic, not much is gained, and so much the less since man has just as great a claim upon the poetic as the moral has a claim upon him. Therefore, let it be said, as it will also be demonstrated, that these books are not only immoral but also unpoetic, for they are irreligious; let it above all be said that anyone can live poetically who truly wants to do so.

If we ask what poetry is, we may say in general that it is victory over the world; it is through a negation of the imperfect actuality that poetry opens up a higher actuality, expands and transfigures the imperfect into the perfect and thereby assuages the deep pain that wants to make everything dark. To that extent, poetry is a kind of reconciliation, but it is not the true reconciliation, for it does not reconcile me with the actuality in which I am living; no transubstantiation of the given actuality takes place by virtue of this reconciliation, but it reconciles me with the given actuality by giving me another, a higher and more perfect actuality. The greater the contrast, the less perfect the actual reconciliation, so that when all is said and done there is often no reconciliation but rather an enmity. Therefore, only the religious is able to bring about the true reconciliation, because it infinitizes actuality for me. Therefore, the poetic is a kind of victory over actuality, but the infinitizing is more of an emigration from actuality than a continuance XIII 367 in it. To live poetically, then, is to live infinitely. But infinity can be either an external infinity or an internal infinity. The person who wants to enjoy infinitely poetically does indeed have an infinity before him, but it is an external infinity, because in my enjoying, I am continually outside myself in that other something. But an infinity such as that must cancel itself. Only when I in my enjoying am not outside myself but am inside myself, only then is my enjoyment infinite, because it is inwardly infinite. Even if he enjoys the whole world, the person who enjoys poetically nevertheless lacks one enjoyment, for he does not enjoy himself. But to enjoy oneself (of course, not in the Stoic or egotistical sense, for there is no true infinity in that, either, but in the religious sense) is the only true infinity.

If after these observations we revert to the demand to live poetically as being identical with enjoying (and precisely because our age is so saturated with reflection, the contrast between the poetic actuality and the given actuality must manifest itself in a far more profound form than it has ever appeared before in the world, inasmuch as poetic development previously went hand in hand with the given actuality, but now the issue is in fact to be or not to be, since one is not satisfied to live poetically once in a while but demands that all life be poetic), it is easy to see that it misses the highest enjoyment, the true bliss in which the subject is not dreaming but possesses himself in infinite clarity, is absolutely transparent[133] to himself, which is possible only for the religious individual, who does not have his infinity outside himself but inside himself. To take revenge, for example, is a poetic enjoyment, and pagans believed that the gods had reserved revenge for themselves[134] because it was so sweet; but even if I had my vengeance absolutely satisfied, even if I were a pagan god before whom all trembled, and whose fiery wrath could consume everything, yet in my revenge I would be enjoying myself only egotistically, my enjoyment would be only an external infinity, and the simplest human being who did not allow his revenge to rage but controlled his wrath would be much closer to having overcome the world,[135] and not until he enjoyed himself in truth, not until he had inward infinity, not until then would he live poetically.

If from this position we were to regard the life as presented in *Lucinde* as a poetic life, we would concede it every possible
XIII 368 enjoyment, but presumably no one will deny us the right to use one predicate concerning it—that it is an infinitely cowardly life. If it is not maintained that to be cowardly is the same as to live poetically, it ought to be possible for this poetic life to manifest itself as somewhat or, more correctly, totally unpoetic, because living poetically is not the same as being in the dark about oneself, as sweating oneself out in loathsome sultriness, but it means becoming clear and transparent to oneself, not in finite and egotistical self-satisfaction but in one's absolute and eternal validity.[136] And if this is not possible

for every human being, then life is lunacy, then it is incomparably stupid for the single individual, even though he may be the most richly endowed person who ever lived, to delude himself into thinking that what is denied to everyone else is reserved for him, because either to be human is the absolute, or all life is nonsense, and despair is the only alternative for anyone not demented enough, not unkind and proud enough, not despairing enough, to believe that he is the chosen one. Consequently, we should not limit ourselves to reciting moral aphorisms against the whole trend that after *Lucinde*—often with great talent, often very enchantingly—has taken it upon itself not to lead people but to mislead them. But we are not to allow it to delude itself and others that it is poetic or that it is the way to attain what every human being has an inalienable claim upon—to live poetically.

But we return again to Julius and Lisette. Lisette ends her life as she had begun it, by carrying out what Julius never had time to decide to do, and by committing suicide seeks to attain the objective of all her endeavors—to be rid of herself. She preserves her esthetic pattern to the end, however, and her last lines, spoken, according to her servant, in a loud voice—"Lisette soll zu Grunde gehen, zu Grunde jetzt gleich: so will es das Schicksal, das eiserne [Lisette must perish, perish now: that is the will of an iron fate]"[137]—must be considered a kind of dramatic idiocy that for someone who had earlier been an actress in a theater and later became one in life would be quite natural.

Lisette's death was, of course, bound to have an impact upon Julius. But I shall let Schlegel himself speak, lest I be accused of distorting it. "Die erste Folge von Lisettens Ruin war, dasz er *ihr Andenken* mit schwärmerischer Achtung *vergötterte* [The first consequence of Lisette's ruin was that he *worshiped her memory* with fanatical respect]" (p. 77).[138] But not even this event was enough to develop Julius: "Diese Ausnahme von dem, was Julius für gewöhnlich hielt beim weiblichen Geschlecht" (ordinarily, according to Julius, they did XIII
not possess the "high energy" that Lisette had), "war zu einzig 369
und die Umgebung, in der er sie fand, zu unrein, als dasz er

dadurch zu einer wahren Ansicht hätte gelangen können [Lisette was too unique an exception to Julius's usual ideas of the female sex, . . . and the surroundings in which he had met her were too unclean for him to have been able to arrive at a true understanding of women by this experience]" (p. 78).[139]

Thereupon Schlegel has Julius, after withdrawing into solitude for a time, come in contact with social life again and in a more mental relation to several feminine members of this social life skim once again through several love affairs until he eventually finds in Lucinde the unity of all the separate elements, finds just as much sensuousness as brilliance. But inasmuch as this erotic liaison has no deeper foundation than a mental sensuousness, since it has no element of resignation—in other words, since it is no marriage, since it maintains the view that passivity and vegetating are perfection—here once again ethics [*Sædelighed*][140] is negated. Therefore, this love affair can acquire no content, in the deeper sense can have no history, and their diversions can be only the same *en deux* as Julius thought were the best to use in his solitude[141]—namely, pondering what one or another brilliant lady would say or reply in this or that piquant situation. Thus it is a love without any real content, and the eternity so frequently talked about is nothing but what could be called the eternal moment of enjoyment, an infinity that is no infinity and as such is unpoetic.

One can scarcely keep from smiling when such a flimsy and weakly constructed erotic liaison fancies that it is able to defy the storms of life, fancies that it has the strength to regard "*die herbeste Laune des Zufalls für schönen Witz und ausgelassene Willkühr* [the bitterest whim of chance as a lovely witticism and an exuberant caprice]" (p. 9),[142] since this love does not belong in the real world at all but in an imaginary world where the lovers themselves are lords of the storms and hurricanes. Inasmuch as everything in such a liaison is meant to be pleasurable, it naturally perceives just as egotistically its relation to the generation that owes its existence to it: "So schlingt die Religion der Liebe unsre Liebe immer inniger und stärker zusammen, wie das Kind die Lust der zärtlichen Eltern dem Echo gleich verdoppelt [So is it that the religion of love weaves

our love ever more closely and tightly together, just as the child, echolike, redoubles the happiness of its tender parents]" (p. 11).[143] Frequently enough one meets parents who with foolish earnestness wish to see their children well settled as soon as possible, perhaps even well settled in the grave. In XIII
contrast, Julius and Lucinde prefer to keep them continually 370
the same age as little Wilhelmine in order to derive amusement from them.

The oddity about *Lucinde* and the whole trend associated with it is that, by starting from the freedom and the constitutive authority of the *I*, one does not arrive at a still higher spirituality but comes only to sensuousness and consequently to its opposite. In ethics [*Sædelighed*],[144] the relation to spirit is implied, but because the *I* wants a higher freedom, it negates the ethical spirit and thereby falls under the laws of the flesh and of drives. But since this sensuousness is not naïve, it follows that the same arbitrariness that installed sensuousness in its presumed rights can shift over the very next instant to assert an abstract and exaggerated spirituality. Now these vibrations can be interpreted both as the play of world irony with the individual and as the individual's attempt to copy world irony.

TIECK[145]

The focus in this discussion will be especially on some of Tieck's satirical dramas and his poetry. His earlier novellas were written before the Schlegels brought him to the knowledge of the truth; his later novellas draw closer and closer to actuality and with a certain latitude at times come to correspond to it. In Tieck, I already breathe more easily, and when I look back at *Lucinde* once again, I seem to be waking from a troubled, uneasy dream in which I simultaneously heard seductive tones of sensuousness and wild, bestial howling intermingled with them. I seem to have been offered a nauseous preparation, brewed in a witch's cauldron, that deprives one of all relish, all appetite for life. Schlegel didacticizes; he turns directly against actuality. This is not the case with Tieck, who

indulges in a poetic abandon, but he maintains this in its indifference toward actuality. Only where he does not do so does he come close to attacking actuality, but even then he still attacks it more indirectly. Surely no one will deny that such a poetic abandon that is utterly inordinate in its excessively ironic capering[146] has its validity. If it has, then Hegel[147] has
XIII 371 frequently wronged Tieck, and I must agree completely with the comment made somewhere by an otherwise ardent Hegelian*: "In Spasz und Heiterkeit fand er (Hegel) sich gleichfalls behaglich, doch die letzte Tiefe des Humors blieb ihm theilweise verschlossen, und die neueste Form der Ironie widerstrebte dermaszen seiner eigenen Richtung, dasz es ihm fast an dem Organ gebrach, auch das Aechte in ihr anzuerkennen oder gar zu genieszen [Equally at home with jest and cheer, he (Hegel) nevertheless remained partly impervious to the ultimate depths of humor, and the most recent form of irony stood in such stark contrast to his own orientation that he completely lacked the wherewithal with which to recognize or appreciate what was genuine in it]."

But the closer such poetizing comes to actuality, the more it becomes intelligible only through a break with actuality, the more polemic it conceals in itself, the more it makes a polemic tendency a condition for the readers' sympathy, so much more that it forgets its poetic indifference, loses its innocence, and acquires an objective. Then it is no longer the poetic license that like Münchhausen collars itself and in this way, without any footing, floating in the air, makes one somersault stranger than another. It is no longer poetry's pantheistic infinity, but it is the finite subject, who applies the ironic lever in order to tip all existence out of its fixed consolidation. Now all existence becomes just a game for the poetizing arbitrariness that rejects nothing, not even the most insignificant thing, but for which nothing endures, either, not even the most significant. In this respect, one need only read the list of characters in a play by Tieck or by any other of the romantic

* Heinrich Gustav Hotho,[148] *Vorstudien für Leben und Kunst* (Stuttgart and Tübingen: 1835), p. 394.

poets to gain a notion of the unheard-of and highly improbable things that take place in their poet-world. Animals talk like human beings, human beings talk like asses, chairs and tables become conscious of their meaning in existence, human beings find existence meaningless. Nothing becomes everything, and everything becomes nothing; everything is possible, even the impossible; everything is probable, even the improbable.

But it must be borne in mind that Tieck and the whole romantic school stepped into or thought they were stepping into an age in which people seemed to be totally fossilized in finite social forms. Everything was completed and consummated in a divine Chinese optimism that let no reasonable longing go unsatisfied, no reasonable desire go unfulfilled. The glorious principles and maxims of habit and custom were the objects of a pious idolatry; everything was absolute, even the absolute. One abstained from polygamy; one wore a stovepipe hat. XIII 372
Everything had its importance. In accordance with his station, everyone felt with nuanced dignity how much he was accomplishing, how great was the importance of his indefatigable efforts to himself and to the whole. People did not live with a rash Quakerish disregard of the hours and the stroke of the hour—attempts on the part of that sort of impiety to insinuate itself were futile. Everything proceeded calmly with measured step, even the person on his way to propose marriage, because he knew, of course, that he was on a licit mission and was taking a very earnest step. Everything occurred according to the stroke of the hour. One reveled in nature on St. John's Eve [Midsummer], one was contrite on the fourth Friday after Easter [Great Day of Prayer]; one fell in love when one turned twenty, went to bed at ten o'clock. One married, one lived for domesticity and one's position in society; one acquired children, acquired family worries. One stood in the full vigor of manhood, started to be noticed in high places for one's benevolent activities, was an associate of the clergyman, under whose eyes one epically developed the many beautiful traits necessary for an honorable posthumous reputation, which one knew the pastor some day would seek in vain to stammer

out with deep emotion. One was a friend in the true sense of the word, a real friend, just as one was a real government officeholder. One knew something about the world and brought up children in the same understanding; one was inspired one evening a week by the poet's praises of the beauty of existence; one was also everything to one's own family, year in and year out with an on-the-dot certainty and precision.

The world was in its dotage and had to be rejuvenated. In that respect, romanticism was beneficial. A cool breeze, refreshing morning air, blows through romanticism from the primeval forests of the Middle Ages or from the pure ether of Greece; it sends a cold shiver down the backs of the philistines, and yet it is necessary to dispel the bestial miasma in which one breathed up to this point. The hundred years are over, the spellbound castle bestirs itself, its inhabitants awaken again, the forest breathes lightly, the birds sing, the beautiful princess once again attracts suitors, the forest resounds with the reverberation of hunters' horns and the baying of hounds, the meadows are fragrant, poems and songs break away from nature and flutter about, and no one knows whence they come or whither they go.

The world is rejuvenated, but as Heine[149] so wittily remarked, it was rejuvenated by romanticism to such a degree that it became a baby again. The tragedy of romanticism is that what it seizes upon is not actuality. Poetry awakens; the powerful longings, the mysterious intimations, the inspir-
XIII 373 ing feelings awaken; nature awakens; the enchanted princess awakens—the romanticist falls asleep. He experiences all this in a dream, and whereas everything was fast asleep around him before, now everything is awakening—but he is sleeping. But dreams do not satisfy. He wakes up tired and torpid, unrefreshed, only to lie down to sleep again, and soon he needs to produce the somnambulant state artificially, but the more art it takes, the more exaggerated also becomes the ideal that the romanticist evokes.

Romantic poetry moves between two poles. On the one side stands the given actuality with all its paltry philistinism;

on the other, the ideal actuality with its dimly emerging shapes. These two elements are indispensable to each other. The more actuality is caricatured, the higher the ideal wells up, but the fountain that wells up here does not well up into an eternal life.[150] The very fact, however, that this poetry moves between two opposites shows that in the deeper sense it is not true poetry. In no way is the true ideal in the beyond—it is behind insofar as it is the propelling force; it is ahead insofar as it is the inspiring goal, but at the same time it is within us, and this is its truth.[151]

The reason this kind of poetry cannot enter into a truly poetic relation to the reader is precisely that the writer himself does not enter into a genuinely poetic relation to what he writes. The poetic position taken by the writer is poetic arbitrariness; the total impact made by the poem is an emptiness in which nothing remains. This arbitrariness appears in the entire design. Now the play speeds ahead, then it stands still; now it stagnates in an episode, then it goes backward; now we are in Peder Madsen's Alley, then in heaven; now something so improbable takes place that the writer knows very well that it is improbable. Now there is a jingling in the distance—it is the pious procession of the three wise men; then comes a solo
for the French horn;* now something is asserted in all earnest- XIII 374
ness and is immediately turned inside out, and the unity of

* Hotho's excellent description on page 412 is appropriate: "Da behält die *abenteuernde Ungebundenheit* der Phantasie einen schrankenlosen Raum zu jederlei Art der Gebilde offen; wo sie nur immer mögen, ranken sich kecke Episoden umher, arabeskenartige Seltsamkeiten schlingen sich zu neckendem
Gelächter bunt durch das lose Gewebe, die Allegorie weitet die sonst so be- XIII 374
gräntzen Gestalten nebelhaft aus, dazwischen spuckt der parodische Scherz in verkehrendem Uebermuth, und diesem genialen Belieben verschwistert sich jene matte Behaglichkeit, die keinen müszigen Einfall zurückweisen kann, weil er auf ihrem Boden erwachsen ist [Here the *adventurous license* of the imagination reserves unlimited room for any kind of image: daring episodes swirl forth at will, arabesquelike curiosities gaudily twist themselves into teasing laughter through the loose fabric, allegory expands otherwise constricted shapes until they turn nebulous, here and there the parodic jest hovers in topsy-turvy abandonment. And this ingenious pleasure is then wedded to that flat indulgence that is unable to refuse any idle whim, because it grows out of the very ground of this indulgence]."

laughter is supposed to reconcile the contrasts, but this laughter is accompanied by the distant flute tones of a deep sadness etc. etc.

But precisely because the entire design is not ordered in a poetic totality, because for the writer the poetic is the freedom in which he has everything at his disposal, because for the reader the poetic is the freedom with which he imitates the writer's caprices, because, I repeat, the entire design is not ordered in a poetic totality, the separate elements stand [*staae*] isolated—or, more correctly, because the separate elements subsist [*bestaae*] in an isolated endeavor, there can never be any poetic unity. The polemic endeavor never finds rest, because the poetic consists precisely in continually freeing itself by means of a new polemic, and it is just as difficult for the writer to find the caricature as it is for him to find the ideal. Every polemical line continually has in it a something more, the possibility of going beyond itself in a still more ingenious depiction. The ideal endeavor in turn has no ideal, since every ideal is instantly nothing but an allegory hiding a higher ideal within itself, and so on into infinity. Thus during all this the writer grants neither himself nor the reader any rest, inasmuch as rest is the very opposite of this kind of writing. The only rest he has is the poetic eternity in which he sees the ideal, but this eternity is a nonentity, since it has no time, and therefore the ideal becomes allegory the very next instant.

Just as Tieck was incomparably ingenious in the interpretation of philistinism, was marvelously expert in skewed perspective, so his ideal endeavor has such artesian depth that the image that is to appear in the sky infinitely vanishes in the infinite. He has a singular gift for making a person feel strange, and because of their singularity the ideal human shapes that sometimes appear can actually make a person very fearful, because at times they resemble remarkable natural cre-
XIII 375 ations, and their wise and unwavering eyes do not inspire confidence but rather a certain *unheimlich* [disquieting] anxiety.*

* If someone desires a sketch in order to form some idea of a shape such as

Since this whole poetic endeavor is essentially a matter of coming closer by way of continual approximation to the mood that nevertheless can never find its perfectly adequate expression, for which reason this poetry is poetry about poetry ad infinitum, and since on the other hand it places the reader in a mood that is incommensurate even with this poetry's own achievements, it naturally has its strength in the lyrical. But this lyric must not become heavy and stiff by way of a deeper content; it must continually become lighter and lighter, must fade away, weaker and weaker, into the distant resounding of a dying echo. The musical element in the lyric is the subjective factor. This is developed very one-sidedly. Thus everything comes to depend on the sound of the verse, the resonance with which one stanza calls to and replies to the other, the graceful intertwining with which the stanza moves in light, supple dance steps and also even sings, as it were.[153] Rhyme becomes a wandering knight seeking adventure, and what Tieck and the whole romantic movement are so busily engaged in—namely, having a strange face suddenly appear that nevertheless seems so familiar that it seems as if one had seen this face long ago in a past that goes far beyond the historical consciousness—the same thing happens to rhyme, which suddenly encounters an old acquaintance from better days and begins to feel very strange about it. Weary and bored with its old associates, rhyme seeks new and interesting acquaintances. Ultimately the musical element isolates itself entirely, and at times romanticism actually succeeds in reconstructing poetry of the kind everyone remembers from childhood in the delightful verse: Eeny meeny, hippity dick, dilya dyelya, dominick.[154] Such poems must now, of course, be considered the ultimate, because here mood—and mood, after all, is all-important—has absolute sway and is utterly free, since all content is negated.

Although Tieck did not negate actuality with as much earnestness as Schlegel did, nevertheless his exaggerated and im-

---

this, I direct him to the picture found in *Des Knaben Wunderhorn, alte deutsche Lieder*, III.[152]

potent ideal, which floats about like a cloud in the sky or like
XIII the cloud's shadow fleetingly flies across the ground, reveals
376 that he has gone astray. Schlegel set his mind at rest in Catholicism; Tieck at times found repose in a kind of deification of all existence whereby everything became equally poetic.

SOLGER[155]

Solger was the one who wanted to become philosophically conscious of the nature of irony. He has presented his view in his lectures on esthetics, published after his death,* also in a few treatises found in his posthumous papers.** Hegel gave considerable attention to Solger's presentation and treats him with a certain partiality. In his oft-mentioned review (p. 486), Hegel says: "Wie sie (die Ironie) gewöhnlich vorkommt, ist sie mehr nur als ein berühmter, vornehm seyn sollender Spuk anzusehen; in Beziehung auf Solger aber kann sie als ein Princip behandelt werden [As it usually appears, irony is rather to be regarded only as a celebrated hobgoblin with aristocratic pretensions. With respect to Solger, however, it may be treated as a principle]."[157] In the introduction to his *Aesthetics* (p. 89), Hegel also discusses Solger ("Solger war nicht wie die Uebrigen mit oberflächlicher Bildung zufrieden, sondern sein ächt speculatives innerstes Bedürfnisz drängte ihn in die Tiefe der philosophischen Idee hinabzusteigen [Solger was not, as the others were, satisfied with a superficial culture. A truly speculative impulse of his innermost nature made him probe the very depths of the philosophical idea]"[158]) and laments that Solger died too early to come to the concrete fulfillment of this.

To explain Solger's views is certainly very difficult, for as Hotho correctly observes (p. 399), he has developed his point of view with *schwerbegreifbarer philosophischer Klarheit* [a philosophical clarity difficult to comprehend]. The point is simply

* K.W.F. Solger, *Vorlesungen über Aesthetik*, edited by K.W.L. Heyse (Leipzig: 1829).[156]

** *Solgers nachgelassene Schriften und Briefwechsel*, I-II, edited by Ludwig Tieck and Friedrich v. Raumer (Leipzig: 1826).

this: Solger has gone completely astray in the negative, and it is not without some hesitation that I set out upon this stormy sea,[159] not so much because I fear for my life as out of concern that it will be very difficult for me to give the reader any reliable information as to what has become of me or where I am at each particular moment. Since the negative always becomes visible only through the positive, but the negative here is the XIII
absolute monarch and is present here in all its unproductive- 377
ness, everything becomes confused, and the moment one hopes for the possibility of having a determination by which to orient oneself, everything vanishes again, because the positive that appeared in the distance is found upon closer inspection to be a new negation. Presumably Solger may have his significance in the development, but no doubt he can best be regarded as a sacrifice Hegel's system demanded. This also explains Hegel's partiality for him; he is the metaphysical knight of the negative. Therefore he does not come into collision with actuality in the sense that the other ironists do, since his irony did not in any way take the shape of opposition to actuality.* His irony is contemplative irony; he perceives the nothingness of everything. Irony is an organ, a sense for the negative.

Solger's efforts are totally within the sphere of scholarship. But since he has nowhere provided a coherently advancing, strictly scholarly discussion but, on the contrary, only aphoristic exclamations that sometimes take us into purely metaphysical observations, then into historical-philosophical, then esthetic, then ethical etc. investigations—exclamations that

* Thus Solger is entirely correct in remarking in his *Nachgelassene Schriften* (II, p. 514): "Aber ist denn nun diese Ironie ein schnödes Hinwegsetzen über Alles, was den Menschen wesentlich und ernstlich interessirt, über den ganzen Zwiespalt in seiner Natur? Keineswegs; dieses wäre eine gemeine Spötterei, die nicht über Ernst und Scherz stände, sondern auf demselben Boden und mit ihren eigenen Kräften sie bestritte [Is this irony an insolent disregard for whatever essentially and seriously interests man, a total disregard for the split in his nature? By no means. That would be a vulgar mockery, which is not superior to earnestness and jest, but rather combats them on their own level with their own weapons]."

are tangential to the whole realm of scholarship—we are already faced with great difficulty.

Add to this the fact that his use of language is frequently more poetic than philosophical (for example, when he says that God in revealing himself sacrifices himself;[160] I am indeed aware that this expression could well be used with a meaning analogous to the metaphysical meaning in modern scholarship of the phrase "God is reconciling himself with the world,"[161] but since even this usage is a volatilization of the concept with respect to Christian terminology, this misuse hardly provides any acceptable defense of Solger's treatment of an even more concrete concept), so that it does not always give a reader a clear idea of the direction in which the movement is proceeding. Such expressions as "to negate," "to destroy," and "to
XIII annul" are frequently used, but in order for the reader to be
378 truly oriented, he must know the laws of motion. The negative has, namely, a double function—it infinitizes the finite and it finitizes the infinite. But if the reader does not know in which current he is or, more correctly, if he is now in one current and then in another, everything is confused. Furthermore, there must be agreement on the importance of that which is declared to be negated, for otherwise the negation (like the caesura in that famous verse[162]) falls in the wrong place. When, for example, it is said that actuality must be destroyed, must be negated, then we must know what is understood by actuality, because in one sense actuality itself did indeed result from a negation. But this is never the case, and thus there is the kind of confusion we find in the statement that man is the *Nichtige* [nullity]* (already here we must be cautious, must agree on the sense in which man is the *Nichtige*, and to what extent there is anything positive and valid in this *Nichtige*), and the *Nichtige* must be destroyed (here again we first must hold a little conference about the extent to which man is himself able to destroy the *Nichtige* within him,

* I have kept this German word because I really do not know any exact Danish equivalent. Even though the reader may be disturbed by this word, he may still benefit from having an established memento of Solger.

whereby in another sense he does not remain the *Nichtige*), and yet the *Nichtige* within ourselves is the divine itself (see *Solgers nachgelassene Schriften*, I, p. 511).

Solger wants to bring about the absolute identity of the finite and the infinite, wants to destroy the partition that in so many ways wants to separate them. Thus he is working toward the absolute, presuppositionless beginning; consequently his striving is speculative. In his posthumous works (I, p. 507), he says: "Das ist doch wohl gewisz, dasz sich seine Wissenschaft (Philosophens) von allen übrigen dadurch wesentlich unterscheidet, dasz sie allumfassend ist. Jede andere hat etwas Vorausgesetztes, Gegebenes, entweder eine bestimmte Form der Erkenntnisz, wie die Mathematik, oder einen bestimmten Stoff, wie Geschichte, Naturkunde und dergl. Sie allein musz sich selbst schaffen [It is surely certain that his science (the philosopher's) differs essentially from every other in that it is all-encompassing. Every other science presupposes something as given, either a specific form of knowledge as in mathematics, or a specific subject matter as in history, natural science, and the like. Philosophy alone XIII
must create itself]." His contemplative irony now sees the fi- 379
nite as the *Nichtige*, as that which must be annulled.*

But, on the other hand, the infinite also must be negated; it must not continue in an otherworldly *an sich* [in itself]. In this way, the true actuality is produced. See the posthumous writings (I, p. 600): "Aber das Endliche, die gemeine Thatsache, ist eben so wenig die wahre Wirklichkeit, wie das Unendliche, die Beziehung auf Begriffe und wechselnde Gegensätze, das Ewige ist. Die wahre Wirklichkeit ist ein Moment der Anschauung, in welchem Endliches und Unendliches, die unser gemeiner Verstand nur in Beziehung auf einander erkennt, völlig aufgehoben werden, indem sich darin Gott oder das Ewige offenbart [But the finite, the ordinary fact, is no more

* Here one will immediately see the essential difference between Solger's irony and that described earlier. Solger's irony is a kind of contemplative devotion, and it is not very important to him to keep the being-for-itself subject in its prudery. All finitude must be negated, the contemplating subject as well—indeed, it actually is already negated in this contemplation.

the true actuality than the infinite, the relation to concepts and alternating opposites, the eternal is. The true actuality is a moment of intuition wherein the finite and the infinite, cognizable by our ordinary understanding only in relation to each other, are completely annulled, inasmuch as God or the eternal discloses itself in it]."

Here, then, we have the idea at the point of the absolute beginning; therefore we have it as the infinite absolute negativity. Now, if this is to become something, the negative must assert itself again in a finitizing of the idea—that is, in making it concrete. The negative is the restlessness of thought, but this restlessness must manifest itself, must become visible; its desire must manifest itself as the desire that actuates the work, its pain as the pain it engenders. If this does not happen, then we have only the unreal actuality of contemplation, devotion, and pantheism. In other words, whether one affirms devotion as an element or will have the whole of life become devotion, the true actuality still does not emerge. If it is only an element, then there is nothing to do but to produce it instantly again; if it is to fill the whole of life, then the actuality never truly comes to exist. Hence it does no good for Solger[163] to explain that we must not, as Plato does, think of the idea in a celestial or supracelestial place; it does no good for him to assure us that he does not, as Spinoza does, have finitude vanish as a mere *modus* [form]; it does no good for him not to have the idea come into existence in an eternal becoming, as Fichte does; it does as little good for him to frown upon Schelling's attempt to show that perfect being is being in existence. All such things are merely introductory studies. Solger is at the beginning, but this beginning is utterly abstract, and now the point is that the dualism that is in existence is to manifest itself
XIII 380 in its truth. But this does not happen. On the contrary, it becomes clear that Solger is unable to achieve the concession of any validity to the finite. He cannot achieve concreteness for the infinite. He sees the finite as the *Nichtige*, as the vanishing, as the *nichtige All* [universe].

Therefore moral qualifications have no validity; all finitude together with its moral and immoral striving vanishes in the metaphysical contemplation that sees it as nothing. See his posthumous writings (I, p. 512): "Dasz wir aber böse seyn können, rührt daher, dasz wir eine Erscheinung, eine gemeine Existenz haben, die an sich weder gut noch böse, weder Etwas noch Nichts ist, sondern eben blos der Schatten, den das Wesen in seinem getrennten Daseyn auf sich selbst wirft, und auf welchen wir, wie auf einen Rauch, das Bild des Guten und des Bösen hinwerfen können. Alle unsere blos moralischen Tugenden sind ein solches reflectirtes Bild des Guten, und wehe dem, der sich auf sie verläszt! Alle unsere blos moralischen Laster sind ein solcher Widerschein des Bösen, und wehe dem, der darüber verzweifelt und sie für etwas hält, das wirklich und wahrhaft ist, und nicht an den glaubt, vor dem sie nichts sind und der sie allein in uns heben kann [That we are capable of evil is due to our phenomenal appearance, is due to having an ordinary existence that in itself is neither good nor evil, neither something nor nothing, but is merely a shadow that casts upon itself the essence in its divided existence and upon which we in turn may cast the image of good and evil as upon a haze. All our moral virtues are but such reflections of the good, and woe to them who trust in them! All our moral vices are but such reflections of evil, and woe to them who despair over them and regard them as actual and true, not believing in that before which they are nothing and that which alone is able to cancel them in us]!"

Here the weakness in Solger is clear. It is indeed true that moral virtues have no worth in and by themselves but only in the humility that allows God to evoke them in us; and it is indeed true that human vices can be canceled only by God and not by one's own powers; but by no means does this say that one is to lose oneself metaphysically and in the one case to disregard the synergism[164] that comes to the aid of the divine and in the other case to disregard the repentance that does not let go of God.[165] In that way the finite is indeed the *Nichtige*, but there is nevertheless something in it with substance.

Therefore the scientific-scholarly effort that is apparent in all this is not carried through, and thus there is more of a pantheistic absorption than a speculative account of the abstract *an sich* of the infinite's and the finite's absolute identity. Pantheism can emerge in two ways—either as I accentuate man or as I accentuate God, by either anthropocentric or theocentric reflection. If I let the human race create God, then there is no conflict between God and man; if I let man disappear in God, then there is no conflict, either. Solger obviously does the latter. To be sure, he does not insist, as Spinoza does, that God be regarded as substance, but this is because he does not wish to annul devotion's identification of the divine and the human.

XIII 381 These metaphysical investigations will be carried no further. Therefore we shall turn to another cycle of observations that belong more to a speculative-dogmatic sphere. Solger as a matter of course uses such concrete concepts as God, to sacrifice, to devote oneself out of love, etc. We find repeated reference to such concepts as God's creating out of nothing, his Atonement, etc. Hegel has carefully considered this part, and therefore I can draw upon him. But first some quotations from Solger. Most of these speculative glimpses are found in the first volume of posthumous writings (I, p. 603), particularly in two letters, one to Tieck and the other to Abeken:[166] "Indem Gott in unserer Endlichkeit existirt oder sich offenbart, opfert er sich selbst auf und vernichtet sich in uns: denn wir sind Nichts [Inasmuch as God exists or reveals himself in our finitude, he sacrifices and annihilates himself in us, for we are nothing]." In the same section (p. 511) it is noted: "Nicht unsere relative Schwäche macht unsere Unvollkommenheit, nicht unser eigenes wesentliches Seyn unsere Wahrheit aus. Wir sind deshalb nichtige Erscheinungen, weil Gott in uns selbst Existenz angenommen und sich dadurch von sich selbst geschieden hat. Und ist dieses nicht die höchste Liebe, dasz er sich selbst in das Nichts begeben, damit wir seyn möchten, und dasz er sich sogar selbst geopfert und sein Nichts vernichtet, seinen Tod getödtet hat, damit wir nicht ein bloszes Nichts bleiben, sondern zu ihm zurückkehren und in ihm seyn möchten? Das Nichtige in uns ist selbst das Göttliche, insofern wir es nämlich als das Nichtige und uns selbst als dieses erkennen. In diesem Sinne ist es auch das Gute, und wir können vor

Gott nur wahrhaft gut seyn durch Selbstopferung [It is not our relative weakness that constitutes our imperfection, and it is not our own essential being that constitutes our truth. We are *nichtige* phenomena because God has assumed existence in us and thereby separated himself from himself. And is this not the greatest love, that he himself has entered into nothing in order that we might be, that he has sacrificed himself and annihilated his nothingness, killed his death, so that we might not remain mere nothing but return to him and be in him? The *Nichtige* in us is itself the divine, insofar as we recognize it as the *Nichtige* and know ourselves as this. In this sense it is also the good, and we can be truly good before God only through self-sacrifice]." Hegel's development of this is found on pages 469 top ff.*[167] Here we promptly see that Solger, despite his speculative energy, still does not orient us as much as he disorients us, and also that since all the middle terms are missing it becomes very difficult to determine whether the negations ensue properly. When it says: "indem Gott in unserer Endlichkeit existirt oder sich offenbart [inasmuch as God exists or reveals himself in our finitude]," we first of all have to know something about how God exists in finitude—we lack here the concept of creation. When it expressly says next that by existing this way in finitude he sacrifices himself, it might seem XIII 382
that here creation is expressed. But if this is the meaning, it is not strictly expressed, for then it would have to read: In sacrificing himself, God creates. This could seem to be confirmed by the corresponding predicate, that God destroys himself. In other words, if we say that God destroys himself, we do, of course, have a negation, but, please note, a negation by means of which the infinite is made finite and concrete. On the other hand, however, the statement that God sacrifices himself, just as the one that God destroys himself, leads thought more to the Atonement. This is confirmed by the very next words: We are nothing, for that, of course, posits the finite, posits it in its

* Incidentally, Hegel's discussion of Solger's observations provides a very interesting contribution to the question: In what relation did Hegel stand to the Christian view?

finitude, its nothingness, and it is this nothingness that must be negated, whereby the negation then infinitizes the finite. But here we lack the middle terms to inform us in what sense man is nothing—middle terms of such scope that the meaning of sin might be construed therein. As a result, we have a speculative unclarity that does justice neither to creation nor to the Atonement, neither to finitude nor to sinfulness.

If we compare this with the remarks in his letter to Tieck, we find a similar speculative twilight. Here we learn that we "deshalb nichtige Erscheinungen sind, weil Gott in uns selbst Existenz angenommen und sich dadurch von sich selbst geschieden hat [are therefore *nichtige* phenomena because God has assumed existence in us and thereby separated himself from himself]."[168] Now this is obviously an intimation of the concept of creation. However, quite apart from the lack of the middle terms that would really enable us to hold fast to the act of creation, not even the pantheistic thought is strictly presented, because it cannot really be said that we are *nightige Erscheinungen* because God has taken up existence within us. In accord with Solger's views and terminology, one ought rather say: Since God destroys himself, the nothing of all finitude comes into existence [*blive til*]; but when God takes up his existence in it, God is not separated from himself (because this he is in the moment of creation) but is in himself, and the nothingness is canceled. When it goes on to say: "Und ist dieses nicht die höchste Liebe, dasz er sich selbst in das Nichts begeben, damit wir seyn möchten [And is this not the greatest love, that he himself has entered into nothing so that we might be]," [169] then here again creation and the Atonement are confused and confounded with each other. In other words, God has not entered into nothing in order that we might be, because we are indeed nothing; but God has entered into nothing in order that we might cease to be nothing. With regard to Solger's wanting to see God's love in this, here again the middle terms are lacking, because the concept of creation must always be a given lest God's love become self-love.

Solger[170] goes on to use even more concrete expressions when he says that God has sacrificed himself and destroyed his

nothingness and killed his death. This makes one think of the XIII
Atonement, of the negation and the return of finitude to God 383
and in God. But since in the previous passage it stated that in his existing in our finitude God destroys himself, we have now had the same expression for both creation and the Atonement. Furthermore, it seems difficult to understand what is meant by the statement that God sacrifices himself if it is to be explained by the following words: He annihilates his nothingness. But the confusion becomes even greater when we learn that the *Nichtige* in us is the divine. We are supposed to be the *Nichtige*, and how then can the *Nichtige* in us (thereby suggesting that there is something else in us that is not the *Nichtige*) be the divine? Finally, it is taught that we ourselves can recognize the *Nichtige* in us. If this means that we ourselves can negate this *Nichtige* by means of this knowledge, then we obviously have here a Pelagian conception of the Atonement.

Throughout this whole investigation, Solger seems to have a dim notion of the negation of the negation, which in itself contains the true affirmation. But since the whole train of thought is not developed, the one negation erroneously slips into the other, and the true affirmation does not result. Hegel has perceived this very clearly and therefore articulates it explicitly on page 470: "das eine Mal sind *wir* darin als das *Nichts* (was das Böse ist) *vorausgesetzt*, dann ist auch wieder von Gott der harte, abstracte Ausdruck gebraucht, dasz *er* sich *vernichte*, also er es sey, der sich als das Nichts setze, und zwar, damit wir *seyen*, und darauf heiszt das *Nichtige* in uns selbst das Göttliche, insofern wir es nämlich als das Nichtige erkennen [at that one point *we* are *presupposed* as *nothing* (that which is evil); the harsh, abstract expression, that *he annihilates* himself, is then in turn predicated of God; hence it is God who posits himself as nothing and does this so that we might be; accordingly, the *Nichtige* in us is called the divine, that is, insofar as we recognize it as the *Nichtige*]."[171]

If I were to give the reader an idea of Solger's view, I would perhaps come closest to it by attaching it to his favorite concept, irony, and would say that Solger actually turns the existence of God into irony: God continually translates himself

into nothing, takes himself back again, translates himself again, etc.—a divine diversion that sets up the most horrible contrasts, as does all irony. In the enormous swinging of this double movement (the centrifugal as well as the centripetal), finitude also participates, and in it at the instant of separation man is the projected shadow of the divine, man sketches his moral virtues and vices into this shadow-existence, which is seen as a nothing only by someone with eyes wide open for irony. Since all finitude is now nothing, then the person who by means of irony sees it as such comes to the aid of divinity. This is as far as I can proceed with this point of view, since I
XIII 384 do not find any information in Solger pertaining to what reality finitude acquires by means of irony. In a few passages,[172] Solger does indeed speak of a mysticism that is the mother of irony when it gazes upon actuality, but when it gazes at the eternal world it is the child of enthusiasm and inspiration. Solger also speaks of an immediate presence of the divine, which manifests itself precisely in the vanishing of our actuality, but here again there is a lack of the middle terms that are required before a more profound, positive, total view can be constructed out of this.

We shall now take a look at how Solger has carried out his position in the sphere of esthetics. Here he came to the aid of the romanticists and became the philosophic spokesman for romanticism and romantic irony. Here again we meet the very same basic view that finitude is a nothing and must perish as the false actuality so that the true actuality may emerge. The truth in this has been pointed out in the appropriate place,[173] but I have also tried to show its incomplete character. Accordingly, one does not see which actuality is supposed to be destroyed, whether it is the false actuality (to this Solger presumably would answer "Yes," but more needs to be known about what he understood by the false actuality, for otherwise his affirmative answer would become a tautology), that is, whether it is the selfishness of the separate elements that must be negated in order for the true actuality to emerge, the actuality of spirit not as something otherworldly but as something present, or whether that divine diversion cannot allow any actuality to remain. Solger seems to want to find in art and poetry the higher actuality that emerges through the negation of finite actuality. But here a new difficulty appears. Since the poetry, the romantic, which Solger in his letters to Tieck[174] so frequently acknowledges as supreme, is quite incapable of pacifying the negation in that higher actuality, inasmuch as in its essential striving it itself seeks to create an awareness that the given actuality is the imperfect one but the higher actuality can be perceived only in the infinite approximation of intimation, then it seems to become necessary to relate ironically once again to every poetic work, because every single work is only an approximation. If so, it is clear that that higher actuality that is supposed to emerge in poetry nevertheless is not in the poetry but is continually becoming.

Do not misunderstand me, as if I meant that becoming is XIII
not a necessary aspect of the actuality of the spirit. The true 385
actuality becomes what it is; the actuality of romanticism merely becomes. Thus faith is victory over the world,[175] and yet it is a struggle, and when it has struggled, it has won the victory over the world; and yet it had won the victory over the world before it struggled. Thus faith becomes what it is. Faith is not an eternal struggle, but it is a victory that is struggling. Consequently, in faith that higher actuality of the spirit is not only becoming but is present, although it is also becoming.

Irony is frequently mentioned in Solger's lectures on esthetics, especially in the section "*Von dem Organismus des künstlerischen Geistes.*"[176] Irony and enthusiasm are presented there as the two factors necessary for artistic production, the two necessary conditions for the artist. What that may mean will be explained in more detail in the appropriate place.[177] May I simply note here that this whole point of view actually belongs to a completely different position, unless irony is allowed to manifest itself in destroying its own work of art and enthusiasm is allowed to designate the mood that has a presentiment of something higher.

At this point, some comments that appear in the review (found in volume II of Solger's posthumous works[178]) of A. W. Schlegel's *Vorlesungen*[179] should be the object of some-

what more detailed consideration. Here there is considerable lack of clarity. In certain passages, Solger describes irony as the limiting power that specifically teaches man to remain in actuality, teaches him to seek his truth in limitation. After protesting on page 514 against the notion that irony is supposed to teach man to place himself above and beyond everything, he adds "die wahre Ironie geht von dem Gesichtspunkte aus, dasz der Mensch, so lange er in dieser gegenwärtigen Welt lebt, seine Bestimmung, auch im höchsten Sinne des Worts, nur in dieser Welt erfüllen kann. Jenes Streben nach dem Unendlichen führt ihn auch gar nicht wirklich, wie der Verfasser meint, über dieses Leben hinaus, sondern nur in das Unbestimmte und Leere, indem es ja, wie er selbst gesteht, blos durch das Gefühl der irdischen Schranken erregt wird,
XIII auf die wir doch ein für allemal angewiesen sind. Alles, womit
386 wir rein über endliche Zwecke hinauszugehen glauben, ist eitle und leere Einbildung [True irony proceeds from the point of view that as long as man lives in the present world, he can fulfill his destiny, even in the highest sense of the word, only in this world. Striving for the infinite does not actually lead man beyond this life, as the author maintains, but merely into indefiniteness and emptiness, because, as the author admits, it is incited merely by the feeling of earthly limitation to which we have been assigned once and for all. Any thought we might entertain of going beyond finite ends is foolish and empty conceit]." This contains a profound truth, to which I shall later return, but I am sure everyone will agree that one would think that Goethe rather than Solger is speaking here. The following words immediately also sound somewhat alarming, teaching as they do that the highest in finite existence perishes just as completely as the lowest, and are not easy to reconcile with the previous statement, teaching as it does that man can fulfill his destiny precisely by limiting himself—unless it is assumed that it is the destiny of man to perish. But the person who evaporates into infinite emptiness seems just as able to achieve this destiny; indeed, he even seems to come to the aid of divinity, whereas the other seems to put obstacles in his way.

Solger's view of actuality as something that must be destroyed is also discussed rather frequently here (for example, on p. 502): "das Irdische musz als solches verzehrt werden, wenn wir erkennen sollen, wie das Ewige und Wesentliche darin gegenwärtig ist [the earthly as such must be consumed if we are to recognize how the eternal and essential is present in it]." We shall now see how far Solger is successful in letting the higher actuality in art and poetry truly manifest itself, to what extent there is, in Solger's opinion, genuine repose in the world of poetry. We quote a passage in which he discusses our relation to poetry (p. 512): "Prüfen wir uns endlich recht genau über das, was wir bei wahren tragischen oder komischen Meisterwerken empfinden, so leuchtet uns wohl ein, dasz in beiden noch auszer der dramatischen Form ein inneres Gemeinsameres ist. Der ganze Widerstreit zwischen dem Unvollkommenen im Menschen und seiner höheren Bestimmung fängt an, uns als etwas Nichtiges zu erscheinen, worin etwas ganz anderes zu walten scheint als dieser Zwiespalt allein. Wir sehen die Helden irre werden an dem Edelsten und Schönsten in ihren Gesinnungen und Gefühlen, nicht blos in Rücksicht des Erfolgs, sondern auch ihrer Quelle und ihres Werthes, ja wir erheben uns an dem Untergange des Besten selbst, und nicht blos, indem wir uns daraus in eine unendliche Hoffnung flüchten. Und wiederum erfreut uns in der Komödie dieselbe Nichtigkeit der menschlichen Dinge, indem sie uns vorkommt wie das, worauf wir ein-für allemal angewiesen sind . . . . . Jene Stimmung aber, worin die Widersprüche sich vernichten und doch eben dadurch das Wesentliche für uns enthalten, nennen wir die *Ironie*, oder im Komischen auch wohl *Laune* und *Humor* [If we examine ourselves carefully as to what we perceive in true tragic or comic masterpieces, it is evident that, in addition to their dramatic form, they have something in common in a more internal sense. The entire conflict between the imperfection in man and his higher destiny begins to take on the appearance of something *Nichtige*, in which something quite other than this preclusive split seems to hold sway. We see heroes growing doubtful about the noblest and finest in their feelings and sentiments, not only with regard to the success of these, but also with regard to their source and worth. Indeed, what lifts us up is the destruction of the best as such, yet not merely by way of taking refuge in an infinite hope. And in comedy we once again derive pleasure from the very same nothingness of human affairs, seemingly the lot to which we have been assigned once and for all . . . . . But that very mood in which contradictions annihilate themselves, thereby nevertheless retaining what is essential for us, we call *irony* or, in the comic sphere, *caprice* and *humor*]."

Here it is apparent to what extent the negation that destroys
XIII actuality is brought to rest in a higher actuality. We are lifted
387 up by the downfall of the best, but this uplifting is of a very negative kind. It is irony's uplifting, resembling here the envy of the gods, yet it is envious not only of what is great and outstanding but is just as envious of what is lowly and insignificant, on the whole, envious of finitude. When the great perishes in the world, this is tragic, but poetry reconciles us to this tragedy by showing us that it is the true that is victorious.[180] Herein lies the uplifting and the upbuilding. Thus we are not uplifted by the destruction of the great but are reconciled to its destruction by the victory of what is true, and we are uplifted by its victory. But if in the tragedy I see only the destruction of the hero and am uplifted by that, if in the tragedy I become aware only of the nothingness of human affairs, if the tragedy pleases me in the same way that comedy does by showing me the nothingness of what is great, just as comedy shows me the nothingness of what is lowly—then the higher actuality has not emerged. Indeed, here the author even seems unwilling to allow the mood to remain that has a presentiment of the higher actuality, because he does say that we lift ourselves up by the downfall of the best and do so not only by flight out of it in an infinite hope. The something more that can come from this dilution[181] in an infinite hope is nothing more or less than the bliss implicit in the perishing of everything, the desolation and the emptiness in which there certainly is far too much peace and quiet.

If we now summarize these comments on Solger, it is apparent that his position, as he himself termed it, was irony, except that his irony was of a speculative nature, and with him the infinite abstract negativity is a speculative element. He does have the negation of negation, but still there is a veil in front of his eyes so that he does not see the affirmation. It is well known that he died at an early age. Whether he would have succeeded in carrying through the speculative ideas he seized with so much energy or whether his energy would instead have been consumed in maintaining the negation, I shall not decide at this point, but the thought that appeals to me most is that Solger was a sacrifice to Hegel's positive system.

XIII
388

Irony as a Controlled Element, the Truth of Irony

It has already been pointed out in the foregoing that in his lectures on esthetics[182] Solger makes irony the condition for every artistic work. When we now in this context say that the poet must be related ironically to his writing, this means something different from what was said about this earlier. Shakespeare has frequently been eulogized as the grand master of irony, and there can be no doubt that there is justification for that. But by no means does Shakespeare allow the substantive worth to evaporate into an ever more fugitive sublimate,[183] and as for the occasional culmination of his lyrics in madness, there is an extraordinary degree of objectivity[184] in this madness. When Shakespeare is related ironically to what he writes, it is precisely in order to let the objective dominate. Irony is now everywhere present; it sanctions every single line so that there will be neither too much nor too little, in order that everything can have its due, in order that the true balance may be achieved in the miniature world of the poem, whereby the poem has the center of gravity in itself. The greater the contrasts in the movement, the more is irony required to direct and control the spirits that willfully want to charge forward. The more irony is present, the more freely and poetically the poet floats above his artistic work. Therefore, irony is not present at some particular point of the poem but is omnipresent in it, so that the irony visible in the poem is in turn ironically controlled. Therefore irony simultaneously makes the poem and the poet free. But in order for this to happen, the poet himself must be master over the irony. But this does not always mean that just because a poet manages to be master over the irony at the time of writing he is master over it in the actuality to which he himself belongs. It is customarily said that the poet's personal life is of no concern to us. This is absolutely right, but in the present undertaking it should not be out of place to point out the misrelation that can often exist in this respect.

In addition, the less the poet remains in the immediate position of genius, the greater becomes the significance of this misrelation. The more the poet has abandoned this, the more necessary it is for him to have a totality-view of the world and in this way to be master over irony in his individual existence, XIII 389
and the more necessary it becomes for him to be a philosopher to a certain degree.[185] If this is the case, then the individual poetic work will not have a merely external relation to the poet; in the individual poem, he will see an element in his own development. The reason Goethe's poet-existence was so great was that he was able to make his poet-life congruous with his actuality. But that in turn takes irony, but, please note, controlled irony. For the romanticist, the individual poetic work is either a darling favorite with which he himself is utterly infatuated and which he cannot explain to himself—how he could possibly have given life to it—or it is an object that arouses his disgust. Both responses, of course, are false; the truth of the matter is that the individual work is an element. In Goethe, irony was in the strictest sense a controlled element; it was a serving spirit to the poet. On the one hand, the individual poem rounds itself off in itself by means of the irony in it; on the other hand, the individual poetic work emerges as an element, and thereby the whole poet-existence rounds itself off by means of irony. As poet, Professor Heiberg takes the same position, and while almost every line of dialogue he has written can provide an example of irony's inner economy in the play, all his plays exhibit the conscious striving to assign to every particular line its place in the whole. Here, then, the irony is controlled, is reduced to an element. The essence is nothing other than the phenomenon; the phenomenon is nothing other than the essence. Possibility is not so prudish as to be unwilling to enter into any actuality, but actuality is possibility. Goethe, both the striving and the victorious Goethe, has always acknowledged this view, has continually articulated this view very energetically.

After all, what holds for the poet-existence holds also in

some measure for every single individual's life. In other words, the poet does not live poetically by creating a poetic work, for if it does not stand in any conscious and inward relation to him, his life does not have the inner infinity that is an absolute condition for living poetically (thus we also see poetry frequently finding an outlet through unhappy individualities—indeed, the painful destruction of the poet is a condition for the poetic production[186]), but he lives poetically only when he himself is oriented and thus integrated in the age in which he lives, is positively free in the actuality to which he belongs. But anyone can live poetically in this way. But the
XIII rare gift, the divine good fortune to be able to let what is po-
390 etically experienced take shape and form itself poetically, remains, of course, the enviable fate of the chosen few.

To be controlled in this way, to be halted in the wild infinity into which it rushes ravenously, by no means indicates that irony should now lose its meaning or be totally discarded. On the contrary, when the individual is properly situated—and this he is through the curtailment of irony—only then does irony have its proper meaning, its true validity. In our age there has been much talk about the importance of doubt for science and scholarship, but what doubt is to science, irony is to personal life. Just as scientists maintain that there is no true science without doubt, so it may be maintained with the same right that no genuinely human life is possible without irony. As soon as irony is controlled, it makes a movement opposite to that in which uncontrolled irony declares its life. Irony limits, finitizes, and circumscribes and thereby yields truth, actuality, content; it disciplines and punishes and thereby yields balance and consistency. Irony is a disciplinarian[187] feared only by those who do not know it but loved by those who do. Anyone who does not understand irony at all, who has no ear for its whispering, lacks *eo ipso* [precisely thereby] what could be called the absolute beginning of personal life; he lacks what momentarily is indispensable for personal life; he lacks the bath of regeneration and rejuvenation, irony's baptism of purification that rescues the soul from having its life in finitude even though it is living energetically and robustly in it. He does not know the refreshment and strengthening that come with undressing when the air gets too hot and heavy and diving into the sea of irony, not in order to stay there, of course, but in order to come out healthy, happy, and buoyant and to dress again.

Therefore, if at times someone is heard talking with great superiority about irony in the infinite striving in which it runs wild, one may certainly agree with him, but insofar as he does not perceive the infinity that moves in irony, he stands not above but below irony. So it is always wherever we disregard the dialectic of life. It takes courage not to surrender to the shrewd or sympathetic counsel of despair that allows a person to erase himself from the number of the living; but this does not necessarily mean that every sausage peddler, fed and fattened on self-confidence, has more courage than the person who succumbed to despair. It takes courage when sorrow would delude one, when it would reduce all joy to sadness, all longing to privation, every hope to recollection—it takes XIII 391
courage to will to be happy; but this does not necessarily mean that every full-grown adult infant with his sweet, sentimental smile, his joy-intoxicated eyes, has more courage than the person who yielded to grief and forgot to smile. So it is also with irony. Even though one must warn against irony as against a seducer, so must one also commend it as a guide.

Particularly in our age, irony must be commended. In our age, scientific scholarship has come into possession of such prodigious achievements that there must be something wrong somewhere; knowledge not only about the secrets of the human race but even about the secrets of God is offered for sale at such a bargain price today that it all looks very dubious. In our joy over the achievement in our age, we have forgotten that an achievement is worthless if it is not made one's own. But woe to him who cannot bear to have irony seek to balance the accounts. Irony as the negative is the way; it is not the truth but the way.[188] Anyone who has a result as such does not possess it, since he does not have the way. When irony now lends a hand, it brings the way, but not the way whereby someone fancying himself to have the achievement comes to possess it, but the way along which the achievement deserts him. Furthermore, if our generation has any task at all, it must be to translate the achievement of scientific scholarship into personal life, to appropriate it personally.[189] For example, when scientific scholarship teaches that actuality has absolute validity, then the point is truly to acquire that validity, and one cannot deny that it would be most ridiculous if someone who in his youth learned and perhaps even taught others that actuality has absolute meaning grew old and died without actuality's ever having had any other validity than his proclaiming in and out of season the wisdom that actuality has validity. When scientific scholarship mediates all the opposites, then the point is that this full-bodied actuality ought truly to become visible.

In another direction there is in our day a prodigious enthusiasm, and, strangely enough, that which makes it enthusiastic seems to be prodigiously little. How beneficial irony can be here. There is an impatience that wants to harvest before it sows—just let irony discipline it. In every personal life there is so much that must be thrown out, so many wild shoots to be pruned. Here again irony is an excellent surgeon, because, as stated, when irony has been put under control, its function
XIII 392 is extremely important in enabling personal life to gain health and truth.

Irony as a controlled element manifests itself in its truth precisely by teaching how to actualize actuality, by placing the appropriate emphasis on actuality. In no way can this be interpreted as wanting to deify actuality in good St. Simon[190] style or as denying that there is, or at least that there ought to be, a longing in every human being for something higher and more perfect. But this longing must not hollow out actuality; on the contrary, life's content must become a genuine and meaningful element in the higher actuality whose fullness the soul craves. Actuality hereby acquires its validity, not as a purgatory—for the soul is not to be purified in such a way that stark naked, so to speak, it runs blank and bare out of life—but as history in which consciousness successively matures, yet in such a way that salvation consists not in forgetting all this but in becoming present in it. Actuality, therefore, will not be rejected, and longing will be a sound and healthy love, not a weak and sentimental sneaking out of the world. The romantic longing for something higher may well be genuine, but just as man must not separate what God has joined together, so man also must not join what God has separated,[191] but a sickly longing such as this is simply a way of wanting to have the perfect prematurely. Therefore actuality acquires its validity through action. But action must not degenerate into a kind of fatuous indefatigableness; it ought to have an apriority in itself so as not to lose itself in a vapid infinity.

So much for the practical side. On the theoretical side, essence must manifest itself as phenomenon. When irony is controlled, it no longer believes, as do certain shrewd people in everyday life, that there is always more than meets the eye; but it also prevents all idol worshiping of the phenomenon. And just as it teaches respect for contemplation, it also rescues it from the verbosity that believes that giving an exposition of world history, for example, should take as long a time as the world has needed to live through it.

Finally, insofar as there may be a question concerning irony's "eternal validity,"[192] this question can be answered only
by entering into the realm of humor.[193] Humor has a far more XIII
profound skepticism than irony, because here the focus is on 393
sinfulness, not on finitude. The skepticism of humor is related to the skepticism of irony as ignorance is related to the old thesis: *credo quia absurdum* [I believe because it is absurd],[194] but it also has a far deeper positivity, since it moves not in human but in theanthropological categories; it finds rest not by making man man but by making man God-man. Yet all this lies beyond the scope of this study, and if anyone should wish food for thought, I recommend Prof. Martensen's review of Heiberg's *Nye Digte*.[195]

Addendum

NOTES OF SCHELLING'S BERLIN LECTURES

NOTES OF SCHELLING'S BERLIN LECTURES

Philosophie
der Offenbarung
[Philosophy of Revelation]

by
Friedrich Wilhelm Joseph Schelling

University of Berlin
November 15, 1841-February 4, 1842

SCHELLING III C 27 XIII 254

[Lectures 1-41]

No. 1

1

. . . . . he wanted to be regarded as one deceased in the Greek understanding, in the Platonic sense.

2

When he spoke of a revelation [*Aabenbaring*], he meant thereby that it contains something that is above reason [*over Fornuft*]; as Kanne[1] has said, it is not worth the trouble to get excited about daily things, and thus revelation would have no interest if it did not contain anything more than reason. —He should strive for clarity and simplicity. Others might have the pleasure of making the simple difficult, and even if it were difficult, το ἀλε[η]θές ῥᾴδιον [the simple truth] would still apply. He would like to begin from the very beginning, presuppose nothing.

PHILOSOPHY AND ACTUALITY[2]

Everything actual has a double aspect: *quid sit* (what it is), *quod sit* (that it is). Consequently philosophy can have a double relation to it; one can have a concept without cognition* [*in mar-* III C 27
gin: *a concept is expressed by *quid sit*, but from this it does XIII 255
not follow that I know *quod sit*,] but not cognition without the concept. In cognition there is a doubleness whereby it is memory. In seeing a plant, I remember it and convert it to the universal by recognizing it as plant. This was also seen in the doubleness implicit in the Latin *cognitio* [knowledge] and in the Hebrew ידע [to know]. *Philosophy and Being* [*Væren*].

3 November 22 [1841]

Philosophy may be called ἐπιστήμη τοῦ ὄντος [knowledge of being], and this is a very suitable designation insofar as it at least anticipates the later development. The question would remain, then, with respect to the above-mentioned doubleness, whether philosophy pertains to both kinds of being, and if it does, whether it then would be in one science, or [whether it would pertain] to only one. One might say: When I know something, I do know it as a being [*et Værende*]. When I know a plant, I know it as a being. Next, objections of a Kantian kind, that being is an accident.[3] But if it were a question of something that does not fall into the category of the accidental but of the necessary, one might reply that it is still only a question of content, not of being. In logic, furthermore, movement takes place not *in Bezug auf quodditas* [with regard to thatness] but *auf quidditas* [to whatness]. Consequently, philosophy became doctrine either about essence, as it has customarily been called, or about existence [*Existents*], as some more recent [thinkers] have called it. That which exists could be known in experience, and to that extent no necessity would be seen for the laborious and nevertheless superfluous expenditures of philosophy. But there was something that could not be experienced. This, then, would have to lie in reason. But to discover this, the entire content of reason would have to be developed and therefore a beginning made with the immediate [*Umiddelbare*]. What is the immediate content of reason? *Reason is the infinite potency* [*Potens*] *of cognition.* As such, it seems to have no content, but still it has a content. However, this is without its *Zuthun* [assistance]—its "*eingeborene* [in-
III C 27 nate], a priori *content.*" *This is the infinite potency of being.* But
XIII 256 all philosophy is action, is activity, aims at itself, is thought, philosophic thought. In this content, thought discovers its mobile nature. In this respect, being might be reminiscent of the old scholastic *ens omnimode indeterminatum* [being entirely undefined], something not existing—not this or that existing entity, but existing in general. But being is not only *aptitudo ad existendum* [an aptitude to exist]—the scholastic *ens* [being]

is completely dead, only a nominal paraphrase. —In Wolff,[4] *ens* became "*non repugnantia ad existendum* [unopposed to existing]," but our *Seyn* [being] is being's infinite concept itself, *ist das ihr*[*er*] *Natur nach in den Begriff Uebergehen* [is the passing over, according to its nature, into the concept]. Yet this is not a matter of any actual passing over. The *Seynkönnen* [ability to be] potency of being passes over into *Seyn* and consequently into thought, but the entire movement is in the direction of *quidditas* [whatness], not of *quodditas* [thatness], and this actuality is in another sense still only possibility. This he illustrated by drawing upon geometry, which has no interest whatever in any particular triangle. The potency of *Seyn* is the source of *Seyn*. But the movements here are again *besondere Möglichkeiten* [particular possibilities] within this possibility. Consequently, we have an a priori science, a science of pure reason—whether or not it is philosophy, I do not know—yet it certainly is included—*philosophia prima, ontologia* [first philosophy, ontology]. This has been the center of concern ever since Kant's critique—but Kant took pure reason only in the subjective sense, not as the infinite potency of cognition, as is done here. Now the question is *whether it is philosophy but not "die" Philosophie* [*"the" philosophy*]—*or whether it is "die" Philosophie—or whether it is not philosophy at all*. But before we move on to this inquiry, it is necessary to examine the content of the science of reason. The content of the infinite potency of cognition is the infinite potency of being. But this potency is transition into being. Potency, therefore, is without *Seyn* but is transition into *Seyn*. If it passes over into *Seyn*, then it is no longer power but *ausser sich* [outside itself], has lost itself, is an ἐφιστάμενον [opposition to itself].[5] It does not cease to be but ceases to be power to be. But potency means to be power to be; consequently, by being it ceases [to] be and is this equivocation [*Tvetydighed*].

4 Nov. 23 III C 27

It began with a repetition. One might ask: What is the im- XIII 257
mediate content of reason? Some have held that it is God, that reason is *Gott-Setzen* [God-positing]. But God is surely some-

thing actual, but the first content of reason is not something actual; its content, that is, *Seyn*, is the opposite of actuality. Reason is, as the derivation of the word also indicates, *Alles-Vernehmen* [all-perceiving], and thus it is filled with something a priori, but not with something actual; it is *omnibus aequa* [all-inclusive], excluding only *Nichts* [nothing]. That this word (*Vernunft* [reason]) is *foemini generis* [feminine gender] also indicates this, this femininity; whereas *Verstand* [understanding] is *masculinum* [masculine]. Therefore its content is *Seyn*, as το περιφερές [the encircling] that momentarily switches over.

Immediate possibility is first and is conceptless possibility, since the concept is potency; the possibility is *begrifflos, macht- und sinnlos, schrankenlos* [conceptless, powerless and meaningless, boundless]. We do not find it in nature, but as ὑποκείμενον [substratum] it is still a presupposition. The potency is defined as infinite, but the true infinity has *Schranken* [bounds] only in itself. Potency allows for two *contradictoria* [contradictions]. He who is healthy only *potentia* [in potency] is also just as sick *potentia*; he who is learned only *potentia* is also just as ignorant *potentia*, and the reverse, he who is ignorant *potentia* is just as learned *potentia*, to whatever extent he can become that. The transition into *Seyn* according to *potentia* does not exclude not to be able to pass over. The potency of *Seyn* is therefore just as much to be able to pass over into *Seyn* as not to be able to pass over. Only when it actually has passed over does it exclude the other but precisely by this posits it, because to exclude it is *ausser-sich-setzen* [to posit outside itself]. This is explained as follows. Capability is a quiet will; a transition *a potentia ad actum* [from potency to actuality] is a transition from not-willing to willing. In this will, one can think of a willing and a not-willing, since the infinite potency does contain both parts and contains the opposites. The *Nicht-Uebergehen-Willende* [*sic*] [not willing to pass over] is actually the im-
III C 27 potent; capability acquires it by exclusion. The *Uebergehen-*
XIII *Willende* [willing to pass over] passes over, but the *Nicht-*
258 *Uebergehen-Willende* is of course inactivity (*Gelassenheit*), but in passing over, the *Uebergehen-Willende* excludes the other from itself and thereby posits it, forces it out of this *Gelassen-*

heit. But when in potency these two (*das Uebergehen-Willende* and *das Nicht-Uebergehen-Willende*) do not exclude each other, then they do not exclude a third possibility, a free vacillation between being and non-being. This is also the case with the first potency, but what we are speaking of here is still more remote from being and becomes a being for itself only by being excluded from the others, *exclusum tertium* [an exclusive third] (there is a wordplay here with *excludere pullos* [to hatch their young],[6] because from this everything emerges). Thus we see that the infinity of potency involves a totality—not an indeterminate series but a *geschlossene Allheit* [closed totality]. The infinite potency is not exhausted by the first possibility; as long as it has not abandoned possibility, it is *instar omnium* [worth them all] (in the sense that it is just as much the impending as it is the opposing), but by abandoning its place it transfers a power to another, becomes the material for its realization [*Realisation*]. It establishes itself by making itself a ὑποκείμενον, does not have its basis in something preceding but in something following, which is indeed not something preceding, and becomes a relative non-being, inasmuch as that which subordinates itself as a ὑποκείμενον *is* not in the same sense as that to which it subordinates itself. Being has excluded non-being. Non-being now will negate, since by this exclusion it is posited; then the first as ὑποκείμενον passes over *ex actu in potentiam* [from actuality into potency].

5 Nov. 24

Nur-Seyn-Können [mere ability to be] in the first potency is only the first; the second is *Nicht-Nur-Seyn-Können* [not mere ability to be]. He was asked the question how it could be posited in the original potency, since it was first posited with the second [potency], as he himself had presented it. —The second potency is pure being. Potency is the opposite of actual III C 27 XIII 259 being. Now, pure being is no more actual being than potency is. By the actual [*det virkelige*] is understood that which has passed over *a potentia ad actum* [from potency to actuality]; otherwise it [pure being] would not be pure being. But it is not potency. No, it is not immediate potency, but it can become mediate potency. Being is potency; a being is not potency. It fulfills itself by a transition from *actu ad potentiam ausser sich* [actuality to potency outside itself].

Therefore the third (*tertium exclusum*) becomes that which in its potency is being. The first potency is only potential *Geist* [spirit], because it can be the opposite—the second is not [*Geist*], because it is not free—but the third is *Geist.*

Nature is completed in *selbstbewusstem Können* [self-conscious ability]. Then it passes into a new process. Thus philosophy has two developments: philosophy of nature and philosophy of spirit.

In margin: Recapitulation

There has always been an inclination to get *hinter* [behind] *das Seyn*; for a long time this was understood only in contradistinction to revelation, but it applies to all actual being. P[otencies] for the manifested *Seyn* [being].[7] (1) *Das unmittelbar-seyn-Können* [the immediate ability to be], (2) *das seyende Seyn* [the being that is]—this constitutes the change *ab actu ad potentiam* [from actuality to potency], (3) the third potency, which is the unity in which potency is being, which has being equal to that of no. 2, potency equal to that of no. 1, but does not have being outside itself.

6

The science we have treated up to this point excludes everything that is foreign to the content of reason, that which must be left to experience as that which goes beyond reason. This arrives at its true content only when it has eliminated everything foreign. The necessary content of reason is potency as that which does not have being outside itself, is not related as ought-to-be being [*Skulde-Væren*] to being outside itself but remains in itself, is essence, *das sich Entaüssernde* [the self-externalizing],[8] which is not *existentia obnoxium* [dependent existence], which can be called the highest essence, which does
III C 27 not have essence as something outside itself but is itself es-
XIII 260 sence, which in *Seyn* remains what it was, which is potency
and *Actus* [actuality] simultaneously. Thought is thereby *bey sich* [present to itself], is *freyes Denken* [free thought], the self-

possessing concept. Idea (idea is on the whole the *gewollte* [the thing sought]). In this science, the new science, that is, it is only concept, not the concept passing over into existence [*Existents*]. Consequently, the first science is negative and does not conceal or deny its kinship with Kant's *Critique*. The idea is not the result but *das Stehenbleibende* [that which persists]. This is also a negative concept. The God-concept is apprehended as the necessary content of reason, as the final, concluding concept of reason. Yet it must not give the appearance of cognition in the sense of existence; it has *quid sit* [what it is], not *quod sit* [that it is]; it is neither stated nor demonstrated that he exists [*existere*]. If one so desired, this system could be called an emanation system, if one keeps in mind that it is reversed, since God is the final logical emanation of the system; here the God-concept has only a regulative role, not constitutive. In this science, one cannot begin with God. In the other science, however, potency cannot be *prius* [antecedent], as in everything finite, but here existence is *prius* and potency *posterius* [subsequent]. Consequently, in the first science the final potency is the reversed *Seynkönnende* [ability to be], which has *Seyn* as *prius*, not as *posterius*. Here we may say that God is necessary existence if he exists. The first science is now at its boundary, and this *Umkehrung* [reversal] paralyzes it. Its object becomes experience. This new science does not proceed along the same line but begins from the beginning and from the opposite end. This philosophy could be called *philosophia secunda* [second philosophy] (an expression Aristotle[9] uses, although by it he meant physics); yes, it is indeed authentic philosophy, and it is difficult to show that the first is also that. It is the *philosophy of identity*.

7

The a priori content of the science of reason is, then, the whole of actuality, but only what it is, not that it is, and it has no temptation in that direction. If it wants to demonstrate existence, then it must turn to another science, and this must re- III C 27
solve to presuppose that which is *ausser der Vernunft* [outside XIII 261
reason]. This science of reason is, then, the philosophy of

identity, whose point of departure is indifference and whose conclusion is the identity of subject and object. Historically, it is related to Fichte and his *Wissenschaftslehre* [theory of knowledge],[10] which, assuming the *I*, established everything out of itself. Through subjective reflection, everything was gradually included, just as in Descartes. Fichte had comprehended *das Seyn in der That* [the being in and through the action], for *Ich* [the *I*] is present only in the act whereby it posits itself and steps forward out of its potency. The error in Fichte was that he took back everything subjectively. Thus it is easy to view the subjective-objective in the all of self-consciousness. The philosophy of identity begins not with *Ich*, but with *Ich* as potency, and thereby nature enters into philosophy. This happens in the *System des transcendentalen Idealismus* [system of transcendental idealism], in which the objective method is applied. The subject of *Seyn* is the potency of *Seyn*—neither subject- nor object-indifference. In immediacy, the subject is the not-yet-being, consequently has *Seyn* ahead of it, and consequently is τὸ μὴ ὄν [the non-being]. After it has made the transition, it is once again non-being, but not in the same sense. This can be explained by Plato's distinction between οὐκ ὄν [absolute non-being] and μὴ ὄν [relative non-being].[11] There has been perplexity about this, but Plutarch explained it well by distinguishing between μὴ εἶναι [is not] and μὴ ὄν εἶναι [is non-being].[12] Thus error and sickness are not altogether *nichts* [nothing], not οὐκ ὄντα [not existing], but μὴ ὄντα [nonexistent]. (Plato's *Sophist*[13] was aimed at the Sophists' attempt to prove that error is a nothing, but if this is true, then truth is just as much a nothing.) Thus when I doubt about sensible things, doubt nevertheless presupposes that they are *quodam modo* [in a certain manner]. —But non-being is still always the subject, not, as Fichte said, *das Nicht-Ich* [*the not-I*];[14] the subject is still in things but in such a way that it is the subject reversed in the object. This philosophy thereby preserves its subjective-objective character throughout. This relative non-being is really the central point in the philosophy of identity,
III C 27 whereby it shows that it has abandoned the subjective orien-
XIII 262 tation in Fichte. In this relative non-being lies doubt also.

Doubt must not be understood in a subjective sense as something that intervenes, but it is in the system—it is movement. Every relative non-being perishes, becomes the basis for something higher. *Der Mensch* [man] is *Seyn*, but relative, and therefore a new world is possible. This higher is the subject-object being, not possibility but actuality [*Virkelighed*], absolute identity as the other for everything other. —Philosophy is now given in this philosophy as the pure concept of reason. This has been misunderstood when its supreme proposition has been taken as something to be demonstrated instead of being regarded as the end point striven toward.

8

The philosophy of identity did not presuppose the truth but arrived at it, proceeded not from an immediate certainty but from the irresolute. Everything between the beginning and the end has only relative truth. Its method was that of ascending but also of descending, in that what appeared as subject through advancing καταβολή [beginning] was made into an object—but everything is still only thought. —If there is to be a system of the actual, everything must be reversed. —Everything in this method was relative; everything was momentarily central and in the next instant became peripheral. But everything was merely brought to *Erkennbarkeit* [perceptibility]. This system has been charged with making everything *Einerlei* [all the same]. This is true in the same sense that everything in the voltaic pile is *einerlei*, a discovery that remarkably enough was contemporary with this philosophy—everything in it is of one kind, one material. —This science is therefore purely a priori.[15] (Kant declared everything to be a priori that can be derived from the *Vermögen* [faculty] for knowledge; we, everything that can be derived from the infinite potency of *Seyn*. The a priori is not to be known from existence. Kant says the a priori is everything one could have *learned* from the cognition of reason without needing to learn it from experience. *Vernunft-Erkenntniss* [rational knowledge] and the a priori are for him one and the same.) —This science is purely logical *durchaus* [throughout]. It might seem, then, that all

progress in thought here is tautological or analytic. (Kant called synthetic that which goes beyond the nature of things.
III C 27 But this became something accidental. It was existence.[16]) Ac-
XIII 263 cordingly, all a priori knowledge was only analytic or tautological, but here it is precisely something whose nature is to change into something else and therefore is synthetic and analytic simultaneously. Yet the change is only in possibility, not into actuality. Thus, as far as the existence of God is concerned, it can be demonstrated that if he exists, he necessarily exists, but not that he exists. Like the philosophy of nature, this science contained only types. It was immanent, not transcendent. It was true, and so true that even if nothing did exist, it would still be true, just like geometry. —Kant's *Critique* was therefore negative philosophy, this expression taken in all its truth (but thereby one expresses at once a positive philosophy, but this was not presented).

9

The pure science of reason is, then, only negative, has nothing to do with existence. But existence can also be the object of science. For example, a revelation that always presupposes a God who actually is, would also belong to this. This science of reason is complete only when it is made to the point of knowing itself as negative, but this is impossible without having the positive outside itself at least as possibility. But if the positive does not come quickly, the negative easily becomes obscured, and the logical is taken for the actual.

The philosophy of identity has been charged with having produced God—it must be the case either that God appeared as its final outcome, but such a God would be devoid of all interest, or that he produced himself in the system. On both counts the philosophy of identity is completely innocent, since it in no way said that the result was the actual God. Kant has been charged with idealism in the invidious sense especially with regard to sensible things. In order to counteract this, he provided a defense in the second edition of *The Cri-*
III C 27 *tique of Pure Reason.*[17] This was a mistake. Kant was idealism,
XIII 264 and the philosophy of identity [was] idealism scientifically

carried out. The philosophy of identity was not a system any more than geometry is.

The philosophy of identity, in its origin as well as in its conclusions, forms a contrast to Spinoza.[18] For him, God is a principle; here he is the end. For him, things are logical emanations from God; here God is the final emanation in the logical process. On the whole, Spinoza first introduced into philosophy the confusion between the positive and the negative. God as blind *existing* nature is made into a principle, and in this way the logical boundary has already been transgressed inasmuch as he has the existent and then he makes things proceed with logical necessity from the nature of God. (The confusion is rooted in making something follow with logical necessity from an existent.) This he has simply asserted and never demonstrated. Inasmuch as the positive science was not presented, one could be tempted to regard potency as God's nature and the last as the victorious God returning into himself. This would be a transfigured, a sublimated Spinozism. The temptation for this would be great, for if the demand of the negative is not fulfilled by the positive, the [negative] itself shifts over into the positive.

Hegel did this; he made the philosophy of identity into positive philosophy, the only philosophy.[19]

One can readily agree with Hegel's definition of philosophy, that it is the science of reason, insofar as it becomes self-conscious as all being, but it must be borne in mind that not *alles Seyn* [all being] is actual *Seyn*; reason appears *der Materie nach* [according to its substance] as *alles Seyn*. This really should not be lacking in the definition. Whether Hegel tacitly included this or he himself was not aware of it is not known.

10

III C 27 XIII 265

Hegel observed quite generally concerning his entire undertaking that he wanted not only to presuppose the absolute as present to intellectual intuition but to achieve it scientifically.[20]

In these lectures the absolute is named now for the first time, and we shall now see what may really be meant by this. The philosophy of identity presupposed the indifference of subject and object or, expressed more simply, presupposed the infinite potency of *Seyn* as the immediate content of reason. In this unity everything lay concealed, more specifically, *das unmittelbar-Seyn-Können* [the immediate ability to be], and then the ensuing possibilities, also the potency that *nicht übergeht* [does not pass over]. This could more specifically be regarded as the absolute, because it was *freigesprochen* [absolved] from making the transition. —The indifference could be called the absolute, because it is *omnibus numeris absolutum* [absolute in all respects]; it is potency to the one (the not-absolute) as to the other. But the indifference is only absolute potency, not the absolute, is the potential and material absolute. What then is the discussion of this in Hegel?[21] The philosophy of identity also has the absolute as the end; therefore Hegel must mean that the philosophy of identity has wanted to have the absolute for the end, but for the conclusion of existence, and for this the intellectual intuition was an inconvenient medium. If the absolute indifference did exist, then everything that emerged would be also an existent. Now, Hegel thinks that the absolute indifference was assumed as existence; he thinks that this philosophy was an existence-system and then set out in the wrong way by appealing to intellectual intuition, of which nothing was known, which perhaps was something accidental, subjective, a *privatissimum* [private matter] for the chosen ones.

The phrase "intellectual intuition" has always been associated with the philosophy of identity, although it has in no way been responsible for it. In the first presentation of the philosophy of identity (and the only one recognized by the author as authentic), which is found in *Zeitschrift für Physik*, II,[22] the expression is not found at all. In an earlier article in volume I
III C 27 of the same journal, it is mentioned. This expression belongs
XIII 266 to Fichte.[23] He appealed to intellectual intuition, the content of which was: *Ich bin* [*I am*]. The expression was chosen in contradistinction to sense intuition, in which subject and object are different. The philosophy of identity called for abstraction from the subjective implicit [in Fichte's view], from immediate *certainty*, inasmuch as *Ich* is the definite form and

consequently not the entire content of reason; only when this is wiped away does one arrive at it, at the pure content and essence of reason. Potency, therefore, is not the existent but the νοούμενον [object of intuition], and that which is the eternal *prius* [antecedent] of all existence surely cannot itself exist [*existere*] in turn. Hegel gave the philosophy of identity the direction toward an existential system.[24] The requirement of the philosophy of identity was to draw back to pure thought and to maintain there an abstraction from all existence outside reason. Potency exists [*existere*] in reason. But the philosophy of identity does not undertake to demonstrate the existence of potency. Hegel criticizes it for not having demonstrated it. But that is unreasonable. If, finally, one wants to employ the expression "intellectual intuition," it can be used differently. In an intuition in which subject and object are one, there could be some point in reason's own intellectual intuition. That the philosophy of identity never did presuppose potency as existing can be seen from the following. How does infinite potency relate to actual thought? Not as object but as substance, as that without which thought cannot take place but which still is not thought in actual thought, as the not-thought in thought.

Therefore Hegel, as he himself said, did not have the bad intellectual intuition.[25] He had, on the other hand, logic as the science that was supposed to demonstrate the existence of the absolute, and thereupon he moved to another science. That this science is part of the entire science is already dubious. Therefore Hegel was in the position of demonstrating the absolute twice, first in the logic, for he had already arrived at existence there, and then in the second science.[26]

11

III C 27
XIII
267

In Hegel, *Seyn* [being] is perhaps what may be called essence,[27] not potency. Not at all—*Seyn* is only as *actus* [actuality], as *purus actus* [pure actuality]. Hegel himself says that *Seyn* is immediate certainty (and here a subjective point of departure is apparent). This cannot be potency but *actus*; according to Hegel, *Seyn* is the most remote from the concept, something like what we call the postulate most ["]external to itself." In this pure being, the conceptual definitions are successively postulated and annulled right up to the idea, which at the outset was excluded. *Seyn* is vitiated, and as soon as this is consumed, the idea comes as the actual actualized idea. This idea is defined almost as the absolute in the philosophy of identity, but it is also the actually existing idea. Here the logical ends and also pure rational philosophy, not to mention negative philosophy, since this expression may be misunderstood. In this way, then, philosophy was made into a system, into a *behauptendes* [affirming], dogmatic system, but the philosophy of identity did not want this at all, and to the extent that one wanted to take the word "system" in another sense, the philosophy of identity was that beforehand. It is, namely, system by way of the method.

Hegel, then, was the founder of a system that finally became too ponderous even for him.

Hegel himself says: Logic is a purely subjective science,[28] outside all content; only philosophy runs through all these stages; its content has nothing actual corresponding in actuality. Thought has only itself as content, has the concretion of all actuality outside itself, is a shadow world until one reaches the idea, pure essentiality without any concretion. In this he differs from other philosophers, for their[29] philosophy was right in the middle of nature even though not in actual nature. All concepts were a priori, such that they correspond to an object; in Hegelian philosophy every relation to actuality is canceled. Other philosophers had in the concept what generally is in intuition; they had experience as confirmation and
III C 27 XIII 268 substantiation, even though they did not draw upon experience. The metaphysics of pre-Kantian philosophy had as its content only the concepts as concepts (ontology), but since Bacon's falling away from ontology such a metaphysics lost its significance; all nations turned to experience. After Kant, metaphysics was maintained but did not exclude experience. The philosophy of identity combined thought with nature; therefore it had an objective logic (Hegel himself calls his subjective logic[30]), because it had a relation to the object. Hegel excluded nature from logic. The objection could be made:

Where then does the philosophy of identity have a place for the treatment of the concepts as concepts? Answer: It has no place for concepts that have the real [*Reale*] outside themselves, but in its successive advances it must come to the point where it has the concepts as *impressa vestigia* [footprints][31] in what preceded, to the point where the concepts show themselves as the free possession of consciousness. The logical forms can be treated as the natural forms whose potencies have disbursed themselves in *Seyn* and now have come to themselves. Here is the place for logic, just as in actuality the concepts first enter with consciousness. Here again is a corresponding actuality. And the abstract cannot be prior to that from which it abstracts. Hegel assigns pure thought to logic; thus it is thought about thought, but such thought finally annuls actual thought. He deals either with concepts that are not actual and do not have actual content, and [*sic*] when he goes over to nature he then says that the concept has lost its power—consequently he really has actual thought nowhere.

12 December 8

The error in Hegel's logic is that it does not go further, that it omits philosophy of nature and philosophy of spirit. He wants to substantiate the Absolute and not regard it as the outcome of another science. Consequently, in Hegel's logic the idea is in process [*Vorden*, becoming].[32] Nature, then, is a world in contrast to logic, but for Hegel nature is not a priori nature,
since this must have a place in logic, but empirical, which III C 27
must be explained. But there is no necessity of movement im- XIII 269
plicit in the idea, not to mention a movement whereby it breaks off from itself. The idea is ideality and reality [*Realitæt*] and does not need to become real in any other way. There is no necessity for nature implicit in the idea; possibility is difficult to discern, and necessity even more difficult. Over against the idea, nature seems to be something superfluous and accidental and thus cannot find a place in a rational science, which must, as Spinoza says, regard everything *modo aeterno* [under the form of eternity].[33] When the idea resolves to posit itself, there is no question of emanating. Here it is clear that H.

wants to present a system of actuality, since a free self-resolving is indeed an existent and not merely a concept. In the philosophy of identity the Absolute is a remaining-in-itself that cannot go further, that consequently cannot become a principle but is the end. Where, then, is the way out? It is this: in the science of pure reason there must be no reference to the existence of nature; there it is found only a priori; it must be left to another science, positive philosophy.

Hegel says in the first edition of the *Encyclopedia:* nature has been defined correctly as the falling away of the idea from itself;[34] in nature, the concept is bereft of all its glory, is untrue to itself, impotent; it is the concept's "*Agoni* [death struggle]." In the second edition of the *Encyclopedia*, it is simply stated that nature is the falling away from the idea; the expression "correctly" is omitted.[35] I have not seen the third edition;[36] perhaps the entire portion has been omitted. But where, one may ask, has nature been defined as the falling away of the idea from itself? It might be in a small work, *Religion und Philosophie*,[37] that appeared in the form of a conversation in which the relation between negative and positive philosophy was taken up (*Bruno* 1802).[38]

Ideas do not fall away from themselves into nature, but rational philosophy falls away from itself when it passes over to it.

But now suppose that the idea has cast itself into nature in order thereby to become spirit as man, where it can shed all the characteristics of subjectivity and become object—God. This is the second main issue. Now let us see what Hegel thinks he has accomplished here. "Earlier philosophy has God
III C 27 XIII 270 only as substance, not as spirit."[39] We have already been instructed by Christianity and the catechism to believe in God as spirit, and to that extent it would scarcely occur to a philosopher to presume to be the first inventor. In the philosophy of identity, the absolute had already been conceived as subject-object, and this is a ὁ ἑαυτὸν νοούμενον [that which conceives itself] and consequently not only substance. Therefore, when this philosophy did not use the word "spirit," it was in order to reserve it for genuine spirit. Furthermore, Hegel begins not

with God but with *Seyn*, and the idea results from the movements. Consequently, the idea is the finale, not principle, and as such only *substantieller Geist* [substantial spirit], not the productive, eternal, absolute spirit, but only according to essence. Such a God comes *post festum* [afterward]; he comes when all is past but is not the *Anfang* [beginning],[40] is not principle.

In the beginning, Hegel himself had had a presentiment that logic is only negative, but later, as the need for the positive became greater, he forgot this and made logic the actual.[41]

13 December 10

H. now moves quickly from logic to empirical nature and here again has God as a conclusion rather than as creator, etc. Now, one may say, "What is present *am Ende* [in the end] is also present *am Anfang* [in the beginning]," but it still cannot be absolutely identical, for then there would be no movement. As the *Anfang* it is *nur Anfang* [only the beginning]; as the *Ende* it is the *Ende seiner selbst* [end of itself]. "Movement is his process of realization [*Realisation*] through an *äussernhaft* [external] series of manifestations between the beginning and the end." Hegel later sought to arrive at a free creation. In the second edition of his logic, there is a remarkable passage: "the absolute spirit, the ground in which everything is included, which at the end the concrete spirit knows as free, *entschliessend* [resolving] upon a creation, which in reverse contains all the preceding results, the absolute turns into a principle from which III C 27 XIII 271
all the preceding now proceeds."[42] If Hegel had done this and not only talked about it, he would have achieved the positive philosophy and recognized the first as the negative philosophy. Here just a remark should be made about the expression that everything is included in the absolute as ground. In the philosophy of identity it was said that everything preceding has its truth only in what follows, that everything preceding is established by becoming the ground of what follows, that it is itself therefore the ground. Thus, heavenly bodies, the nature of which is to fall, find their ground by becoming the ground for something else. So much for this expression. Hegel's final attainment was therefore a free activity, but it must

be insisted upon that this is perceived not *am Ende* [in the end], when everything is over, which in a sense it is not, since it is only so in the moment when it is ended. In this way, then, he has the absolute as the final cause, since everything has tended toward it. But the entire series is a succession, a chain of final causes, each for its successor. Thus inorganic nature [is the final cause] for matter, organic nature for inorganic, animals for plants, man for animal. If now everything is to be turned around so that the ultimate final cause becomes creative, so must all the intermediate final causes also become freely productive. He would readily have seen the difficulties in this. He did not, however, make an attempt in this respect, since the expression was merely tossed off loosely, but intimated that the absolute is the freely determining, prior to nature, not to mention prior to history, that it is the freely self-*entäussernde* [externalizing] to nature.

This aspect of Hegel, particularly when he encroaches upon religious interests, has become popularized: "It is not the Idea, as in the philosophy of identity, but the Absolute Spirit that *sich entäussert* [externalizes itself] in nature"; this presentation has thereby sought to give itself a historical form, but when it adds that it has always happened and always will happen, it is canceled again. God is free insofar as he always brings his freedom as sacrifice; he is *im Process* [in the process] and is *Selbst-Process* [self-process], who always makes what he has always made: a cycle. This is reminiscent of Aristotle, who
III C 27 taught that God acts ὡς τέλος [as end, goal], himself ἀκίνητος
XIII 272 [unmoved].[43] Or this presentation goes like this: "God is indeed *an sich* [in himself] the Absolute *zuvor* [beforehand] (where does this expression come from in a purely rational science), but, in order to become conscious, *entäussert er sich* [he externalizes himself], sets himself over against a world, man, whose God-consciousness is his self-consciousness." Now, if Christianity also should be reformed, it would be particularly the doctrine of the Trinity. "God must reveal himself, because his essence is process; this revelation is the world, and his essence is the Son; he must return to himself, and this occurs through man and takes place through art, religion, and

philosophy; the human spirit is the Holy Spirit." What such a philosophy wants is not apparent, since Christ cannot possibly satisfy it; the fact that it has sought to relate itself to Christianity must offend the philosophers. If I were to reproach it for anything, it would be that it wants to be Christian; it did not need to go to that trouble, since it is a pure rational science and does not need to be that any more than geometry does.

An *interpolation* regarding the trilogy: art, religion, and philosophy. The philosophy of identity has been reproached for having rather exclusively affirmed art, because the one and the other do not erase the sensate. Forgotten, however, is the fact that the philosophy of identity also named religion, since it would be strange not to mention it at all in an inclusive philosophy. The difference, then, is that it forgot to place philosophy above religion or that it did not include the final reflection whereby philosophy establishes itself.

The philosophy of identity presupposed nature and arrived at freedom, at individual action and the individuality of history, arrived at the power that does not lose itself in the process, arrived at God as the *über dem Seyn bleibende* [that which remains above being]. But this concept is not like the others. It cannot be referred to experience, and yet it does not leave us indifferent; a subjective and moral necessity insists upon finding it. The pure science of reason has no basis for going beyond itself, but this necessity will lead to a seeking outside itself for that which it does not have in itself, and here come *religion*, *art*, and *philosophy*.

14 December 13 III C 27 XIII 273

The human spirit cannot be indifferent to this potency that is *über Seyn* [beyond being] but seeks to demonstrate its existence.

The first possibility. This occurs when the subject, the individual, seeks to annihilate, as far as possible, everything accidental in himself and outside himself and thereby to bring that *über-Seyende* [beyond being] into existence. This is religion in the subjective sense, so that not even asceticism is excluded. Religion is thereby not yet excluded. Rational science does not recognize a religion of reason. Religion can appear in rational science but as something transcending its boundary.

The second possibility. This occurs by way of objective works, actual production, i.e., art, especially in poetry, in tragedy, in which an attempt is made, so to speak, to conjure the prodigious spirit forth from ὕλη [matter]. Even sculpture is not art, for the reason that it produces a likeness to creation. Art means particularly poetry, tragedy. Rational science can recognize these efforts as necessary and take them as identical with itself.

The third is philosophy. That philosophy places this not only outside itself but within itself, but in turn within itself not like the preceding, not merely as possibility, but as something in which it becomes as if identical with itself, which, therefore, it does not place *ausser sich* [outside itself] but *über sich* [above itself]. Negative philosophy ends in requiring positive philosophy, in which the *über-Seyende* appears objective, in the same way that it is in art, and subjective, as in religion.

Hegel therefore gives these three instances: (a) religion of art, (b) revealed religion, (c) philosophy. (In the second edition of the *Encyclopedia*, however, the expression "religion of art" is changed to "art"[44] alone, but in any case it is really only in an improper sense that this expression can be justified.) The difference, then, is that "religion" appears twice here. But ra-
III C 27 tional science knows nothing of religion, of genuine religion,
XIII 274 which it does not include even as possibility. Hegel knows nothing of what here has been called subjective religion.

And now what kind of philosophy occupies the third place? It is obviously the one that he presupposes, the one from which he proceeds, and consequently not a new philosophy. With religion and art, the science of reason has already transcended its boundaries; how can it now fall back into itself? Rational philosophy, as we interpret it, also posits a philosophy, but *ausser sich* as another philosophy. Hegel should have left the third place open, because he really had nothing with which to fill it.

Positive philosophy, therefore, is required by negative philosophy. Negative philosophy posits positive philosophy outside itself.

Consequently, it is important that negative philosophy be formulated properly, that it receive its due and enjoy the satisfaction that it in its true modesty, which will not encroach upon positive philosophy, deserves. In this respect, too, I differ from Hegel, since by him negative philosophy was not adequately formulated either.

In the Kantian period, the expression "dogmatism" was used. This subsequently fell *in Verruf* [into disrepute]. A distinction must be made, however, between a dogmatizing and a dogmatic philosophy. The older metaphysics was dogmatizing and therefore never achieved what it aimed at, a rational demonstration of existence, and therefore it was merely dogmatizing. It was completely and forever demolished by Kant. But pure rationalism is nevertheless contained only indirectly in Kant's critique. This should be set forth. Only when this has been done will it be possible for positive philosophy to appear.

15

Positive philosophy, then, has now become possible, and he challenged everyone to work toward it in his own discipline. Those who occupied themselves with defending Hegelian philosophy presumably did not think that this philosophy already had it but that through this it could be achieved. Then this Hegelian philosophy was supposed to be used to take up positive philosophy. This conduct disclosed a total misunderstanding of Hegelian philosophy, because it had already done III C 27
this, and therein lay, as we have seen, precisely its error. The XIII 275
aim of these efforts to spread Hegelian philosophy was to introduce the personality of God into rational science. Presumably the basis for this was that positive philosophy was said to tend particularly in that direction. Thus, H.'s Absolute Spirit was not personality, and yet H. allowed it to decide freely on creation. This, then, was a new misunderstanding. But the question was: Is a rational science in and by itself necessary? Quite right, the one (negative philosophy) is just as necessary

as the other. But positive philosophy has an entirely new method; positive philosophy does not need to be based on negative philosophy. Negative philosophy does not have a *prius* [antecedent] in this sense, as does positive philosophy; in negative philosophy its *prius* is a *posterius* [subsequent]. Negative philosophy has need for positive philosophy, but positive philosophy has no need to be based on negative philosophy. Negative philosophy delivers its conclusion to positive philosophy not as a conclusion but as a task for it, and positive philosophy must itself provide means for carrying it out. Its beginning, according to its concept, is the absolute beginning and needs no other basis.

Consequently, there are two philosophies and the unity is broken. So it is, and there is no need to be afraid of this thought, because there has really always been dual philosophy. This is apparent already in the difficulty that has always been involved in arriving at a complete definition of philosophy. If, for example, one says that it is a science that goes back to pure thought in itself, this is a rather good definition of negative philosophy. But if this is supposed to be all of philosophy, everything in actuality has only logical coherence, and the illogical in actuality rebels against this. —Add to this that it can be shown that these two lines have always been present in philosophy. Aristotle names two kinds of philosophers.[45] The first he calls "theologians." By this he means primarily those who were under the influence of the oracles etc. But
III C 27 since he also uses this name to designate some of the living
XIII 276 philosophers of the time, it seems clear that he wants to designate them as dogmatic or positive philosophers. Among the other philosophers, he reckons especially the Ionian physicists, [for example,] Heraclitus (τὰ πάντα ἰέναι, καὶ μενει οὐδέν [all things flow, and nothing abides]). By this the science of reason is designated, because what is subject at one moment becomes object the next etc. Then he refers to other philosophers, the Eleatics, who, as he says, promote a fraud and in whom there is nothing helpful as soon as they try to explain actuality. They promote a fraud, just as does every uninterrupted movement at one point.[46] Socrates' dialectic was di-

rected as much against the subjective untruths of the Sophists as against that more objective turgidity, which was, as Plutarch says, like smoke that Socrates blew back upon them.[47]

16

If Socrates had called himself ignorant in the sense that he actually was ignorant, such an expression would amount to a triviality, since it is, after all, not particularly surprising that an ignorant person is actually ignorant; in that case it would be more surprising if he were knowledgeable. Lawyers say: *Quisque praesumitur bonus, donec probatur contrarium* [Everyone is presumed to be good, until the contrary is proved]; thus philosophers say: *Quisque praesumitur insciens, donec* [Everyone is presumed to be ignorant, until] etc. Therefore Socrates' ignorance was *docta ignorantia* [learned ignorance]. But then what knowledge did he attribute to others that he denied to himself? Not every thought is knowledge. What he seemed to have in mind was a *Denk-Wissenschaft* [discursive science]. In this sense, geometry is a science, but not a cognitive science [*vidende Videnskab*], and that is why in the ranking in Plato's *Republic*, Book VI, geometry is classed with διάνοια [understanding] and not with ἐπιστήμη [knowledge].[48] It is what we call pure science of reason, which Socrates knew just as well as the Eleatics did. Therefore by his ignorance he had to posit a genuinely cognitive science. Was he ignorant here, too? Inasmuch as he would say so, it again must not have been that he was ignorant in the direct sense, for then it would be point- III C 27 XIII 277
less to say so, but that he was ignorant only intimates the *überschwengliche* [exuberant]. How far Socrates came is difficult to decide, but that he always gives his presentation a mythical garb is a mark of his leaning toward the historical. His disciple Plato also becomes historical in his last work, *Timaeus*, so that it is difficult to find the scientific transition. Socrates and Plato are more prophetically related. Aristotle shows, however, that he is their *Schüler* [pupil] by turning from the purely logical to the empirical; *dass es ist* [that it is] is the main thing for him; what it is, is the second. He censures those who want to grasp actuality ἐν τοῖς λόγοις [in the discourses]. He censures Plato's

doctrine of the participation of things in the idea and calls this κενολόγειν [using empty words].[49] To say that the particular beautiful thing is beautiful only by reason of its participation in the idea has meaning only with respect to a possible explanation. He reproaches and censures a confusion of the logical order and the order of *Seyn*. Nevertheless, Aristotle is akin to negative philosophy. This is apparent in the method of both. Negative philosophy is not logical in the Aristotelian sense, because the a priori is no empty logic and *dem Inhalt nach* [with regard to content] necessarily passes over into the empirical. Potency continually thrusts being away from itself until it comes to itself thinking and becomes free thought; previously it was only necessary thought. Therefore it is not in opposition to experience; on the contrary, where experience ceases, it also ceases, since it always points away from itself to experience. On the other hand, experience also contains the a priori. Therefore there is also a path from the empirical to the logical. Aristotle entered upon this path and climbed up step by step to his first science or first philosophy, for both names appear (πρώτη ἐπιστήμη, πρώτη φιλοσοφία [first science, first philosophy]).[50] His system is an analysis prepared out of actuality. Here he must continually coincide with negative philosophy. Nature raises itself stepwise out of potency's possibility; the *Ziel* [goal] of the antecedent is in each subsequent;
III C 2 everything is in its place a final cause just as the last is that.
XIII The series, says Aristotle, cannot lose itself in the infinite.[51]
278 ὕλη, matter (in Aristotle it is potency and must not be understood as merely physical; thus there is mention of matter also in a conclusion) is successively cast away. The ultimate he also regards as an existent, since his science is the science of the actual. Nevertheless, what he has in mind especially is not *das* [that], but *was* [what]. Nor does he make use of the ultimate as a principle; for him it is only the final cause, not productive, not τέλος ποιητικόν [creative end]. This ultimate is τέλος [end], itself ἀκίνητον [unmoved].[52] Everything is drawn to it; it is itself unmoved, just as that which is requested is the object of the request but itself remains still. Aristotle defines the ultimate in many ways. He says that this ultimate entity is also

the most blessed, but inasmuch as to think is the most blessed *actus* [activity] of all *actus*, its *actus* must be thought. But what does this thought think—only itself—everything else is unworthy of it. (This, however, is not only thought about thinking, for this entity thinks itself.)[53]

Then the neo-Platonists sought a positive philosophy. Aristotle cannot satisfy, because to end in God in this way is not enough. This is important not only because Christianity has developed in the world; even before that, Aristotle could not comprehend mythology, which after all did have historical reality [*Realitæt*], and did not know how to explain it other than as the remains of an *Urwissen* [primordial knowledge].

The question has been brought up: Why did Charlemagne introduce Aristotle's writings into his *schola palatina*?[54] Aristotle was indeed charged with atheism and justifiably so, inasmuch as he has no God as a principle. He excludes every active providence, inasmuch as he merely teaches that everything strives toward God, that everything proceeds toward this *Endziel* [final goal]. A writer in the seventeenth century answered this question very naïvely by saying that it is always good for theologians to have something to find fault with in philosophy; if a union between these two powers were possible, then the devil could tempt people to think that Christianity is a human invention. There is, however, another answer, and Aristotelian philosophy has never been presented in its pure form.

17 III C 27 XIII 279

What the Christian school needed was a God who was beginning and principle. This it had in scholastic philosophy, which continued essentially up to Kant, even though somewhat diluted. Scholasticism recognized three sources of all knowledge: (1) experience; (2) κοινὰς ἐννοίας [universal ideas], (a) *angeborne Begriffe* [innate concepts], the first of which was *ens universale* [universal being], (b) universal principles, of which *principium causalitatis* [principle of causality] was the most important; (3) *ratiocinium, Vernunft-Schluss* [reasoning], as the source of a special kind of knowledge. For example, conclusions beyond experience drawn from the givens of experience. All rational knowledge was formal, and neither rationalism nor empiricism could move. Everything was held together under the authority of the Church. After the Reformation, this was shaken metaphysically on the one hand by Descartes and on the other by Locke and Hume. The last-named extended empiricism to the point that all concepts became merely the results of experience, as when he taught that cause and effect are acquired through long practice,[55] something, incidentally, that the simplest observation contradicts, because, for example, when a child in his cradle hears a noise, he turns his head toward the point of origin (certainly without any practice), and this is obviously an expression of cause and effect. All dogmatic rationalism was thereby destroyed. Then came Kant and brought pure rationalism; over against this stands pure empiricism, which began with Bacon. In its grand efforts, something of the divine must be acknowledged, for otherwise what explanation is there for the religious conscientiousness, the enthusiasm, with which researchers expose themselves to dangers, unless there is a presentiment that there is really something more to it, that this empiricism must indeed be countered by a higher system.

What relation is there between empiricism and positive philosophy? The usual meaning of "experience" is the certainty about an external object that we acquire through external sensation or the certainty about an internal object that we acquire through the internal senses, therefore something that belongs either to the external or to the internal sense-world. If empir-
III C 27 icism is carried through in this sense, it ultimately denies all
XIII 280 concepts. But the concept of empiricism need not be connected to such notions or exclusively to them; it does not need to be limited to the sense-world. A freely acting intelligence, for example, does not fall within the sense-world, and yet he is to be known only empirically. Thus, also, a free intelligence beyond the world will be knowable only through *Thatsachen* [facts]. Consequently, there is an empiricism that is supra-sensible and nevertheless is empiricism, a metaphysical [empiricism] that is not merely sense-empiricism. It would seem that

this agrees with positive philosophy. Therefore there is empirical metaphysical theory. Manifestations of this are: a[56] theory that bases all philosophy on divine revelation, a theory that goes beyond every merely historical fact and traces everything to inner experience and maintains that reason is atheistic; a theory of the secrets of the divine essence that makes these into objects of intuition (theosophy, mysticism, speculative mysticism), which gives itself a scientific form but still lays claim to objective knowledge. Pure rationalism has been unable to overcome all this. These require a positive philosophy, which up to this time they themselves have replaced, but in addition they point out that modern philosophy also has this contrast between negative philosophy and positive philosophy. What, then, is the relation of positive philosophy to this? It must have a relation to experience. Since we have only the two expressions, "philosophy" and "empiricism," positive philosophy also must stand in a relation to empiricism. The common element in all these theories is that they are based upon something occurring and given in experience, for example, Christ's *Erscheinung* [appearance] and miracles or an *überschwenglich* [exuberant] feeling or an immediate intuition. Positive philosophy is not based solely on the given in thought any more than on the given in experience. Its principle can be neither in experience nor in pure thought. Its principle is the absolute transcendence that comes *zuvor* [before] thought as well as experience. Its *prius* is not a relative *prius* as in pure thought, because the *nichtseiende* [not that which is] potency has within itself the necessity of changing into *Seyn* III C 27 XIII 281
and pulling thought along with it. It is an absolute *prius* that has no necessity of changing over into *Seyn*, that is therefore not the *prius des Seyns* [antecedent of being] but the *prius des Begriffs* [antecedent of the concept]. Concept in contrast to *Seyn* is potency. Therefore, the change is from *Seyn* as *prius* to *Begriff als Posterius* [concept as subsequent]. Therefore, potency is *Posterius*, but potency thereby becomes the *Ueberseiende* [beyond-being]. Change from *Seyn* to potency is not necessary change. That which follows the absolute *prius* as a consequent does not follow with necessity.

18

Positive philosophy, therefore, is not empiricism in the sense that it is based *upon* experience; neither does it have an immediate given upon which it is based, nor does it draw itself from a given by way of conclusions, but it *goes to* experience and demonstrates its *prius* a posteriori. This adequately shows its difference from empiricism, but then is it not on a par with negative philosophy? Negative philosophy has being in experience as the object of possible knowledge; it leaves the a posteriori, which it has found a priori, standing outside itself; if it tallies with experience, that is fine, but the truth of its constructions depends upon an inner immanence. Positive philosophy goes to and into experience. The a posteriori is not taken up from experience; it is based upon the absolute *prius* and from this by way of free thought (negative philosophy has necessary thinking) derives the a posteriori as the actual, not merely as the possible. It is not the absolute *prius* that *soll erwiesen werden* [ought to be demonstrated] but the consequence of it; this consequence may be demonstrated as becoming through a free *Fortgang* [advance], yet not out of experience but into it. This, then, is a priori empiricism; negative philosophy is pure a priorism. In positive philosophy, experience is a collaborator. Of course, experience in this connection is to be understood not as some particular experience but as a totality. Positive philosophy is also a priori with respect to the world; with respect to the concept, to God, it is a posteriori. The demonstration it makes is rooted in the totality of expe-
III C 27 rience. But the realm of actuality is not complete; therefore it
XIII
282 is not concluded. On the preceding level, the object of positive philosophy is not concluded and completed, since one cannot know what freedom will bring to light. Positive philosophy is therefore philosophy in the sense implicit in the word itself—it seeks after wisdom. Its demonstration of God is therefore only for those who are willing; only the intelligent learn from experience. The proof of God, therefore, does not have the necessity such that it can almost be forced upon the stupid. Negative philosophy is a system completed within itself; pos-

itive philosophy is not a system in this sense. If, however, positive *Behauptungen* [affirmations] are demanded of a system, then, [positive philosophy is very much a system, negative philosophy not], since it is *nichts behauptend* [affirming nothing].

But now what is the position of positive philosophy toward revelation? It arrives at revelation just as it arrives at everything else. It is for positive philosophy a relative *terminus ad quem* [point to which]; for positive philosophy, it has no authority different from that of any other object. The observed motions of the planets are also an authority for positive philosophy. Therefore, positive philosophy is not religious philosophy. If this predicate is adopted, it might seem to imply indirectly that negative philosophy is irreligious. But this is completely untrue, although negative philosophy certainly has religion *ausser sich* [outside itself]. Neither can it be called irreligious for this reason, because a truly irreligious theory can never claim to be philosophy. If, on the other hand, positive philosophy wanted to claim to be religious, it would be much too vague a definition to mean anything. Then it would have designated itself more specifically as Christian, Catholic, Protestant, etc., which can occur only to those who desire a privileged philosophy. In contrast to this, however, one could point to the dependence of all philosophy upon Christianity. One could say, "Philosophy never would have gone so far without Christianity," but then philosophy could just as well be called empirical, since no philosophy would have come into being without the existence [*Tilvær*] of this world. But Christianity must not be conceived so *engherzig* [narrow-mindedly] as merely historical fact; Christianity is much more, from the beginning of the world. I would like to express this relation III C 27
between philosophy and revelation figuratively. As is known, XIII 283
the four satellites of Jupiter are visible only through a telescope, yet there are men who can see them with the naked eye and others who cannot readily see a fixed star with the naked eye but can do it only if they have seen it through a telescope first. In the same way, philosophy would presumably not have seen much without revelation, but now it can see with the na-

ked eye. Christianity has indeed been incorporated in Christianity [*miswriting for "philosophy"*] lately, but it is so diluted in negative philosophy that it is hardly detectable. But in stressing Christianity we have come back to the point where the contrast between negative and positive philosophy again becomes conspicuous, as all history shows. Kant has provided the most striking example of this contrast.

19

This contrast in Kant between negative and positive philosophy is very clear in his antinomies or antitheses of reason,[57] which are neither more nor less than just so many expressions for the relation between negative and positive philosophy. That which is the thesis could just as well be made the antithesis and vice versa. It is remarkable, however, that his thesis is always positive, always belongs to what we call positive philosophy. Thus when the antithesis affirms that the world cannot have any limits, this belongs essentially to negative philosophy, because to predicate that it has a limit is first a genuine predication, is first a positive predication, belongs first to positive philosophy; on the other hand, that it has no limits belongs to negative philosophy and means only that in the idea of the world there is no necessity to think of it as limited. —It is rather curious that Kant finds this contradiction only in cosmological ideas (Kant had two kinds of antinomies, the mathematical and the dynamic).[58] If it happens, then, that is, if one
III C 27 XIII 284 makes an error in thought, as Kant did, then the same contradiction runs through all the transcendental ideas, philosophy of mind and theology as well. Thus the contrast between freedom and necessity, the soul is eternal or mortal, God is a blind necessary being or freedom. K.'s antinomies, however, are not so very dangerous, for inasmuch as the antithesis always pertains to a world (of pure thought) different from that (the actual world) of the thesis, they do not contradict one another.

But are we willing to let this distinction between positive and negative philosophy stand? In order to consider this, one must take the position (from which the matter is viewed) that approaches philosophy without anything preceding. Philosophy is different from all other sciences in that it provides itself with its object, must acquire it itself. It cannot exclude anything in advance; it goes through all possibilities until it finds its object, but it must not accept these possible objects in a fortuitous way or allow them to be given from elsewhere. It can acquire them only by proceeding from the universal possibility of reason and now seeing how everything changes therefrom into *Seyn*, and consequently by taking the position of possibility and a priority. Philosophy, therefore, is identical with a priori science. By continuing in this way, it comes to something final beyond which it cannot go and which it has not brought to *Erkennbarkeit* [cognizability], but this is the very thing that is most valuable to know and the purest knowledge to be known, because here potency is pure actuality. This ultimate it reserves for itself. As the science of sciences, it places all knowledge outside itself in the sciences of which it is the science, but now it no longer places them outside itself.

Positive philosophy does not have the truth only as a conclusion, as negative philosophy does; für sich [by itself] *negative philosophy cannot be called philosophy; it becomes philosophy only in connection with positive philosophy; negative philosophy is prima scientia* [first science]; *positive philosophy is the highest science; negative philosophy has primum cogitabile* [the first object conceivable]; *positive philosophy has summum cogitabile* [the highest object conceivable]. Between the first and the highest sciences lie all other sciences; just as negative philosophy precedes all other sciences, so positive philosophy concludes them. Perhaps nega- III C 27 XIII 285
tive philosophy would never have developed so vigorously if it had not imagined itself to be all of philosophy. There is, then, only one philosophy, since negative philosophy, in becoming conscious of positive philosophy, does not in this consciousness have positive philosophy outside itself but is itself within positive philosophy.

20

Negative philosophy is misjudged if it is regarded merely as an introduction to positive philosophy; within positive philos-

ophy, it may very well appear foreshortened, but nevertheless it cannot for that reason give up its claim to be independent. Negative philosophy will belong particularly to the school, will be metaphysics. It will always occupy a place of honor as man's own invention. It is not a *besondere Wissenschaft* [special science]; it has all the sciences outside itself; it is the science of sciences. On the other hand, positive philosophy is a *besondere Wissenschaft.* Positive philosophy is essentially in negative philosophy as potency, seeks itself in negative philosophy. Negative philosophy is merely *hinwegschaffende* [way-clearing], that is, it gets out of the way everything that is not philosophy; only at the final point is it positive philosophy. It rightfully honors itself with the proud name: science of reason. Its content, however, is really the continual overthrowing of reason, since reason has no content in itself. Positive philosophy brings to cognition what is indiscernible in negative philosophy; it straightens up the reason stooped in negative philosophy. Negative philosophy is the abased state of reason; positive philosophy is its elevated state. In negative philosophy alone, it would have had no yield, but by requiring positive philosophy it has a positive yield. In positive philosophy, negative philosophy triumphs. Positive philosophy is always the *ursprünglich gewollte* [originally intended] philosophy, and the development also shows how much later the purely rational issues begin to be of concern, but positive philosophy usually follows along; then critique arises, which negative philosophy itself has evoked by this mistake. Negative philosophy could very well be alone, but then it would abandon all actual knowledge, but how should it desire to remain completely empty this way? To that extent Kant very properly calls his philosophy critique, not philosophy. How, then, would negative philosophy be able to answer the justified claims made
III C 27 upon it? Or would it not be obliged to turn the entire content
XIII 286 of feeling and conception into psychological oddities and no more? It has actually been thought that negative philosophy provides the basis for positive philosophy; it is more correct to say the opposite, that positive philosophy provides the basis

for negative philosophy. In negative philosophy, the lesser mysteries are presented; in positive philosophy, the greater mysteries. (As is known, the Eleusinian Mysteries[59] were divided in this way.) The neo-Platonists made a similar [*end of first section of notebook; text continues in second section of notebook*]

No. 2[60]

distinction and called Aristotelian philosophy the Lesser Mysteries in contrast to Platonic philosophy, the Greater.[61] The contrast did not fit there, but here it does.—

But how is the transition made from negative philosophy to positive philosophy? Negative philosophy deals not with the actually existent but with the *Existiren-Könnende* [being able to exist]. Its ultimate is potency that is not disturbed by any *actus* [actuality] but where potency itself is *actus*, and therefore *actus* is not disturbing. This is the *seyende* [that which is] potency, but it is first possessed only in the concept, since it is always about the *Existiren-Könnende*, about which everything revolves. Science looks around after existence. The *seyende* potency does not have *Seyn* as *posterius*; when it exists [*existerer*], it has *Seyn* only as *prius*; it is a priori. Thus the *seyende* potency is the *Seyn-Könnende* [being able to be] reversed. In negative philosophy, the first *Seyn-Könnende* has *Seyn* following it. So far, then, negative philosophy goes. The earlier metaphysics also went so far, as was shown particularly by the ontological argument, which was advanced by Anselm but rejected by Thomas Aquinas[62] and the Thomists. It is curious that Kant[63] did not present its defects better. The demonstration runs something like this. The highest being (this
III C 27 XIII 287 obviously is nothing other than the highest potency) cannot possibly exist accidentally, and consequently it exists necessarily—note, however, if it exists. This can also be elucidated in another way. The major premise is only about necessary existence; therefore there can be nothing in the conclusion about existence in general. The conclusion is: consequently he exists necessarily—if he exists. God cannot result from a *transitus a potentia ad actum* [passage from potentiality to actuality]; then he would not be *das aufrecht stehende* [the upright] *Seyn-Könnende*. He is the *an* and *vor sich* [in and before itself] being (not "*für sich*" [for itself], which also violates language usage

by placing two very different concepts together); *das heisst er ist das vor seiner Gottheit Seyende, also das seinem Begriffe und damit allen Begriffen voraus Seyende* [that is, he is the that which is before his divinity, consequently the that which is antecedent to his concept and thereby all concepts]. But he is thereby *das blind Seyende, das nothwendig Seyende* [the blind that which is, the necessary that which is], and it becomes doubtful whether *God* exists. Therefore I cannot presuppose that *God* is the *an* and *vor sich Seyende* [that which is in and prior to itself]; I must forego the concept "God" until later. I must proceed from *das blind Seyende* and see if I can come to the concept and thereby to God. Potency or concept is the a priori; therefore *das blind Seyende* is the a posteriori. Negative philosophy also arrives at the *Seyn-Könnende*, but it arrives at it in the wrong way, since it arrives at it from potency. If I am to bring it into knowledge, I must arrive at it as the *posterius*, and everything is hereby turned around. This can take place only in a new science. Here we really have Spinoza's principle, *das allem Denken voraus Existirende* [that which exists antecedent to all thought].[64]

Just as all philosophy will be destroyed in the eccentric extension of empiricism, so also positive philosophy is present in all building of philosophy, and it can be said in this connection that recent philosophy is a preparation for it. Descartes' question was not about concept but about *Seyn*. The *I* became his point of departure,[65] but it was subjective. The truth in the ontological argument is that it leads to positive philosophy and appears in this way in Spinoza.[66] However, he grasped only the beginning in order to move straightway into necessary thinking. But because he had this orientation toward being, he had such a strong and great influence, particularly on the best and the most religious minds; he had influence by way of his absolute transcendence that exploded the contrast III C 27
between thought and being. Jacobi[67] himself struggles in vain XIII 288
with the abyss into which Spinoza pulls him down. The relationship between Spinoza and Jakob Boehme[68] has never really been explained. This tendency can be called the reaction of Orientalism against Occidentalism and Aristotelianism.

What is the relation between positive philosophy and reason?

21

Positive philosophy, therefore, proceeds from *dem geradezu Seienden* [the that which simply is]. In negative philosophy, it is the thought preceding *Seyn* that everything revolves around; in positive philosophy, *Seyn* precedes thought. This *geradezu Seiende* could also be called the *nothwendig Seyende* [that which necessarily is], but in modern philosophy this expression has so frequently been identified automatically with the concept "God" that for this reason it is not advisable to use it. By way of a prior concept, it usually means something on which is enjoined the necessity to exist; God is regarded as such a something. But by *das blind Seyende* [the blind that which is] is understood that which is outside all prior concepts. This expression is now used as a matter of course for the highest essence. The highest essence can be only the necessarily existing, but not only is God the *nothwendig Seyende*, but he is *das nothwendig nothwendig-Seyende* [the necessary that which necessarily is]. This indicates the difference from *das blind Seyende*, which is only the *einfach* [simply] *nothwendig-Seyende*. —It does not, however, prove that he exists. The *nothwendig Seyende ist allein des höchsten Wesens Seyn-Können* [that which necessarily is is solely the ability to be of the highest being]. As an objection, the old thesis could be offered: *in deo nil potentiale* [in God there is no potentiality].[69] To this one might reply: Here it is a question not of the nature of God—according to his nature, God is sheer actuality—but of existence. Here it is a question not of potency that changes into *Seyn* but of *purus actus* [pure actuality]; the ultimate *Existiren-Könnende* [being able to exist] is itself potency that consequently has *Seyn* not after itself but before. —*Das geradezu Seyende* could also be called *das nothwendig Seyende*. This needs no justification and does not even permit it; it is independent of all ideas. Positive philosophy drops the concept and detaches itself from negative philosophy and could just as well
III C 27 begin without negative philosophy, just as Spinoza began
XIII 289 with infinite existence. This *geradezu Existerende* [which simply exists] does have a relation to reason. Is this now *geradezu*

Existerende, is it idea, concept? If "idea" is taken in the sense in which it must be taken in negative philosophy, where it is *das gewollte* [the willed], then this *geradezu Existerende* is not idea; in another sense it is idea insofar as it "*behauptet* [affirms]" nothing. Existence cannot be predicated of it, because it is itself the *Existerende*. It is ὄντω τὸ ὄν [the truly being], but ὄν is to be taken not substantively but verbally; *Seyn* cannot be used attributively of it. One is reminded of the ancient Indian saying that it *weder ist noch nicht ist* [neither is nor is not]; it [is] a pure *quid* [what], not a *quod* [that]. It is a concept of reason, but one *der nicht sich Seyn vorsetzt, sondern Seyn sich* [that does not place being before itself, but itself before being]. Reason acquires it as its content a posteriori, but it is that which is placed outside reason, ecstatic. *Das unbedingt* [unconditioned] *Seyende* has no condition except the negative: that reason leaves itself *(sich lässt)*. In negative philosophy, reason is the self-observing, the objective for itself. This is the unconditioned concept of reason and changes into thought; it is the immediate concept of reason.

Kant said that what the older metaphysics sought was a conclusion to prove the necessary existence of a thing, but this was an impossibility.[70] He is perfectly right about this. —The question has been raised whether *Etwas existerendes* [something existing] could demonstrate it is a necessary existence. This is a foolish question, because by *Etwas* a particular has already been designated.

Das blind Seyende and the concept certainly always stand in relation to each other, just as it already appears in the relation between negative and positive philosophy, for negative philosophy ends in the concept and positive philosophy begins with *das blind Seyende*.

Das bloss [pure] *Seyende* is absolute transcendence, but transcendence is always relative, i.e., with respect to something else. Now it must be remembered that we place this before all ideas; we do not place the idea first and then seek to arrive at it—this was the transcendence of the older metaphysics, which is a relative transcendence and is untrue. Our tran-

scendence is absolute and thus none. If I first have made myself immanent, then it is the transcendent to go over to absolute *Seyn*. Kant forbids reason to reach this transcendence by
III C 27 way of inference, but he does not forbid and cannot forbid
XIII 290 inferring the highest essence from necessary being, since such a thing never occurred to him. Reason posits this being outside itself in order that this being can become its content, since a posteriori it becomes God. —Negative philosophy has the a priori conceivable *Seyn* as its content; positive philosophy has the a priori inconceivable *Seyn*. —Philosophy is indeed the science of reason. If one is again to make a distinction between positive and negative philosophy, one may say that in negative philosophy reason is *only* in itself (this "only" is obviously a negative definition); in positive philosophy, reason has a relation to actual being. The science of reason applied to negative philosophy is used in a material sense, inasmuch as reason is itself its substance and material; applied to positive philosophy, it is used in a more formal sense.

With this, the introduction is concluded.

22 January 3 [1842]

In negative philosophy, nothing is fixed, but everything is flowing until it comes to the principle. In this, one can already see the defect of negative philosophy, that it has the principle in reverse order, as the end and not as the beginning. Consequently, it ends in the principle. The principle is, namely, potency, which does not *vorausgeht* [precede] its *Seyn* but which presupposes *Seyn*. The principle is really only that which is assured against all consequent possibilities. The Pythagoreans distinguished and contrasted δυάς [dyad] and μόνας [unit, monad][71] and by the first understood more this double movement [*dobbelt Bevægelse*], the flowingness, and by μόνας the true being. In true science, that is, positive science, *monas* must be prior to *düas*. This *monas* is partly sheer idea, as in negative philosophy, partly actual existence. Insofar as it is the latter, we can proceed not from potency but from *Seyn*, the *Seyn* that has never changed *a potentia ad actum* [from potency to actuality], that is *actus* forthwith and always *actus*. Now it might be

objected: "Such an actuality preceding all possibility is incon- III C 27
ceivable." There is some truth in this, and therefore it may also XIII
be said of this *Seyn* that it is *das unvordenkliche Seyn* [the being 291
absolutely antecedent to thought].[72] As such it is the beginning for all thought, but this is not thought; it is the first object of thinking (*primum quod se objicit cogitationi* [that which reveals itself first for cognition]), which is not the content of thought but can become that. It may be objected that it can never be imagined, either, but to this the reply might be given that there are many possibilities of imagining such a possibility prior to the actuality, such as a machine, a work of art. Presumably there are other possibilities in which the content is first given with the actuality, and only such concepts are truly original. Thus far Aristotle's dictum holds true: *initium philosophiae est admiratio* [the beginning of philosophy is wonder],[73] and Plato's: τὸ πάθος τοῦ φιλοσοφοῦ ἐστι τὸ θαυμάζειν [the pathos of the philosopher is wonder].[74] Philosophy now comprehends a posteriori the incomprehensible a priori. —The main point is to maintain that pure being is pure being in the verbal sense, *in actu puro* [in pure actuality], and its essence is only to be the purely existing. In this regard, one is reminded of the numerous formulations that appeared in earlier theology and later in dogmatics: *in deo essentia et existentia unum est idemque* [in God essence and existence are one and the same]—which means: God's essence and concept consist in this, that he is, he is being; *est ipse suum esse* and *suum esse est ipse* [he himself is his own being . . . his own being is he himself], i.e., his essence is to be; *in deo non differunt esse et quod est* [in God being and that which is do not differ]. His essence consists in being, just as with other things their essence is non-being, the accidental. *A se esse* is not *von sich Seyn* [being from himself] but *von selbst Seyn, ultro esse, geradezu Seyn* [being of himself, being of its own accord, simply being]. *Asseitas* [Underived existence] is therefore always recognized as the highest; Spinoza also made it a principle: *id quod cogitari non potest nisi existens* [that which cannot be thought unless it exists].[75] God is that which cannot be preceded by the thought of non-

being; yes, God cannot even precede himself with the thought that he is not.

III C 27 Being, then, is motionless and immovable, and yet we must
XIII 292 try to move away from it. This is the first, and, to use this expression, at one time there was nothing but this being. We shall now attempt[76] this. We have rejected only the potency preceding *Seyn*; before it is, it cannot be potency—that is a contradiction. But from this it does not follow at all that it cannot become that *nach der Hand, post actum* [by and by, after actuality]; *nachher* [afterward] it can become the *Seyn-Könnende* [being able to be]. If, then, we assume this (here we express ourselves purely hypothetically and shall give the justification later), the *Seyende* is raised to *potentia potentiae* [the potency of potency] and in this way first becomes truly the *Seyn-Könnende*. It is truly the *Seyn-Könnende*, because it has its *Urseyn* [primordial being] as an a priori in itself prior to all possibility. Here, then, a possibility appears. It is a matter of indifference to pure being whether it takes up this other being into itself or not. But this possibility appears as something new, unexpected, because it comes after *Seyn*, but although it appears in this way, *so erscheint es doch zugleich dem Seyn von Ewigkeit her* [at the same time it nevertheless appears to being from all eternity]. That which comes before everything eternally is, even before thought. Eternity belongs to the qualities of God that the dogmaticians call negative, without which God cannot be but by which he still is not. Spinoza's substance is also eternal in this way, but yet not God. This eternity is now *terminus a quo* [the point from which], which therefore is also called *von Ewigkeit* [from eternity]. Science cannot stop with that but moves straightway from it. Now something thereby appears for being; it can will. This cannot apply to pure being itself, for it is sheer *Gelassenheit* [inactivity]. Here being manifests itself as lord, different from the *unvordenkliche Seyn* [the being absolutely antecedent to thought], whose lord it was not. But more takes place. That which is really an object for a will is always the accidental, not being. If we call the *unvordenkliche Seyn* A and the accidental B, then being, in positing B, which it is lord over, is its lord, but it is also A's lord.

In positing B, it turns A out of its *Gelassenheit* and becomes its lord. Now being has a negation within itself and no longer is pure being, but only *der Potenz nach* [with regard to potency] is it *actus purus*.

23 January 5 III C 27

XIII 293

The expression for the beginning of positive philosophy is basically the formulation presented in the last lecture, a being that is identical with essence or whose essence by itself is being. The concept of this being is found only later. In the context of our present discussion, such a being is not perfection, and we are still dealing only with what dogmaticians call negative attributes. Dogmaticians often take being as something positive, as a perfection, but in taking it this way they exclude themselves from the scientific path by which one can go from the negative to the positive. Therefore, the identity of essence and *Seyn* must be understood in a negative sense so that essence is not an essence isolated from *Seyn* but [is] being; existing is essence. We do not stop with this negation but posit it only as the beginning. As Spinoza's example shows, there is nothing to be done with sheer *actus purus* [pure actuality]; one can move away from it insofar as it is possible to move away from it through a subsequent potency. We say it is a possibility, and the subsequent potency is itself also only a possibility, here enunciated simply as a possibility. That which always has its *Seyn* before is really the sole *Wollende* [that which wills], the only one that can begin something. Thus a man whose existence is disturbed in some way is said to be unable to begin. A priori being, which begins with being being, is first actual potency. The truth of potency is therefore rooted in the preceding being. If we wanted to state a predicate for the existent and not merely state tautologically that it is this existent, then we might say that it is the *Existiren-Könnende, Seyn-Könnende* [being able to exist, being able to be], namely, not in the sense of before but in the sense of afterward. But it still remains only a possibility; that it is actual must be shown a posteriori. We see not what it is but that it is. A priori it is only *possible*; that it can become the *Seyn-Könnende* is a hypothesis. Being is the

III C 27 XIII 294 thesis; that it is the *Seyn-Könnende* is the antithesis in the sense in which rhetoricians use the word. We have said earlier that positive philosophy has to do with thinking freely, and this is apparent here, for it proceeds from *actus purus*, and one can move from it only through freedom; there is no necessary transition from *actus* to potency. If we suppose now that for this essence identical with *Seyn* or, as we may express it, that for *Seyn*'s subject (which is no different from *Seyn*, is not essence for itself)—that for this there appears a possibility of being something other than it is according to its *unvordenkliche Seyn* [being absolutely antecedent to thought]—then this possibility, insofar as it is possible, will continually manifest itself, that is, from all eternity. The first consequence of this is that being becomes *gegenständlich* [objective] to its own *unvordenkliches Seyn*. Earlier, being has its *unvordenkliches Seyn an sich* [in itself] (just as we say of a man that he has a defect *an sich*, that he is not conscious of it). Second. The *actus* of its existence is necessary only as long as it is not *gegenständlich* to itself, as long as it is *an sich*. As soon as this possibility manifests itself, it separates the necessary by nature and the necessary only *actu* [in actuality] and to that extent the only accidentally necessary.

The necessarily existing brings with itself *actus* for existing before it thinks itself; *der actus des Existirens kommt sich selbst zuvor* [the actuality of existing precedes itself]. No potentiality precedes this existence, but from this it does not follow that being is not meant to achieve something afterward, even beyond *unvordenkliches Seyn*. Earlier it does not achieve anything beyond; it submits to it, *wovor es nicht kann* [which is why it cannot]. But in relation to its essence, this is something accidental, something that happens to it. —*Das unvordenkliche Seyn* is = *a se esse* [being of itself], *primum constitutivum* [the first constitutive]. *A se esse* must not be translated as *von sich seyn* [being from itself]—that would lead either to the concept *causa sui* [cause of itself] (as Descartes understood it, Spinoza, too, although in Spinoza it is a deceptive expression, because in his usage he really falls into the contradiction with himself that God as *causa sui* becomes potency, δύναμις [power], and

thus God as potency precedes himself as *actus*) or to the self-revealing or the self-positing—but as *ultro, sponte*, αὐτομάτως ὄν [of its own accord, voluntarily, being of its own accord]. Thus *das unvordenkliche Seyn* manifests itself as the accidental. III C 27
When I plant a seed in a particular place, I do not think it XIII 295
strange that it comes up there, because I have a concept of it prior to its being. If, however, a plant comes up in a place where I have not sown, I am amazed, because to me it is something accidental. If potency preceded *das unvordenkliche Seyn*, it is not the necessary; if it is only *actu* [in actuality], then neither is it the necessary.

24 January 7

Das unvordenkliche Seyn [the being absolutely antecedent to thought] is not existence but precedes it. Its essence is not as essence; it is completely ecstatic; it has not *sich entäussert* [externalized itself] but is *entäussert* [externalized]; it is antipodal to the idea but on the very basis of this contrast is itself idea. —nothing precedes this *actus purus* [pure actuality], but therefore it is eternal, like everything before which nothing can come. All negative attributes are exclusions of every preceding potency.

Das unvordenkliche Seyn has *Seyn an sich* [being in itself], is the *an sich Seyende* [that which is in itself], the *an und vor sich Seyende* [that which is in and prior to itself]. But an existent only *actu* [in actuality], without being qualified according to its nature, is accidental blind existence.

This is not the place to develop the many meanings of the accidental, but I refer to the portion on the accidental in Aristotle's *Metaphysics*.[77] Here only the remark that the accidental is the unwilled or the unforeseen, but the unforeseen is that blind being, *prae quo nihil potest* [before which nothing is possible].

It may also be said that the blind *Seyende* is that which precedes its possible opposite. If I choose between +A and −A and I choose +A, then −A is absolutely excluded. If, however, I am thereby +A *actu*, then −A is indeed excluded, but not absolutely. *Das Andersseyn* [the contrariety], as we pointed

out earlier, is not surmounted; it can come afterward. A doubt can arise afterward, *post actum* [after actuality], and render the
III C 27 *unvordenkliche Seyn* accidental, demand of it that it must man-
XIII 296 ifest itself as the necessary, which, if one may put it this way, it previously did not have time for. It will also manifest itself as necessary if this contrast intervenes. —This law is the ultimate ground in everything, this law that nothing is to remain untried, undisclosed. This law is indeed not above God but first places God in freedom in opposition to his *unvordenkliches Seyn*. Thus it is God's own law; only because *das unvordenkliche Seyn* precedes all thinking does this law appear as something foreign to God. It is only God's own idea that introduces this law. —The dialectic of this world does not want anything to remain doubtful anywhere. Hegel has advanced dialectic again, but primarily in negative philosophy. Plato calls dialectic the royal art,[78] an expression to be understood rather as if he had said the divine. —Dialectic really belongs in freedom and therefore in positive philosophy. God lets that principle of contrast apply until the final possibility is exhausted; it is not merely once for all but always.

The possibility of an advance away from the motionless depends upon this accidentality. An existent only *actu* [in actuality] is something accidental, but since it is something accidental there is the possibility of a potency that cancels that possibility. The accidental is material potency, and thereby an *Andersseyn* is *zugelassen* [admitted] as a possibility.

The *Seyn-Könnende* [being able to be] is that which transcends the *Seyende*. The concepts turn around. The *Seyende* appeared as positive, but it is also only the *actu Seyende*, the impotent, and therefore negative; the *Seyn-Könnende* appeared as negative but is positive; this is his strength. With the *Seyn-Könnende* his divinity begins, in that he can transcend the *unvordenkliche Seyn*. So it is in a human being, too. The deeper and more complete his turning around and his *Entäusserung* [externalization] of his *Seyn*, the freer, the more divine; to free himself from his being is the task of all education. God is the living God, therefore not shut up in *Seyn*. If one does not discern this, one ends either in pantheism—or abstract theism, which assumes an intelligent world-source but interprets creation as an incomprehensibility to reason.

Yet it may be objected that that we are assuming *ein ungött-* III C 27
liches Seyn [a nondivine being] in God and in this way do not XIII 297
arrive at pantheism but rather materialism, naturalism. This would be the case, too, if God were not placed in anything but this *Andersseyn*, for then he would fall completely within being. But (1) *Andersseyn* is not a blindly changing potency, and (2) he has it solely in himself as a presupposition of being God.

25 January 10

In the preceding lectures, we have shown the possibility of an *Aufheblichkeit des unvordenklichen Seyns* [a suspension of the being absolutely antecedent to thought]. In place of the existence *actu* [in actuality], we have the existence not *actu* but *natura* [in nature], therefore the essential existence. It is thereby beyond mere *actus* and free toward existence, but it has its place in this *actu*. If the necessary existence *natura* preceded existence *actu*, it would be a necessitated existence, but it is not this *actus purus* [pure actuality]; it is *a se esse* [being of itself]. The best picture of this kind of existence is always innocence. If a concept preceded, it would not be innocence. The necessary existence *natura* is the true essence of the existence *actu* but not its cause; on the contrary, it is intrinsically the opposite in the existence *actu*. When the accidentality of the first is shown, then the true necessary existence comes forth without need for this *actus*, [then it] is the necessary existence even with the annulment of this *actus*, since it is the necessary existence *natura*. It sees itself as the *Seyn-Könnende* [being able to be], beyond this *actu Seyende* [that which is in actuality], as free. [It sees itself] as lord over the *Seyn* posited in contrast to the *unvordenkliche Seyn*, which it can will or not, as well as lord over the *unvordenkliche Seyn* itself, not, however, as that which posits it, since the *unvordenkliche Seyn* always precedes the necessary existence *natura*. In the appearance of the first possibility, the *unvordenkliche Seyn* was moved from its position (*loco motus*), lifted into the air, because possibility and the *unvordenkliche Seyn*

cannot be *uno eodemque loco* [in one and the same place]; by a negation it was posited in the sense not of something preceding but of something following. The necessary existence *natura* is divine existence. This expression can now be used of
III C 27 being, since it has manifested itself as lord, but the concept of
XIII 298 God is precisely *Herrlichkeit* [lordship, majesty, glory], i.e., to be lord, and therefore, as Newton says, *deus est vox relativa, includens dominationem* [God is a relative word, including dominion].[79] But where should that which it is lord over come from, if not from the *unvordenkliche Seyn*? Through the positing of possibility, the *unvordenkliche Seyn* is excluded and placed back into itself, pressed back into itself[80] as potency. In this way there is imposed the necessity of working to place itself back into *actus purus*, because potency is something completely foreign to it. Thus it must negate the new *Seyende*. — It now manifests itself as lord of another possibility, namely, that of hypostatizing the *unvordenkliche Seyn* and taking it away from itself precisely by showing it to be something accidental. —The third possibility is to manifest itself as being free from necessary *seienden Seyn* [that which is being], to posit itself as spirit [*Aand*]. On the whole, spirit is that which is free to express itself or not to express itself. Posited as essence, it is the *Seyn-Könnende*, is that which cannot become unlike itself. In *Seyn* it persists and continues to be the *Seyn-Könnende*, just as it continues as the *Seyn-Könnende* to be *Seyn*. I say that which is "posited *as* essence," and this is of great importance. The particle *als* [as] is very important. Pure being is not posited *als* being; it is just *einfach* [simple] but precisely thereby admits the opposite potency outside itself. Now, however, it is posited *as* being, since it cannot cease to be being. Thus essence is here posited as essence, but hitherto only by way of ideal exclusion. This is spirit. It may be put also in this way. It cannot be the immediate *Seyn-Könnende*, because its place is occupied; it cannot be the *Seyn-Müssende* [being that must be], either, because it is taken; consequently it is the *Seyn-Könnende* that is also the *Seyn-Müssende*. The third possibility appears to the *unvordenkliche Seyn* as the *Seyn-Sollende* [being that ought to be] proper; it appears as *Schluss* [conclu-

sion]. The *unvordenkliche Seyn* must now elevate itself to the necessary existence *natura*; this gives it the power to posit free being instead of *das blind Seyende*. God is not only spirit; he is more than spirit. He is not the necessary spirit but the absolutely free spirit. Thus Christianity, too, teaches that spirit is a person, and yet God is spirit. It is the same with spirit as with essence, because essence manifests itself prior to existence, but [also] after it, in that it appears as the *überexistirende* [that which exists above].

26 January 13 III C 27

The necessary existence *natura* [in nature] has the same relation XIII 299 to the necessary existence merely *actu* [in actuality] as essence to *Seyn*, concept to *Seyn*, but in such a way that the concept does not precede *Seyn* but exists as *überexistirend* and consequently is more than essence, is *Ueberwesen* [above-essence] as this word is commonly understood. For this reason, and quite rightly, dogmaticians in an earlier period pointed out that when the word "essence" is used about God, one must remember that he is more than essence, is ὑπερουσία [above-essence].

The *unvordenkliche Seyn* [being absolutely antecedent to thought] elevates itself to idea and now is really God; previously it was only substantially God or God according to possibility. Not until now is this the real God. To move from the *unvordenkliche Seyn* to this point is possible only for a very exhaustive dialectic. Dialectic belongs essentially to positive philosophy. The concept of God is essence as *actus purus* [pure actuality]. Now the formulae presented earlier (*in deo essentia et existentia non differunt* [in God, essence and existence do not differ] etc.) take the opposite form: in God, *actus* is his essence. The negative attributes are a priori attributes that come prior to his *Gottheit* [divinity]. —There is no transition from the negative to the positive attributes; it cannot be a necessity. —Without the *unvordenkliche Seyn*, God could not be, because he could not be lord and neither could he be personality, because lordship over *Seyn* is exactly what personality is; absolute personality is beyond *Seyn schlechthin* [totally]. —God's existence cannot be demonstrated, but the *Gottheit des Existi-*

renden [divinity of the existing] [can be demonstrated], and this only a posteriori. —God knows himself beyond existence *actu*, that he is the necessary existence *natura*; this transcendence is his very divinity, *qua existentiam transcendit* [by which he transcends existence]. From all eternity, he sees himself as lord, able to annul his *unvordenkliches Seyn* or, more accurately, to suspend it.

Now we come to something new. Why does God suspend this *unvordenkliche Seyn*, why does he actualize this possibility, since he is indeed lord beforehand—why, then, does he actualize this possibility? One could reply that it is in order to
III C 27 XIII 300 transform his blind affirmation into a conscious affirmation. But for whom, then, does he do this? For himself—he knows that. He can decide on this process only for something that is outside himself (*praeter se*). Aristotle says God continuously thinks only himself, and discussion of the eternal subject-object is to be understood in the same way. Aristotle[81] seeks the happiness of God in precisely this. But might it not rather be considered the greatest limitation not to be able to get away from oneself? Man desires to get away from himself and feels that his happiness consists in that; Joh. v. Müller[82] says that he is satisfied only when he is productive. God is therefore happy because he is away from himself. —Between this suspension and return lies the whole world, or the world exists precisely because of this *suspendirte Aktus des göttlichen Seyns* [suspended actuality of the divine being]. —God *entäussert sich* [externalizes himself] not to nature—he is that *auf unvordenkliche Weise* [in ways absolutely antecedent to thought]—but since he *entäussert sich* in this, he enters his concept and he suspends the *unvordenkliche Seyn* in order to posit another *Seyn* instead. —In positive philosophy, God has the same indifference in *Seyn-* and *Nicht-Seyn-Können* [ability to be . . . not to be] as in negative philosophy, and in this he has the real ground from which he puts forth all these possibilities as actualities. The same potencies come again here as in negative philosophy, but they come as those having *Seyn* as their presupposition. If we imagine the advancement of this process beforehand, it will [be], apart from the actuality comprehending all a priori pos-

sibilities in itself, a πᾶν [all], an all-being, from which the accidental is not excluded but is subordinated to necessity. This world is not only logical but also real, but still also logical, because the accidental is subordinated to necessity. This connection of the real and the logical is the most difficult to comprehend.

It is a question of demonstrating accidental existence, appearance *ex improviso* [unexpected]. That which necessarily exists has its place directly in *Seyn*, which no potency precedes. But possibility is therefore not excluded; only the actual excludes by way of actuality, but possibility insinuates itself everywhere. This possibility is due to the *unvordenkliche Seyn*, for if it were not, possibility could not be, either.—

27 January 14 III C 27

XIII 301

A genuine possibility always presupposes a being. Potency for all existence, as in negative philosophy, is not genuine potency. The possibility that appears for the *unvordenkliche Seyn* [being absolutely antecedent to thought] can appear for it only as its potency; it has no place outside it; in God [it] evokes a corresponding will over which he is still lord. If he posits it, it is an intention, and the only way it can come about is as a means. The *unvordenkliche*[83] *Seyn* must also be posited in this intention. —God is God as he who is lord over his own substantiality and the unity in which the *unvordenkliche Seyn* and the accidental are held together. The *unvordenkliche Seyn* is indeed posited *ex actu* [from actuality], but still not absolutely annulled, for not even God is capable of that. *Der actus* is annulled and is thereby itself posited as the potency of *actus* and must work to place itself back in *actus prius* [antecedent actuality]. The ὑποκείμενον [substratum] of creation is *Nichts* [nothing], which means that it has its ground solely in the will of God—will is *Urseyn* [primordial being]. —There is in human life an analogy to what is involved in the overcoming of this accidental. In the individual, anger posits a foreign will but with the effect that the individual's true will reacts and the subject again feels his freedom.

This overcoming could take place all at once, but here the

previously discussed leniency toward the contrary intervenes; just like persuasion, to recall an expression in Plato, it must be traced back. If we assume such an overcoming step by step, we must assume a principle that determines the steps, a principle that must be independent of the contrary as well as of that which conjures it up, so to speak, stepwise; it must be independent of both, because the first wants unconditionally to endure and the second unconditionally to subordinate. — This third is given in that third potency, i.e., spirit, a principle that is undivided, dispassionate.

Thus we have three potencies. The effective cause of the whole movement is the first, which we shall call B. This *Seyn*, which opposes the *unvordenkliche Seyn*, is self-contrasting *Seyn*, is blind and mindless will. It works exclusively upon *Urseyn*, which we must think of in the form of complete ne-
III C 27 XIII 302 gation. If that will is quieted, a third is posited that belongs to both wills. (It should be remembered here that creation really falls into two elements: (1) the positing of the *schrankenlose Seyn* [boundless being] and (2) *die Verinnerlichung* [the internalization], because a potency is posited in *Seyn*. Therefore, creation is not only positive, but it has a negative concept in itself.) The third that comes forth is a thing, something concrete. The second potency as the original could not actualize itself; this is the genuine negative and consequently is not the first—there must be something beforehand. If we assume the whole process to have taken place, B is *entwirklicht* [deactualized]; A is *actus purus* again. The third potency is destined to enter into actuality when the others have withdrawn. Spirit alone is the *Seyn-Sollende* [that which ought to be]. There is really a fourth independent of all these three, which, like all potencies, are excluding potencies. We can also bring to mind here the old classification: B is therefore *causa materialis* [material cause], the second potency is *causa efficiens* [efficient cause], the third potency is *causa in quam* [final cause]. The third potency, simply with its will, keeps every becoming at its level; therefore, "he commanded and it was there" means not that it came into existence [*blev til*] but that it remained standing.

28 January 17

Therefore the third potency is the genuine *Seyn-Sollende* [that which ought to be]. From this it seems to follow that the first potency is the not-*Seyn-Sollende*, and consequently an evil principle, something that should not be included. Now, it must be borne in mind that there is a great difference between saying that something is not the *Seyn-Sollende* and saying that it is the not-*Seyn-Sollende*, whereby it is posited as something. In every action that is not momentary, that which is the means is not the *Seyn-Sollende*, but it nevertheless is not to be cast aside and is a genuine *Gewolltes* [something willed]. If this is denied, it is tantamount to saying that God does not use means. That, however, is the most unreasonable of all, for God always works through means or, as a Greek has expressed it, always through τὸ ἐναντίον (the opposite). One can go further and say that *das entgegengesetzte Seyn* [the opposed being] is really the *Seyn-Sollende* at the beginning of the process, that is, in that moment. After the process, the situation is altered; III C 27
if it now affirms itself, it is the *Wider-Göttliche* [anti-divine].[84] XIII 303

The content of the process is the bringing forth of a world in which all possibilities are actualities. The true God is first one who creates. Without potency and *die Herrlichkeit* [the lordship], he is not true God. It is something else to say that God is not God without the world, for as the "*Herr dieser weltschöpfenden Potenz* [Lord of this world creating potency]" he is God and does not need the world. Before the world is, he is lord over it; that is, he is lord over positing it and over not positing it. The world is not a logical consequence of God's nature in the sense that the idea that it has arisen from his will is thereby excluded. Neither is what is here developed synonymous with what is often said, that God indeed has freedom to *entäussern sich* [externalize himself] to nature but in such a way that he himself is included in the process. He is the cause that remains outside; he is *causa causarum* [cause of causes], the ground of the *Spannung* [tension] of the potencies.

Creation necessarily requires an explanation. To stop with saying that it is incomprehensible is certainly of no help; therefore those escapes are seized upon. If creation is not an emanation, it must be something in the middle between the divine, eternal *Seyn* and the being of the world. The world must have existed in *Entschluss* [resolve] before it actually came into existence [*blev til*], must have existed as possibility and future. —It is this *Urmöglichkeit* [primordial possibility] that frees the creator from the *Seyn* he cannot get rid of. But the *entgegengesetzte Seyn* is negated not all at once but *im verschiedenen* [to a varying] degree, and thus the second potency actualizes itself *im verschiedenen* degree and likewise the corresponding third. Here, then, is an infinite multiplicity of possible positions of the potencies toward one another, and the lord over these potencies has the power to try them and place them in opposition to one another, power to let them pass him.

This is the theory of ideas and archetypes as known from Greek culture. "Idea" means the seeing as well as that which is seen. It is vision before it becomes actual. That primal potency has therefore been the object of attention for all peoples at all times. It is that *fortuna primigenia* [primal fortune] worshiped in Praeneste[85] and in whose arms Zeus lies. *Mater*
III C 27 [mother] and *materia* [matter] have a close relation to each
XIII 304 other—that primordial potency is ὑποκείμενον [substratum]—the world's nurse is also a well-known conception—*Maya* to the Indians is related to the German *Macht* [power] and the *Machia* of the Persians—*Maya* is that which stretches *die Netze des Scheins* [the nets of semblance] in order to hold fast to the creator and force him to create. —In Solomon's proverbs it is called wisdom.[86] It might be objected, when I also discern in this a designation of that primal potency, that this is saying too much for it, is too concrete an expression. It must be remembered that this primordial potency, which is the original *Seyn-Könnende* [being-able to be] is now no longer merely the *Seyn-Könnende*; it has in fact passed through *Seyn*, since it emerged in this way, but this necessarily has some meaning, because otherwise it would end with nothing more coming out of the process than entered into the process, or everything would emerge unaltered from the process. After having passed through *Seyn*, it is no longer merely the *Seyn-Könnende*

but is the *posited Seyn-Könnende*, which has control over itself and is also a something that has become.

This is the only way in which consciousness can arise; there is no immediate consciousness. This is knowledge of the process, i.e., wisdom. From this the purpose of the process is also apparent, inasmuch as God can will it only for the sake of such a co-knowing will. —Concerning this designation, it must also be remembered that frequently a principle is named for that to which it is destined in the end. —In proceeding from matter, one notes that it bears only the stamp of understanding and successively develops it more and more until in man it asserts itself. In madness, on the other hand, there is potency *ausser sich gesetzt* [posited outside itself]. When it is said that there is an element of madness in everything great, this really means that there is a controlled madness; the poetic is precisely an example of such control. The opposite of *Wahnsinn* [insanity] is *Blödsinn* [idiocy], in which the understanding lacks inner substance on which it works.

29 January 18 III C 27 XIII 305

Understanding [*Forstand*] and will are frequently contrasted; this is correct when taken abstractly. On the other hand, the will that has control over itself is understanding. The primordial potency, when it is brought back to itself, is understanding in this way. Earlier it is blind will. Will is the subject (*subjectum*) of understanding and can be called understanding *potentia* [in potency]. From this it is seen that primordial potency can be called wisdom, and to what extent. *Verstand* [understanding] could also be called *Vorstand* [before-standing] in the sense of *Urstand* [under-standing] (J. Böhme[87]); it is that to which the entire process is linked. When it is brought to rest, it is the actual subject, *der wirkliche Unterstand der gottlichen Existents* [the actual under-standing of divine existence]. It is spirit's *Verstand* that has become its subject, that is, *Unterstand*. The same double meaning is present in the Greek ἐπιστήμη [knowledge], from ἐφίσταμαι [I know]: I remain standing (primordial potency brought to the point of standing), and I gain power over it. Bacon says: *scientia est potentia* [knowledge

is power].[88] The German word *"Können"* is also used in the sense of *"Wissen* [knowledge]." —The portion previously mentioned from Solomon's proverbs fits primordial potency perfectly. "He had me before his path";[89] he had me before he proceeded from his *unvordenkliches Seyn*, because whatever has a path must also move. It is before all his works; although not God, it is nevertheless not creature and therefore is the midway between God and man. "The lord had it"; *er bekam sie* [he obtained it], since it was not beforehand but came gradually. He did not have it as *Möglichkeit seiner selbst* [the possibility of himself] but *Alles Anderen* [of all else]. Varro (the Roman)[90] distinguishes between *principes dii* [the first gods] and *summi dii* [the highest gods]. Thus the world is co-posited as the *prius allen Werdens* [of all becoming]. Now the thought is broadened poetically. The following must be translated "like a child," not, as usually happens, *"als Werkmeister* [like a master workman]" (the Hebrew word [אמון] means both). Potency was not yet *ausgesetzt* [posited apart]; therefore it was like a child in his father's house: "I played before him," showed him (the father) everything that could come, since it is all-possibility, "but my joy was in the children of men."[91] That the crea-
III C 27 XIII 306 tor carries it out cannot be perceived a priori. It becomes manifest through experience that the necessary being is God. If with respect to God the actual positing is a matter of indifference, if for him it is the same whether he stops with the intention or lets it come forth, what, then, can move him to create? Although lord, he still lacks something, namely, to be known, and we dare attribute this need to God. —He can be creator not as one but as one in many. And this he is, since he is *causa causarum* [cause of causes] and the unity of *causa materialis, efficiens, et in quam* [material cause, efficient, and final]. Here we acknowledge monotheism. In speaking absolutely of God, I presuppose his *Einzigkeit* [uniqueness]. This is already implicit in the language itself. If one does not go further, this may be called the *absolute Einzigkeit*. But the content of a dogma must be something more than a tautology that signifies itself. *Das reine Seyn* [The pure being] cannot have any likeness, because it can [have] nothing at all. The particular

existent always has within itself the potency for something else, because it does not exhaust its concept (thus, for example, each particular plant has within itself the potency of all plants of the same species). The *reine Seyn* has no possibility prior to itself, and therefore it is the *einzige* [unique one] according to its own nature. Pure *Seyn* is Spinoza's substance,[92] but in this way Spinoza did indeed become a monotheist. Hegel[93] even regards the Eleatic position as monotheism and speaks of several monotheisms. God's *Einzigkeit* is treated among the negative characteristics. These negative attributes are the ones declared of God as substance. The one God is infinite substance. If one cannot go further, one can continue claiming to be a monotheist and put up with being called an atheist, both with equal justification.

30 January 20

The general thesis of monotheism does not go beyond the mere concept of God, does not reach the one God; this is theism, not monotheism. By elemental theism is meant the view that regards God simply as infinite substance. As sub- III C 27
stance, he is indeed God *potentia* [in potency]. In the old the- XIII 307
ologians, a theist and an atheist are the same. If, however, one stops with this bare substance, nothing can be defined regarding God's relation to things and to the world. If this is to be done and defining is done in such a way that things are only qualifications of substance, this is pantheism. Theism, therefore, is by no means the true contrast to pantheism, since theism itself, as soon as it wants to get involved in this question, must define itself in the direction of pantheism. Monotheism, therefore, is the doctrine of God as God *nach seiner Gottheit* [according to his divinity]. The living God is he who steps out of his *unvordenkliches Seyn* [being absolutely antecedent to thought], posits an other in contrast to it, makes this a potency, frees his essence from the *unvordenkliche Seyn* as free essence, and thereby is creator. Here is not only unity of substance; the substantial has disappeared in potency. Potency is called potency because it first manifests itself as the possibility of a future movement; in actuality, they are actual elements.

God is neither one, nor two, nor three, but unity, and not many Gods, but one God. The same development that leads to creation leads also not only to the *einzige* [the unique one] but to the *gott-einzige* [divine unique one]. Monotheism does not teach that God is *der eine* [the one] but *der all-eine* [the all-one]; *nach den Gestalten seines Seyns* [according to the forms of his being], he is not one and yet he is one; when one looks away from his *Gottheit* [divinity], he is not one. Monotheism must be not only negative, and it is that only when it actually says that he is one; it must be positive, and it is that only when it says that he is many. The immediately *behauptete* [asserted] in monotheism is multiplicity. John of Damascus[94] says that God is more than *einzig*. In the Old Testament, it says not that the Lord our God is one, but that *er ist ein einziger* יהוה [he is a unique Jehovah], not that he is one, but that he is the sole one as Jehovah. On the whole, monotheism is a restrictive concept; unity is only with regard to *die Gottheit*. It is the true contrast to pantheism, where God is still bare being. Bare being is the presupposition that makes monotheism possible, because this necessity of his *Seyn* places him in a position to become free. Monotheism posits genuine surmounted
III C 27 pantheism. It has not only God but the definite God, ὁ θεός
XIII [the God]. Theism is in a sense a mere deficiency insofar as it
308 has not yet reached the true God, but if it opposes the movement to monotheism, it is false. One cannot stop with theism; it is the indefinite, the potential, which goes over either into pantheism or into monotheism. Jacobi[95] boasted of being a pure theist, declaims against pantheism and now translates this word as the doctrine of *Alleinheit* [all-oneness], ἓν τὸ πᾶν [all is one].[96] This, however, is also monotheism. Therefore the distinction does not lie here, because here there is likeness. The distinction is that pantheism thinks only a principle, blind being, and out of this no system can be formed. Alongside *Einheit* [oneness], he places an *Allheit* [allness]. So it was for Spinoza;[97] his substance was not an empty *Eins* [one], but he posits two characteristics, *ausgedehntes* and *denkendes Seyn* [extended . . . thinking being]. The first is *Seyn*'s potency changing *a potentia ad actum* [from potency to actuality], which has

lost itself, our *Seyn-Könnendes* [being-able to be], the first potency. *Das denkende Seyn* is our second potency, but actually the whole thing is formulated solely according to Descartes.[98] Where we have the third potency, he falls back into the substantial. Thus the error is not his doctrine of *Alleinheit* but that his *Alleinheit* is dead. From two sides, opposite charges can be brought against him—he can be charged with not being a monotheist, and he can be charged with being more than a theist, that for him God is not empty. The latter is, of course, the objection of theism.

31 January 24

Pantheism is impotency and has its essence more in nonknowledge than in knowledge; pantheism is negative, monotheism positive. Jacobi has always maintained the scientific rightness of pantheism. The only science, he says, is Spinozism, in which God etc. cannot be comprehended by reason [*Fornuft*]. In our time, theism is really an improved edition of deism, and there is always something suspicious that it is this in particular that has undertaken to battle against pantheism. Theism is the opposite only of atheism, if by this is understood a system that completely denies God, for example, Epicureanism, which puts chance in place of providence. Atheism is not at all closer to pantheism than to theism. In negative philosophy, theism III C 27
is the only possible expression for the highest idea; if one does XIII
not go beyond negative philosophy, one has only theism. The- 309
ism is the common element of pantheism and monotheism, and therefore the potency of both, but really is not potency for pantheism but only for monotheism. Eternal is that before which nothing comes, not even a thought; it is the *primum constitutivum* [first constitutive]. True theism must acknowledge this *Seyn*; only then can it meet pantheism. The distinction between true and false theism is that the false does not see anything in the *unvordenkliche Seyn* [being absolutely antecedent to thought] except *bruta existentia* [brute existence]; true theism also sees freedom in the *an und vor sich Seyende* [that which is in itself and present to itself], simply because it has *Seyn* before. If theism has come so far, it is no longer really

monotheism but is still *potentia* [*in potency*]. In monotheism, philosophy comes in touch with Christian ideas; God's *Alleinheit* [all-oneness] has its more specific expression in the trinity of God and, vice versa, the trinity in *Alleinheit*. In order to preclude misunderstanding, one must remember that *Alleinheit* is still not the Christian Trinity. Here it should be observed (1) how *Alleinheit* is different from the Trinity [and] (2) what qualifications must be added. —Before creation, God already had the three potencies; in creation they are in effect; consequently there is a multiplicity of potencies, of effective causes, which do not, however, have independence, but [God] is that which works in everything, absolute personality. Christian doctrine affirms a multiplicity not only of potencies but of persons, who, each of them, are Gods; we have only one person, three potencies, not three persons. What we call absolute personality could be compared to what Paul calls ὁ θεός καὶ πατήρ [the God and Father], what the Church calls *principium divinitatis* [the principle of divinity]; he can set B and all other potencies in motion. —If we look at the end of the entire process, our first potency can more definitely be designated as Father. By his will, he posits another, merely possible *Seyn* (B) *entgegen* [in opposition to] his *unvordenkliches Seyn*, thereby posits his *unvordenkliches Seyn ex actu* [being absolutely antecedent to thought according to actuality] and makes it a task, by surmounting the contrast, to return to *actus purus* [pure actuality]. Language has no other expression for this
III C 27 movement than "to give birth," *generare* [to generate], and the
XIII 310 expression used here is used not figuratively but very literally. By his will, absolute personality is the cause of the contrasting *Seyn* and thereby gives birth to the other. To give birth is not to posit an other but to posit an other in such a way that it must actualize itself. The second potency (A^2) fulfills itself by overcoming B, is now its lord in the same sense as the Father, but as lord over *Seyn* is not only potency but personality. This is the Son and is of the same *Herrlichkeit* [lordship, majesty, glory] as the Father in lordship over B. Thus it is the same with the Son as it was originally with the Father. The divinity of the Son is one with the Father. —The same holds true of

the third potency, in which God posits his essence free from the *unvordenkliche Seyn.* The overcome B is given to the third potency for its possession. The second potency has B through continuous overcoming; the third potency has B, now in possession of this overcoming.

32 January 25

The first personality is the one who has power to put no. 2 and 3 into action without entering into the process himself, so that they remain outside as effective causes. B is not the Father but is the generative *Kraft* [power]; the Father is Father only in and with the Son, the actualized Son, just as the Son in turn also actualizes the Father. Here in the conclusion, *Seyn* [being] is now common for Father and Son. The same holds true of the Spirit. We do not have three Gods, because the same *Seyn* is common to all and thus also *die Herrlichkeit* [the lordship, majesty, glory]. As long as the potencies are active, they are only personalities *potentia* [in potency]. —We hereby elevate ourselves into another world. With personality, the divine world opens up for us. Here, too, the meaning of the process for God is apparent. *Seyn* is first with the Father as possibility; then it is transferred to the Son, to whom, as it is said, the Father has given life. Then the Son gives back[99] to the Father *Seyn* as overcome. Christ says somewhere that he who loves me loves the Father, and we shall come to him and μόνην ποιήσομεν [we shall make (our) abode].[100] The same is said elsewhere of the Spirit, that by the Spirit we know that he is in III C 27
us.[101] XIII 311

Here it is not a question of the truth of the Christian religion, but here it is a question of understanding it. The acceptance is something else. The *Spannung* [tension] of the three potencies goes throughout all of nature; nothing expresses perfect unity. Every *Entstehen* [generating] is a fourth among the three potencies. But this *Spannung* lasts only until the end of nature. Man, original man, as such has a relation to personalities; nature has relation only to potencies. In the Mosaic creation story, the one Elohim always speaks, but when man is to be created, they (consequently plural) take counsel and say:

Let us create a man, i.e., for ourselves. The Son is indeed in the process, but as potency, not as personality. If the divine is first absolute in the three personalities, then in relation to things the process is the process *der Schöpfung* [of the creation], and in relation to God it is a theogony. Scriptures say that everything is created by the Father through the Son;[102] therefore the Son is involved in the process of the creation. The Father is not in the process; the process strives only toward the manifestation of his divinity. Earlier, Dionysius the Areopagite[103] used the phrase θεόγονος θεότης [god-begotten deity]. Basil M.[egas][104] calls the Son αἰτία δημιουργικόν [creative cause], the Spirit αἰτία τελειοτίκω [perfecting cause]. The Scriptures [Romans 11:36] distinguish among ἐκ ὃυ, δι ὃυ, εἶσ ὅν [from whom, through whom, to whom]. Unity is the common divinity of the three persons. Man is inclosed not by the three potencies but by the three personalities. Therefore it says in the Scriptures (Genesis 2:15) that after creation man was in a divine inclosure, which is implicit in the meaning of the Hebrew and of the German word *Garten* [garden], inclosed by Elohim. In that primal relation, there was more than a revelation. What we lack, however, up to now is an *aussergöttliches Seyn* [being outside the divine]; we do indeed have something *praeter deum* [aside from God] but nothing *extra deum* [outside God]; up to now creation is immanent. God goes beyond *unvordenkliches Seyn* [being absolutely antecedent to thought] but incloses it within himself. We must, however, have a free relation to God; we must be in an *aussergöttliches Seyn*; and on the other hand we must have freedom with this world, which would not be possible if it were the divine, or in
III C 27 that case it would be stupidity on our part. Our development
XIII
312 has its conclusion in this, that in God the creation is concluded, but we see how *der Kreis des Geschehens* [the sphere of events] opens up right here. Beyond nature, which cannot step further, we find a human race, divided into peoples, and spirit and movement, whereas nature stands still. Whence this new world? It was not implicit in the original intention, the immediate purpose of the creation; consequently, it must lie within man himself. But how was it in man's power to make

everything totter after everything was complete, at rest? Another question is: What change has taken place and how has *die aussergöttliche Welt* [the world outside the divine] appeared, which we already recognize in paganism, an *aussergöttliche Welt* that also is the only possibility of explaining revelation—otherwise for what purpose?—and possible in such a way without a break in God's unity, which cannot proceed from God? Where did man get this power? In contrast to an infinite causality, an infinite passivity must always be supposed. We must know that creation is not *einfach Akt* [simply an act]; it is positive and negative, and these two cannot both be posited with the same elements.

33 January 26

If the creation arose *einfach* [simply], solely by the infinite causality of God, freedom cannot be saved—there are several causes, each of which in itself is infinite, but in relation to each other finite. From all eternity there is a potency, *ein entzündbare[r] Wille* [an inflammable will], in the creator himself. This will is boundless, therefore impotent, is matter, substratum. The cause that posits the form is not the same as that which posits matter. Matter as such is indeterminate. There are not many creators, since the causes in themselves produce nothing. There is only one creator; he teaches, as it were, the causes to work together. Consequently, that which appears as the final result of the creation is free from the first cause through the other, is free from B through A, just as the weight, as the beam, in a scale. It also has a relation to the third potency (*in quam* [final]), to which only a free relation is possible. With the final production of creation, all *Spannung* [tension] is canceled. It stands among the three potencies, inde- III C 27
pendent of all, hovering as pure motion, sheer freedom. The XIII 313
material lies in the *Spannung* of the potencies, and the immateriality of the human soul is already apparent here. The final production of creation is not a thing but *Leben, Hauch* [life, breath], yet only conditioned; it possesses it only at that place, when it remains there. Man is established in it, but as absolute mobility, and consequently has the possibility of placing him-

self outside it. Therefore man was commanded to keep to that point. —Man possesses B but possesses B only as a creature and consequently only as possibility, not as God possesses it in order to make it actual. Yet this possibility appears as the potency of a second becoming. He is commanded not to move B. In Midrash Koheleth,[105] it says that the creator addresses newly created man: "Take care that you do not shake my world, for if you shake it, nothing (nothing new) can calm it." —This prohibition shows man the very possibility of doing it. —For man, therefore, B is the *Nicht-Seyn-Sollende* [that which ought not to be], the forbidden fruit. —It would take a supranatural will to withstand the temptation; to this extent the occurred change is a natural one. The consequence did not turn out to be what man wanted. Like God, he had wanted to set the potencies in motion; *er wollte mit ihnen walten* [he wanted to rule with them]—but this is not his to do, and therefore he was ὑστερούμενος τῆς δόξης τõυ θεοῦ [lacking in the glory of God] (not glory for God but the glory of God), because he would have God's *Herrlichkeit* [lordship, majesty, glory]. What man wanted was the same turning about or turning out *(Auswendung)* of the potencies that God brought about, the same as could be called *universio* [turned about]. In God's self-concept, B is the most negated and turned inward, that which in creation is most outwardly turned. This is divine irony, which turns out another side in this way, and therefore we must be prudent. The world is *unum versum, universum:* that which is turned about. Thus man thought he would get eternal life by turning this principle outward. Man did not become lord over it but became mastered by it. This principle is now not only *aussergöttlich* [outside the divine] but *widergöttlich* [anti-divine]. The world alienated from God is bereft of its
III C 27 XIII 314 *Herrlichkeit*, has no center of unity, which man is supposed to be, is completely subsumed under externality; the one has steadily lost its significance as a factor; everything falls apart as *Einzelnes* [particulars]. This external world continually seeks its end and never finds it in this eternal appearance. Through this principle, man thought to achieve a divine eternal life. Of course, he could not annul the substance of the

world, but [he could] alter its form; instead of unity in God, there was *Zerissenheit* [fragmentation]. Through this annulled unity there is a new movement, a new *Spannung* of the potencies; what preceded was divinely willed, but this is humanly established. God is, as it were, expelled from potency by man's putting himself in his place. "Behold, the man has become like one of us."[106] There has been a desire to translate this as *ist gewesen* [has been], but this goes against linguistic usage. There has been a desire to explain Elohim as pertaining to his natures, but such a communicative *pluralis*, in which God establishes himself among his natures, is impossible. A plurality of potencies is indeed designated, in which God knows himself, i.e., in his divinity. It is the potency that is entrusted to man for safe keeping. In that calm of creation, in the calm of that principle, the second and the third personalities were posited; through a change of that principle, these must again be evicted from their *Herrlichkeit* in man's consciousness so that the second personality is related only as potency, not as divine personality, likewise the third as πνεῦμα τοῦ κοσμοῦ [spirit of the universe].[107]

34 January 28

We must now consider in more detail the historical relation among these three personalities as presented in the New Testament. Here the Son speaks of obedience to the Father and thus attributes to himself a free, independent will, at least as possibility. This passage cannot be understood with reference only to Christ's human nature, inasmuch as human becoming is itself presented as voluntary. Such a relation at the end of the creation is unthinkable. There was only one personality, the Father; the Son had no independent *Seyn* [being], only a mutual *Seyn*. Therefore our view needs something before it completely agrees with Christianity. We have seen that that unity did not come into being at the end of the creation; it
remained only idea, and something new appeared, B brought III C 27
back to itself, which is man. Man possessed B as mere possi- XIII 315
bility, could elevate it to actuality. It cannot be shown a priori that he has actually done this. On the assumption that it has

happened, it follows that the second and third personality in divinity as such are *entwirklicht* [deactualized] and excluded from the consciousness in which B is lord, and they are thereby in one *Seyn*, independent of the Father, which they have from man when they return to their *Herrlichkeit* [lordship, majesty, glory]; [they] have it not simply as given by the Father but as self-acquired. The second personality is especially important to us. The Son's being is now suspended by man's activity, as it was in creation by the Father's. In that unity of the end of creation, the Son was only in the Father, not independent of him. Now he is the Son of man; as the Son of God [he is] υἱὸς τοῦ ἀνθρώπου [Son of man]. Since Kant's time, this expression has been understood as pertaining to original man, man par excellence, but in the N.T. this is used not as a title of honor but as a title of degradation.

Now a new process arises, in which the excluded second potency posits itself in its *actus*, a process that is not divinely willed, yes, is even against God's will. Yet this must be said with great caution, not unconditionally, because then God might not have willed the world at all, but he has also foreseen the Son as personality independent of him. The Father's activity went only as far as that unity; if it were broken, he would not be able to unite it again. A static world was possible through the Father and the Son *begriffen* [comprehended] in him (as demiurgic cause), but not a free world outside God, *extra deum*. This world is possible only through the Son. In the creation, the Son was counted on to save that which unavoidably must fall away from him. "All is entrusted to me by the Father."[108] This does not refer to the original entrusting in the creation; τὰ πάντα [all things] is here the created order that is left to him. *Ohne Voraussicht des Sohnes* [Without the prevision of the Son], there would be no world of freedom. An *aussergöttliche* [outside the divine] world is necessary in order to gain freedom over against God. When by that *Ur-That* [primordial act] (sin) the world is placed outside God, how does it endure and how do the potencies keep this power, for they are, nevertheless, only through the will of that which wills all in all? The will continues, but as *Unwille* [displeasure], as *Zorn* [wrath].

35 January 29 III C 27

Consequently, B had mastered itself, and thereby the purpose of creation was achieved, but man had the possibility of establishing himself anew as B. Even at the conclusion of the creation, God's unity is and is not, namely, if man wants it. In the final moment of the creation, therefore, unity was posited as possibility placed before man. —After that *Ur-That* [primordial act], God effects this world's substance, not its form, since the world [is] the object of *Unwille*; he effects not as Father; this is possible only when the Son is. It was in the creator's power to take back the *Seyn* of the entire world, but then he would not have created it at all. Consequently, there are two periods: (1) Father eon; the Son is not outside the Father, but only in the Father; (2) the Son's period, which is the entire time of this world; the Son is as an independent person outside the Father. Here again there are two periods. Man has fallen into the power of B, the divine displeasure apparent in the whole race. In the beginning, when the power of this principle is unbroken, the *vermittelnde* [mediating] person is in his highest negation and suffering (these words mean the same); he is *aus seiner* δόξα *und Herrlichkeit gesetzt* [placed outside his glory and lordship] in the deepest abasement, finds no place in consciousness, is unfree, works not according to will but according to nature, is the *Wirken-Müssende* [that which must work].[109] This is *paganism*, where the *vermittelnde* personality does not work according to his will. This is the suffering of the second personality, as it is expressed in the Old Testament, in Isaiah, for example. The Messiah is the Lord's Anointed, but the Anointed is still not king. The Old Testament depicts not so much his coming suffering as his present suffering; he is in suffering from the beginning of creation, as a[110] potency posited in the deepest degradation, excluded from *Seyn*. When this potency has made itself lord over *Seyn*, he can then lead it back to God. With the freedom of the second person a new period of time begins; now he can do what he wants with *Seyn* according to his divine will. This is Christianity. The content of this sequence is the content of revelation.

XIII 316

When man awakens this principle, the higher potencies are *entwirklicht* [deactualized]. Inwardly, they do indeed retain
III C 27 divine meaning; outwardly, they are *aussergöttliche* [outside-
XIII 317 God] powers. The process that now takes place is distinguished by two things. (1) It takes place only in man's consciousness (the *Spannungen* [tensions] are here), and man's all has to do with consciousness, and it takes place in a process analogous to the first process. (2) This process is purely natural; divinity does not participate in it—indeed, it is excluded. The two personalities do participate, but since they are outside God they are related only as potencies and natural power. Nevertheless, this process is also a theogonic process. Paganism lacks this theogonic ground; therefore, the apostle's words "He in whom σπέρμα τοῦ θεοῦ [the seed of God] remains does not sin"[111] come to mind if it is remembered that ἁμαρτία [sin] is used in the N.T. essentially about paganism as idolatry. In its new form, B is the God-denying principle; when it is brought back into itself, it is the God-positing, *actu*-positing. This return would be impossible if the potency, which according to its nature is destined to overcome B, did not keep its relationship to the process, did not participate in the process, if it did not become lord over it through its own activity, no longer through the Father's, and have the ability to do with it what it willed. The Apostle Paul says of the pagans that they are ἄθεοι ἐν τῷ κοσμῷ [without God in the world];[112] ἐν τῷ κοσμῷ is a more detailed explanation: they are without God and are subject to the cosmic potencies. Here is the point at which the transition must be made to the *Philosophie der Mythologie* [philosophy of mythology], which must precede. The mediating personality, excluded from *Seyn*, must make himself lord before he can appear as personality and act in freedom. His *Thun* [work] as free *That* [act] is the content of revelation. The deeper presupposition of revelation is mythology. A *Philosophie der Mythologie* can present the mythological conceptions as well as the causes of these conceptions. These are found primarily in the mysteries, which form a *Corollarium* [corollary] to mythology and the immediate transition to the *Philosophie der Offenbarung* [philosophy

of revelation]. The *Anlass, das Vermittelnde*, and *Ziel* [motive, the mediating, . . . goal] are the same as in the first theogonic process.

36 January 31 III C 27 XIII 318

The creation was complete but built upon moving ground. In looking out over the elements of the preceding process, one must say that everything presses on toward the world, where God first has a free world outside himself, to the world in which we live. All the traversed elements are indeed actualities, but prior to this world they are still only thoughts. The personalities cannot be posited entirely without any relation to themselves; they have only withdrawn from their divinity, working in potency and necessity; they must follow man, cannot avoid it, but must enter into the *widergöttliche* [anti-divine] process. This process is simply a repetition of the first process. Three things are to be noted: (1) the universal, (2) the various elements, (3) the causes.

The elements of the second theogonic process are the same as in the first theogonic process. It is distinguished by being in consciousness. After commencing, it is a [process] independent of man's freedom. It declares itself only in representations. These are the mythological representations. They can be explained not as inventions or as accidental confusion (presenting a previous revelation or science) but only as necessary *Erzeugnisse* [products] of the consciousness fallen under the cosmic potencies. They do not come from the outside but are the results of a distinctive life-process. Neither are they accidental interior[113] productions (for example, of a particular mental power, of imagination); they are the productions of substance. An explanation is thereby given of (1) the faith, which mankind, captivated in this process, bestows on them. They are not merely conceived powers [*Magter*] but the theogonic powers themselves, not merely ideas but the same powers that operate in nature and have also seized possession of consciousness; (2) its relation to nature and its *Erscheinung* [appearance]. Mythology has been regarded as theory of nature.

But this is not the case. The same world-creating potencies operate in nature and in mythology.

The question might be raised: What did man do in that prehistoric time—and the answer must be: Man was occupied
III C 27 with the movements that accompany mythology. Peoples ac-
XIII 319 quired external history only after that inward process was completed. Until then, mankind was in a kind of ecstatic state, from which it later moved over into a more *besonnen* [reflective] [state]. In that state, mankind had no sense of external relations. With each new people, the process advanced a stage further. The mythologies of the various peoples have a similarity, for what is past is present in a later stage or it is present as past. The mythologies are, therefore, not independent; they are elements in the common mythology-producing process.

How is the shifting, which is the beginning of all mythology, reflected in the beginning of mythological consciousness? In man, this principle is brought back (at the conclusion of the creation) into its *an sich* [in itself] and should reside in man as the intransitive *Seyn-Könnende* [being-able to be], should remain as potency. Since man did not do that, this principle presented itself to him as *Seyn-Können* [ability to be]. This possibility is capable of nothing; man must decide to will it. In this condition (i.e., as long as this possibility merely stands before man without man's having made his choice), this possibility can appear only as *feminine*, as something attracting the will, as the alluring. This element is depicted in mythology by a feminine being. Persephone,[114] who corresponded also to the *duas* of the Pythagoreans.[115] Yet Persephone is only a reflection of the beginning of the beginning of this condition. The beginning itself is a surprise; only in the conclusion does consciousness become clear. Something similar is taught in Genesis. Three elements in particular should be noted: (1) man's first sin is beguilement; (2) the accessible side is woman; (3) the seductive principle is the serpent.[116] The serpent is a metaphor for eternity, which becomes corruptible as soon as it is broken, which is suggested by the upright walk of the serpent, its standing on end.[117] This is a *natura anceps* [twofold nature]. In the Greek mysteries, it is also taught that

Zeus[118] approaches Persephone as a serpent, because, as it is said, the Persephone who remains entirely within is a maiden, and the one who comes out is a mother. The mythological process is a common fate that the entire human race undergoes.

37 and 38 February 1 III C 27 XIII

[*In margin:* (he lectures two hours each time)] 320

The Epochs in the Mythological Process

Epoch I. A. The process begins with the *schrankenlose Seyn* [boundless being] of that principle in whose power B finds itself. The principle itself, not representations, has seized possession of consciousness, which does not have freedom against it. Man's essence is posited far back in time prior to all nature, because that principle is nature's *prius* [antecedent], and to that extent this principle is a *natur-widriges* [anti-nature] [principle] that does not want to have anything to do with nature, since it would become the basis of nature by being limited. It is a principle that consumes everything, allows nothing to endure. The permanent *prius* that magically draws all potencies to itself (as *ruhender Wille* [reposing will]). If, however, it steps forth, it thrusts the higher potencies away from itself and yet wants to maintain itself in its centrality and not admit that it is *entgeistet* [devoid of spirit]. The battle is between this principle, which wants to be *über-material* [supra-material], and the higher potencies. It is the same element as in the becoming of nature. Every element wants to make itself the center, although a higher power posits it as peripheral. It is an astral system; nature's primal principle becomes the world-system. Sabianism[119] (from *Seba*, host), the heavenly host. The object of devotion is not the physical aspect of the stars but the genuinely astral, which is the *Ueberkörperliche* [supracorporal], the fundamental basis for all sidereal movements, not a particular manifestation, for example, the beneficent power of the sun. This system is not reached either by sense perception or by thought, but man's inner being was posited with and in that sidereal principle. Therefore man led a roaming, nomadic life.

The same necessity was the ground of the sidereal principle and of their nomadic life. In the sidereal relation, they saw a prototype of their own life. The oldest religion is thus in a certain sense monotheism, insofar as it was only one principle that was the object of worship.

B. The subordination of the hitherto reigning principle under the higher powers simply means that the principle makes
III C 27 itself conquer*able* without actually being overcome. Previ-
XIII 321 ously, the principle was Uranus,[120] as heaven, lord. Now the principle becomes feminine, Urania.[121] Sabianism is not mythology. Mythology first arises through successive polytheism. Another god follows another, since Urania was merely a transition. Here we have the first historical people for whom star worship becomes material, as when the Persians worship particular heavenly bodies, the sun and moon. It is the material. They also sacrificed to Urania. Babylonians, Assyrians, Arabs. Among the Babylonians it is called Melita. The second god was already suggested by the Babylonian custom that in honor of Melita every woman had to commit public adultery in her temple. Among the Arabs, the second god appears as Dionysus, Urania's son.[122] It is our second potency, which surmounts that principle; it is the liberating god, but he can be operative only successively. Hence the various conceptions of the god, different with respect to the moment in which he is first born into actuality, different with respect to the beginning of his activity, [different] in perfection. The time we are now describing is [that of] the peaceful existence of Urania and this second god. It is the god of true human life.

C. The battle between the principle that has become conquerable and the potency that leads it back to its *an sich* [in-itself]. Here are new sections with respect to the sequence of the struggle.

(1) Consciousness opposes the activity of the liberating god. It was feminine toward the other god only as long as he was not active, but this principle now resists the other god as active. Phoenicians, Syrians, Carthaginians. Baal, the original name of Uranus. He does not acknowledge the other god but nevertheless has him alongside himself. Likewise Moloch,[123]

Cronus.[124] The liberating god manifests himself only after he overcomes that principle. The liberating god becomes an intermediary being; here he is like a negated god; he must gain his divinity. Heracles[125] of the Phoenicians. Heracles is a forerunner of Dionysus. He is the son of god displaced from his divinity. Cronus is the false god; he can exclude him from lordship and kingdom but not from *Seyn*, just as the Messiah is presented in the O.T. as one suffering in the form of a servant.[126] Among the Greeks, Heracles, having endured hard- III C 27 XIII 322
ships, actually elevates himself to [the position of] god.

(2) The transition here is provided by a feminine being. Cronus turns feminine; it is Cybele.[127] Here are the peoples who follow the Phoenician and Canaanite tribes. The Phrygians, the Greeks, the Romans (where the worship of Cybele still remained *religio peregrina* [a foreign religion]). Through Urania, the process became possible; through Cybele, it becomes actual in a definite polytheism.

(3) Full-blown polytheism.
Egyptian, Indian, Greek.

The principle of mythology is a successive appearance of potencies. At first, there is only one potency (Uranus), then a second potency destined to overcome. The first overcoming of B, or what could be called its basic καταβολή [beginning], is Urania. From Urania to Cybele, there are only two principles; now there is genuine overcoming; now it becomes the substratum for that which actually is supposed to be, and thus we are dealing with the totality of potencies. —The entire mythological process revolves around only these three potencies. They are the causes, and as lords and gods of consciousness they are essential causes. In A (Epoch I) there is the excluding god, in B the arrival of the second god, his birth, in C the arrival of the third potency. Spirit can come only when the unspiritual has been brought to the point of expiration. Genuine overthrow.

The material gods must be separated from the potencies; they arose along with the real causes, θεοῦ γεννητοῦ [begotten of god].[128] The formal and the material gods must be sepa-

rated. In the first period, when the principle wants to maintain its centrality but cannot, it splits into numerous elements for consciousness; from these [come] the sidereal gods that are brought about and do not belong to the causes. —In the second period, Urania and Dionysus are the formal gods, the truly active gods. The material gods are the star gods, the remains of Sabianism; they tend more and more toward the material category. —In the third epoch, Cronus and Heracles are the active gods. Cronus is inorganic. The Greeks, too, have
III C 27 gone through this inorganic period. Fetishism proper belongs
XIII 323 to the inorganic period; it is stupid worship. —In the following phase, Cybele and Dionysus are side by side. Cybele is *magna deorum mater* [the great mother of the gods]. She is the mother of the material gods, who arise when the process begins. *Götter-Vielheit* [god-plurality] is simultaneous polytheism; *Viel-Götterei* [plurality of gods] is successive polytheism. —The real inner understanding of mythology is contained in these three potencies. Mythology attains this esoteric understanding only at the conclusion. From Cybele onward, the third potency is included as soon as the first potency is powerful enough to overcome the second. From now on, every mythology has all the potencies. But how, then, are the differences to be explained? They arise because the totality of the potencies always manifests itself differently. Here again three versions are possible, although every mythology has all three [potencies]. *Egyptian* [mythology] has the hardest battle with the blind principle, which is indeed combated, but its utmost strength is taxed. It is the death struggle of Typhon,[129] the material principle. Osiris[130] is the good divinity. Victory is uncertain—now Typhon is trampled down, then Osiris. Only when Horus appears, the third potency, is Typhon overcome. Isis is the god-bound principle that hovers between Typhon and Osiris until it gives birth to Horus. Typhon himself becomes Osiris. He is, in fact, only in contrast to Osiris; changed into Osiris, he is invisible, the god of the underworld. The other is Osiris himself. The third is Horus, who is *Geist* [spirit]. These are the formal gods. The material

[gods] arise in and through the battle and are like trembling limbs.

39 and 40 February 2

Indian [mythology]. In Egyptian [mythology], consciousness still holds painfully to the material principle; here, however, consciousness is eccentric turmoil without any understanding; that principle is overwhelmed by the higher potencies. Brahma,[131] which is that principle, has in a way disappeared, is *verschollen, Gott der Vergangenheit* [lost in oblivion, a god of
the past], without a temple and without worship (similarly, III C 27
although not wholly so, Typhon was *Gott der Vergangenheit*), XIII 324
enjoys no adoration, has completely disappeared without any relation to consciousness. Shiva, the god of destruction, reigns in his place—there is also the third potency, Vishnu. These three do not unite in the Indian consciousness as the three do in the Egyptian, still less than in the Christian consciousness. Vishnu has his characteristic adherents, who exclude Shiva, and in return Shiva has his. The masses of people affirm Shiva alone, the higher classes Vishnu. The Indian consciousness shifts over to fable, the legends about Vishnu's incarnations, particularly in Krishna. This is no mythology; this is simply *Ausgeburt einer haltungslosen Imagination* [a product of an unstable imagination]. Buddha is of no further concern to us, partly because he is really foreign to the Indians and partly because this teaching is only a reaction against mythology. Buddhism and the mysticism, idealism, and spiritualism awakened by it serve to complete the unhappy Indian consciousness.

Greek mythology does not give up the god who has been overcome, like the Indian Brahma; it keeps him spiritually. The process in Indian mythology also has its crisis, but it is only unto destruction. Shiva is only the disturber, not the liberator. The crisis ends in decay; there is no abiding achievement. Now a fictive mythology appears or that false tendency toward unity: spiritualism. The consciousness of unity remains in Greek mythology and embodies all its elements; whereas with the Indians it deteriorates into this desperate ni-

hilism. The Indian gods are *verzerrte* [deformed]; the Greek are beautiful, blessed visions in which the material principle disappears but collaborates. The Greek gods are representatives of eternal elements, the gentle strain of the material principle, which in its disappearing leaves behind a beautiful world, but they are still only *Erscheinungen* [appearances]; they do not have flesh and blood; they are like imaginings, and yet they are for consciousness the most real beings. Animality has now disappeared. In the world of the Greek gods, it is the same as when the principle of nature, after the hard battle with animality, ends in man's gentle tone. Just as when the material principle entirely *verscheidet* [expires] so that the potencies,
III C 27 XIII 325 held in *Spannung* [tension] by this principle, annul the tension and touch each other in unity, so it also is the case with the god-creating potencies in consciousness. The first principle is the material principle. It is *hergestellt* [established] in its *an sich* [in itself]; thus it is the invisible god, αἰδής, Hades,[132] in the moment it becomes invisible and thus still belongs to the material gods. He is the third, the deepest ground for *Göttervielheiten* [god-pluralities]; only when he is overcome, becomes invisible, does *Göttervielheit*, the whole Olympus, arise. He is invisible among the material gods; if he could become visible, everything would have to disappear. His dwelling is therefore a terror even to the gods. Likewise, all nature would perish if the invisible *prius* in nature were to become visible. There is something similar in Egyptian mythology, where the gods fear that Typhon may become visible. Hades, however, is not only this element; he is *Alles an sich* [all in itself] or matter, the common ground of the gods, not only those who appear with Zeus (as pure potency, pure cause), also in the time of Cronus and Uranus. Consciousness comes to a universal concept of this god, who has become the stuff for all gods. He is no particular god; he is universal god and can have only one of the formal gods over against himself; he no longer excludes the other potencies. The Greeks have a consciousness of this spiritual principle. Their gods are not partial gods but universal; like man, they lie at the end of creation, inclosed among all three potencies. There is a difference between an exoteric and

an esoteric god-doctrine. But these two god-doctrines are contemporary and do not annul each other. The esoteric god-doctrine arose by way of the return of the material principle to the inner realm; it arose through the process that posits the external. Without the esoteric, the exoteric is annulled, for if the emergent exoteric god did not become esoteric, then the external, exoteric plurality would be impossible. —The mysteries contain the genuine esoteric god-doctrine. We have two transitional elements: (1) the material principle renders itself conquerable; (2) it actually is overcome. Both transitions are indicated by a feminine god. Is there not a third element, in which the material principle is not the object of actual overcoming but actually is overcome, in which consciousness stands in the middle between a past (in which the material principle disappears) and a present, in which it *aufgeht* III C 27
[emerges]? In any case, consciousness represents the feminine XIII 326
element. At every moment, god is a specific [god] succeeded by another. Likewise, consciousness is in every phase a definite [consciousness], but it is also more, since it is god-positing in general. In this way the goddesses, too, are more. Rhea and Gaea[133] are devoted to the future. The consciousness that stands between mythology and mystery is Demeter, a feminine being. Demeter (Ceres of the Romans) continually sides with the material principle, which in the overcoming is the *Begriffene* [comprehended], but still only the *Begriffene.* The feminine god is always consciousness, either of the god who stands just opposite or of the one who is to come, is either consort or mother. Later, Demeter is mother; now she is Poseidon's[134] consort. Poseidon corresponds to Dionysus, is the material prototype. Later, Demeter is consciousness devoted to the influences of Dionysus as the actually overcome. Demeter [is] what Urania and Cybele [were] earlier.

The material principle is now overcome; consciousness must now give up the excluding god, isolate this principle from itself; consciousness does indeed feel bound to it but feels also that this bond does not have reality [*Realitæt*]. Persephone is this consciousness. The material principle is isolated as belonging to the *Vergangenheit* [past], as belonging to the *Gott der Vergangenheit*—it is forcibly isolated as plundering; this is the significance of the kidnapping of Persephone. Demeter is not willing to acknowledge it, holds fast to the material principle, is grieved; therefore, she will not acknowledge the emergent *Göttervielheit*, either, the Dionysian polytheism (somewhere Dionysus is depicted with the attributes of Zeus). Consequently, Demeter must be reconciled.

This is as far as exoteric mythology goes. With Demeter's pacification and the restitution for her loss, there is the initial manifestation of the genuine *Seyn-Sollende* [that which ought to be], which cannot enter into that plurality. Here we have the mysteries, the Eleusinian Mysteries. The mysteries of Demeter. Their content is not agricultural or physical truths, as a French writer has thought, saying, among other things, that the whole thing was a course in agriculture. With agriculture, the unstable life ceased and true human life began, but because
III C 27 of this the astral also ceased. Therefore, the point here is the
XIII moral significance of agriculture. Therefore, Demeter is also
327 called θεσμοφόρος [law-giving]. Isocrates names the mysteries and agriculture together as the gifts of Demeter.[135] Sabianism is always where there are no fixed buildings; Tacitus describes the Germans in this way.[136] Since man turns away from the universal god, from the boundless, he demands limitation, but when he has experienced the deficiencies of civic life, he longs again for the infinite, for the vast dome of heaven. In this view, among the Greeks and also the Romans, Uranus and Cronus merged. When thoughts were turned from the restrictions of civic life to infinity, this was conceived of as the golden age, and Cronus was the god of the golden age—"then it was not allowed to limit one's fields"—and thus the Romans assigned the golden age to Saturn. —For the Phrygians, Cybele was the founder of agriculture. —It is curious that whereas the Babylonians put so much emphasis on buildings and land, the peoples who followed them (Phoenicians etc.) detached themselves completely from these and turned to the sea. The Egyptians, however, regarded the sea as the Typhonic element. —Demeter, therefore, expressed this two-

sidedness of the destruction of the astral principle and the rise of agriculture.

Perhaps one could go further. None of the proper types of seeds is found growing wild. A Spanish writer who has traveled much in South America points out that certain plants that are otherwise not found there come of themselves when men reside there. Thus human nature seems to stand in a secret relation to nature, seems to have a kindling power. Perhaps Demeter has been used to indicate this. —Persephone does not have a physical significance, either. Indeed, there is a similarity between her and the seed grain, but Persephone does not signify seed grain; it must rather be said that seed grain signifies Persephone. Persephone is *die Potenz des Gottsetzens in dem Bewusstseyn* [the potency of god-positing in the consciousness], varying according to its being purely inward or appearing externally, just as Persephone concealed herself in the inner realm and at other times appeared. In primal consciousness,
true monotheism existed as potency, because its opposite was III C 27
possible. Its opposite appeared in relative monotheism, in or- XIII 328
der that true unity could manifest itself as actual.

41 February 3

Persephone is, therefore, the genuine establishing principle of mythology, is its germ; she really must be concealed. When she appears, she herself becomes an element in a theogonic process. She nevertheless remains only a natural monotheism, distinguished from revealed monotheism.

We learn of Demeter's reconciliation from Homer's hymns.[137] Demeter says: I shall establish the mysteries so that you will be able to reconcile my mind. The mysteries are also called Dionysian. Previously Dionysus was only the second potency, the liberating god. Customarily, the manifestation of his activity was orgiasm; liberated from the material principle, consciousness becomes *Taumel* [frenzy]. At first, he is contemporary with Urania. These debaucheries are also called "Sabazia," which indicates the destruction of the older religion (the word itself alludes to Sabianism, which perishes here, whereby the transition is made to genuine mythology), yet they were not a common thing but only side ceremonies. In Egypt, there is an analogy, the phallic celebrations. Dionysus is an element that goes through all the mythologies, and without this element there would be no mythology. Therefore Sabianism is really not mythology. The idea of Dionysus, however, goes beyond Dionysus himself, and only then does the idea appear in all its magnificence. This Dionysus is the son of Semele, a mortal mother, whose mortal part is consumed by her relation to Zeus. Although the cause of all the material gods, Dionysus is the youngest in mythology; he was concealed in Zeus after his birth. His first opponent was King Lycurgus, who is mentioned in the *Iliad*,[138] and it is curious, after all, that in Homer Dionysus is not the complete god but the growing god.[139] —Then Pentheus,[140] king of Thrace, and finally Orpheus.[141] He was torn to pieces by the Maenads. Orpheus is a representative of time past, which struggles against Dionysus's own time. This consciousness shatters. Homer himself is the supreme consummation of exoteric mythology. Homer's power consists precisely in the power with which he excludes the past. In that always lies the power to suppress the past. Homer is beautiful youth. Homer belongs to the time in which the Hellenic people isolate themselves from the universally human, so that they are really not even a people. Dionysus is Occidentalism; Orpheus is still Orientalism (perhaps Orpheus has a connection with ὀρφναῖος, the dark).

42 February 4 [1842]

[End of the lecture notes][142]

SUPPLEMENT

KEY TO REFERENCES

Marginal references alongside the text of *The Concept of Irony* are to volume and page [XIII 100] in *Søren Kierkegaards samlede Værker*, I-XIV, edited by A. B. Drachmann, J. L. Heiberg, and H. O. Lange (1 ed., Copenhagen: Gyldendal, 1901-06). The same marginal references are used in Sören Kierkegaard, *Gesammelte Werke, Abt.* 1-36 (Düsseldorf, Cologne: Diederich, 1952-69).

References to Kierkegaard's works in English are to this edition, *Kierkegaard's Writings* [*KW*], I-XXVI (Princeton: Princeton University Press, 1978-). Specific references to the *Writings* are given by English title and the standard Danish pagination referred to above [*Either/Or*, I, p. 120, *KW* III (*SV* I 100)].

Marginal references alongside the text of Kierkegaard's *Notes of Schelling's Berlin Lectures* [III C 27; XIII 300] and other references to the *Papirer* [*Pap.* I A 100; note the differentiating letter A, B, or C, used only in references to the *Papirer*] are to *Søren Kierkegaards Papirer*, I-XI, edited by P. A. Heiberg, V. Kuhr, and E. Torsting (1 ed., Copenhagen: Gyldendal, 1909-48), and 2 ed., photo-offset with two supplemental volumes, XII-XIII, edited by Niels Thulstrup (Copenhagen: Gyldendal, 1968-70), and with index, XIV-XVI (1975-78), edited by Niels Jørgen Cappelørn. References to the *Papirer* in English [*JP* II 1500] are to the volume and serial entry number in *Søren Kierkegaard's Journals and Papers*, I-VII, edited and translated (and amended in the Supplement) by Howard V. Hong and Edna H. Hong, assisted by Gregor Malantschuk (Bloomington: Indiana University Press, 1967-78).

References to correspondence are to the serial numbers in *Breve og Aktstykker vedrørende Søren Kierkegaard*, I-II, edited by Niels Thulstrup (Copenhagen: Munksgaard, 1953-54), and to the corresponding serial numbers in *Kierkegaard: Letters and*

Documents, translated by Henrik Rosenmeier, *Kierkegaard's Writings*, XXV [*Letters*, Letter 100, *KW* XXV].

References to books in Kierkegaard's own library [*ASKB* 100] are based on the serial numbering system of *Auktionsprotokol over Søren Kierkegaards Bogsamling* [Auction-catalog of Søren Kierkegaard's Book-collection], edited by H. P. Rohde (Copenhagen: Royal Library, 1967).

In the Supplement, references to page and lines in the text are given as: 100:1-10.

In the notes, internal references to the present work are given as: p. 100.

Three spaced periods indicate an omission by the editors; five spaced periods indicate a hiatus or fragmentariness in the text.

Wherever possible, translations of German, Latin, and Greek quotations are from standard English versions. Bibliographical information is given in the notes. Occasional divergences from these translations are indicated by (ed. rev.). Heise's Danish translations of Plato in *Om Begrebet Ironi* are all ed. tr. In a few instances, the transcribed Danish text of the Schelling lecture notes does not agree with the manuscript microfilm. In such cases, the manuscript text is followed and the variant in the printed text is given in a note.

Om

Begrebet Ironi

med stadigt Hensyn til Socrates.

Udgivet for Magistergraden

af

S. A. Kierkegaard,
theologisk Candidat.

Kjøbenhavn.
Paa Boghandler P. G. Philipsens Forlag.
Trykt i Bianco Lunos Bogtrykkeri.
1841.

ON

THE CONCEPT OF IRONY

WITH CONTINUAL REFERENCE TO SOCRATES.

Published for the M.A. degree

by

S. A. Kierkegaard,
theological candidate.

Copenhagen.
Available at Bookseller P. G. Philipsen Publishing House.
Printed by Bianco Luno Press.
1841.

Om Begrebet Ironi

med stadigt Hensyn til Socrates.

Af

S. A. Kierkegaard.

ἀλλὰ δὴ ὧδ᾽ ἔχει· ἄν τέ τις εἰς κολυμβήθραν σμικρὰν ἐμπέσῃ ἄν τε εἰς τὸ μέγιστον πέλαγος μέσον, ὅμως γε νεῖ οὐδὲν ἧττον. Πάνυ μὲν οὖν. Ὀυκοῦν καὶ ἡμῖν νευστέον καὶ πειρατέον σώζεσθαι ἐκ τοῦ λόγου, ἤτοι δελφῖνά τιν᾽ ἐλπίζοντας ἡμᾶς ἀπολαβεῖν ἄν ἤ τινα ἄλλην ἄπορον σωτηρίαν.

De republica L. 5 § 453 D

Kjøbenhavn.

Paa Boghandler P. G. Philipsens Forlag.

Trykt i Bianco Lunos Bogtrykkeri.

1841.

ON

THE CONCEPT OF IRONY

WITH CONTINUAL REFERENCE TO SOCRATES.

By

S. A. Kierkegaard.

> but the fact is that whether one tumbles into a little diving pool or plump into the great sea he swims all the same. By all means. Then we, too, must swim and try to escape out of the sea of argument in the hope that either some dolphin will take us on its back or some other desperate rescue.
>
> *Republic*, I, 5 § 453 D.

Copenhagen.

Available at Bookseller P. G. Philipsen Publishing House.

Printed by Bianco Luno Press.

1841.

N: 1

1.

Han vilde betragte [illegible] som en Stat i høiere Forstand, i platonisk Betydning.

2.

Man har kaldet enhver Afhandling for meget fordømmet, at den indeholdt noget som var mod Fornuften, det var som Kanne sagde, ikke længere var at blive begribeligt for det Dybsindige, saaledes havde Aabenb. ingen Interesse naar den ikke indeholdt mod Fornuften. – Han skulde bevare sig for Tydelighed og Simpelhed; Andre maatte have den Glæde, at de gjøre det simpelt, og om det nu var nærdeligt han gjelde det dog endnu de aldeles Ideer. Han vilde begynde at dele saaledes, hvilket han stille.

Philosophie og Virkelighed.

Alt Virkeligt har en dobbelt Side: quid sit (hvad det er) quod sit (at det er). Altsaa kan Philosophien være: at dobbelt Arbeide; man kan sige at Begreb uden Erkjendelsen(x), men ikke Erkjendelsen uden Begrebet. I Erkjendelsen er nemlig det Dobbelte, hvorved den er Erindring. Naar jeg seer en Plante, gjenkjender jeg den og fører den hen til det Almindelige, det jeg anerkjender den som Plante. Det har man ogsaa i den Dobbelthed der kan: det latinske cognitio og i den Dobbelthed i det hebraiske [illegible].

(x) at Begreb er nemlig udtrykt ved quid sit, men deraf følger ikke, at jeg erkjender: quod sit.

Philosophie og Væren.

3.

d. 22 Novb.

Man kunde kalde Philosophien Videnskaben for [illegible] og dette er og forhaabentlig en meget passende Benævnelse, som dog forøvrigt ikke er hans Udvikling. Spørgsmaalet blev, da m. H. t. den i det Foregaaende viste Dobbelthed om Philosoph. til begge Arter af Væren, og hvis den gjorde det, om det da var i een Videnskab, eller i to. Man kunde nu sige, naar jeg erkjender noget saa erkjender jeg det jo ogsaa som et Værende, naar jeg erkjender en Plante erkjender jeg den som en Værende. Dog er Tilbøieligheden i Sproget, at Væren er et Afhængende. Men naar der nu var Tale om Noget, der ikke var nødvendig Tilfældighed, men Nødv:, man maatte sige, at der blev en Tale om Indhold ikke om Væren. Ogsaa i det Logiske staae Begreberne ikke in Bezug auf quodditas, nur auf quidditas. Altsaa blev Philosophien enten Lære om Væsen, som man var vant til at sige det, eller om Begrebet, som nyere nyere sagde det. Det Existerende kunde

SCHELLING No. 1

1.

he wanted to be regarded as one deceased in the Greek understanding, in the Platonic sense.

2.

When he spoke of a revelation, he meant thereby that it contains something that is above reason; as Kanne has said, it is not worth the trouble to get excited about daily things, and thus revelation would have no interest if it did not contain anything more than reason. —He should strive for clarity and simplicity. Others might have the pleasure of making the simple difficult, and even if it were difficult, το ἀληθές ῥᾴδιον would still apply. He would like to begin from the very beginning, presuppose nothing.

Philosophy and Actuality

Everything actual has a double aspect: *quid sit* (what it is), *quod sit* (that it is). Consequently philosophy can have a double relation to it; one can have a concept without cognition,* but not cognition without a concept. In cognition there is a doubleness whereby it is memory. In seeing a plant, I remember it and convert it to the . . .

*a concept is expressed by *quid sit*, but from this it does not follow that I know *quod sit*

SELECTED ENTRIES FROM KIERKEGAARD'S JOURNALS AND PAPERS PERTAINING TO *THE CONCEPT OF IRONY*

See Historical Introduction, p. vii:

I am amazed that (as far as I know) no one has ever treated *the idea of a "master thief"*[1] . . . .[2]—*JP* V 5061 (*Pap.* I A 11) September 12, 1834

People often say that someone is a Don Juan or a Faust but rarely say that someone is the Wandering Jew.[3] Should there not also be individuals of this kind who have embodied in themselves too much of the essence of the Wandering Jew? — Is it right for Sibbern in Gabrielis's *Efterladte Breve*[4] to have the hero say that he would like very much to roam around as the Wandering Jew? To what extent is it proper in and by itself—that is, to what extent is it to be preferred to the life his hero leads—and to what extent is it proper in the character of this hero, or does it involve a contradiction?—*JP* II 2206 (*Pap.* I C 66) March 28, 1835

From draft of a letter:[5]

. . . The majority will get to try out in life what the Hege- I
lian dialectic really means. Incidentally, it is altogether proper A 72 46
that wine ferments before it becomes clear; nevertheless the
particular aspects of this condition are often unpleasant, although regarded in its totality, of course, it has its own pleas- I
antness, inasmuch as it still has its relative results in the con- A 72 47
text of the universal doubt. It is especially significant for the
person who through this comes to realize his destiny, not only
because of the contrasting tranquillity that follows the preced-

ing storm but also because then *life has* an entirely different meaning than previously. This is the Faustian element that in part asserts itself more or less in every intellectual development, which is why I have always been of the opinion that world-significance ought to be attributed to the idea of Faust. . . .

I A 72 51 —As far as little annoyances are concerned, I will say only that I am in the process of studying for the theological examination,[6] a pursuit that does not interest me in the least and that therefore does not get done very fast. I have always preferred free, perhaps therefore also a bit indefinite, studying to the boarding house where one knows beforehand who the guests will be and what food will be served each day of the week. Since it is, however, a requirement, and one scarcely gets permission to enter into the scholarly pastures without being branded, and since in view of my present state of mind I regard it as advantageous, plus the fact that I know that by going through with it I can make my father[7] happy (he thinks that the real land of Canaan lies on the other side of the theological diploma, but in addition, like Moses of old, ascends Mount Tabor[8] and declares that I will never get in—yet I hope that it will not be fulfilled this time), so I had better dig in. How lucky you are to have found an enormous field of investigation in Brazil, where every step offers some new oddities, where the screaming of the rest of the Republic of Scholars does not disturb your peace. To me the scholarly theological world is like Strandveien[9] on Sunday afternoon during the Dyrehaug season—they dash by each other, yelling and shouting, laugh and make fools of each other, drive their horses to death, tip over and are run over, and when they finally come—covered with dust and out of breath—to Bakken—well, they just look at each other, turn around, and go home. . . .—*JP* V 5092 (*Pap*. I A 72) June 1, 1835

See 286-301:

Schleiermacher, "Vertraute Briefe über die Lucinde." Mit einer Vorrede v. Karl Gutzkov.[10] Hamburg, 1835.

These letters are written about a book *Lucinde* published at one time by F. Schlegel. It is not known for sure whether or not this book is by Schl.[eiermacher],[11] but Gutzkov puts the burden upon everyone to prove that it is not by him. Surely on the basis of internal evidence alone it is incontestable; the characteristically Schl. dialectical-polemical language is unmistakable throughout, just as in, for example, "*Versuch über die Schamhaftigkeit.*"[12] It is probably a model review and also an example of how such a thing can be most productive, in that he constructs a host of personalities out of the book itself and through them illuminates the work and also illuminates their individuality, so that instead of being faced by the reviewer with various points of view, we get instead many personalities who represent these various points of view.[13] But they are complete beings, so that it is possible to get a glance into the individuality of the single individual and through numerous yet merely relatively true judgments to draw up our own final judgment. Thus it is a true masterpiece.—*JP* IV 3846 (*Pap*. I C 69) In October 1835

It is interesting that Faust (whom I perhaps more properly place in the third stage as the more mediate) embodies both Don Juan and the Wandering Jew (despair).—

It must not be forgotten, either, that Don Juan must be interpreted lyrically (therefore with music); the Wandering Jew epically, and Faust dramatically.—*JP* II 1179 (*Pap*. I C 58) December 1835

The irony of life must of necessity be most intrinsic to childhood, to the age of imagination; this is why it is so striking in the Middle Ages; this is why it is present in the romantic school. Adulthood, the more it becomes engrossed in the world, does not have so much of it.—*JP* II 1669 (*Pap*. I A 125) February 1836

Humor in contrast to irony—and yet as a rule they can be united in one individual, since both components are contingent on one's not having compromised with the world. This noncompromise with the world is modified in humor by one's not giving two hoots for it, and in the other [irony], however, by one's trying to influence the world and for precisely this reason being ridiculed by the world. They are the two opposite ends of a teeter-totter (wave motions). The humorist, when the world makes fun of him, feels for a time like the other, who must often go under in his battle with life and then again often rises above it and smiles at it. (When, for example, Faust does not understand the world and yet smiles at the world, which does not understand him.)—*JP* II 1671 (*Pap.* I A 154) April 1836

One who walked along contemplating suicide—at that very moment a stone fell down and killed him,[14] and he ended with the words: Praise the Lord!—*JP* II 1672 (*Pap.* I A 158) *n.d.*, 1836

Irony, the ignorance Socrates began with, the world created from nothing, the pure virgin who gave birth to Christ— —*JP* II 1673 (*Pap.* I A 190) *n.d.*, 1836

Does not the irony in Christianity lie in this, that it made an attempt to encompass the entire world, but the seeds of the impossibility of doing this lay within itself, and this is connected with the other, the humorous, its view of what it actually calls the world (this concept properly belongs to it and therefore in a sense it stops halfway), because everything that hitherto had asserted itself in the world and continued to do so was placed in relation to the presumably single truth of the Christian, and therefore to the Christian the kings and the princes, power and glory, philosophers and artists, enemies and persecutors, etc., etc. appeared to be nothing and to be laughable because of their opinions of their own greatness.—*JP* II 1674 (*Pap.* I A 207) July 19, 1836

It is quite curious that, after being occupied so long with the concept of the romantic, I now see for the first time that the romantic becomes what Hegel calls the dialectical, the other position where

Stoicism—fatalism
Pelagianism—Augustinianism
humor—irony
etc.

are at home, positions that do not have any continuance by themselves, but life is a constant pendulum-movement between them.

I now perceive also that when Heiberg transferred Hegelianism to esthetics and believed that he had found the triad: lyric—epic—lyric-epic (dramatic),[15] he was right; but [I also perceive] that this can be carried through on a far greater scale: classical–romantic–absolute beauty, and in such a way that precisely the Heiberg-triad becomes meaningful, since the classical, as well as the romantic and absolute beauty, has its lyrical—its epical—its dramatic.

To what extent, for that matter, is it right to begin with the lyrical; the history of poetry seems to indicate a beginning with the epic.—*JP* II 1565 (*Pap*. I A 225) August 19, 1836

Precisely because it actually is mood that dominates in Holberg, at many points his dramas (*Erasmus Montanus*, *Jeppe*, etc.) slip over into tragedy, skip over the ironical point of view that moderates it, just as tragedy based on immediacy easily takes on a tinge of comedy (through accidentals that as such become ridiculous) or irony lies dormant from the outset, as in the hero stories, for example.—*JP* II 1675 (*Pap*. I A 238) *n.d.*, 1836

August, 1836

For the ancients the divine was continually merged with the world; therefore no irony.—*JP* II 1677 (*Pap*. I A 256) August 1836

Irony is native only to the immediate (where, however, the individual does not become conscious of it as such) and to the dialectical position; whereas in the third position (that of character) the reaction to the world does not appear as irony, since resignation has now developed in the individual, which is precisely the consciousness of the limitation every effort must have, insofar as it is to continue in a structure of world-order, because as striving it is infinite and unlimited. Irony and resignation are two opposite poles, the two opposite directions of motion.[16] —*JP* II 1676 (*Pap.* I A 239) September 13, 1836

What is involved in the concept *myth* and *mythology*—does not every age have its mythology—Novalis etc.—how is it different from poetry (the subjunctive—the novel, poetic prose)—a hypothetical proposition in the indicative.—*JP* III 2798 (*Pap.* I A 241) September 13, 1836

Mythology is the compacting (suppressed being) of eternity (the eternal idea) in the categories of time and space—in time, for example, Chiliasm or the doctrine of a kingdom of heaven that begins in time*; in space, for example, an idea construed as being a finite personality. Just as the poetic is the subjunctive but does not claim to be more (poetic actuality), mythology, on the other hand, is a hypothetical statement in the indicative (see p. 1 of this book [*Pap.* I A 141]) and lies in the very middle of the conflict between them, because the ideal, losing its gravity, is compacted in earthly form.—

*Therefore it is in a certain sense basically comical to think of Pastor Stiefel (contemporary with Luther), who predicted the end of the world at a certain hour and gathered his congregation in the church, but nothing happened; however, it could easily have become the end of him, because the people became so embittered that they nearly killed him.—*JP* III 2799 (*Pap.* I A 300) *n.d.*, 1836

Does not some of what I have called irony approach what the Greeks called Nemesis—for example, the overrating of an individual the very moment he feels most distressed about some guilt—for example, the scene in *Faust*[17] where the jubilant peasants receive him and thank him for his and his father's skill during the epidemic, likewise often the Wagner-type admiration.—*JP* II 1678 (*Pap.* I A 265) October 27, 1836

The quiet and the security one has in reading a classic or in associating with a fully matured person is not found in the romantic; there it is something like watching a man write with hands that tremble so much that one fears the pen will run away from him any moment into some grotesque stroke. (This is dormant irony.)—*JP* II 1679 (*Pap.* II A 37) *n.d.*, 1837

In margin of Pap. II A 37:

The development of the concept of irony has to begin here where the fantastic, grandiose ideas are gratified and reflection has not yet disturbed the ingenuousness of this position. But now one observes that it does not go this way in the world, and since he is unable to surrender his lofty ideals, he likewise has to feel in some manner the world's ridicule (irony—romantic, the previous was not romantic but a gratification in the form of achievement) (this irony is the world's irony over the individual and is different from what the Greeks called irony, which was the ironical gratification in which the single individual hovered above the world and which with Socrates began to develop as the idea of the state disappeared more and more; but in the romantic position, where everything is striving, irony cannot gain entrance in the individual but lies outside him; I believe this distinction has been too much overlooked), and finally the third position, where irony is outlived.—*JP* II 1680 (*Pap.* II A 38) *n.d.*

How unhappy I am—Martensen has written an essay on Lenau's *Faust*![18]—*JP* V 5225 (*Pap.* II A 597) *n.d.*, 1837

The whole attitude of the Greek nature (harmony) had the effect that even though battle divided them, the struggle never became acute—then there was harmony in nature—irony in the individual—now comes the revenge—irony in nature and humor in the individual. If someone says that irony and humor are identical, only different in degrees, I will say what Paul says of the relationship of Christianity to Judaism: "All is new."[19]—*JP* II 1711 (*Pap*. II A 608) *n.d.*, 1837

If I have conceived (see another sheet [*Pap*. I A 154])[20] of the romantic position as a teeter-totter, the ends of which are characterized by irony and humor, then it follows naturally that the path of its oscillation is extremely varied, all the way from the most heaven-storming humor to the most desperate bowing down in irony, just as there is also a certain rest and equilibrium in this position (Wieland's "Irony"[21]), for irony is first surmounted when the individual, above everything and looking down from this position, is finally elevated beyond himself and from this dizzy height sees himself in his nothingness, and thereby he finds his true elevation. —See *Prindsessinn Brambilla*.[22]

June 2, 1837

This self-overcoming of irony is the crisis of the higher spiritual life; the individual is now acclimatized—the bourgeois mentality, which really only hides in the other position, is conquered, and the individual is reconciled.

The ironical position as such is: *nil admirari* [to admire nothing]; but irony, when it slays itself, has *disdained* everything with humor, itself included.—*JP* II 1688 (*Pap*. II A 627) June 2, 1837

How close the *immediate, spontaneous* expression often lies to irony, and yet how far away. For example, Oehlenschlaeger:

O flower, as it goes with you
so it goes with me.
Like a cornflower the wretched poet
stands and grieves.
He only stands in the way of the *nourishing grain*—
What does he achieve etc.[23]

Is it the same immediacy, although far more profound, that keeps Christ's discourses and for the most part the whole

New Testament from having an ironical and humorous imprint, although one single stroke would immediately give the expression the strongest possible coloring of irony and humor?—*JP* II 1689 (*Pap*. II A 101) June 30, 1837

Irony presumably can also produce a certain tranquillity II A 102 62 (which then must correspond to the peace following a humorous development), which, however, is a long way from being Christian redemption[a] (brothers in Christ—every other distinction completely disappears, becomes nothing in proportion to being brothers in Christ—but did not Christ make distinctions, did he not love John more than the others—Poul Møller[24] in a most interesting conversation on the evening of June 30). It can produce a certain love,[b] the kind with which Socrates, for example, encompassed his pupils (spiritual pederasty, as Hamann[25] says), but it is still *egotistical*, because he stood as their deliverer, expanded their narrow expressions and views in his higher consciousness, in his perspective; the diameter of the movement is not as great as in the case of the humorist[c] (heaven—hell—the Christian has to despise all things—the ironist's highest polemical movement is *nil admirari* [to admire nothing]). Irony is *egotistical* (it contends with the bourgeois, philistine mentality and yet retains it even though in the individual it mounts in the air like a songbird,[d] little by little throwing out its cargo, until it runs the risk of ending with an egotistical "Go to the devil," for irony has not yet slain itself by looking at itself, in the sense that the individual sees himself in the light of the irony). Humor is *lyrical* (it is the most profound earnestness about life—profound poetry, which cannot form itself as such and therefore crystallizes in the most baroque forms—it is hemorrhoidal *non fluens* [nonflowing]—the *molimina* [exertions] of the higher life).

The whole attitude of the Greek nature (harmony—beauty) II A 102 63 was such that even if the individual disengaged himself and the battle began, there was still the imprint of having arisen from this harmonious view of life, and therefore it soon came to an end without having described a large circle (Socrates). But now there appeared a view of life that taught that all nature is corrupt (the deepest polemic, the widest wing-stretching), but nature took revenge—and now I get *humor* in the individual and *irony*[e] in nature, and they meet in that humor wants to be a fool in the world and the irony in the world accepts them [men of humor] as actually being that.

Some say that irony and humor are basically the same with only a degree of difference. I will answer with Paul, where he talks about the relationship of Christianity to Judaism: *Everything is new in Christ.*[26]

The Christian humorist is like a plant of which only the roots are visible, whose flower unfolds for a loftier sun.—*JP* II 1690 (*Pap.* II A 102) July 6, 1837

[a]*In margin of Pap.* II A 102:

Therefore Socrates' influence was simply to awaken—midwife that he was—not redeeming except in an inauthentic sense.—*JP* II 1691 (*Pap.* II A 103) October 30, 1837

In margin of Pap. II A 102:

[b]and therefore so enormously different from the more recent idealistic-philosophical go-to-the-devil.—*JP* II 1692 (*Pap.* II A 104) *n.d.*

[c]*In margin of Pap.* II A 102:

Humor can therefore approach blasphemy; Hamann[27] would rather hear wisdom from Balaam's ass or from a philosopher against his will than from an angel or an apostle.—*JP* II 1693 (*Pap.* II A 105) *n.d.*

[d]*In margin of Pap.* II A 102:

It is no heavenly ladder on which angels *descend* from the *opened* heaven,[28] but it is an assault-ladder, gigantic, which Christianly means to take God's kingdom by force.—*JP* II 1694 (*Pap.* II A 106) *n.d.*

In margin of Pap. II A 102:

[e]Irony in nature must be worked out, such as the ironical juxtapositions (man and monkey) etc. found in various forms in Schubert's *Symbolik*;[29] this was something the Greeks knew nothing about, as far as I know.

The medieval fairy story has capricious humor, for example, a man who, standing two miles away from a windmill, makes it go by *laying his finger on one nostril* and blowing through the other.[30] —*JP* II 1695 (*Pap.* II A 107) *n.d.*

In margin of Pap. II A 102:

Jean Paul[31] is the greatest humorist *capitalist.*—*JP* II 1696 (*Pap.* II A 108) *n.d.*

Irony no longer stands out the way it used to. I have often thought it was a kind of irony of the world[32] when, for example, a horsefly sat on a man's nose the very moment he made his last running leap to throw himself into the Thames, when in the story of Loki and the dwarf,[33] after Eitri has gone away and Brock stands by the bellows, a fly settles on his nose three times—here the ironical appears as one of Loki's intrigues to prevent him from winning the wager, and in the other case it is a grandiose human plan which is horridly ridiculed by a horsefly.—*JP* II 1697 (*Pap.* II A 112) July 8, 1837

See this book, pp. 10 and 11 [*Pap.* II A 101-08].

Humor is irony carried through to its maximum oscillations. Even though the essentially Christian is the real *primus motor* [prime mover], nevertheless there are those in Christian Europe who have not achieved more than irony and for that reason have also not been able to accomplish the absolutely isolated, independently personal humor. Therefore they either seek rest in the Church, where in united humor over the *world* the solidarity of individuals develops a *Christian irony*, as was the case with Tieck[34] and others, or, if the religious is not in motion, form a club (*Serapions Brüder*[35]—which in Hoffmann's case was nevertheless not something palpable, actual, but ideal). No, Hamann[36] is still the greatest and most authentic humorist, the genuinely humorous Robinson Crusoe, not on a desert island but in the noise of life; his humor is not an esthetic concept but life, not a hero in a controlled drama.—*JP* II 1699 (*Pap*. II A 136) August 4, 1837

See pages 10 and 11 and 19 [*Pap*. II A 101-08, 136].

Now I perceive why genuine humor cannot be caught, as irony can, in a novel and why it thereby ceases to be a life-concept, simply because not-to-write is part of the nature of the concept, since this would betray an all too conciliatory position toward the world (which is why Hamann remarks somewhere that fundamentally there is nothing more ludicrous than to write for the people[37]). Just as Socrates left no books, Hamann left only as much as the modern period's rage for writing made relatively necessary, and furthermore only occasional pieces.—*JP* II 1700 (*Pap*. II A 138) *n.d.*, 1837

The ancients' use of irony is completely different from that of the moderns. First of all there is its relation to a harmonic language, the compact Greek in contrast to modern reflective prolixity, but the irony of the Greeks is also *plastic*, for example, Diogenes,[38] who does not merely make the observation that when a poor marksman shoots the best thing is for him to stand close to the target, but he walks ahead and stands close to the target. Oh, I would like to have heard Socrates ironize!—*JP* II 1703 (*Pap*. II A 141) *n.d.*, 1837

Irony in relation to ancient linguistic structure—before the modern reflected prolixity.—*JP* II 1714 (*Pap*. II A 659) *n.d.*, 1837

See Historical Introduction, pp. vii-xiii:

Now I know a suitable subject for a dissertation: concerning the concept of satire among the ancients, the reciprocal relation of the various Roman satirists to each other.—*JP* V 5262 (*Pap*. II A 166) September 25, 1837

In Clausen and Hohlenberg's *Tidsskrift for udenlandsk theologisk Litteratur*, 1837, no. 3, pp. 485-534,[39] there is a fragment of an article by Baur[40] on the *Christian elements in Platonism* that drives right into my own study of irony and humor; this must be the case particularly with the portion omitted from the journal, since one of its particular tasks is to develop the concept "irony." (To what extent Baur has become conscious of the Christian contrast in humor I still do not know, of course, as I have not read the article.) In his parallel between Christ and Socrates on page 529 [p. 528] there are some very good things. Just as in paganism the divine belongs on the whole only to the subjective representation, and thus always has the human [p. 529] as its presupposition and foundation, so that precisely this, the human subjectivity of the divine, is paganism's greatest characteristic, just so even such a remarkable personality as Socrates is regarded only from the standpoint of the human.—*JP* IV 4243 (*Pap*. II A 186) November 1, 1837

Humor is first of all really reflective—in the face of all empiricism it is an unshakable, authentic frame of mind related to genius; whereas irony at every moment exempts itself from a new dependence—which from another angle means that it is dependent at every moment.—*JP* II 1707 (*Pap*. II A 192) November 9, 1837

When irony (humor) in its polemic has put the whole world, heaven and earth, under water and in compensation has enclosed a little world in itself—it lets a raven fly out when it is ready to be reconciled with the world again—and then a dove, which returns with an olive leaf.[41]—*JP* II 1708 (*Pap*. II A 195) November 15, 1837

But humor is also the joy that has overcome the world.[42]—*JP* II 1716 (*Pap*. II A 672) *n.d.*, 1837

I would like to write a novel in which the main character would be a man who had gotten a pair of glasses, one lens of which reduced images as powerfully as an oxyhydrogen microscope and the other magnified on the same scale, so that he perceived everything very relatively.—*JP* V 5281 (*Pap.* II A 203) December 10, 1837

I am utterly dismayed upon reading the essay with which Fichte[43] begins his journal. When we see a man with his abilities arm himself for battle with such earnestness, such "fear and trembling" (Philippians[44]), what is there for the rest of us to say? I think I will give up my studies, and now I know what I will be—I will become a witness in the office of a notary public.—*JP* V 5282 (*Pap.* II A 204) December 12, 1837

Irony is an abnormal development that, like the abnormality of the livers of Strasburger geese, ends by killing the individual.—*JP* II 1717 (*Pap.* II A 682) January 1, 1838

Die Ironien in den Reden Jesu, by F. Joseph Grulich. Leipzig: 1838.—*JP* V 5317 (*Pap.* II A 737) *n.d.*, 1838

For a dedication copy of my treatise:[45] Since I know that you probably will not read it, and if you did would not understand it, and if you understood it would take exception to it, may I direct your attention only to the externals: gilt-edges and morocco binding.—*JP* V 5322 (*Pap.* II A 749) *n.d.*, 1838

There is an *indescribable joy* that glows all through us just as inexplicably as the apostle's exclamation breaks forth for no apparent reason: "Rejoice, and again I say, Rejoice."[46] Not a joy over this or that, but the soul's full outcry "with tongue and mouth and from the bottom of the heart":[47] "I rejoice for my joy, by, in, with, about, over, for, and with my joy"—a heavenly refrain that, as it were, suddenly interrupts our other singing, a joy that cools and refreshes like a breath of air, a breeze from the trade winds that blow across the plains of Mamre to the everlasting mansions.[48]—*JP* V 5324 (*Pap.* II A 228) 10:30 A.M. May 19, 1838

How I thank you, Father in heaven, for having kept an earthly father present for a time here on earth, where I so greatly need him; with your help I hope that he will have greater joy in being my father the second time than he had the first time. [49]—*JP* V 5328 (*Pap*. II A 231) July 9, 1838

I hope that my contentment with my life *here at home*[50] will turn out to be like that of a man I once read about.[51] He, too, was fed up with home and wanted to ride away from it. When he had gone a little way, his horse stumbled and he fell off, and as he got up on his feet he happened to see his home, which now looked so beautiful to him that he promptly mounted his horse, rode home, and stayed home. It depends on getting the right perspective.—*JP* V 5330 (*Pap*. II A 233) July 10, 1838

My father[52] died on Wednesday (the 8th) at 2:00 A.M. I so deeply desired that he might have lived a few years more, and I regard his death as the last sacrifice of his love for me, because in dying he did not depart from me but he *died for me*, in order that something, if possible, might still come of me. Most precious of all that I have inherited from him is his memory, his transfigured image, transfigured not by my poetic imagination (for it does not need that), but transfigured by many little single episodes I am now learning about, and this memory I will try to keep most secret from the world. Right now I feel there *is* only *one* person (E. Boesen[53]) with whom I can really talk about him. He was a "faithful friend."—*JP* V 5335 (*Pap*. II A 243) August 11, 1838

Much of my suffering occurred because the doubt, concern, and restlessness, which my real self wanted to forget in order to form a view of the world, my reflective self seemed to try to impress upon me and sustain, partly as a necessary and partly as an interesting feature of transition, in the fear that I might have shammed a result.

For example, now when my life has shaped up in such a way

that it seems that I am destined to study for the examination[54] *in perpetuum* [forever] and that no matter how long I live I will never get beyond the point where I once voluntarily stopped (just as one occasionally sees mentally deranged people who forget their whole intermediate life and remember only their childhood, or forget everything but one single moment in their lives)—it seems that the very thought of being a student of theology must remind me simultaneously of that happy period of possibilities (which might be called one's preexistence) and of my stopping there, feeling somewhat like the child who does not grow because he had been given alcohol. Now when my energetic self tries to forget it in order to act, my reflective self wants very much to hang on to it, because it seems interesting, and, as reflection raises itself to the power of a universal consciousness, abstracts from my personal consciousness.—*JP* V 5432 (*Pap.* II A 807) *n.d.*, 1838

I have no alternative than to suppose that it is God's will that I prepare for my examination[55] and that it is more pleasing to him that I do this than actually coming to some clearer perception by immersing myself in one or another sort of research,[56] for obedience is more precious to him than the fat of rams.[57]—*JP* V 5385 (*Pap.* II A 422) May 13, 1839

Preface[58]

Whether this preface is going to be long or short, I simply do not know at this moment. My soul is filled with but one thought, a longing, a thirsting, really to run wild in the lyrical underbrush of the preface, really to rumble about in it, for just as the poet at times must feel lyrically stirred and then again relishes the epical, so I as a prose writer feel at present an indescribable joy in surrendering all objective thinking and really exhausting myself in wishes and hopes, in a secret whispering with the reader, a Horatian *sussuratio* [low whisper][59] in the evening hours, for the preface always ought to be conceived in twilight, which also is undeniably the most beautiful; no wonder, therefore, that we read that the Lord God walked in the cool of the evening (Genesis),[60] an evening hour when the pressure of reflection is a solemn distant sound, like the laughter of the harvesters.—*JP* V 5387 (*Pap*. II A 432) May 17, 1839

The trouble with me is that while other authors usually think less of what they have written in the past, I am just the opposite and always think better of what I have written[61] prior to what I am writing at present.[62]—*JP* V 5391 (*Pap*. II A 476) July 14, 1839

I would like to write a dissertation on suicide dealing with statistical information on suicide and its relation to the ancient world-view and the modern, its pathological Chladni figures,[63] etc.—*JP* V 5393 (*Pap*. II A 482) July 20, 1839

It is with me as with Sarah: νενεκρωμένος [as good as dead][64]; I will come up for examination παρὰ καιρὸν ἡλικίας [past the appropriate age].—*JP* V 5394 (*Pap*. II A 490) *n.d.*, 1839

See 198:10:

For the period of a year, a mile in time, I will plunge underground like the river Guadalquibir—but I am sure to come up again!—*JP* V 5397 (*Pap*. II A 497) *n.d.*, 1839

If only I could have my examination soon so that I could become a *quodlibetarius* [one who does as he pleases] once again.—*JP* V 5406 (*Pap*. II A 534) August 8, 1839

See 35:2-8:

It is strange what hate, conspicuous everywhere, Hegel has for the upbuilding or the edifying, but that which builds up is not an opiate that lulls to sleep; it is the amen of the finite spirit and is an aspect of knowledge that ought not to be ignored.—*JP* II 1588 (*Pap*. III A 6) July 10, 1840

The view that Hegel is a parenthesis in Schelling seems to be more and more manifest; we are only waiting for the parenthesis to be closed.—*JP* II 1589 (*Pap*. III A 34) *n.d.*, 1840

I have always been charged with using long parentheses. Studying for my final examination[65] is the longest parenthesis I have experienced.—*JP* V 5446 (*Pap*. III A 35) *n.d.*, 1840

I sit here all alone (I have frequently been just as alone many times, but I have never been so aware of it) and count the
III A73 36 hours until I shall see Sæding.[66] I cannot recall any change in my father, and now I am about to see the places where as a poor boy he tended sheep, the places for which, because of his descriptions, I have been so homesick. What if I were to get sick and be buried in the Sæding churchyard![67] What a strange idea! His last wish[68] for me is fulfilled—is that actually to be the sum and substance of my life? In God's name! Yet in relation to what I owed to him the task was not so insignificant. I learned from him what fatherly love is, and through this I gained a conception of divine fatherly love, the one single unshakable thing in life, the true Archimedean point.[69]—*JP* V 5468 (*Pap*. III A 73) *n.d.*, 1840

Preface[70]

Its significance. Probably it is irrelevant to the dissertation but it is a necessary factor in the personality.

See EE, p. 18 [*JP* V 5387 (*Pap*.. II A 432)]

I have worked on this dissertation with fear and trembling lest my dialectic swallow too much.

The ease of style will be censured. One or another half-educated Hegelian robber will say that the subjective is too prominent. First of all, I will ask him not to plague me with a rehash of this new wisdom that I must already regard as old, also not to place such great claims upon me: that the idea's own movements should take place through me, that the idea should break out in me (for most young people burst forth, like the woman in *Ludlams Hule*,[71] with a rustic region behind them), and, finally, that one cannot write about a negative concept except in this way; and I ask him, instead of continually giving assurances that doubt is overcome, irony conquered, to permit it to speak for once. Moreover, whether I may have been too prolix at times, and since Hegel says with authority that the mind is the best epitomizer (see the introduction to his *Philosophie der Geschichte*, p. 8[72]), let me be judged modestly and without any demands, but I will not be judged by boys.[73]—*JP* V 5484 (*Pap*. III B 2) *n.d.*, 1840-41

. . . . . and if it should seem to one or another that this is madness, I will reply with Soc. (*Phaedrus*, 244 a): ἐι μὲν γὰϱ ἦν ἁπλοῦν τὸ μανίαν κακὸν εἶναι, καλῶς ἂν ἐλέγετο. νῦν δὲ τὰ μέγιστα τῶν ἀγαθῶν ἡμῖν γίγνεται διὰ μανίας, θείᾳ μέντοι δόσει διδομένης [That would be right if it were an invariable truth that madness is an evil, but in reality, the greatest blessings come by way of madness, indeed of madness that is heaven-sent].[74]

And if something should be found, particularly in the first part of the dissertation, that one is generally not accustomed to come across in scholarly writings, the reader must forgive my jocundity, also that I, in order to lighten the burden, sometimes sing at my work.—*Pap*. III B 3 *n.d.*, 1840-41

See 82:6-26:

When Socrates says at the end of the *Apology* that it is impossible to call death the greatest evil since we do not know really what it is, this is still spoken with irony—but with a little modification the same thing could be said humorously.—*JP* II 1723 (*Pap*. III B 4) *n.d.*, 1840-41

See 241:1-245:14:

Introduction

That it [irony] is not an esthetic concept—but the *molimina* [exertions] for a life-view—the relation of paradox* to thought—personality—the style is the man—Socrates came to himself by standing still—the Middle Ages by journeying around the world—there is humor in Clement of Alexandria's praise of writing allegories so that the heathens could not understand.[75]—*JP* II 1724 (*Pap.* III B 5) *n.d.*, 1840-41

Addition to Pap. III B 5:

*The significance of the polemical—the comic has the polemical as a necessary element.—*JP* II 1726 (*Pap.* III B 7) *n.d.*, 1840-41

Immediacy—Whimsy—

To what extent there is immediacy in the comic—after all, there is really nothing immediate—to what extent it points back to something of the sort— —*JP* II 1725 (*Pap.* III B 6) *n.d.*, 1840-41

In the case of Socrates it was an irony of fate or of life that Xanthippe frequently made him celebrated, that he was more or less henpecked.

Also his similarity to his most ill-tempered enemies, the Sophists, with whom he could easily be confused.

Socrates was the ugliest of men.[76]—*JP* IV 4244 (*Pap.* III B 8) *n.d.*, 1840-41

In the case of Swift, it was an irony of fate that in his old age he entered the insane asylum he himself had erected in his early years.[77]—*JP* II 1727 (*Pap.* III B 9) *n.d.*, 1840-41

Irony conceived according to its definition becomes a factor understood by the Greeks as σωφροσύνη [soundness of mind]—which shears away fieriness and gets insipidity.—*JP* II 1728 (*Pap.* III B 10) *n.d.*, 1840-41

Humor by definition becomes a polemical factor in the Christian view of life.[78]—*JP* II 1729 (*Pap.* III B 11) *n.d.*, 1840-41

See 9:2-19:

If there is anything to be praised in modern philosophical endeavor in its magnificent manifestation, it certainly is the power of genius with which it seizes and vigorously *holds on to* the phenomenon. Although it is fitting for the phenomenon (which as such is always *foeminini generis* [of the feminine gender]) by reason of its feminine nature to surrender* to the stronger sex, yet among the knights of the modern age there is frequently a lack of deferential propriety, profound enthusiasm, in place of which one sometimes hears too much the jingle of spurs etc.—and at times it shrivels before the fellows.

In margin: *And with justification one nevertheless—in contrast to what has often been said, that the observer ought to surrender himself—ought to remember that it is rather up to the phenomenon; and we will say that history, so to speak, rejoices at the prospect of this embrace.

However sterile history is, its embrace is fertile, like that of the old witch in the fairy tale by Musaeus,[79] and just as those three armor bearers of Roland's with a certain aversion decided to share the bed with the old crone, yet they did not regret it afterward.

In the arms of philosophy, history rejuvenates itself unto divine youthfulness.—*JP* III 3283 (*Pap.* III B 12) *n.d.*, 1840-41

In margin of Pap. III B 12:

halb zog sie ihn
halb sank er hin
[she half dragged him
he half sank down].[80]

—*Pap.* III B 13 *n.d.*, 1840-41

It requires a trained eye to see what is round, because it cannot be seen all at once and the inner sense must exercise diligent control over the external eye's hasty, inquisitive, and desultory observations lest one mistake a sphere for a polygon. The same is true when considering the cycle of history—lest the observation of multiplicity weaken the impression of continuity. That everything is new[81] is the angle of refraction;[*] that nothing is new is the bond of unity; but these must be in and with each other—only in this does the truth lie. Yet this likeness among the different is not to be conceived abstractly, not as the Sophist Protagoras[82] did.[**] This observation is the sophism comparable to the idea of mediation.

[*]*In margin:* the infinite tangential possibilities of the periphery.

[**]*In margin:* Heise,[83] II, p. 152: that all things are like each other.—*JP* II 1633 (*Pap*. III B 14) *n.d.*, 1840-41

See 329:17-21:

When I speak of the stillness and silence of contemplation, I do not mean, for example, that one should use just as much time (or even longer) to comprehend history as history itself covers.—*JP* II 1634 (*Pap*. III B 15) *n.d.*, 1840-41

The demonic humor that attempts to draw even the divine along into the humoristic "Go to the devil" (thus Heine: the heavenly family[84] etc.).—*JP* II 1730 (*Pap*. III B 16) *n.d.*, 1840-41

Hamann's relationship to his contemporaries—Socrates' to the Sophists (who could say something about *everything*).—*JP* II 1547 (*Pap*. III B 17) *n.d.*, 1840-41

Hoffmann, who himself would have artistically conceived of Kreisler's going mad—the presumed part three of *Kater Murr*.[85] The confounding of first person and third person.—*Pap*. III B 18 *n.d.*, 1840-41

See 328:25-329:30:

Irony is the birth-pangs of the objective mind (based upon the misrelationship, discovered by the *I*, between existence [*Existentsen*] and the idea of existence).

Humor is the birth-pangs of the absolute mind (based upon

the misrelationship, discovered by the *I*, between the *I* and the idea of the *I*).—*JP* II 1731 (*Pap*. III B 19) *n.d.*, 1840-41

The dogmatic thesis around which everything turns in Hamann πάντα θεῖα καὶ πάντα ἀνθρώπινα [everything divine and everything human][86]—yet it still has not become the center, but the thoughts spill out chaotically.

Irony becomes aristocratic. (The philosophers.) Humor reconciled with all existence (πάντα θεῖα καὶ πάντα ἀνθρώπινα).—*JP* II 1548 (*Pap*. III B 20) *n.d.*, 1840-41

There is irony in the identity of asking and answering only insofar as people are permitted to remain in their ignorance (such as when someone said to me that it must be hard to take a shower bath in the winter when the water is many degrees colder, and I answered—as if conceding the worth of the remark—that as yet it had not happened to me).—*JP* II 1732 (*Pap*. III B 21) *n.d.*, 1840-41

Irony is *negative* creation.—blowing soap bubbles—.—*JP* II 1733 (*Pap*. III B 22) *n.d.*, 1840-41

The concept of divine irony. Attempts were made to emancipate the divine, but this was possible only by means of the idea that it floated freely above all finite qualifications, denying them all, but the concept of *positive freedom* was not achieved, that it divinely moved freely within all these finite qualifications. Because the divine and the human were confused, a similar attempt arose from the human side.

When trust and faith in the gods were lost, it became no longer possible to maintain the divine except in its purely negative form—the reflex of this in the realm of consciousness is *ignorance*, and the corresponding factor in the realm of action is irony.

Earlier the divine was maintained as the individually human; now this has been annihilated and has been replaced by the abstractly human—the pure "I."—*JP* II 1734 (*Pap*. III B 23) *n.d.*, 1840-41

See 329:26-31:

We recognize humor immediately only in such a reply as *credo quia absurdum* [I believe because it is absurd].[87] Ignorance, however, is something quite different.—*JP* II 1735 (*Pap*. III B 24) *n.d.*, 1840-41

See 191:13-25:

The great picture in *Phaedrus*,[88] in which the fourth kind of madness—the madness of love—is described, a description that is just as chaste as it is voluptuous, because voluptuousness is at all times conquered by the chasteness; the voluptuousness is the strong coloring.

It ends with a prayer.

The whole passage must be examined. Para. 244-57.

Hegel touches on this picture. *Gesch. d. Ph.*, II, pp. 208ff.[89]

Also Schleiermacher[90] in the preface to *Phaedrus*, but [he] thinks it ought not be insisted upon.

What is expressed here is love's moment of stimulation, which is so incomparably described.—*JP* III 3323 (*Pap*. III B 26) *n.d.*, 1840-41

See 220:18-30:

How abstract Socrates' dialectic was can also be seen in the basic law for the dialectical movement, which is that only two things can be the opposite of each other (*principium exclusi medii inter duo contradictoria* [the principle of the excluded middle between two contradictories]). See *Phaedrus*, p. 218;[91] *Protagoras*, p. 155;[92] *Republic*, Schleiermacher, pp. 245, 246, etc.[93] (the dichotomous throughout the *Sophist*).—*JP* IV 4245 (*Pap*. III B 27) *n.d.*, 1841

On bottom of p. 272 of copy of Om Begrebet Ironi; *see 259:1-2:*

Hegel has an analogy to this section in vol. II of his *Aesthetik*,[94] where he develops the significance of satire.—*Pap*. III B 28 October 17, 1841

On bottom of p. 322 of copy of Om Begrebet Ironi; *see 303:9-13:*

In defense of this entire passage, which has met with so much opposition, I could refer to Hegel's *Aesthetik*, II, p. 217.[95]—*Pap*. III B 29 October 17, 1841

On front end-sheet of a copy of Om Begrebet Ironi:

Caricature. III B 30

Socrates was the ugliest man in Athens and had the most shrewish wife around—one more reason for him to spend so much time on the streets. He was first a sculptor but gave up this profession when he began playing the genius. He had a little property (perhaps he had invested it on good terms with one or another of the businessmen or shopkeepers with whom he associated); no doubt he ate into his capital later, and therefore it was no wonder that he always was at hand when a banquet took place (for this reason both Xenophon and Plato have a symposium, however different their interpretations otherwise are); he did not wish to have any fixed occupation and therefore, in order to have his future secured nevertheless, he wanted to be maintained as a pensioner in the Prytaneum, and in this way he would pass through the two categories vagabonds are accustomed to pass through—that of being a capitalist and of being a pensioner. 121

He was an idler who never left the city (see *Crito*, Hey[i]se, p. 150 middle and bottom;[96] see *Phaedrus*, Ast, I, p. 133, Phaedrus's speech[97]).

He was very absentminded; for this reason some have wanted to explain the ambiguous passage in Aristophanes' *Clouds* as an absentminded error. See Rötscher, p. 284 etc.[98]

The whole collection of quotations in Süvern, p. 3 etc.,[99] Rötscher, p. 277 etc.[100]

He was discontented with the established order; therefore he loafed around everywhere; this also had a basis in his unfortunate marriage, for although he had the benefit of his wife as riding masters have of wild horses by learning to constrain them (see Forchhammer, p. 49, bottom[101]), it was nevertheless natural that he often sought out strangers, all the more because he seldom saw strangers at home (the story about Xanthippe's getting angry; see Plutarch, 11, 41 A, B[102]).

III B 30 122 He was not constituted like other men, was never sick, not even during the horrible plague during the time of the Peloponnesian War. See Heinsius, p. 5.[103]

He learned to dance when he was sixty years old because the motion was so superb. (See Diogenes Laertius.[104])—*JP* IV 4246 (*Pap.* III B 30) *n.d.*, 1842-43

In a copy of Om Begrebet Ironi, *p. 60; see 59:19-29:*

It is a shame I did not know at that time the skepticism that Sextus Empiricus maintains with respect to teaching. See Tennemann, V, p. 294.[105]—*JP* II 2280 (*Pap.* IV A 198) *n.d.*, 1842-43

On inside front cover of a copy of Om Begrebet Ironi:

Actually it was Cato who first declared that Socrates was a *Schwatzer* [babbler] who wanted to turn things topsy-turvy for his people. See Plutarch in *Life of Cato*, ch. 23.

(found in the Danish translation, III, p. 450.[106])—*JP* IV 4247 (*Pap.* IV A 199) *n.d.*, 1842-43

On inside front cover of a copy of Om Begrebet Ironi:

In his *De genio Socratis*, Plutarch[107] tells that Socrates' father had received the oracle about his son stating that he must compel him in no way but allow him to follow his inclinations completely.

See Tennemann, *Geschichte der Philosophie*, II, p. 30 note.—*JP* IV 4248 (*Pap.* IV A 200) *n.d.*, 1842-43

On inside front cover of a copy of Om Begrebet Ironi:

Ritter and Preller[108] have included a good selection of quotations from Plato in their history of Greek philosophy. They

are noted in my copy.—*JP* V 5577 (*Pap.* IV A 201) *n.d.*, 1842-43

On inside front cover of a copy of Om Begrebet Ironi:

Two quotations concerning his relation to Xanthippe, which I have never seen referred to otherwise but found in Antoninus, *Philosophus ad se ipsum*, XI, para. 23 and 28.[109]

Moreover, I have indicated the best of *Diogenes Laertius*[110] in my copy of the Danish translation. The article in Bayle[111] also contains a few things.—*JP* IV 4249 (*Pap.* IV A 202) *n.d.*, 1842-43

On inside front cover of a copy of Om Begrebet Ironi:

Something of the former in the dialogue *Alcibiades primus*[112] (about how Socrates went looking for Alcibiades), although Schleiermacher rightly assumes this dialogue to be spurious[113] and the interpretation of Socrates incorrect but useful.[114]—*JP* IV 4250 (*Pap.* IV A 203) *n.d.*, 1842-43

On inside front cover of a copy of Om Begrebet Ironi:

That Socrates is supposed to have stood up in the theater during the performance of *The Clouds* is told by Aelian, *Var. hist.*, II, ch. 13 (found in Flögel, *Geschichte der comischen Literatur*, IV, p. 64[115]).—*JP* IV 4251 (*Pap.* IV A 204) *n.d.*, 1842-43

On front end-sheet of a copy of Om Begrebet Ironi:

Socrates is mentioned as using the parable

Aristotle, *Rhetoric*, II, ch. 20.[116] The same passage is usually cited as an example of an incorrect analogical conclusion. See Trendlenburg [*sic*], *Erläuterungen zu den Elementen der aristotelischen Logik*, Berlin, 1842, p. 79.[117]—*JP* IV 4252 (*Pap.* IV A 205) *n.d.*, 1842-43

On front end-sheet of a copy of Om Begrebet Ironi:

Socrates' discourse on death in Plato's *Apology*[118] is mentioned in Plutarch's *Consolations to Apollonius*, para. 12 etc.[119]—*JP* IV 4253 (*Pap*. IV A 206) *n.d.*, 1842-43

On front end-sheet of a copy of Om Begrebet Ironi:

Socrates' answer to Archelaus

Aristotle's *Rhetoric*, II, ch. 23 (in the little translation, p. 199[120]); see also Antoninus, *Philosophus*, the portion cited in this volume.[121]—*JP* IV 4254 (*Pap*. IV A 207) *n.d.*, 1842-43

On front end-sheet of a copy of Om Begrebet Ironi:

There are very important passages in Flögel, *Geschichte der Hofnarren*, pp. 96, 97.[122]—*JP* IV 4255 (*Pap*. IV A 208) *n.d.*, 1842-43

On back end-sheet of a copy of Om Begrebet Ironi:

See the conclusion of Aristophanes' *The Frogs*.

For it is excellent not to sit
With Socrates, gossiping
And denigrating the art of poetry etc.[123]

—*JP* IV 4256 (*Pap*. IV A 209) *n.d.*, 1842-43

On back end-sheet of a copy of Om Begrebet Ironi:

In *The Wasps*, ll. 1075-79,[124] Aristophanes himself names the evil of which he wanted to cleanse the state with *The Clouds:* idleness and legal trickery.—*JP* IV 4257 (*Pap*. IV A 210) *n.d.*, 1842-43

On back end-sheet of a copy of Om Begrebet Ironi:

Socrates has also been depicted by two other comic poets: Ameipsias in the comedy *Konnos* and Eupolis.[125] See Krag's translation, p. 272.[126]

See the same book, p. 268 note: it is impossible to repudiate completely the Roman's harsh words[127] declaring that he talked about virtue, corrupted the morals, and as a citizen was dangerous to public freedom.—*JP* IV 4258 (*Pap*. IV A 211) *n.d.*, 1842-43

On back end-sheet of a copy of Om Begrebet Ironi:

Plutarch relates (*vitae paralelae: Aristides*, ch. 1)[128] that Demetrius of Phaleron reports that Socrates not only owned his own house but also had accumulated funds amounting to 70 minas, which he had deposited at interest with Crito.—*JP* IV 4259 (*Pap*. IV A 212) *n.d.*, 1842-43

When I am not *reus voti* [one bound by a vow],[129] nothing happens for me. Because of it I passed my theological examination, because of it I wrote my dissertation, because of it I was all through with *Either/Or*[130] in eleven months. . . .—*JP* V 5626 (*Pap*. IV A 70) *n.d.*, 1843

When Father died,[131] Sibbern[132] said to me, "Now you will never get your theological degree," and then I did get it. If Father had lived, I would never have gotten it. [133]—When I broke the engagement, Peter[134] said to me, "Now you are lost." And yet it is clear that if I have indeed amounted to something, I did it through that step.—*JP* V 5769 (*Pap*. VI A 8) *n.d.*, 1844-45

Definition of Irony

Irony is the unity of ethical passion, which in inwardness infinitely accentuates the private self, and of development, which in outwardness (in association with people) infinitely abstracts from the private self. The effect of the second is that no one notices the first; therein lies the art, and the true infinitizing of the first is conditioned thereby.[135]—*JP* II 1745 (*Pap*. VI A 38) *n.d.*, 1845

From draft of Postscript:

VI B 35:24 118 This is what Socrates develops in the *Symposium*. In his dissertation, Magister Kierkegaard was alert enough to discern the Socratic but is considered not to have understood it, probably because, with the help of Hegelian philosophy, he has become super-clever and objective and positive or has not had the courage to acknowledge the negation. Finitely understood, of course, the continued and perpetually continued striving toward a goal without attaining it is to be rejected, but, infinitely understood, striving is life itself and is essentially the life of that which is composed of the infinite and the finite. An imaginary positive accomplishment is a chimera. It
VI B 35:24 119 may well be that logic has it, although before this can be regarded as true it needs to be more precisely explained than has been done up to now, but the subject is an existing [*existerende*] subject, consequently is in contradiction, consequently is in the process of becoming, and if he is, consequently is in the process of striving.[136]—*JP* V 5796 (*Pap*. VI B 35:24) *n.d.*, 1845

. . . The last two months have been very rewarding for my observations. What I said in my dissertation[137] about irony making phenomena stand revealed is so true. First of all, my ironic leap into *The Corsair*[138] helps make it perfectly clear that *The Corsair* is devoid of idea. Seen from the point of view of idea, it is dead, even if it did get a few thousand subscribers. It wants to be ironical and does not even understand irony. Generally speaking, it would have been an epigram over my whole life if it might ever be said: Contemporary with him there existed a bungling ironic journal that sang his praises; no, hold on—he was abused, and he himself asked for it. — Secondly, my ironic leap into *The Corsair* shows up the self-contradiction of the environing world. Everyone has been going around saying: It is nothing; who cares about *The Corsair* etc. What happens, when one does it, is that he is charged with being rash; they say he has deserved all this (now, you see, it is "all this") because he prompted it himself; they hardly dare walk in the street with me—fearing they too will be in

The Corsair. . . . —*JP* V 5887 (*Pap*. VII^1 A 98, p. 43) March 9, 1846

A Passage in My Dissertation

Influenced as I was by Hegel and whatever was modern, without the maturity really to comprehend greatness, I could not resist pointing out somewhere in my dissertation[139] that it was a defect on the part of Socrates to disregard the whole and only consider numerically[140] the individuals.

What a Hegelian fool I was! It is precisely this that powerfully demonstrates what a great ethicist Socrates was.—*JP* IV 4281 (*Pap*. X^3 A 477) *n.d.*, 1850

Inversion

was already known to Socrates, but of course a whole quality lower than in Christianity, and, also a quality lower, he practiced the philosophy of inversion.

Aelianus (in *Variae historiae*[141]) tells of an artist who was commissioned to paint a horse rolling. The artist painted a horse in full jump. When the owner complained and said that was not what he had ordered, the artist replied: Turn the picture upside down and you will have what you asked for. — This, says Aelianus, is the way Socrates talks; he must be understood inversely.

This is excellent! When I wrote my dissertation on irony I had not read Aelianus, but how remarkable that nobody brought him to my attention!—*JP* IV 4289 (*Pap*. X^4 A 490) *n.d.*, 1852

The State

That the state in a Christian sense is supposed to be what XI^2 A 108
Hegel[142] taught—namely, that it has moral significance, that 114
true virtue can appear only in the state (something I also childishly babbled after him in my dissertation[143]), that the goal of the state is to improve men—is obviously nonsense.

The state is of the evil rather than of the good, a necessary evil, in a certain sense a useful, expedient evil, rather than a good.

XI^2 A 108 115 The state is human egotism on a large scale and in great dimensions—so far off was Plato[144] when he said that in order to become aware of the virtues we should study them in the state.

The state is human egotism in great dimensions, very expediently and cunningly composed so that the egotisms of individuals intersect each other correctively. To this extent the state is no doubt a safeguard against egotism by manifesting a higher egotism that copes with all the individual egotisms so that these must egotistically understand that egotistically it is the most prudent thing to live in the state. Just as we speak of a calculus of infinitesimals, so also the state is a calculus of egotisms, but always in such a way that it egotistically appears to be the most prudent thing to enter into and to be in this higher egotism. But this, after all, is anything but the moral abandoning of egotism.

The state cannot go beyond this; so to be improved by living in the state is just as doubtful as being improved in a prison. Perhaps an individual becomes much shrewder about his egotism, his enlightened egotism, that is, his egotism in relation to other egotisms, but less egotistic he does not become, and what is worse, he is spoiled by regarding this official, civic, authorized egotism as virtue—this, in fact, is how demoralizing civic life is, because it reassures one in being a shrewd egotist.

Higher than this the state cannot go, and considered as moral upbringing and growth this must be regarded as very dubious.

Thus the state is continually subject to the same sophistry that engrossed the Greek Sophists—namely, that injustice on a vast scale is justice, that in a very peculiar manner the concepts turn around or flop over,[145] that what counts is to practice it on a vast scale. Furthermore, the state is continually subject to the skepticism that quantity or the numerical defines the concept, that the greatest number is equivalent to the truth.

And then the state is supposed to be counted on to develop men morally, to be the proper medium for virtue, the place where one really can become virtuous! In fact, for such a purpose this place is just as strange as would be the claim that the best place for a watchmaker or an engraver to work is aboard XI^2 A 108 116
a ship in a heavy sea.

Christianity therefore does not believe that the Christian is to remain in the body politic for the purpose of being morally improved—no, in fact it tells him in advance that it will mean suffering.

But in thieves' slang, of course, the state is said to be morally ennobling—thus we are perfectly secure against anyone's suspecting that the authorized egotism is not virtue.

Generally speaking, it can never be emphasized strongly enough that the immediate, the unrefined, the imprudent, etc. are never as corrupt as the shrewdly prudent. A brazen lecher, blazingly licentious, is perhaps not as corrupt as the lecher who observes decorum. A swindler who, as the saying goes, skins another man is perhaps not as corrupt as the person who knows precisely how far he dares to go with his swindling and still preserve the reputation and esteem of being a highly respectable man.—*JP* IV 4238 (*Pap*. XI^2 A 108) *n.d.*, 1854

EDITORIAL APPENDIX

ACKNOWLEDGMENTS

Preparation of manuscripts for *Kierkegaard's Writings* is supported by a genuinely enabling grant from the National Endowment for the Humanities. The grant includes gifts from the Dronning Margrethe og Prins Henrik Fond, the Danish Ministry of Cultural Affairs, the Augustinus Fond, the Carlsberg Fond, the Konsul George Jorck og Hustru Emma Jorcks Fond, the Lutheran Brotherhood Foundation, and the A. P. Møller og Hustru Chastine Mc-Kinney Møllers Fond.

The translators-editors are indebted to Grethe Kjær and Julia Watkin for their knowledgeable observations on crucial concepts and terminology.

John Elrod, Per Lønning, and Sophia Scopetéa, members of the International Advisory Board for *Kierkegaard's Writings*, have given valuable criticism of the manuscript on the whole and in detail. Catherine Gjerdingen, Craig Mason, Robert L. Perkins, Jack Schwandt, Pamela Schwandt, and Julia Watkin have helpfully read the manuscript. The translations of German passages are by Rune Engebretsen and the Greek and Latin passages by James May and Christopher Smith. Robert F. Brown checked and corrected the special Schelling expressions. Kathryn Hong, copyeditor for *KW*, Kierkegaard Library, scrutinized the manuscript and prepared the index.

Acknowledgment is made to Gyldendals Forlag for permission to use the text and to absorb notes in *Søren Kierkegaard's samlede Værker* and *Søren Kierkegaards Papirer*. The texts for the Schelling lecture notes are the manuscript in the Kierkegaard Arkiv (*Pap*. III C 27, *Kollegie til Schellings Forelæsninger i Berlin over Aabenbaringen's Filosofi*, C. Pk. 4. Læg. 4), a transcript of the manuscripts, and, with the permission of the editor, Niels Thulstrup, *Pap*. III C 27 in supplemental vol. *Pap*. XIII, pp. 254-329.

Inclusion in the Supplement of entries from *Søren Kierke-*

gaard's Journals and Papers is by arrangement with Indiana University Press.

The book collection and the microfilm collection of the Kierkegaard Library, St. Olaf College, have been used in preparation of the text, notes, Supplement, and Editorial Appendix. Gregor Malantschuk's annotated set of *Kierkegaards samlede Værker* has been used in the preparation of the Supplement and notes.

The original manuscript was typed by Dorothy Bolton. Word processing of the final manuscript was done by Kennedy Lemke and Francesca Lane Rasmus. The volume has been guided through the press by Cathie Brettschneider.

COLLATION OF *THE CONCEPT OF IRONY* IN THE DANISH EDITIONS OF KIERKEGAARD'S COLLECTED WORKS

Vol. XIII Ed. 1 Pg.	*Vol. XIII Ed. 2 Pg.*	*Vol. 1 Ed. 3 Pg.*
95	103	59
96	104	60
97	105	61
99	107	63
100	107	63
101	109	65
105	113	69
106	114	69
107	115	70
108	116	71
109	118	73
110	118	73
111	119	74
112	121	75
113	122	76
114	123	77
115	124	78
116	126	79
117	126	79
118	127	80
119	128	81
120	129	82
121	130	83
122	131	84
123	132	85
124	133	85
125	134	86
126	135	87
127	136	88
128	137	89
129	139	90
130	139	91
131	140	92
132	141	92
133	142	93
134	143	94
135	144	95
136	145	96
137	146	97
138	148	98
139	149	99
140	150	100
141	151	101
142	152	102
143	153	103
144	155	104
145	156	105
146	157	106
147	158	106
148	159	107
149	160	108
150	161	109
151	162	110
152	163	111
153	164	112
154	166	113
155	167	114
156	168	115
157	169	116
158	170	117
159	171	118
160	173	119
161	174	120
162	175	121
163	176	122
164	177	123

Vol. XIII Ed. 1 Pg.	Vol. XIII Ed. 2 Pg.	Vol. 1 Ed. 3 Pg.	Vol. XIII Ed. 1 Pg.	Vol. XIII Ed. 2 Pg.	Vol. 1 Ed. 3 Pg.
165	178	124	207	223	161
166	179	125	208	224	162
167	180	125	209	225	163
168	181	126	210	226	164
169	183	127	211	228	165
170	184	128	212	229	166
171	185	129	213	230	167
172	186	130	214	231	168
173	187	131	215	232	169
174	188	132	216	233	170
175	189	133	217	234	171
176	190	133	218	235	172
177	191	134	219	236	172
178	192	135	220	237	173
179	193	136	221	238	174
180	194	137	222	240	175
181	196	138	223	241	176
182	197	139	224	242	177
183	197	140	225	243	178
184	198	141	226	243	178
185	199	142	227	245	179
186	201	143	228	245	180
187	202	143	229	247	181
188	202	144	230	247	181
189	203	145	231	248	182
190	204	146	232	249	183
191	205	147	233	250	184
192	207	147	234	252	185
193	208	148	235	253	186
194	209	149	236	253	187
195	210	150	237	254	187
196	211	151	238	256	188
197	212	152	239	257	189
198	213	153	240	258	190
199	215	154	241	259	191
200	215	155	242	260	192
201	216	156	243	260	192
202	218	157	244	261	193
203	219	158	245	263	194
204	220	159	246	264	195
205	221	160	247	265	196
206	222	160	248	266	197

Vol. XIII Ed. 1 Pg.	Vol. XIII Ed. 2 Pg.	Vol. 1 Ed. 3 Pg.	Vol. XIII Ed. 1 Pg.	Vol. XIII Ed. 2 Pg.	Vol. 1 Ed. 3 Pg.
249	267	198	291	313	236
250	268	199	292	313	237
251	269	200	293	315	238
252	270	200	294	316	239
253	271	201	295	317	240
254	272	202	296	318	241
255	273	203	297	319	242
256	274	204	298	321	243
257	275	205	299	321	244
258	276	206	300	322	244
259	277	206	301	323	245
260	278	207	302	324	246
261	280	208	303	325	247
262	281	209	304	327	248
263	282	210	305	328	249
264	283	211	306	329	250
265	284	212	307	330	251
266	285	213	308	331	252
267	286	214	309	332	252
268	288	215	310	333	253
269	289	216	311	335	254
270	290	217	312	336	255
271	291	218	313	337	256
272	292	219	317	341	259
273	293	220	318	342	259
274	294	221	319	343	260
275	295	221	320	344	261
276	296	222	321	345	262
277	298	223	322	346	263
278	299	224	323	347	264
279	300	226	324	348	265
280	300	226	325	350	266
281	302	227	326	351	267
282	303	228	327	352	268
283	304	229	328	353	269
284	305	230	329	354	270
285	306	231	330	355	271
286	307	232	331	356	271
287	309	233	332	357	272
288	309	234	333	359	274
289	311	235	334	360	275
290	311	235	335	361	276

Vol. XIII Ed. 1 Pg.	*Vol. XIII Ed. 2 Pg.*	*Vol. 1 Ed. 3 Pg.*
336	362	276
337	363	277
338	364	278
339	365	279
340	367	280
341	368	281
342	369	282
343	370	283
344	371	284
345	372	285
346	374	286
347	375	287
348	376	288
349	377	289
350	378	290
351	379	291
352	380	292
353	382	293
354	383	294
355	384	295
356	385	296
357	386	297
358	387	298
359	388	298
360	390	299
361	391	300
362	392	301
363	393	302
364	394	303
365	395	304
366	396	305
367	398	306
368	399	307
369	400	308
370	401	309
371	402	310
372	403	311
373	405	312
374	406	313
375	407	314
376	408	314
377	409	315
378	410	316
379	411	317
380	412	318
381	414	319
382	415	320
383	416	321
384	417	322
385	418	323
386	420	324
387	421	325
388	422	326
389	423	327
390	424	328
391	426	329
392	427	330
393	428	331

NOTES

THE CONCEPT OF IRONY

TITLE PAGE. For a range of entries on irony and on Socrates, see *JP* II 1669-1769; IV 4243-4304; VII, pp. 51-52, 88-89.

Part One

1. The date is a misprint for MDCCCXLI.

2. Frederik Christian Sibbern (1785-1872), professor of philosophy (1813-1870), University of Copenhagen, and dean of the philosophy faculty when Kierkegaard's dissertation was submitted. See *Letters*, Letters 55, 132, *KW* XXV. In 1838, Sibbern wrote a critique of Hegel's philosophy in the form of an extended review of Johan Ludvig Heiberg's *Perseus* (Copenhagen: 1837; *ASKB* 569) under the title *"Perseus, Journal for den speculative Idee. Udgiven af Johan Ludvig Heiberg. Nr. 1, Juni 1837. . . .—(Med stadigt Hensyn til Dr. Rothes: 'Læren om Treenighed og Forsoning'),"* *Maanedsskrift for Litteratur*, XIX-XX, 1838, pp. 283-360, 424-60, 546-82; 20-60, 103-36. The first three parts were published later the same year as a book under the title *Bemærkninger og Undersøgelser, fornemmelig betreffende Hegels Philosophie, betragtet i Forhold til vor Tid* (Copenhagen: 1838; *ASKB* 778).

3. On the degree, see Historical Introduction, pp. xii-xiii.

4. *XXIX* and *hora 10* (ten o'clock) are handwritten in the official copies containing the Latin theses. Copies available to the public do not contain the Latin theses. The colloquium was conducted in Latin and ran from 10:00 to 2:00 and from 4:00 to 7:30.

5. See Historical Introduction, p. xi; Corsair *Affair*, p. 91, *KW* XIII.

6. A misprint for MDCCCXLI (1841).

7. In his own copy of *Om Begrebet Ironi* (now in the Royal Library, Copenhagen), Kierkegaard wrote the following references to the theses (pagination adapted to the present volume and *Søren Kierkegaards samlede Værker*, 1 ed.): Thesis I, pp. 14, 220-21, 271 (*SV* XIII 110, 300, 344); II, pp. 15-27 (*SV* XIII 111-23); III, p. 127 (*SV* XIII 212); IV, pp. 32-40 (*SV* XIII 127-36); V, pp. 79-96 (*SV* XIII 171-84); VI, pp. 195-96 (*SV* XIII 277); VII, p. 154 fn. (*SV* XIII 238 fn.); XV, pp. 326-27 (*SV* XIII 390).

8. See Supplement, p. 443 (*Pap.* III B 12).

9. Cf., for example, Hegel, *Die Phänomenologie des Geistes, Georg Wilhelm Friedrich Hegel's Werke. Vollständige Ausgabe*, I-XVIII, ed. Philipp Marheineke et al. (Berlin: 1832-45: *ASKB* 549-65), II, p. 72; *Sämtliche Werke. Jubiläumsausgabe* [*J.A.*], I-XXVI, ed. Hermann Glockner (Stuttgart: Frommann, 1927-40), II, p. 80; *The Phenomenology of Mind* (tr. based primarily on *P.G.*, 3

ed., 1841; Kierkegaard had 2 ed., 1832), tr. J. B. Baillie (New York: Harper, 1967), p. 145:

> In pressing forward to its true form of existence, consciousness will come to a point at which it lays aside its semblance of being hampered with what is foreign to it, with what is only for it and exists as an other; it will reach a position where appearance becomes identified with essence, where, in consequence, its exposition coincides with just this very point, this very stage of the science proper of mind. And, finally, when it grasps this its own essence, it will connote the nature of absolute knowledge itself.

10. See pp. 5-6, Thesis X.

11. Cf., for example, Hegel, *Wissenschaft der Logik*, I, *Die objektive Logik*, *Werke*, III, p. 60; *J.A.*, IV, p. 70; *Hegel's Science of Logic* (tr. of *W.L.*, Lasson ed., 1923; Kierkegaard had 2 ed., 1833), tr. A. V. Miller (New York: Humanities, 1976), p. 67:

> It is only in recent times that thinkers have become aware of the difficulty of finding a beginning in philosophy, and the reason for this difficulty and also the possibility of resolving it has been much discussed. What philosophy begins with must be either *mediated* or *immediate*, and it is easy to show that it can be neither the one nor the other; thus either way of beginning is refuted.
>
> The *principle* of a philosophy does, of course, also express a beginning, but not so much a subjective as an *objective* one, the beginning of *everything*. . . . Thus the principle ought also to be the beginning, and what is the first [*prius*] for thought ought also to be the first in the *process* of thinking.

12. *Mellemværende* literally means "something between," an issue, a difference, an unsettled account. In a letter (8, p. 52) to Emil Boesen, Kierkegaard exploits aspects of the term. He also coined a word from it, *Mellemhverandre*, literally "between each other." The word is used in *Irony* on pp. 147, 180, 292. It also appears in a few other places, for example: *From the Papers*, *KW* I (*SV* XIII 68, 69 fn.); *Either/Or*, I, p. 126, *KW* III (*SV* I 105); *Two Ages*, p. 39, *KW* XIV (*SV* VIII 36); *Fear and Trembling*, p. 243 and note, *KW* VI; *JP* I 803; V 5659 (*Pap*. III A 94; IV B 78, provisional title of *Fear and Trembling*). The meaning of the term varies according to the context.

13. In Greek mythology, Lethe was the stream of oblivion in the lower world, from which souls drank before passing to Elysium, in order that they might forget all earthly sorrows. See Virgil, *Aeneid*, VI, 703-17; *Virgils Æneide*, tr. Johan Henrik Schønheyder (Copenhagen: 1812), pp. 291-92; *Virgil*, I-II, tr. H. Rushton Fairclough (Loeb, Cambridge: Harvard University Press, 1978), I, p. 555.

14. See Matthew 12:36; Hebrews 4:12.

15. Cf. *Schelling Lecture Notes*, p. 350 and note 37.

16. See, for example, Hegel, *Wissenschaft der Logik*, II, *Werke*, V, p. 45; *J.A.*, V, p. 45; *Science of Logic*, p. 607:

With respect to completeness, we have seen that the determinate side of particularity is *complete* in the difference of the *universal* and the *particular*, and that these two alone constitute the particular species. In *nature*, of course, there are to be found more than two species in a genus, just as between these many species there cannot exist the relationship we have just indicated. This is the impotence of nature, that it cannot adhere to and exhibit the strictness of the Notion and runs wild in this blind irrational [*begrifflos*] multiplicity. We can *wonder* at nature's manifold genera and species and the endless diversity of her formations, for *wonderment* is *unreasoning* and its object the irrational.

17. See J. L. Heiberg's review of Waldemar Henrik Rothe, *Læren om Treenighed og Forsoning*, in *Perseus*, 1 (see note 2 above), pp. 29-30 (ed. tr.): "But since the infinite cannot be realized in a progression through space and time, since, on the other hand, it may be realized intellectually, the place of the globe in the universe cannot stand in relation to or be the basis of its inhabitants' realization of the infinite . . . ." See also Heiberg, *"Gudstjeneste. En Foraars-Phantasie," Nye Digte* (Copenhagen: 1841; *ASKB* 1562), pp. 1-27, which closes with lines about nature and the poet who "in lyrics sings forth its longings [*Længseler*]." The last sentence in *Irony* is a reference to Heiberg's *Nye Digte* and H. L. Martensen's review of the work.

18. Cf. I Corinthians 13:12.

19. See, for example, Plato, *Symposium*, 220 c-d; *Platonis quae exstant opera*, I-XI, ed. Friedrich Ast (Leipzig: 1819-32; *ASKB* 1144-54), III, pp. 540-41; *Udvalgte Dialoger af Platon*, I-VIII, tr. Carl Johan Heise (Copenhagen: 1830-59; *ASKB* 1164-67, 1169 [I-VII]), II, pp. 97-98; *The Collected Dialogues of Plato*, ed. Edith Hamilton and Huntington Cairns (Princeton: Princeton University Press, 1963), p. 571 (Alcibiades speaking):

> And now I must tell you about another thing 'our valiant hero dared and did' in the course of the same campaign. He started wrestling with some problem or other about sunrise one morning, and stood there lost in thought, and when the answer wouldn't come he still stood there thinking and refused to give it up. Time went on, and by about midday the troops noticed what was happening, and naturally they were rather surprised and began telling each other how Socrates had been standing there thinking ever since daybreak. And at last, toward nightfall, some of the Ionians brought out their bedding after supper—this was in the summer, of course—partly because it was cooler in the open air, and partly to see whether he was going to stay there all night. Well, there he stood till morning, and then at sunrise he said his prayers to the sun and went away.

In the dissertation, some Plato quotations are from the Heise Danish translations available at the time (English translations from the Danish are by the editors). Other Plato quotations in the text are in Greek (English translations are from the Hamilton-Cairns edition).

20. See, for example, *JP* I 648-57 (*Pap.* VIII² B 79, 81-89), drafts of lectures on communication.

21. See, for example, the opening lines of *Either/Or*, I, p. 3, *KW* III (*SV* I v); Hegel, *Wissenschaft der Logik*, I, *Werke*, IV, pp. 177-80; *J.A.*, IV, pp. 655-58; *Science of Logic*, pp. 526-28, especially p. 528:

> Conversely, it follows from this that each of the differences of form, the inner and outer, is posited within itself as the totality of itself and its other; the inner, as simple identity reflected into itself, is the immediate and accordingly is as much being and externality as essence; and the outer, as manifold, determinate being is only an outer, that is, is posited as unessential and as withdrawn into its ground, hence as an inner. This transition of each into the other is their immediate identity as substrate; but it is also their mediated identity; for it is precisely through its other that each is what it is in itself, the totality of the relation.

22. See Supplement, pp. 443-44 (*Pap.* III B 14).

23. See, for example, Hegel, *Vorlesungen über die Aesthetik*, I, *Werke*, X[1], p. 87; *J.A.*, XII, p. 103; *The Philosophy of Fine Art*, I-IV (tr. of *V.A.*, 1 ed., 1835-38; Kierkegaard had this ed.), tr. F.P.B. Osmaston (London: Bell, 1920), I, pp. 90-91:

> The proximate form of this negativity which has been called irony is, then, on the one hand, the illusory nature of all that is matter of fact, or moral, or of substantive content, the nothingness of all that is objective and of essential and independent worth. So long as the Ego adheres to such a standpoint as this, everything appears to be null and void, the personal subjectivity alone excepted, which thereby becomes hollow and empty, and nothing but conceit itself.

24. In Scandinavia, an elflike household creature, benevolent if treated properly, vexatious otherwise, and, according to some traditions, invisible when wearing his pointed red stocking cap.

25. Ferdinand Christian Baur, *Tübinger Zeitschrift für Theologie*, 3, 1837 (*ASKB* 422), pp. 90-154 (excerpts ed. tr.).

26. Xenophon, *Memorabilia*, III, 14, 1-3; *Xenophontis memorabilia Socratis cum apologia Socratis*, ed. Friedrich A. Bornemann (Leipzig: 1829; *ASKB* 1211), p. 247; *Xenophon Memorabilia and Oeconomicus*, tr. E. C. Marchant (Loeb, New York: Putnam, 1923), p. 259:

> Whenever some of the members of a dining-club brought more meat than others, Socrates would tell the waiter either to put the small contribution into the common stock or to portion it out equally among the diners. So the high batteners felt obliged not only to take their share of the pool, but to pool their own supplies in return; and so they put their own supplies also into the common stock. And since they thus got no more than those who brought little with them, they gave up spending much on meat.
>
> He observed on one occasion that one of the company at dinner had

> ceased to take bread, and ate the meat by itself. Now the talk was of names and the actions to which they are properly applied. "Can we say, my friends," said Socrates, "what is the nature of the action for which a man is called greedy? For all, I presume, eat meat with their bread when they get the chance: but I don't think there is so far any reason for calling them greedy?"
>
> "No, certainly not," said one of the company.
>
> "Well, suppose he eats the meat alone, without the bread, not because he's in training, but to tickle his palate, does he seem a greedy fellow or not?"
>
> "If not, it's hard to say who does," was the reply.
>
> Here another of the company queried, "And he who eats a scrap of bread with a large helping of meat?"
>
> "He too seems to me to deserve the epithet," said Socrates.

27. See p. 159.

28. Cf. *Philosophical Fragments, or a Fragment of Philosophy*, passim, especially ch. IV, *KW* VII (*SV* IV).

29. See John 14:6.

30. See Luke 10:24; Matthew 13:17.

31. Erasmus writes that Socrates was supposed to have said this to a boy. See *Apophthegmata*, III, 70, *Opera*, I-VIII (Basel: 1540), IV, p. 148 (ed. tr.):

> Quum diues quidam filium adolescentulum ad Socratem misisset, ut indolem illius inspiceret, ac paedagogus diceret, Pater ad te, O Socrates, misit filium, ut eum videres: tum Socrates ad puerum, Loquere igitur, inquit, adolescens, ut te videam: significans, ingenium hominis non tam in uultu relucere, quam in oratione, quod hoc sit certissimum [When a certain wealthy man had sent his very young son to Socrates to observe his genius, and his slave said, "His father sent his son to you in order that you might see him, Socrates": thereupon Socrates said to the boy, "Speak, lad, so that I may see you": thus signifying that the character of a man comes to light not so much in his countenance as in his manner of speaking, in that this is most certain] . . ..

See also Johann Georg Hamann, *Aesthetica in Nuce, Hamann's Schriften*, I-VIII, ed. Friedrich Roth and G. A. Wiener (Berlin, Leipzig: 1821-43; *ASKB* 536-44), II, pp. 261-62 (ed. tr.): "*Rede, daszich Dichsehe!* . . . *Reden ist übersetzen* [*Speak, so that I may see you!* . . . Speaking is *translating*]." See *Either/Or*, II, p. 275, *KW* IV (*SV* II 246); *Stages on Life's Way*, pp. 398, 484, *KW* XI (*SV* VI 371, 450); *Letters*, Letter 8, *KW* XXV; *JP* II 2115 (*Pap.* VI B 53:16).

32. A wish that was fulfilled in *Fragments*, *KW* VII (*SV* IV 173-272).

33. See pp. 5-6, Thesis I.

34. See, for example, Xenophon, *Memorabilia*, I, 1, 20-I, 2, 1 and I, 2, 62; Bornemann, pp. 13-14, 40; Loeb, pp. 13, 43:

I wonder, then, how the Athenians can have been persuaded that Socrates was a freethinker, when he never said or did anything contrary to sound religion, and his utterances about the gods and his behaviour towards them were the words and actions of a man who is truly religious and deserves to be thought so.

No less wonderful is it to me that some believed the charge brought against Socrates of corrupting the youth.

Such was the character of Socrates. To me he seemed to deserve honour rather than death at the hands of the State. And a consideration of his case in its legal aspect will confirm my opinion.

35. An allusion to Gottfried Wilhelm Leibniz, *Monadology*, 78; *God. Guil. Leibnitii opera philosophica*, I-II, ed. Johann Eduard Erdmann (Berlin: 1840; *ASKB* 620), II, p. 711; *Leibniz: The Monadology and Other Philosophical Writings*, tr. Robert Latta (London: Oxford University Press, 1965), pp. 262-63:

These principles have given me a way of explaining naturally the union or rather the mutual agreement . . . of the soul and the organic body. The soul follows its own laws, and the body likewise follows its own laws; and they agree with each other in virtue of the *preestablished harmony* between all substances, since they are all representations of one and the same universe.

See pp. 27, 172; *Either/Or*, I, p. 359, *KW* III (*SV* I 328); II, p. 20, *KW* IV (*SV* II 19); *Fear and Trembling*, p. 45, *KW* VI (*SV* III 95).

36. See John 5:2-9.

37. See pp. 149-51.

38. Presumably an allusion to the Pythagoreans' idea of "the music of the spheres," the cosmic harmony of the octave of the earth, sun, moon, and the five then-known planets.

39. See Plutarch, "Aristides," 7, *Lives*; *Plutark's Levnetsbeskrivelser*, I-IV, tr. Stephan Tetens (Copenhagen: 1800-11; *ASKB* 1197-1200), III, pp. 339-43; *Plutarch's Lives*, I-XI, tr. Bernadotte Perrin (Loeb, Cambridge: Harvard University Press, 1968-84), II, pp. 233-35:

Now at the time of which I was speaking, as the voters were inscribing their *ostraka*, it is said that an unlettered and utterly boorish fellow handed his *ostrakon* to Aristides, whom he took to be one of the ordinary crowd, and asked him to write *Aristides* on it. He, astonished, asked the man what possible wrong Aristides had done him. "None whatever," was the answer, "I don't even know the fellow, but I am tired of hearing him everywhere called 'The Just.' "

See also *Two Ages*, p. 83, *KW* XIV (*SV* VIII 78).

40. Cf. a letter from Ludwig Tieck to Karl Wilhelm Ferdinand Solger, March 24, 1817, *Solgers nachgelassene Schriften und Briefwechsel*, I-II, ed. Ludwig Tieck and Friedrich v. Raumer (Leipzig: 1826; *ASKB* 1832-33), I, p. 558.

Tieck writes of his dialogue with Friedrich Heinrich Jacobi, in which "we heard the echo more than our words." Hegel touches on this letter in his review of the Solger edition in *Vermischte Schriften aus der Berliner Zeit, Werke*, XVI, p. 458; *J.A.*, XX, p. 154.

41. *Dansk Folkeblad*, a paper published by the Society for the Proper Use of Freedom of the Press, 1835-48.

42. An allusion to Per Degn, a comic character in Ludvig Holberg's *Erasmus Montanus eller Rasmus Berg*. In I, 4, Per Degn boasts that he had sung the *Credo* more loudly than any of ten other contestants. See Holberg, *Den Danske Skue-Plads*, I-VII (Copenhagen: 1788; *ASKB* 1566-67), V, no pagination; *Comedies by Holberg*, tr. Oscar James Campbell, Jr., and Frederic Schenck (New York: American-Scandinavian Foundation, 1914), pp. 126-27.

43. Xenophon, *Memorabilia*, I, 1, 8; Bornemann, pp. 6-7; Loeb, pp. 5-6.

44. See I Corinthians 3:9.

45. See Xenophon, *Memorabilia*, I, 2, 36; Bornemann, p. 29; Loeb, p. 29.

46. See pp. 147-48.

47. See Xenophon, *Memorabilia*, I, 2, 32-38; Bornemann, pp. 28-29; Loeb, pp. 27-31:

> When the Thirty were putting to death many citizens of the highest respectability and were encouraging many in crime, Socrates had remarked: "It seems strange enough to me that a herdsman who lets his cattle decrease and go to the bad should not admit that he is a poor cowherd; but stranger still that a statesman when he causes the citizens to decrease and go to the bad, should feel no shame nor think himself a poor statesman." This remark was reported to Critias and Charicles, who sent for Socrates, showed him the law and forbade him to hold conversation with the young. . . .
>
> "But you see, Socrates," explained Critias, "you will have to avoid your favourite topic,—the cobblers, builders and metal workers; for it is already worn to rags by you in my opinion."
>
> "Then must I keep off the subjects of which these supply illustrations, Justice, Holiness, and so forth?"
>
> "Indeed yes," said Charicles, "and cowherds too: else *you* may find the cattle decrease."
>
> Thus the truth was out: the remark about the cattle had been repeated to them: and it was this that made them angry with him.

48. See p. 12, note 22 above, and *JP* IV 4392 (*Pap.* I A 313).

49. This phrase reappears with crucial significance in Kierkegaard's later writing. See, for example, *Sickness unto Death*, pp. 99, 117, 121, *KW* XIX (*SV* XI 210, 227, 231); *JP* III 3645-50 (*Pap.* X^2 A 296; X^3 A 23; X^4 A 258; XI^1 A 2, 67, 495); VII, p. 78.

50. Aristippus (c. 425-366 B.C.), Greek hedonistic philosopher who taught that prudence should govern the search for pleasure lest pain be the result.

51. See, for example, the launching of the extended discussion of justice in

Plato, *Republic*, I, 328 e-331 c; *Opera*, IV, pp. 6-13; *Dialogues*, pp. 578-80 (Socrates conversing with Cephalus, an old man):

> Why, yes, Cephalus, said I, and I enjoy talking with the very aged. For to my thinking we have to learn of them as it were from wayfarers who have preceded us on a road on which we too, it may be, must sometime fare—what it is like. Is it rough and hard-going or easy and pleasant to travel? And so now I would fain learn of you what you think of this thing, now that your time has come to it, the thing that the poets call 'the threshold of old age.' Is it a hard part of life to bear or what report have you to make of it?
>
> Yes, indeed, Socrates, he said, I will tell you my own feeling about it. . . .
>
> And I was filled with admiration for the man by these words, and desirous of hearing more I tried to draw him out and said, I fancy, Cephalus, that most people, when they hear you talk in this way, are not convinced but think that you bear old age lightly not because of your character but because of your wealth, for the rich, they say, have many consolations. . . .
>
> May I ask, Cephalus, said I, whether you inherited most of your possessions or acquired them yourself? . . .
>
> But tell me further this. What do you regard as the greatest benefit you have enjoyed from the possession of property? . . .
>
> It is for this, then, that I affirm that the possession of wealth is of most value, not it may be to every man but to the good man. Not to cheat any man even unintentionally or play him false, not remaining in debt to a god for some sacrifice or to a man for money, so to depart in fear to that other world—to this result the possession of property contributes not a little. It has also many other uses. But, setting one thing against another, I would lay it down, Socrates, that for a man of sense this is the chief service of wealth.
>
> An admirable sentiment, Cephalus, said I. But speaking of this very thing, justice, are we to affirm thus without qualification that it is truth-telling and paying back what one has received from anyone, or may these very actions sometimes be just and sometimes unjust?

52. Literally, the Danish *slet* and the German *schlecht* mean "bad." Hegel translators use "spurious" (Miller), "wrong" (Wallace), and "false" (Haldane and Simson). See, for example, Hegel, *Encyclopädie der philosophischen Wissenschaften im Grundrisse*, I, *Die Logik*, 94 and *Zusatz*, *Werke*, VI, pp. 184-85; *J.A.*, VIII, pp. 222-23; *Hegel's Logic* (tr. of *L.*, 3 ed., 1830; Kierkegaard had this ed.), tr. William Wallace (Oxford: Oxford University Press, 1975), pp. 137-38:

> This **Infinity** is the wrong or negative infinity: it is only a negation of a finite: but the finite rises again the same as ever, and is never got rid of and absorbed. In other words, this infinite only expresses the *ought-to-be* elimination of the finite. The progression to infinity never gets further than a

statement of the contradiction involved in the finite, viz. that it is somewhat as well as somewhat else. It sets up with endless iteration the alternation between these two terms, each of which calls up the other.

If we let somewhat and another, the elements of determinate Being, fall asunder, the result is that some becomes other, and this other is itself a somewhat, which then as such changes likewise, and so on *ad infinitum*. This result seems to superficial reflection something very grand, the grandest possible. But such a progression to infinity is not the real infinite. That consists in being at home with itself in its other, or, if enunciated as a process, in coming to itself in its other. Much depends on rightly apprehending the notion of infinity, and not stopping short at the wrong infinity of endless progression. When time and space, for example, are spoken of as infinite, it is in the first place the infinite progression on which our thoughts fasten. We say, Now, This time, and then we keep continually going forwards and backwards beyond this limit. The case is the same with space, the infinity of which has formed the theme of barren declamation to astronomers with a talent for edification. In the attempt to contemplate such an infinite, our thought, we are commonly informed, must sink exhausted. It is true indeed that we must abandon the unending contemplation, not however because the occupation is too sublime, but because it is too tedious. It is tedious to expatiate in the contemplation of this infinite progression, because the same thing is constantly recurring. We lay down a limit: then we pass it: next we have a limit once more, and so on for ever. All this is but superficial alternation, which never leaves the region of the finite behind. To suppose that by stepping out and away into that infinity we release ourselves from the finite, is in truth but to seek the release which comes by flight. But the man who flees is not yet free: in fleeing he is still conditioned by that from which he flees. If it be also said that the infinite is unattainable, the statement is true, but only because to the idea of infinity has been attached the circumstance of being simply and solely negative. With such empty and other-world stuff philosophy has nothing to do.

53. Xenophon, *Memorabilia*, IV, 7, 2, treats geometry; IV, 7, 4, astronomy; IV, 7, 6, is a warning against Anaxagoras. Bornemann, pp. 314-15, 316, 318; Loeb, pp. 347, 349, 349-51.

54. Plato, *Republic*, 526 d-e; *Opera*, IV, pp. 404-05; *Dialogues*, p. 758 (Glaucon and Socrates conversing):

> So much of it [geometry], he [Glaucon] said, as applies to the conduct of war is obviously suitable. For in dealing with encampments and the occupation of strong places and the bringing of troops into column and line and all the other formations of an army in actual battle and on the march, an officer who had studied geometry would be a very different person from what he would be if he had not.
>
> But still, I said, for such purposes a slight modicum of geometry and calculation would suffice. What we have to consider is whether the greater

and more advanced part of it tends to facilitate the apprehension of the idea of good. That tendency, we affirm, is to be found in all studies that force the soul to turn its vision round to the region where dwells the most blessed part of reality, which it is imperative that it should behold.

You are right, he said.

Then if it compels the soul to contemplate essence, it is suitable; if genesis, it is not.

So we affirm.

55. Most likely *Memorabilia*, I, 3, 14 should read III, 11, 5.

56. Plato, *Phaedrus*, 249 a; *Opera*, I, pp. 176-77; *Dialogues*, p. 495.

57. See Plato, *Symposium*, 177 d-e; *Opera*, III, pp. 442-43; Heise, II, p. 14; *Dialogues*, p. 532:

> The motion is carried, Eryximachus, said Socrates, unanimously, I should think. Speaking for myself, I couldn't very well dissent when I claim that love is the one thing in the world I understand—nor could Agathon and Pausanias; neither could Aristophanes, whose whole life is devoted to Dionysus and Aphrodite; no more could any of our friends who are here with us tonight.

58. See Plato, *Symposium*, 220 a; Heise, II, p. 97; cf. *Dialogues*, p. 571.

59. See Plato, *Symposium*, 223 c-d; *Opera*, III, pp. 546-48; Heise, II, pp. 103-04; *Dialogues*, pp. 573-74.

60. See Xenophon, *Socrates' Defense to the Jury* [*Apology*], 2-7; Bornemann, pp. 333-37; *Xenophon Anabasis Symposium and Apology*, tr. Carleton L. Brownson and O. J. Todd (Loeb, New York: Putnam, 1922), pp. 489-91:

> Hermogenes, the son of Hipponicus, however, was a companion of his and has given us reports of such a nature as to show that the sublimity of his speech was appropriate to the resolve he had made. For he stated that on seeing Socrates discussing any and every subject rather than the trial, he had said: "Socrates, ought you not to be giving some thought to what defence you are going to make?" That Socrates had at first replied, "Why, do I not seem to you to have spent my whole life in preparing to defend myself?" Then when he asked, "How so?" he had said, "Because all my life I have been guiltless of wrong-doing; and that I consider the finest preparation for a defence." Then when Hermogenes again asked, "Do you not observe that the Athenian courts have often been carried away by an eloquent speech and have condemned innocent men to death, and often on the other hand the guilty have been acquitted either because their plea aroused compassion or because their speech was witty?" "Yes, indeed!" he had answered; "and I have tried twice already to meditate on my defence, but my divine sign interposes." And when Hermogenes observed, "That is a surprising statement," he had replied, "Do you think it surprising that even God holds it better for me to die now? Do you not know that I would refuse to concede that any man has lived a better life than I have up to now? For I

> have realized that my whole life has been spent in righteousness toward God and man,—a fact that affords the greatest satisfaction; and so I have felt a deep self-respect and have discovered that my associates hold corresponding sentiments toward me. But now, if my years are prolonged, I know that the frailties of old age will inevitably be realized,—that my vision must be less perfect and my hearing less keen, that I shall be slower to learn and more forgetful of what I have learned. If I perceive my decay and take to complaining, how," he had continued, "could I any longer take pleasure in life? Perhaps," he added, "God in his kindness is taking my part and securing me the opportunity of ending my life not only in season but also in the way that is easiest. For if I am condemned now, it will clearly be my privilege to suffer a death that is adjudged by those who have superintended this matter to be not only the easiest but also the least irksome to one's friends and one that implants in them the deepest feeling of loss for the dead."

See also Xenophon, *Memorabilia*, IV, 8, 4-8; Bornemann, pp. 322-26; Loeb, pp. 355-57; *For Self-Examination*, *KW* XXI (*SV* XII 301-02).

61. Christiansfeld is a small Danish town in southern Jutland. There the colony of Moravian Brethren (*Herrnhuter Brüdergemeinde*) established schools to which members sent their children. Kierkegaard's father and the family of Emil Boesen, Kierkegaard's closest friend, were associated with the group in Copenhagen during Kierkegaard's early years.

62. See Plato, *Symposium*, 179 d; *Opera*, III, pp. 446-49; Heise, II, pp. 17-18; *Dialogues*, pp. 533-34:

> Thus heaven itself has a peculiar regard for ardor and resolution in the cause of Love. And yet the gods sent Orpheus away from Hades empty-handed, and showed him the mere shadow of the woman he had come to seek. Eurydice herself they would not let him take, because he seemed, like the mere minstrel that he was, to be a lukewarm lover, lacking the courage to die as Alcestis died for love, and choosing rather to scheme his way, living, into Hades. And it was for this that the gods doomed him, and doomed him justly, to meet his death at the hands of women.

See p. 412 and note 141.

63. A sound picture produced in sand by the nodal lines of a vibrating plate. Named after the German physicist Ernst Florens Friedrich Chladni (1756-1827). See *Entdeckungen über die Theorie des Klanges* (Leipzig: 1787), plates I-XI at end.

64. See Hegel, *Aesthetik*, I, *Werke*, X^1, pp. 89-90, 205; *J.A.*, XII, pp. 105-06, 221; *Philosophy of Fine Art*, I, pp. 93-94, 217:

> Solger was not, as the others were, satisfied with a superficial philosophical culture. A truly speculative impulse of his innermost nature made him probe the very depths of the philosophical idea. And in doing so he came upon the dialectical phase of the Idea, that transition point which I call the

infinite absolute negativity, the activity of the idea in its negation of itself as infinite and universal, in order to pass into finiteness and particularity, and with no less truth once more in order to annul this negation, and in so doing to establish again the universal and infinite within the finite and particular. Solger did not get beyond this negativity; and unquestionably it is a *phase* in the speculative idea; but nevertheless, as exclusively conceived in this dialectic unrest and dissolution of the infinite no less than the finite, it is *only* such a phase contributory, and not, as Solger imagined, the *Entire Idea*.

No doubt we find in irony that absolute principle of negativity, in which the subject of consciousness becomes self-centred through the annihilation of definite relations and particulars; but in this case the act of annihilation of definite relations and particulars, as we have already pointed out when discussing the principle, is not, as in comedy, essentially in its right place, simply exposing its own want of substance, but is directed quite as often against everything else excellent in itself and of sterling worth. Whether we regard irony, then, as this art of universal destruction, or as the yearning of which we have spoken in contrast with the true Ideal, it betrays a secret lack of proportion and restraint which is detrimental to the artist.

65. Should be Callicles. See next note.

66. Plato, *Gorgias*, 490 d-491 a; *Opera*, I, pp. 372-73; Heise, III, p. 111; *Dialogues*, p. 273:

SOCRATES: Well then, the best and wisest expert in shoes should obviously have the advantage in them. The cobbler, I suppose, should have the largest and most numerous shoes in which to walk around.

CALLICLES: Shoes! You keep talking nonsense.

SOCRATES: Well, if that is not what you mean, here it is perhaps. A farmer for instance who is an expert with good sound knowledge about the soil should have a larger share of seed and use the most seed possible on his own land.

CALLICLES: How you keep saying the same things, Socrates!

SOCRATES: Not only that, Callicles, but about the same matters.

67. See J. L. Heiberg, *Alferne*, II, *J. L. Heibergs samlede Skrifter. Skuespil*, I-VII (Copenhagen: 1833-41; *ASKB* 1553-59), VI, pp. 24-30.

68. Xenophon, *Memorabilia*, IV, 4; Bornemann, pp. 286-99; Loeb, pp. 309-25.

69. See note 35 above.

70. See James 1:17, Kierkegaard's favorite Biblical text; *JP* VI 6965 (*Pap.* XI^3 B 291:4). See also *Two Upbuilding Discourses* (1843), II, and *Four Upbuilding Discourses* (1843), II, III, in *Eighteen Upbuilding Discourses, KW* V (*SV* III 35-52; IV 24-53); *The Changelessness of God*, in The Moment *and Late Writings, KW* XXIII (*SV* XIV 277-94); *JP* III 3395; VI 6666, 6769, 6800 (*Pap.* IV B 175; X^3 A 391; X^4 A 323, 540).

71. An adaptation of lines from Abraham à St. Clara (Ulrich Megerle, 1644-1709), *Abraham à St. Clara's sämmtliche Werke*, I-XXII (Passau, Lindau: 1835-54; *ASKB* 294-311), VIII, p. 14, which is cited in a note to *JP* I 265 (*Pap.* II A 12). Cf. a letter from Lessing to his brother Karl Gotthelf Lessing, January 5, 1778, *Gotthold Ephraim Lessing's sämmtliche Schriften*, I-XXXII (Berlin, Stettin: 1825-28; *ASKB* 1747-62), XXVIII, pp. 327-28. See also *Either/Or*, I, p. 40, *KW* III (*SV* I 24).

72. See p. 201 fn.; Supplement, pp. 438-39 (*Pap.* III B 2). The manuscript preface may have been intended provisionally for the section on Plato.

73. Sallust, *Catalina*, X, 5; *Sallusts Catilinariske Krig*, tr. Rasmus Møller (Copenhagen: 1811; *ASKB* 1273), pp. 15-16; *Sallust*, tr. J. C. Rolfe (Loeb, New York: Putnam, 1921), p. 19: "Ambition drove many men to become false; to have one thought locked in the breast, another ready on the tongue; to value friendships and enmities not on their merits but by the standard of self-interest, and to show a good front rather than a good heart."

74. In grammar, *casus* [case] is the form that governs the relation of a word to another word. In Hebrew grammar, the idea of the genitive or possessive case is indicated by placing the noun possessed directly before the noun that is the possessor, as in the English construction "the hand of the man." The noun possessed is said to be in the *status constructus*; the second noun or possessor is in the *status absolutus*. See *Fragments*, p. 100, *KW* VII (*SV* IV 262); *Pap.* V B 6:22.

75. On this important term and category in later writings and in the *Papirer*, see, for example, *Fear and Trembling*, p. 36 and note 20, *KW* VI (*SV* III 87); *Fragments*, p. 43, *KW* VII (*SV* IV 211); *JP* III 2338-59 and p. 794; VII, p. 56. See also Lessing, "*Ueber den Beweis des Geistes und der Kraft*," *Schriften*, V, pp. 82-83; *Lessing's Theological Writings*, ed. and tr. Henry Chadwick (Stanford: Stanford University Press, 1967), p. 55.

76. See John 20:22.

77. See Matthew 9:5.

78. Plato, *Symposium*, 181 d; Heise, II, p. 21; cf. *Dialogues*, p. 535.

79. See John 4:14.

80. See Plato, *Theaetetus*, 149 a-b, 150 b-d; *Opera*, II, pp. 22-25, 26-27; *Dialogues*, pp. 853-55:

> SOCRATES: How absurd of you, never to have heard that I am the son of a midwife, a fine buxom woman called Phaenarete!
>
> THEAETETUS: I have heard that.
>
> SOCRATES: Have you also been told that I practice the same art?
>
> THEAETETUS: No, never.
>
> SOCRATES: It is true, though; only don't give away my secret. It is not known that I possess this skill; so the ignorant world describes me in other terms as an eccentric person who reduces people to hopeless perplexity. Have you been told that too?
>
> THEAETETUS: I have.
>
> SOCRATES: Shall I tell you the reason?

THEAETETUS: Please do.

SOCRATES: Consider, then, how it is with all midwives; that will help you to understand what I mean. I dare say you know that they never attend other women in childbirth so long as they themselves can conceive and bear children, but only when they are too old for that. . . .

SOCRATES: All this, then, lies within the midwife's province, but her performance falls short of mine. It is not the way of women sometimes to bring forth real children, sometimes mere phantoms, such that it is hard to tell the one from the other. If it were so, the highest and noblest task of the midwife would be to discern the real from the unreal, would it not?

THEAETETUS: I agree.

SOCRATES: My art of midwifery is in general like theirs; the only difference is that my patients are men, not women, and my concern is not with the body but with the soul that is in travail of birth. And the highest point of my art is the power to prove by every test whether the offspring of a young man's thought is a false phantom or instinct with life and truth. I am so far like the midwife that I cannot myself give birth to wisdom, and the common reproach is true, that though I question others, I can myself bring nothing to light because there is no wisdom in me. The reason is this. Heaven constrains me to serve as a midwife, but has debarred me from giving birth. So of myself I have no sort of wisdom, nor has any discovery ever been born to me as the child of my soul. Those who frequent my company at first appear, some of them, quite unintelligent, but, as we go further with our discussions, all who are favored by heaven make progress at a rate that seems surprising to others as well as to themselves, although it is clear that they have never learned anything from me. The many admirable truths they bring to birth have been discovered by themselves from within. But the delivery is heaven's work and mine.

81. See Plato, *Phaedo*, 75 b-e; *Meno*, 81 c-d; *Opera*, I, pp. 514-15; IX, pp. 224-25; Heise, I, pp. 37-38 (*Phaedo*; Heise does not include *Meno*); *Dialogues*, pp. 58-59 (Socrates and Simmias conversing), 364 (Socrates speaking):

Did we not begin to see and hear and possess our other senses from the moment of birth?

Certainly.

But we admitted that we must have obtained our knowledge of equality before we obtained them.

Yes.

So we must have obtained it before birth.

So it seems.

Then if we obtained it before our birth, and possessed it when we were born, we had knowledge, both before and at the moment of birth, not only of equality and relative magnitudes, but of all absolute standards. Our present argument applies no more to equality than it does to absolute beauty, goodness, uprightness, holiness, and, as I maintain, all those characteristics which we designate in our discussions by the term 'absolute.' So we must have obtained knowledge of all these characteristics before our birth.

That is so.

And unless we invariably forget it after obtaining it we must always be born *knowing* and continue to *know* all through our lives, because 'to know' means simply to retain the knowledge which one has acquired, and not to lose it. Is not what we call 'forgetting' simply the loss of knowledge, Simmias?

Most certainly, Socrates.

Thus the soul, since it is immortal and has been born many times, and has seen all things both here and in the other world, has learned everything that is. So we need not be surprised if it can recall the knowledge of virtue or anything else which, as we see, it once possessed. All nature is akin, and the soul has learned everything, so that when a man has recalled a single piece of knowledge—*learned* it, in ordinary language—there is no reason why he should not find out all the rest, if he keeps a stout heart and does not grow weary of the search, for seeking and learning are in fact nothing but recollection.

And if it is true that we acquired our knowledge before our birth, and lost it at the moment of birth, but afterward, by the exercise of our senses upon sensible objects, recover the knowledge which we had once before, I suppose that what we call learning will be the recovery of our own knowledge, and surely we should be right in calling this recollection.

See, for example, *Fragments*, pp. 9-21, 96, *KW* VII (*SV* IV 179-90, 259); *Stages*, pp. 8-19, *KW* XI (*SV* VI 15-24); *Postscript*, *KW* XII (*SV* VII 229-32, 465-68).

82. Diogenes Laertius, *Lives of Eminent Philosophers*, III, 49-50; *Diogenis Laertii de vitis philosophorum libri X*, I-II (Leipzig: 1833; *ASKB* 1109), I, pp. 161-63; *Diogen Laërtses filosofiske Historie*, I-II, tr. Børge Riisbrigh (Copenhagen: 1812; *ASKB* 1110-11), I, pp. 138-39; *Lives of Eminent Philosophers*, I-II, tr. R. D. Hicks (Loeb, Cambridge: Harvard University Press, 1979-80), I, p. 321:

Of the Platonic dialogues there are two most general types, the one adapted for instruction and the other for inquiry. And the former is further divided into two types, the theoretical and the practical. And of these the theoretical is divided into the physical and logical, and the practical into the ethical and political. The dialogue of inquiry also has two main divisions, the one of which aims at training the mind and the other at victory in controversy. Again, the part which aims at training the mind has two subdivisions, the one akin to the midwife's art, the other merely tentative. And that suited to controversy is also subdivided into one part which raises critical objections, and another which is subversive of the main position.

I am not unaware that there are other ways in which certain writers classify the dialogues. For some dialogues they call dramatic, others narrative, and others again a mixture of the two. But the terms they employ in their classification of the dialogues are better suited to the stage than to philosophy.

83. See p. 13 fn.

84. See p. 13 fn.

85. See, for example, J. L. Heiberg, *Ledetraad ved Forelæsningerne over Philosophiens Philosophie eller den speculative Logik*, 13-16 (pr. as ms., Copenhagen: 1831-32), *Johan Ludvig Heibergs Prosaiske Skrifter*, I-XI (Copenhagen: 1861-62), I, pp. 120-22; Hegel, *Wissenschaft der Logik*, II, *Werke*, V, pp. 344-45; *J.A.*, V, pp. 344-45; *Science of Logic*, pp. 836-37:

> In this turning point of the method, the course of cognition at the same time returns into itself. As self-sublating contradiction this negativity is the *restoration* of the *first immediacy*, of simple universality; for the other of the other, the negative of the negative, is immediately the *positive*, the *identical*, the *universal*. If one insists on *counting*, this *second* immediate is, in the course of the method as a whole, the *third* term to the first immediate and the mediated. It is also, however, the third term to the first or formal negative and to absolute negativity or the second negative; now as the first negative is already the second term, the term reckoned as *third* can also be reckoned as *fourth*, and instead of a *triplicity*, the abstract form may be taken as a *quadruplicity*; in this way, the negative or the difference is counted as a *duality*. The third or fourth is in general the unity of the first and second moments, of the immediate and the mediated. That it is this *unity*, as also that the whole form of the method is a *triplicity*, is, it is true, merely the superficial external side of the mode of cognition; but to have demonstrated even this, and that too in a more specific application—for it is well known that the abstract number form itself was advanced at quite an early period, but, in the absence of the Notion, without result—must also be regarded as an infinite merit of the Kantian philosophy. . . .
>
> Now more precisely the *third* is the immediate, but the immediate *resulting from sublation of mediation*, the simple resulting from *sublation of difference*, the positive resulting from sublation of the negative, the Notion that has realized itself by means of its otherness and by the sublation of this reality has become united with itself, and has restored its absolute reality, its *simple* relation to itself. This *result* is therefore the *truth*.

86. See pp. 100-09.

87. Cf. Plato, *Protagoras*, 337 e-338 a; Heise, II, p. 167; *Dialogues*, p. 332 (Hippias speaking):

> Socrates should not insist on the strict forms of discussion, carried on through the briefest of exchanges, if it is unwelcome to Protagoras, but should give way and slacken the reins of his discourse, so that it may wear for us a more dignified and elegant air, and Protagoras should refrain from shaking out every reef and running before the wind, launching out on a sea

of words till he is out of sight of land. Let both take a middle course. Do this, take my advice, and appoint an arbitrator, referee, or president to preserve a moderate length in the speeches of both of you.

88. See, for example, Plato, *Gorgias*, 447 b-448 d, 471 d-e; *Opera*, I, pp. 256-61, 320-21; Heise, III, pp. 4, 63-64; *Dialogues*, pp. 230-32, 254:

CALLICLES: What, Chaerephon? Is Socrates anxious to hear Gorgias?
CHAEREPHON: That is the very reason why we are here.
CALLICLES: Any time you like to come home with me, then, for Gorgias is staying with me and will give you an exhibition.
SOCRATES: Most kind of you, Callicles, but would he also be willing to converse with us? I want to learn from him what is the scope of his art and just what he professes and teaches. As for the exhibition, let him give us that, as you suggest, on some other occasion. . . .
SOCRATES: It is plain, Gorgias, that Polus is well equipped to make speeches, but he fails to accomplish what he promised to Chaerephon.
GORGIAS: Pray, how is that, Socrates?
SOCRATES: It seems that he does not quite answer the question asked.
GORGIAS: Well, if you prefer it, you may ask him yourself.
SOCRATES: No, not if you are ready to answer instead; I would much rather question you. For it is obvious from what Polus has said that he is much better versed in what is called rhetoric than in dialogue.

SOCRATES: At the very beginning of our discussion, Polus, I praised you for being in my opinion well trained in rhetoric, though you had neglected dialectic. And now is this the argument whereby even a child might refute me, and have I now, as you imagine, been refuted by it when I claim that the wrongdoer is not happy? How so, my good fellow? Indeed I do not admit a word of what you say.
POLUS: You refuse to, though you really think as I do.
SOCRATES: My dear sir, you are trying to refute me orator-fashion, like those who fancy they are refuting in the law courts.

89. Horace, *The Art of Poetry*, 322 ("*inopes rerum*" is cited in reverse order); *Q. Horatii Flacci opera* (Leipzig: 1828; *ASKB* 1248), p. 693; *Horace Satires, Epistles and Ars Poetica*, tr. H. Rushton Fairclough (Loeb, Cambridge: Harvard University Press, 1978), pp. 476-77.

90. Plato, *Symposium*, 201 c; Heise, II, pp. 60-61; cf. *Dialogues*, p. 553.

91. Plato, *Protagoras*, 331 b-c; Heise, II, p. 152; cf. *Dialogues*, p. 326.

92. Plato, *Protagoras*, 334 c-d; Heise, II, p. 160; cf. *Dialogues*, p. 329.

93. Plato, *Gorgias*, 454 b-c; Heise, III, p. 21; cf. *Dialogues*, pp. 237-38.

94. Plato, *Gorgias*, 473 d-e; Heise, III, p. 68; cf. *Dialogues*, p. 256.

95. Plato, *Gorgias*, 473 c-474 a; Heise, III, p. 68; cf. *Dialogues*, p. 256.

96. Plato, *Symposium*, 194 d; Heise, II, p. 47; cf. *Dialogues*, p. 547.

97. Plato, *Phaedrus*, *Dialogues*, p. 485.

98. A famous peasant clown in northern Germany in the fourteenth or fif-

teenth century. The perennial interest in Till Eulenspiegel in Scandinavia is suggested by two volumes that Kierkegaard had: *En gandske ny og lystig Historie om Ulspils Overmand, Eller Robertus von Agerkaal* (Copenhagen: 1724; *ASKB* 1467) and *Underlig og selsom Historie, Om Tiile Ugelspegel* (Copenhagen: 1781; *ASKB* 1469).

99. For Kierkegaard's use of sewing as an analogy, see *Sickness unto Death*, p. 93, *KW* XIX (*SV* XI 204); *On My Work as an Author*, with *Point of View*, *KW* XXII (*SV* XIII 508); Moment, *KW* XXIII (*SV* XIV 138); *JP* III 3540, 3689; VI 6760, 6803 (XI² A 281; X⁴ A 190, 285, 557).

100. See, for example, Hegel, *Wissenschaft der Logik*, I, *Werke*, III, p. 43; *J.A.*, IV, p. 53; *Science of Logic*, pp. 55-56:

> That which enables the Notion to advance itself is the already mentioned *negative* which it possesses within itself; it is this which constitutes the genuine dialectical element. Dialectic in this way acquires an entirely different significance from what it had when it was considered as a separate part of logic and when its aim and standpoint were, one may say, completely misunderstood. Even the *Platonic* dialectic, in the Parmenides itself and elsewhere even more directly, on the one hand, aims only at abolishing and refuting limited assertions through themselves, and, on the other hand, has for result simply nothingness. Dialectic is commonly regarded as an external, negative activity which does not pertain to the subject matter itself, having its ground in mere conceit as a subjective itch for unsettling and destroying what is fixed and substantial, or at least having for result nothing but the worthlessness of the object dialectically considered.

101. See Lessing, *"Eine Duplik," Schriften*, V, p. 98 (ed. tr.): "*ein andres ist, **auf etwas antworten**; ein andres, **etwas beantworten*** [it is one thing **to reply to something**; something else **to answer something**]."

102. See Horace, *Odes*, I, 4, 7; *Opera*, p. 15: "*Junctaeque Nymphis Gratiae decentes / Alterno terram quatiunt pede*"; *Horace The Odes and Epodes*, tr. C. E. Bennett (Loeb, Cambridge: Harvard University Press, 1978), p. 17: "The comely Graces linked with Nymphs tread the earth with tripping feet."

103. All cases except the nominative.

104. Plato, *Gorgias*, 461 d-e; Heise, III, p. 38; cf. *Dialogues*, p. 244. The opening phrase and Polus's name are transitional additions by Kierkegaard.

105. Plato, *Protagoras*, 328 e, 329 b; Heise, II, pp. 145, 147; cf. *Dialogues*, p. 324.

106. Plato, *Apology*, 17 a; *Opera*, VIII, p. 98; *Dialogues*, p. 4.

107. Plato, *Symposium*, 198 b, d; Heise, II, pp. 54-55; cf. *Dialogues*, pp. 550-51.

108. Plato, *Protagoras*, 339 e-340 a; Heise, II, pp. 170-71; cf. *Dialogues*, pp. 333-34.

109. See Plato, *Apology*, 36 b-38 b; *Opera*, VIII, pp. 144-49; *Dialogues*, pp. 21-23 (Socrates speaking):

> However, we must face the fact that he demands the death penalty. Very good. What alternative penalty shall I propose to you, gentlemen? Ob-

viously it must be adequate. Well, what penalty do I deserve to pay or suffer, in view of what I have done?

I have never lived an ordinary quiet life. I did not care for the things that most people care about—making money, having a comfortable home, high military or civil rank, and all the other activities, political appointments, secret societies, party organizations, which go on in our city. I thought that I was really too strict in my principles to survive if I went in for this sort of thing. So instead of taking a course which would have done no good either to you or to me, I set myself to do you individually in private what I hold to be the greatest possible service. I tried to persuade each one of you not to think more of practical advantages than of his mental and moral well-being, or in general to think more of advantage than of well-being in the case of the state or of anything else. What do I deserve for behaving in this way? Some reward, gentlemen, if I am bound to suggest what I really deserve, and what is more, a reward which would be appropriate for myself. Well, what is appropriate for a poor man who is a public benefactor and who requires leisure for giving you moral encouragement? Nothing could be more appropriate for such a person than free maintenance at the state's expense.[*] He deserves it much more than any victor in the races at Olympia, whether he wins with a single horse or a pair or a team of four. These people give you the semblance of success, but I give you the reality; they do not need maintenance, but I do. So if I am to suggest an appropriate penalty which is strictly in accordance with justice, I suggest free maintenance by the state. . . .

. . . If I had money, I would have suggested a fine that I could afford, because that would not have done me any harm. As it is, I cannot, because I have none, unless of course you like to fix the penalty at what I could pay. I suppose I could probably afford a mina. I suggest a fine of that amount.

One moment, gentlemen. Plato here, and Crito and Critobulus and Apollodorus, want me to propose thirty minas, on their security. Very well, I agree to this sum, and you can rely upon these gentlemen for its payment.

[*] In Athens, the prytanes (presidents), as well as citizens of high merit and foreign ambassadors, dined daily in the city hall (Prytaneum) at public expense.

110. See Plato, *Apology*, 39 c-40 a; *Opera*, VIII, pp. 150-53; *Dialogues*, p. 24 (Socrates speaking):

Having said so much, I feel moved to prophesy to you who have given your vote against me, for I am now at that point where the gift of prophecy comes most readily to men—at the point of death. I tell you, my executioners, that as soon as I am dead, vengeance shall fall upon you with a punishment far more painful than your killing of me. You have brought about my death in the belief that through it you will be delivered from submitting your conduct to criticism, but I say that the result will be just the opposite. You will have more critics, whom up till now I have restrained without your knowing it, and being younger they will be harsher to you and will cause you more annoyance. If you expect to stop denunciation of your wrong way of life by putting people to death, there is something amiss with your reasoning. This way of escape is neither possible nor creditable. The best and easiest way is not to stop the mouths of others, but to make yourselves as good men as you can. This is my last message to you who voted for my condemnation.

As for you who voted for my acquittal, I should very much like to say a few words to reconcile you to the result, while the officials are busy and I am not yet on my way to the place where I must die. I ask you, gentlemen, to spare me these few moments. There is no reason why we should not exchange fancies while the law permits. I look upon you as my friends, and I want you to understand the right way of regarding my present position.

111. See note 60 above; Diogenes Laertius, II, 40-41; *Vitis*, I, p. 79; Riisbrigh, I, p. 74; Loeb, I, p. 171:

The philosopher then, after Lysias had written a defence for him, read it through and said: "A fine speech, Lysias; it is not, however, suitable to me." For it was plainly more forensic than philosophical. Lysias said, "If it is a fine speech, how can it fail to suit you?" "Well," he replied, "would not fine raiment and fine shoes be just as unsuitable to me?"

112. See, for example, Homer, *Odyssey*, XI, 13-14; *Homers Odyssee*, tr. Christian Wilster (Copenhagen: 1837), p. 147; *Homer The Odyssey*, I-II, tr. A. T. Murray (Loeb, Cambridge: Harvard University Press, 1976-80), I, p. 387:

"So when we had made fast all the tackling throughout the ship, we sat down, and the wind and the helmsman made straight her course. All the day long her sail was stretched as she sped over the sea; and the sun set and all the ways grew dark.

"She came to deep-flowing Oceanus, that bounds the Earth, where is the land and city of the Cimmerians, wrapped in mist and cloud."

113. See Plato, *Apology*, 23 b-c; *Opera*, VIII, pp. 112-13; *Dialogues*, p. 9 (Socrates speaking):

That is why I still go about seeking and searching in obedience to the divine command, if I think that anyone is wise, whether citizen or stranger, and when I think that any person is not wise, I try to help the cause of God [the god] by proving that he is not. This occupation has kept me too busy to do much either in politics or in my own affairs. In fact, my service to God [the god] has reduced me to extreme poverty.

114. Plato, *Apology*, 30 a; *Opera*, VIII, p. 128; *Dialogues*, p. 16.
115. Plato, *Apology*, 33 c; *Opera*, VIII, p. 136; *Dialogues*, p. 19.
116. Plato, *Gorgias*, 485 d; Heise, III, p. 99; cf. *Dialogues*, p. 268.
117. Plato, *Apology*, 41 b; *Opera*, VIII, p. 156; *Dialogues*, p. 25.

118. Plato, *Symposium*, 175 e; Heise, II, p. 10; cf. *Dialogues*, p. 530.

119. Plato, *Apology*, 23 a; *Opera*, VIII, p. 112; *Dialogues*, p. 9.

120. See Judges 16:25-30.

121. See p. 32.

122. See Plato, *Symposium*, 201 c-d; *Opera*, III, pp. 496-97; Heise, II, p. 61; *Dialogues*, p. 553 (Socrates speaking):

> And now I'm going to leave you in peace, because I want to talk about some lessons I was given, once upon a time, by a Mantinean woman called Diotima—a woman who was deeply versed in this and many other fields of knowledge. It was she who brought about a ten years' postponement of the great plague of Athens on the occasion of a certain sacrifice, and it was she who taught me the philosophy of Love.

123. See Plato, *Symposium*, 212 b; *Opera*, III, pp. 520-21; Heise, II, p. 82; *Dialogues*, p. 563 (Socrates speaking):

> This, Phaedrus—this, gentlemen—was the doctrine of Diotima. I was convinced, and in that conviction I try to bring others to the same creed, and to convince them that, if we are to make this gift our own, Love will help our mortal nature more than all the world.

124. See Plato, *Symposium*, 214 e-215 a; *Opera*, III, pp. 526-29; Heise, II, p. 87; *Dialogues*, p. 566:

> Then here goes, said Alcibiades. There's one thing, though. If I say a word that's not the solemn truth I want you to stop me right away and tell me I'm a liar—but I promise you it won't be my fault if I do. On the other hand, you mustn't be surprised if I tell them about you just as it comes into my head, and jump from one thing to another. You can't expect anyone that's as drunk as I am to give a clear and systematic account of all *your* eccentricities.

125. See p. 32.

126. For the series of speeches, see Plato, *Symposium*, 178 a-180 b (Phaedrus), 180 c-185 c (Pausanias), 185 e-188 e (Eryximachus), 189 c-193 d (Aristophanes), 194 e-197 e (Agathon), 199 c-212 c (Socrates); *Opera*, III, pp. 442-49, 448-61, 460-67, 468-79, 480-89, 492-521; Heise, II, pp. 15-19, 19-29, 30-35, 36-45, 47-53, 56-82; *Dialogues*, pp. 532-34, 534-39, 539-42, 542-46, 547-50, 551-63.

127. See Plato, *Symposium*, 186 e-187 a; *Opera*, III, pp. 462-63; Heise, II, p. 32; *Dialogues*, p. 540 (Eryximachus speaking):

> And so, gentlemen, I maintain that medicine is under the sole direction of the god of love, as are also the gymnastic and the agronomic arts. And it must be obvious to the most casual observer that the same holds good of music—which is, perhaps, what Heraclitus meant us to understand by that rather cryptic pronouncement, 'The one in conflict with itself is held together, like the harmony of the bow and of the lyre.'

Cf. Philip Wheelwright, *Heraclitus* (Princeton: Princeton University Press, 1959), p. 102: "People do not understand how that which is at variance with itself agrees with itself. There is a harmony in the bending back, as in the case of the bow and the lyre."

128. Cf. Hegel, *Vorlesungen über die Geschichte der Philosophie*, I, *Werke*, XIII, p. 336; *J.A.*, XVII, p. 352; *Hegel's Lectures on the History of Philosophy*, I-III (tr. of *G.P.*, 2 ed., 1840-44; Kierkegaard had 1 ed., 1833-36), tr. E. S. Haldane and Frances H. Simson (New York: Humanities, 1974), I, p. 285:

> But this does not contradict Heraclitus, who means the same thing. That which is simple, the repetition of a tone, is no harmony; difference is clearly necessary to harmony, or a definite antithesis; for it is the absolute becoming and not mere change. The real fact is that each particular tone is different from another—not abstractly so from any other, but from *its* other—and thus it also can be one. Each particular only is, in so far as its opposite is implicitly contained in its Notion. Subjectivity is thus the "other" of objectivity and not a piece of paper, which would be meaningless; since each is the "other" of the "other" as its "other," we here have their identity. This is Heraclitus' great principle; it may seem obscure, but it is speculative. And this to the understanding which maintains the independence of Being and non-being, the subjective and objective, the real and the ideal, is always difficult and dim.

129. See Plato, *Symposium*, 190 d-191 a; *Opera*, III, pp. 470-73; Heise, II, pp. 39-40; *Dialogues*, p. 543 (Aristophanes speaking):

> At last, however, after racking his brains, Zeus offered a solution.
>
> I think I can see my way, he said, to put an end to this disturbance by weakening these people without destroying them. What I propose to do is to cut them all in half, thus killing two birds with one stone, for each one will be only half as strong, and there'll be twice as many of them, which will suit us very nicely. They can walk about, upright, on their two legs, and if, said Zeus, I have any more trouble with them, I shall split them up again, and they'll have to hop about on one.
>
> So saying, he cut them all in half just as you or I might chop up sorb apples for pickling, or slice an egg with a hair. And as each half was ready he told Apollo to turn its face, with the half-neck that was left, toward the side that was cut away—thinking that the sight of such a gash might frighten it into keeping quiet—and then to heal the whole thing up. So Apollo turned their faces back to front, and, pulling in the skin all the way round, he stretched it over what we now call the belly—like those bags you pull together with a string—and tied up the one remaining opening so as to form what we call the navel. As for the creases that were left, he smoothed most of them away, finishing off the chest with the sort of tool a cobbler uses to smooth down the leather on the last, but he left a few puckers round about the belly and the navel, to remind us of what we suffered long ago.
>
> Now, when the work of bisection was complete it left each half with a

desperate yearning for the other, and they ran together and flung their arms around each other's necks, and asked for nothing better than to be rolled into one.

130. Plato, *Symposium*, 191 d; Heise, II, p. 41; cf. *Dialogues*, p. 544: ". . . this love is always trying to redintegrate our former nature, to make two into one, and to bridge the gulf between one human being and another."

131. Plato, *Symposium*, 198 d-e; Heise, II, p. 55; cf. *Dialogues*, pp. 550-51:

> But the truth, it seems, is the last thing the successful eulogist cares about; on the contrary, what he does is simply to run through all the attributes of power and virtue, however irrelevant they may be, and the whole thing may be a pack of lies, for all it seems to matter.
>
> I take it then that what we undertook was to flatter, rather than to praise, the god of love . . ..

132. See, for example, Hegel, *Aesthetik*, II, *Werke*, X², pp. 178-86; *J.A.*, XIII, pp. 178-86; *Philosophy of Fine Art*, II, pp. 337-45. The expression is Hegelian in the sense of being appropriate to Hegel's discussion of love but is not used in that particular form by Hegel.

133. An arithmetical expression used to designate the "carrying" of a number from one column to the next in addition and multiplication, hence, here, an important point to be carried or kept in mind throughout the discussion.

134. See pp. 96-109.

135. Plato, *Symposium*, 222 b; Heise, II, p. 101; cf. *Dialogues*, pp. 572-73. See *Fragments*, p. 24, *KW* VII (*SV* IV 193); *JP* IV 4262-63 (*Pap*. V B 4:3, 23:1).

136. The Corybantes were priests of the Phrygian goddess Cybele, whose rites were conducted with loud, wild music and frenzied dancing.

137. Plato, *Symposium*, 215 d-e; Heise, II, p. 89; cf. *Dialogues*, p. 567.

138. See Homer, *Odyssey*, XII, 40-49, 172-79; Wilster, pp. 166, 169-70; Loeb, I, pp. 435, 445:

> Whoso in ignorance draws near to them and hears the Sirens' voice, he nevermore returns, that his wife and little children may stand at his side rejoicing, but the Sirens beguile him with their clear-toned song, as they sit in a meadow, and about them is a great heap of bones of mouldering men, and round the bones the skin is shrivelling. But do thou row past them, and anoint the ears of thy comrades with sweet wax, which thou hast kneaded, lest any of the rest may hear.

> Meanwhile the well-built ship speedily came to the isle of the two Sirens, for a fair and gentle wind bore her on. Then presently the wind ceased and there was a windless calm, and a god lulled the waves to sleep. But my comrades rose up and furled the sail and stowed it in the hollow ship, and thereafter sat at the oars and made the water white with their polished oars of fir. But I with my sharp sword cut into small bits a great round cake of wax, and kneaded it with my strong hands, and soon the wax grew warm, forced by the strong pressure and the rays of the lord Helios Hyperion.

> Then I anointed with this the ears of all my comrades in turn; and they bound me in the ship hand and foot, upright in the step of the mast, and made the ropes fast at the ends to the mast itself; and themselves sitting down smote the grey sea with their oars.

139. See Homer, *Odyssey*, IV, 414-24; Wilster, p. 53; Loeb, I, p. 137 (the goddess Eidothea, daughter of Proteus, the sea god, speaking to Menelaus):

> Now so soon as you see him [Proteus] laid to rest, thereafter let your hearts be filled with strength and courage, and do you hold him there despite his striving and struggling to escape. For try he will, and will assume all manner of shapes of all things that move upon the earth, and of water, and of wondrous blazing fire. Yet do ye hold him unflinchingly and grip him yet the more. But when at length of his own will he speaks and questions thee in that shape in which you saw him laid to rest, then, hero, stay thy might, and set the old man free, and ask him who of the gods is wroth with thee, and of thy return, how thou mayest go over the teeming deep.

See also Virgil, *Georgics*, IV, 387-414, for a slightly different version of the story; Loeb, I, pp. 222-25.

140. François Alexandre La Rochefoucauld-Liancourt, *Maximes*, 271; *Maximes* (in Greek, French, and English) (Paris: 1828), pp. 152-53: "*La jeunesse est une ivresse continuelle: C'est la fievre de la raison*. . . . (Youth is continual intoxication: It is the fever of season [*sic*])."

141. Plato, *Symposium*, 216 d-217 a; Heise, II, p. 90 ("Socrates says" added in text and "his" in line two omitted); cf. *Dialogues*, p. 568. Silenus, the oldest of the Satyrs and the teacher, trainer, and companion of Dionysus, was often represented in openable small statues as a pot-bellied, hairy old man with pointed ears.

142. A term in Lutheran theology pertaining to the way in which Christ used his divine qualities.

143. Plato, *Symposium*, 221 d-e; Heise, II, p. 100. See *Dialogues* (221 e-222 a), p. 572:

> Anyone listening to Socrates for the first time would find his arguments simply laughable; he wraps them up in just the kind of expressions you'd expect of such an insufferable satyr. He talks about pack asses and blacksmiths and shoemakers and tanners, and he always seems to be saying the same old thing in just the same old way, so that anyone who wasn't used to his style and wasn't very quick on the uptake would naturally take it for the most utter nonsense. But if you open up his arguments, and really get into the skin of them, you'll find that they're the only arguments in the world that have any sense at all, and that nobody else's are so godlike, so rich in images of virtue, or so peculiarly, so entirely pertinent to those inquiries that help the seeker on his way to the goal of true nobility.

On Silenus, see note 141 above.

144. Plato, *Symposium*, 219 b-d; Heise, II, pp. 95-96 (text compacted and adapted); cf. *Dialogues*, p. 570.

145. Plato, *Symposium*, 222 c-d; Heise, II, p. 101; cf. *Dialogues*, p. 573.

146. Cf. Hegel, *Wissenschaft der Logik*, I, *Werke*, III, p. 124; *J.A.*, IV, p. 134; *Science of Logic*, p. 118:

> *Thirdly*, therefore, the other is to be taken as isolated, as in relation to itself, *abstractly* as the *other*; the τὸ ἕτερον of Plato, who opposes it as one of the moments of totality to the One, and in this way ascribes to the other a *nature* of its own. Thus the other, taken solely as such, is not the other of something but the other in its own self, that is, the other of itself. Such an other, determined as other, is physical nature; it is the other of spirit. This its determination is thus at first a mere relativity by which is expressed, not a quality of nature itself, but only a relation external to it. However, since spirit is the true something and nature, consequently, in its own self is only what it is as contrasted with spirit, the quality of nature taken as such is just this, to be the *other* in its own self, that which is *external to itself* (in the determinations of space, time and matter).
>
> The other simply by itself is the other in its own self, hence the other of itself and so the other of the other—it is, therefore, that which is absolutely dissimilar within itself, that which negates itself, *alters* itself. But in so doing it remains identical with itself, for that into which it alters is the other, and this is its sole determination; but what is altered is not determined in any different way but in the same way, namely, to be an other; in this latter, therefore, it only unites with its own self.

147. See Baur, *Das Christliche des Platonismus oder Sokrates und Christus*, p. 108. Baur cites David Strauss, *Das Leben Jesu*, I-II (Tübingen: 1835), II, p. 276; *The Life of Jesus Critically Examined* (tr. of 4 ed., 1892), tr. George Eliot (Philadelphia: Fortress, 1972), pp. 545-46, fn. 19:

> Plato also in the Symposion (p. 223, B. ff. Steph.), glorifies his Socrates by arranging in a natural manner, and in a comic spirit, a similar group to that which the Evangelists here present in a supernatural manner, and in a tragic spirit. After a bacchanalian entertainment, Socrates outwatches his friends, who lie sleeping around him: as here the disciples around their master; with Socrates there are awake two noble forms alone, the tragic and the comic poet, the two elements of the early Grecian life, which Socrates united in himself: as, with Jesus, the lawgiver and prophet, the two pillars of the Old Testament economy, which in a higher manner were combined in Jesus; lastly, as in Plato both Agathon and Aristophanes at length sleep, and Socrates remains alone in possession of the field: so in the gospel, Moses and Elias at last vanish, and the disciples see Jesus left alone.

148. *Platons Werke*, I-III, tr. Friedrich Ernst Daniel Schleiermacher (Berlin: 1817-28; *ASKB* 1158-63), I[1], pp. 45, 48-50; *Schleiermacher's Introductions to the Dialogues of Plato*, tr. William Dobson (1836; New York: Arno, 1973), pp. 40-41, 44-45:

> . . . here we can only give an account of the principles which are the basis of the general plan.

If then, to continue, we keep to the somewhat contracted selection of the more important Platonic works in which alone the main thread of this connection, as has been already mentioned, is to be found perfect, there are some of them distinguished above all the rest by the fact that they alone contain an objective scientific exposition; the *Republic* for instance, the *Timaeus* and the *Critias*.

As then, these constructive dialogues are indisputably the last, some, on the other hand, of the remaining ones distinguish themselves as clearly as the first; for instance, continuing to adhere only to those of the first rank, the *Phaedrus*, *Protagoras*, and *Parmenides*. . . . But the most important thing yet in them is their internal matter, for in them are developed the first breathings of what is the basis of all that follows, of Logic as the instrument of Philosophy, of Ideas as its proper object, consequently of the possibility and the conditions of knowledge. These therefore, in conjunction with some dialogues attaching to them of the lesser kind, form the first, and, as it were, elementary part of the Platonic works. The others occupy the interval between these and the constructive, inasmuch as they treat progressively of the applicability of those principles, of the distinction between philosophical and common knowledge in their united application to two proposed and real sciences, that of Ethics, namely, and of Physics. In this respect also they stand in the middle between the constructive in which the practical and the theoretical are completely united, and the elementary, in which the two are kept separate more than any where else in Plato. These, then, form the second part, which is distinguished by an especial and almost difficult artificiality, as well in the construction of the particular dialogues as in their progressive connection, and which might be named for distinction's sake, the indirect method, since it commences almost universally with the juxtaposition of antitheses. In these three divisions therefore, the works of Plato are here to be given to the reader; so that while each part is arranged according to its obvious characteristics, the dialogues also of the second rank occupy precisely the places which, after due consideration of every point, seems to belong to them.

149. Plato, *Gorgias*, 466 a-c; Heise, III, pp. 48-49; cf. *Dialogues*, p. 248.

150. Plato, *Gorgias*, 523 a-527 e; *Opera*, I, pp. 456-69; Heise, III, pp. 190-201; *Dialogues*, pp. 303-07.

151. Plato, *Crito*, 50 c; Heise, I, p. 146; cf. *Dialogues*, p. 35.

152. Plato, *Apology*, 27 a-b; *Opera*, VIII, p. 122; *Dialogues*, p. 13.

153. See Plato, *Republic*, III, 396 c-397 b; *Opera*, IV, pp. 146-49; *Dialogues*, pp. 641-42 (Socrates conversing with Glaucon):

If, then, I understand your meaning, said I, there is a form of diction and narrative in which the really good and true man would narrate anything that he had to say, and another form unlike this to which the man of the opposite birth and breeding would cleave and in which he would tell his story.

What are these forms? he said.

A man of the right sort, I think, when he comes in the course of his narrative to some word or act of a good man will be willing to impersonate the other in reporting it, and will feel no shame at that kind of mimicry, by preference imitating the good man when he acts steadfastly and sensibly, and less and more reluctantly when he is upset by sickness or love or drunkenness or any other mishap. But when he comes to someone unworthy of himself, he will not wish to liken himself in earnest to one who is inferior, except in the few cases where he is doing something good, but will be embarrassed both because he is unpracticed in the mimicry of such characters, and also because he shrinks in distaste from molding and fitting himself to the types of baser things. His mind disdains them, unless it be for jest.

Naturally, he said.

Then the narrative that he will employ will be of the kind that we just now illustrated by the verses of Homer, and his diction will be one that partakes of both, of imitation and simple narration, but there will be a small portion of imitation in a long discourse—or is there nothing in what I say?

Yes, indeed, he said, that *is* the type and pattern of such a speaker.

Then, said I, the other kind of speaker, the more debased he is the less will he shrink from imitating anything and everything. He will think nothing unworthy of himself, so that he will attempt, seriously and in the presence of many, to imitate all things, including those we just now mentioned—claps of thunder, and the noise of wind and hail and axles and pulleys, and the notes of trumpets and flutes and Panpipes, and the sounds of all instruments, and the cries of dogs, sheep, and birds—and so his style will depend wholly on imitation in voice and gesture, or will contain but a little of pure narration.

That too follows of necessity, he said.

These, then, said I, were the two types of diction of which I was speaking.

There are those two, he replied.

154. *Platons Werke*, III[1], p. 8; *Schleiermacher's Introductions*, pp. 354–55.

155. See *Platons Werke*, III[1], p. 7; *Schleiermacher's Introductions*, p. 354:

Thus the first book does indeed conclude with the victory of Socrates over the sophists, but also with the lamentation of the conquerer himself, that the nature of justice has still not been yet discovered, consequently, that the question started remains where it was, perfectly untouched. And by this conclusion the book is clearly enough marked as an introduction, so that the arguments up to this point can only have any value as preparatory to what is to follow.

And by this conclusion the same also is virtually maintained of all the Socratic dialogues previously given in this translation, as many of them at least as discussed any virtue whatever, inasmuch as they all failed to discover the correct explanation.

156. See *Platons Werke*, I[1], p. 228; *Schleiermacher's Introductions*, p. 91:

> Now whoever attends not only to this or that point, in this dialogue, but to every thing, to the frequently interspersed and cursory hints which in Plato least of any writer admit of being overlooked, to the change of the *form* in the different sections, to what is continually recurring in and between these sections, notwithstanding all the multiplicity of subjects—whoever does this will recognize, in this very dispute respecting the form and method, the main purpose of the whole; the purpose, namely, to praise and ennoble the dialogistic form of Socrates, and to proclaim it as the proper form of all genuine philosophical communication, in opposition to all sophistical forms, all of which therefore make their appearance, not even the method of commentating upon passages of poets excepted. If we place ourselves in this true centre point of the work, we see first, in the most decided manner, how very closely this dialogue connects itself by manifold ramifications with the *Phaedrus*. For as there the inward spirit of the philosophizing process was exhibited, so the outward form is here discovered, and what results, as such, is criticised.

157. Philippe Néricault Destouches, *Le Dissipateur* (Paris: 1808), V, 7, p. 65 (Marquis to Cleon): "*Te voilà vraiment libre, et vis-à-vis de rien.*"

158. The source has not been located.

159. Plato, *Protagoras*, 361 a-c; Heise, II, p. 216. See *Dialogues*, p. 351 (Socrates speaking):

> It seems to me that the present outcome of our talk is pointing at us, like a human adversary, the finger of accusation and scorn. If it had a voice it would say, 'What an absurd pair you are, Socrates and Protagoras. One of you, having said at the beginning that virtue is not teachable, now is bent upon contradicting himself by trying to demonstrate that everything is knowledge—justice, temperance, and courage alike—which is the best way to prove that virtue *is* teachable. If virtue were something other than knowledge, as Protagoras tried to prove, obviously it could not be taught. But if it turns out to be, as a single whole, knowledge—which is what you are urging, Socrates—then it will be most surprising if it cannot be taught. Protagoras on the other hand, who at the beginning supposed it to be teachable, now on the contrary seems to be bent on showing that it is almost anything rather than knowledge, and this would make it least likely to be teachable.'
>
> For my part, Protagoras, when I see the subject in such utter confusion I feel the liveliest desire to clear it up. I should like to follow up our present talk with a determined attack on virtue itself and its essential nature.

The movements of Protagoras and Socrates are epitomized in the salt-weighing metaphor below, which refers to a game in which two persons stand back to back, lock arms, and then tip back and forth as a kind of human teeter-totter.

160. From a story by Johann Peter Hebel (1760-1826), German dialect poet and popular author. Before Kierkegaard began working on his dissertation, a selection of Hebel's stories had appeared in Danish, *Udvalgte Fortællinger af J. P. Hebel*, tr. Tage Algreen-Ussing (Copenhagen: 1835).

161. Plato, *Republic*, IV; *Opera*, IV, p. 248; *Dialogues*, p. 688.

162. Plato, *Republic*, IV, 444 e; *Opera*, IV, p. 246; *Dialogues*, p. 687.

163. See Schleiermacher, *Der christliche Glaube*, I-II (3 ed., Berlin: 1835-36; *ASKB* 258), I, 56, 2, p. 305; *The Christian Faith* (tr. of 2 ed., 1830-31), ed. H. R. Mackintosh and J. S. Stewart (Edinburgh: Clark, 1960), p. 229:

> And first as to the *Unity* of God—strictly taken it can never be an attribute of a thing that it only exists in a definite number. It is not an attribute of the hand to be dual; but it is the attribute of a man to have two hands, and of a monkey to have four. In the same way it could be an attribute of the world to be ruled by One God only, but not of God to be One only. And so if a divine attribute is here in question, we must turn away from mere number; and in that case what we have first to insist upon is the general expression that God has no equal, which, of course, our language can more distinctly express by 'uniqueness.' And inasmuch as many similars are always of the same kind or species, the individual beings representing the existence of the species and the species the essence of the individuals, it might be said that the unity or uniqueness of God is that attribute in virtue of which there is no distinction of essence and existence. Now this as such could belong only to speculative theology. But if, on the other hand, we abstract from what in strictness must be understood by an attribute, and if we consider that the excitations of the religious consciousness are individual moments, while that upon which in those excitations we feel ourselves absolutely dependent is not objectively given, then this term 'unity' expresses the fact that all those excitations are meant and comprehended as indications of One, and not of many.

164. See *Fragments*, pp. 9-10, *KW* VII (*SV* IV 179-80).

165. A character in Ludwig Tieck, *Der gestiefelte Kater* (1797), *Ludwig Tieck's sämmtliche Werke*, I-II (Paris: 1837; *ASKB* 1848-49), I, pp. 466-90.

166. Pelagius, a British monk (fl. 400), maintained a view that affirmed perfect human freedom and responsibility and man's capability of spiritual good unaided by divine grace and that denied original sin.

167. Literally, "May it agree with you," a customary response to "*Tak for Mad* [Thanks for the food]" after a meal. See *JP* III 2586 (*Pap*. III A 117).

168. *Platons Werke*, II³, pp. 5-6; *Schleiermacher's Introductions*, pp. 293-94:

> Thus, then, the immortality of the soul is the condition of all true knowledge as regards men, and conversely, the reality of knowledge is the ground upon which the immortality of the soul is most certainly and easily understood. Hence, in the former dialogues also, in which knowledge was inves-

tigated, immortality was always presupposed and investigated simultaneously; and one may say, that, from the *Gorgias* and *Theaetetus* downwards, the two subjects are continually approximating in their progress, until they are at last in this dialogue most closely combined. Whoever then comprehends the connection of these two points in the sense in which Plato meant it, will certainly no longer hesitate to place the *Phaedon* and the *Symposium* together, and to recognise the reciprocal relation of the two. For, as the love there described exhibits the endeavour to connect the immortal with the mortal, that pure contemplation here represented is the endeavour to withdraw the immortal, as such, away from the mortal; and the two are manifestly in necessary connection with one another.

169. Heise, II, pp. 224-30.

170. Gottfried Stallbaum, *Platonis dialogos selectos* (Gotha, Erfurt: 1827).

171. See note 170 above.

172. Friedrich Ast's biography and study of Plato is not included in the auction catalog (*ASKB*). Excerpts from the work are ed. tr.

173. See, for example, *Three Discourses on Imagined Occasions*, *KW* X (*SV* V 26-53).

174. Plato, *Phaedo*, 70 b-c; Heise, I, p. 27; cf. *Dialogues*, pp. 52-53.

175. Plato, *Phaedo*, 77 d-e; Heise, I, p. 42; cf. *Dialogues*, p. 61.

176. Plato, *Phaedo*, 115 d; Heise, I, 119; cf. *Dialogues*, p. 95.

177. Cf. *JP* II 1186; III 2338 (*Pap.* I C 50; IV C 11) on Johann Gottlieb Fichte.

178. See Plato, *Phaedo*, 62 b; *Opera*, I, pp. 484-85; Heise, I, pp. 10-11; *Dialogues*, p. 45 (Socrates speaking):

> The allegory which the mystics tell us—that we men are put in a sort of guard post, from which one must not release oneself or run away—seems to me to be a high doctrine with difficult implications. All the same, Cebes, I believe that this much is true, that the gods are our keepers, and we men are one of their possessions. Don't you think so?

179. See I Corinthians 3:9.

180. See Plato, *Phaedo*, 62 c-e; *Opera*, I, pp. 484-87; Heise, I, pp. 11-12; *Dialogues*, p. 45 (Cebes speaking):

> But what you were saying just now, that philosophers would be readily willing to die—that seems illogical, Socrates, assuming that we were right in saying a moment ago that God is our keeper and we are his possessions. If this service is directed by the gods, who are the very best of masters, it is inexplicable that the very wisest of men should not be grieved at quitting it, because he surely cannot expect to provide for himself any better when he is free. On the other hand a stupid person might get the idea that it would be to his advantage to escape from his master. He might not reason it out that one should not escape from a good master, but remain with him as long as possible, and so he might run away unreflectingly. A sensible man

would wish to remain always with his superior. If you look at it in this way, Socrates, the probable thing is just the opposite of what we said just now. It is natural for the wise to be grieved when they die, and for fools to be happy.

181. See Plato, *Phaedo*, 63 b-c; *Opera*, I, pp. 486-87; Heise, I, pp. 12-13; *Dialogues*, p. 46 (Socrates speaking):

> Very well then, let me try to make a more convincing defense to you than I made at my trial. If I did not expect to enter the company, first, of other wise and good gods, and secondly of men now dead who are better than those who are in this world now, it is true that I should be wrong in not grieving at death. As it is, you can be assured that I expect to find myself among good men. I would not insist particularly on this point, but on the other I assure you that I shall insist most strongly—that I shall find there divine masters who are supremely good. That is why I am not so much distressed as I might be, and why I have a firm hope that there is something in store for those who have died, and, as we have been told for many years, something much better for the good than for the wicked.

182. The last line of Kierkegaard's first upbuilding discourse is almost exactly the same as "in order . . . soul." See *Eighteen Upbuilding Discourses*, *KW* V (*SV* III 34).

183. The relation between contemporary and later witnesses is a major theme in *Fragments*, *KW* VII (*SV* IV 173-272).

184. See Plato, *Phaedo*, 60 a; *Opera*, I, pp. 478-79; Heise, I, p. 6; *Dialogues*, p. 43 (Phaedo speaking):

> After a short interval he came back and told us to go in. When we went inside we found Socrates just released from his chains, and Xanthippe—you know her!—sitting by him with the little boy on her knee. As soon as Xanthippe saw us she broke out into the sort of remark you would expect from a woman, Oh, Socrates, this is the last time that you and your friends will be able to talk together!
>
> Socrates looked at Crito. Crito, he said, someone had better take her home.
>
> Some of Crito's servants led her away crying hysterically.

185. Plato, *Phaedo*, 60 c; Heise, I, p. 7; cf. *Dialogues*, p. 43.

186. Plato, *Phaedo*, 60 c; Heise, I, pp. 6-7, cf. *Dialogues*, p. 43.

187. Plato, *Phaedo*, 117 a-c; Heise, I, p. 123; cf. *Dialogues*, p. 97.

188. See Plato, *Phaedo*, 65 c-d; *Opera*, I, pp. 492-93; Heise, I, p. 17; *Dialogues*, p. 48 (Socrates speaking):

> Surely the soul can best reflect when it is free of all distractions such as hearing or sight or pain or pleasure of any kind—that is, when it ignores the body and becomes as far as possible independent, avoiding all physical contacts and associations as much as it can, in its search for reality.

That is so.

Then here too—in despising the body and avoiding it, and endeavoring to become independent—the philosopher's soul is ahead of all the rest.

It seems so.

Here are some more questions, Simmias. Do we recognize such a thing as absolute uprightness?

Indeed we do.

And absolute beauty and goodness too?

Of course.

Have you ever seen any of these things with your eyes?

Certainly not, said he.

Well, have you ever apprehended them with any other bodily sense? By 'them' I mean not only absolute tallness or health or strength, but the real nature of any given thing—what it actually is.

189. See Plato, *Phaedo*, 66 e-67 b; *Opera*, I, pp. 494-97; Heise, I, pp. 19-20; *Dialogues*, p. 49 (Socrates speaking):

It seems, to judge from the argument, that the wisdom which we desire and upon which we profess to have set our hearts will be attainable only when we are dead, and not in our lifetime. If no pure knowledge is possible in the company of the body, then either it is totally impossible to acquire knowledge, or it is only possible after death, because it is only then that the soul will be separate and independent of the body. It seems that so long as we are alive, we shall continue closest to knowledge if we avoid as much as we can all contact and association with the body, except when they are absolutely necessary, and instead of allowing ourselves to become infected with its nature, purify ourselves from it until God himself gives us deliverance. In this way, by keeping ourselves uncontaminated by the follies of the body, we shall probably reach the company of others like ourselves and gain direct knowledge of all that is pure and uncontaminated—that is, presumably, of truth. For one who is not pure himself to attain to the realm of purity would no doubt be a breach of universal justice.

Something to this effect, Simmias, is what I imagine all real lovers of learning must think themselves and say to one another. Don't you agree with me?

Most emphatically, Socrates.

190. See Plato, *Phaedo*, 66 a-b; *Opera*, I, pp. 492-95; Heise, I, pp. 18-19; *Dialogues*, p. 49 (Socrates speaking):

Don't you think that the person who is likely to succeed in this attempt most perfectly is the one who approaches each object, as far as possible, with the unaided intellect, without taking account of any sense of sight in his thinking, or dragging any other sense into his reckoning—the man who pursues the truth by applying his pure and unadulterated thought to the pure and unadulterated object, cutting himself off as much as possible from his eyes and ears and virtually all the rest of his body, as an impediment which by its presence prevents the soul from attaining to truth and clear thinking? Is not this the person, Simmias, who will reach the goal of reality, if anybody can?

What you say is absolutely true, Socrates, said Simmias.

All these considerations, said Socrates, must surely prompt serious philosophers to review the position in some such way as this. It looks as though this were a bypath leading to the right track. So long as we keep to the body and our soul is contaminated with this imperfection, there is no chance of our ever attaining satisfactorily to our object, which we assert to be truth.

191. See Plato, *Phaedo*, 81 c-d; *Opera*, I, pp. 530-33; Heise, I, p. 50; *Dialogues*, p. 64 (Socrates speaking):

> On the contrary, it will, I imagine, be permeated by the corporeal, which fellowship and intercourse with the body will have ingrained in its very nature through constant association and long practice.
>
> Certainly.
>
> And we must suppose, my dear fellow, that the corporeal is heavy, oppressive, earthly, and visible. So the soul which is tainted by its presence is weighed down and dragged back into the visible world, through fear, as they say, of Hades or the invisible, and hovers about tombs and graveyards. The shadowy apparitions which have actually been seen there are the ghosts of those souls which have not got clear away, but still retain some portion of the visible, which is why they can be seen.

192. See note 189 above.

193. See Plato, *Phaedo*, 70 c-72 d; *Opera*, I, pp. 504-09; Heise, I, pp. 27-32; *Dialogues*, pp. 53-55 (Socrates speaking to Cebes):

> There is an old legend, which we still remember, to the effect that they *do* exist there, after leaving here, and that they return again to this world and come into being from the dead. If this is so—that the living come into being again from the dead—does it not follow that our souls exist in the other world? They could not come into being again if they did not exist, and it will be sufficient proof that my contention is true if it really becomes apparent that the living come from the dead, and from nowhere else. But if this is not so, we shall need some other argument. . . . For example, if 'falling asleep' existed, and 'waking up' did not balance it by making something come out of sleep, you must realize that in the end everything would make Endymion look foolish. He would be nowhere, because the whole world would be in the same state—asleep. And if everything were combined and nothing separated, we should soon have Anaxagoras' 'all things together.' In just the same way, my dear Cebes, if everything that has some share of life were to die, and if after death the dead remained in that form and did not come to life again, would it not be quite inevitable that in the

end everything should be dead and nothing alive? If living things came from other living things, and the living things died, what possible means could prevent their number from being exhausted by death?

None that I can see, Socrates, said Cebes. What you say seems to be perfectly true.

Yes, Cebes, he said, if anything is true, I believe that this is, and we were not mistaken in our agreement upon it. Coming to life again is a fact, and it is a fact that the living come from the dead, and a fact that the souls of the dead exist.

194. See Plato, *Phaedo*, 72 e-77 e; *Opera*, I, pp. 508-23; Heise, I, pp. 32-42; *Dialogues*, pp. 55-60 (Socrates, Cebes, and Simmias conversing):

Besides, Socrates, rejoined Cebes, there is that theory which you have often described to us—that what we call learning is really just recollection. If that is true, then surely what we recollect now we must have learned at some time before, which is impossible unless our souls existed somewhere before they entered this human shape. So in that way too it seems likely that the soul is immortal.

How did the proofs of that theory go, Cebes? broke in Simmias. Remind me, because at the moment I can't quite remember.

One very good argument, said Cebes, is that when people are asked questions, if the question is put in the right way they can give a perfectly correct answer, which they could not possibly do unless they had some knowledge and a proper grasp of the subject. And then if you confront people with a diagram or anything like that, the way in which they react is an unmistakable proof that the theory is correct. . . .

Well, how do we stand now, Simmias? If all these absolute realities, such as beauty and goodness, which we are always talking about, really exist, if it is to them, as we rediscover our own former knowledge of them, that we refer, as copies to their patterns, all the objects of our physical perception—if these realities exist, does it not follow that our souls must exist too even before our birth, whereas if they do not exist, our discussion would seem to be a waste of time? Is this the position, that it is logically just as certain that our souls exist before our birth as it is that these realities exist, and that if the one is impossible, so is the other?

It is perfectly obvious to me, Socrates, said Simmias, that the same logical necessity applies to both. . . .

Quite right, Simmias, said Cebes. It seems that we have got the proof of one half of what we wanted—that the soul existed before birth—but now we need also to prove that it will exist after death no less than before birth, if our proof is to be complete.

195. See Plato, *Phaedo*, 73 e-75 e; *Opera*, I, pp. 512-17; Heise, I, pp. 33-38; *Dialogues*, pp. 56-59 (Socrates conversing with Simmias):

So by recollection we mean the sort of experience which I have just described, especially when it happens with reference to things which we had not seen for such a long time that we had forgotten them.

Quite so. . . .

Here is a further step, said Socrates. We admit, I suppose, that there is such a thing as equality—not the equality of stick to stick and stone to stone, and so on, but something beyond all that and distinct from it—absolute equality. Are we to admit this or not?

Yes indeed, said Simmias, most emphatically. . . .

Then we must have had some previous knowledge of equality before the time when we first saw equal things and realized that they were striving after equality, but fell short of it.

That is so. . . .

And at the same time we are agreed also upon this point, that we have not and could not have acquired this notion of equality except by sight or touch or one of the other senses. I am treating them as being all the same.

They are the same, Socrates, for the purpose of our argument.

So it must be through the senses that we obtained the notion that all sensible equals are striving after absolute equality but falling short of it. Is that correct?

Yes, it is.

So before we began to see and hear and use our other senses we must somewhere have acquired the knowledge that there is such a thing as absolute equality. Otherwise we could never have realized, by using it as a standard for comparison, that all equal objects of sense are desirous of being like it, but are only imperfect copies.

That is the logical conclusion, Socrates. . . .

Then if we obtained it before our birth, and possessed it when we were born, we had knowledge, both before and at the moment of birth, not only of equality and relative magnitudes, but of all absolute standards. Our present argument applies no more to equality than it does to absolute beauty, goodness, uprightness, holiness, and, as I maintain, all those characteristics which we designate in our discussions by the term 'absolute.' So we must have obtained knowledge of all these characteristics before our birth.

That is so. . . .

And if it is true that we acquired our knowledge before our birth, and lost it at the moment of birth, but afterward, by the exercise of our senses upon sensible objects, recover the knowledge which we had once before, I suppose that what we call learning will be the recovery of our own knowledge, and surely we should be right in calling this recollection.

196. Plato, *Phaedo*, 75 d; Heise, I, pp. 37-38; cf. *Dialogues*, p. 58. See note 194 above.

197. Plato, *Phaedo*, 76 a; Heise, I, pp. 38-39; cf. *Dialogues*, p. 58.

198. See note 133 above.

199. See Plato, *Phaedo*, 75 e; *Opera*, I, pp. 516-17; Heise, I, p. 38; *Dialogues*, p. 59. See note 195 above.

200. See Plato, *Phaedo*, 78 c-d; Heise, I, p. 44; *Dialogues*, pp. 61-62 (Socrates and Cebes conversing):

> Then let us return to the same examples which we were discussing before. Does that absolute reality which we define in our discussions remain always constant and invariable, or not? Does absolute equality or beauty or any other independent entity which really exists ever admit change of any kind? Or does each one of these uniform and independent entities remain always constant and invariable, never admitting any alteration in any respect or in any sense?
>
> They must be constant and invariable, Socrates, said Cebes.

201. Plato, *Phaedo*, 79 a; Heise, I, p. 45 (compactly quoted). Cf. *Dialogues*, p. 62.

202. See Plato, *Phaedo*, 80 a-b; *Opera*, I, pp. 528-29; Heise, I, p. 47; *Dialogues*, p. 63 (Socrates conversing with Cebes):

> Now, Cebes, he said, see whether this is our conclusion from all that we have said. The soul is most like that which is divine, immortal, intelligible, uniform, indissoluble, and ever self-consistent and invariable, whereas body is most like that which is human, mortal, multiform, unintelligible, dissoluble, and never self-consistent. Can we adduce any conflicting argument, my dear Cebes, to show that this is not so?
>
> No, we cannot.

203. See Plato, *Phaedo*, 87 b; *Opera*, I, pp. 544-45; Heise, I, pp. 61-62; *Dialogues*, p. 69 (Socrates speaking):

> Well, here is my answer. I want you to consider whether there is anything in what I say—because like Simmias I must have recourse to an illustration. Suppose that an elderly tailor has just died. Your theory would be just like saying that the man is not dead, but still exists somewhere safe and sound, and offering as proof the fact that the coat which he had made for himself and was wearing has not perished but is still intact.

204. Plato, *Phaedo*, 104 b-c; Heise, I, p. 97; cf. *Dialogues*, p. 85.

205. See I John 3:2.

206. See Plato, *Phaedo*, 114 c; *Opera*, I, pp. 608-11; Heise, I, p. 117; *Dialogues*, p. 94 (Socrates speaking):

> But those who are judged to have lived a life of surpassing holiness—these are they who are released and set free from confinement in these regions of the earth, and passing upward to their pure abode, make their dwelling upon the earth's surface. And of these such as have purified themselves sufficiently by philosophy live thereafter altogether without bodies,

and reach habitations even more beautiful, which it is not easy to portray—nor is there time to do so now.

207. In Greek mythology, Zeus punished Ixion for making love to Hera (Roman Juno) by sending him a cloud resembling Hera. From this union came the centaurs. See Paul Friedrich A. Nitsch, *neues mythologisches Wörterbuch*, I-II, rev. Friedrich Gotthilf Klopfer (Leipzig, Sorau: 1821; *ASKB* 1944-45), II, pp. 122-23.

208. See Karl Rosenkranz, review of Schleiermacher, *Der christliche Glaube* (2 ed., 1830-31), *Jahrbücher für wissenschaftliche Kritik*, 1831, col. 949.

209. Notably Achilles. See Homer, *Odyssey*, XI, 489-91; Wilster, p. 160; Loeb, I, p. 421: " 'I should choose, so I might live on earth, to serve as the hireling of another, of some portionless man whose livelihood was but small, rather than to be lord over all the dead that have perished.' "

210. See, for example, John 12:24-26; Romans 8:9-17, 12:1-2.

211. Cf. Genesis 1:26: "Let us make man in our image, after our likeness" (*RSV*). Danish: "*lader os gjøre et Menneske i vort Billede, efter vor Lignelse.*"

212. In the early Church, the day of a martyr's death was celebrated as his birthday. See, for example, *Martyrium Polycarpi*, 18; "The Martyrdom of St. Polycarp," *Ancient Christian Writers*, ed. and tr. James A. Kleist (Westminster, Md.: Newman, 1948), p. 99: "Then the Lord will permit us . . . to assemble in rapturous joy and celebrate his martyrdom—his birthday."

213. See Plato, *Phaedo*, 63 e-64 a; *Opera*, I, pp. 488-89; Heise, I, p. 14; *Dialogues*, p. 46 (Socrates speaking to Simmias and Cebes):

> I want to explain to you how it seems to me natural that a man who has really devoted his life to philosophy should be cheerful in the face of death, and confident of finding the greatest blessing in the next world when his life is finished. I will try to make clear to you, Simmias and Cebes, how this can be so.
>
> Ordinary people seem not to realize that those who really apply themselves in the right way to philosophy are directly and of their own accord preparing themselves for dying and death. If this is true, and they have actually been looking forward to death all their lives, it would of course be absurd to be troubled when the thing comes for which they have so long been preparing and looking forward.

214. Johan Herman Wessel, "*Gravskrifter over Digteren, af ham selv,*" *Samlede Digte* (Copenhagen: 1832), p. 269 (ed. tr.).

215. See Genesis 1:3-14.

216. Plato, *Phaedo*, 91 a-b; Heise, I, p. 69; cf. *Dialogues*, p. 73.

217. See Friedrich Ast, *Platon's Leben und Schriften* (Leipzig: 1816), pp. 474-91.

218. *Platons Werke*, I[2], p. 185; *Schleiermacher's Introductions*, p. 138.

219. Stallbaum, *Platonis dialogos*.

220. See Ast, *Platon's Leben*, p. 482. Although Ast regards Xenophon's

Apology as inauthentic, he does consider the presentation in *Memorabilia* to be superior to Plato's.

221. This is the first appearance of "either/or" in Kierkegaard's writings. The Latin form was used by philosophy professor Frederik Christian Sibbern in his long review of Johan Ludvig Heiberg's *Perseus, Journal for den speculative Idee, Nr. 1*, in *Maanedskrift for Litteratur*, XIX, 1838, p. 432, in a section on the principle of contradiction. The phrase was used also by Bishop Jakob Peter Mynster in his discussion of the principle of contradiction, in opposition to Hegel, Johan Alfred Bornemann, and Johan Ludvig Heiberg, in *Tidsskrift for Litteratur og Critik*, I, 1839, p. 267; see also Mynster, *Blandede Skrivter*, I-VI (Copenhagen: 1852-57), II, p. 114. See *Postscript*, *KW* XIII (*SV* VII 261).

222. See p. 52 on the unity of the comic and the tragic in the *Symposium*, also pp. 67-68 on pleasure and pain in the *Phaedo*.

223. See Plato, *Apology*, 28 e; *Opera*, VIII, p. 126; *Dialogues*, p. 15.

224. See Plato, *Apology*, 29 a; *Opera*, VIII, p. 126; *Dialogues*, p. 15.

225. See Supplement, p. 441 (*Pap.* III B 4).

226. Plato, *Dialogues*, p. 22.

227. Ibid., p. 25.

228. King Minos and his brother Rhadamanthus from Crete; Aeacus, son of Zeus, from Aegina; and Triptolemus, legendary hero who taught the Greeks the cultivation of grain. See *Apology*, 41 a; *Opera*, VIII, pp. 154-55; *Dialogues*, p. 25.

229. See p. 40.

230. Plato, *Opera*, VIII, p. 158; *Dialogues*, p. 26.

231. Ast, *Platon's Leben*, pp. 487-88.

232. Cf. Plato, *Apology*, 35 e-36 a; *Opera*, VIII, pp. 142-43 ("τρεῖς," "*tres*"); *Platons Werke*, I^2, p. 220 ("*drei*"); *Dialogues*, p. 21 ("thirty"):

> There are a great many reasons, gentlemen, why I am not distressed by this result—I mean your condemnation of me—but the chief reason is that the result was not unexpected. What does surprise me is the number of votes cast on the two sides. I should never have believed that it would be such a close thing, but now it seems that if a mere thirty votes had gone the other way, I should have been acquitted. Even as it is, I feel that so far as Meletus' part is concerned I have been acquitted, and not only that, but anyone can see that if Anytus and Lycon had not come forward to accuse me, Meletus would actually have forfeited his one thousand drachmas for not having obtained one fifth of the votes.

233. See Matthew 20:1-16.

234. See Ast, *Platon's Leben*, pp. 477-80.

235. Plato, *Gorgias*, 521 e; Heise, III, p. 188; cf. *Dialogues*, p. 302.

236. Jens Baggesen, *"Kallundborgs Krønike," Jens Baggesens danske Værker*, I-XII (Copenhagen: 1827-32; *ASKB* 1509-20), I, p. 236 (ed. tr.). Jens Skovfogd, whose home was about to be plundered, in the ensuing struggle

apparently killed one thief, who thereby was saved from a worse death by hanging.

237. See Plato, *Gorgias*, 473 e-474 a; *Opera*, I, pp. 526-27; Heise, III, pp. 68-69; *Dialogues*, p. 256:

> POLUS: Do you not consider yourself already refuted, Socrates, when you put forward views that nobody would accept? Why, ask anyone present!
>
> SOCRATES: I am no politician, Polus, and last year when I became a member of the Council and my tribe was presiding and it was my duty to put the question to the vote, I raised a laugh because I did not know how to. And so do not on this occasion either bid me put the question to those present, but if you can contrive no better refutation than this, then leave it to me in my turn, as I suggested just now, and try out what I consider the proper form of refutation. For I know how to produce one witness to the truth of what I say, the man with whom I am debating, but the others I ignore. I know how to secure one man's vote, but with the many I will not even enter into discussion.

238. See note 232 above.

239. See note 110 above.

240. See p. 183 and note 426.

241. Presumably a copy of the *Sistine Madonna*, a painting by Raphael (1483-1520). See, for example, H. Knackfuz, *Raffael* (Bielefeld, Leipzig: 1905), plate 104.

242. In the following quotations from Ast's *Platon's Leben*, there are a few minor variations from Ast's text that do not impair the substance.

243. Ast's Greek quotations and pagination thereof in the German text are from *Platonis Euthyphro Apologia Socratis Crito Phaedo*, ed. Johann Friedrich Fischer (Leipzig: 1783).

244. From the title of Matthias Claudius's *ASMUS omnia sua SECUM portans, oder Sämmtliche Werke des Wandsbecker Bothen, Werke*, I-IV (Hamburg: 1838; *ASKB* 1631-32). Kierkegaard omitted *sua* [his], presumably because it did not apply to Socrates, who in his ignorance had nothing.

245. Ast, *Platon's Leben*, p. 479. See Plato, *Apology*, 21 a, 30 c, 20 e; cf. 17 c, 27 b, 31 e; *Opera*, VIII, pp. 106, 130-31, 106; cf. 98-99, 122-23, 132-33; *Dialogues*, pp. 7, 16, 7; cf. 4, 13, 17.

246. Plato, *Apology*, 30 d-e; *Opera*, VIII, pp. 130-31; *Dialogues*, pp. 16-17.

247. Plato, *Protagoras*, 320 c; Heise, II, p. 130; cf. *Dialogues*, p. 318.

248. Plato, *Protagoras*, 328 c; Heise, II, p. 145; cf. *Dialogues*, p. 324.

249. See Plato, *Gorgias*, 461 b-c, 482 c-d; *Opera*, I, pp. 292-93, 352-53; Heise, III, pp. 38, 93-94; *Dialogues*, pp. 244, 265-66:

> POLUS: What, Socrates? Is what you are saying your true opinion about rhetoric? Or do you imagine just because Gorgias was ashamed not to admit that the rhetorician will know the just also and the honorable and the good, and that, if any man came to him without this knowledge, he himself would instruct him, and then, as result, I suppose, of this admission a con-

tradiction arose in the argument—which is just what you love and you yourself steer the argument in that direction—why, who do you think will deny that he himself knows the right and will teach it to others? But it is the height of bad taste to lead discussions into such channels.

CALLICLES: Socrates, it seems to me that you run wild in your talk like a true mob orator, and now you are haranguing us in this way because Polus fell into the very error which he blamed Gorgias for being drawn into by you. Gorgias, he said, was asked by you whether, in case a prospective pupil of rhetoric came to him without a knowledge of justice, he himself would teach him, and he was shamed into saying he would do so, because the general conventional view demanded it and men would be vexed if one refused. It was through this admission that he was forced to contradict himself, and that is just what you like. And Polus, in my opinion, was quite right in laughing at you at the time, but now he himself in turn has been caught in the same way. And I do not think much of Polus for the very reason that he agreed with you that it is more disgraceful to do than to suffer injustice, for it was as a result of this admission that he was caught in the toils of your argument and silenced, because he was ashamed to say what he thought.

250. See Plato, *Gorgias*, 523 a-526 d; *Opera*, I, pp. 456-65; Heise, III, pp. 190-97; *Dialogues*, pp. 303-06.

251. See Plato, *Phaedo*, 107 d-114 d; *Gorgias*, 523 a-526 d; *Republic*, X, 614 b-621 b; *Opera*, I, pp. 595-611, 456-65, V, pp. 92-107; Heise, I, pp. 104-17, III, pp. 190-97; *Dialogues*, pp. 89-95, 303-06, 838-44.

252. Johann August Eberhard, *Neue vermischte Schriften* (Halle: 1788).

253. See W. Ackermann, *Das Christliche in Plato und in der platonischen Philosophie* (Hamburg: 1835), p. 52.

254. See Plato, *Republic*, IV, 427 b-c; *Opera*, IV, pp. 208-09; *Dialogues*, pp. 668-69 (Adimantus and Socrates conversing):

> What part of legislation, then, he said, is still left for us?
>
> And I replied, For us nothing, but for the Apollo of Delphi, the chief, the fairest, and the first of enactments.
>
> What are they? he said.
>
> The founding of temples, and sacrifices, and other forms of worship of gods, daemons, and heroes, and likewise the burial of the dead and the services we must render to the dwellers in the world beyond to keep them gracious. For of such matters we neither know anything nor in the founding of our city if we are wise shall we entrust them to any other or make use of any other interpreter than the god of our fathers. For this god surely is in such matters for all mankind the interpreter of the religion of their fathers who from his seat in the middle and at the very navel of the earth delivers his interpretation.

255. The highest level of initiation in the rites of the Eleusinian Mysteries, the principal Mysteries of Greece, which centered on the legends of Demeter, Kore (Persephone), and Dionysus, who symbolized the annual death and renewal of life. The rites included ceremonial purification, sacred drama, and a procession from Athens to Eleusis.

256. See, for example, Plato, *Republic*, II, 377 b-c, 380 c, III, 392 a-b, 401 b-d; *Opera*, IV, pp. 108-11, 116-17, 136-39, 156-59; *Dialogues*, pp. 624, 627, 637, 646 (Adimantus and Socrates conversing):

> We must begin, then, it seems, by a censorship over our storymakers, and what they do well we must pass and what not, reject. And the stories on the accepted list we will induce nurses and mothers to tell to the children and so shape their souls by these stories far rather than their bodies by their hands. But most of the stories they now tell we must reject.
>
> I cast my vote with yours for this law, he said, and am well pleased with it.
>
> This, then, said I, will be one of the laws and patterns concerning the gods to which speakers and poets will be required to conform, that God is not the cause of all things, but only of the good.
>
> What type of discourse remains for our definition of our prescriptions and proscriptions? We have declared the right way of speaking about gods and daemons and heroes and that other world?
>
> We have.
>
> Speech, then, about men would be the remainder.
>
> Obviously.
>
> It is impossible for us, my friend, to place this here.
>
> Why?
>
> Because I presume we are going to say that so it is that both poets and writers of prose speak wrongly about men in matters of greatest moment, saying that there are many examples of men who, though unjust, are happy, and of just men who are wretched, and that there is profit in injustice if it be concealed, and that justice is the other man's good and your own loss, and I presume that we shall forbid them to say this sort of thing and command them to sing and fable the opposite. Don't you think so?
>
> Nay, I well know it, he said.
>
> Is it, then, only the poets that we must supervise and compel to embody in their poems the semblance of the good character or else not write poetry among us, or must we keep watch over the other craftsmen, and forbid them to represent the evil disposition, the licentious, the illiberal, the graceless, either in the likeness of living creatures or in buildings or in any other product of their art, on penalty, if unable to obey, of being forbidden to practice their art among us, that our guardians may not be bred among symbols of evil, as it were in a pasturage of poisonous herbs, lest grazing freely and cropping from many such day by day they little by little and all

unawares accumulate and build up a huge mass of evil in their own souls. But we must look for those craftsmen who by the happy gift of nature are capable of following the trail of true beauty and grace, that our young men, dwelling as it were in a salubrious region, may receive benefit from all things about them, whence the influence that emanates from works of beauty may waft itself to eye or ear like a breeze that brings from wholesome places health, and so from earliest childhood insensibly guide them to likeness, to friendship, to harmony with beautiful reason.

Yes, he said, that would be far the best education for them.

257. See, for example, Plato, *Republic*, X, 602 b-c, 605 a-c; *Opera*, V, pp. 64-65, 70-73; *Dialogues*, pp. 827, 830 (Glaucon and Socrates conversing):

On this, then, as it seems, we are fairly agreed, that the imitator knows nothing worth mentioning of the things he imitates, but that imitation is a form of play, not to be taken seriously, and that those who attempt tragic poetry, whether in iambics or heroic verse, are all altogether imitators.

By all means.

In heaven's name, then, this business of imitation is concerned with the third remove from truth, is it not?

Yes.

This consideration, then, makes it right for us to proceed to lay hold of him and set him down as the counterpart of the painter, for he resembles him in that his creations are inferior in respect of reality, and the fact that his appeal is to the inferior part of the soul and not to the best part is another point of resemblance. And so we may at last say that we should be justified in not admitting him into a well-ordered state, because he stimulates and fosters this element in the soul, and by strengthening it tends to destroy the rational part, just as when in a state one puts bad men in power and turns the city over to them and ruins the better sort. Precisely in the same manner we shall say that the mimetic poet sets up in each individual soul a vicious constitution by fashioning phantoms far removed from reality, and by currying favor with the senseless element that cannot distinguish the greater from the less, but calls the same thing now one, now the other.

By all means.

But we have not yet brought our chief accusation against it. Its power to corrupt, with rare exceptions, even the better sort is surely the chief cause for alarm.

258. Cf. Hegel, *Vorlesungen über die Philosophie der Religion*, I, *Werke*, XI, p. 142; *J.A.*, XV, p. 158; *Lectures on the Philosophy of Religion*, I-III (tr. of *P.R.*, 2 ed., 1840, which Kierkegaard obtained eventually, although he may not have had it at the time *Irony* was being written), I-III, tr. E. B. Speirs and J. Burdon Sanderson (New York: Humanities, 1974), I, p. 146: "There are, it is true, myths in which the external form in which they appear is of the most

importance, but usually such a myth contains an allegory, like the myths of Plato." See also *JP* III 2799 (*Pap*. I A 300).

259. See Plato, *Phaedrus*, 246 a-d; *Opera*, I, pp. 168-71; *Dialogues*, p. 493.

260. See Plato, *Gorgias*, 523 e-524 a; *Opera*, I, pp. 458-61; Heise, III, pp. 192-93; *Dialogues*, p. 304.

261. See Plato, *Phaedo*, 107 d-114 c; *Opera*, I, pp. 594-613; Heise, I, pp. 104-17; *Dialogues*, pp. 89-94.

262. See Hegel, *Vorlesungen über die Philosophie der Geschichte*, *Werke*, IX, p. 171; *J.A.*, XI, pp. 193-94; *The Philosophy of History* (tr. of *P.G.*, 2 ed., 1840; Kierkegaard had 1 ed., 1837), tr. J. Sibree (New York: Dover, 1956), p. 141: "The Indian view of things is a Universal Pantheism, a Pantheism, however, of Imagination, not of Thought." See also *Aesthetik*, I, *Werke*, X[1], pp. 468, 486; *J.A.*, XII, pp. 485, 502; *Philosophy of Fine Art*, II, pp. 89, 106: "The Pantheism of Art," "the imagination of pantheism."

263. See Supplement, p. 428 (*Pap*. I A 241, 300). See also *Stages*, pp. 204-05, *KW* XI (*SV* VI 194); *JP* III 2309-15 (*Pap*. II A 155-61).

264. See note 277 below.

265. See John 3:8.

266. Henrich Steffens, *Caricaturen des Heiligsten*, I-II (Leipzig: 1819-21; *ASKB* 793-94), I, pp. 1-15.

267. *ASKB* 576.

268. See note 122 above.

269. Cf., for example, Hegel, *Wissenschaft der Logik*, preface to 1 ed., 1812, *Werke*, III, p. 7; *J.A.*, IV, p. 17; *Science of Logic*, p. 28:

> The understanding *determines*, and holds the determinations fixed; reason is negative and *dialectical*, because it resolves the determinations of the understanding into nothing; it is positive because it generates the universal and comprehends the particular therein. Just as the understanding is usually taken to be something separate from reason as such, so too dialectical reason is usually taken to be something distinct from positive reason. But reason in its truth is *spirit* which is higher than either merely positive reason, or merely intuitive understanding. It is the negative, that which constitutes the quality alike of dialectical reason and of understanding; it negates what is simple, thus positing the specific difference of the understanding; it equally resolves it and is thus dialectical.

270. Plato, *Symposium*, 211 e; Heise, II, p. 81; cf. *Dialogues*, p. 563.

271. See, for example, Immanuel Kant, *Critik der reinen Vernunft* (4 ed., Riga: 1794; *ASKB* 595), pp. xxv-vi; *Immanuel Kant's Critique of Pure Reason* (tr. of *C.V.*, 2 ed., 1787), tr. Norman Kemp Smith (London: Macmillan, 1950), p. 27:

> That space and time are only forms of sensible intuition, and so only conditions of the existence of things as appearances; that, moreover, we have no concepts of understanding, and consequently no elements for the knowledge of things, save in so far as intuition can be given corresponding

> to these concepts; and that we can therefore have no knowledge of any object as thing in itself, but only in so far as it is an object of sensible intuition, that is, an appearance—all this is proved in the analytical part of the Critique. Thus it does indeed follow that all possible speculative knowledge of reason is limited to mere objects of *experience*. But our further contention must also be duly borne in mind, namely, that though we cannot *know* these objects as things in themselves, we must yet be in position at least to *think* them as things in themselves; otherwise we should be landed in the absurd conclusion that there can be appearance without anything that appears.

Cf. *Postscript*, *KW* XII (*SV* VII 282-83).

272. See, for example, Kant, *Religion innerhalb der Grenzen der bloszen Vernunft* (Leipzig: 1838), pp. 19-45; *Religion within the Limits of Reason Alone*, tr. Theodore M. Greene and Hoyt H. Hudson (Chicago: Open Court, 1934), pp. 15-39. See also *JP* III 3089 (*Pap.* VIII[1] A 11).

273. Ast, *Platon's Leben*, pp. 312-13 fn.

274. Baur, *Sokrates und Christus*, p. 96.

275. See Plato, *Gorgias*, 523 a, 524 a, 526 d; *Opera*, I, pp. 456-57, 460-61; 464-65; Heise, III, pp. 190, 193, 197; *Dialogues*, pp. 303, 304, 306.

276. Plato, *Gorgias*, 527 a; Heise, III, p. 198; cf. *Dialogues*, p. 306.

277. Plato, *Phaedo*, 114 d; Heise, I, p. 117; cf. *Dialogues*, pp. 94-95.

278. Cf. *Schleiermacher's Introductions*, pp. 355-56.

279. Plato, *Republic*, I, 348 c-d; *Opera*, IV, p. 50; *Dialogues*, p. 598.

280. See Plato, *Republic*, I, 336 b-c; *Opera*, IV, pp. 25-26; *Dialogues*, p. 586 (Socrates speaking):

> Now Thrasymachus, even while we were conversing, had been trying several times to break in and lay hold of the discussion but he was restrained by those who sat by him who wished to hear the argument out. But when we came to a pause after I had said this, he couldn't any longer hold his peace. But gathering himself up like a wild beast he hurled himself upon us as if he would tear us to pieces. And Polemarchus and I were frightened and fluttered apart.
>
> He bawled out into our midst, What balderdash is this that you have been talking, and why do you Simple Simons truckle and give way to one another?

281. See Plato, *Gorgias*, 461 b-c, 481 b-c; Heise, III, pp. 37, 91; *Opera*, I, pp. 292-93, 350-51; *Dialogues*, pp. 244 (see n. 249 above), 265:

> CALLICLES: By heaven, that is just what I am anxious to do. Tell me, Socrates, are we to consider you serious now or jesting? For if you are serious and what you say is true, then surely the life of us mortals must be turned upside down and apparently we are everywhere doing the opposite of what we should.

282. Plato, *Republic*, I, 336 d-e; *Opera*, IV, pp. 24-25; *Dialogues*, pp. 586-87.

283. See Plato, *Gorgias*, 473 d; *Opera*, I, pp. 326-27; Heise, III, p. 68; *Dialogues*, p. 256 (Socrates speaking to Polus): "Now you are trying to make my flesh creep, my noble friend, instead of refuting me, and just now you were appealing to witnesses. However, refresh my memory a trifle. Did you say 'criminally plotting to make himself a tyrant'?"

284. Plato, *Republic*, I, 338 c; *Opera*, IV, p. 28; *Dialogues*, p. 588.

285. Plato, *Gorgias*, 490 d-e; Heise, III, pp. 110-11 (Kierkegaard compresses the intervening dialogue into "I understand . . . clothes"); cf. *Dialogues*, pp. 272-73.

286. Plato, *Republic*, I, 350 c-d; *Opera*, IV, pp. 54-57; *Dialogues*, p. 600.

287. This June festival celebrated Bendis, a Thracian goddess, recently introduced into Greece, who was identified with the Olympian goddess Artemis, goddess of chastity and marriage and of the moon.

288. See Plato, *Republic*, I, 331 e, 332 b-c; *Opera*, IV, pp. 14-15; *Dialogues*, pp. 580, 581 (Socrates and Cephalus conversing):

> Tell me, then, you the inheritor of the argument, what it is that you affirm that Simonides says and rightly says about justice.
>
> That it is just, he replied, to render to each his due. In saying this I think he speaks well.

> It was a riddling definition of justice, then, that Simonides gave after the manner of poets, for while his meaning, it seems, was that justice is rendering to each what befits him, the name that he gave to this was 'the due.'

289. Plato, *Republic*, I, 338 c; *Opera*, IV, pp. 28-29; *Dialogues*, p. 588.

290. Plato, *Republic*, I, 341 b; *Opera*, IV, pp. 34-35; *Dialogues*, p. 591.

291. Plato, *Republic*, I, 343 a; *Opera*, IV, pp. 38-39; *Dialogues*, p. 593.

292. Plato, *Republic*, I, 354 a; *Opera*, IV, pp. 64-65; *Dialogues*, p. 605. See also note 287 above.

293. Plato, *Republic*, I, 354 b; *Opera*, IV, pp. 64-65; *Dialogues*, p. 605.

294. See note 155 above.

295. See Plato, *Republic*, I, 346 a-e; *Opera*, IV, pp. 44-49; *Dialogues*, pp. 595-96 (Socrates and Thrasymachus conversing):

> We ordinarily say, do we not, that each of the arts is different from others because its power or function is different? And, my dear fellow, in order that we may reach some result, don't answer counter to your real belief.
>
> Well, yes, he said, that is what renders it different.
>
> And does not each art also yield us benefit that is peculiar to itself and not general, as for example medicine health, the pilot's art safety at sea, and the other arts similarly?
>
> Assuredly. . . .
>
> Then, Thrasymachus, is not this immediately apparent, that no art or office provides what is beneficial for itself—but as we said long ago it pro-

vides and enjoins what is beneficial to its subject, considering the advantage of that, the weaker, and not the advantage of the stronger?

296. See Ast, *Platon's Leben*, p. 53.
297. See ibid., pp. 157-59.
298. Pp. 62-64.
299. Schleiermacher, *"Ueber den Werth des Sokrates als Philosophen," Abhandlungen der philosophischen Klasse der königlich-preussischen Akademie der Wissenschaften aus den Jahren 1814-1815* (Berlin: 1818), pp. 63-66.
300. See Aristotle, *Sophistical Refutations*, 183 a-b; *Aristoteles graece*, I-II, ed. Immanuel Bekker (Berlin: 1831; *ASKB* 1074-75), I, p. 183; *The Complete Works of Aristotle*, I-II, ed. Jonathan Barnes (rev. Oxford tr., Princeton: Princeton University Press, 1984), I, p. 313:

> Our programme was, then, to discover some faculty of reasoning about any theme put before us from the most reputable premisses that there are. For that is the essential task of the art of dialectic and of examination. Inasmuch, however, as there is annexed to it, on account of its affinity to the art of sophistry, that it can conduct an examination not only dialectically but also with a show of knowledge, we therefore proposed for our treatise not only the aforesaid aim of being able to exact an account of any view, but also the aim of ensuring that in defending an argument we shall defend our thesis in the same manner by means of views as reputable as possible. The reason of this we have explained [165 a]; for this was why Socrates used to ask questions and not to answer them—for he used to confess that he did not know.

301. See pp. 28-29.
302. On "being beyond" or "going further," see, for example, Hans Lassen Martensen's review (*Maanedsskrift for Litteratur*, XVI, 1836, p. 527, ed. tr.) of Johan Ludvig Heiberg, *Indlednings-Foredrag til det i November 1834 begyndte logiske Cursus paa den kongelige militaire Høiskole* (1835), in which Martensen states that if Hegel sought "the eternal word" rather than "the eternal idea," "the objective point of departure of philosophy would have gone beyond the abstract category." See also, for example, *Soap-Cellars*, *KW* I (*Pap*. II B 19, p. 300); *Fear and Trembling*, pp. 5-7, *KW* VI (*SV* III 57-59); *JP* V 5200 (*Pap*. II A 7); VII, p. 41.
303. See *Repetition*, p. 131, *KW* VI (*SV* III 173).
304. See Luke 11:24.
305. See *JP* IV 4066, 4067, 4775 (*Pap*. I A 285, 288; II A 291).
306. See, for example, Claudius Aelianus, *Variae historiae*, II, 13; *Werke*, I-IX, tr. Ephorus Wunderlich and Friedrich Jacobs (Stuttgart: 1839-42; *ASKB* 1042-43), I, p. 51.
307. Pp. 43-50. See *Postscript*, *KW* XII (*SV* VII 95).
308. Cleon, a demagogue, is attacked by Aristophanes in *The Knights*, Euripides in *The Frogs* and *Thesmophoriazusae*, and Socrates in *The Clouds*.
309. Johann Georg Sulzer, *Nachträge zu Sulzers allgemeiner Theorie der*

schönen Künste, I-VIII, ed. Christian Gottfried Schütz (Leipzig: 1792-1808) (excerpts ed. tr.).

310. Heinrich Theodor Rötscher, *Aristophanes und sein Zeitalter* (Berlin: 1827), pp. 272-88, provides a survey of interpretations, and pp. 319-22 present Rötscher's own view.

311. In 1827, Süvern published *Ueber Aristophanes Drama benannt das Alter.*

312. Cf. Hegel, *Aesthetik*, III, *Werke*, X³, p. 547; *J.A.*, XIV, p. 547; *Philosophy of Fine Art*, IV, p. 315:

> . . . the chorus is, in truth, there as a substantive and more enlightened intelligence, which warns us from irrelevant oppositions, and reflects upon the genuine issue. But, granting this to be so, it is by no means a wholly disinterested person, at leisure to entertain such thoughts and ethical judgments as it likes as are the spectators, which, uninteresting and tedious on its own account, could only be attached for the sake of such reflections. The chorus is the actual substance of the heroic life and action itself: it is, as contrasted with the particular heroes, the common folk regarded as the fruitful heritage, out of which individuals, much as flowers and towering trees from their native soil, grow and whereby they are conditioned in this life. Consequently, the chorus is peculiarly fitted to a view of life in which the obligations of State legislation and settled religious dogmas do not, as yet, act as a restrictive force in ethical and social development, but where morality only exists in its primitive form of directly animated human life . . ..

313. Aristophanes, *The Clouds*, ll. 510-633. All quoted passages from *The Clouds* are in Greek. In *Irony*, although no reference is made to the text used, Kierkegaard's line numbers correspond to those given in *Aristophanis Comoediae*, I-II, ed. Guilielmo Dindorf (Leipzig: 1830; *ASKB* 1051), I, and in the English translations of the Greek in *Aristophanes*, I-III, tr. Benjamin Bickley Rogers (Loeb, Cambridge: Harvard University Press, 1979-82), I, pp. 266-401.

314. See Aristophanes, *Clouds*, ll. 269-74; Dindorf, p. 239; Loeb, I, p. 289:

> Come forth, come forth, dread Clouds, and to earth
>   your glorious majesty show;
> Whether lightly ye rest on the time-honoured crest
>   of Olympus environed in snow,
> Or tread the soft dance 'mid the stately expanse
>   of Ocean, the nymphs to beguile,
> Or stoop to enfold with your pitchers of gold,
>   the mystical waves of the Nile,
> Or around the white foam of Maeotis ye roam,
>   or Mimas all wintry and bare,
> O hear while we pray, and turn not away
>   from the rites which your servants prepare.

315. See Aristophanes, *Clouds*, l. 379; Dindorf, I, p. 185; Loeb, I, p. 301.

316. See Aristophanes, *Clouds*, ll. 339-57; Dindorf, I, pp. 182-83; Loeb, I, pp. 295-97.

317. Cf. *Point of View*, *KW* XXII (*SV* XIII 547).

318. Hegel, *Werke*, XIV, p. 70 (ed. tr.); *J.A.*, XVIII, p. 70; cf. *History of Philosophy*, I, p. 406.

319. Rötscher, *Aristophanes*, p. 325.

320. Cf. *Soap-Cellars*, *KW* I (*Pap.* II B 10, p. 289).

321. See Aristophanes, *Clouds*, ll. 217-27; Dindorf, I, pp. 175-76; Loeb, I, pp. 283-85 (student and Strepsiades speaking):

Hallo! who's that? that fellow in the basket?
STU. That's HE.
ST. Who's HE?
STU. Socrates.
ST. Socrates!
You sir, call out to him as loud as you can.
STU. Call him yourself: I have not leisure now.
ST. Socrates! Socrates!
Sweet Socrates!
SOCRATES. Mortal! why call'st thou me?
ST. O, first of all, please tell me what you are doing.
SO. I walk on air, and contem-plate [*sic*] the Sun.
ST. O then from a basket you contemn the Gods,
And not from the earth, at any rate?

322. See Aristophanes, *Clouds*, ll. 852-61; Dindorf, I, pp. 207-08; Loeb, I, p. 343 (Strepsiades and his son, Pheidippides, conversing):

PH. . . . These then are the mighty secrets
You have picked up amongst those earth-born fellows.
ST. And lots besides: but everything I learn
I straight forget: I am so old and stupid.
PH. And this is what you have lost your mantle for?
ST. It's very absent sometimes: 'tisn't lost.
PH. And what have you done with your shoes, you dotard you?
ST. Like Pericles, all for the best, I've lost them.
Come, come; go with me: humour me in this,
And then do what you like.

323. See Aesop, *"Vulpis et Ciconia," Phaedri Augusti Liberti Fabularum Aesopiarum Libri* V (Leipzig: 1828), XXVI, pp. 12-13; "The Fox and the Stork," *Babrius and Phaedrus*, ed. and tr. Ben Edwin Perry (Loeb, Cambridge: Harvard University Press, 1965), pp. 221-23.

324. *ASKB* 1055 (ed. tr.).

325. See note 221 on contemporary Danish discussion of the principle of contradiction.

326. See pp. 140-41 fn.

327. Rötscher, *Aristophanes*, pp. 284-88.

328. See Süvern, *Ueber Aristophanes*, p. 186.

329. Karl C. Reisig (1792-1829), German philologist.

330. *Aristophanis Nubes cum scholiis*, ed. Johann Gottfried Jakob Hermann (Leipzig: 1798), p. 33.

331. See Kant, *Critik der reinen Vernunft*, p. 627; *Critique of Pure Reason*, p. 505:

> A hundred real thalers do not contain the least coin more than a hundred possible thalers. For as the latter signify the concept, and the former the object and the positing of the object, should the former contain more than the latter, my concept would not, in that case, express the whole object, and would not therefore be an adequate concept of it. My financial position is, however, affected very differently by a hundred real thalers than it is by the mere concept of them (that is, of their possibility). For the object, as it actually exists, is not analytically contained in my concept, but is added to my concept (which is a determination of my state) synthetically; and yet the conceived hundred thalers are not themselves in the least increased through thus acquiring existence outside my concept.

Cf. Hegel, *Wissenschaft der Logik*, I, *Werke*, III, pp. 84-88; *J.A.*, IV, pp. 94-98; *Science of Logic*, pp. 86-89.

332. See Hegel, *Geschichte der Philosophie*, II, *Werke*, XIV, p. 85; *J.A.*, XVIII, p. 85; *History of Philosophy*, I, p. 426.

333. Rötscher, *Aristophanes*, pp. 276-88, 312-19.

334. See Plato, *Apology*, 33 a; *Opera*, VIII, pp. 136-37; *Dialogues*, p. 18:

> I have never countenanced any action that was incompatible with justice on the part of any person, including those whom some people maliciously call my pupils. I have never set up as any man's teacher, but if anyone, young or old, is eager to hear me conversing and carrying out my private mission, I never grudge him the opportunity; nor do I charge a fee for talking to him, and refuse to talk without one.

335. See Plato, *Phaedo*, 97 b-98 d; *Opera*, I, pp. 568-73; Heise, I, pp. 82-85; *Dialogues*, pp. 79-80:

> However, I once heard someone reading from a book, as he said, by Anaxagoras, and asserting that it is mind that produces order and is the cause of everything. This explanation pleased me. Somehow it seemed right that mind should be the cause of everything, and I reflected that if this is so, mind in producing order sets everything in order and arranges each individual thing in the way that is best for it. . . .
>
> These reflections made me suppose, to my delight, that in Anaxagoras I had found an authority on causation who was after my own heart. I assumed that he would begin by informing us whether the earth is flat or round, and would then proceed to explain in detail the reason and logical

necessity for this by stating how and why it was better that it should be so. . . .

It was a wonderful hope, my friend, but it was quickly dashed. As I read on I discovered that the fellow made no use of mind and assigned to it no causality for the order of the world, but adduced causes like air and aether and water and many other absurdities. It seemed to me that he was just about as inconsistent as if someone were to say, The cause of everything that Socrates does is mind—and then, in trying to account for my several actions, said first that the reason why I am lying here now is that my body is composed of bones and sinews, and that the bones are rigid and separated at the joints, but the sinews are capable of contraction and relaxation, and form an envelope for the bones with the help of the flesh and skin, the latter holding all together, and since the bones move freely in their joints the sinews by relaxing and contracting enable me somehow to bend my limbs, and that is the cause of my sitting here in a bent position.

336. See Aristophanes, *Clouds*, ll. 367-71; Dindorf, I, p. 184; Loeb, I, p. 299:

SO. Zeus, indeed! there's no Zeus: don't you be so obtuse.
ST. No Zeus up aloft in the sky!
Then, you first must explain, who it is sends the rain;
or I really must think you are wrong.
SO. Well then, be it known, these send it alone:
I can prove it by arguments strong.
Was there ever a shower seen to fall in an hour
when the sky was all cloudless and blue?
Yet on a fine day, when the Clouds are away,
he might send one, according to you.

337. See p. 10 and note 12.

338. Prodicus of Ceos (fl. 340-400 B.C.), an eminent Sophist and author of *The Choice of Hercules*. See Aristophanes, *Clouds*, ll. 361-62; Dindorf, I, p. 183; Loeb, I, p. 299.

339. See, for example, Xenophon, *Symposium*, V, 5-8; *Xenophontis Opera, graece et latine*, I-IV, ed. Carl August Thieme (Leipzig: 1801-04; *ASKB* 1207-10), IV, pp. 472-74; Loeb, pp. 447-49 (Socrates and Critobulus conversing):

SOC. "Do you know the reason why we need eyes?"

CRIT. "Obviously to see with."

"In that case, it would appear without further ado that my eyes are finer ones than yours."

"How so?"

"Because, while yours see only straight ahead, mine, by bulging out as they do, see also to the sides."

CRIT. "Do you mean to say that a crab is better equipped visually than any other creature?"

SOC. "Absolutely; for its eyes are also better set to insure strength."

CRIT. "Well, let that pass; but whose nose is finer, yours or mine?"

SOC. "Mine, I consider, granting that Providence made us noses to smell with. For your nostrils look down toward the ground, but mine are wide open and turned outward so that I can catch scents from all about."

"But how do you make a snub nose handsomer than a straight one?"

SOC. "For the reason that it does not put a barricade between the eyes but allows them unobstructed vision of whatever they desire to see; whereas a high nose, as if in despite, has walled the eyes off one from the other."

"As for the mouth," said Critobulus, "I concede that point. For if it is created for the purpose of biting off food, you could bite off a far bigger mouthful than I could. And don't you think that your kiss is also the more tender because you have thick lips?"

SOC. "According to your argument, it would seem that I have a mouth more ugly even than an ass's. But do you not reckon it a proof of my superior beauty that the River Nymphs, goddesses as they are, bear as their offspring the Seileni,[*] who resemble me more closely than they do you?"

[*] See note 143 above.

340. See Rötscher, *Aristophanes*, pp. 319-30.

341. See Aristophanes, *Clouds*, ll. 889-1104; Dindorf, I, pp. 209-20; Loeb, I, 347-67, a debate between Right Logic and Wrong Logic.

342. According to the Loeb edition, Socrates is speaking to Strepsiades. However, in *Des Aristophanes Werke*, I-III, ed. Johann Gustav Droysen (Berlin: 1835-38; *ASKB* 1052-54), III, pp. 72-73, ll. 696-722 are between Strepsiades and the chorus.

343. See Ludvig Holberg, *Erasmus Montanus*, I, 2; III, 4; *Danske Skue-Plads*, V, no pagination; *Comedies by Holberg*, pp. 122, 147-49.

344. See Aristophanes, *Clouds*, ll. 483-85; Dindorf, I, p. 339; Loeb, I, p. 311:

Two ways, by Zeus:
If I'm owed anything, I'm mindful, very:
But if I owe, (Oh, dear!) forgetful, very.

345. See p. 137.

346. *Irische Elfenmärchen* (tr. of Thomas Crofton Croker, *Fairy Legends and Traditions of the South of Ireland*, I-III [London: 1825]), tr. Jakob Ludwig and Wilhelm Karl Grimm (Leipzig: 1826; *ASKB* 1423), p. xxxvii. See p. 255; *JP* IV 4089 (*Pap*. II A 775).

347. Attributed to Archimedes: Give me a place to stand (that is, a fulcrum and a lever), and I will move the world. See Plutarch, "Marcellus," 14, *Lives*; Tetens, III, p. 272; Loeb, V, p. 473. See also, for example, *Either/Or*, I, pp. 294-95, *KW* III (*SV* I 266); *JP* V 5099 (*Pap*. I A 68).

348. See Rötscher, *Aristophanes*, pp. 247-57. Cf. the conception of subjectivity found, for example, throughout *Either/Or*, II, *Fragments*, *Postscript*, and *Sickness unto Death*, *KW* IV, VII, XII, XIX (*SV* II, IV, VII, XI).

349. See Hegel, *Werke*, XIV, p. 85; *J.A.*, XVIII, p. 85; *History of Philosophy*, I, p. 426:

> Aristophanes regarded the Socratic philosophy from the negative side, maintaining that through the cultivation of reflecting consciousness, the idea of law had been shaken, and we cannot question the justice of this conception. Aristophanes' consciousness of the one-sidedness of Socrates may be regarded as a prelude to his death; the Athenian people likewise certainly recognized his negative methods in condemning him.

350. Xenophon, *Memorabilia*, I, 2, 6-8; Bornemann, pp. 16-17; Loeb, p. 15:

> Nor, again, did he encourage love of money in his companions. For while he checked their other desires, he would not make money himself out of their desire for his companionship. He held that this self-denying ordinance insured his liberty. Those who charged a fee for their society he denounced for selling themselves into bondage; since they were bound to converse with all from whom they took the fee. He marvelled that anyone should make money by the profession of virtue, and should not reflect that his highest reward would be the gain of a good friend; as though he who became a true gentleman could fail to feel deep gratitude for a benefit so great. Socrates indeed never promised any such boon to anyone; but he was confident that those of his companions who adopted his principles of conduct would throughout life be good friends to him and to one another.

351. See p. 186 fn.

352. Cf. Job 1:21.

353. See p. 140 fn.

354. See Rötscher, *Aristophanes*, p. 20, concerning also the other comedies by Aristophanes that were sent to Dionysius.

355. Danish: *Tredje mod Een*. See "third party" (*Trediemand*, "arbitrator," "mediator"), p. 16.

356. Cf., for example, Hegel, *Wissenschaft der Logik*, I, *Werke*, IV, pp. 163-70; *J.A.*, IV, p. 641-48; *Science of Logic*, pp. 513-18.

357. Adam Gottlob Oehlenschläger, *"Skattegraveren,"* st. 2, ll. 3-4, *Digte* (Copenhagen: 1803), p. 28.

358. C. Philip Funcke, *Neues Real-Schullexikon*, I-V (Braunschweig: 1800-05).

359. *Xenophons Sokratiske Mærkværdigheder*, tr. Jens Bloch (Copenhagen: 1802), pp. 36-37.

360. Theodor Heinsius, *Sokrates nach dem Grade seiner Schuld* . . . (Leipzig: 1839), p. 19 fn. In the quotation from Lelut, Heinsius has *language* instead of the French *langage*.

361. Ast, *Platon's Leben*, p. 483; pp. 484-85 in the following paragraph.

362. Presumably an allusion to the Old Testament spelling of the name of

God with only consonants so the unpronounceability would signify ineffability and transcendence.

363. The complete edition of Plutarch was published in Paris, 1572, by H. Stephanus (Henri Estienne). Kierkegaard's library contained six editions of the *Moralia* and the *Lives* but not the Stephanus edition. See Plutarch, "The Sign of Socrates," 10-12, *Moralia*, 580 c-582 c; *Plutarchs moralische Abhandlungen*, I-IX, tr. Johann F. S. Kaltwasser (Frankfurt/M: 1783-1800; *ASKB* 1192-96), V, pp. 127-32; *Plutarch's Moralia*, I-XV, tr. Frank Cole Babbitt et al. (Loeb, Cambridge: Harvard University Press, 1967-84), VII, pp. 405-17.

364. See *M. Tullii Ciceronis opera omnia*, I-IV and index, ed. Johann August Ernesti (Halle: 1756-57; *ASKB* 1224-29), IV, p. 651; *Cicero De senectute, De amicitia, De divinatione*, tr. William Armistead Falconer (Loeb, Cambridge: Harvard University Press, 1979), pp. 357-59.

365. See Plato, *Apology*, 31 c-32 a; *Opera*, VIII, pp. 132-35; *Dialogues*, p. 17:

> It may seem curious that I should go round giving advice like this and busying myself in people's private affairs, and yet never venture publicly to address you as a whole and advise on matters of state. The reason for this is what you have often heard me say before on many other occasions—that I am subject to a divine or supernatural experience, which Meletus saw fit to travesty in his indictment. It began in my early childhood—a sort of voice which comes to me, and when it comes it always dissuades me from what I am proposing to do, and never urges me on. It is this that debars me from entering public life, and a very good thing too, in my opinion, because you may be quite sure, gentlemen, that if I had tried long ago to engage in politics, I should long ago have lost my life, without doing any good either to you or to myself. Please do not be offended if I tell you the truth. No man on earth who conscientiously opposes either you or any other organized democracy, and flatly prevents a great many wrongs and illegalities from taking place in the state to which he belongs, can possibly escape with his life. The true champion of justice, if he intends to survive even for a short time, must necessarily confine himself to private life and leave politics alone.

366. See Plato, *Apology*, 27 b-e; *Opera*, VIII, pp. 122-25; *Dialogues*, pp. 13-14:

> Is there anyone in the world, Meletus, who believes in human activities, and not in human beings? Make him answer, gentlemen, and don't let him keep on making these continual objections. Is there anyone who does not believe in horses, but believes in horses' activities? Or who does not believe in musicians, but believes in musical activities? . . . Is there anyone who believes in supernatural activities and not in supernatural beings?
>
> No. . . .
>
> As for your prospect of convincing any living person with even a smattering of intelligence that belief in supernatural and divine activities does

not imply belief in supernatural and divine beings, and vice versa, it is outside all the bounds of possibility.

367. See Matthew 23:24.

368. Hegel, *Werke*, IX, pp. 328-29; *J.A.*, XI, pp. 350-51; *Philosophy of History*, pp. 269-70.

369. Rötscher, *Aristophanes*, p. 254 (ed. tr.).

370. Hegel, *Grundlinien der Philosophie des Rechts oder Naturrecht und Staatswissenschaft im Grundrisse*, *Werke*, VIII, p. 369; *J.A.*, VII, p. 385; *Hegel's Philosophy of Right* (tr. of *P.R.*, 1 ed., 1821, with reference also to 2 ed., 1833, and later editions; Kierkegaard had 2 ed.), tr. T. M. Knox (London: Oxford University Press, 1978), p. 184.

371. See Hegel, *Werke*, XIV, pp. 94-99, 103-07; *J.A.*, XVIII, pp. 94-99, 103-07; *History of Philosophy*, I, 421-26, 431-35.

372. Hegel, *Geschichte der Philosophie*, II, *Werke*, XIV, pp. 95-96, 99 (ed. tr.); *J.A.*, XVIII, pp. 95-96, 99; cf. *History of Philosophy*, I, p. 425.

373. Hegel, *Geschichte der Philosophie*, II, *Werke*, XIV, p. 96 (ed. tr.); *J.A.*, XVIII, p. 96; cf. *History of Philosophy*, I, pp. 422-23.

374. Hegel, *Geschichte der Philosophie*, II, *Werke*, XIV, p. 97 (ed. tr.); *J.A.*, XVIII, p. 97; cf. *History of Philosophy*, I, p. 423.

375. Hegel, *Geschichte der Philosophie*, II, *Werke*, XIV, pp. 95, 96, 99 (ed. tr.); *J.A.*, XVIII, pp. 95, 96, 99; cf. *History of Philosophy*, I, pp. 422, 423, 425.

376. Hegel, *Geschichte der Philosophie*, II, *Werke*, XIV, pp. 98-99 (ed. tr.); *J.A.*, XVIII, pp. 98-99; cf. *History of Philosophy*, I, p. 424.

377. Hegel, *Geschichte der Philosophie*, II, *Werke*, XIV, p. 106 (ed. tr.); *J.A.*, XVIII, p. 106; cf. *History of Philosophy*, I, pp. 424-25.

378. See Plutarch, "Caesar," 38, *Lives*; *Plutarchs Levnetsbeskrivelser*, ed. Niels Lang Nissen (Copenhagen: 1826), p. 274 ("Caesar" not included in Tetens ed.); Loeb, VII, pp. 535-37. See also *The Crisis and a Crisis in the Life of an Actress*, with *Christian Discourses*, *KW* XVII (*SV* X 328).

379. See Hegel, *Geschichte der Philosophie*, II, *Werke*, XIV, pp. 94-96; *J.A.*, XVIII, pp. 94-96; *History of Philosophy*, I, pp. 421-22.

380. See II Corinthians 10:5.

381. See Hegel, *Geschichte der Philosophie*, II, *Werke*, XIV, p. 53; *J.A.*, XVIII, p. 53; *History of Philosophy*, I, p. 392:

> His philosophy, which asserts that real existence is in consciousness as a universal, is still not a properly speculative philosophy, but remained individual; yet the aim of his philosophy was that it should have a universal significance. Hence we have to speak of his own individual being, of his thoroughly noble character, which usually is depicted as a complete catalogue of the virtues adorning the life of a private citizen; and these virtues of Socrates are certainly to be looked at as his own, and as made habitual to him by his own will.

382. See Tacitus, *Annals*, I, 1; *Des C. Cornelius Tacitus Sämmtliche Werke*, I-III, tr. Johann Samuel Müllern (Hamburg: 1765-66; *ASKB* 1283-85), I, p.

9. Note 7 explains the expression by adding *nec beneficio, nec injuria* (because he had known "neither favor nor injury" at the hands of Tiberius and his successor). See *Tacitus The Histories The Annals*, I-IV, tr. Clifford Moore and John Jackson (Loeb, New York: Putnam, 1931-57), II, pp. 244-45.

383. Plato, *Apology*, 20 c; *Opera*, VIII, pp. 106-07; *Dialogues*, p. 6.

384. Kierkegaard presumably had in mind Hegel's writings and works such as Peter Wilhelm Forchhammer, *Die Athener und Sokrates, die Gesetzlichen und der Revolutionär* (Berlin: 1837), which he subsequently cites in the dissertation.

385. Diogenes Laertius, II, 40; *Vitis*, I, p. 79; Riisbrigh, I, p. 74; Loeb, I, p. 171.

386. Among them was Anaxagoras. See Diogenes Laertius, II, 12-14; *Vitis*, I, pp. 66-67; Riisbrigh, I, p. 62; Loeb, I, pp. 143-45.

387. See Plato, *Apology*, 26 d; *Phaedo*, 97 b-98 b; *Opera*, VIII, pp. 120-21; I, pp. 570-73; *Dialogues*, pp. 13, 79-80.

388. See Plato, *Republic*, VII, 531 c-534 d; *Opera*, I, pp. 414-21; *Dialogues*, pp. 763-66.

389. For the ascent of Eros, see Plato, *Symposium*, 209 e-212 a; *Opera*, III, pp. 516-21; Heise, II, pp. 77-81; *Dialogues*, pp. 561-63.

390. Plato, *Apology*, 20 d; *Opera*, VIII, pp. 106-07; *Dialogues*, p. 7.

391. Plato, *Apology*, 20 e; *Opera*, VIII, pp. 106-07; *Dialogues*, p. 7.

392. Xenophon, *Apology*, 15; Bornemann, pp. 339-40; Loeb, p. 497.

393. Plato, *Apology*, 23 a-b; *Opera*, VIII, pp. 112-13; *Dialogues*, p. 9.

394. Hegel, *Werke*, XIV, p. 173; *J.A.*, XVIII, p. 173; *History of Philosophy*, II, pp. 4-5.

395. See note 35 above.

396. Plato, *Apology*, 23 a; *Opera*, VIII, pp. 112-13; *Dialogues*, p. 9.

397. Cf. John 3:17.

398. See Plato, *Apology*, 23 b; *Opera*, VIII, pp. 112-13; *Dialogues*, p. 9.

399. See Plato, *Apology*, 29 c-d; *Opera*, VIII, pp. 130-31; *Dialogues*, p. 15 (Socrates speaking in the court):

> Suppose that, in view of this, you said to me, Socrates, on this occasion we shall disregard Anytus and acquit you, but only on one condition, that you give up spending your time on this quest and stop philosophizing. If we catch you going on in the same way, you shall be put to death.
>
> Well, supposing, as I said, that you should offer to acquit me on these terms, I should reply, Gentlemen, I am your very grateful and devoted servant, but I owe a greater obedience to God than to you, and so long as I draw breath and have my faculties, I shall never stop practicing philosophy and exhorting you and elucidating the truth for everyone that I meet.

400. Cf. Matthew 5:26.

401. See Plato, *Timaeus*, 29 a-e; *Opera*, V, pp. 136-39; Heise, VII, pp. 23-25; *Dialogues*, p. 1162 (Timaeus speaking):

If the world be indeed fair and the artificer good, it is manifest that he must have looked to that which is eternal, but if what cannot be said without blasphemy is true, then to the created pattern. Everyone will see that he must have looked to the eternal, for the world is the fairest of creations and he is the best of causes. And having been created in this way, the world has been framed in the likeness of that which is apprehended by reason and mind and is unchangeable, and must therefore of necessity, if this is admitted, be a copy of something. . . . Let me tell you then why the creator made this world of generation. He was good, and the good can never have any jealousy of anything. And being free from jealousy, he desired that all things should be as like himself as they could be.

402. See Augustine, *De dilegendo Deo*, 6, *Sancti Aurelii Augustini Opera*, I-XVIII (Bassano: 1797-1807; *ASKB* 117-34), XVII, col. 1705 ("*felix culpa*"). *Beata culpa* is a variation of *felix culpa*, which is found, for example, in the *Exsultet* on Holy Saturday of the Roman missal:

O felix culpa, quae talem ac tantum meruit habere Redemptorem
[O happy fault, which has deserved to have such and so mighty a Redeemer].

403. Rötscher, *Aristophanes*, p. 253, (ed. tr.).

404. Hegel, *Geschichte der Philosophie*, II, *Werke*, XIV, pp. 60-61; *J.A.*, XVIII, pp. 60-61; *History of Philosophy*, I, p. 399.

405. See Schleiermacher, *Der christliche Glaube*, I, 36-39, pp. 183-92; *The Christian Faith*, pp. 143-49.

406. See p. 20 fn.

407. See *Alcibiades II*, 138 b-c; *Opera*, VIII, pp. 300-03; Heise, I, pp. 159-60; *The Dialogues of Plato*, I-II, tr. Benjamin Jowett (New York: Random, 1937), II, p. 793. See also *JP* IV 4250 (*Pap*. IV A 203). Kierkegaard knew that *Alcibiades I* (and presumably *Alcibiades II*) was not by Plato.

408. *Alcibiades II*, 143 a; *Opera*, VIII, pp. 312-13; Heise, I, p. 170; Jowett, p. 798.

409. One of the epigraphs on the temple of Apollo at Delphi. See Plato, *Phaedrus*, 230 a; *Opera*, I, pp. 130-31; *Dialogues*, p. 478:

I can't as yet 'know myself,' as the inscription at Delphi enjoins, and so long as that ignorance remains it seems to me ridiculous to inquire into extraneous matters. Consequently I don't bother about such things, but accept the current beliefs about them, and direct my inquiries, as I have just said, rather to myself, to discover whether I really am a more complex creature and more puffed up with pride than Typhon, or a simpler, gentler being whom heaven has blessed with a quiet, un-Typhonic nature.

See, for example, *Fragments*, pp. 37, 39, *KW* VII (*SV* IV 204, 206).

410. See Plato, *Apology*, 28 e; *Opera*, VIII, pp. 126-27; *Dialogues*, p. 15.

411. See Plato, *Apology*, 32 b; *Opera*, VIII, pp. 134-35; *Dialogues*, p. 18; Xenophon, *Memorabilia*, I, 1, 18; Bornemann, pp. 12-13; Loeb, pp. 10-11.

412. The Danish text is a free and compacted translation of *Memorabilia*, I, 6, 15. The text is not from *Xenophons Sokratiske Mærkvaerdigheder*, tr. Jens Bloch, which is cited on p. 157. See Bornemann, p. 74; Loeb, p. 75:

> On yet another occasion Antiphon asked him: "How can you suppose that you make politicians of others, when you yourself avoid politics even if you understand them?"
>
> "How now, Antiphon?" he retorted, "should I play a more important part in politics by engaging in them alone or by taking pains to turn out as many competent politicians as possible?"

413. See p. 159 and note 365.

414. See Heinsius, p. 8.

415. See Forchhammer, p. 6 (ed. tr.).

416. Plato, *Apology*, 36 b-c; *Opera*, VIII, pp. 144-45; *Dialogues*, p. 21. See paragraph 2 in note 109 above.

417. See Plato, *Apology*, 28 d; *Opera*, VIII, pp. 126-27; *Dialogues*, p. 15: "The truth of the matter is this, gentlemen. Where a man has once taken up his stand, either because it seems best to him or in obedience to his orders, there I believe he is bound to remain and face the danger, taking no account of death or anything else before dishonor."

418. See Cicero, *Tusculan Disputations*, V, 10; *Opera*, IV, p. 425; *Cicero Tusculan Disputations*, tr. J. E. King (Loeb, Cambridge: Harvard University Press, 1971), p. 435:

> But from the ancient days down to the time of Socrates, who had listened to Archelaus the pupil of Anaxagoras, philosophy dealt with numbers and movements, with the problem whence all things came, or whither they returned, and zealously inquired into the size of the stars, the spaces that divided them, their courses and all celestial phenomena; Socrates on the other hand was the first to call philosophy down from the heavens and set her in the cities of men and bring her also into their homes and compel her to ask questions about life and morality and things good and evil . . ..

419. See p. 13.

420. Plato, *Phaedrus*, 230 d; *Opera*, I, pp. 132-33; *Dialogues*, p. 479.

421. See note 416 above.

422. An allusion to political opposition to the absolute monarchy of King Christian VIII. Cf. *Two Ages*, pp. 60-112, *KW* XIV (*SV* VIII 57-105).

423. Forchhammer, pp. 54-60.

424. The source has not been located.

425. See Schleiermacher, "*Sokrates als Philosoph,*" p. 52.

426. See Plato, *Apology*, 26 a; *Opera*, VIII, pp. 118-19; *Dialogues*, p. 12:

> Either I have not a bad influence, or it is unintentional, so that in either case your accusation is false. And if I unintentionally have a bad influence, the correct procedure in cases of such involuntary misdemeanors is not to summon the culprit before this court, but to take him aside privately for in-

struction and reproof, because obviously if my eyes are opened, I shall stop doing what I do not intend to do. But you deliberately avoided my company in the past and refused to enlighten me, and now you bring me before this court, which is the place appointed for those who need punishment, not for those who need enlightenment.

427. See Hegel, *Geschichte der Philosophie*, II, *Werke*, XIV, pp. 107-13; *J.A.*, XVIII, pp. 107-13; *History of Philosophy*, I, pp. 435-40.

428. Xenophon, *Memorabilia*, I, 2, 49; Bornemann, pp. 34-35; Loeb, p. 37:

"But," said his accuser, "Socrates taught sons to treat their fathers with contempt: he persuaded them that he made his companions wiser than their fathers: he said that the law allowed a son to put his father in prison if he convinced a jury that he was insane; and this was a proof that it was lawful for the wiser to keep the more ignorant in gaol."

429. Xenophon, *Apology*, 20; Bornemann, pp. 344-45; Loeb, pp. 499-501:

"But, by Heaven!" said Meletus: "there is one set of men I know,—those whom you have persuaded to obey you rather than their parents." "I admit it," he reports Socrates as replying, "at least so far as education is concerned; for people know that I have taken an interest in that. But in a question of health, men take the advice of physicians rather than that of their parents; and moreover, in the meetings of the legislative assembly all the people of Athens, without question, follow the advice of those whose words are wisest rather than that of their own relatives. Do you not also elect for your generals, in preference to fathers and brothers,—yes, by Heaven! in preference to your very selves,—those whom you regard as having the greatest wisdom in military affairs?" "Yes," Meletus had said; "for that is both expedient and conventional."

430. See p. 143.

431. Xenophon, *Apology*, 29-31; Bornemann, pp. 350-51; Loeb, pp. 505-07:

It is said also that he remarked as he saw Anytus [one of Socrates' accusers, a tanner by trade] passing by: "There goes a man who is filled with pride at the thought that he has accomplished some great and noble end in putting me to death, because, seeing him honoured by the state with the highest offices, I said that he ought not to confine his son's education to hides. What a vicious fellow," he continued, "not to know, apparently, that whichever one of us has wrought the more beneficial and noble deeds for all time, *he* is the real victor. But," he is reported to have added, "Homer has attributed to some of his heroes at the moment of dissolution the power to foresee the future; and so I too wish to utter a prophecy. At one time I had a brief association with the son of Anytus, and I thought him not lacking in firmness of spirit; and so I predict that he will not continue in the servile occupation that his father has provided for him; but through want of a worthy adviser he will fall into some disgraceful propensity and will surely go far in the career of vice." In saying this he was not mistaken; the young man, delighting in wine, never left off drinking night or day, and at last turned out worth nothing to his city, his friends, or himself. So Anytus, even though dead, still enjoys an evil repute for his son's mischievous education and for his own hard-heartedness.

432. See note 429 above.

433. Xenophon, *Memorabilia*, I, 2, 51; Bornemann, p. 35; Loeb, p. 37: " 'But,' said his accuser, 'Socrates caused his companions to dishonour not only their fathers, but their other relations as well, by saying that invalids and litigants get benefit not from their relations, but from their doctor or their counsel.' "

434. Hegel, *Geschichte der Philosophie*, II, *Werke*, XIV, pp. 109-10; *J.A.*, XVIII, pp. 109-10; *History of Philosophy*, I, p. 437:

> On the whole not much can be said on this point, for all depends on the mode of intervention, and if it is necessary in certain cases, it need not take place generally, and least of all when some private individual takes that liberty. Children must have the feeling of unity with their parents; this is the first immediately moral relationship; every teacher must respect it, keep it pure, and cultivate the sense of being thus connected. Hence, when a third person is called into this relation between parents and children, what happens through the new element introduced, is that the children are for their own good prevented from confiding in their parents, and made to think that their parents are bad people who harm them by their intercourse and training; and hence we find this revolting.

435. See Aristophanes, *Clouds*, ll. 1145-49; Dindorf, I, p. 222; Loeb, I, p. 371 (Socrates and Strepsiades conversing):

> SO. I clasp Strepsiades.
> ST. And I clasp you: but take this meal-bag first.
> 'Tis meet and right to glorify one's Tutors.
> But tell me, tell me, has my son yet learnt
> That Second Logic which he saw just now?
> SO. He hath.
> ST. Hurrah! great Sovereign Knavery!

436. See Plato, *Apology*, 19 d, 31 b, 33 a; *Euthyphro*, 3 d; *Opera*, VIII, pp. 102-05, 131-33, 136-37, 56-59; *Dialogues*, pp. 6, 16, 18, 171. See also Xenophon, *Memorabilia*, I, 2, 5-8 and 60; I, 6, 13-14; Bornemann, pp. 16-17, 39, 72-75; Loeb, pp. 15, 43, 73-75.

437. Plato, *Gorgias*, 511 e-512 a; Heise, III, p. 165 (ed. tr.); cf. *Dialogues*, p. 293: ". . . and the man who possesses this art and achieves these results goes ashore and walks alongside his ship with modest bearing. For I suppose he is capable of reflecting that it is uncertain which of his passengers he has benefited and which he has harmed by not suffering them to be drowned . . .."

438. See p. 47.

439. Plato, *Apology*, 33 a; *Opera*, VIII, pp. 134-36; *Dialogues*, p. 18.

440. Cf. Matthew 5:28.

441. An allusion to part of the process of refining silver. See *Johannes Climacus, or De omnibus dubitandum est*, p. 122, *KW* VII (*Pap*. IV B 1, p. 108); *Stages*, p. 60, *KW* XI (*SV* VI 61).

442. See I Corinthians 15:52.

443. The source has not been located.

444. See p. 29 and note 80.

445. Plato, *Phaedrus*, 249 a; *Opera*, I, p. 176; *Dialogues*, p. 495 (ed. rev.).

446. Gesner, *Socrates* (Göttingen: 1753).

447. Plato, *Symposium*, 181 b-c; Heise, II, p. 21. Cf. *Dialogues*, p. 535:

> For, first, they are as much attracted by women as by boys; next, whoever they may love, their desires are of the body rather than of the soul . . . . For this is the Love of the younger Aphrodite, whose nature partakes of both male and female.
>
> But the heavenly Love springs from a goddess whose attributes have nothing of the female, but are altogether male, and who is also the elder of the two . . . . And so those who are inspired by this other Love turn rather to the male, preferring the more vigorous and intellectual bent.

448. Hegel, *Aesthetik*, I, *Werke*, X^1, pp. xviii, 213-22; *J.A.*, XII, pp. 14, 213-22; *Philosophy of Fine Art*, I, pp. xix, 209-18; *Philosophie der Geschichte*, *Werke*, IX, p. 292; *J.A.*, XI, p. 314; *Philosophy of History*, pp. 238-39:

> In Man, the side of his subjective existence which he owes to Nature, is the Heart, the Disposition, Passion, and Variety of Temperament: this side is then developed in a spiritual direction to free Individuality; so that the character is not placed in a relation to universally valid moral authorities, assuming the form of duties, but the Moral appears as a nature peculiar to the individual—an exertion of will, the result of disposition and individual constitution. This stamps the Greek character as that of *Individuality conditioned by Beauty*, which is produced by Spirit, transforming the merely Natural into an expression of its own being. The activity of Spirit does not yet possess in itself the material and organ of expression, but needs the excitement of Nature and the matter which Nature supplies: it is not free, self-determining Spirituality, but mere naturalness formed to Spirituality—Spiritual Individuality. The Greek Spirit is the plastic artist, forming the stone into a work of art. In this formative process the stone does not remain mere stone—the form being only superinduced from without; but it is made an expression of the Spiritual, even contrary to its nature, and thus *trans*formed. Conversely, the artist *needs* for his spiritual conceptions, stone, colors, sensuous forms to express his idea. . . . Such are the qualities of that *Beautiful Individuality*, which constitutes the centre of the Greek character.

449. See Xenophon, *Symposium*, II, 10; Thieme, IV, pp. 434-35; Loeb, p. 393:

> "If that is your view, Socrates," asked Antisthenes, "how does it come that you don't practise what you preach by yourself educating Xanthippe, but live with a wife who is the hardest to get along with of all the women there are—yes, or all that ever were, I suspect, or ever will be?"
>
> "Because," he replied, "I observe that men who wish to become expert horsemen do not get the most docile horses but rather those that are high-mettled, believing that if they can manage this kind, they will easily handle any other. My course is similar. Mankind at large is what I wish to deal and associate with; and so I have got her, well assured that if I can endure her, I shall have no difficulty in my relations with all the rest of human kind."
>
> These words, in the judgment of the guests, did not go wide of the mark.

See also Diogenes Laertius, II, 36-37; *Vitis*, I, pp. 77-78; Riisbrigh, I, pp. 72-73; Loeb, I, p. 167.

450. Forchhammer, pp. 49-50. Note 43 refers to Xenophon, *Symposium*, II, 10, and to Diogenes Laertius, II, 37. See note 449 above.

451. Hegel, *Geschichte der Philosophie*, II, *Werke*, XIV, pp. 113-21; *J.A.*, XVIII, pp. 113-21; *History of Philosophy*, I, pp. 440-48.

452. See Plato, *Apology*, 38 a-b; *Opera*, VIII, pp. 148-49; *Dialogues*, p. 23.

453. See Plato, *Apology*, 36 a-38 b; *Opera*, VIII, pp. 142-49; *Dialogues*, pp. 21-23.

454. See p. 86 and note 232.

455. Cf. the story of the sword of Damocles, Cicero, *Tusculan Disputations*, V, 61-62; *Opera*, IV, pp. 443-44; Loeb, pp. 487-89.

456. See Horace, *Odes*, III, 24, 6; *Opera*, p. 218; Loeb, p. 253: "Though thou be richer than the unrifled treasuries of the Arabs or rich India, and with thy palaces encroach on all the land and the public sea, if dire Necessity plant her nails of adamant in thy topmost roof, thou shalt not free thy soul from fear nor thy head from the snare of Death."

457. See Plato, *Apology*, 29 a-b; *Opera*, VIII, pp. 126-31; *Dialogues*, p. 15.

458. Plato, *Apology*, 38 a; *Opera*, VIII, pp. 148-49; *Dialogues*, p. 23.

459. Romantic irony, discussed in Part Two.

460. See *JP* V 5397; VI 6416, 6431, 6445, 6461 (*Pap*. II A 497; X[1] A 422, 510, 546, 593).

461. Danish: *Tankestreg*, which means, literally, "thought line."

462. See, for example, Hegel, "World History," 341-43, *Philosophie des Rechts*, *Werke*, VIII, pp. 430-32; *J.A.*, VII, pp. 446-48; *Philosophy of Right*, pp. 216-17; *Philosophie der Geschichte*, *Werke*, IX, pp. 31-32; *J.A.*, XI, pp. 53-54; *Philosophy of History*, p. 25:

> The History of the World begins with its general aim—the realization of the Idea of Spirit—only in an *implicit* form (*an sich*) that is, as Nature; a hidden, most profoundly hidden, unconscious instinct; and the whole process of History (as already observed), is directed to rendering this uncon-

> scious impulse a conscious one. Thus appearing in the form of merely natural existence, natural will—that which has been called the subjective side—physical craving, instinct, passion, private interest, as also opinion and subjective conception—spontaneously present themselves at the very commencement. This vast congeries of volitions, interests and activities, constitute the instruments and means of the World-Spirit for attaining its object; bringing it to consciousness, and realizing it.

463. Two scholastic ways of defining God: the denial of all imperfections and the affirmation of all perfections. See p. 236; *Fragments*, p. 44, *KW* VII (*SV* IV 212).

464. Hegel, *Werke*, IX, p. 185; *J.A.*, XI, p. 207; *Philosophy of History*, p. 151.

465. Hegel, *Geschichte der Philosophie*, II, *Werke*, XIV, p. 42; *J.A.*, XVIII, p. 42; *History of Philosophy*, I, p. 384.

466. See note 462 above. Socrates "is not only a most important figure in the history of Philosophy—perhaps the most interesting in the philosophy of antiquity—but is also a world-famed personage. For a mental turning-point exhibited itself in him in the form of philosophic thought."

467. Plato, *Apology*, 30 d; *Opera*, VIII, pp. 130-31; *Dialogues*, p. 16 (ed. rev.).

468. Plato, *Apology*, 31 a; *Opera*, VIII, pp. 132-33; *Dialogues*, p. 17.

469. Cf. *Soap-Cellars*, *KW* I (*Pap.* II B 1-21).

470. See p. 199 and note 466.

471. Rötscher, *Aristophanes*, pp. 85-89.

472. See, for example, Hegel, *Philosophie des Rechts*, 139-40, *Werke*, VIII, pp. 184-207; *J.A.*, VII, pp. 200-23; *Philosophy of Right*, pp. 92-103.

473. See Mark 5:9.

474. See Hegel, *Werke*, XIV, pp. 5-42; *J.A.*, XVIII, pp. 5-42; *History of Philosophy*, I, pp. 352-84.

475. See Hegel, *Philosophie der Geschichte*, *Werke*, IX, p. 8; *J.A.*, XI, p. 30; *Philosophy of History*, p. 5:

> A history which aspires to traverse long periods of time, or to be universal, must indeed forego the attempt to give individual representations of the past as it actually existed. It must foreshorten its pictures by abstractions; and this includes not merely the omission of events and deeds, but whatever is involved in the fact that Thought is, after all, the most trenchant epitomist. A battle, a great victory, a siege, no longer maintains its original proportions, but is put off with a bare mention. When Livy *e.g.* tells us of the wars with the Volsci, we sometimes have the brief announcement: "This year war was carried on with the Volsci."

See also Supplement, pp. 440-41 (*Pap.* III B 2).

476. Hegel, *Philosophie der Geschichte*, *Werke*, IX, pp. 327-28; *J.A.*, XI, pp. 349-50; *Philosophy of History*, pp. 268-69.

477. See Ludwig Achim v. Arnim and Clemens Brentano, *"Doktor Faust"*

(with subtitle *"Fliegendes Blatt aus Köln"*), *Des Knaben Wunderhorn*, I-III (Heidelberg: 1819; *ASKB* 1494-96), I, p. 214; Hamann, *Schriften*, VII, p. 121: "*fliegende Blatt meiner Muse* [fly sheet of my muse]." See also *JP* V 5159, 5200 (*Pap.* I C 101; II A 7), where "*ein fliegendes Blatt aus München* [a fly sheet from Munich]" is used with reference to Hans Lassen Martensen, who had been in Munich for a time during a two-year study tour.

478. Cf. *Either/Or*, I, p. 25, *KW* III (*SV* I 9).

479. See Plato, *Protagoras*, 309 c-314 b; *Opera*, I, pp. 5-17; Heise, II, pp. 108-18; *Dialogues*, pp. 309-13.

480. See Johann Wolfgang v. Goethe, *Faust*, I, 4, ll. 1868-1925, *Goethe's Werke. Vollständige Ausgabe letzter Hand*, I-LX (Stuttgart, Tübingen: 1828-42; *ASKB* 1641-68 [I-LV]), XII, pp. 95-97; *Faust*, tr. Bayard Taylor (New York: Modern Library, 1950), pp. 65-66.

481. See Plato, *Gorgias*, 456 a-457 b; *Opera*, I, pp. 280-85; Heise, III, pp. 26-27; *Dialogues*, pp. 239-40 (Gorgias speaking):

> Ah, if only you knew all, Socrates, and realized that rhetoric includes practically all other faculties under her control. And I will give you good proof of this. . . . The rhetorician is competent to speak against anybody on any subject, and to prove himself more convincing before a crowd on practically every topic he wishes, but he should not any the more rob the doctors—or any other craftsmen either—of their reputation, merely because he has this power.

482. Peter Wessel (1691-1720), Norwegian-Danish naval hero knighted with the name Tordenskjold (Thunder-shield). For many years, the most widely sold brand of Danish matches has carried a picture of Tordenskjold on the boxes.

483. Cf. *Fragments*, p. 7, *KW* VII (*SV* IV 177).

484. A term used by Hegel for the method and view of the Sophists. See, for example, *Encyclopädie*, *Die Logik*, 121, *Werke*, VI, p. 248; *J.A.*, VIII, p. 286; *Hegel's Logic*, p. 178:

> To get no further than mere grounds, especially on questions of law and morality, is the position and principle of the Sophists. Sophistry, as we ordinarily conceive it, is a method of investigation which aims at distorting what is just and true, and exhibiting things in a false light. Such however is not the proper or primary tendency of Sophistry: the standpoint of which is no other than that of *raisonnement*. The Sophists came on the scene at a time when the Greeks had begun to grow dissatisfied with mere authority and tradition and felt the need of intellectual justification for what they were to accept as obligatory. That desideratum the Sophists supplied by teaching their countrymen to seek for the various points of view under which things may be considered: which points of view are the same as grounds. But the ground, as we have seen, has no essential and objective principles of its own, and it is as easy to discover grounds for what is wrong and immoral as for what is moral and right. Upon the observer therefore it

> depends to decide what points are to have most weight. The decision in such circumstances is prompted by his individual views and sentiments. Thus the objective foundation of what ought to have been of absolute and essential obligation, accepted by all, was undermined: and Sophistry by this destructive action deservedly brought upon itself the bad name previously mentioned.

485. See Exodus 1:14, 5:17-19.

486. Hegel, *Werke*, XIV, p. 5; *J.A.*, XVIII, p. 5; *History of Philosophy*, I, p. 352.

487. See, for example, Hegel, *Geschichte der Philosophie*, II, *Werke*, XIV, pp. 30-31; *J.A.*, XVIII, pp. 30-31; *History of Philosophy*, I, pp. 373-74:

> The main point in his system of knowledge he [Protagoras] expressed thus: "Man is the measure of all things; of that which is, that it is; of that which is not, that it is not." On the one hand, therefore, what had to be done was to grasp thought as determined and as having content; but, on the other, to find the determining and content-giving; this universal determination then becomes the standard by which everything is judged. Now Protagoras' assertion is in its real meaning a great truth, but at the same time it has a certain ambiguity, in that as man is the undetermined and many-sided, either he may in his individual particularity, as this contingent man, be the measure, or else self-conscious reason in man, man in his rational nature and his universal substantiality, is the absolute measure. If the statement is taken in the former sense, all is self-seeking, all self-interest, the subject with his interests forms the central point; and if man has a rational side, reason is still something subjective, it is "he." But this is just the wrong and perverted way of looking at things which necessarily forms the main reproach made against the Sophists—that they put forward man in his contingent aims as determining[*]; thus with them the interest of the subject in its particularity, and the interest of the same in its substantial reason are not distinguished.
>
> The same statement is brought forward in Socrates and Plato, but with the further modification that here man, in that he is thinking and gives himself a universal content, is the measure. Thus here the great proposition is enunciated on which, from this time forward, everything turns, since the further progress of Philosophy only explains it further: it signifies that reason is the end of all things.

[*]The German text is "*den Menschen . . . zum Zwecke setzten*," which literally means "make man the goal."

488. The Danish *Maal* means both "measure" and "goal" or "end."

489. Plato, *Theaetetus*, 152 a; *Opera*, II, 50; *Dialogues*, p. 856.

490. Pp. 52-62.

491. See, for example, Plato, *Meno*, 95 c; *Opera*, IX, pp. 262-65; *Dialogues*, p. 379:

> SOCRATES: And what about the Sophists, the only people who profess to teach it [virtue]? Do you think they do?
>
> MENO: The thing I particularly admire about Gorgias, Socrates, is that you will never hear him make this claim; indeed he laughs at the others when he hears them do so. In his view his job is to make clever speakers.

492. See Heinrich Ritter, *Geschichte der Philosophie*, I-IV (Hamburg: 1836-39; *ASKB* 735-38), I, p. 596; *The History of Ancient Philosophy*, I-IV, tr. Alexander J. W. Morrison (Oxford: Talboys, 1838-46), I, p. 583: "For instance, he endeavours first to shew that nothing is; secondly, that if any thing is, it cannot be an object of knowledge; and finally, that even if any thing is, and can be known, it cannot be imparted to others."

493. Hegel, *Geschichte der Philosophie*, II, *Werke*, XIV, pp. 41-42; *J.A.*, XVIII, pp. 41-42; *History of Philosophy*, I, p. 384.

494. The exact phrase is not found in the *Gorgias*. It is, however, pertinent, for example, to 489 b-c; *Opera*, I, pp. 368-69; Heise, II, p. 107; *Dialogues*, p. 271 (Callicles speaking): "Will this fellow never stop driveling? Tell me, Socrates, are you not ashamed to be captious about words at your age, considering it a godsend if one makes a slip in an expression? Do you imagine that by the more powerful I mean anything else but the better? Did I not tell you long ago that I identify the better and the more powerful?"

495. For the two theses, see Plato, *Gorgias*, 483 a-d; *Opera*, I, pp. 354-55; Heise, III, pp. 95-96; *Dialogues*, p. 266 (Callicles speaking):

> For by nature everything that is worse is more shameful, suffering wrong for instance, but by convention it is more shameful to do it. For to suffer wrong is not even fit for a man but only for a slave, for whom it is better to be dead than alive, since when wronged and outraged he is unable to help himself or any other for whom he cares. But in my opinion those who framed the laws are the weaker folk, the majority. And accordingly they frame the laws for themselves and their own advantage, and so too with their approval and censure, and to prevent the stronger who are able to overreach them from gaining the advantage over them, they frighten them by saying that to overreach others is shameful and evil, and injustice consists in seeking the advantage over others. For they are satisfied, I suppose, if being inferior they enjoy equality of status. That is the reason why seeking an advantage over the many is by convention said to be wrong and shameful, and they call it injustice. But in my view nature herself makes it plain that it is right for the better to have the advantage over the worse, the more able over the less. And both among all animals and in entire states and races of mankind it is plain that this is the case—that right is recognized to be the sovereignty and advantage of the stronger over the weaker.

496. Cf. *Two Ages*, pp. 97-100, 103, *KW* XIV (*SV* VIII 91-93, 96).

497. Cf., for example, Hegel's use of the term "hero" in *Philosophie der Geschichte*, *Werke*, IX, p. 38; *J.A.*, XI, p. 60; *Philosophy of History*, p. 30:

> Such are all great historical men—whose own particular aims involve those large issues which are the will of the World-Spirit. They may be called Heroes, inasmuch as they have derived their purposes and their vocation, not from the calm, regular course of things, sanctioned by the existing order; but from a concealed fount—one which has not attained to phenomenal, present existence—from that inner Spirit, still hidden beneath the surface, which, impinging on the outer world as on a shell, bursts it in pieces, because it is another kernel than that which belonged to the shell in question. They are men, therefore, who appear to draw the impulse of their life from themselves; and whose deeds have produced a condition of things and a complex of historical relations which appear to be only *their* interest, and *their* work.
>
> Such individuals had no consciousness of the general Idea they were unfolding, while prosecuting those aims of theirs; on the contrary, they were practical, political men. But at the same time they were thinking men, who had an insight into the requirements of the time—*what was ripe for development.* This was the very Truth for their age, for their world; the species next in order, so to speak, and which was already formed in the womb of time. It was theirs to know this nascent principle; the necessary, directly sequent step in progress, which their world was to take; to make this their aim, and to expend their energy in promoting it. World-historical men—the Heroes of an epoch—must, therefore, be recognized as its clear-sighted ones; *their* deeds, *their* words are the best of that time.

498. See Matthew 11:15; Mark 8:18.

499. See Plato, *Apology*, 30 e; *Opera*, VIII, pp. 130-31; *Dialogues*, pp. 16-17:

> It is literally true, even if it sounds rather comical, that God has specially appointed me to this city, as though it were a large thoroughbred horse which because of its great size is inclined to be lazy and needs the stimulation of some stinging fly. It seems to me that God has attached me to this city to perform the office of such a fly, and all day long I never cease to settle here, there, and everywhere, rousing, persuading, reproving every one of you.

500. See Cicero, *Tusculan Disputations*, IV, 37; *Opera*, IV, p. 419; Loeb, p. 419:

> Zopyrus, who claimed to discern every man's nature from his appearance, charged Socrates in company with a number of vices which he enumerated, and when he was ridiculed by the rest who said they failed to recognize such vices in Socrates, Socrates himself came to his rescue by saying that he was naturally inclined to the vices named, but had cast them out of him by the help of reason.

501. *Zeitschrift für Philosophie und spekulative Theologie*, ed. Immanuel Hermann Fichte (*ASKB* 877-911).

502. See Sextus Empiricus, *Outlines of Pyrrhonism*, I, 30; *Sexti Empirici opera quae extant*, ed. P. and J. Chouet (Orleans: 1621; *ASKB* 146), I, 22, p. 9; *Sextus Empiricus*, I-IV, tr. R. G. Bury (Loeb, Cambridge: Harvard University Press, 1961-68), I, pp. 20-21: "Hence we say that, while in regard to matters of opinion the Sceptic's End is quietude, in regard to things unavoidable it is 'moderate affection.' But some notable Sceptics have added the further definition 'suspension of judgement in investigations.' " Cf. Hegel, *Phänomenologie des Geistes*, *Werke*, II, p. 156; *J.A.*, II, p. 164; *Phenomenology of Mind*, p. 248:

> Sceptical self-consciousness thus discovers, in the flux and alternation of all that would stand secure in its presence, its own freedom, as given by and received from its own self. It is aware of being this ἀταραξία of self-thinking thought, the unalterable and genuine certainty of its self. This certainty does not arise as a result out of something extraneous and foreign which stowed away inside itself its whole complex development; a result which would thus leave behind the process by which it came to be.

See also *Fragments*, pp. 82-83, *KW* VII (*SV* IV 245-46).

503. See Galatians 3:23-24.

504. Presumably the period between Kant and Hegel. See pp. 272-323.

505. See p. 324; cf. *From the Papers*, *KW* I (*SV* XIII 57); *JP* II 1587 (*Pap*. III A 1).

506. See, for example, Wilhelm Traugott Krug, *Geschichte der Philosophie alter Zeit* (Leipzig: 1815), pp. 152-63; *Allgemeines Handwörterbuch der philosophischen Wissenschaften*, I-V (Leipzig: 1827-29; *ASKB* 604-08), III, pp. 711-29. There are, however, sections on Socrates in *Geschichte* (2 ed., Leipzig: 1827), pp. 157-68, and in *Handwörterbuch* (2 ed., Leipzig: 1832), III, pp. 791-801; V, pp. 308-09.

507. See Ast, *Platon's Leben*.

508. See Lucius Firmianus Lactantius, *Institutiones divinae*, III, 19; *Firmiani Lactantii opera*, I-II, ed. Otto Fridolin Fritzsche (Leipzig: 1842-44; *ASKB* 142-43), I, p. 152; *The Divine Institutes*, tr. Mary Francis McDonald, *The Fathers of the Church*, I-LXIX, ed. Roy J. Deferrari (Washington, D.C.: Catholic University of America Press, 1943-78), XLIX, pp. 218-19:

> Cicero in his *Consolation* [fragment 11] says it is 'best by far not to be born, and not to come up against these rocks of life, but, if you are born, it is next best to escape as it were from the fire of fortune as quickly as possible.' It is clear that he believed that very foolish saying, because he added something of his own that he might adorn it. I wonder, therefore, for whom he thinks it is best not to be born, since there is no one at all who may be sensible of it, for the senses effect that something be good or bad. Then, why did he think that all life was nothing else than rocks and burning? As if it were in our power either not to be born, or that chance bestowed life on us, not God, or that the plan of living might seem to have some similarity to a burning.

> That theory of Plato's is not dissimilar, because he said that he was thankful to nature, first, because he was born a man rather than a dumb beast; then, because he was a man rather than a woman, a Greek rather than a foreigner; and, finally, because he was an Athenian and of the time of Socrates.

See also Plutarch, "Caius Marius," 46, *Lives*; Tetens, IV, pp. 338-39; Loeb, IX, p. 595.

509. Brandis, *Rheinisches Museum für Jurisprudenz, Philologie, Geschichte und griechische Philosophie, Ersten Jahrganges erstes und zweites Heft, Abtheilung für Philologie, Geschichte und Philosophie*, pp. 118-19 (ed. tr.).

510. Hegel, *Werke*, XIV, p. 126; *J.A.*, XVIII, p. 126; *History of Philosophy*, I, p. 449: "The most varied schools and principles proceeded from this doctrine of Socrates, and this was made a reproach against him, but it was really due to the indefiniteness and abstraction of his principle. And in this way it is only particular forms of this principle which can at first be recognized in philosophic systems which we call Socratic."

511. Hegel, *Werke*, XIV, p. 127; *J.A.*, XVIII, p. 127; *History of Philosophy*, I, p. 452: "Of those Socratics who hold a place of their own, there are, according to this, three schools worthy of consideration; first the Megaric School, at whose head stands Euclid of Megara, and then the Cyrenaic and Cynic Schools; and from the fact that they all three differ very much from one another, it is clearly shown that Socrates himself was devoid of any positive system."

512. Hegel, *Geschichte der Philosophie*, II, *Werke*, XIV, p. 124 (ed. tr.); *J.A.*, XVIII, p. 124; cf. *History of Philosophy*, I, p. 449.

513. Hegel, *Geschichte der Philosophie*, II, *Werke*, XIV, pp. 127-28; *J.A.*, XVIII, pp. 127-28; *History of Philosophy*, I, pp. 452-53:

> The Megarics were most abstract, because they held to the determination of the good which, as simple, was to them the principle; the unmoved and self-related simplicity of thought becomes the principle of consciousness as individual, as it is of conscious knowledge. The Megaric school associated with the assertion of the simplicity of the good, the dialectic, that all that was defined and limited is not true. . . .
>
> The Cyrenaics take knowledge in its subjective signification, and as signifying individuality as certainty of self, or feeling; to this as to that which is essential, they restrict the exercise of consciousness, and, generally speaking, make existence for consciousness consist therein. Now because they thereby sought to define the Good more closely, they called it simply pleasure or enjoyment, by which, however, anything can be understood. . . .
>
> The Cynics also further defined the principle of the Good, but in another way from the Cyrenaics; its content, they said, lay in man's keeping to what is in conformity with nature and to the simple needs of nature. They simi-

larly call all that is particular and limited in the aims of men that which is not to be desired.

514. See p. 146 fn.

515. Probably an allusion to Hans Lassen Martensen.

516. See, for example, Jakob Brucker, *Historia critica philosophiae a mundi incunabulis ad nostram usque aetatem deducta*, I-V (Leipzig: 1776-77; *ASKB* 446-50), I, pp. 522-83.

517. See, for example, Thomas Christian Tychsen, *"Ueber den Process des Sokrates," Bibliothek der alten Litteratur und Kunst, erstes Stück* (Göttingen: 1786), pp. 1-53; *zweites Stück* (1787), pp. 1-60.

518. See Krug, *"Sokrates' Dämon oder Genius," Handwörterbuch*, III, pp. 711-18; *Geschichte der Philosophie*, pp. 152-63.

519. See pp. 174-75, also pp. 166-67, 219, 221, 224, 227.

520. Schleiermacher, *"Sokrates als Philosoph,"* p. 61.

521. See Plato, *Phaedrus*, 265 d-266 b; *Opera*, I, pp. 216-19; *Dialogues*, pp. 511-12:

> PHAEDRUS: What procedures do you mean?
>
> SOCRATES: The first is that in which we bring a dispersed plurality under a single form, seeing it all together—the purpose being to define so-and-so, and thus to make plain whatever may be chosen as the topic for exposition. For example, take the definition given just now of love. Whether it was right or wrong, at all events it was that which enabled our discourse to achieve lucidity and consistency.
>
> PHAEDRUS: And what is the second procedure you speak of, Socrates?
>
> SOCRATES: The reverse of the other, whereby we are enabled to divide into forms, following the objective articulation; we are not to attempt to hack off parts like a clumsy butcher, but to take example from our two recent speeches. The single general form which they postulated was irrationality; next, on the analogy of a single natural body with its pairs of like-named members, right arm or leg, as we say, and left, they conceived of madness as a single objective form existing in human beings. Wherefore the first speech divided off a part on the left, and continued to make divisions, never desisting until it discovered one particular part bearing the name of 'sinister' love, on which it very properly poured abuse. The other speech conducted us to the forms of madness which lay on the right-hand side, and upon discovering a type of love that shared its name with the other but was divine, displayed it to our view and extolled it as the source of the greatest goods that can befall us.
>
> PHAEDRUS: That is perfectly true.
>
> SOCRATES: Believe me, Phaedrus, I am myself a lover of these divisions and collections, that I may gain the power to speak and to think, and whenever I deem another man able to discern an objective unity and plurality, I follow 'in his footsteps where he leadeth as a god.' Furthermore—whether

I am right or wrong in doing so, God alone knows—it is those that have this ability whom for the present I call dialecticians.

See also Supplement, p. 446 (*Pap.* III B 27).

522. Baur, *Sokrates und Christus*, pp. 90-154.

523. Suspension of judgment or withholding of assent in Greek skeptical philosophy. See *Fragments*, pp. 82-83, *KW* VII (*SV* IV 245-46 and notes). The usual Danish translation is *Tilbageholdenhed* [a holding back] rather than *Paaholdenhed* [a holding on, close-handedness], but both denote reserve, a principle of parsimony.

524. See pp. 5-6, Thesis I.

525. See Colossians 2:9.

526. See Ephesians 5:30.

527. See, for example, Brandis, "*Grundlinien der Lehre des Sokrates*," p. 126.

528. See p. 107 and note 271.

529. See Livy, *Fragments*, XIX, 12; *Livy*, I-XIV, tr. B. O. Foster et al. (Loeb, Cambridge: Harvard University Press, 1965-84), XIV, p. 181: "Servius, note on *Aeneid* VI. 198: The story is told in Livy that when a certain consul [Publius Claudius Pulcher, son of Appius Claudius] who was anxious to conduct a campaign was prevented from departing by a tribune of the commons, the consul ordered the chickens to be brought. When these failed to eat the grain scattered before them, the consul, mocking the omen, said, 'Let them drink, then', and flung them into the Tiber. After that as he was triumphantly returning in his fleet to Africa he lost his life at sea, along with all his men." See *JP* III 3279 (*Pap.* II A 529).

530. See pp. 226-27.

531. Plato, *Meno*; *Opera*, IX, pp. 193-277; *Dialogues*, pp. 353-84.

532. Hegel, *Geschichte der Philosophie*, II, *Werke*, XIV, p. 69; *J.A.*, XVIII, p. 69; *History of Philosophy*, I, p. 406 (ed. rev.). The last line is in *Werke*, 1833, and *J.A.* but not in 2 ed. of *G.P.* and *History*. The sentence "*Diese Verwirrung . . . Sokrates*" is altered in 2 ed. of *G.P.* and *History:* "Philosophy must, generally speaking, begin with a puzzle in order to bring about reflection; everything must be doubted, all presuppositions given up, to reach the truth as created through the Notion."

533. The following five quotations are from Hegel, *Geschichte der Philosophie*, II, *Werke*, XIV, pp. 179, 184, 222, 226, 230; *J.A.*, XVIII, pp. 179, 183-84, 222, 226, 230; *History of Philosophy*, II, pp. 10 (ed. rev.), 13 (ed. rev.), 51, 52, 56 (the parenthetical clauses are Kierkegaard's additions).

534. Hegel, *Werke*, XIV, pp. 42-122; *J.A.*, XVIII, pp. 42-122; *History of Philosophy*, I, pp. 384-448.

535. Hegel, *Werke*, XIV, pp. 93-94 (ed. tr.); *J.A.*, XVIII, pp. 93-94; cf. *History of Philosophy*, I, p. 420.

536. Hegel, *Werke*, XIV, p. 95 (ed. tr.); *J.A.*, XVIII, p. 95; cf. *History of Philosophy*, I, p. 422.

537. Hegel's *Geschichte der Philosophie* and some other works were compiled after his death by his students on the basis of lecture notes.

538. The Danish *Moralen* in the text corresponds to Hegel's *Moralität*, which Hegel associates with Socrates, in contrast to *Sittlichkeit* [custom, law, "ethical life," or social morality]. In later writing (see, for example, "The Balance of the Esthetic and the Ethical in the Development of the Personality," *Either/Or*, II, pp. 155-333, *KW* IV [*SV* II 141-299]), Kierkegaard does not follow Hegel's usage but instead associates Socrates with the ethical, the ethical consciousness, the normative universally human, as distinguished from *Sædelighed*, social morality, custom. For Hegel's conception, see, for example, *Philosophie des Rechts*, 33, *Werke*, VIII, pp. 68-69; *J.A.*, VII, pp. 84-85; *Philosophy of Right*, pp. 35-36:

Division of the Subject

In correspondence with the stages in the development of the Idea of the absolutely free will, the will is

A. immediate; its concept therefore is abstract, namely personality, and its embodiment is an immediate external thing—the sphere of *Abstract* or *Formal Right*;

B. reflected from its external embodiment into itself—it is then characterized as subjective individuality in opposition to the universal. The universal here is characterized as something inward, the good, and also as something outward, a world presented to the will; both these sides of the Idea are here mediated only by each other. This is the Idea in its division or in its existence as particular; and here we have the right of the subjective will in relation to the right of the world and the right of the Idea, though only the Idea implicit—the sphere of *Morality*;

C. the unity and truth of both these abstract moments—the Idea of the good not only apprehended in thought but so realized both in the will reflected into itself and in the external world that freedom exists as substance, as actuality and necessity, no less than as subjective will; this is the Idea in its absolutely universal existence—*Ethical Life*.

But on the same principle the ethical substance is

(*a*) natural mind, the *Family*;

(*b*) in its division and appearance, *Civil Society*;

(*c*) the *State* as freedom, freedom universal and objective even in the free self-subsistence of the particular will. This actual and organic mind (α) of a single nation (β) reveals and actualizes itself through the inter-relation of the particular national minds until (γ) in the process of world-history it reveals and actualizes itself as the universal world-mind whose right is supreme.

The translator of *Hegel's Lectures on the History of Philosophy* adds a note on this theme (I, pp. 387-88):

The distinction between these two words is a very important one. Schwegler, in explaining Hegel's position in his "History of Philosophy," states that Hegel asserts that Socrates set *Moralität*, the subjective morality of individual conscience, in the place of *Sittlichkeit*, "the spontaneous, natural, half-unconscious (almost instinctive) virtue that rests in obedience to established custom (use and wont, natural objective law, that is at bottom, according to Hegel, rational, though not yet subjectively cleared, perhaps, into its rational principles)." As Dr. Stirling says in his Annotations to the same work (p. 394), "There is a period in the history of the State when people live in tradition; that is a period of unreflected *Sittlichkeit*, or natural observance. Then there comes a time when the observances are questioned, and when the right or truth they involve is reflected into the subject. This is a period of *Aufklärung*, and for *Sittlichkeit* there is substituted *Moralität*, subjective morality: the subject will approve nought but what he finds inwardly true to himself, to his conscience."

539. Hegel, *Geschichte der Philosophie*, II, *Werke*, XIV, p. 43 (ed. tr.); *J.A.*, XVIII, p. 43; cf. *History of Philosophy*, I, p. 385.

540. See Hegel, *Geschichte der Philosophie*, II, *Werke*, XIV, p. 85; *J.A.*, XVIII, p. 85; *History of Philosophy*, I, p. 426:

> Aristophanes regarded the Socratic philosophy from the negative side, maintaining that through the cultivation of reflecting consciousness, the idea of law had been shaken, and we cannot question the justice of this conception. Aristophanes' consciousness of the one-sidedness of Socrates may be regarded as a prelude to his death; the Athenian people likewise certainly recognized his negative methods in condemning him.

541. Hegel, *Geschichte der Philosophie*, II, *Werke*, XIV, p. 89; *J.A.*, XVIII, p. 89; *History of Philosophy*, I, p. 430. The second part of the quotation ("*Sokrates . . . galt*"; ed. tr.) is not found on p. 430 of the English translation, which is based on 2 ed.

542. See Hegel, *Geschichte der Philosophie*, II, *Werke*, XIV, pp. 50-57; *J.A.*, XVIII, pp. 50-57; *History of Philosophy*, I, pp. 392-96 (tr. of 2 ed., with variations from 1 ed.).

543. Hegel, *Geschichte der Philosophie*, II, *Werke*, XIV, p. 58 (ed. tr.); *J.A.*, XVIII, p. 58; cf. *History of Philosophy*, I, pp. 396-97.

544. See Hegel, *Geschichte der Philosophie*, II, *Werke*, XIV, p. 59; *J.A.*, XVIII, p. 59; *History of Philosophy*, I, pp. 397-98:

> Thus it can be said that in content his philosophy had an altogether practical aspect, and similarly the Socratic method, which is essential to it, was distinguished by the system of first bringing a person to reflection upon his duty by any occasion that might either happen to be offered spontaneously, or that was brought about by Socrates. By going to the work-places of tailors and shoemakers, and entering into discourse with them, as also with youths and old men, Sophists, statesmen, and citizens of all kinds, he in the first place took their interests as his topic—whether these were household interests, the education of children, or the interests of knowledge or of

truth. Then he led them on from a definite case to think of the universal, and of truths and beauties which had absolute value, since in every case, from the individual's own thoughts, he derived the conviction and consciousness of that which is the definite right. This method has two prominent aspects, the one the development of the universal from the concrete case, and the exhibition of the notion which implicitly exists in every consciousness, and the other is the resolution of the firmly established, and, when taken immediately in consciousness, universal determinations of the sensuous conception or of thought, and the causing of confusion between these and what is concrete.

545. See note 538 above.

546. See Hegel, *Philosophie des Rechts*, 105-41, 142-360, *Werke*, VIII, pp. 148-209, 210-440; *J.A.*, VII, pp. 164-225, 226-456; *Philosophy of Right*, pp. 75-104, 105-223.

547. See Hegel, *Philosophie des Rechts*, 139-40, *Werke*, VIII, pp. 184-207; *J.A.*, VII, pp. 200-23; *Philosophy of Right*, pp. 92-103.

548. Hegel, *Philosophie des Rechts*, 139, *Werke*, VIII, p. 184 (ed. tr.); *J.A.*, VII, p. 200; cf. *Philosophy of Right*, p. 92.

549. Hegel, *Geschichte der Philosophie*, II, *Werke*, XIV, p. 77; *J.A.*, XVIII, p. 77; *History of Philosophy*, I, p. 412 (ed. rev.). Cf. Aristotle, *Magna Moralia*, I, 1, 1182 a; Bekker, II, p. 1182; *Works*, II, pp. 1868-69.

550. See note 549 above; Hegel, *History of Philosophy*, I, p. 413.

551. Hegel, *Geschichte der Philosophie*, II, *Werke*, XIV, p. 55; *J.A.*, XVIII, p. 55; *History of Philosophy*, I, p. 394 (ed. rev.).

552. Hegel, *Geschichte der Philosophie*, II, *Werke*, XIV, p. 56; *J.A.*, XVIII, p. 56; *History of Philosophy*, I, p. 395.

553. Hegel, *Geschichte der Philosophie*, II, *Werke*, XIV, pp. 78-79; *J.A.*, XVIII, pp. 78-79; *History of Philosophy*, I, p. 414 (*Logous* [*sic*] translated as "perceptions" rather than as "reason" or "rational principle"). See Aristotle, *Nicomachean Ethics*, VI, 13, 1144 b; Bekker, II, p. 1144; *Works*, II, p. 1808.

554. Cf. *Sickness unto Death*, pp. 87-96, *KW* XIX (*SV* XI 199-207).

555. For the three Hegel references, see *Geschichte der Philosophie*, II, *Werke*, XIV, pp. 71, 79, 70; *J.A.*, XVIII, pp. 71, 79, 70; *History of Philosophy*, I, pp. 407, 414, 406.

556. Hegel, *Geschichte der Philosophie*, II, *Werke*, XIV, pp. 70-71; *J.A.*, XVIII, pp. 70-71; *History of Philosophy*, I, pp. 406-07 (ed. rev.).

557. For this quotation and the Hegel quotations and references in the next two paragraphs, see *Geschichte der Philosophie*, II, *Werke*, XIV, pp. 79, 79, 81, 82, 83-84 (ed. tr.), 85 (ed. tr.), 90 (ed. tr.); *J.A.*, XVIII, pp. 79, 79, 81, 82, 83-84, 85, 90; *History of Philosophy*, I, pp. 414, 414, 415, 416; cf. pp. 417-18, 418, 421.

558. See Bornemann, pp. 292-94, 299; Bloch, pp. 356-58, 363-64; Loeb, pp. 314-19, 324-25.

559. See, for example, Hegel, *Geschichte der Philosophie*, II, *Werke*, XIV, p. 63; *J.A.*, XVIII, p. 63; *History of Philosophy*, I, p. 401: "This irony is thus only

a trifling with everything, and it can transform all things into show: to this subjectivity nothing is any longer serious, for any seriousness which it has, immediately becomes dissipated again in jokes, and all noble or divine truth vanishes away or becomes mere triviality."

560. See p. 170.

561. See p. 122 fn.

562. See pp. 198-99 and note 463.

563. Charon, son of Erebus (the son of Chaos) and Nox, ferried the souls of the dead over the River Styx in Hades. See Lucian, *Dialogues of the Dead*, II, XIV; *Luciani Samosatensis opera*, I-IV (Leipzig: 1829; *ASKB* 1131-34), I, pp. 193-99; *Lucian*, I-VIII, tr. A. M. Harmon, K. Kilburn, and M. D. Macleod (Loeb, Cambridge: Harvard University Press, 1913-41), VII, pp. 9-15, 73-79; "Charon, or the Inspectors," XIV, *Opera*, I, pp. 275-76; Loeb, II, p. 427 (Charon to Hermes): "In the meantime let them be exalted, only to have a sorrier fall from a higher place. For my part I shall laugh when I recognize them aboard my skiff, stripped to the skin, taking with them neither purple mantle nor tiara nor throne of gold." See also Virgil, *Aeneid*, VI, 298-315; Schønheyder, pp. 266-67; Loeb, I, 526-29; *JP* V 5296 (*Pap*. II A 691).

564. See Hegel, *Geschichte der Philosophie*, II, *Werke*, XIV, pp. 58-70; *J.A.*, XVIII, pp. 58-70; *History of Philosophy*, I, pp. 397-406.

Part Two

1. Friedrich v. Schlegel (1772-1829), one of the founders of the romantic school in Germany and author of the novel *Lucinde* (1799), the handbook of Young Germany. See p. 275 and note 73.

2. Johann Ludwig Tieck (1773-1853), one of the founders of the romantic school in Germany, writer of the influential *Gedichte* (1823) and other poetry marked by an appreciation of nature and an interest in medieval legends.

3. Karl Wilhelm Ferdinand Solger (1780-1819), esthetician, student of Fichte and Schelling, professor of philosophy in Berlin, and author of *Erwin, vier Gespräche über das Schöne und die Kunst*, I-II (1815), and *Vorlesungen über Aesthetik* (1829).

4. See, for example, Hegel, *Die Phänomenologie des Geistes*, II; *Grundlinien der Philosophie des Rechts oder Naturrecht und Staatswissenschaft im Grundrisse*; *Vorlesungen über die Aesthetik*, I; *Vorlesungen über die Philosophie der Religion*, II; *Vorlesungen über die Geschichte der Philosophie*, II, III; *"Ueber 'Solger's nachgelassene Schriften und Briefwechsel',"* *Vermischte Schriften aus der Berliner Zeit*, *Georg Wilhelm Friedrich Hegel's Werke. Vollständige Ausgabe*, I-XVIII, ed. Philipp Marheineke et al. (Berlin: 1832-45; *ASKB* 549-65), II, pp. 476-505; VIII, pp. 200-04; X^1, pp. 84-90, 205-06, 312-13; XII, pp. 388-90; XIV, pp. 42-122; XV, p. 642; XVI, pp. 436-506; *Sämtliche Werke. Jubiläumsausgabe* [*J.A.*], I-XXVI, ed. Hermann Glockner (Stuttgart: Frommann, 1927-40), II, pp. 484-513; VII, pp. 216-20; XII, pp. 100-06, 221-22, 328-29; XVI, pp. 388-90; XVIII, pp. 42-122; XIX, pp. 644-76; XX, pp. 132-202; *The Phenomenology of Mind* (tr. based primarily on 3 ed. of *P.G.*, 1841; Kierkegaard had 2 ed., 1832), tr. J. B. Baillie

(New York: Harper, 1967), pp. 644-76; *Hegel's Philosophy of Right* (tr. of *P.R.*, 1 ed., 1821, with reference also to 2 ed., 1833, and later editions; Kierkegaard had 2 ed.), tr. T. M. Knox (London: Oxford University Press, 1978), pp. 101-03; *The Philosophy of Fine Art*, I-IV (tr. of *V.A.*, 1 ed., 1835-38; Kierkegaard had this ed.), tr. F.P.B. Osmaston (London: Bell, 1920), I, pp. 90-94, 217-18, 324-25; *Lectures on the Philosophy of Religion*, I-III (tr. of *P.R.*, 2 ed., 1840; Kierkegaard eventually had this ed.), tr. E. B. Speirs and J. Burdon Sanderson (New York: Humanities, 1962), III, pp. 183-85; *Hegel's Lectures on the History of Philosophy*, I-III (tr. of *G.P.*, 2 ed., 1840-44; Kierkegaard had 1 ed., 1833-36), tr. E. S. Haldane and Frances H. Simson (New York: Humanities, 1974), I, pp. 384-448; III, pp. 507-08.

5. *Solgers nachgelassene Schriften und Briefwechsel*, I-II, ed. Ludwig Tieck and Friedrich v. Raumer (Leipzig: 1826; *ASKB* 1832-33) (ed. tr.).

6. August Wilhelm v. Schlegel, *Ueber dramatische Kunst und Litteratur*, I-II (Heidelberg: 1809-11; *ASKB* 1392-94).

7. Hegel, *"Ueber 'Solger's nachgelassene Schriften und Briefwechsel',"* *Werke*, XVI, p. 492; *J.A.*, XX, p. 188 (ed. tr.).

8. Leading figures (named Brunhild and Siegfried in the German *Nibelungenlied*) in the Norse-Icelandic *Volsungasaga* and the second half of the elder *Edda*. Sigurd rides through the flames and awakens Brynhild (Odin had thrust a sleep-thorn into her), who had vowed she would never wed one who knew the name of fear. See Nicolai Frederik Severin Grundtvig, *Optrin af Norners og Asers Kamp*, III, *Optrin af Nordens Kæmpeliv*, I-II (Copenhagen: 1809-11), I, pp. 90-106; *Nordiske Kæmpe-Historier*, I-III, tr. Carl Christian Rafn (Copenhagen: 1821-26; *ASKB* 1993-95), I, pp. 66-82; *The Volsunga Saga*, tr. Eirikr Magnusson and William Morris (New York: Norrœna Society, 1907), pp. 84-86.

9. See Jean Paul (J. P. Friedrich Richter), *Vorschule der Aesthetik*, I-III (Stuttgart, Tübingen: 1813; *ASKB* 1381-83), I, 37-38, pp. 176-88; *Jean Paul's sämmtliche Werke*, I-LX (Berlin: 1826-28; *ASKB* 1777-99), XLI, pp. 199-207.

10. See Franz Xaver v. Baader, *Revision der Philosopheme der Hegel'schen Schule bezüglich auf das Christenthum. Nebst zehn Thesen aus einer religiösen Philosophie* (Stuttgart: 1839; *ASKB* 416), pp. 7-28 (*"Exposition einiger Elementarprincipien der Philosophie J. Böhms"*), 72-75.

11. See John 16:33; *JP* I 742; II 1327; IV 3915, pp. 54-55 (*Pap.* III A 238, 131, C 1).

12. See Ephesians 2:19.

13. See *Two Ages*, pp. 68-112, *KW* XIV (*SV* VIII 64-105).

14. See *Soap-Cellars*, in *Early Polemical Writings*, *KW* I (*Pap.* II B 16, p. 96).

15. See Plato, *Sophist*, 263 e; *Platonis quae exstant opera*, I-XI, ed. Friedrich Ast (Leipzig: 1819-32; *ASKB* 1144-54), II, pp. 348-49; *The Collected Dialogues of Plato*, ed. Edith Hamilton and Huntington Cairns (Princeton: Princeton University Press, 1963), p. 1011 (stranger speaking to Theaetetus): "Well, thinking and discourse are the same thing, except that what we call thinking

is, precisely, the inward dialogue carried on by the mind with itself without spoken sound."

16. Horace, *Epistles*, I, 18, 71; *Q. Horatii Flacci opera* (Leipzig: 1828; *ASKB* 1248), p. 605; *Horace Satires, Epistles and Ars Poetica*, tr. H. Rushton Fairclough (Loeb, Cambridge: Harvard University Press, 1978), pp. 374-75.

17. The source has not been located.

18. See, for example, Hegel's references to Tieck and associates, *Aesthetik*, I, *Werke*, X[1], pp. 86-87, 90; *J.A.*, XII, pp. 102-03, 106; *Philosophy of Fine Art*, I, pp. 90, 94:

> It is thus that this virtuosity of your ironical artist's life comes to be credited as some *god-like geniality*, for which every conceivable thing is a purely spectral creature, to which the free creator, knowing himself to be absolutely unattached, does not yoke himself, for he can ever annihilate the same no less than create it. Whoever has reached such a standpoint of god-like geniality consequently looks down in his superior fashion on all other mortals. . . . This irony was the discovery of Herr Fried. von Schlegel, and many have chattered about it after him, or it may be are giving us a fresh sample of such chatter.
>
> With regard to Ludwig Tieck, his culture, too, dates from that period in which Jena was the literary centre. Tieck and others who belonged to these superior people are on excellent terms with such modes of expression, without being able to tell us much what they mean. Thus Tieck always insists on the importance of Irony. But when it comes to delivering judgment on great works of art, though his recognition and description of their greatness is no doubt beyond reproach, yet if one imagines that in any particular example—let us say "Romeo and Juliet"—we have the opportunity put for an explanation of that in which here the irony consists, we are wide of the mark. We hear nothing more whatever about Irony.

19. See, for example, Hegel's references to modern romantic irony, *Geschichte der Philosophie*, II, III, *Werke*, XIV, pp. 63-64; XV, pp. 642-44; *J.A.*, XVIII, pp. 63-64; XIX, pp. 642-44; *History of Philosophy*, I, pp. 401-02; III, pp. 507, 509:

> The divine is said to be the purely negative attitude, the perception of the vanity of everything, in which my vanity alone remains. Making the consciousness of the nullity of everything ultimate, might indeed indicate depth of life, but it only is the depth of emptiness, as may be seen from the ancient comedies of Aristophanes. From this irony of our times, the irony of Socrates is far removed; as is also the case with Plato, it has a significance which is limited. Socrates' premeditated irony may be called a manner of speech, a pleasant rallying; there is in it no satirical laughter or pretence, as though the idea were nothing but a joke.
>
> It can make a pretence of knowing all things, but it only demonstrates vanity, hypocrisy, and effrontery. Irony knows itself to be the master of every possible content; it is serious about nothing, but plays with all forms.

They outbid one another in conceits of fancy, in ardent poetry. But before the Truth vanity turns pale, spitefully sneering it sneaks back into itself. Ask not after a criterion of the truth, but after the Notion of the truth in and for itself; on that fix your gaze.

20. The text has "Arv," the name of a naïve character who appears in a number of Ludvig Holberg's plays. See, for example, *Jule-Stue*, *Den Danske Skue-Plads*, I-VII (Copenhagen: 1788; *ASKB* 1566-67) II, no pagination; *The Christmas Party*, *Seven One-Act Plays by Holberg*, tr. Henry Alexander (Princeton: Princeton University Press for the American-Scandinavian Foundation, 1950), pp. 81-102.

21. See I Corinthians 1:27.

22. Peder Erichsen (patronymic), son of Erich Madsen, a character in Ludvig Holberg's play *Den Stundesløse*, II, 7-8; *Danske Skue-Plads*, V, no pagination; *The Fussy Man*, *Four Plays by Holberg*, tr. Henry Alexander (Princeton: Princeton University Press for the American-Scandinavian Foundation, 1946), pp. 14-16.

23. See I Thessalonians 5:2.

24. In some medieval French churches, there were processions and dramatic presentations in which an ass played a role. The Feast of Fools was a remnant of the ancient Saturnalias and in the twelfth century was celebrated by the clergy, who read parodies on ecclesiastical activities. Easter Comedy was an old practice of presenting comical stories from the pulpit during Easter week and later the practice of including such tales in the Easter service.

25. Lucian (2 cent.), celebrated Greek prose writer, is best known for his satirical works primarily on ancient mythology and contemporary philosophers.

26. Charles M. de Talleyrand (1754-1838) is supposed to have said this to a Spanish diplomat. See *Stages*, p. 339, *KW* XI (*SV* VI 317); *JP* I 623; III 2322; IV 3870 (*Pap*. V A 19; B 115:2; XI[2] A 117).

27. See, for example, *JP* V 5938 (*Pap*. VII[1] A 148).

28. See p. 26 and note 64.

29. Gotthilf Heinrich v. Schubert, *Die Symbolik des Traumes* (Bamberg: 1821; *ASKB* 776), p. 38 (ed. tr.). See *Repetition*, p. 155, *KW* VI (*SV* III 195); *Fragments*, p. 108, *KW* VII (*SV* IV 269); *JP* II 1695; III 2307, 3623; IV 3992 (*Pap*. II A 107, 62; XI[1] A 247; II A 19).

30. *Irische Elfenmärchen* (tr. of Thomas Crofton Croker, *Fairy Legends and Traditions of the South of Ireland*, I-III [London: 1825]), tr. Jakob Ludwig and Wilhelm Karl Grimm (Leipzig: 1826; *ASKB* 1423). *"Risen fra Letraberg,"* st. 77, *Færøiske Qvæder*, ed. and tr. Hans Christian Lyngbye (Randers: 1822; *ASKB* 1484). Literally, *Dvergmaal* and *Bergmaal* mean "dwarf language" and "mountain language."

31. See Supplement, pp. 431-32 (*Pap*. II A 102).

32. Theophrastus, *Characters*, I; *Theophrasti Characteres*, ed. Friedrich Ast (Leipzig: 1816; *ASKB* 1204), p. 4; *The Characters of Theophrastus*, ed. and tr. J. M. Edmonds (Loeb, New York: Putnam, 1929), p. 41: "Now Dissembling would seem, to define it generally, to be an affectation of the worse in word

and deed; and the Dissembler will be disposed rather to go up to an enemy and talk with him than to show his hatred; he will praise to his face one he has girded at behind his back; he will commiserate even his adversary's ill-fortune in losing his case to him."

33. Cf. Hegel, *Philosophie des Rechts*, *Werke*, VIII, pp. 192-96; *J.A.*, VII, pp. 208-12; *Philosophy of Right*, pp. 95-98, especially pp. 97-98:

> To this context there also belongs the notorious maxim: 'The end justifies the means.' In itself and prima facie this expression is trivial and pointless. Quite so, one may retort in terms equally general, a just end of course justifies the means, while an unjust end does not. The phrase: 'If the end is right, so is the means' is a tautology, since the means is precisely that which is nothing in itself but is for the sake of something else, and therein, i.e. in the end, has its purpose and worth—provided of course it be truly a means.
>
> But when someone says that the end justifies the means, his purport is not confined to this bare tautology; he understands by the words something more specific, namely that to use as means to a good end something which in itself is simply not a means at all, to violate something in itself sacrosanct, in short to commit a crime as a means to a good end, is permissible and even one's bounden duty.

34. See Hegel, *Phänomenologie*, *Werke*, II, pp. 463-76; *J.A.*, II, pp. 471-84; *Phenomenology*, pp. 629-41.

35. See p. 254 and note 29.

36. See *JP* II 1581 (*Pap*. II A 808).

37. See Ecclesiastes 1:2.

38. See *JP* III 2796 (*Pap*. III A 70).

39. The Danish *spøge* means both "to haunt" and "to jest."

40. Presumably a paraphrase of Cleanthes' "Hymn to Zeus" via Seneca, "On Obedience to the Universal Will," *Epistles*, 107; *L. Annaei Senecae . . . Opera omnia*, I-II, ed. A. Schotto (Geneva: 1626; *ASKB* 1274), II, p. 829; *Seneca ad Lucilium epistulae morales*, I-III, tr. Richard M. Gummere (Loeb, Cambridge: Harvard University Press, 1962), III, p. 229:

> Let us address Jupiter, the pilot of this world-mass, as did our great Cleanthes in those most eloquent lines—lines which I shall allow myself to render in Latin, after the example of the eloquent Cicero. If you like them, make the most of them; if they displease you, you will understand that I have simply been following the practice of Cicero:
>
> Lead me, O Master of the lofty heavens,
> My Father, whithersoever thou shalt wish.
> I shall not falter, but obey with speed.
> And though I would not, I shall go, and suffer,
> In sin and sorrow what I might have done
> In noble virtue. Aye, the willing soul
> Fate leads, but the unwilling drags along.

41. Acts 5:9.

42. Cf. John 2:17.

43. Tamerlane, or Timur (c. 1336-1405), the Mongol conqueror, extended his power from the Volga to the Great Wall of China and left a broad trail of destruction and slaughter in the invasion of India in 1398.

44. See Matthew 24:2; Mark 13:2; Luke 19:44, 21:6.

45. Hieronymus Cardanus (1501-1576), philosopher and mathematician (see *JP* II 2188; V 5611, 5612; *Pap.* VIII[1] A 97; IV A 36, 37); Tommaso Campanella (1568-1639), Dominican friar, philosopher (see *JP* I 246; III 3312; *Pap.* VIII[1] A 167, 166); Giordano Bruno (1548-1600), philosopher, victim of the Inquisition (see *JP* II 1221, 1357; III 3048; *Pap.* X[2] A 516; VIII[1] A 148, 118). See Hegel, *Geschichte der Philosophie*, III, *Werke*, XV, pp. 219-20; *J.A.*, XIX, pp. 219-20; *History of Philosophy*, III, pp. 115-16.

46. Desiderius Erasmus (1467-1536), Dutch humanist scholar. See *JP* III 3163 (*Pap.* X[4] A 332).

47. Cf. *JP* I 284 (*Pap.* II A 595).

48. Hegel, *Werke*, XIV, p. 62 (ed. tr.); *J.A.*, XVIII, p. 62; cf. *History of Philosophy*, I, p. 400.

49. Cf. Exodus 20:6; Deuteronomy 5:10.

50. See Luke 7:19.

51. See Luke 17:33.

52. See pp. 5-6, Thesis VIII. On subjectivity and Greek substantiality, see "The Tragic in Ancient Drama Reflected in the Tragic in Modern Drama," *Either/Or*, I, pp. 139-47, *KW* III (*SV* I 117-24).

53. See Hegel, *Geschichte der Philosophie*, II, *Werke*, XIV, p. 64; *J.A.*, XVIII, p. 64; *History of Philosophy*, I, pp. 401-02.

54. See p. 248 and note 18.

55. Ibid.

56. Cf. Hegel, *Phänomenologie*, *Werke*, II, p. 9; *J.A.*, II, p. 17; *Phenomenology*, pp. 73-74:

> This easy contentment in receiving, or stinginess in giving, does not suit the character of science. The man who only seeks edification, who wants to envelop in mist the manifold diversity of his earthly existence and thought, and craves after the vague enjoyment of this vague and indeterminate Divinity—he may look where he likes to find this: he will easily find for himself the means to procure something he can rave over and puff himself up withal. But philosophy must beware of wishing to be edifying.

57. Hegel, *Werke*, XIV, pp. 59-67 (the following excerpts ed. tr.); *J.A.*, XVIII, pp. 59-67; cf. *History of Philosophy*, I, pp. 397-406.

58. See note 48 above.

59. Hegel, "*Ueber 'Solger's nachgelassene Schriften',*" *Werke*, XVI, pp. 436-506; *J.A.*, XX, pp. 132-202.

60. Ibid., *Werke*, XVI, p. 488; *J.A.*, XX, p. 184.

61. See Luke 15:12.

62. Tithonus, husband of Eos (Aurora, dawn), was given immortality but not youth and therefore wasted away to almost nothing but his voice. Eos finally changed him into a grasshopper. See *JP* II 1189 (*Pap*. I A 302).

63. From Aesop's fables. See Aesop, *"Vulpis et Corvus," Phaedri August Liberti Fabularum Aesopiarum Libri V* (Leipzig: 1828), pp. 7-8; "The Fox and the Crow," *Babrius and Phaedrus*, ed. and tr. Ben Edwin Perry (Loeb, Cambridge: Harvard University Press, 1965), pp. 207-09.

64. See p. 107 and note 271.

65. The school of Paschasius Radbertus (c. 785-860), Benedictine theologian and author of the first doctrinal monograph on the Eucharist, *De corpore et sanguine Domini* (831), which emphasizes the real presence of Christ in the Eucharist. See Ferdinand Christian Baur, *Die christliche Kirche des Mittelalters* (Tübingen: 1861), p. 59.

66. See, for example, J. G. Fichte, *Die Bestimmung des Menschen* (Berlin: 1838; *ASKB* 500), pp. 79-81, 117; *Johan Gottlieb Fichte's sämmtliche Werke*, I-VIII (Berlin: 1845-46; *ASKB* 492-99), II, pp. 224-25, 249-50; *The Vocation of Man, The Popular Works of Johann Gottlieb Fichte*, I-II, tr. William Smith (London: Trübner, 1889), I, pp. 381-82, 406-07:

> *Spirit*. Thou observest well—but do not rush too hastily to a conclusion. If that whereon we have already agreed remains true, and thou canst be immediately conscious of thyself only; if the consciousness now in question be not a consciousness of thine own passivity, and still less a consciousness of thine own activity;—may it not then be an *unrecognised* consciousness of thine own being?—of thy being in so far as thou art a *knowing* being,—an Intelligence?
>
> *I*. I do not understand thee; but help me once more, for I wish to understand thee.
>
> *Spirit*. I must then demand thy whole attention, for I am here compelled to go deeper, and expatiate more widely, than ever.——What art thou?
>
> *I*. To answer thy question in the most general way,—I am I, myself.
>
> *Spirit*. I am well satisfied with this answer. What dost thou mean when thou sayest "I";—what lies in this conception,—and how dost thou attain it?
>
> *I*. On this point I can make myself understood only by contrast. External existence—*the thing*, is something out of me, the cognitive being. *I* am *myself* this cognitive being, one with the object of my cognition. As to my consciousness of the former, there arises the question,—Since the thing cannot know itself, how can a knowledge of it arise?—how can a consciousness of the thing arise *in me*, since I myself am not the thing, nor any of its modes or forms, and all these modes and forms lie within the circle of its own being, and by no means in mine? How does the thing reach me? What is the tie between me, the subject, and the thing which is the object of my knowledge? But as to my consciousness of *myself*, there can be no such question. In this case, I have my knowledge within myself, for I am intelligence. What I am, I know because I am it; and that whereof I know im-

mediately that I am it, that I am because I immediately know it. There is here no need of any tie between subject and object; my own nature is this tie. I am subject and object:—and this *subject-objectivity*, this return of knowledge upon itself, is what I mean by the term "I," when I deliberately attach a definite meaning to it.

Spirit. Thus it is in the identity of subject and object that thy nature as an intelligence consists?

I. Yes.

Spirit. Canst thou then comprehend the possibility of thy becoming conscious of this identity, which is neither subject nor object, but which lies at the foundation of both, and out of which both arise?

I. By no means. It is the condition of all my consciousness, that the conscious being, and what he is conscious of, appear distinct and separate. I cannot even conceive of any other consciousness. In the very act of recognising myself, I recognise myself as subject and object, both however being immediately bound up with each other.

There is within me an impulse to absolute, independent self-activity. Nothing is more insupportable to me than to be merely by another, for another, and through another; I must be something for myself and by myself alone. This impulse I feel along with the perception of my own existence, it is inseparably united to my consciousness of myself.

I explain this feeling to myself by reflection; and, as it were, endow this blind impulse with the gift of insight by the power of thought. According to this impulse I must act as an absolutely independent being:—thus I understand and translate the impulse. I must be independent. Who am I? Subject and object in one,—the conscious being and that of which I am conscious, gifted with intuitive knowledge and myself revealed in that intuition, the thinking mind and myself the object of the thought—inseparable and ever present to each other. As both, must I be what I am, absolutely by myself alone;—by myself originate conceptions,—by myself produce a condition of things lying beyond these conceptions.

Cf. Hegel, *"Darstellung des Fichteschen Systems," "Differenz des Fichteschen und Schellingschen Systems . . .," Aufsätze aus dem kritischen Journal der Philosophie und andere Schriften aus der Jenenser Zeit, Werke*, I, pp. 205-49; *J.A.*, I, pp. 77-121; *The Difference between Fichte's and Schelling's System of Philosophy*, tr. H. S. Harris and Walter Cerf (Albany: State University of New York Press, 1977), pp. 119-54; *Wissenschaft der Logik*, I, *Werke*, III, pp. 94-95, 272-73; IV, p. 11; *J.A.*, IV, pp. 104-05, 282-83, 489; *Hegel's Science of Logic* (tr. of *W.L.*, Lasson ed., 1923; Kierkegaard had 2 ed., 1833), tr. A. V. Miller (New York: Humanities, 1976), pp. 95, 232-33, 396-97; *"Ueber 'Solger's nachgelassene Schriften'," Werke*, XVI, pp. 487-88; *J.A.*, XX, pp. 183-84.

67. See J. G. Fichte, *Nachgelassene Werke*, I-III, ed. Immanuel Hermann Fichte (Bonn: 1834-35; *ASKB* 489-91), II, p. 2.

68. See Colossians 3:3.

69. See Matthew 10:39; Mark 8:35; Luke 9:24; John 12:25.

70. Johann Tauler, *Nachfolgung des armen Lebens Christi* (Frankfurt/M: 1821; *ASKB* 282), p. 254 (ed. tr.).

71. Cf. Colossians 2:2.

72. See p. 273 and note 67.

73. A name given to a group of writers who were politically active in the 1830s and influential in literary criticism, the novel, and social commentary. The principal reason for the emergence of the movement was an order from the Diet of Frankfurt, December 10, 1833, that suppressed the past and future writings of Ludwig Börne, Karl Gutzkow, Heinrich Heine, Heinrich Laube, and Theodor Mundt. See note 1 above.

74. Cf. Matthew 16:19.

75. *Dichtung und Wahrheit* (Poetry and Truth). An allusion to the subtitle of Goethe's autobiography, *Aus meinem Leben, Dichtung und Wahrheit, Goethe's Werke. Vollständige Ausgabe letzter Hand*, I-LX (Stuttgart, Tübingen: 1828-42; *ASKB* 1641-68 [I-LV]), XXIV-XXVI, XLVIII.

76. Lessing, *Nathan der Weise*, III, 7, *Gotthold Ephraim Lessing's sämmtliche Schriften*, I-XXXII (Berlin, Stettin: 1825-28; *ASKB* 1747-62), XXII, pp. 132-38; *Nathan the Wise*, tr. Patrick Maxwell (New York: Bloch, 1939), p. 250.

77. Hegel, *"Ueber 'Solger's nachgelassene Schriften',"* *Werke*, XVI, p. 465; *J.A.*, XX, p. 161.

78. See Psalm 104:26.

79. See Hebrews 7:7.

80. Cf. *Either/Or*, I, p. 304, *KW* III (*SV* I 276).

81. See I Corinthians 3:9; Philippians 1:6.

82. Most likely from the title *Aus dem Leben eines Taugenichts*, *Joseph Freiherrn von Eichendorff's Werke*, I-IV (Berlin: 1841), IV, pp. 3-113.

83. See I Corinthians 3:18.

84. The followers of the Greek philosopher Pythagoras (582-c. 507 B.C.) held the view that individual souls return in bodies appropriate to the previous lives (reincarnation, transmigration, metempsychosis).

85. See Lucian, "The Dream, or the Cock," 15-20; *Luciani Samosatensis opera*, I-IV (Leipzig: 1829; *ASKB* 1131-34), III, pp. 188-93; *Lucian*, I-VIII, tr. A. M. Harmon, K. Kilburn, and M. D. Macleod (Loeb, Cambridge: Harvard University Press, 1913-41), II, pp. 203-15.

86. See Psalm 3:18.

87. A rhyme used, for example, in counting a child's buttons in order to find out what his occupation will be; freely translated: rich man, poor man, beggar man, thief. See *Postscript*, *KW* XII (*SV* VII 84 fn.), which has "nobleman, beggar, doctor, pastor, shoemaker, tailor."

88. The chair reserved for the leading Roman official.

89. See "The Seducer's Diary," *Either/Or*, I, pp. 301-445, *KW* III (*SV* I 273-412), which is an elaboration in epistolary novel form of the double poetizing discussed here.

90. See p. 225 and note 538.

91. See Solger, *Nachgelassene Schriften*, II, p. 514.

92. Cf. *Either/Or*, I, pp. 305-06, *KW* III; II, pp. 229-31, *KW* IV (*SV* I 277; II 206-07); *JP* I 1069 (*Pap*. III C 13).

93. According to legend, Venus held court in certain mountains (Venusberg: Venus Mountain) in Germany, particularly in Swabia (southwest Bavaria), and presided over revelries that lured men astray from the path of salvation.

94. Ed. tr. of Danish summary of Hegel's quotations from Tieck's correspondence with Solger. See Hegel, *"Ueber 'Solger's nachgelassene Schriften',"* *Werke*, XVI, pp. 458-64; *J.A.*, XX, pp. 154-60.

95. Cf. *Either/Or*, I, pp. 281-300, *KW* III (*SV* 253-72).

96. In Norse mythology, Loki was an evil, or at least arbitrary and mischievous, god who caused Balder's death and reproached the gods at Ægir's feast. He was ultimately captured by the gods in the Fraananger Cascade. See Jacob Bærent Møinichen, *Nordiske Folks Overtroe, Guder, Fabler og Helte* (Copenhagen: 1800; *ASKB* 1947), pp. 291-92 (ed. tr.): "Loke Laufeiason or Loptur, a very ambivalent person, who was counted among the gods although he was rather a devil or a perfect blending of evil and good, continually in the company of gods, did all possible roguish things to them but just as frequently benefited them and assisted them out of many predicaments by his unrivaled craftiness."

97. Berlin: 1799. After Schleiermacher's death, Karl Gutzkow republished (1835) Schleiermacher's long defensive review, *Vertraute Briefe über Friedrich Schlegels Lucinde* (1 ed., anon., Lübeck, Leipzig: 1800). Therefore, the second editions of both *Lucinde* and *Vertraute Briefe* appeared while Kierkegaard was a university student. An adequate treatment of the relation between *Lucinde* and "The Seducer's Diary" in *Either/Or*, I, has yet to appear. See Supplement, pp. 424-25 (*Pap*. I C 69).

98. See p. 275 and note 73.

99. See Hegel, *Philosophie des Rechts*, *Werke*, VIII, p. 229; *J.A.*, VII, p. 245; *Philosophy of Right*, p. 263; *Aesthetik*, II, *Werke*, X², p. 108; *J.A.*, XIII, p. 109; *Philosophy of Fine Art*, II, p. 269; *"Ueber 'Solger's nachgelassene Schriften',"* *Werke*, XVI, p. 446; *J.A.*, XX, p. 142 (ed. tr.):

> Friedrich von Schlegel in his *Lucinde. Ein Roman*, and a follower of his in the *Briefe eines Ungenannten* [Schleiermacher, 1800], have put forward the view that the wedding ceremony is superfluous and a formality that might be discarded. Their reason is that love is, so they say, the substance of marriage and that the celebration therefore detracts from its worth. Surrender to sensual impulse is here represented as necessary to prove the freedom and inwardness of love—an argument not unknown to seducers. . . . the wanton disregard of things that are sacred and of the highest excellence such as marks the period of Friedrich von Schlegel's "Lucinde." . . . the most brazen and flourishing period of irony . . . .

100. See, for example, *JP* II 1280; III 3065, 3067 (*Pap*. II A 23; XI[1] A 195, 210).

101. The page number and the numbers in the rest of the Schlegel section are from *Lucinde* (2 ed., Stuttgart: 1835). The English translation is from *Friedrich Schlegel's* Lucinde *and the Fragments*, tr. Peter Firchow (Minneapolis: University of Minnesota Press, 1971), p. 128.

102. Firchow, p. 74.

103. Ibid., p. 75.

104. Possibly an allusion to J. L. Heiberg, *Julespøg og Nytaarsløier* (Copenhagen: 1817, a parody of Bernhard Severin Ingemann, *Blanca*), in which the hero's and heroine's numerous "holy, sentimental, and Platonic children" have neither muscles nor legs, and their skin is moonlight; they are "only the fruits of our frequent public embraces." Heiberg, *Julespøg*, I, 3; *J. L. Heibergs Skuespil*, I-VII (Copenhagen: 1833-41; *ASKB* 1553-59), I, p. 223 (ed. tr.).

105. See "The Esthetic Validity of Marriage," *Either/Or*, II, pp. 3-154, *KW* IV (*SV* II 3-140), for Judge William's elaboration of this theme.

106. See Luke 14:20.

107. See p. 225 and note 538.

108. See Firchow, p. 52.

109. Ibid., pp. 50 (impertinence), 53-63 (impudence).

110. See p. 225 and note 538.

111. The text is a Danish paraphrase. See Firchow, p. 98.

112. Ibid., p. 64.

113. Ibid., pp. 58-59.

114. Cf. Matthew 3:17, 17:5; Mark 9:7. For this quotation and the two following quotations see Firchow, pp. 62, 57, 50.

115. The story about Archimedes and his discovery, while bathing, of the principle of specific gravity. See *Two Ages*, p. 66, *KW* XIV (*SV* VIII 62).

116. See Firchow, p. 44.

117. Ibid., p. 45.

118. Ibid., p. 128.

119. In Roman mythology, Minerva (identified with the Olympian Pallas Athena), the goddess of wisdom and crafts, sprang full-grown and fully armed from the brow of Jupiter after he had swallowed her mother, Metis. See Paul Friedrich A. Nitsch, *neues mythologisches Wörterbuch*, I-II, rev. Friedrich Gotthilf Klopfer (Leipzig, Sorau: 1821; *ASKB* 1944-45), II, p. 251; Lucian, *Dialogues of the Gods*, VIII; *Opera*, I, pp. 115-16; Loeb, VII, pp. 305-08.

120. Firchow, p. 77.

121. Presumably an allusion to Mozart's *Don Giovanni*. See *Either/Or*, I, pp. 45-135, *KW* III (*SV* I 29-113).

122. See Firchow, p. 80.

123. Ibid., pp. 82-93.

124. The text is a Danish paraphrase. See Firchow, pp. 87-88.

125. In his writings, Caesar refers to himself in the third person.

126. See Firchow, pp. 63-68.

127. Ibid., p. 66.

128. The text here is in Danish, a faithful rendition of the German except for the omission of italics in the last two words. Cf. Firchow, p. 66.

129. Ibid., pp. 48-49.

130. Ibid., p. 126.

131. Ibid., p. 127.

132. See "Diapsalmata," *Either/Or*, I, pp. 17-43, *KW* III (*SV* I 1-27).

133. Cf., for example, *Sickness unto Death*, p. 14, *KW* XIX (*SV* XI 128).

134. In Greek mythology, Nemesis was the goddess of chastisement and vengeance. See *JP* II 1678 (*Pap.* I A 265).

135. See John 16:33.

136. See, for example, *Either/Or*, II, pp. 206, 209, 231, 266, 269, *KW* IV (*SV* II 185, 188, 207, 239, 241); *JP* II 1587 (*Pap.* III A 1).

137. Firchow, p. 87.

138. Ibid.

139. Ibid., p. 88.

140. See p. 225 and note 538.

141. Firchow, p. 63.

142. Ibid., p. 48.

143. Ibid., p. 49.

144. See p. 225 and note 538.

145. Ludwig Tieck (1773-1853), a prominent German novelist of the romantic school and translator of Shakespeare.

146. Danish: *Hopsasa*, the name of a kind of waltz. See *JP* III 3280 (*Pap.* II A 814).

147. See, for example, Hegel, *"Ueber 'Solger's nachgelassene Schriften',"* *Werke*, XVI, pp. 447-51, 456-64; *J.A.*, XX, pp. 143-47, 152-60.

148. *ASKB* 580 (excerpt ed. tr.). Hotho was the editor of Hegel's posthumously published *Aesthetik*, I-III, *Werke*, X; *J.A.*, XII-XIV.

149. See Heinrich Heine, *Die romantische Schule* (Hamburg: 1836; *ASKB U* 63), pp. 43-44; *The Prose Writings of Heinrich Heine*, ed. Havelock Ellis (London: 1887), pp. 87-88.

150. See John 4:14.

151. See Supplement, pp. 440-41 (*Pap.* III B 2); *JP* I 132 (*Pap.* II A 636). Cf. *JP* II 2177 (*Pap.* II A 580).

152. Ludwig Achim v. Arnim and Clemens Brentano, *Des Knaben Wunderhorn*, I-III (Heidelberg: 1819; *ASKB* 1494-96). On the title page of volume III there is a picture of a young man and young woman dressed in medieval apparel and playing stringed instruments.

153. See *JP* I 132 (*Pap.* II A 636).

154. Danish: *Ulen Dulen Dorf.* For this counting-off verse used in designating who is "it" in a children's game, see *Danske Folkesagn*, I-IV, ed. Just Matthias Thiele (Copenhagen: 1819-23; *ASKB* 1591-92), III, p. 140:

> Ulen, dulen, doff,
> Fingen, Fangen, Foff,

Foff for alle Mærkepande,
E. B. ba, buff.
Kaalvippen, kaalvappen, Der slap En.

155. See p. 242 and note 3.

156. *ASKB* 1387.

157. Hegel, *"Ueber 'Solger's nachgelassene Schriften',"* *Werke*, XVI, pp. 486-87 (ed. tr.); *J.A.*, XX, pp. 182-83.

158. Hegel, *Aesthetik*, I, *Werke*, X[1], p. 89; *J.A.*, XII, p. 105; *Philosophy of Fine Art*, I, p. 93.

159. See Supplement, epigraph on original title page, pp. 418-19.

160. See Solger, *Nachgelassene Schriften*, I, p. 603.

161. See II Corinthians 5:19.

162. See J. H. Wessel, *"Jeg synger om en Mand," Johan Herman Wessels samtlige Skrivter*, I-II (Copenhagen: 1787), II, p. 131 (ed. tr.):

Jeg synger om en Kone. Hemistichen faldt,
Som synes Læseren en Smule splittergalt
[I sing of a woman. The caesura falls,
As the reader thinks, not right at all].

163. See Solger, *Nachgelassene Schriften*, I, p. 605.

164. A semi-Pelagian doctrine that asserts that human effort cooperates with divine grace, a view variously represented by Erasmus, Melanchthon, and the Council of Trent.

165. See Genesis 32:26.

166. Bernhard Rudolf Abeken (1780-1866), German philologist and tutor of Schiller's children.

167. See Hegel, *"Ueber 'Solger's nachgelassene Schriften',"* *Werke*, XVI, pp. 469-74; *J.A.*, XX, pp. 165-70.

168. See Solger, *Nachgelassene Schriften*, I, p. 511.

169. Ibid., p. 512.

170. Ibid., p. 514.

171. Hegel, *"Ueber 'Solger's nachgelassene Schriften',"* *Werke*, XVI, p. 470; *J.A.*, XX, p. 166 (ed. tr.).

172. See Solger, *Nachgelassene Schriften*, I, pp. 652, 689; II, p. 515. Cf. Hegel, *"Ueber 'Solger's nachgelassene Schriften',"* *Werke*, XVI, pp. 489-91; *J.A.*, XX, pp. 185-87.

173. See pp. 259-60.

174. See Solger, *Nachgelassene Schriften*, I, pp. 293-95, 350, 428.

175. See I John 5:4.

176. See Solger, *Vorlesungen über Aesthetik*, ed. Karl Wilhelm Ludwig Heyse (Leipzig: 1829; *ASKB* 1387), pp. 183-256.

177. See pp. 324-25.

178. Solger, *Nachgelassene Schriften*, II, pp. 493-524.

179. Schlegel, *Ueber dramatische Kunst und Litteratur*.

180. Cf. Hegel, *Philosophie des Rechts, Werke*, VIII, pp. 201-02 fn.; *J.A.*, VII, pp. 217-18 fn.; *Philosophy of Right*, pp. 101-02 fn.:

> My colleague, the late Professor Solger, adopted the word 'irony' which Friedrich von Schlegel brought into use at a comparatively early period of his literary career and enhanced to equivalence with the said principle of subjectivity knowing itself as supreme. But Solger's finer mind was above such an exaggeration; he had philosophic insight and so seized upon, emphasized, and retained only that part of Schlegel's view which was dialectic in the strict sense, i.e. dialectic as the pulsating drive of speculative inquiry. His last publication, a solid piece of work, a thorough *Kritik über die Vorlesungen des Herrn August Wilhelm von Schlegel über dramatische Kunst und Literatur* (Wiener Jahrbuch, vol. vii, pp. 90 ff.), I find somewhat obscure, however, and I cannot agree with the argument which he develops. 'True irony', he says (p. 92), 'arises from the view that so long as man lives in this present world, it is only in this world that he can fulfil his "appointed task" no matter how elevated a sense we give to this expression. Any hope we may have of transcending finite ends is foolish and empty conceit. Even the highest is existent for our conduct only in a shape that is limited and finite.' Rightly understood, this is Platonic doctrine, and a true remark in rejection of what he has referred to earlier, the empty striving towards the (abstract) infinite. But to say that the highest is existent in a limited and finite shape, like the ethical order (and that order is in essence actual life and action), is very different from saying that the highest thing is a *finite* end. . . . The *tragic* destruction of figures whose ethical life is on the highest plane can interest and elevate us and reconcile us to its occurrence only in so far as they come on the scene in opposition to one another together with equally justified but different ethical powers which have come into collision through misfortune, because the result is that then these figures acquire guilt through their opposition to an ethical law. Out of this situation there arises the right and wrong of both parties and therefore the true ethical Idea, which, purified and in triumph over this one-sidedness, is thereby reconciled in *us*. Accordingly, it is not the highest in us which perishes; we are elevated not by the destruction of the best but by the triumph of the true.

181. Although the Danish text is *Udvanding* [dilution] in the first edition and in the three editions of the *Samlede Værker* (drafts and the final ms. of *Irony* are not extant), this may be a misprint for *Udvandring* [exodus, emigration], which would be consistent with the idea of flight in the preceding sentence and would be a repetition of *Udvandring* in a similar context on p. 297.

182. See Solger, *Vorlesungen über Aesthetik*, pp. 199, 242-44.

183. See p. 293 and note 505.

184. Cf. Solger, *Vorlesungen über Aesthetik*, pp. 199, 214: "*Gleichgültigkeit* . . . auch wohl *Objectivität* gennant"; "Gleichgültigkeit oder sogennante *Objectivität* [*indifference* . . . also called *objectivity*; indifference or so-called *objectivity*]." "Indifference" or "objectivity" is interpreted along the lines of Kant's

stipulation of "disinterestedness." See Immanuel Kant, *Critik der Urtheilskraft* (Berlin: 1793; *ASKB* 594), I, 5, p. 16; *Critique of Judgement*, tr. James Creed Meredith (Oxford: Oxford University Press, 1964), p. 50: "*Taste* is the faculty of estimating an object or a mode of representation by means of a delight or aversion *apart from any interest*. The object of such a delight is called *beautiful*."

185. Cf. J. L. Heiberg, *Om Philosophiens Betydning for den nuværende Tid* (Copenhagen: 1833; *ASKB* 568), p. 45 (ed. tr.), where Goethe's poetry is said to "present the philosophy that the age seeks. Not only are some of his most important works, such as *Wilhelm Meister*, *Tasso*, and especially *Faust*, didactic poetry in the previously established sense, but the speculative idea penetrates the composition of almost all his works . . . ."

186. Cf. the opening paragraph of "Diapsalmata," *Either/Or*, I, p. 19, *KW* III (*SV* I 3).

187. See *Either/Or*, I, p. 120, *KW* III (*SV* I 100).

188. Cf. John 14:6.

189. On the further development of the view that "subjectivity is truth," see especially *Postscript*, *KW* XII (*SV* VII 157-211). See also *JP* IV 4534-74, 4842-89, and pp. 712-15, 749-52.

190. Claude-Henri de Rouvroy, Comte de Saint-Simon (1760-1825), French social philosopher and advocate of socialism.

191. Cf. Mark 10:9.

192. See pp. 263-64, 326-29.

193. See, for example, *Postscript*, *KW* XII (*SV* VII 229-32, 248-50, 257, 260, 434-54, 464, 480-84); *JP* II 1669-1769; VII, pp. 46-47, 51-52.

194. A common version of Tertullian, *De carne Christi*, 5: "*Mortuus est dei filius; credible est, quia ineptum est*"; *On the Flesh of Christ, The Ante-Nicene Fathers*, I-IX, ed. Alexander Roberts and James Donaldson (Buffalo: Christian Literature Publishing Co., 1885-97), III, p. 525: "And the Son of God died; it is by all means to be believed, because it is absurd [*ineptum*]."

195. J. L. Heiberg, *Nye Digte* (Copenhagen: 1841; *ASKB* 1562), reviewed by Hans Lassen Martensen, *Fædrelandet*, 398-400, January 10-12, 1841, col. 3205-24.

NOTES OF SCHELLING'S BERLIN LECTURES

1. Presumably Johann Arnold Kanne, *Leben und aus dem Leben merkwürdiger und erweckter Christen aus der Protestantischen Kirche*, I-II (Bamberg, Leipzig: 1816-17). The reference has not been located. See *Pap*. I C 5.

2. Cf. *Either/Or*, I, p. 31, *KW* III (*SV* I 16).

3. Accidental (nonessential) in the Aristotelian sense. Cf. *Fragments*, p. 39, *KW* VII (*SV* IV 207).

4. Christian Wolff (1679-1754), German rationalist philosopher of the En-

lightenment who joined scholastic tradition with the metaphysical theories of Descartes and Leibniz.

5. The edition of Schelling's lectures pirated prior to publication has ἐξισταμενον [standing outside its place]. See *Die endlich offenbar gewordene positive Philosophie der Offenbarung oder Enstehungsgeschichte, wörtlicher Text, Beurtheilung und Berichtigung der v. Schellingischen Entdeckungen über Philosophie überhaupt, Mythologie und Offenbarung des dogmatischen Christenthums im Berliner Wintercursus von 1841-42. Der allgemeinen Prüfung vorgelegt von Dr. H.E.G. Paulus*, ed. Heinrich Eberhard Gottlob Paulus (Darmstadt: 1843; Frankfurt/M: Suhrkamp, 1977), p. 225.

6. See Cicero, *On the Nature of the Gods*, II, 52, 129; *M. Tullii Ciceronis opera omnia*, I-IV and index, ed. Johann August Ernesti (Halle: 1756-57), IV, p. 556; *Cicero De natura deorum Academica*, tr. H. Rackham (Loeb, Cambridge: Harvard University Press, 1979), pp. 246-47.

7. Although not altogether unambiguous, the manuscript seems to read: *P for det gezeigte Seyn*.

8. Cf. Paulus, p. 258: "Sie kann sich nicht mehr entäussern, sondern bleibt bei sich; sie kann *das Wesen* genannt werden [It cannot externalize itself anymore; it can be called *the essence*] . . .."

9. See Aristotle, *Metaphysics*, 1026 a, 1037 a; *Aristoteles graece*, I-II, ed. Immanuel Bekker (Berlin: 1831), II, pp. 1026, 1037; *The Complete Works of Aristotle*, I-II, ed. Jonathan Barnes (rev. Oxford tr.; Princeton: Princeton University Press, 1984), II, pp. 1620, 1637:

> We answer that if there is no substance other than those which are formed by nature, natural science will be the first science; but if there is an immovable substance, the science of this must be prior and must be first philosophy, and universal in this way, because it is first. And it will belong to this to consider being *qua* being—both what it is and the attributes which belong to it *qua* being.
>
> Whether there is, apart from the matter of such substances, any other substance, and one should look for some substance other than these, e.g. numbers or something of the sort, must be considered later. For it is for the sake of this that we are trying to determine the nature of perceptible substances, since in a sense the inquiry about perceptible substances is the work of natural science, i.e. of second philosophy; for the natural scientist must not only know about the matter, but also about the substance in the sense of the formula, and even more than about the other.

10. See, for example, J. G. Fichte, *Die Bestimmung des Menschen* (Berlin: 1838), pp. 85-87, 116; *Johann Gottlieb Fichte's sämmtliche Werke*, I-VIII (Berlin: 1845-46), II, pp. 228-30, 249; *The Vocation of Man, The Popular Works of Johann Gottlieb Fichte*, I-II, tr. William Smith (London: Trübner, 1889), I, pp. 385-87, 406 (Spirit speaking):

In all consciousness I contemplate myself, for I am myself:—to the subjective, conscious being, consciousness is self-contemplation. And the objective, that which is contemplated and of which I am conscious, is also myself,—the same self which contemplates, but now floating as an objective presentation before the subjective. In this respect, consciousness is an active retrospect of my own intuitions; an observation of myself from my own position; a projection of myself out of myself by means of the only mode of action which is properly mine,—perception. I am a living faculty of vision. I see (*consciousness*) my own vision (*the thing of which I am conscious*).

Hence this object is also thoroughly transparent to thy mind's eye, because it is thy mind itself. Thou dividest, limitest, determinest, the possible forms of things, and the relations of these forms, previous to all perception. No wonder,—for in so doing thou dividest, limitest, and determinest thine own knowledge, which undoubtedly is sufficiently known to thee. Thus does a knowledge of things become possible; it is not in the things, and cannot proceed out of them. It proceeds from thee, and is indeed thine own nature.

There is no outward sense, for there is no outward perception. There is, however, an outward intuition;—not of things, but this outward intuition—this knowledge apparently external to the subjective being, and hovering before it,—is itself the thing, and there is no other. By means of this outward intuition are perception and sense regarded as external. It remains eternally true, for it is proved,—that I see or feel a surface,—my sight or feeling takes the shape of the sight or feeling of a surface. Space,—illuminated, transparent, palpable, penetrable space,—the purest image of my knowledge, is not seen, but is an intuitive possession of my own mind; in it even my faculty of vision itself is contained. The light is not out of, but in me, and I myself am the light. Thou hast already answered my question, "How dost thou know of thy sensations, of thy seeing, feeling, &c.?" by saying that thou hast an immediate knowledge or consciousness of them. Now, perhaps, thou wilt be able to define more exactly this immediate consciousness of sensation.

I. It must be a two-fold consciousness. Sensation is itself an immediate consciousness; for I am sensible of my own sensation. But from this there arises no knowledge of outward existence, but only the feeling of my own state. I am however, originally, not merely a sensitive, but also an intuitive being; not merely a practical being, but also an intelligence. I intuitively contemplate my sensation itself, and thus there arises from myself and my own nature, the *cognition of an existence*. Sensation becomes transformed into its own object; my affections, as red, smooth, and the like, into a *something* red, smooth, &c. out of myself. . . .

"Not merely TO KNOW, but according to thy knowledge TO DO, is thy vocation:"—thus is it loudly proclaimed in the innermost depths of my soul, as soon as I recollect myself for a moment, and turn my observation inward upon myself. "Not for idle contemplation of thyself, not for brooding over devout sensations;—no, for action art thou here; thine action, and thine action alone, determines thy worth."

11. See, for example, Plato, *Sophist*, 241 d, 256 d-e, 258 a-c; *Platonis quae exstant opera*, I-XI, ed. Friedrich Ast (Leipzig: 1819-32), II, pp. 280-82, 326-29, 332-33; *The Collected Dialogues of Plato*, ed. Edith Hamilton and Huntington Cairns (Princeton: Princeton University Press, 1963), pp. 985, 1003, 1005:

STRANGER: We shall find it necessary in self-defense to put to the question that pronouncement of father Parmenides, and establish by main force that what is not in some respect has being, and conversely that what is, in a way is not.

STRANGER: It must, then, be possible for 'that which is not' [i.e., is different from existence] to be [to exist], not only in the case of motion but of all the other kinds. For in the case of them all the nature of difference makes each one of them different from existence and so makes it a thing that 'is not,' and hence we shall be right to speak of them all on the same principle as things that in this sense '*are not*,' and again, because they partake of existence, to say that they '*are*' [exist] and call them things that have being [existence].

THEAETETUS: No doubt.

STRANGER: So, in the case of every one of the forms there is much that it *is* and an indefinite number of things that it *is not*.

THEAETETUS: So it appears.

STRANGER: And, moreover, existence itself must be called different from the rest.

THEAETETUS: Necessarily.

STRANGER: We find, then, that existence likewise 'is not' in as many respects as there are other things, for, not being those others, while it *is* its single self, it *is not* all that indefinite number of other beings.

STRANGER: So, it seems, when a part of the nature of the different and a part of the nature of the existent [existence] are set in contrast to one another, the contrast is, if it be permissible to say so, as much a reality as existence itself; it does not mean what is contrary to 'existent,' but only what is different from that existent.

THEAETETUS: That is quite clear.

STRANGER: What name are we to give it, then?

THEAETETUS: Obviously this is just that 'what-is-not' which we were seeking for the sake of the Sophist.

STRANGER: Has it then, as you say, an existence inferior to none of the rest in reality? May we now be bold to say that 'that which is not' unquestionably *is* a thing that has a nature of its own—just as the tall was tall and the beautiful was beautiful, so too with the not-tall and the not-beautiful—and in that sense 'that which is not' also, on the same principle, both was and *is* 'what is not,' a single form to be reckoned among the many realities? Or have we any further doubts with regard to it, Theaetetus?

12. See Plutarch, "Reply to Colotes in Defense of the Other Philosophers," *Moralia*, 1115 d-f; *Plutarchs moralische Abhandlungen*, I-IX, tr. Johann F. S. Kaltwasser (Frankfurt/M: 1783-1800), VIII, p. 398 fn.; *Plutarch's Moralia*, I-XV, tr. Frank Cole Babbitt et al. (Loeb, Cambridge: Harvard University Press, 1967-84), XIV, pp. 239-41:

"But in Plato's view there is a world of difference between 'is not' and 'is non-being,' for by the former is meant the denial of any kind of being, by the latter the otherness of the participant and what it participates in, an otherness that later philosophers brought under the head of a mere difference of genus and species or between characters shared and characters not shared, and went no higher, as they became involved in problems more purely dialectical. The relation of the partaken in to the partaker is that of cause to matter, model to copy, power to effect. And it is chiefly by this relation that the absolute and always identical differs from what is caused by something else and is never in the same state. The former will never be non-being and has never come to be, and is therefore in the full and true sense 'being'; whereas the latter has no firm hold even on such participation in being as it incidentally has from something else, but is too weak to preserve its identity, inasmuch as matter sits loosely to its form and admits into its copy of being many effects and alterations that lead to movement and instability."

13. See, for example, Plato, *Sophist*, 240 d-e, 260 b-261 b; *Opera*, II, pp. 278-79, 338-41; *Dialogues*, pp. 984, 1007-08:

STRANGER: When we say that he deceives with that semblance we spoke of and that his art is a practice of deception, shall we be saying that, as the effect of his art, our mind thinks what is false, or what shall we mean?

THEAETETUS: Just that. What else could we mean?

STRANGER: And false thinking, again, will be thinking things contrary to the things that are?

THEAETETUS: Necessarily.

STRANGER: Does that mean thinking that things that are not are not, or that things that are not in any way, in some way are?

THEAETETUS: It must at least mean thinking that things that are not, are in some way, if anyone is ever to be in error even to the smallest extent.

STRANGER: And also surely thinking that things which certainly are, are not in any way at all?

THEAETETUS: Yes.

STRANGER: That also is error?

THEAETETUS: Yes, that also.

STRANGER: And a false statement, I suppose, is to be regarded in the same light, as stating that things that are, are not, and that things that are not, are.

STRANGER: We saw that 'not-being' is a single kind among the rest, dispersed over the whole field of realities.

THEAETETUS: Yes.

STRANGER: We have next to consider whether it blends with thinking and discourse.

THEAETETUS: Why that?

STRANGER: If it does not blend with them, everything must be true, but if it does, we shall have false thinking and discourse, for thinking or saying 'what is not' comes, I suppose, to the same thing as falsity in thought and speech.

THEAETETUS: Yes.

STRANGER: And if falsity exists, deception is possible.

THEAETETUS: Yes.

STRANGER: And once deception exists, images and likenesses and appearance will be everywhere rampant.

THEAETETUS: Of course.

STRANGER: And the Sophist, we said, had taken refuge somewhere in that region, but then he had denied the very existence of falsity; no one could either think or say 'what is not,' because what is not never has any sort of being.

THEAETETUS: So he said.

STRANGER: But now that 'what is not' has been found to have its share in existence, perhaps he will not fight with us further on that point.

On the other hand, he may perhaps say that some things partake of not-being, some do not, and that speech and thinking are among those that do not, and so once more he might contend that the art of creating images and semblances, where we say he is to be found, has no existence at all, since thought and speech have no share in not-being, and without that combination there is no such thing as falsity.

That is why we must begin by investigating the nature of discourse and thinking and appearance, in order that we may then make out their combination with non-being and so prove that falsity exists, and by that proof pin down the Sophist there, if he is amenable to capture, or else let him go and pursue our search in some other kind.

THEAETETUS: Certainly, sir, what we said at the outset about the Sophist seems true—that he is a hard sort of beast to hunt down. Evidently he possesses a whole armory of problems, and every time that he puts one forward to shield him, we have to fight our way through it before we can get at him. So now, hardly have we got the better of his defense that 'what is not' cannot exist, when another obstacle is raised in our path. We must, it seems, prove that falsity exists both in speech and thought, and after that perhaps something else, and so on. It looks as if the end would never be in sight.

14. See, for example, J. G. Fichte, *Die Bestimmung des Gelehrten*, *Werke*, VI, p. 296; *The Vocation of the Scholar*, *Works*, I, p. 152:

> That which he is in this respect, he is, not primarily because he himself exists, but because something other than himself exists. The empirical self-consciousness,—that is, the consciousness of a determinate vocation,—is not possible except on the supposition of a Non-Ego, as we have already said, and in the proper place will prove. This Non-Ego must approach and influence him through his passive capacity, which we call *sense*. Thus in so far as man possesses a determinate existence, he is a *sensuous* being. But still, as we have already said, he is also a reasonable being;—and his Reason must not be superseded by Sense, but both must exist in harmony with each other. In this connexion the principle propounded above,—*Man is because he is*,—is changed into the following,—*Whatever Man is, that he should be solely because he is;*—*i.e.* all that he is should proceed from his pure Ego,—from his own simple personality;—he should be all that he is, absolutely because he is an Ego,—and whatever he cannot be solely upon that ground, he should absolutely not be. This as yet obscure formula we shall proceed to illustrate.
>
> The pure Ego can only be conceived of negatively,—as the opposite of the Non-Ego, the character of which is multiplicity . . ..

15. See, for example, Immanuel Kant, *Critik der reinen Vernunft* (4 ed., Riga: 1794), pp. 2-3, 148-49; *Immanuel Kant's Critique of Pure Reason* (tr. of *C.V.*, 2 ed., 1787), tr. Norman Kemp Smith (London: Macmillan, 1950), pp. 43, 188:

> In what follows, therefore, we shall understand by *a priori* knowledge, not knowledge independent of this or that experience, but knowledge absolutely independent of all experience. Opposed to it is empirical knowledge which is knowledge possible only *a posteriori*, that is, through experience. *A priori* modes of knowledge are entitled pure when there is no admixture of anything empirical. Thus, for instance, the proposition, 'every alteration has its cause', while an *a priori* proposition, is not a pure proposition, because alteration is a concept which can be derived only from experience.

> Principles *a priori* are so named not merely because they contain in themselves the grounds of other judgments, but also because they are not themselves grounded in higher and more universal modes of knowledge. But this characteristic does not remove them beyond the sphere of proof. This proof cannot, indeed, be carried out in any objective fashion, since such principles [do not rest on objective considerations but] lie at the foundation of all *knowledge* of objects. This does not, however, prevent our attempting a proof, from the subjective sources of the possibility of knowledge of an object in general. Such proof is, indeed, indispensable, if the propositions are not to incur the suspicion of being merely surreptitious assertions.

16. See, for example, Kant, *Critik der reinen Vernunft*, pp. 265-66; *Critique of Pure Reason*, pp. 503-04:

> There is already a contradiction in introducing the concept of existence—no matter under what title it may be disguised—into the concept of a thing which we profess to be thinking solely in reference to its possibility. If that be allowed as legitimate, a seeming victory has been won; but in actual fact nothing at all is said: the assertion is a mere tautology. We must ask: Is the proposition that *this or that thing* (which, whatever it may be, is allowed as possible) *exists*, an analytic or a synthetic proposition? If it is analytic, the assertion of the existence of the thing adds nothing to the thought of the thing; but in that case either the thought, which is in us, is the thing itself, or we have presupposed an existence as belonging to the realm of the possible, and have then, on that pretext, inferred its existence from its internal possibility—which is nothing but a miserable tautology. The word 'reality', which in the concept of the thing sounds other than the word 'existence' in the concept of the predicate, is of no avail in meeting this objection. For if all positing (no matter what it may be that is posited) is entitled reality, the thing with all its predicates is already posited in the concept of the subject, and is assumed as actual; and in the predicate this is merely repeated. But if, on the other hand, we admit, as every reasonable person must, that all existential propositions are synthetic, how can we profess to maintain that the predicate of existence cannot be rejected without contradiction? This is a feature which is found only in analytic propositions, and is indeed precisely what constitutes their analytic character. . . .
>
> '*Being*' is obviously not a real predicate; that is, it is not a concept of something which could be added to the concept of a thing. It is merely the positing of a thing, or of certain determinations, as existing in themselves. Logically, it is merely the copula of a judgment.

17. See Kant, *Critik der reinen Vernunft*, pp. xxxix-xli; *Critique of Pure Reason*, pp. 34-36 fn.:

> The only addition, strictly so called, though one affecting the method of proof only, is the new refutation of psychological *idealism* (cf. below, p. 244), and a strict (also, as I believe, the only possible) proof of the objective reality of outer intuition. However harmless idealism may be considered in respect of the essential aims of metaphysics (though, in fact, it is not thus harmless), it still remains a scandal to philosophy and to human reason in general that the existence of things outside us (from which we derive the whole material of knowledge, even for our inner sense) must be accepted merely on *faith*, and that if anyone thinks good [*sic*] to doubt their existence, we are unable to counter his doubts by any satisfactory proof. Since there is some obscurity in the expressions used in the proof, from the third line to the sixth line, I beg to alter the passage as follows: "*But this permanent cannot be an intuition in me. For all grounds of determination of my existence which are to be met with in me are representations; and as representations themselves re-*

quire a permanent distinct from them, in relation to which their change, and so my existence in the time wherein they change, may be determined." To this proof it will probably be objected, that I am immediately conscious only of that which is in me, that is, of my *representation* of outer things; and consequently that it must still remain uncertain whether outside me there is anything corresponding to it, or not. But through inner *experience* I am conscious of *my existence* in time (consequently also of its determinability in time), and this is more than to be conscious merely of my representation. It is identical with the *empirical consciousness of my existence*, which is determinable only through relation to something which, while bound up with my existence, is outside me. This consciousness of my existence in time is bound up in the way of identity with the consciousness of a relation to something outside me, and it is therefore experience not invention, sense not imagination, which inseparably connects this outside something with my inner sense. For outer sense is already in itself a relation of intuition to something actual outside me, and the reality of outer sense, in its distinction from imagination, rests simply on that which is here found to take place, namely, its being inseparably bound up with inner experience, as the condition of its possibility. If, with the *intellectual consciousness* of my existence, in the representation 'I am', which accompanies all my judgments and acts of understanding, I could at the same time connect a determination of my existence through *intellectual intuition*, the consciousness of a relation to something outside me would not be required. But though that intellectual consciousness does indeed come first, the inner intuition, in which my existence can alone be determined, is sensible and is bound up with the condition of time. This determination, however, and therefore the inner experience itself, depends upon something permanent which is not in me, and consequently can be only in something outside me, to which I must regard myself as standing in relation. The reality of outer sense is thus necessarily bound up with inner sense, if experience in general is to be possible at all; that is, I am just as certainly conscious that there are things outside me, which are in relation to my sense, as I am conscious that I myself exist as determined in time. In order to determine to which given intuitions objects outside me actually correspond, and which therefore belong to outer *sense* (to which, and not to the faculty of imagination, they are to be ascribed), we must in each single case appeal to the rules according to which experience in general, even inner experience, is distinguished from imagination—the proposition that there is such a thing as outer experience being always presupposed. This further remark may be added. The representation of something *permanent* in existence is not the same as *permanent representation*. For though the representation of [something permanent] may be very transitory and variable like all our other representations, not excepting those of matter, it yet refers to something permanent. This latter must therefore be an external thing distinct from all my representations, and its existence must be included in the *determination* of my own existence, constituting with it but a single experience such as would not take place even inwardly if it were not also at the same time, in part, outer. How this should be possible we are as little capable of explaining further as we are of accounting for our being able to think the abiding in time, the co-existence of which with the changing generates the concept of alteration.

18. See, for example, Spinoza, *Ethics*, Part I, Def. 1-6, Prop. 25; Benedicti de Spinoza, *Opera philosophica omnia*, ed. August Gfroerer (Stuttgart: 1830), pp. 278, 300; *The Collected Works of Spinoza*, ed. and tr. Edwin Curley (Princeton: Princeton University Press, 1985), pp. 408-09, 431:

D1: By cause of itself I understand that whose essence involves existence, *or* that whose nature cannot be conceived except as existing.

D2: That thing is said to be finite in its own kind that can be limited by another of the same nature.

For example, a body is called finite because we always conceive another that is greater. Thus a thought is limited by another thought. But a body is not limited by a thought nor a thought by a body.

D3: By substance I understand what is in itself and is conceived through itself, i.e., that whose concept does not require the concept of another thing, from which it must be formed.

D4: By attribute I understand what the intellect perceives of a substance, as constituting its essence.

D5: By mode I understand the affections of a substance, *or* that which is in another through which it is also conceived.

D6: By God I understand a being absolutely infinite, i.e., a substance consisting of an infinity of attributes, of which each one expresses an eternal and infinite essence.

P25: *God is the efficient cause, not only of the existence of things, but also of their essence.*

Dem.: If you deny this, then God is not the cause of the essence of things; and so (by A4) the essence of things can be conceived without God. But (by P15) this is absurd. Therefore God is also the cause of the essence of things, q.e.d.

Schol.: This Proposition follows more clearly from P16. For from that it follows that from the given divine nature both the essence of things and their existence must necessarily be inferred; and in a word, God must be called the cause of all things in the same sense in which he is called the cause of himself. This will be established still more clearly from the following corollary.

Cor.: Particular things are nothing but affections of God's attributes, *or* modes by which God's attributes are expressed in a certain and determinate way. The demonstration is evident from P15 and D5.

19. See, for example, Hegel, *Grundlinien der Philosophie des Rechts*, *Georg Wilhelm Friedrich Hegel's Werke*, I-XVIII, ed. Philipp Marheineke et al. (Berlin: 1832-45), p. 19; *Sämtliche Werke. Jubiläumsausgabe* [*J.A.*], I-XXVI, ed. Hermann Glockner (Stuttgart: Frommann, 1927-40), VII, p. 35; *Hegel's Philosophy of Right* (tr. of *P.R.*, 1 ed., 1821), tr. T. M. Knox (London: Oxford University Press, 1978), p. 12:

> What lies between reason as self-conscious mind and reason as an actual world before our eyes, what separates the former from the latter and prevents it from finding satisfaction in the latter, is the fetter of some abstraction or other which has not been liberated [and so transformed] into the concept. To recognize reason as the rose in the cross of the present and thereby to enjoy the present, this is the rational insight which reconciles us to the actual, the reconciliation which philosophy affords to those in whom there has once arisen an inner voice bidding them to comprehend, not only to dwell in what is substantive while still retaining subjective freedom, but also to possess subjective freedom while standing not in anything particular and accidental but in what exists absolutely.
>
> It is this too which constitutes the more concrete meaning of what was described above rather abstractly as the unity of form and content; for form in its most concrete signification is reason as speculative knowing, and content is reason as the substantial essence of actuality, whether ethical or natural. The known identity of these two is the philosophical Idea.

20. See, for example, Hegel, *Wissenschaft der Logik*, I, *Werke*, III, p. 73; *J.A.*, IV, p. 83; *Hegel's Science of Logic* (tr. of *W.L.*, Lasson ed., 1923), tr. A. V. Miller (New York: Humanities, 1976), p. 77:

> But what, at the *beginning* of the science, is *actually present* of intellectual intuition—or of the eternal, the divine, the absolute, if its object be so named—cannot be anything else than a first, immediate, simple determination. Whatever richer name be given to it than is expressed by mere *being*, the consideration of such absolute must be restricted solely to the way in which it enters into our knowing as *thought* and is enunciated as such.

21. See Hegel, *Wissenschaft der Logik*, I, *Werke*, III, pp. 456-66; *J.A.*, IV, pp. 466-76; *Science of Logic*, pp. 375-85.

22. Schelling was editor of the journal *Zeitschrift für Spekulative Physik* in 1800-01.

23. See, for example, J. G. Fichte, *Die Bestimmung des Menschen*, pp. 104-05; *Werke*, II, p. 242; *The Vocation of Man*, *Works*, I, pp. 399-400:

> This perceiving, thinking, willing, intelligent entity, or whatever else thou mayest name that which possesses the faculties of perception, thought, and so forth;—that in which these faculties inhere, or in whatever other way thou mayest express this thought;—how do I attain a knowledge of it? Am I immediately conscious of it? How can I be? It is only of actual and specific *acts* of perception, thought, will, &c., as of particular occur-

> rences, that I am immediately conscious; not of the capacities through which they are performed, and still less of a being in whom these capacities inhere. I perceive, directly and intuitively, this specific thought which occupies me during the present moment, and other specific thoughts in other moments; and here this inward intellectual intuition, this immediate consciousness, ends. This inward intuitive thought now becomes itself an object of thought . . ..

24. See note 19 above.

25. See, for example, Hegel, *Encyclopädie der Philosophischen Wissenschaften*, III, *Die Philosophie des Geistes*, 449, *Zusatz*, *Werke*, VII², pp. 318-19; *J.A.*, X, pp. 324-25; *Hegel's Philosophy of Mind* (tr. of *P.G.*, 3 ed., 1830, plus *Zusätze*), tr. William Wallace and A. V. Miller (Oxford: Oxford University Press, 1971), p. 199:

> In the broadest sense of the word, one could of course give the name of intuition to the immediate or sensuous consciousness considered in para. 418. But if this name is to be taken in its proper significance, as rationally it must, then between that consciousness and intuition the essential distinction must be made that the former, in the *unmediated*, quite abstract certainty of itself, relates itself to the *immediate* individuality of the object, an individuality sundered into a multiplicity of aspects; whereas intuition is consciousness *filled* with the certainty of Reason, whose object is *rationally* determined and consequently not an individual torn asunder into its various aspects but a totality, a unified fullness of determinations. It was in this sense that Schelling formerly spoke of intuition. Mindless intuition is merely sensuous consciousness which remains external to the object. Mindful, true intuition, on the contrary, apprehends the genuine substance of the object.

26. See, for example, Hegel, *Wissenschaft der Logik*, I, *Werke*, III, p. 35; *J.A.*, IV, pp. 49-50; *Science of Logic*, pp. 49-50:

> The Notion of pure science and its deduction is therefore presupposed in the present work in so far as the *Phenomenology of Spirit* is nothing other than the deduction of it. Absolute knowing is the *truth* of every mode of consciousness because, as the course of the *Phenomenology* showed, it is only in absolute knowing that the separation of the *object* from the *certainty of itself* is completely eliminated: truth is now equated with certainty and this certainty with truth.
>
> Thus pure science presupposes liberation from the opposition of consciousness. It contains *thought in so far as this is just as much the object in its own self, or the object in its own self in so far as it is equally pure thought.* As science, truth is pure self-consciousness in its self-development and has the shape of the self, so that the absolute truth of being is the known Notion and the Notion as such is the absolute truth of being.
>
> This objective thinking, then, is the content of pure science. Conse-

quently, far from it being formal, far from it standing in need of a matter to constitute an actual and true cognition, it is its content alone which has absolute truth, or, if one still wanted to employ the word matter, it is the veritable matter—but a matter which is not external to the form, since this matter is rather pure thought and hence the absolute form itself. Accordingly, logic is to be understood as the system of pure reason, as the realm of pure thought. This realm is truth as it is without veil and in its own absolute nature. It can therefore be said that this content is the exposition of God as he is in his eternal essence before the creation of nature and a finite mind.

27. See, for example, Hegel, *Wissenschaft der Logik*, I, *Werke*, IV, p. 3; *J.A.*, IV, p. 481; *Science of Logic*, p. 389:

The truth of *being* is *essence*.

Being is the immediate. Since knowing has for its goal knowledge of the true, knowledge of what being is *in and for itself*, it does not stop at the immediate and its determinations, but penetrates it on the supposition that at the back of this being there is something else, something other than being itself, that this background constitutes the truth of being. This knowledge is a mediated knowing for it is not found immediately with and in essence, but starts from an other, from being, and has a preliminary path to tread, that of going beyond being or rather of penetrating into it. Not until knowing *inwardizes, recollects* [*erinnert*] itself out of immediate being, does it through this mediation find essence. The German language has preserved essence in the past participle [*gewesen*] of the verb *to be*; for essence is past—but timelessly past—being.

When this movement is pictured as the path of knowing, then this beginning with being, and the development that sublates it, reaching essence as a mediated result, appears to be an activity of knowing external to being and irrelevant to being's own nature.

But this path is the movement of being itself. It was seen that being inwardizes itself through its own nature, and through this movement into itself becomes essence.

If, therefore, the absolute was at first defined as *being*, now it is defined as *essence*.

28. See, for example, Hegel, *Encyclopädie der philosophischen Wissenschaften im Grundrisse*, I, *Die Logik*, *Werke*, VI, 19, p. 28; *J.A.*, VIII, p. 66; *Hegel's Logic* (tr. of *L.*, 3 ed.), tr. William Wallace (Oxford: Oxford University Press, 1975), p. 25:

Logic is the science of the pure Idea; pure, that is, because the Idea is in the abstract medium of Thought.

This definition, and the others which occur in these introductory outlines, are derived from a survey of the whole system, to which accordingly they are subsequent. The same remark applies to all prefatory notions whatever about philosophy.

Logic might have been defined as the science of thought, and of its laws and characteristic forms. But thought, as thought, constitutes only the general medium, or qualifying circumstance, which renders the Idea distinctively logical. If we identify the Idea with thought, thought must not be taken in the sense of a method or form, but in the sense of the self-developing totality of its laws and peculiar terms. These laws are the work of thought itself, and not a fact which it finds and must submit to.

29. The manuscript text reads: *deres* [their]. Cf. *Pap*. XIII, p. 267.

30. See, for example, Hegel, *Wissenschaft der Logik*, I, *Werke*, III, p. 55; *J.A.*, IV, p. 65; *Science of Logic*, pp. 63-64:

> The objective logic, then, takes the place rather of former *metaphysics* which was intended to be the scientific construction of the world in terms of *thoughts* alone. If we have regard to the final shape in the elaboration of this science, then it is first and immediately *ontology* whose place is taken by objective logic—that part of this metaphysics which was supposed to investigate the nature of *ens* in general; *ens* comprises both *being* and *essence*, a distinction for which the German language has fortunately preserved different terms. But further, objective logic also comprises the rest of metaphysics in so far as this attempted to comprehend with the forms of pure thought particular substrata taken primarily from figurate conception, namely the soul, the world and God; and the *determinations of thought* constituted what was *essential* in the mode of consideration. Logic, however, considers these forms free from those substrata, from the subjects of figurate conception; it considers them, their nature and worth, in their own proper character. Former metaphysics omitted to do this and consequently incurred the just reproach of having employed these forms *uncritically* without a preliminary investigation as to whether and how they were capable of being determinations of the thing-in-itself, to use the Kantian expression—or rather of the Reasonable. Objective logic is therefore the genuine critique of them—a critique which does not consider them as contrasted under the abstract forms of the *a priori* and the *a posteriori*, but considers the determinations themselves according to their specific content.
>
> The subjective logic is the logic of the *Notion*, of essence which has sublated its relation to being or its illusory being [*Schein*], and in its determination is no longer external but is subjective—free, self-subsistent and self-determining, or rather it is the subject itself.

31. Cf. Cicero, *Orator*, III, 12; *M. Tullii Ciceronis opera omnia*, I-IV and index, ed. Johann August Ernesti (Halle: 1756-57), I, p. 656 ("*primum impressa sunt vestigia*"); *Orator*, tr. H. M. Hubbell (Loeb, Cambridge: Harvard University Press, 1952), pp. 313-15; "There indeed is the field for manifold and varied debate, which was first trodden by the feet of Plato."

32. See, for example, Hegel, *Encyclopädie*, I, *Logik*, 215, *Werke*, VI, p. 390; *J.A.*, VIII, p. 428; *Hegel's Logic*, p. 278:

> The Idea is essentially a process, because its identity is the absolute and free identity of the notion, only in so far as it is absolute negativity and for that reason dialectical. It is the round of movement, in which the notion, in the capacity of universality which is individuality, gives itself the character of objectivity and of the antithesis thereto; and this externality which has the notion for its substance, finds its way back to subjectivity through its immanent dialectic.

33. See Spinoza, *Ethics*, Part V, Prop. 36; *Opera*, p. 427; *Works*, p. 612:

> P.36: *The Mind's intellectual Love of God is the very Love of God by which God loves himself, not insofar as he is infinite, but insofar as he can be explained by the human Mind's essence, considered under a species of eternity; i.e., the Mind's intellectual Love of God is part of the infinite Love by which God loves himself.*

34. See Hegel, *"Die Philosophie der Natur,"* 193, *Encyclopädie der philosophischen Wissenschaften im Grundrisse und andere Schriften aus der Heidelberger Zeit* (Heidelberg: 1817), p. 128; *J.A.*, VI, p. 148:

> "—Mit Recht ist die Natur überhaupt als der *Abfall* der Idee von sich selbst bestimmt worden, weil sie in dem Elemente der Aeusserlichkeit die Bestimmung der Unangemessenheit ihrer selbst mit sich hat."

35. Hegel, *Encyclopädie der philosophischen Wissenschaften im Grundrisse* (Heidelberg: 1827).

36. See ibid. (Heidelberg: 1830), 248; *Werke*, VII[1], p. 29; *J.A.*, IX, p. 55; *Hegel's Philosophy of Nature* (tr. of Nicolin-Pöggeler ed., 1959, based on 3 ed., 1930), tr. A. V. Miller (Oxford: Oxford University Press, 1970), p. 17. The sentence Schelling refers to is omitted in the third edition of *Encyclopädie*.

37. F.W.J. v. Schelling, *Philosophie und Religion* (Tübingen: 1804). This work, although differing in form from that of *Bruno* (1802; 2 ed., Berlin: 1842; *ASKB* 765), is (according to the preface) substantively the same as *Bruno*. The expression *Abfall* [falling away] is found in *Philosophie und Religion*, p. 35 (ed. tr.): "The absolute is the only real; finite things, on the other hand, are not real; their ground, therefore, cannot be in an *impartation* from reality to them or to their substratum; it can lie only in a *removal*, in a *falling away* from the absolute." See also pp. 37-38. *Abfall* has not been located in *Bruno*, although other similar terms are used frequently: *Entfernung, Trennung, absondert* [removal, separation, detached]. Paulus (p. 131) states that Schelling referred to a "third dialogue" that was to have appeared as a resolution of the contradiction. This third was in fact the distinction between negative and positive philosophy.

38. See note 37 above.

39. The source of the sentence as quoted has not been located. The sentence and the remainder of the paragraph, as well as the opening lines of notes to

lecture 13, seem to be a compaction of Hegel, *Encyclopädie*, III, *Philosophie des Geistes*, 573-77; *Werke*, VII², pp. 458-75; *J.A.*, X, pp. 458-75; *Philosophy of Mind*, pp. 302-15.

40. The manuscript reads: *Anfang* [beginning]. Cf. *Pap*. XIII, p. 270 (Dan. *Omfang* [extension, dimension]). Note the repetition of *Anfang* in the second and third sentences of lecture 13.

41. See, for example, notes 26, 28, and 30 above.

42. The reference may be to a passage (which does not contain the sentence exactly as quoted) at the end of Hegel, *Wissenschaft der Logik*, II; *Werke*, V, pp. 352-53; *J.A.*, V, pp. 352-53; *Science of Logic*, pp. 843-44:

> The Idea, namely, in positing itself as absolute *unity* of the pure Notion and its reality and thus contracting itself into the immediacy of *being*, is the *totality* in this form—*nature*. But this determination has not *issued from a process* of *becoming*, nor is it a *transition*, as when above, the subjective Notion in its totality *becomes objectivity*, and the *subjective end becomes life*. On the contrary, the pure Idea in which the determinateness or reality of the Notion is itself raised into Notion, is an absolute *liberation* for which there is no longer any immediate determination that is not equally *posited* and itself Notion; in this freedom, therefore, no transition takes place; the simple being to which the Idea determines itself remains perfectly transparent to it and is the Notion that, in its determination, abides with itself. The passage is therefore to be understood here rather in this manner, that the Idea *freely releases* itself in its absolute self-assurance and inner poise. By reason of this freedom, the form of its determinateness is also utterly free—the *externality of space and time* existing absolutely on its own account without the moment of subjectivity. In so far as this externality presents itself only in the abstract immediacy of being and is apprehended from the standpoint of consciousness, it exists as mere objectivity and external life; but in the Idea it remains essentially and actually [*an und für sich*] the totality of the Notion, and science in the relationship to nature of divine cognition. But in this next resolve of the pure Idea to determine itself as external Idea, it thereby only posits for itself the mediation out of which the Notion ascends as a free Existence that has withdrawn into itself from externality, that completes its self-liberation in the *science of spirit*, and that finds the supreme Notion of itself in the science of logic as the self-comprehending pure Notion.

43. See Aristotle, *Metaphysics*, 1012 b; Bekker, II, p. 1012; *Works*, II, p. 1599: ". . . there is something which always moves the things that are in motion, and the first mover must itself be unmoved."

44. Hegel, *Encyclopädie*, III (Heidelberg: 1817), heading above 456, p. 280: "*Die Religion der Kunst*," *J.A.*, VI, p. 302; *Encyclopädie* (2 ed., Heidelberg: 1827), heading above 556: "*Die Kunst*," *Werke*, VII² (3 ed. text), p. 441; *Philosophy of Mind*, heading above 556, p. 293: "ART."

45. See Aristotle, *Metaphysics*, 1000 a-1001 b; Bekker, II, pp. 1000-01; *Works*, II, pp. 1579-82.

46. Cf. Schelling, *Philosophie der Offenbarung*, I-II (Stuttgart, Augsburg: 1858; Darmstadt: Wissenschaftliche Buchgesellschaft, 1955), I, pp. 96-97.

47. Cf. Plutarch, "Platonic Questions," I, *Moralia*, 1000; Kaltwasser, VII, p. 515; Loeb, XIII[1], pp. 24-25.

48. See Plato, *Republic*, 511 c-d; *Opera*, IV, pp. 574-77; *Dialogues*, pp. 746-47 (Glaucon speaking):

> I understand, he said, not fully, for it is no slight task that you appear to have in mind, but I do understand that you mean to distinguish the aspect of reality and the intelligible, which is contemplated by the power of dialectic, as something truer and more exact than the object of the so-called arts and sciences whose assumptions are arbitrary starting points. And though it is true that those who contemplate them are compelled to use their understanding and not their senses, yet because they do not go back to the beginning in the study of them but start from assumptions you do not think they possess true intelligence about them although the things themselves are intelligibles when apprehended in conjunction with a first principle. And I think you call the mental habit of geometers and their like mind or understanding and not reason because you regard understanding as something intermediate between opinion and reason.

49. See Aristotle, *Metaphysics*, 991 a; Bekker, II, p. 991; *Works*, II, p. 1566:

> Above all one might discuss the question what on earth the Forms contribute to sensible things, either to those that are eternal or to those that come into being and cease to be. For they cause neither movement nor any change in them. But again they help in no way towards the *knowledge* of the other things (for they are not even the substance of these, else they would have been in them), nor towards their being, if they are not *in* the particulars which share in them; though if they were, they might be thought to be causes, as white causes whiteness in that with which it is mixed. But this argument, which first Anaxagoras and later Eudoxus and certain others used, is too easily upset; for it is not difficult to collect many insuperable objections to such a view.
>
> But further all other things cannot come from the Forms in any of the usual senses of 'from'. And to say that they are patterns and the other things share them is to use empty words and poetical metaphors.

50. See Aristotle, *Metaphysics*, 1026 a; Bekker, II, p. 1026; *Works*, II, p. 1620:

> —That natural science, then, is theoretical, is plain from these considerations. Mathematics also is theoretical; but whether its objects are immovable and separable from matter, is not at present clear; it is clear, however, that it considers some mathematical objects *qua* immovable and *qua* separable from matter. But if there is something which is eternal and immov-

able and separable, clearly the knowledge of it belongs to a theoretical science,—not, however, to natural science (for natural science deals with certain movable things) nor to mathematics, but to a science prior to both. For natural science deals with things which are inseparable from matter but not immovable, and some parts of mathematics deal with things which are immovable, but probably not separable, but embodied in matter; while the first science deals with things which are both separable and immovable. Now all causes must be eternal, but especially these; for they are the causes of so much of the divine as appears to us. There must, then, be three theoretical philosophies, mathematics, natural science, and theology, since it is obvious that if the divine is present anywhere, it is present in things of this sort. And the highest science must deal with the highest genus, so that the theoretical sciences are superior to the other sciences, and this to the other theoretical sciences. One might indeed raise the question whether first philosophy is universal, or deals with one genus, i.e. some one kind of being; for not even the mathematical sciences are all alike in this respect,—geometry and astronomy deal with a certain particular kind of thing, while universal mathematics applies alike to all. We answer that if there is no substance other than those which are formed by nature, natural science will be the first science; but if there is an immovable substance, the science of this must be prior and must be first philosophy, and universal in this way, because it is first.

51. See Aristotle, *Metaphysics*, 994 a-b; Bekker, II, p. 994; *Works*, II, pp. 1570-72:

> Evidently there is a first principle, and the causes of things are neither an infinite series nor infinitely various in kind. . . . Similarly the final causes cannot go on *ad infinitum*,—walking for the sake of health, this for the sake of happiness, happiness for the sake of something else, and so one thing always for the sake of another. . . .
>
> At the same time it is impossible that the first cause, being eternal, should be destroyed; for while the process of becoming is not infinite in the upward direction, a first cause by whose destruction something came to be could not be eternal.
>
> Further, the *final cause* is an end, and that sort of end which is not for the sake of something else, but for whose sake everything else is; so that if there is to be a last term of this sort, the process will not be infinite; but if there is no such term, there will be no final cause. But those who maintain the infinite series destroy the good without knowing it. Yet no one would try to do anything if he were not going to come to a limit. Nor would there be reason in the world; the reasonable man, at least, always acts for a purpose; and this is a limit, for the end is a limit. . . .
>
> But if the *kinds* of causes had been infinite in number, then also knowledge would have been impossible; for we think we know, only when we

have ascertained the causes, but that which is infinite by addition cannot be gone through in a finite time.

52. See note 43 above.

53. See, for example, Aristotle, *Nicomachean Ethics*, 1178 b; Bekker, II, p. 1178; *Works*, II, pp. 1862-63:

> But that complete happiness is a contemplative activity will appear from the following consideration as well. We assume the gods to be above all other beings blessed and happy; but what sort of actions must we assign to them? Acts of justice? Will not the gods seem absurd if they make contracts and return deposits, and so on? Acts of a brave man, then, confronting dangers and running risks because it is noble to do so? Or liberal acts? To whom will they give? It will be strange if they are really to have money or anything of the kind. And what would their temperate acts be? Is not such praise tasteless, since they have no bad appetites? If we were to run through them all, the circumstances of action would be found trivial and unworthy of gods. Still, every one supposes that they *live* and therefore that they are active; we cannot suppose them to sleep like Endymion. Now if you take away from a living being action, and still more production, what is left but contemplation? Therefore the activity of God, which surpasses all others in blessedness, must be contemplative; and of human activities, therefore, that which is most akin to this must be most of the nature of happiness.

54. To encourage learning, Charlemagne founded the Palace School (781) with the English scholar Alcuin as its head.

55. See David Hume, *An Enquiry concerning Human Understanding*, V, 1; *Enquiries*, ed. L. A. Selby-Bigge (2 ed., Oxford: Oxford University Press, 1946), pp. 42-43:

> Suppose a person, though endowed with the strongest faculties of reason and reflection, to be brought on a sudden into this world; he would, indeed, immediately observe a continual succession of objects, and one event following another; but he would not be able to discover anything farther. He would not, at first, by any reasoning, be able to reach the idea of cause and effect; since the particular powers, by which all natural operations are performed, never appear to the senses; nor is it reasonable to conclude, merely because one event, in one instance, precedes another, that therefore the one is the cause, the other the effect. Their conjunction may be arbitrary and casual. There may be no reason to infer the existence of one from the appearance of the other. And in a word, such a person, without more experience, could never employ his conjecture or reasoning concerning any matter of fact, or be assured of anything beyond what was immediately present to his memory and senses.
>
> Suppose, again, that he has acquired more experience, and has lived so long in the world as to have observed familiar objects or events to be constantly conjoined together; what is the consequence of this experience? He

immediately infers the existence of one object from the appearance of the other. Yet he has not, by all his experience, acquired any idea or knowledge of the secret power by which the one object produces the other; nor is it, by any process of reasoning, he is engaged to draw this inference. But still he finds himself determined to draw it: And though he should be convinced that his understanding has no part in the operation, he would nevertheless continue in the same course of thinking. There is some other principle which determines him to form such a conclusion.

This principle is Custom or Habit. For wherever the repetition of any particular act or operation produces a propensity to renew the same act or operation, without being impelled by any reasoning or process of the understanding, we always say, that this propensity is the effect of *Custom*. By employing that word, we pretend not to have given the ultimate reason of such a propensity. We only point out a principle of human nature, which is universally acknowledged, and which is well known by its effects.

56. The manuscript reads: *ere: en*. Cf. *Pap*. XIII, p. 280 (*rene* [pure]).

57. See Kant, *Critik der reinen Vernunft*, pp. 398, 449-50, 454-55, 462-63, 472-73, 480-81; *Critique of Pure Reason*, pp. 328, 394, 396, 402, 409, 415:

There are, then, only three kinds of dialectical syllogisms—just so many as there are ideas in which their conclusions result. In the *first* kind of syllogism I conclude from the transcendental concept of the subject, which contains nothing manifold, the absolute unity of this subject itself, of which, however, even in so doing, I possess no concept whatsoever. This dialectical inference I shall entitle the transcendental *paralogism*. The *second* kind of pseudo-rational inference is directed to the transcendental concept of the absolute totality of the series of conditions for any given appearance. From the fact that my concept of the unconditioned synthetic unity of the series, as thought in a certain way, is always self-contradictory, I conclude that there is really a unity of the opposite kind, although of it also I have no concept. The position of reason in these dialectical inferences I shall entitle the *antinomy* of pure reason. Finally, in the *third* kind of pseudo-rational inference, from the totality of the conditions under which objects in general, in so far as they can be given me, have to be thought, I conclude to the absolute synthetic unity of all conditions of the possibility of things in general, *i.e.* from things which I do not know through the merely transcendental concept of them I infer an *ens entium*, which I know even less through any transcendental concept, and of the unconditioned necessity of which I can form no concept whatsoever. This dialectical syllogism I shall entitle the *ideal* of pure reason.

A dialectical doctrine of pure reason must therefore be distinguished from all sophistical propositions in two respects. It must not refer to an arbitrary question such as may be raised for some special purpose, but to one which human reason must necessarily encounter in its progress. And secondly, both it and its opposite must involve no mere artificial illusion such as at once vanishes upon detection, but a natural and unavoidable illusion, which even after it has ceased to beguile still continues to delude though not to deceive us, and which though thus capable of being rendered harmless can never be eradicated.

Such dialectical doctrine relates not to the unity of understanding in empirical concepts, but to the unity of reason in mere ideas. Since this unity of reason involves a synthesis according to rules, it must conform to the understanding; and yet as demanding absolute unity of synthesis it must at the same time harmonise with reason. But the conditions of this unity are such that when it is adequate to reason it is too great for the understanding; and when suited to the understanding, too small for reason. There thus arises a conflict which cannot be avoided, do what we will.

These pseudo-rational assertions thus disclose a dialectical battlefield in which the side permitted to open the attack is invariably victorious, and the side constrained to act on the defensive is always defeated.

THE ANTINOMY OF PURE REASON
FIRST CONFLICT OF THE TRANSCENDENTAL IDEAS

Thesis	*Antithesis*
The world has a beginning in time, and is also limited as regards space.	The world has no beginning, and no limits in space; it is infinite as regards both time and space.

THE ANTINOMY OF PURE REASON
SECOND CONFLICT OF THE TRANSCENDENTAL IDEAS

Thesis	*Antithesis*
Every composite substance in the world is made up of simple parts, and nothing anywhere exists save the simple or what is composed of the simple.	No composite thing in the world is made up of simple parts, and there nowhere exists in the world anything simple.

THE ANTINOMY OF PURE REASON
THIRD CONFLICT OF THE TRANSCENDENTAL IDEAS

Thesis	*Antithesis*
Causality in accordance with laws of nature is not the only causality from which the appearances of the world can one and all be derived. To explain these appearances it is necessary to assume that there is also another causality, that of freedom.	There is no freedom; everything in the world takes place solely in accordance with laws of nature.

THE ANTINOMY OF PURE REASON
FOURTH CONFLICT OF THE TRANSCENDENTAL IDEAS

Thesis	*Antithesis*
There belongs to the world, either as its part or as its cause, a being that is absolutely necessary.	An absolutely necessary being nowhere exists in the world, nor does it exist outside the world as its cause.

58. See Kant, *Critik der reinen Vernunft*, p. 559; *Critique of Pure Reason*, p. 463: "Inasmuch as the dynamical ideas allow of a condition of appearances outside the series of the appearances, . . . we arrive at a conclusion altogether different from any that was possible in the case of the mathematical antinomy." The first two antinomies are called "mathematical" by Kant because both the objects to be established and the objects that count as evidence for them are conditioned by space and time. The branch of mathematics called geometry is the science of space, and the branch called arithmetic is the science of time. Both the theses and the antitheses of the mathematical antinomies presuppose the possibility of completing an infinite series of observations. The third and fourth antinomies, the "dynamical" antinomies, are different, however, and, according to Kant, this difference permits both the thesis and the antithesis to be true. The dynamical antinomies involve a heterogeneity between what is to be established (i.e., a necessary being) and what is to be regarded as evidence (i.e., contingent facts). These two dynamical antinomies can employ a notion of what is "purely intelligible" and existent apart from any possible observation, because their objects are not assumed to be objects of appearance.

59. The Eleusinian Mysteries, the principal religious mysteries of Greece, were celebrated in Eleusis (twelve miles northwest of Athens) from ancient times. The Greater Mysteries centered on the legends of death and renewal (Demeter, Persephone, and Dionysus). The Lesser Mysteries, celebrated in the spring, were a preparation for the Greater Mysteries, celebrated in September-October.

60. Part two of the notebook in which the lecture notes were written.

61. With varying degrees of distinction, some of the later Neo-Platonic schools (Syrian: Iamblichus; Pergamanian: Aedisius; Athenian: Plutarch, Syrianius, Prochus, Marinus) regarded Aristotle's thought as preparation for the study of Plato.

62. See, for example, Thomas Aquinas, *Summa Theologica*, I, 2, 1; *Basic Writings of Saint Thomas Aquinas*, I-II, ed. Anton C. Pegis (New York: Random House, 1945), I, pp. 18-20:

> *Obj. 2.* Further, those things are said to be self-evident which are known as soon as the terms are known, which the Philosopher says is true of the first principles of demonstration. Thus, when the nature of a whole and of a part is known, it is at once recognized that every whole is greater than its

part. But as soon as the signification of the name *God* is understood, it is at once seen that God exists. For by this name is signified that thing than which nothing greater can be conceived. But that which exists actually and mentally is greater than that which exists only mentally. Therefore, since as soon as the name *God* is understood it exists mentally, it also follows that it exists actually. Therefore the proposition *God exists* is self-evident. . . .

Reply Obj. 2. Perhaps not everyone who hears this name *God* understands it to signify something than which nothing greater can be thought, seeing that some have believed God to be a body. Yet, granted that everyone understands that by this name *God* is signified something than which nothing greater can be thought, nevertheless, it does not therefore follow that he understands that what the name signifies exists actually, but only that it exists mentally. Nor can it be argued that it actually exists, unless it be admitted that there actually exists something than which nothing greater can be thought; and this precisely is not admitted by those who hold that God does not exist.

63. See, for example, Kant, *Critik der reinen Vernunft*, pp. 629-30; *Critique of Pure Reason*, pp. 506-07:

> Whatever, therefore, and however much, our concept of an object may contain, we must go outside it, if we are to ascribe existence to the object. In the case of objects of the senses, this takes place through their connection with some one of our perceptions, in accordance with empirical laws. But in dealing with objects of pure thought, we have no means whatsoever of knowing their existence, since it would have to be known in a completely *a priori* manner. Our consciousness of all existence (whether immediately through perception, or mediately through inferences which connect something with perception) belongs exclusively to the unity of experience; any [alleged] existence outside this field, while not indeed such as we can declare to be absolutely impossible, is of the nature of an assumption which we can never be in a position to justify.
>
> The concept of a supreme being is in many respects a very useful idea; but just because it is a mere idea, it is altogether incapable, by itself alone, of enlarging our knowledge in regard to what exists. It is not even competent to enlighten us as to the *possibility* of any existence beyond that which is known in and through experience. The analytic criterion of possibility, as consisting in the principle that bare positives (realities) give rise to no contradiction, cannot be denied to it. But since the realities are not given to us in their specific characters; since even if they were, we should still not be in a position to pass judgment; since the criterion of the possibility of synthetic knowledge is never to be looked for save in experience, to which the object of an idea cannot belong, the connection of all real properties in a thing is a synthesis, the possibility of which we are unable to determine *a priori*. And thus the celebrated Leibniz is far from having succeeded in what

he plumed himself on achieving—the comprehension *a priori* of the possibility of this sublime ideal being.

The attempt to establish the existence of a supreme being by means of the famous ontological argument of Descartes is therefore merely so much labour and effort lost; we can no more extend our stock of [theoretical] insight by mere ideas, than a merchant can better his position by adding a few noughts to his cash account.

64. See, for example, Spinoza, *Ethics*, Part II, Prop. 7; *Opera*, pp. 312-13; *Works*, pp. 451-52:

P7: *The order and connection of ideas is the same as the order and connection of things.*

Dem.: This is clear from IA4. For the idea of each thing caused depends on the knowledge of the cause of which it is the effect.

Cor.: From this it follows that God's [NS: actual] power of thinking is equal to his actual power of acting. I.e., whatever follows formally from God's infinite nature follows objectively in God from his idea in the same order and with the same connection.

Schol.: Before we proceed further, we must recall here what we showed [NS: in the First Part], viz. that whatever can be perceived by an infinite intellect as constituting an essence of substance pertains to one substance only, and consequently that the thinking substance and the extended substance are one and the same substance, which is now comprehended under this attribute, now under that. So also a mode of extension and the idea of that mode are one and the same thing, but expressed in two ways. Some of the Hebrews seem to have seen this, as if through a cloud, when they maintained that God, God's intellect, and the things understood by him are one and the same.

For example, a circle existing in nature and the idea of the existing circle, which is also in God, are one and the same thing, which is explained through different attributes. Therefore, whether we conceive nature under the attribute of Extension, or under the attribute of Thought, or under any other attribute, we shall find one and the same order, *or* one and the same connection of causes, i.e., that the same things follow one another.

When I said [NS: before] that God is the cause of the idea, say of a circle, only insofar as he is a thinking thing, and [the cause] of the circle, only insofar as he is an extended thing, this was for no other reason than because the formal being of the idea of the circle can be perceived only through another mode of thinking, as its proximate cause, and that mode again through another, and so on, to infinity. Hence, so long as things are considered as modes of thinking, we must explain the order of the whole of nature, *or* the connection of causes, through the attribute of Thought alone. And insofar as they are considered as modes of Extension, the order of the whole of nature must be explained through the attribute of Extension alone. I understand the same concerning the other attributes.

> So of things as they are in themselves, God is really the cause insofar as he consists of infinite attributes. For the present, I cannot explain these matters more clearly.

65. See, for example, Descartes, *Discourse on Method*, IV; *Renati Des-Cartes opera philosophica*, I-II (Amsterdam: 1685), I, pp. 20-21; *Descartes' Philosophical Writings*, tr. Norman Kemp Smith (London: Macmillan, 1952), pp. 140-41:

> But I immediately became aware that while I was thus disposed to think that all was false, it was absolutely necessary that I who thus thought should be somewhat; and noting that this truth *I think, therefore I am*, was so steadfast and so assured that the suppositions of the sceptics, to whatever extreme they might all be carried, could not avail to shake it, I concluded that I might without scruple accept it as being the first principle of the philosophy I was seeking.

66. See, for example, Spinoza, *Ethics*, Part I, Prop. 7, 11; *Opera*, pp. 289, 291; *Works*, pp. 412, 417:

> P7: *It pertains to the nature of a substance to exist.*
> Dem.: A substance cannot be produced by anything else (by P6C); therefore it will be the cause of itself, i.e. (by D1), its essence necessarily involves existence, *or* it pertains to its nature to exist, q.e.d.

> P11: *God*, or *a substance consisting of infinite attributes, each of which expresses eternal and infinite essence, necessarily exists.*
> Dem.: If you deny this, conceive, if you can, that God does not exist. Therefore (by A7) his essence does not involve existence. But this (by P7) is absurd. Therefore God necessarily exists, q.e.d.

67. Friedrich Heinrich Jacobi (1743-1819), German philosopher and a major critic of Kant.

68. Jakob Boehme (1575-1624), German contemplative who exercised some influence on Schelling's thought. It is said that while he was looking at a pewter dish in the sunlight he saw the Being of Beings, the Byss of the Abyss.

69. See, for example, Thomas Aquinas, *Summa*, I, 3, 4: "*in Deo nihil sit potentiale*"; *Basic Writings*, I, p. 30 ("*in God there is no potentiality*"). See also Aristotle, *Metaphysics*, 1050 b; Bekker, II, p. 1050; *Works*, II, p. 1659: "But actuality is prior in a higher sense also; for eternal things are prior in substance to perishable things, and no eternal thing exists potentially." See also *Summa*, I, 3, 2; *Basic Writings*, I, p. 28; *Metaphysics*, 1072 b-1073 a; Bekker, II, pp. 1072-73; *Works*, II, pp. 1694-95.

70. See, for example, the fourth antinomy in note 57 above.

71. See, for example, Diogenes Laertius, *Lives of Eminent Philosophers*, VIII, 24-25; *Diogenis Laertii de vitis philosophorum libri X*, I-II (Leipzig: 1833), II, p. 100; *Diogen Laërtses filosofiske Historie*, I-II, tr. Børge Riisbrigh (Copen-

hagen: 1812), I, p. 374; *Lives of Eminent Philosophers*, I-II, tr. R. D. Hicks (Loeb, Cambridge: Harvard University Press, 1979-80), II, pp. 341-43:

> Alexander in his *Successions of Philosophers* says that he found in the Pythagorean memoirs the following tenets as well. The principle of all things is the monad or unit; arising from this monad the undefined dyad or two serves as material substratum to the monad, which is cause; from the monad and the undefined dyad spring numbers; from numbers, points; from points, lines; from lines, plane figures; from plane figures, solid figures; from solid figures, sensible bodies, the elements of which are four, fire, water, earth and air; these elements interchange and turn into one another completely, and combine to produce a universe animate, intelligent, spherical, with the earth at its centre, the earth itself too being spherical and inhabited round about.

72. See *Letters*, Letter 63, *KW* XXV.

73. Aristotle, *Metaphysics*, 982 b; Bekker, II, p. 982; *Works*, II, p. 1554:

> For it is owing to their wonder that men both now begin and at first began to philosophize; they wondered originally at the obvious difficulties, then advanced little by little and stated difficulties about the greater matters, e.g. about the phenomena of the moon and those of the sun and the stars, and about the genesis of the universe. And a man who is puzzled and wonders thinks himself ignorant (whence even the lover of myth is in a sense a lover of wisdom, for myth is composed of wonders); therefore since they philosophized in order to escape from ignorance, evidently they were pursuing science in order to know, and not for any utilitarian end.

The particular Latin formulation has not been located. Ast, *Platonis opera*, II, p. 41, in a Latin translation of the Plato quotation in this sentence, uses *admiratio* for wonder. See *Fragments*, p. 80 and note 35, *KW* VII (*SV* IV 244); *JP* III 3284 (*Pap*. IV A 107).

74. A free but essentially faithful quotation from Plato, *Theaetetus*, 155 c-d; *Opera*, II, p. 41; *Dialogues*, p. 860:

> THEAETETUS: No, indeed it is extraordinary how they set me wondering whatever they can mean. Sometimes I get quite dizzy with thinking of them.
>
> SOCRATES: That shows that Theodorus was not wrong in his estimate of your nature. This sense of wonder is the mark of the philosopher. Philosophy indeed has no other origin, and he was a good genealogist who made Iris the daughter of Thaumas.

75. A free but essentially faithful version of Spinoza, *Ethics*, Part I, Def. 1; *Opera*, p. 287; *Works*, p. 408: "By cause of itself I understand that whose essence involves existence, *or* that whose nature cannot be conceived except as existing."

76. The manuscript reads: *forsøge*. Cf. *Pap*. XIII, p. 292 (*forsage* [forsake]).

77. See Aristotle, *Metaphysics*, 1025 a; Bekker, II, p. 1025; *Works*, II, p. 1619:

> We call an accident that which attaches to a something and can be truly asserted, but neither of necessity nor usually, e.g. if one in digging a hole for a plant found treasure. This—the finding of treasure—happens by accident to the man who digs the hole; for neither does the one come of necessity from the other or after the other, nor, if a man plants, does he usually find treasure. And a musical man might be white; but since this does not happen of necessity nor usually, we call it an accident. Therefore since there are attributes and they attach to a subject, and some of them attach in a particular place and at a particular time, whatever attaches to a subject, but not because it is this subject, at this time or in this place, will be an accident. Therefore there is no definite cause for an accident, but a chance cause, i.e. an indefinite one. Going to Aegina was an accident, if the man went not in order to get there, but because he was carried out of his way by a storm or captured by pirates. The accident has happened or exists,—not in virtue of itself, however, but of something else; for the *storm* was the cause of his coming to a place for which he was not sailing, and this was Aegina.
>
> 'Accident' has also another meaning, i.e. what attaches to each thing in virtue of itself but is not in its substance, as having its angles equal to two right angles attaches to the triangle. And accidents of this sort may be eternal, but no accident of the other sort is. This is explained elsewhere.

78. The particular phrase has not been located. Cf. "philosophy is the greatest of the arts" (Plato, *Phaedo*, 60 e-61 a; *Opera*, I, pp. 480-81; *Dialogues*, p. 43); "set dialectic above all other studies to be as it were the coping stone" *(Republic*, 534 e; *Opera*, IV, pp. 420-21; *Dialogues*, p. 766); "a gift of the gods" (*Philebus*, 16 c; *Opera*, III, pp. 278-79; *Dialogues*, p. 1092).

79. See *Sir Isaac Newton's Mathematical Principles*, tr. Andrew Motte, rev. Florian Cajori (Berkeley: University of California Press, 1946), p. 544: "This Being governs all things, not as the soul of the world, but as Lord over all; and on account of his dominion he is wont to be called *Lord God* παντοκράτωρ, or *Universal Ruler*; for *God* is a relative word, and has a respect to servants; and *Deity* is the dominion of God not over his own body, as those imagine who fancy God to be the soul of the world, but over servants." In a fragment titled "Of the faith which was once delivered to the Saints," Newton wrote: "If the father or son be called *God*, they take the name in a metaphysical sense, whereas it relates only to God's dominion to teach us obedience. The word *God* is relative and signifies the same thing with Lord and King but in a higher degree" (Jerusalem: Jewish National and University Library, Yahuda ms. 7, 7, folio 16r, in Frank E. Manuel, *The Religion of Isaac Newton* [Oxford: Oxford University Press, 1974], p. 21). Newton's scientific and extrascientific Latin terminology was well known in learned circles in Germany.

80. At this point, the text in *Pap*. XIII, p. 298, reads: *tilbage sc. i sig selv*. The abbreviation *sc.* does not appear in the manuscript.

81. See note 53 above.

82. Johannes v. Müller (1752-1809), prominent German historian whose *Sämmtliche Werke*, I-XXVII (Stuttgart: 1810-19), in itself exemplifies his Faustian view of man.

83. The manuscript text reads: *unv.*, an abbreviation of *unvordenkliche*.

84. The manuscript text reads: *Wider-Göttliche*. Cf. *Pap*. XIII, p. 303 (*Wieder-Göttliche* [again divine]). See also pp. 396, 401.

85. Praeneste (Palestrina) was one of the most ancient and important cities in Latium (Italy) and was especially famous for its Temple of Fortune and its associated oracle.

86. See Proverbs 8:22-31.

87. See note 68 above. *Urstand* pertains to Boehme's view of the *Ungrund*, the primordial "unground" in its "under-standing." See, for example, *Von sechs Puncten* (with circular subtitle in German: Unground. Eternal Freedom. God outside Nature and Creatures. The Mirror of Wisdom) (Amsterdam: 1682), I, 22, p. 9; *Six Theosophic Points and Other Writings*, tr. John R. Earle (Ann Arbor: University of Michigan Press, 1970), pp. 10-11:

> 22. Thus, we understand eternity: (1) How it was before the times of the creation of this world [the *Urstand]*. (2) What the divine Essence is in itself without a principle. (3) What the eternal beginning in the unground is, and the eternal end in its own ground generated in itself, viz. the centre to the word, which word is the centre itself. (4) And yet the eternal birth of the Word in the will, in the mirror of the eternal wisdom, in the virgin, continually takes place from eternity to eternity without a genetrix or without bringing forth.

88. See, for example, Francis Bacon, *Novum Organum*, I, aphorism 3; *Francis Bacon's neues Organ der Wissenschaften*, tr. Anton T. Brück (Leipzig: 1830), p. 26; *The Philosophical Works of Francis Bacon*, ed. John M. Robertson (Ellis and Spedding tr.) (New York: Dutton, 1905), p. 259:

> Human knowledge and human power meet in one; for where the cause is not known the effect cannot be produced. Nature to be commanded must be obeyed; and that which in contemplation is as the cause is in operation as the rule.

89. See Proverbs 8:22.

90. Cf. Terentius Varro, *De lingua latina*, V, 57 ("*principes dei*," the first gods), V, 58 ("*dei magni*," great gods); *Varro on the Latin Language*, I-II, tr. Roland G. Kent (Loeb, Cambridge: Harvard University Press, 1938-51), I, pp. 53-55.

91. Proverbs 8:31.

92. See notes 64 and 75 above.

93. See Hegel, *Encyclopädie*, III, *Philosophie des Geistes*, *Werke*, VII², p. 463; *J.A.*, X, p. 469; *Philosophy of Mind*, pp. 309-10:

I refrain from accumulating further examples of the religious and poetic conceptions which it is customary to call pantheistic. Of the philosophies to which that name is given, the Eleatic, or Spinozist, it has been remarked earlier (para. 50, note) that so far are they from identifying God with the world and making him finite, that in these systems this 'everything' has no truth, and that we should rather call them monotheistic, or, in relation to the popular idea of the world, acosmical. They are most accurately called systems which apprehend the Absolute only as substance. Of the oriental, especially the Mohammedan, modes of envisaging God, we may rather say that they represent the Absolute as the utterly universal genus which dwells in the species or existences, but dwells so potently that these existences have no actual reality. The fault of all these modes of thought and systems is that they stop short of defining substance as subject and as mind.

These systems and modes of pictorial conception originate from the one need common to all philosophies and all religions of getting an idea of God, and, secondly, of the relationship of God and the world. (In philosophy it is specially made out that the determination of God's nature determines his relations with the world.)

94. See John of Damascus, *De fide orthodoxa*, I, 5, *Opera omnia quae exstant*, I-II, ed. Michaelis Lequien (Venice: 1748), I, p. 129; *Saint John of Damascus Writings*, ed. Frederic H. Chase, Jr., tr. S.D.F. Salmand (New York: Fathers of the Church, 1958), p. 167:

> Now, we both know and confess that God is without beginning and without end, everlasting and eternal, uncreated, unchangeable, inalterable, simple, uncompounded, incorporeal, invisible, impalpable, uncircumscribed, unlimited, incomprehensible, uncontained, unfathomable, good, just, the maker of all created things, all-powerful, all-ruling, all-seeing, the provider, the sovereign, and the judge of all. We furthermore know and confess that God is one, that is to say, one substance, and that He is both understood to be and is in three Persons—I mean the Father and the Son and the Holy Ghost—and that the Father and the Son and the Holy Ghost are one in all things save in the being unbegotten, the being begotten, and the procession.

95. See, for example, F. H. Jacobi, *Von den Göttlichen Dingen und ihrer Offenbarung*, *Friedrich Heinrich Jacobi's Werke*, I-VI (Leipzig: 1812-25), III, pp. 348, 354 (ed. tr.):

> Nicht ohne Grund rühmt sich das neueste System der *Alleinheit* oder absoluten Identität, zu der ältesten *Philosophie* (die man aber nicht für die älteste *Lehre* halten musz) zurückzuführen [It is not entirely unfounded for the most recent system of *singleness* or absolute identity to pride itself on being traceable to the most ancient *philosophy* (which nevertheless should not be considered the most ancient *theory*)].

Von der Kantischen Entdeckung aus: dasz wir nur das vollkommen einsehen und begreifen, was wir zu construiren im Stande sind—war nur ein Schritt bis zum Identitätssystem. Der mit strenger Consequenz durchgeführte Kantische Kriticismus muszte die *Wissenschaftslehre*, diese, wiederum streng durchgeführt, *Alleinheitslehre*, einen umgekehrten oder verklärten Spinozismus, *Idealmaterialismus* zur Folge haben [From the Kantian discovery—that we perceive and conceive perfectly only that which we are capable of constructing—to the identity-system was but a short step. Kantian criticism, carried through with such rigorous consistency, had to issue in the *theory of science*, in that *doctrine of singleness*, which, once again rigorously sustained, is a reversed or transfigured Spinozism, an *ideal-materialism*].

96. The manuscript text reads: ἓν τὸ πᾶν. Cf. *Pap*. XIII, p. 308 (εν και παν).

97. See, for example, Spinoza, *Ethics*, Part II, Prop. 1, 2; *Opera*, p. 311; *Works*, pp. 448-49:

> P1: *Thought is an attribute of God*, or *God is a thinking thing*. . . .
> P2: *Extension is an attribute of God*, or *God is an extended thing*.

98. See, for example, Descartes, *Principles of Philosophy*, I, 53-54; *Opera*, I, pp. 14-15; *Philosophical Writings*, ed. and tr. Elizabeth Anscombe and Peter Thomas Geach (Indianapolis: Bobbs-Merrill, 1971), pp. 192-93:

> LIII. Any attribute gives us knowledge of substance; but every substance has a principal property that constitutes its essential nature, and all others are reduced to this. Extension in length, breadth, and depth is what constitutes the very nature of corporeal substance; consciousness is what constitutes the very nature of a conscious substance. For any other possible attribute of body presupposes extension and is, so to say, an aspect (*modus*) of an extended thing; and likewise whatever is found in the mind is merely one aspect or another of consciousness (*diversi modi cogitandi*). For example, shape is not conceivable except in an extended thing, nor motion except in an extended space; whereas imagination, sensation and will are inconceivable except in a conscious being. But on the other hand extension is conceivable apart from shape or motion, and so is consciousness apart from imagination and sense, and so on; this is clear to anyone on reflection. LIV. We can thus readily get two clear and distinct notions or ideas: one of created conscious substance, the other of corporeal substance; provided that we carefully distinguish all attributes of consciousness from attributes of extension.
>
> We can likewise get a clear and distinct idea of uncreated and independent conscious substance, that is, God; provided that we do not suppose that this idea is an adequate manifestation of all that exists in God, and do not falsely imagine that something is comprised in it, but merely observe what it really does involve—what we evidently see belongs to the nature of a supremely perfect being. And assuredly nobody can deny that there is

within us such an idea of God, unless he should think that there is no knowledge of God in the human mind at all.

99. The manuscript reads: *tilbage*. Cf. *Pap*. XIII, p. 310 (*tillige* [also]).

100. See John 14:21-23.

101. See Romans 8:16.

102. See John 1:3.

103. See, for example, *Dionysius the Areopagite on the Divine Names and the Mystical Theology*, tr. C. E. Rolt (New York: Macmillan, 1966), II, 11, p. 80: "περὶ θείων ὀνομάτων."

104. Basil the Great. See August Hahn, *Lehrbuch des christlichen Glaubens* (Leipzig: 1828; *ASKB* 535), p. 284.

105. A Hebrew homiletical interpretation (Midrash) of Ecclesiastes.

106. Genesis 3:22.

107. The manuscript reads: πνευμα. Cf. *Pap*. XIII, p. 314 (πνευμα).

108. See John 16:15; Romans 11:36.

109. The manuscript reads: *Wirken-Müssende*. Cf. *Pap*. XIII, p. 316 (*Virken-Müssende*).

110. The manuscript reads: *en*. Cf. *Pap*. XIII, p. 316 (*er* [is]).

111. See I John 3:9.

112. Ephesians 2:12.

113. The manuscript reads: *indre*. Cf. *Pap*., XIII, p. 318 (*andre* [other]).

114. In Greek mythology, Persephone was the daughter of Zeus and Demeter (L. Ceres), the wife of Hades (Pluto), and the queen of the infernal regions. The worship of Persephone was associated with the Eleusinian Mysteries and was related to the change of seasons.

115. See note 71 above.

116. See Genesis 3:1-6.

117. See Genesis 3:14.

118. In Greek mythology, Zeus, son of Cronus and Rhea, was the supreme Olympian god.

119. The Sabians were a sect in ancient Persia and Chaldea who acknowledged the unity of God but worshiped intelligences in the heavenly bodies and in some groups worshiped the heavenly bodies themselves.

120. In Greek mythology, Uranus, son and husband of Gaea, the earth goddess, was the god who personified heaven.

121. In Greek mythology, Urania was the muse of astronomy. The name was used for Aphrodite (L. Venus), the goddess of vegetation, beauty, and love. According to early legends, she was the daughter of Zeus and Dione. Later legends told of her springing from the sea, into which the blood of Uranus was shed when he was wounded by Cronus.

122. In Greek mythology, Dionysus (L. Bacchus), originally the god of vegetation, was the god of wine and drama.

123. In Phoenician mythology, Moloch was a god associated with Baal and characterized especially by a total lack of benevolence. Worship of Moloch involved human sacrifice and self-mutilation.

124. In Greek mythology, Cronus, the youngest Titan, was the son of Uranus and Gaea (see note 120), the husband of Rhea, and the father of Zeus, Hades, Poseidon, Demeter, Hera, and Hestia. He led the Titans in their revolt against Uranus and was overthrown by the Olympian gods led by Zeus. His reign on earth was a time of peace and prosperity. In Roman mythology, he was identified with Saturn.

125. In Greek mythology, Heracles (more frequently called Hercules), the son of Zeus and Alcmena, represented manly strength and patient endurance. Among his legendary feats were the cleansing of the Augean stables and the temporary relief of Atlas in the task of supporting the world.

126. See, for example, Isaiah 53.

127. In Phrygian mythology, Cybele was the Great Mother, the source of all living things. The Greeks identified her with Rhea.

128. The manuscript reads: θεου γεννητου. Cf. *Pap*. XIII, p. 322 (θεοι γεννητοι).

129. In Greek mythology, Typhon, a personification of the powerful volcanic forces of the earth, was the son of the monster Typhoeus (also the father of Cerberus) and was later identified with him. In Egyptian mythology, he was identified with an evil god called Set.

130. Osiris was the most popular of the Egyptian gods and represented the sun, the Nile, and the vicissitudes of life. He was slain by Set, avenged by Horus, and became judge of the dead. Isis, the principal goddess in Egyptian mythology, was the wife and sister of Osiris and the mother of Horus. She taught men the arts and crafts and symbolized fecundity.

131. In Hindu thought, Brahma is the primordial essence from which all things emanate and to which all return. Brahma, Shiva (destroyer of life), and Vishnu (preserver of life) form the Hindu triad.

132. In Greek mythology, Hades was the ruler of the underworld and the kidnapping husband of Persephone. Hades was also the name of the underworld.

133. In Greek mythology, Rhea, daughter of the earth goddess Gaea and the sky god Uranus, was the mother of the gods and wife of her brother Cronus. At times she was identified with Cybele, the Great Mother. Among her children was Demeter, the Olympian goddess who personified the fruitfulness of the earth.

134. In Greek mythology, Poseidon, son of Cronus and Rhea and brother of Zeus, was the god of the sea.

135. See Isocrates, *Panegyricus*, 28-30; *Isocrates Werke*, I-IV, tr. Adolph Heinrich Christian (Stuttgart: 1832), I, pp. 173-74; *Isocrates*, I-III, tr. George Norlin and LaRue Van Hook (Loeb, New York: Putnam, 1928-61), I, p. 135:

> Now, first of all, that which was the first necessity of man's nature was provided by our city; for even though the story has taken the form of a myth, yet it deserves to be told again. When Demeter came to our land, in her wandering after the rape of Korê, and, being moved to kindness to-

wards our ancestors by services which may not be told save to her initiates, gave these two gifts, the greatest in the world—the fruits of the earth, which have enabled us to rise above the life of the beasts, and the holy rite which inspires in those who partake of it sweeter hopes regarding both the end of life and all eternity,—our city was not only so beloved of the gods but also so devoted to mankind that, having been endowed with these great blessings, she did not begrudge them to the rest of the world, but shared with all men what she had received. The mystic rite we continue even now, each year, to reveal to the initiates; and as for the fruits of the earth, our city has, in a word, instructed the world in their uses, their cultivation, and the benefits derived from them. This statement, when I have added a few further proofs, no one could venture to discredit.

136. See Tacitus, *Germania*, IX; *Des C. Cornelius Tacitus Sämmtliche Werke*, I-III, tr. Johann Samuel Müllern (Hamburg: 1765-66), III, pp. 604-05; *Cajus Cornelius Tacitus*, I-III, tr. Jacob Baden (Copenhagen: 1773-97), III, p. 541; *Tacitus: The Historical Works, Germania and Agricola*, I-II, tr. Arthur Murphy (Everyman, New York: Dutton, 1907), II, p. 317:

In some parts of the country of the Suevians, the worship of Isis [identified with Demeter by the Greeks] is established. To trace the introduction of ceremonies, which had their growth in another part of the world, were an investigation for which I have no materials: suffice it to say, that the figure of a ship (the symbolic representation of the goddess) clearly shows that the religion was imported into the country. Their deities are not immured in temples, nor represented under any kind of resemblance to the human form. To do either, were, in their opinion, to derogate from the majesty of superior beings. Woods and groves are the sacred depositories; and the spot being consecrated to those pious uses, they give to that sacred recess the name of the divinity that fills the place, which is never profaned by the steps of man. The gloom fills every mind with awe; revered at a distance, and never seen but with the eye of contemplation.

137. See Homer, "To Demeter," 470-79, *The Homeric Hymns*; *Hesiod The Homeric Hymns and Homerica*, tr. Hugh G. Evelyn-White (Loeb, Cambridge: Harvard University Press, 1982), p. 323.

138. See Homer, *Iliad*, VI, 130-43; *Homers Iliade*, I-II, tr. Christian Wilster (Copenhagen: 1836), I, pp. 98-99; *Homer The Iliad*, I-II, tr. A. T. Murray (Loeb, Cambridge: Harvard University Press, 1976-78), I, pp. 271-73.

139. See, for example, Homer, *Iliad*, VI, 132-36; XIV, 325; Wilster, I, pp. 98-99; II, pp. 36-37; Loeb, I, pp. 271-73; II, p. 91.

140. In Greek mythology, Pentheus, king of Thebes, imprisoned Dionysus when he came to Thebes to teach his new religion of freedom and joy. Pentheus was killed by a group of women led by his mother when he went to a forest to observe the revelries of the followers of Dionysus.

141. In Greek mythology, Orpheus, the son of Calliope and Zeus or Oea-

grus, was a legendary musician and hero. He met his death by being torn to pieces by Thracian women during their orgiastic worship of Dionysus. He was regarded as the founder of the Orphic mysteries, which celebrated Dionysus.

142. See Kierkegaard's letters to his brother and to Emil Boesen, *Letters*, Letter 68 (February 6, 1842), 69 (February 27, 1842), and 70 (February 1842), *KW* XXV; *JP* V 5532 (*Pap*. III A 176).

SUPPLEMENT

TITLE PAGE. The Danish version (*Om*) of the conventional Latin *De* in titles is omitted in the English translation.

EPIGRAPH. Plato, *Republic*, 453 d; *Platonis quae exstant opera*, I-XI, ed. Friedrich Ast (Leipzig: 1819-32; *ASKB* 1144-54), IV, p. 453; *The Collected Dialogues of Plato*, ed. Edith Hamilton and Huntington Cairns (Princeton: Princeton University Press, 1963), p. 692. The reference to a dolphin is an allusion to Arion, a legendary Greek poet and musician, who was compelled by sailors to leap into the sea after they had robbed him. A dolphin rescued him and carried him to Taenarus.

1. Cf. *JP* V 5062, 5073, 5074, 5081, 5205 (*Pap*. I A 13-15, 18; II A 20).

2. This is the earliest dated entry indicating a theme for investigation, probably as the subject of an essay or a dissertation. See Historical Introduction, pp. vii-viii; *JP* VII, p. 60.

3. Along with the Master Thief, these are the three main themes on which Kierkegaard considered writing. See Historical Introduction, p. vii. On Don Juan, see *Either/Or*, I, pp. 45-135, *KW* III (*SV* I 29-113); Corsair *Affair*, pp. 28-37, *KW* XIII (*SV* XIII 447-56); *JP* I 769 (*Pap*. II A 55); VII, p. 28. On Faust, see *Either/Or*, I, pp. 204-15, *KW* III (*SV* I 180-89); *JP* II 1177-85; VII, p. 37. On the Wandering Jew, see *JP* VII, p. 100.

4. *Efterladte Breve af Gabrielis* (Copenhagen: 1826), p. 32. The book, autobiographical in nature, was written by Frederik Christian Sibbern, who is named as the editor.

5. From references to Brazil, the letter was apparently intended for the paleontologist Peter Wilhelm Lund (1801-1880), brother of Johan Christian Lund and Henrik Ferdinand Lund (married to Kierkegaard's sisters Nicoline Christine and Petrea Severine, respectively). He returned to Brazil in January 1833. Emanuel Hirsch regards the entry as part of an unfinished and unpublished series of "Faustian Letters" (*Kierkegaard-Studien*, I-II [Gutersloh: 1933; repr. Vaduz, Liechtenstein: Topus Verlag, 1978], II, pp. 490-92). See *Either/Or*, I, p. ix and note 12, *KW* III; *JP* V 5181 and note 245.

6. See Historical Introduction, pp. vii, ix-x.

7. Michael Pedersen Kierkegaard (1756-1838). See Historical Introduction, p. ix.

8. See Deuteronomy 34:1-4, which refers to Mount Nebo rather than to Tabor, and Numbers 14:20-23.

9. The coastal road running north from Copenhagen and the main highway to *Dyrehaven (Dyrehaug)*, a large woods with deer. Part of it is *Dyrehavsbakken*, a carnival-type amusement park that operates from May through September, a time period both earlier and later than the original traditional period called *Dyrehavstiden*, Midsummer Day (June 24, *Sankt Hans Dag*) to Visitation Day (July 2, *Mariæ Besøgelsesdag*). See *Fragments*, p. 6, *KW* VII (*SV* IV 177); *Stages*, p. 480, *KW* XI (*SV* VI 446); *Postscript*, *KW* XII (*SV* VII 410, 429, 430).

10. Karl Ferdinand Gutzkov (1811-1851), German writer and a leading figure in a politically active group of romantic writers called Young Germany. See p. 275 and note 73.

11. "This book" refers not to *Lucinde* but to *Vertraute Briefe über Friedrich Schlegels Lucinde*, the first edition of which (Lübeck, Leipzig: 1800, printed in Jena) was anonymous. The second edition, published shortly after Schleiermacher's death, carried the author's name.

12. Schleiermacher, *Vertraute Briefe*, pp. 46-68.

13. This entry is the earliest hint of what came to be Kierkegaard's indirect method in the pseudonymous works. See *Repetition*, p. 357, *KW* VI, note on subtitle.

14. The world's irony over the individual. Cf. *Either/Or*, I, p. 24, *KW* III (*SV* I 9).

15. See Johan Ludvig Heiberg, *Kjøbenhavns flyvende Post*, 8, 1828; *JP* V 5192 (*Pap*. I C 124).

16. Cf. *Fear and Trembling*, p. 51, *KW* VI (*SV* III 101).

17. Johann Wolfgang v. Goethe, *Faust*, I, 2; *Goethe's Werke. Vollständige Ausgabe letzter Hand*, I-LX (Stuttgart, Tübingen: 1828-42; *ASKB* 1641-68 [I-LV]), XII, pp. 55-56; *Faust*, tr. Bayard Taylor (New York: Modern Library, 1950), pp. 35-36.

18. Martensen, *Ueber Lenau's Faust. Von Johannes M. . . . .n* (Stuttgart: 1836). A Danish version, *"Betragtninger over Ideen af Faust,"* appeared in J. L. Heiberg's *Perseus*, I (*ASKB* 569), June 1837, pp. 91-164.

19. Cf. Supplement, pp. 431-32 (*Pap*. II A 102).

20. See Supplement, pp. 425-26.

21. Possibly a reference to the ironic sayings of Diogenes of Sinope. See ΣΩΚΡΑΤΗΣ ΜΑΙΝΟΜΕΝΟΣ *oder die Dialogen des Diogenes von Sinope*, tr. Christoph Martin Wieland (Leipzig: 1770; *ASKB* 474); *Nachlass des Diogenes von Sinope, C. M. Wielands sämmtliche Werke*, I-XXXVIII (Leipzig: 1794-1805), XIII.

22. Ernst Theodor Amadeus Hoffmann, *Prindsessinn Brambilla, E.T.A. Hoffmann's ausgewählte Schriften*, I-X (Berlin: 1827-28; *ASKB* 1712-16), IX, pp. 127-282. See *Pap*. I C 92.

23. Adam Gottlob Oehlenschläger, *"Morgen-Vandring," Poetiske Skrifter*, I-II (Copenhagen: 1805; *ASKB* 1597-98), I, p. 364.

24. Poul Martin Møller (1794-1838), Kierkegaard's favorite professor of philosophy at the University of Copenhagen.

25. Johann Georg Hamann, *Fünf Hirtenbriefe über das Schuldrama, Hamann's Schriften*, I-VIII, ed. Friedrich Roth and G. A. Wiener (Berlin, Leipzig: 1821-43; *ASKB* 536-44), II, p. 434: *"heiligen Päderastie."*

26. See II Corinthians 5:17.

27. Cf. Hamann, letter to J.G. Lindner, Oct. 12, 1759, *Schriften*, I, p. 497.

28. See Genesis 28:10-12.

29. See Gotthilf Heinrich v. Schubert, *Die Symbolik des Traumes* (Bamberg: 1821; *ASKB* 776), p. 155.

30. See *"Sechse kommen durch die ganze Welt," Kinder- und Haus-Märchen, gesammelt durch die Brüder Grimm*, I-III (Berlin: 1819-22; *ASKB* 1425-27), I, 71, pp. 378-85; "How Six Men Got On in the World," *The Complete Grimm's Fairy Tales*, ed. Padraic Colum (New York: Pantheon, 1972), p. 345. See also *Letters*, Letter 195, *KW* XXV.

31. Jean Paul (J. P. Friedrich Richter, 1763-1825), prominent German thinker and novelist. See *Jean Paul's sämmtliche Werke*, I-LXV (Berlin: 1826-38; *ASKB* 1777-99 [I-LX]).

32. Cf. *Either/Or*, I, p. 24, *KW* III (*SV* I 9); *Repetition*, p. 170, *KW* VI (*SV* III 209); *JP* V 5100, 5187 (*Pap*. I A 75, pp. 57-58, 335).

33. See Thomas Keightley, *Mythologie der Feen und Elfen vom Ursprunge dieses Glaubens bis auf die neuesten Zeiten aus dem Englischen übersetzt*, tr. Oscar Ludwig Bernhard Wolff, I-II (Weimar: 1828), I, pp. 131-32.

34. Johann Ludwig Tieck (1773-1853), a leading German novelist of the romantic school. *Ludwig Tieck's sämmtliche Werke*, I-II (Paris: 1837; *ASKB* 1848-49).

35. Hoffmann, *Die Serapions Brüder, Schriften*, I-IV.

36. See note 25 above and note 37 below.

37. See *Schriften*, I, p. VIII. The editor, Friedrich Roth, states (I, p. VIII) that Hamann's activity as an author was as hidden and modest as his life (1730-1788). Hamann's collected writings, most of them unpublished during his lifetime, were edited and published (1821-43) about half a century after his death. See Supplement, p. 434 (II A 138).

38. See Diogenes Laertius, *Lives of Eminent Philosophers*, VI, 67; *Diogenis Laertii de vitis philosophorum libri X*, I-II (Leipzig: 1833; *ASKB* 1109), I, pp. 277-78; *Diogen Laërtses filosofiske Historie*, I-II, tr. Børge Riisbrigh (Copenhagen: 1812; *ASKB* 1110-11), I, p. 258; *Lives of Eminent Philosophers*, I-II, tr. R. D. Hicks (Loeb, Cambridge: Harvard University Press, 1979-80), II, p. 69.

39. *Tidsskrift for udenlandsk theologisk Litteratur*, ed. Henrik Nikolai Clausen and Matthias Hagen Hohlenberg, V, 1837, 3, pp. 485-533.

40. Ferdinand Christian Baur, *"Das Christliche des Platonismus oder Sokrates und Christus," Tübinger Zeitschrift für Theologie*, 3, 1837.

41. See Genesis 8:6-11.

42. Cf. I John 5:4.

43. Johann Gottlieb Fichte, "*Speculation og Aabenbaring,*" Danish translation in *Tidsskrift for udenlandsk theologisk Litteratur*, V, 1837, 4, pp. 747-77.

44. See Philippians 2:12.

45. The reference (*Afhandling:* treatise, essay, dissertation) is unclear. The publication of *Om Begrebet Ironi* is about three years away, but the first part may have been written before the writing of *From the Papers of One Still Living* (pub. September 7, 1838). Although the term could refer to either or both or to any other work, the formula does not appear in any extant dedication copies.

46. See Philippians 2:12.

47. From the watchman's midnight call. See *Instruction for Natte-Vægterne i Kiøbenhavn* (Copenhagen: 1784), p. 20; Thomas Hansen Kingo, *Psalmer og aandelige Sange af Thomas Kingo*, ed. Peter Andreas Fenger (Copenhagen: 1827; *ASKB* 203), 231 (based on Psalm 51), p. 521.

48. This entry intimates a religious experience akin to Pascal's and is the counterpart of *JP* V 5430 (*Pap*. II A 805).

49. There had been a period of estrangement between father and son. The entry mirrors a wholehearted reconciliation. See Supplement, p. 437 (*Pap*. II A 233); Historical Introduction, pp. ix-x.

50. See Supplement, p. 437 (*Pap*. II A 231).

51. This may be a reference to Gunnar in *Njals Saga*, ch. 75. Kierkegaard's library included *Nordiske Kæmpe-Historier*, I-III, tr. Carl Christian Rafn (Copenhagen: 1821-26; *ASKB* 1993-95), and *Oldnordiske Sagaer*, I-XII, tr. Rafn (Copenhagen: 1826-37; *ASKB* 1996-2007). See *Repetition*, p. 171, *KW* VI (*SV* III 209), where the episode is attributed to Justinus Kerner.

52. See note 7 above.

53. Emil Ferdinand Boesen (1812-1881), Kierkegaard's close friend from childhood.

54. See Historical Introduction, pp. vii, ix-x.

55. See ibid., pp. ix-x.

56. During his student days, Kierkegaard had begun studies of the Master Thief, Faust, Don Juan, and the Wandering Jew. See note 3 above and various entries interspersed in the Supplement.

57. See I Samuel 15:22.

58. See Supplement, pp. 440-41 (*Pap*. III B 2).

59. See Horace, *Odes*, I, 9, 19; *Q. Horatii Flacci opera* (Leipzig: 1828; *ASKB* 1248), p. 30; *Horace The Odes and Epodes*, tr. C. E. Bennett (Loeb, Cambridge: Harvard University Press, 1978), pp. 28-29.

60. See Genesis 3:8.

61. *From the Papers of One Still Living* was published September 7, 1838.

62. The reference is ambiguous. Although it may pertain in part to dissertation work, it more likely refers to writing done in connection with Kierkegaard's preparation for the final comprehensive examination, which took place about one year later (July 3, 1840).

63. See p. 26 and note 63.

64. See Hebrews 11:11-12. The term is used for Abraham because of his age; the second expression is used for Sarah.

65. July 3, 1840.

66. After the final comprehensive examination, Kierkegaard journeyed (July 19-August 6, 1840) to his father's boyhood home in Sæding, Jutland. See *JP* V 5451-74.

67. Danish: *Kirkegaard* [churchyard, cemetery]. *Gaard* denotes a circumscribed piece of land. Therefore, the name *Ki[e]rkegaard* was also used to designate the two farms [*Gaard*] belonging to the Sæding parish. The family name "Kierkegaard" (with an added "e") is a place name and comes from "church farm," not from "cemetery."

68. Kierkegaard had entered the university on October 30, 1830. By the time his father died, he had been a student for about eight years. His father's wish was that he settle down and complete his university studies. See Historical Introduction, pp. vii, ix-x.

69. To Archimedes (287?-212 B.C.) is attributed the saying: Give me a place to stand and I will move the world. See Plutarch, "Marcellus," 14, *Lives*; *Plutark's Levnetsbeskrivelser*, I-IV, tr. Stephan Tetens (Copenhagen: 1800-11; *ASKB* 1197-1200), III, p. 272; *Plutarch's Lives*, I-XI, tr. Bernadotte Perrin (Loeb, Cambridge: Harvard University Press, 1968-84), V, p. 473: ". . . Archimedes, who was a kinsman and friend of King Hiero [tyrant of Syracuse], wrote to him that with any given force it was possible to move any given weight; and emboldened, as we are told, by the strength of his demonstration, he declared that, if there were another world, and he could go to it, he could move this." See also, for example, *Either/Or*, I, p. 294, *KW* III (*SV* I 266); *Repetition*, p. 186, *KW* VI (*SV* III 221); *JP* III 3426; V 5099 (*Pap*. IX A 115; I A 68); VII, p. 7.

70. *Irony* has an introduction but no preface. *Pap*. III B 2-27 are presumably sketched items related to the writing of *Om Begrebet Ironi*.

71. See Jens Baggesen, "*Kritisk Vurdering*" of *Ludlams Hule* by Adam Oehlenschläger, *Danfana*, I, March 1816 (*ASKB* 1508), p. 266.

72. See p. 201.

73. Cf. Isaiah 3:4,12.

74. Plato, *Opera*, I, pp. 164-65; *Dialogues*, p. 491.

75. See *Repetition*, p. 225, *KW* VI (*SV* III 259).

76. See Supplement, pp. 447-48 (*Pap*. III B 30).

77. See *Either/Or*, I, p. 20, *KW* III (*SV* I 5); *Stages*, p. 199, *KW* XI (*SV* VI 189).

78. See, for example, *Postscript*, *KW* XII (*SV* VII 455-58, 480-84).

79. See Johann Karl August Musäus, "*Rolands Knappen*," *Volksmärchen der Deutschen*, I-V (Vienna: 1815; *ASKB* 1434-38), I, pp. 103-05; "*Rolands Vaabendragere*," *Musaeus' Folkeæventyr*, I-III, tr. Frederik Schaldemose (Copenhagen: 1840), I, pp. 116-18.

80. "The water nymph enticed the angler into the water . . . and he never

was seen again." Goethe, *"Der Fischer," Werke*, I, p. 186; *Goethe*, ed. David Luke (Harmondsworth, Middlesex: Penguin, 1964), p. 80.

81. See note 26 above.

82. See Plato, *Protagoras*, 331 d-e; *Opera*, I, pp. 52-55; *Udvalgte Dialoger af Platon*, I-VIII, tr. Carl Johan Heise (Copenhagen: 1830-59; *ASKB* 1164-67, 1169 [I-VII]), II, pp. 152-53; *Dialogues*, pp. 326-27 (Protagoras and Socrates conversing):

> Well of course, he [Protagoras] replied, justice does have some resemblance to holiness. After all, everything resembles everything else up to a point. There is a sense in which white resembles black, and hard soft, and so on with all other things that present the most contrary appearances. Even the parts of the face, which we described earlier as having different functions and not being like each other, have a certain resemblance and are like each other in some way. So by your method you can prove, if you want to, that they too all resemble one another. But it is not right to call things similar because they have some one point of similarity, even when the resemblance is very slight, any more than to call things dissimilar that have some point of dissimilarity.
>
> At this I said in some surprise, And is this how you suppose justice to be related to holiness, that there is only a slight resemblance between them?

83. Plato, *Protagoras*, 331 d; *Opera*, I, pp. 52-53; Heise, II, p. 152. Cf. *Dialogues*, p. 326.

84. See Heinrich Heine, *"Die Heimkehr,"* 66, *Buch der Lieder* (Hamburg: 1837), pp. 232-34; *The Poetry and Prose of Heinrich Heine*, ed. Frederic Ewen (New York: Citadel, 1948), pp. 90-91:

> I dreamed: I am the dear Lord God
> Enthroned in Heaven's palace:
> The angels sit surrounding me
> And sweetly praise my ballads.
>
> I ask for costly cakes and sweets,
> And nibble them all day,
> And drink them down with rare old wine,
> And have no debts to pay.
>
> But boredom plagues me terribly;
> I have an urge to revel;
> And were I not the dear Lord God
> I'd go and join the Devil.

See also *Sickness unto Death*, p. 130, *KW* XIX (*SV* XI 239).

85. Hoffmann, *Lebens-Ansichten des Katers Murr*, 1-2, *Schriften*, VIII. The character Kreisler was considered by many readers to represent Hoffmann himself.

86. Cf. Hamann, *Schriften*, IV, p. 23.

87. See p. 329 and note 194.

88. See Plato, *Phaedrus*, 244 a-257 b; *Opera*, I, pp. 164-95; Heise, I, pp. 164-94; *Dialogues*, pp. 491-502.

89. Hegel, *Vorlesungen über die Geschichte der Philosophie*, I-III, *Georg Wilhelm Friedrich Hegel's Werke*, I-XVIII, ed. Philipp Marheineke et al. (Berlin: 1832-45; *ASKB* 549-65), XIV, pp. 208-12; *Sämtliche Werke. Jubiläumsausgabe* [*J.A.*], I-XXVI, ed. Hermann Glockner (Stuttgart: Frommann, 1927-40), XVIII, pp. 38-41; *Hegel's Lectures on the History of Philosophy*, I-III (tr. of *G.P.*, 2 ed., 1840-44; Kierkegaard had 1 ed., 1833-36), tr. E. S. Haldane and Frances H. Simson (New York: Humanities, 1974), II, pp. 38-41.

90. See *Platons Werke*, I-III, tr. Friedrich Daniel Ernst Schleiermacher (Berlin: 1817-28; *ASKB* 1158-63), I[1], pp. 79-82; *Schleiermacher's Introductions to the Dialogues of Plato*, tr. William Dobson (1836; New York: Arno, 1973), pp. 71-73.

91. Plato, *Phaedrus*, 265 e-266 b; *Opera*, I, p. 218; *Dialogues*, p. 511.

92. Plato, *Protagoras*, 322 a-c; *Opera*, I, pp. 32-35; Heise, II, p. 155; *Dialogues*, pp. 319-20.

93. Plato, *Republic*, 436 a-437 a; *Platons Werke*, III, pp. 245-46; *Opera*, IV, pp. 228-31; *Dialogues*, pp. 677-78.

94. Hegel, *Vorlesungen über die Aesthetik*, II, *Werke*, X[2], pp. 113-19; *J.A.*, XIII, pp. 113-19; *The Philosophy of Fine Art*, I-IV (tr. of *V.A.*, 1 ed., 1835-38; Kierkegaard had this ed.), tr. F.P.B. Osmaston (London: Bell, 1920), II, pp. 272-79.

95. Hegel, *Aesthetik*, II, *Werke*, X[2], pp. 217-40; *J.A.*, XIII, pp. 217-40; *Philosophy of Fine Art*, II, pp. 377-401.

96. Plato, *Crito*, 52 b; Heise, I, p. 150; *Opera*, VIII, pp. 186-87; *Dialogues*, p. 37.

97. Plato, *Phaedrus*, 230 c-d; *Opera*, I, pp. 132-33; *Dialogues*, p. 479.

98. Heinrich Theodor Rötscher, *Aristophanes und sein Zeitalter* (Berlin: 1827).

99. Johann Wilhelm Süvern, *Ueber Aristophanes Wolken* (Berlin: 1826).

100. See note 98 above.

101. Peter Wilhelm Forchhammer, *Die Athener und Sokrates, die Gesetzlichen und der Revolutionär* (Berlin: 1837).

102. See Plutarch, "On the Control of Anger," *Moralia*, 461 d-e; *Plutarchs moralische Abhandlungen*, I-IX, tr. Johann F. S. Kaltwasser (Frankfurt/M: 1783-1800; *ASKB* 1192-96 [I-V]), IV, pp. 279-80; *Plutarch's Moralia*, I-XV, tr. Frank Cole Babbitt et al. (Loeb, Cambridge: Harvard University Press, 1967-84); VI, p. 143:

> Once when Socrates took Euthydemus home with him from the palaestra, Xanthippe came up to them in a rage and scolded them roundly, finally upsetting the table. Euthydemus, deeply offended, got up and was about to leave when Socrates said, "At your house the other day did not a hen fly in and do precisely this same thing, yet we were not put out about it?"

See also *JP* IV 4545 (*Pap*. IX A 363).

103. Theodor Heinsius, *Sokrates nach dem Grade seiner Schuld* . . . (Leipzig: 1839).

104. Diogenes Laertius, II, 32; *Vitis*, I, p. 76; Riisbrigh, I, p. 71; Loeb, I, p. 163.

105. Wilhelm Gottlieb Tennemann, *Geschichte der Philosophie*, I-XI (Leipzig: 1798-1819; *ASKB* 815-26), V, p. 294. Tennemann refers to *Adversus mathematicos*, I, 10-14; *Sexti Empirici opera quae extant*, ed. P. and J. Chouet (Orleans: 1621; *ASKB* 146), pp. 488-89; *Against the Professors, Sextus Empiricus*, I-IV, tr. R. G. Bury (Loeb, Cambridge: Harvard University Press, 1961-68), IV, pp. 9-11:

> CHAPTER II.—CONCERNING THE SUBJECT TAUGHT
>
> Now in dealing with the first point first we assert that if anything is taught either the existent *qua* existent is taught or the non-existent *qua* non-existent. But, as we shall establish, neither is the existent *qua* existent taught nor the non-existent *qua* non-existent; therefore nothing is taught. Now the non-existent *qua* non-existent will not be taught; for if it is taught it is teachable, and being teachable it will become an existent, and because of this it will be both non-existent and existent. But it is not possible for the same thing to be both existent and non-existent; therefore the non-existent *qua* non-existent is not taught. . . . Therefore the non-existent is not capable of being taught.—Nor, indeed, is the existent *qua* existent capable of being taught, for, since existents are equally evident to all men, they will all be incapable of being taught. Wherefrom it will follow that nothing is capable of being taught; for something untaught must be assumed in order that the learning of it may be derived from what is known. Neither, then, is the existent *qua* existent taught.

106. Plutarch, "Cato," *Lives*, 23; Tetens, III, p. 450; Loeb, II, pp. 371-73: "He says, for instance, that Socrates was a mighty prattler, who attempted, as best he could, to be his country's tyrant, by abolishing its customs, and by enticing his fellow citizens into opinions contrary to the laws."

107. Plutarch, "On the Sign of Socrates," *Moralia*, 589 e-f; Kaltwasser, V, pp. 169-70; Loeb, VII, pp. 457-59: "It bade him let the child do whatever came into his mind, and not do violence to his impulses or divert them, but allow them free play, taking no further trouble about him than to pray to Zeus Agoraeus and the Muses, surely implying by this that he had a better guide of life in himself than a thousand teachers and attendants."

108. See Heinrich Ritter and Ludwig Preller, *Historia philosophiae graecoromanae ex fontium locis contexta* (Hamburg: 1838; *ASKB* 726), pp. 139-49.

109. Marcus Aurelius Antoninus, *Meditations*, XI, 23, 28; *Marc. Aurel. Antonin's Unterhaltungen mit sich selbst*, tr. Johann M. Schultz (Schleswig: 1799; *ASKB* 1219), pp. 174, 175; *The Communings with Himself of Marcus Aurelius Antoninus*, tr. C. R. Haines (Loeb, Cambridge: Harvard University Press, 1953), pp. 315, 317:

Socrates used to nickname the opinions of the multitude *Ghouls*, bogies to terrify children.

Think of Socrates with the sheepskin wrapped round him, when Xanthippe had gone off with his coat, and what he said to his friends when they drew back in their embarrassment at seeing him thus accoutred.

110. See note 38 above.

111. See "Agesilaus, II," note (I), Pierre Bayle, *Dictionaire historique et critique*, I-IV (Amsterdam: 1740), I, p. 94; *Herrn Peter Baylens . . . Historisches und Critisches Wörterbuch*, I-IV, tr. Johann Christoph Gottsched (Leipzig: 1741-44; *ASKB* 1961-64), I, p. 95. There is no article on Socrates. For scattered references, see index, "Socrates," *Dictionaire*, IV, p. 795; *Worterbuch*, IV, n.p.

112. See Plato, *Alcibiades I*, 104 c-d, 106 a, 135 d; *Opera*, VIII, pp. 198-99, 200-03, 296-97; *Platons Werke*, II^3, pp. 307, 310, 370; *The Dialogues of Plato*, I-II, tr. Benjamin Jowett (New York: Random House, 1937), II, pp. 734, 735, 772.

113. Plato, *Platons Werke*, II^3, pp. 295-96; *Schleiermacher's Introductions*, pp. 329-30.

114. See Plato, *Platons Werke*, II^3, pp. 302-03; *Schleiermacher's Introductions*, pp. 334-35.

115. Carl [Karl] Friedrich Flögel, *Geschichte der komischen Litteratur*, I-IV (Liegnitz, Leipzig: 1784-87; *ASKB* 1396-99).

116. Aristotle, *Rhetoric*, 1393 b; *Aristoteles graece*, I-II, ed. Immanuel Bekker (Berlin: 1831; *ASKB* 1074-75), II, p. 1393; *The Complete Works of Aristotle*, I-II, ed. Jonathan Barnes (rev. Oxford tr.; Princeton: Princeton University Press, 1984), II, p. 2220.

117. Friedrich Adolf Trendelenburg, *Erläuterungen* (*ASKB* 845).

118. See Plato, *Apology*, 29 a-b, 40 b-42 a; *Opera*, VIII, pp. 126-29, 152-59; *Dialogues*, pp. 15, 24-26.

119. Plutarch, *Moralia*, 107 d-108 e; Kaltwasser, I, pp. 350-54; Loeb, II, pp. 137-45.

120. Aristotle, *Rhetoric*, 1398 a; *Rhetorik*, tr. Karl L. Roth (Stuttgart: 1833; *ASKB* 1092); Bekker, II, p. 1398, *Works*, II, p. 2228.

121. See Supplement, p. 449 (*Pap*. IV A 202).

122. Karl Friedrich Flögel, *Geschichte des Hofnarren* (Liegnitz, Leipzig: 1789; *ASKB* 1401).

123. *Aristophanes's Komedier*, I (no more published), tr. Johan Krag (Odense: 1825; *ASKB* 1055), p. 118 (ed. tr.). Cf. *The Frogs*, ll. 1491-95, *Aristophanes*, I-III, tr. Benjamin Bickley Rogers (Loeb, Cambridge: Harvard University Press, 1979-82), II, pp. 433-35:

RIGHT it is and befitting,
Not, by Socrates sitting,
Idle talk to pursue,
Stripping tragedy-art of
All things noble and true.

124. Aristophanes, *The Wasps*; Krag, p. 271; ll. 1038-42, Loeb, I, p. 507:

> But He, when the monstrous form he saw,
> no bribe he took and no fear he felt,
> For you he fought, and for you he fights:
> and then last year with adventurous hand
> He grappled besides with the Spectral Shapes,
> the Agues and Fevers that plagued our land;
> That loved in the darksome hours of night
> to throttle fathers, and grandsires choke,
> That laid them down on their restless beds,
> and against your quiet and peaceable folk
> Kept welding together proofs and writs
> and oath against oath, till many a man
> Sprang up, distracted with wild affright,
> and off in haste to the Polemarch ran.

125. Ameipsias, Athenian comic writer, was the author of *Konnos* (423 B.C.), which placed second in drama competition and above *The Clouds*. Socrates is a character in the play. Konnos was a harpist who taught Socrates (see Plato, *Euthydemus*, 272 c) and is the name of a dissolute musician in Aristophanes, *The Knights* and *The Wasps*. Eupolis, a tragic poet mentioned in Aristophanes, *The Clouds*, ll. 553-54 (Loeb), was regarded in antiquity as one of the three greatest Old Comedy writers.

126. See note 123 above.

127. See Supplement, p. 448 (*Pap*. IV A 199) and note 106.

128. Plutarch, *Lives*; Tetens, III, p. 327; Loeb, II, p. 215.

129. See Supplement, p. 451 (*Pap*. VI A 8).

130. *Either/Or*, I-II, was published February 20, 1843, twenty months after the publication of the dissertation.

131. August 9, 1838.

132. See p. 2 and note 2.

133. See Hans Brøchner, *Erindringer over Søren Kierkegaard* (Copenhagen: 1953), 6, pp. 21-22; "The Recollections," *Glimpses and Impressions of Kierkegaard*, tr. T. H. Croxall (Digswell Place, Welwyn, Herts.: Nisbet, 1959), p. 10:

> Shortly after Kierkegaard had taken his theological degree, he told me in conversation that his father had always wished him to take the theological examination, and that they had very frequently discussed the matter. 'So long as father lived, however, I was able to defend my thesis that I ought not to take it. But when he was dead, I had to take over his part in the debate as well as my own, and then I could no longer hold out, but had to decide to read for the examination.' He did so, with great energy.

See Historical Introduction, pp. vii, ix-x.

134. His brother Peter Christian (1805-1888).

135. See *Postscript*, *KW* XII (*SV* VII 437-38).

136. See *SV* VII 72-73.

137. See p. 9.

138. See Corsair *Affair*, Historical Introduction, pp. xiii, xix, *KW* XIII.

139. See pp. 234-35.

140. Danish: *numerisk*. Cf. Supplement, pp. 453-55 (*Pap*. XI^2 A 108).

141. See Claudius Aelianus, *Vermischte Nachrichten*, *Werke*, I-IX, tr. Ephorus Wunderlich and Friedrich Jacobs (Stuttgart: 1839-42; *ASKB* 1042-43), III, pp. 318-19.

142. See, for example, Hegel, *Philosophie des Rechts*, 257-360 (especially 257-58); *Werke*, VIII, pp. 312-440 (312-20); *J.A.*, VII, pp. 328-456 (328-36); *Hegel's Philosophy of Right* (tr. of *P.R.*, 1 ed., 1821, with reference also to 2 ed., 1833, which Kierkegaard had, and to later editions), tr. T. M. Knox (Oxford: Oxford University Press, 1967), pp. 155-223 (155-60).

143. See pp. 228-35.

144. See Plato, *Republic*, 368 d-369 a; *Opera*, IV, pp. 90-91; *Dialogues*, p. 615 (Adimantus and Socrates speaking):

> Quite so, said Adimantus, but what analogy to this do you detect in the inquiry about justice?
>
> I will tell you, I said. There is a justice of one man, we say, and, I suppose, also of an entire city?
>
> Assuredly, said he.
>
> Is not the city larger than the man?
>
> It is larger, he said.
>
> Then, perhaps, there would be more justice in the larger object, and more easy to apprehend. If it please you, then, let us first look for its quality in states, and then only examine it also in the individual, looking for the likeness of the greater in the form of the less.

145. See *Fragments*, p. 6, *KW* VII (*SV* IV 177).

BIBLIOGRAPHICAL NOTE

For general bibliographies of Kierkegaard studies, see:

Jens Himmelstrup, *Søren Kierkegaard International Bibliografi*. Copenhagen: Nyt Nordisk Forlag Arnold Busck, 1962.

Aage Jørgensen, *Søren Kierkegaard-litteratur 1961-1970*. Aarhus: Akademisk Boghandel, 1971. *Søren Kierkegaard-litteratur* 1971-80. Aarhus: privately printed, 1983.

François Lapointe, *Søren Kierkegaard and His Critics: An International Bibliography of Criticism*. Westport, Connecticut: Greenwood Press, 1980.

Kierkegaard: A Collection of Critical Essays, ed. Josiah Thompson. New York: Doubleday (Anchor Books), 1972.

Søren Kierkegaard's Journals and Papers, I, ed. and tr. Howard V. Hong and Edna H. Hong, assisted by Gregor Malantschuk. Bloomington, Indiana: Indiana University Press, 1967.

For topical bibliographies of Kierkegaard studies, see *Søren Kierkegaard's Journals and Papers*, I-IV, 1967-75.

INDEX

ADVISORY BOARD

KIERKEGAARD'S WRITINGS